The Great World War 1914-45

1914-45

Volume 2

The Great World War 1914-45

Volume 2
The peoples' experience

Edited by
Dr Peter Liddle
Dr John Bourne
Dr Ian Whitehead

To the generations who experienced
the lightning strikes
1914-1945

HarperCollinsPublishers
77-85 Fulham Palace Road
Hammersmith
London W6 8JB

First published in Great Britain by HarperCollinsPublishers 2001

1 3 5 7 9 10 9 6 4 2

ISBN 0 00 711633 0

British Library Cataloguing in Publication Data:
A catalogue record for this book is available from the British Library.

Printed and bound in England by Clays Ltd, St Ives plc

Contents

Acknowledgements

We are grateful to all the scholars who have contributed to this volume, which, like its predecessor, has been a thoroughly collaborative effort in which we, as editors, have been blessed with friends and colleagues whose unfailing levels of commitment and support ensured that the editorial process was always smooth and enjoyable. We extend special thanks to those contributors who overcame illness, including cancer, bronchial pneumonia, a heart attack, and an appalling mountain-climbing accident to complete their chapters.

We are also grateful to those authors who helped with the provision of illustrations: Joan Beaumont; Bob Bushaway; Irene Guerrini; Sergei Kudryashov; Marco Pluviano; Nicholas Saunders; Naoko Shimazu; Michael Snape; Edward Spiers; and Bernard Waites. Our appreciation in this regard is also due to Claire Harder and Matthew Richardson. Many friends and contributors gave advice on the development of the book, and in this respect we gratefully acknowledge Bob Bushaway, Hugh Cecil, James Cooke, John Erickson, Imanuel Geiss, Werner Rahn, Gary Sheffield, Dennis Showalter and Frank Vandiver. We should also like to thank Dr Mark Wheeler for his helpful advice.

We wish to thank all the relevant archives and authorities for granting permission to quote from material held in their care and for sanctioning the reproduction of photographs. If there were to be any instance of omission of appropriate accreditation, the editors express in advance their regret and their readiness in a later edition to repair such omission. Particular thanks are owed to the Trustees of the Mass Observation Archive, University of Sussex. The editors also thank the following institutions for permission to reproduce photographs and illustrative material: *Birmingham Post and Mail*; Foreign Policy Archives of the Russian Federation; *Fujin Kôron*, Chuokoronsha, Tokyo; Glamorgan Archives Service; *Herald and Evening Times*, Glasgow; Imperial War Museum; Liddle Collection, University of Leeds; Museum of Lincolnshire Life; and the Second World War Experience Centre, Leeds. Once more, thanks are due to Louise Liddle for liaising with Media Studies: Photography in the University of Leeds, and to all the staff at the latter, including David Dixon, Colin Butterfield, and David Bailey, for the excellent reproduction of the photographs.

The editors wish to acknowledge the continued support of the Trustees of the Second World War Experience Centre, Leeds. We appreciate the support and encouragement received from Claire Harder, especially given her own responsibilities as Business Director of the Centre. The task of deciphering Peter's script was ably and cheerfully taken up again by Tracey Craggs – surely work worthy of a medal. The army of committed volunteers at the Centre has also given further gratefully accepted assistance. Amongst these, thanks are specifically due to Robert Carrington for his work on the illustrations.

Finally, the editors wish to express their thanks to all at HarperCollins, notably Will Adams, for their work on this and the earlier volume. Above all we are grateful to our Commissioning Editor, Ian Drury, who has remained throughout a source of much-appreciated advice and assistance.

John Bourne
Peter Liddle
Ian Whitehead
October 2000

Editors' Introduction

The emphasis of this book, like that of the preceding volume, *The Great World War, 1914-45: Lightning Strikes Twice* (HarperCollins, 2000), is on the human experience that binds together the history of the two World Wars. The editors have been conscious throughout of the need for breadth in terms of geographical scope, and have made an effort to cover the experience of widely diverse peoples. In this respect we regret that, although there are chapters on the peoples of India and China, there is no chapter specifically dedicated to the Japanese occupation of Asia, even though there is no First World War counterpart for this.

Part I examines the implications for civilian populations of the increasingly 'total' nature of these conflicts. It discusses the experiences of women and children; the targeting of civilians by aerial bombardment; and the increasing importance of propaganda as a means of galvanising popular support for war. For some societies, such as Italy, it appears that the two wars are part of a single process of national development. We learn that for South Africa conduct of the Second War was essentially a re-run of the first. In Germany and Russia during the Second War we see a striving for better solutions to the same challenges that had faced them in the earlier conflict. However, in terms of national mythology, in Russia there is no sense of comparability between the two conflicts – memory of 20th-century warfare is dominated by the Great Patriotic War against Nazi Germany, while the First World War remains largely forgotten, buried under the historical weight of the Bolshevik Revolution. Conversely, in Australia, despite the fact that the Second World War presented a real threat to the country's independence, in a way that the First World War did not, it is the 1914-18 conflict that remains paramount in the national consciousness.

The book demonstrates the truly global nature of these wars; a fact perhaps more readily recognised in the case of 1939-45 than 1914-18, understanding of which has been dominated by an overwhelming concentration on the Western Front. Some continents and regions, such as Asia, were left largely untouched by the First World War. On the other hand, it is clear that, even for Asia, the Great War was to have immense consequences resulting from the rise of Japanese power. Although the Second World War had a wider global impact there were some regions, like the Middle East, for which the First World War had greater significance.

Part II examines the attitudes of those writers, musicians and artists whose work was shaped by their war experiences. Paintings, literature and music are considered as a record of war experience, revealing the similarities and the contrasts between the First World War and the Second, and exposing a diversity of motivations and reactions: patriotism; elation; optimism; boredom; moral outrage; grief; and despair. However, it is equally important that we recall the lighter side of wartime cultural experience. Music, sport and recreational activities provided civilians and servicemen alike with a welcome diversion from wartime realities.

Part III investigates the moral and ethical questions with which the wartime generations had to grapple. What is revealed is a picture of the moral complexity of the wars – one that does not conform to the idea that the Second World War was freer from ethical dilemmas than its 'unjust' predecessor. The implications of industrialised conflict for the concept of 'civilised' warfare are discussed, and the impact of total war is placed in the context of earlier conflicts. While state intervention during the Second World War was on a greater scale than that witnessed in the First, the liberal democracies in the Second World War were far more ready to tolerate the opponents of war. In both wars, however, it is clear that no single pacifist ideology developed – those who opposed war were motivated by a variety of ethical, religious, political or selfish considerations. The only common bond between these individuals was their willingness to make a stand against the state.

Mechanised warfare ensured that the character of the fighting in the two World Wars was largely remote and impersonal. The unseen enemy, 'silent' weapons such as gas, the remoteness of bomber crews from the civilian deaths and destruction that they wrought – these aspects of modern warfare challenged traditional ideas and expectations concerning the nature of war, and the rules that should govern its conduct, and led individuals to question the purpose of their actions. Yet it is evident that many of those who fought in these conflicts continued to see warfare in terms of accepted notions of chivalrous conduct. It is also clear that spiritual faith continued to sustain many individuals through the emotional and ethical turmoil of war. In Britain, where the 20th century witnessed a decline in organised Christian religious observance, the wars revealed the depth and breadth of individual religious conviction.

Part IV discusses the legacy of the World Wars. The experience of 'total' war is compared with earlier conflicts, alongside an examination of its repercussions for the conduct of warfare in the second half of the 20th century. Chapters on material culture and commemoration discuss the factors that have moulded individual and collective memories of the wars, and reveal the extent to which perceptions of 1914-18 and 1939-45 have been transformed by changing social and cultural attitudes.

The conclusions offered by the book demonstrate that there is much that unites the two conflicts, in terms of the development of modern warfare, its challenges and its impact. For those who lived through and fought in both conflicts the imagery of 'lightning strikes twice', the sub-title of the companion volume, provides an appropriate description of popular reaction to the outbreak of another global war, just 21 years after the Armistice of 1918. But, in international terms, lightning did not always strike twice. In Europe it certainly did and the second strike proved even more destructive than the first. Other regions, however, were variously struck just the once, on the other occasion hearing just the thunder from abroad, although not always escaping the violent aftermath of the storm.

PART I
THE PEOPLES'
EXPERIENCE

Chapter 1

British children in wartime

Eric Hopkins

The experiences of children in Britain during the two World Wars provide a striking study in contrasts: in the four years of the First War, more and more children woke one day to find their father missing from the house. In many cases, apart from brief subsequent glimpses of him on leave, they were never to see him again. In the six years of the Second War, this was rather less likely to happen, especially during the first three years, when more women and children were killed than soldiers. During the First World War, enemy activity in the skies over Britain was limited[1], whereas in the Second it was intense, especially in 1940 and 1941, and again towards the end, in 1944, with the German employment of flying bombs and rockets. In both wars, schooling suffered interruption, though only in the Second World War were children evacuated from cities and towns en masse, and schools themselves suffered severe physical damage. Both wars led to the passing of Education Acts, though the results of the Education Act 1944 were more far-reaching than those of the 1918 Act. Lastly, the First World War left an aftermath of grief and loss that inescapably affected the school life of the inter-war period, with its war memorial tablets in school halls to the Fallen, the wreaths of poppies on Armistice Day each November, and the poignancy of the Two Minutes Silence.

The First World War brought an extraordinary flood of volunteers to the colours. However, large though it was, it still became necessary to introduce conscription in 1916. The result of the massive demand for recruits to the Army was an acute shortage of manpower in industry, where the production of armaments and ammunition was vital for the war effort. As a consequence, women flooded into industry, especially into the manufacture of munitions. It is sometimes said that working-class children were also affected by the manpower shortage, with a marked increase in early school-leaving during the war. This view seems to be based on a statement made by the President of the Board of Education, H. A. L. Fisher, in the House of Commons on 10 August 1917. According to Fisher, 600,000 children 'had been drawn prematurely from school and had become immersed in industry'.[2] However, he did not say whether this number had left illegally before the minimum leaving age of 12, or had left between the ages of 12 and 14, when it was possible to leave early, either to become a half-timer, or because the leaver had reached the educational standard necessary to start work, or had made the minimum number of attendances necessary. These were all legitimate ways of leaving early. In fact, before the war, about half in the age range

12 to 14 seem to have left school before 14, though a contemporary estimate of the situation in London by R. H. Tawney suggested that most children stayed on till 14.[3]

A case study of the situation in Birmingham – the second largest city in England – shows that although prosecutions of employers for the illegal employment of children numbered 325 in 1915, the number fell to only 196 in 1916, to 93 in 1917, then to only four in 1918. On the other hand, prosecutions of parents for non-attendance rose from 2,818 in 1915 to 4,706 in 1917, falling to 4,202 in 1918. Working outside school hours was another matter, of course. This kind of part-time employment had always been widespread in Birmingham, and in September 1917 there were still many working over 30 hours per week, in addition to their 27 hours in school. All the same, attendance in Birmingham in the war years remained at over 87 per cent, and the numbers of 12- and 13-year-olds in elementary schools actually increased slightly between 1914 and 1918. Thus, there is not much to show any great increase in Birmingham in the numbers of school children leaving between 12 and 14, though the temptation to do so obviously existed in a great industrial city, as the figures for prosecutions of parents and employers demonstrate clearly enough.

The Birmingham Education Committee stood firm in the matter. When a Memorandum from Parents and Employers was presented to them in 1916, urging that the school leaving age be reduced for the duration, it was rejected, it being pointed out that a child between 12 and 14 could work full-time only if he passed the Labour Examination in Standard VII and obtained a Labour Certificate; if the employment was under the Factory & Workshops Acts, he had to be 13 before being employed full-time. If employment was to be in farming, the farmer had to be able to show that he could not obtain other labour owing to the war, whereupon the Committee might permit full-time employment between 13 and 14 provided they were satisfied as to conditions of work.

If Birmingham is anything to go by, there was certainly no mass leaving from the elementary schools during the war years, though obviously enough, incentives to leave early did exist. For example, separation allowances for the wives of servicemen were small (and so were widow's pensions), so some extra income from children's earnings would not come amiss. Nevertheless, poverty seems to have declined during the war for the reason that jobs were plentiful, and unemployment fell. Numbers on poor relief declined markedly to two-thirds of what they had been in 1914. In general terms, the physical condition of children appears to have improved.

Against this view must be set the opinion expressed in one of the older authorities on the history of elementary education, which has it that during the war 'most children of school age suffered grievously, that they were on near-starvation rations and experienced deterioration, their clothing becoming threadbare'.[4] This opinion seems quite mistaken: it is clear enough that the standard of working-class living was maintained during the war, and even improved for the families of unskilled workers. The Board of Education's Report for 1914-15 refers to children in many areas as being better-fed and clothed than ever before, while the number of school meals provided for poor children declined during the war; in the year to March 1915 the number of meals served nationally was 422,401, and this figure dropped to 65,301 for the year ending March 1917, falling again to 60,582 for the year ending March 1918.[5] Thus, greater prosperity seems to have helped to reduce malnutrition. It might be added that food rationing was not introduced till 1917, and then at first on a voluntary basis only; rationing never became severe before the war ended, so that any suggestion that rations were on a near-starvation basis is very wide of the mark.

What of conditions in school itself? Both public schools and local authority schools suffered from increasing shortages of staff. In the public schools younger men were more and more difficult to appoint, while military training in the OTC (Officers Training Corps) in the schools took on a new and grim meaning; possession of Certificate 'A' was a passport to a commission, and a speedy entry into the Army at the age of 18. In the state schools there was a marked scarcity of young male teachers, though at first women who had retired compulsorily on marriage were brought back into the schools, and helped to fill vacancies – so also retired male teachers, and even occasionally disabled ex-servicemen. It is difficult to draw a national picture of staffing shortages, though some figures are available for Birmingham. There the number of teachers serving in the forces on 21 December 1916 was 422, together with 103 local government officers in the Education Department, and 56 school caretakers.[6] By the end of the war, the total number of Education Committee employees who had served in the war was 757; at a guess, 500 of these were probably teachers.[7] Some of this number were secondary school teachers, of course, but the majority would have been teachers in elementary schools. Given the fact that there were 189 elementary schools in Birmingham in 1918, the average number of vacancies to be filled during the war would have been between two and three per school. These vacancies would have caused inconveniences, of course, dependent on the size of the school; larger schools with bigger staffs had greater flexibility in timetabling. Towards the end of 1915 it was decided to ask headmasters with an average attendance of not more than 350 to take a class while the war lasted. The peripatetic science staff was also re-arranged.[8] All in all, there were clearly problems arising from the shortage of male teachers, but they were hardly insurmountable.

Other problems arising from war conditions were the cessation of all school building, and the cuts in the school medical and dental services. Certainly, some schools were overcrowded and additional buildings were required. Fortunately, relatively few school buildings were occupied by the military. In 1914 there were 21,500 elementary schools in England and Wales. By July 1916, only 109 were in use as hospitals, and another 61 were used as accommodation for troops. By the end of the war, the total figure in military use was about 200.[9] In some areas overcrowding in schools was a much more serious problem than military occupation. This was true of Birmingham, where there was a pre-war shortage of elementary school accommodation, so that permission had been given before the war for classes to be taught in the school hall in a number of schools.[10] Even before the war came to an end, plans were being made in Birmingham for additional school building.

Nationally, there were certainly some cuts in the school medical and dental services due to the high demand for doctors and dentists in the military hospitals. Thus, in 1916 the number of children medically examined in schools was cut by 28 per cent, but it was observed by the Board of Education that the work of medical treatment was well maintained in some places and even developed.[11] In the year 1917-18, about 70 per cent of normal numbers were inspected.[12] To draw on Birmingham again as an example, the city was clearly one of the areas in which medical services were well maintained and even developed. Dental treatment for 6- to 8-year-olds had started in early 1913, and tonsil operations in October 1913, these operations being performed three times a week. Unlike some authorities, Birmingham kept the children overnight after the operation, and brought them back three weeks later for breathing exercises.[13] The number of operations for tonsils and adenoids went up from 468 in the year ending 31 March 1915 to 1,209 in the year ending 31 March 1918; the number of spectacles prescribed also went up, as did dental treatments (from 11,792 to 17,071 in the same three years), and also X-rays for ringworm (from 220 to 331 in the same period). Inspections for vermin continued, though on a reduced scale; prosecutions rose from 309 in 1915 to 628 in 1917.[14] Such was the Birmingham record that it was commended in the Annual Report of the Chief Medical Officer of the Board of Education in 1917; and after the war, in 1924, the Education Committee thought that it was probably true that there had been greater progress in the school medical services during the previous ten years than in any other branch of the Committee's activities.[15]

Play centres were a new enterprise begun during the war. They were based on the centres in London organised by the novelist Mrs Humphry Ward, with the idea of keeping children off the streets, and reducing the level of juvenile crime that had increased somewhat during the war. One cause of this, it was thought, was the absence of fathers on military service, and also of mothers engaged on war work. In January 1917 the Board of Education issued Circular 980, which authorised grants of up to half the cost of maintaining the centres.[16] How far these play centres had any success in achieving their objective is hard to say. Some cities took the idea very seriously. In Birmingham, for example, it was planned to open five centres in schools on 1 October 1917, while the Birmingham Street Children's Union proposed to open no fewer than 47 Junior Clubs on the lines of play centres, mostly on their own premises. Rooms were made available to this body by the Birmingham Education Committee in an additional nine schools.[17] It is not clear exactly when these centres closed down, though one source states that they ended on 16 April 1919, after a most successful session, with average attendance of 230 in each of the mixed centres, and 120 in the others (there were ten centres in all by the time the scheme ended, opening two evenings a week).[18]

One other educational development is to be noted: this was the passing of the Education Act 1918. This had its origins in a Bill introduced in 1917 that had to be withdrawn in the face of the opposition to it displayed by the local education authorities. In a revised form it became the Fisher Education Act 1918. This Act is generally regarded as disappointing, in that its educational reforms were severely affected by the economy cuts of the early 1920s, especially the 'Geddes Axe' of 1922. Certainly, one major reform – the setting up of day continuation schools up to the age of 18 – was almost entirely abandoned as trade depression set in during

1921. Another reform, the abolition of part-timers between the ages of 12 and 14, did take effect in those few counties where the scheme operated (such as Lancashire and Yorkshire, where there was still a demand for juvenile labour in the mills); but there were very few part-timers in other counties, and in Birmingham, for example, the system of part-timers was not employed at all, and early leaving by means of the Labour Certificate was very limited. In that city it was not thought that the abolition of all leaving before the age of 14 would necessitate any appointment of additional staff.[19] Another proposed reform – the raising of the school leaving age to 15 – was put off till, in 1936, it was at last decided to implement this part of the Act with effect from September 1939. The outbreak of the Second World War led to another postponement of this reform.

So what was the overall effect of the Great War on the children of the country? For many, no doubt, depending on their age, it was part of the mysteries of Growing Up, a dim apprehension of something rather forbidding and frightening going on in France and elsewhere, the reality of which was only brought home by the realisation that Dad was not going to come home any more. Occasionally there would be disturbing glimpses of wounded soldiers in hospital blue (London children might see injured soldiers carried from the hospital trains arriving at Charing Cross, while soldiers on leave came home at Victoria Station; Enoch Powell caught sight of wounded soldiers at New Street Station, Birmingham, and remembered his parents pulling down the blinds in a railway carriage during a Zeppelin raid. He also saw prisoners of war at work in the City.[20]) Life in school did not show many changes, other than the shortage of younger male teachers, and in playtime games the enemy would automatically be 'Jerries'.

However, the effect of wartime conditions was not expunged immediately from childhood consciousness once peace had returned in 1918. This is certainly true of many of the more than 300,000 children who lost their fathers during the war (160,000 wives lost their husbands, too).[21] Some children would know their fathers only by the sepia photographs taken of him in uniform before he left for the front. Their one solid souvenir of him would be his war medals. Even those not touched by personal loss in their families could hardly fail to have the war brought to mind by the reminders of the conflict set up in parks and public places, the war memorials, with their lists of the dead, some 723,000 in all. Parties of schoolchildren in London's Whitehall would gaze with wonder at the Cenotaph, the curiously shaped 'empty tomb' designed by Lutyens as an impressive memorial to the dead (children would not need to be reminded to remove their caps as they passed). It was there, of course, that the greatest memorial service of the year was held on 11 November, with wreaths laid by members of the Royal Family and leading politicians, followed by the nationally observed (and scrupulously observed) Two Minutes Silence. The Silence ended with the sounding of the Last Post. Visitors to Westminster Abbey, not far away, could see another solemn reminder of the war: the tomb of the Unknown Soldier. Other cities had their own way of honouring the dead: Birmingham constructed its own miniature temple, a Hall of Memory, containing the names of the Fallen in large volumes.

Thus, the generation of children growing up between the wars could hardly fail to be reminded of the Great War in a number of ways. Images of the war were inescapable, in magazines, books and films, and, every November, in the newspapers. The *London Evening News*, for example, for years ran a competition for the best letters printed about experiences in the war: the winners were rewarded with prizes of 5 shillings for their efforts. In the schools, ex-servicemen returning to duty as teachers might speak grimly from time to time of their experiences. Some bore visible reminders of the war – a limp and a walking stick, or a missing hand replaced by a false hand concealed in a dark leather glove. All this made a powerful impression on more thoughtful children, and certainly contributed to the fear of war, and its rejection by many adults as an instrument of policy in the 1930s.

As the threat of another European war grew, so the Labour Party was ever more insistent on the need to secure collective security not through rearmament but through disarmament. The Peace Pledge Union, founded in 1934, had 100,000 members by 1936, all pledged never to support or approve another war. In the League of Nations Peace Ballot of 1934-35, although 6.25 million voted to stop an aggressor, if necessary, by war, 2 million disagreed, and another 2 million did not answer. In February 1933, just after Hitler had gained power as Chancellor in Germany, the Oxford Union passed the famous resolution, 'That this House will not fight for King and Country'. The principal speaker was C. E. M. Joad, afterwards famous during the war as a member of the Brains Trust, who on this occasion made a pacifist speech. Most of those present, of course, had been children in the immediate post-war years. Fear of bombing was widespread, and Baldwin's sombre prediction that 'the bomber will always get through' added to the general apprehension.

What might almost be called folk memories of the Great War were strong among the children who grew up in the 1920s and '30s – they were difficult to avoid – and they contributed to the doubts, uncertainties and fears of the inter-war years. At King Edward's High School, Birmingham, which he entered in 1925, Enoch Powell observed the effect the war had on his masters, and, according to his biographer, 'felt a shadow of sorts being cast over him and his generation, with the memory of the war saturating everyday life'.[22] Certainly they help to explain the great outburst of public emotion and profound thankfulness that greeted Chamberlain's announcement of the Munich Agreement in September 1938, and of his having achieved 'peace for our time'.

Against this background, it is understandable that the declaration of war against Germany on 3 September 1939 led the nation to brace itself against the expected onslaught from the skies (especially as the declaration of war was followed almost immediately by the sounding of the air raid sirens, though it proved a false alarm). In 1937 the experts had predicted an attack lasting 60 days, with casualties of 600,000 deaths and 1,200,000 injured. In the light of figures such as these, the Ministry of Health calculated that between one and three million hospital beds would be required once war broke out.[23] As a consequence of forecasts of this kind, the evacuation of children and mothers with children under 5 from the largest cities was begun two days before war began; in all, about 764,000 were moved, all voluntarily, complete with gas masks and under Government supervision, while large numbers of adults made their own arrangements to move out. Thus the outbreak of war had an immediate impact on the lives of many town children as they found themselves separated from their parents and housed temporarily with strangers. Efforts were made to billet like with like, but some middle- and upper-class hosts were horrified at the behaviour of some of the children they had offered to take in. Oliver Lyttleton (later to become Lord Chandos) wrote after the war that he had had a shock:

> 'I had little dreamt that English children could be so completely ignorant of the simplest rules of hygiene, and that they would regard the floors and carpets as suitable places upon which to relieve themselves.'[9]

A letter printed in *The Times* on 22 September 1939 referred to complaints about 'half-savage, verminous, and wholly illiterate children' and of 'mattresses and carpets polluted, of wilful despoilation and dirt one would associate only with untrained animals'.[25]

Incidents of this kind received a good deal of unfavourable publicity in the early days of the war, though they were by no means typical; and of course it is not surprising that children transported suddenly from their own homes into unfamiliar surroundings miles away should be under nervous strain, so that in such circumstances bed-wetting was not unlikely. For children left at home, most city schools were completely closed at first, but re-opened gradually on a voluntary basis as the expected bombing failed to materialise. As an alternative to attendance at school, many authorities organised Home Teaching, that is teaching of small groups of children not necessarily in their homes but more usually in church balls and elsewhere, the aim being to avoid having children together in large numbers.

Early in 1940 the Government decided to take of stock of the situation. In January a nationwide survey showed that of 1,493,967 elementary school children, only 47 per cent were attending school. Another 24 per cent were in Home Teaching, while 27.9 per cent were not being taught at all. Another survey in March 1940 showed that full-time attendance was still less than normal, and varied from place to place; in Birmingham the figure for elementary schools was 74.5 per cent, but in Liverpool it was only 24 per cent, and in Manchester 23.6 per cent. The Government then notified local authorities that they could make attendance compulsory again from 1 April 1940. By this time large numbers of evacuees had returned home; by the end of 1939, 344,900 were already back home – nearly half of those originally evacuated.[26] In Birmingham, by December 1939 there were only 10,352 elementary school children officially evacuated under the Government scheme, and this figure had dropped to 7,200 by June 1940.[27]

The national situation changed dramatically after the withdrawal of the British Army from Dunkirk in June 1940, and after the Battle of Britain that followed shortly after. The Blitz on London and other major cities began in September 1940. Not only was there a further wave of evacuation from London (some 100,000 children left in June 1940), but there was also a further evacuation from Portsmouth, Southampton, and towns on the North East coast. Local schools were all closed along the threatened invasion coasts of Suffolk, Norfolk, Essex and Kent. Some 37,000 children were evacuated from these areas to the Midlands and South

Wales.[28] A Children's Overseas Reception Board was also set up in June, and it received applications from the parents of 211,000 children aged between 10 and 16. However, there were difficulties in arranging shipping, and on 17 September 1940 the *City of Benares* was sunk with the loss of 73 children. Subsequently the scheme lost impetus, and only 2,664 children were evacuated in the final outcome – 1,502 to Canada, 577 to Australia, 353 to South Africa, and 202 to New Zealand. In addition, private evacuation overseas (for example, to the USA) also took place, amounting to the larger total of 13,603 children, in the period from June to December 1940; however, this private evacuation by middle-class parents who could afford it caused some adverse criticism.[29]

The years 1940 and 1941 were to prove a particularly testing time for schoolchildren, especially those in the cities and in the coastal areas threatened with invasion. London, of course, took a great battering from the Luftwaffe from September onwards, its worst attack coming on 10 May 1941, when 1,436 were killed and 1,790 injured. Other cities heavily bombed included Coventry, Birmingham, Liverpool, Southampton, Bristol, Portsmouth and Plymouth. The city that suffered worst after London was Birmingham, where 400 were killed in a raid on 19 November 1940. Three days later another 113 were killed, then on 11 December a further 263, while on 9 April 1941 the worst raid of all took place, resulting in a death toll of 1,121.[30] The German invasion of Russia in June 1941 brought a limited respite from the Blitz, though the so-called Baedeker raids were directed at historic cities such as Exeter, Bath, Norwich, York and Canterbury from April 1942 onwards, together with occasional hit-and-run raids. After D-Day in June 1944 bomber raids as such ceased altogether, but were replaced by attack by flying bombs (V1s) and by rockets (V2s). Some 60,000 deaths in all resulted from bombing, with about 56,000 seriously injured and 151,000 suffering minor injuries.

The effect of all this enemy activity on the schools is easily imagined. In the coastal areas of Kent and East Sussex the schools were closed altogether till the end of 1940, when some Home Teaching began. In London, as early as the third week of October 1940, more than half the London County Council's school buildings were either demolished or damaged, or out of use on account of unexploded bombs. Of the remainder, 96 were in use as rest centres, with another 39 being prepared for this use. As for London teachers, of whom there were 4,893 in all, less than half (1,961) were actually teaching; 1,102 were running rest centres, 555 helping with emergency meal services, 646 on evacuation and registration duties, 14 on standby, 34 on reserve, and 285 on sick leave.[31] In these circumstances, school attendance fell to extraordinarily low levels; in Southwark, south London, it varied from 0 to 5 per cent, and the same was generally true of schools in the East End of London. In the outer London schools, on the east and south-east side, the average attendance was better. In December 1940 an average attendance figure of 13 authorities taken together was 47 per cent, ranging from the highest in Ilford (59 per cent) to the lowest in Hornchurch (31 per cent), where there was a busy fighter station.[32] All these figures improved subsequently, of course, and in early 1941 the LCC began to attempt to enforce compulsory attendance; but undoubtedly the first few months of the Blitz were the most difficult time for the

London schools. Indeed, in November 1940 the Deputy Secretary of the Board of Education feared that the school system in London was near to total collapse, and that about 100,000 children were running loose[33], an exaggeration, perhaps, but quite understandable in the circumstances.

Similar fears were expressed by the Birmingham HMI, T. F. Arnold, after the two heavy raids on Birmingham in November 1940. Writing to his superiors, who had moved to the safety of Bournemouth, Arnold informed them that 40 schools had received heavy damage, most of them direct hits, while another 100 had suffered minor damage. After the severe raid of 22 November 1940, 75 per cent of the schools had been closed all week, the water supply having been disrupted over two-thirds of the city. Arnold concluded:

'To sum up: the educational machine as it was functioning up to November 20th has been smashed beyond repair. An emergency machine will have to be created.'[34]

The educational system in Birmingham did survive, of course, but by the second half of 1941 other worries began to emerge, especially the increasing shortage of teachers. The age of reservation bar had already gone up from 21 to 30 in August 1940, and in 1941 the Ministry of Labour actually proposed the complete de-reservation of male teachers by October 1941. Strong protests by the Board of Education resulted in the age of reservation being fixed at 35, with a further 10 per cent of assistant teachers also being reserved. This still left the 30-35 age group, the cream of the profession, open to call-up. In April 1941 Birmingham was already regarded as severely understaffed, with a staffing ratio of 1:16. In September 1941, Arnold calculated that there would probably be fewer than 400 male assistants left in the Birmingham schools. Writing again to Bournemouth, he declared:

'All this proves my assertion up to the hilt that shortage of staff is doing more damage to education than all Goering's bombs, and is far and away the most serious problem confronting us.'[35]

It is interesting to note that by this time Arnold thought staff shortages a more serious threat than bomb damage to schools or casualties. In the same letter he went on to speak pessimistically of the situation in the great cities:

'...evacuated children have probably lost the blessings of Hadowisation [that is, separate secondary schools] but have gained a wealth of new and stimulating experiences ... but for the children who remain in the cities, it is all loss. Their environment is even more hellish than it was in peacetime.'

How in fact did children react to war conditions and in particular to the bombing? In all probability, children living in rural areas remote from the great cities were relatively untouched by the war, during the first two or three years at least. Their fathers might be in the forces, but casualties were nowhere as heavy as in the early years of the First War (the exception was among air crew, where the death rate was very high). In some areas, after the entry of the USA into the war, children had to get used to American forces, usually cheery enough, and a great source of chewing gum ('Got any gum, chum?'). The blackout was rigidly enforced, and food rationing became stricter as the war went on. There were many minor inconveniences, such as the need to carry around one's gas mask during the early years of the war; but life was tolerable enough. Schools nearer the cities might have to accommodate trekkers overnight from a neighbouring city who came out every night to escape the bombing. This happened to Lancashire schools near Liverpool. The schools had to be disinfected and cleaned every morning.[36]

In the early days of the war country areas had also to find accommodation for evacuees, and rural children often found themselves having to share schools with newcomers from the towns and cities; but this difficulty was easing as increasing numbers went home during the latter years of the war. All in all, rural areas escaped the bombing visited on the big cities, though they suffered from the jettisoning of bombs from passing aircraft and from occasional so-called tip-and-run raids. Schools might be bombed as a result. For example, Petworth Church of England School for Boys in Sussex (80 boys on roll) was bombed in September 1942, the teacher, an assistant master and 29 boys being killed. (There was a similar bombing of a South London school – Sandhurst Road School, Lewisham – on 20 January 1943, resulting in the deaths of 6 teachers and 37 children.[37])

In London the problems were different, and were largely the result of continuous night-time bombing. Many parents who had participated in the first wave of evacuation and later brought their children home, decided that their children should take their chances with them once bombing began in earnest. As a result nights were spent with the family either at home in an Anderson shelter in the garden, or indoors in a reinforced table-shelter (the Morrison), or away from home in a local communal shelter or in the Underground. In central London 79 Underground stations were open all night for shelter; by the end of September 1940 there were 170,000 people sleeping in them. Not all stations were bombproof. In October 1940 four stations suffered direct hits in three nights. In January 1941 Bank Station, just outside the Bank of England and opposite the Mansion House, suffered a direct hit, and 111 were killed.[38]

Undoubtedly, the nightly ordeal left its mark on many children (and there were daytime alerts from time to time as well). In these strange circumstances attendance at school must have been seen by some as a relatively insignificant matter; it must have seemed more important to stay at home if Father was on leave, or to help Mother do domestic work, or to visit bombed-out relatives, in hospital or in temporary rest centres. No wonder there were large numbers of truants. When in 1942 some sort of order had returned to the school system, and attendance had improved (schools now had their windows taped against blast, sandbagged protection, and surface brick shelters in the playground), the children were showing signs of strain. Their powers of concentration had suffered, they were generally more restless, they were noisier, and long periods in shelters resulted in some neglect in personal cleanliness.[39]

Similar developments were noted in Birmingham, the result of loss of sleep and the nervous tension engendered by the raids. The annual report of the

Birmingham Child Guidance Clinic for 1940 at first claimed that the war had not caused any increase in neurosis and maladjustment, but went on to say that greater excitability and aggressive behaviour had been noticed following air raids, together with diminished powers of memory and concentration. The 1941 report made the same points – the children were standing up well to the strain, and that although noisier and less controlled than formerly, the anticipated increase in nervous disorders had not shown up to any degree. Soothing words, but the report went on to suggest that the general impression that war had little effect on the mental health of the children should be accepted with caution and doubt, as little was known about 'possible disturbances in the deeper layers of the personality', or about what the long-term effects of the war might prove to be.[40]

Certainly, after 1941 the school system nationally appears to have settled down. For example, whereas the average attendance figure of 90 per cent or so was typical in 1938-39 in elementary schools in large urban centres, the following attendance figures were attained in March/April 1943: Leeds, 89.4; Liverpool, 86.5; Newcastle, 85.9; Sheffield, 81.5; Hull, 83.8; Manchester, 83.0; and Bradford, 81.1.[41] Attendance at Birmingham for the four weeks ending 24 September 1943 was 87.0 for council schools, 84.6 for Special Schools, and 85.4 for Voluntary (Church) schools.[42] There was also a major increase in the provision of nursery schools, which would permit more mothers to undertake war work. Birmingham is a good example here: there were places for only 410 nursery children in 1939; by December 1945 there were 59 nursery classes in 41 centres, with 1,551 children on roll, and three pre-war nursery classes with 437 children on roll – a total of 1,988 children in all.[43]

There was a further massive increase in the supply of milk in the nation's schools. By February 1942 about 80 per cent of elementary children were receiving milk in special third-of-a-pint bottles. Again, to quote the Birmingham statistics, in March 1939 only 55 per cent of elementary children took milk; by 1944 83 per cent were receiving it. The schools meal service also shot ahead from May 1943 onwards. In Birmingham the total number of meals served in 1940 was 694,092. By 1944 the total had jumped to 4.2 million.[44] Thus, the original provision of free meals for necessitous children gave way to the idea of providing for the majority of normal children as standard practice.[45] There was also a distinct rise in the numbers in secondary schools sitting both the School Certificate and the Higher Schools Certificate. The School Certificate entries rose from 80,673 to 91,853 in 1945. Entries for the Higher Certificate increased from 12,811 in 1940 to 19,206 in 1945.[46]

This settling down of the school system, accompanied by a significant increase in welfare services in the schools, saw also an increasing demand for post-war reform of the whole apparatus of state education. First, there was the so-called Green Book, issued by the Board of Education, setting out possible reforms. Next, there was a White Paper in July 1943, and the Norwood Report in the same year on the curriculum and examinations. Finally, the Butler Education Act 1944 was passed, which made all education free in local authority schools, divided educational provision into three stages, Primary, Secondary and Further, and proposed that the school leaving age be raised to 15. County colleges providing part-time education to the age of 18 were also to be established.

The beneficial effect of all these changes – the increased nursery provision, the welfare reforms in school, the improved public examination results, and the Butler Act – may all too readily be taken as evidence that after the upsets of evacuation and the air raids, the school system actually expanded and flourished. This would be very misleading, for it would be to ignore the increasing problems of the schools during the last three or four years of war. Of these problems, the teacher shortage became acute. As a result, class sizes increased dramatically. In the summer of 1944 Liverpool had 496 classes of over 50 children (in 1938, the figure was 293); Sheffield had 406 classes of over 50 (in 1938, only two); and Birmingham had 279 classes over 50, compared with 72 in 1938.[47] The recommended class size in Birmingham elementary schools was 40. This meant that over-large classes were being taught by more and more elderly teachers, some of whom had come back after retirement. Books and paper were in increasingly short supply, and many textbooks were out of print, due also to shortage of paper. The curriculum itself was not much affected, though young Physical Education staff were hard to find, and in some cases playing fields had been ploughed up and used to grow vegetables. It must also be remembered that though air raids were less of a threat in the last years of the war (with the exception of flying bombs and rockets in 1944), teachers had still to continue as fire-watchers and, in many cases, as members of the Home Guard, so they, too, suffered from strain and tiredness.

The children themselves were more difficult to control in the large classes of the last years of the war. In Birmingham, the Reports of the School Medical Officers for 1944 and 1945 both mention this. In 1941 it was said that an increased number of children got out of control because the father was in the services and the mother was out at work. Some of these children had already been disturbed by evacuation, and had been evacuated at between the ages of 5 and 7, when the effects could be more severe. The number of children referred to the Child Guidance Clinic in 1944 was 363, an increase of 61 on the previous year.[48] The 1945 Report made similar observations: there was a marked increase among the groups aged 6 to 8 who were considered uncontrollable at home or school, or both. This, it was thought, was to be expected, owing to evacuation and return to comparative strangers.[49] One suspects that the behavioural problems were not solely the fault of evacuation, but the fact of ill behaviour seems evident enough.

It is therefore suggested that the schools had their problems, even after the early days of evacuation and air raids were over. Some areas even had to face new problems of receiving evacuees after D-Day. Although the official scheme was wound up in September 1944, Birmingham had to provide accommodation for 6,000 children from London and the South East, then being attacked by the flying bombs and rockets. There was also some deterioration in the school medical and dental services towards the end of the war due to staffing shortages. No doubt the worst set-backs in the school system are to be found in the earlier years. Army tests in 1946 on recruits who had spent their last three years of school between 1939 and 1942 showed an all-round drop in scholastic attainment, and a serious increase in those graded backward and retarded, up to a year in London.[50]

More nursery schools, improved welfare services and better exam results in secondary schools should not be allowed to obscure the realities of life in the elementary schools, where the overwhelming majority of the nation's children were being educated. The reality was of over-large classes of fractious children being taught by elderly teachers with inadequate teaching materials in school buildings made awkward and dingy by bomb damage, blast walls and shelters in the playground, and lacking proper repair and decoration.

According to Professor Gosden, during the war there were both gains and losses – some decline in standards, but also a general reassessment of the importance of the national system of education that led to the Butler Act. He considers that the war increased the proportion of children who got very little education (children of socially inadequate groups), and of children who had supportive families, who gained a lot, and took public examinations.[51] This seems to avoid quantifying the first group, which presumably could have been quite large, given the difficulties of the time, and also estimating the size of the second group, which must have been relatively small. Indeed, it slides too easily over the school experience of the great mass of children in between the two groups who simply soldiered on, come what may.

What in fact did the children themselves think of it all in the Second World War? Evacuation stories are plentiful. Clearly, experience varied from one family to another. There are plenty of stories of callous treatment at the hands of receiving families who were more interested in what they were being paid than in the welfare of their young charges. There are other stories of kind treatment, and of tears on parting when the evacuees had to return home. Tradition has it that there were slum children who had never seen green fields before, and did not know that milk came from cows rather than from bottles in the shops. Some evacuees undoubtedly benefited from the healthier environment, put on weight, and, as HMI Arnold put it, gained a 'wealth of new stimulating experiences'. But it must be remembered that the number who stayed in the reception areas for any length of time was limited, and that rural schools suffered as much as urban schools from staff shortages and inadequate supplies of paper, text-books, and other materials.

It seems fair to assume that the children who suffered the greatest trauma (apart, that is, from those who lost a parent) were those who remained with their parents in the big cities during the bombing of the early years of the war, and later during the era of the flying bombs and rockets. Raids were less frequent and somehow less frightening during the daylight hours, but nights could be very long and exhausting with little sleep. The sirens would usually sound soon after dark, and sometimes the all-clear would not be heard till dawn. Meanwhile, there would be eerie periods of quiet broken by the furious racket of anti-aircraft fire, the whistle and explosion of falling bombs, the clatter of shell fragments in the streets, and an occasional glimpse through the blackout curtains of the intense white light given off by incendiary bombs. These were the common experiences of many thousands of children at the height of the Blitz.

Going to school on the day following a raid, sometimes crunching through broken glass, and sometimes by a new route dictated by road closures due to unexploded bombs, could be something of an anti-climax, but could still be unnerving enough; and, of course, the school might no longer be there except as a heap of smouldering rubble, or might simply be closed for repairs. Deaths at school were unusual, since schools were closed at night, but they could occur in daylight raids, as at Petworth and Lewisham. In Birmingham alone the numbers of children under 16 killed by enemy action was 210, with 420 injured.[52]

However, only a minority of the nation's children actually experienced air raids during the Second World War. Far more, and indeed the majority, were affected by what happened in the schools during the six years of war as a whole. Here the record is uneven, but it is fair to emphasise again that at the beginning of the war the schools were closed and many children were left to roam the streets. The schools had not been re-opened long before the Blitz began, and attendance fell off steeply in the cities, in London even to vanishing point. After 1941 conditions certainly improved, and attendance rose again. But it is still hard to imagine that in the elementary schools anything like normal pre-war conditions were restored. All the difficulties already mentioned – teacher shortages, large classes, and the lack of educational materials – were real problems; more nursery classes, and more milk and school dinners were hardly compensatory factors. It is worth pointing out that any children starting school in September 1939 might have had no school to go to for some months and during the worst Blitz areas in London and other cities spent much time in truanting. Having made a nominal start in September 1939, he or she would leave school nine years later, having spent two-thirds of his or her entire school career under wartime conditions.

Childhood is a special episode in all our lives in which we gradually come to terms with the life going on around us, and is a matter of continuous adaptation, with moments of joy and elation, and at other times moods of dejection and despair. It is a bold historian who is prepared to generalise confidently about the private world of childhood as it was experienced at some point in the past. Still, it seems reasonable to suppose that children kept in touch with what was going on in the war by listening to their parents' conversation, or to the radio, or by skimming the headlines in the daily newspaper (if the household took one). There might also be wall maps in school. For the rest, they got on with their own preoccupations, playing the usual playground games, swapping bits of anti-aircraft shells found in the streets after raids (the brass nose-cones were a collector's item, as was anything recognisable as part of an aeroplane). Comics were read as usual; together with *The Hotspur* and *The Wizard*, *The Magnet* and *The Gem* were considered rather superior reading. In common with the vast majority of the adult population, children went often to the cinema, where after some months of the Blitz, performances continued in spite of air raid warnings. Toys were in short supply, and were sometimes improvised.[53] Sweets were rationed to 2 ounces or so a week, which would permit the purchase of a tuppenny bar of chocolate, though some shops might still offer the pre-war box of penny and ha'penny sweets for younger children to choose from, including sticks or twists of liquorice and Bassett's Sherbet Fountains (still on sale today). London teenagers would frequent milk bars, amusement arcades, and temperance billiard balls. The oldest might visit the Hammersmith Palais. There, Ted Heath and his Band played in the style of the American swing bands.[54] So, away from school, children got on with their own lives, within the limits imposed by the war, sometimes almost indifferent to it (the younger ones knew no other kind of life), absorbed in their own affairs, though they could be pierced to the heart by news of the death of a loved one.

Older readers may recall that in the days of their youth history examiners would require candidates to 'compare and contrast'. If at this point we undertake such an exercise, it is obvious that many children in Britain in both World Wars had one thing in common – the numbing loss or disablement of fathers and male relatives – more especially in the First World War than in the Second. The First World War also left an aftermath of melancholy and sadness that permeated life between the wars. In spite of evacuation, far more children were exposed to the trauma of air raids during the Blitz and after than in the First World War. After the Second World War there was less a sense of mourning and loss than after the first, Great War. The Second World War, of course, remained (and still remains) vividly in the popular memory as a great moral victory. Yet the Two Minutes Silence observed between the wars on 11 November was moved to the nearest Sunday and dropped from the school calendar (a development that has been partly reversed in very recent times). Schooling suffered in both World Wars, but more especially in the Second. Many working-class children at school between 1939 and 1945 had to contend with an increasingly impaired educational system, and among their ranks may be numbered the educational casualties of the Second World War.

Recommended reading

Charles, David and Wharton, Janet (eds), *Children in War: Reminiscences of the Second World War* (Nottingham: University of Nottingham, 1989)
Gosden, P. H. J. H., *Education in the Second World War* (London: Methuen, 1976)
Johnson, B. S., *The Evacuees* (London: Victor Gollancz, 1968)

Notes

[1] There were 5,611 civilian casualties, including 1,570 deaths, all but 157 of these being in air raids; Eric Hopkins, *Social History of the English Working Classes 1815-1945* (London: Edward Arnold, 1979) p223
[2] Hansard Parliamentary Reports, 10 August 1917
[3] Cited in J. S. Hurt, *Elementary Education and the Working Classes 1860-1918* (London: Routledge & Kegan Paul, 1979) p188
[4] G. A. N. Lowndes, *The Silent Social Revolution* (London: Oxford University Press, 2nd ed 1969) p189
[5] Reports of the Board of Education for the years 1916-17 (1918) and 1917-18 (1919)
[6] Attendance, Finance, and General Purposes Committee Minutes, 26 January 1917
[7] Ibid, 28 November 1919
[8] Ibid, 29 October 1915, 26 November 1915
[9] Report of the Board of Education for 1915-16 (1917), p10; and for 1917-18 (1919)
[10] City of Birmingham LEA Scheme (1920), p1
[11] Report of the Board of Education for 1916-17 (1918), p5
[12] Report of the Board of Education for 1917-18 (1919), p8
[13] Report of the City of Birmingham Education Committee, 1914-24, pp62, 63
[14] Ibid for all the figures quoted here, pp72, 67
[15] Minutes of the Hygiene Committee, 26 October 1917
[16] Report of the Board of Education for 1915-16 (1917), p5, and for 1917-18 (1919), p8

[17] Minutes of the Finance and General Purposes Sub-Committee, 23 May 1917; Minutes of the Education Committee, 28 September 1917

[18] Minutes of the Attendance, Finance, and General Purposes Committee, 21 December 1917, and the City of Birmingham Scheme (1920), p26; Minutes of the Continuation Schools Sub-Committee, 30 May 1919

[19] City of Birmingham Scheme (1920), p57

[20] Simon Heffer, *Like the Roman: The Life of Enoch Powell* (London: Weidenfeld & Nicolson, 1998), p5

[21] J. M. Bourne, *Britain and the Great War 1914-1918* (London: Edward Arnold, 1991) pp1, 178

[22] Simon Heffer, op cit, p6

[23] A. J. P. Taylor, *English History 1914-1945* (Oxford: Oxford University Press, 1965) p411

[24] Viscount Chandos, *The Memoirs of Lord Chandos* (London: Bodley Head, 1962) p152

[25] *The Times*, 22 September 1939, p6. See also S. Isaacs, *The Cambridge Evacuation Survey* (London: Methuen, 1941); R. Padley and M. Cole, *Evacuation Survey* (London: Routledge, 1940); R. M. Titmuss, *Problems of Social Policy* (London: HMSO, 1950); and B. S. Johnson, *The Evacuees* (London: Gollancz, 1968)

[26] For all the figures in this paragraph, see Eric Hopkins, *The Rise and Decline of the English Working Class 1918-1990* (New York: St Martin's Press, 1991) pp75-6

[27] Anne E. Houghton, 'Birmingham's Evacuation in the Second World War', BA dissertation, The University of Birmingham, 1985

[28] P. H. J. H. Gosden, *Education in the Second World War* (London: Methuen, 1976) pp36, 37

[29] Ibid, p37

[30] A. Sutcliffe and R. Smith, *History of Birmingham 1939-1970* (London: Oxford University Press, 1974) pp25-39

[31] P. H. J. H. Gosden, op cit, p42

[32] Ibid, pp41, 44

[33] Ibid, p42

[34] Letter from Arnold, 30 November 1941, PRO ED 134/143

[35] PRO ED 134/143

[36] P. H. J. H. Gosden, op cit, p46

[37] Ibid, p58

[38] Eric Hopkins, *Social History*, op cit, pp260-6

[39] P. H. J. H. Gosden, op cit, p43

[40] Report of the Birmingham School Medical Officer for the year ended 31 December 1940, p16; and Report for year ended 31 December 1941, p18

[41] P. H. J. H. Gosden, op cit, p68

[42] Birmingham Education Committee Minutes, 1941-45

[43] Report of the Birmingham School Medical Officer for year ended 31 December 1945, p17

[44] Report of the Birmingham School Medical Officer for the year ended 31 December 1944, p11

[45] P. H. J. H. Gosden, op cit, p196

[46] Ibid, pp87, 88

[47] Ibid, p103

[48] Report of the Birmingham School Medical Officer for the year ended 31 December 1944, p12

[49] Report of the Birmingham School Medical Officer for the year ended 31 December 1945, p17

[50] P. H. J. H. Gosden, op cit, pp73-4

[51] Ibid, pp3, 72

[52] Harold J. Black, *History of the Corporation of Birmingham* (Birmingham: Corporation of Birmingham, 1967) VI (1936-50) pp331, 333

[53] See Geoff Robinson, 'Inspired by Hollywood and Pulp Fiction' in David Charles and Janet Wharton (eds), *Children in War: Reminiscences of the Second World War* (Institute of German, Austrian and Swiss Affairs, University of Nottingham, 1989)

[54] Ibid

Chapter 2

The British experience of bombing

Adam Smith

In the first years of the 20th century a small band of experimenters scattered across the globe was making rapid progress towards a centuries-held ambition: the achievement of practical, powered flight. In the lighter-than-air field, Count Ferdinand von Zeppelin's experimental airship LZ.I hovered ominously over Lake Constance for the first time in July 1900. A little over three years later, at Kitty Hawk, the Wright Brothers' Flyer made the first powered, controlled and sustained flight by a heavier-than-air craft.

It was clear to all the early pioneers of aviation that their work held potential to bring great change to human society, and so it transpired. As the centenary year of powered flight approaches, we can look back and begin to appreciate the fact that aviation had an enormous impact on the 20th century. The ability to fly unhindered from country to country, eventually continent to continent, revolutionised world travel, trade, leisure, communications and, not least, war. The military possibilities of aviation had been obvious for centuries and were not lost on the likes of Zeppelin, whose primary aim throughout was to provide Germany with a new and potent weapon. The Wright Brothers, too, for all their belief that the aeroplane would bring great benefit to society, understood (and attempted to exploit) the military potential of their invention.

In the summer of 1909 Louis Blériot succeeded in flying across the English Channel from France to England. This feat sent shock waves (out of all proportion to the flight's significance as such) across Europe, the United States and the British Empire. For the first time people sensed that a new way of life was about to break upon them. H. G. Wells was one of many commentators who understood that there now existed, albeit in rudimentary form, a means of circumventing the Royal Navy's supremacy: '…in spite of our fleet, Britain is no longer, from the military point of view, an island,' he wrote shortly after Blériot's flight.[1] As with so many other things, Wells was proved prescient – twice within the next 35 years Britain was subjected to a serious campaign of bombing against its towns and cities.

The two World Wars remain the only time the people of mainland Britain have been attacked from the air. On the face of it, the two experiences appear so different as to make serious comparison almost impossible. Whatever measure we care to apply – be it casualties, material damage, social effects or military impact – the Second World War appears in every case to have been vastly more intense.

Bombing barely occupies a place in the popular consciousness of the First World War. This is quite understandable because, for all the attention Zeppelin airships and Gotha bombers aroused at the time, the vast majority of Britons were not in serious danger from air attack. In four years of war there were about 110 air raids, the large majority on London and South East England. A total of 350 tons of bombs were dropped, causing 1,414 deaths.

Although these figures are not entirely trivial the crucial point is that, compared to the land campaigns in Europe and elsewhere, they pale into insignificance. Looking back at a war where several thousand military casualties were commonly sustained per day, air raids seem almost inconsequential. Even during the war itself *Punch* felt moved to comment: 'The space which our Press allots to Air Raids moves Mr Punch to wonder and scorn. Our casualties from that source are never one-tenth so heavy as those in France on days when GHQ reports "everything quiet on the Western front".'[2] And so it is that a modern British schoolchild might easily study the First World War in some detail and learn little or nothing of the German strategic bombing offensive.

The same could hardly be said for the Second World War, where bombing – commonly known as 'the Blitz' – forms an intrinsic part of the popular imagery and teaching of the entire conflict. This is not without good reason. In over 1,300 serious air raids (12 times the 1914-18 total) an estimated 70,000 tons of bombs (200 times the 1914-18 total) were dropped, destroying half a million houses, damaging 4 million others and killing 67,000 British civilians (60 times the 1914-18 total). The large majority of these casualties were sustained in just one year of serious bombing, between mid-1940 and mid-1941. During this period it was not uncommon for the entire First World War tonnage and casualty totals to be exceeded in just one night.

The importance of domestic bombing relative to the armed conflict abroad was also far greater during the Second World War than the First. Strikingly, for the first five years of conflict the total number of civilian casualties exceeded total casualties in the armed forces – only after D-Day did the military bear the heavier burden.

In view of this it is hardly surprising that history judges the two experiences in vastly different ways. The essence of bombing in the First World War (both attack and defence) was ineffective, immature, experimental and peripheral to the overall conduct of the war. In comparison, bombing in the Second World War was intense, developed and a central part of war strategy for every one of the main combatant nations.

It is not the intention of this chapter to disregard these overriding facts. Nevertheless, for all the obvious contrasts between the two wars, a comparative study of Britain's exposure to aerial bombardment is a far from pointless academic exercise. In the first place, knowledge of one can help inform the other – for instance, First World War experiences often had a strong influence on responses to bombing in the Second.

There are also interesting parallels and observations to be drawn from the reactions of British society to being bombed. These are of interest not only to students of history, but also tell us much that is of relevance today. Bombing is still very much with us, and despite the progress in technology since the first half of the 20th century, past experiences can be instructive. It is doubtful whether the apprehension felt by Londoners in 1915 at the approach of the first Zeppelins, and the similar anxiety felt 30 years later as V2 rockets dropped without warning from the heavens, are very different from more recent feelings in Baghdad or Belgrade as residents contemplated the approach of cruise missiles, smart bombs and 'stealth' aircraft.

Compare an 11-year-old child's experience of bombing in Southend, on 12 August 1917...:

'...the third bomb fell within ten feet; fortunately it fell in the flower bed and I was blown down and found myself with two others in the crater burnt by heat and coughing up cordite, one like me still alive. I got out and ran, unfortunately taking the same direction as the planes – the next one fell in front of the Technical School, and a Salvation Army girl and also a man trying to get protection along a low one-foot wall were both killed. The girl was mutilated beyond recognition. I was not so lucky this time getting a piece of shrapnel in my neck... The sights in the hospital (a small cottage type) were terrible to behold. Only two doctors, so the nurses had to operate on the minor cases. Two ladies were helping in a third whose breasts were completely shot away, she was singing "Abide With Me". Australian soldiers billeted in the town brought in children in their arms with legs shattered, some with limbs missing. The sights in that hospital were terrible to behold.'[3]

...with that of an 18-year-old RAF cadet's experience of bombing in London, 20 February 1944:

'My elder sister and I got into the habit of watching nightly London air raids from the front porch of our parent's house, via its view south towards the capital with Alexandra Palace silhouetted on the horizon. Ever exciting as a teenager were the flashes and staccato detonations of the anti-aircraft batteries at the top of our hill. We stayed under the porch to avoid the jagged shrapnel from the exploded AA shells which hissed down all round, often breaking pieces of glass in my father's greenhouse... A Dornier 215 dropped a stick of three HE bombs across East Barnet. One landed on the main road surface twenty feet in front of us. All I remember was a blue flash out of the corner of my eye before I woke up spitting ceiling plaster out of my mouth as I lay on the hall floor. I had caught the full bomb blast on my left side and that arm felt funny, whilst my left leg looked at a peculiar angle on the floor beside me in the torchlight flashes from the air raid wardens who had appeared. My sister was lying beside me but I didn't know she'd been killed outright until about a fortnight later in hospital when I had recovered sufficiently to be told.'[4]

It is an obvious point to make, perhaps, but in whatever war we might choose to study the direct victims of bombing, those people unfortunate enough to find themselves under the path of a falling bomb will share a similarly violent and devastating experience.

There is sometimes an amateurish and vaguely comical perception of bombing in the First World War, perhaps influenced by old film footage of tiny bombs being hand-dropped from light aeroplanes. This may have been true of some early attacks, but, especially as the war went on, it should not be imagined that air raids were necessarily light in either their ferocity or casualty rates. The following extract, from a letter written by a nurse, describes the aftermath of the first daylight raid on London, on 13 June 1917. Twenty Gotha aeroplanes had attacked Liverpool Street Station and East End docks and warehouses:

'It was the most ghastly experience I've ever had & I hope I'll never have another. We had no warning that they were coming at all – we suddenly heard the guns going & then the bombs began to fall … the students cleared the hospital square of the beds and patients in just over 5 minutes – I've never seen anything like the way they worked – & then the casualties began to pour in – we filled every bed & had 7 theatres working till after midnight and we none of us went off duty until after that time. It was colossal & the surgery was just like a battle-field – they were all brought in there to be sorted and the floor for a little bit was strewn with dead & dying.'[5]

This raid resulted in 162 killed and 432 injured – figures that bear comparison with all but the worst of the Blitz. Indeed, relative to the weight of bombs dropped, casualty rates in the whole of the First World War were significantly higher than in the Second. Every ton of bombs that landed on Britain from 1914 to 1918 killed an average of four civilians, whereas every ton dropped between 1939 and 1945 resulted in just under one death. These are interesting statistics. Instinctively one might assume casualty rates in the Second World War to have been greater – bombs were generally larger and contained more destructive power, whilst navigation, target location and bomb-aiming were infinitely more sophisticated.

There are a number of reasons for this apparent decline in the relative effectiveness of bombing, but the most fundamental is the significant difference in preparedness for air raids, in both the military and civil sense, between the two wars. The following eyewitness account was written in July 1917 by a 10-year-old child in London, the day after a raid of 22 Gothas killed 57 people and injured 193 (the spelling and grammar have been left uncorrected; the emphasis is mine):

'My Dear Grannie. I hope you are well. On Saterday we were just looking for some chepe pealoes [potatoes] when we saw 20 German earplains up over our heds and the english were shooting at them and they flew right over our house and we could see all the pufs of smoke and now and then one of them would be covered with smoke and then came out again quite safe *and all the traffic were flying along and all the people were standing out on the street and every boddy stopped buying and ran out in the street and the streets were full of people*.'[6]

During the First World War the bomber had the important advantage of novelty and surprise, and this is reflected strongly in the high casualty rates on the ground. In the example quoted above, the Gothas were able to fly over London in broad daylight and drop their bombs with virtual impunity – and this despite a top speed of less than 100mph. The defending anti-aircraft guns were few in number and primitive in effectiveness, and although almost a hundred British aeroplanes were scrambled, their performance was so poor (particularly the inability to climb quickly to the altitude of the bombers) that no successful interception was made. Once over the city, the bomber crews had little trouble in finding inviting targets. The words '…and the streets were full of people' are a common feature of eyewitness accounts of both day and night raids in the First World War. In the absence of a well-organised system of air raid warning or shelter many people were caught out in the open, with unfortunate results.

It is possible to find examples in the First World War of almost every single one of the well-known responsive measures employed during the Second World War – including air raid warnings, shelters, blackouts, gas masks, evacuation, searchlights, barrage balloons, anti-aircraft guns and airborne fighter defences. However, we should not misinterpret this as evidence of any great national preparedness for bombing. The British response to air raids in the First World War began as a series of improvised measures taken at local level, and there was rarely any national consistency or co-ordination. Particularly at the start of the war, the weight of emphasis was on the individual. If you wanted shelter you could find it yourself; if you wanted a gas mask, well there was plenty of advice in the newspapers on how to make one. The following describes something of the 'do it yourself' atmosphere in London in late 1914:

> 'People began to make preparations for Zeppelin raids: one big wine dealer was reported to have let several of his cellars, and people we knew had furnished theirs and slept with big coats and handbags for valuables by the bedside. Most people had water or buckets of sand or fire extinguishers on every landing. We rather laughed at this at first but by degrees everyone came round to taking certain precautions.'[7]

Matters did improve a little as time went on, and throughout the First World War – as in many other areas of domestic life – intervention from both local and national government in air raid precautions increased gradually. A blackout was enforced in certain areas, policemen and other volunteers were employed to warn the public of raids, and public information posters, leaflets and press notices were distributed concerning appropriate action to be taken in the event of a raid.

Nevertheless, precautions in the First World War are best characterised as having been hastily improvised in the face of a new form of warfare and were usually conceived at a local level. In comparison, Britain in the Second World War was infinitely better prepared and organised, and although policy was often implemented by local government, it was conceived and driven at national level. By 1939-45 there had been significant improvements to both military defences and civil precautions against the bomber, which had lost its advantage of surprise.

Defence was now informed by a degree of past experience. In addition, most technological advances since 1918 – such as improvements to fighter performance and anti-aircraft guns, and particularly the development of radar – assisted defending rather than attacking forces.

The scale of organisation in preparation for air raids during the Second World War took on immense proportions. At the height of the Blitz, in December 1940, there were several million people recorded as employed in some sort of precautionary work. This included 1,050,000 people employed in Air Raid Precautions (ARP) as wardens, rescue and first aid party members, report and control centre staff and messengers; 265,000 people employed in the National Fire Service; 230,000 people employed in Casualty Services; and 35,000 members of the Observer Corps. A massive number of people were also employed as fire-watchers, protecting important buildings and factories against incendiary attack. Although the actual numbers involved appear to be unrecorded, it was a compulsory duty for any male between the age of 16 and 60 not otherwise employed. There were also national schemes to provide adequate public and private shelters, widespread distribution of gas masks and other anti-gas devices, proper early warning sirens, evacuation of women and children from urban areas, and a sustained and co-ordinated programme of public education about air raids, including practice air raid drills.

The differences between the two wars were often a direct result of learning from previous experience. For example, an analysis of casualties in the First World War revealed that the majority of deaths and injuries were due to wounds in the body caused by flying glass. Thus, in urban areas during the Second World War it became almost universal practice to paste strips of scrim across windows, a measure designed to reduce injuries from this source. The civilian population was also made more generally aware of the danger of flying glass, and that being out on the streets during an air raid could be extremely hazardous. This more safety-conscious state of mind, policed by the national network of vigilant wardens, helped to minimise casualties.

Although there was no formal policy for evacuation during the First World War, there was a degree of unofficial evacuation from threatened areas. This was particularly the case in late 1917 when, in response to stiffening defences, the Gotha bombers switched to moonlight raids. A London doctor's diary entry is typical of the mood at that time:

'Monday, September 24th: Decided to leave my house for six days before the full moon and for six days afterwards. My maids were very panicky and wanted to be with their own people. The Friars is in a very dangerous position, being near the Bridge, the Castle and the Aeroplane Works.'[8]

A report to the Cabinet on 17 October 1917 referred to production being disrupted by large numbers of workers leaving the East End of London owing to air raids. A visitor to Brighton in September reported it packed with thousands of people who had left London until the end of the harvest moon, so as to be out of danger.[9]

The trend of unofficial evacuation recommenced at the outbreak of the Second

World War, when advertisements appeared in newspapers offering 'immune from air raid' accommodation in places such as Bath, Bognor Regis and North Wales. Once the air raids began, during periods of heavy attack there were often large movements of people – for example, police estimated as many as 100,000 people (approximately 40 per cent of the population) left Coventry each night as the city suffered in November 1940.

But once again the Second World War saw a much greater degree of state intervention, with official schemes for voluntary evacuation. At the outbreak of war about 1.5 million women and children were moved from cities into 'reception areas'. Apart from its positive effect on casualty rates, evacuation had a social impact on families and communities, both rural and urban, which is still felt and debated.

For those remaining in areas under attack, exhaustion – from a combination of anxiety and lack of sleep – was a factor in both wars. The worst any area suffered in the First World War was three or four consecutive nights of bombing, and there were usually lengthy gaps between raids to recover. Even so, there are ample references in contemporary documents to people feeling 'washed out', 'completely fagged' and 'war fatigued'.

Here, however, the sheer intensity of operations in the Second World War far surpassed anything previously experienced. Commencing on 7 September 1940, for example, London was raided on 68 consecutive nights. The following account was written just a week into this campaign, but even at this early stage the strain was beginning to show:

> 'For Londoners there are no longer such things as good nights; there are only bad nights, worse nights and better nights. Hardly anyone has slept at all in the past week. The sirens go off at approximately the same time every evening, and in the poorer districts, queues of people carrying blankets, thermos flasks and babies begin to form quite early outside the air-raid shelters. The Blitzkrieg continues to be directed against such military objectives as the tired shopgirl, the red-eyed clerk, and the thousands of tired and weary families patiently trundling their few belongings in perambulators away from the wreckage of their homes.'[10]

It is said that sleep – or lack of it – almost replaced the weather as a topic of conversation; strangers in the street would greet each other thus:

'Tired this morning?'

'Dreadful, isn't it?'

Of course it was not just falling bombs that kept everybody awake all night, but few people complained about the sound of the big anti-aircraft guns. Quite the opposite, in fact, for one of the most politically sensitive issues of both wars was the whole topic of 'giving it back' to the enemy. One RAF veteran of the Second World War recalls:

> 'The AA guns were grand to hear at night… To give the impression that we had more AA guns than the pitifully few we actually had, the Bofors would

fire off from one street then dash to another and repeat the procedure giving the impression of a large battery.'[11]

It is worth pointing out here that the gun crews in question were unlikely to have been trying to impress the Luftwaffe – it has been estimated that 30,000 shots were fired for every German plane shot down in September 1940. Rather, a more important function of anti-aircraft artillery was to boost civilian morale. Here is an extract from a letter written in September 1916, describing the barrage that met a Zeppelin raider over Lowestoft:

> 'Star shells; red hot hotchkiss tracers arching in great curved sweeps through the sky; shrapnel; pompoms; six inch guns; five or six land batteries of 12 pounders and every conceivable thing afloat for miles around, blazing, banging, roaring, shrieking and barking at it for all they were worth, Hades for leather one on top of the other all over the place for minutes on end. It was the fair limit and talk about hornet's nests! It will learn them to come here I guess.'[12]

It clearly mattered not to the writer that the airship was unharmed and went on to bomb London; there was something psychologically satisfying about the barrage, perhaps as an antidote to fear, that can be detected in both wars. I now recall watching TV footage of a massive barrage over Baghdad during the Gulf War and wondering how on earth they expected to hit supersonic aircraft and cruise missiles with Second World War technology artillery pieces. In retrospect, perhaps that was not the point.

Incidentally, the spent shells and falling shrapnel that emanated from AA guns are likely to have killed and wounded more civilians than they did German airmen. Even so, most people would still have opted for firing the guns at whatever cost rather than feeling impotent under the bombs of an enemy.

This strong public desire to hit back manifested itself in many other ways – for example, in the First World War there was public pressure for pre-emptive air strikes on German airship bases, and the colourful Noel Pemberton Billing was elected to Parliament as the self-appointed 'Member for Air', advocating a policy of reprisal raids against Germany. In the Second World War there were demands for action against V1 and V2 launch sites, and few greater boosts to national morale than the first 'thousand bomber raid' on Cologne.

For many people, in both wars the principal inconvenience of enemy bombing was not the threat of falling bombs but the deeply unpopular lighting restrictions. A survey of public morale, conducted annually through the Second World War, ranked the blackout as the most disliked aspect of the entire war effort, and there is little to suggest that the First World War blackout was any more popular – in some parts of the country the approach of winter stimulated protests against the compulsory darkness.

Apart from the sheer inconvenience of being unable to see, many faced the indignity of a court appearance for failing correctly to observe the blackout – there were over a million prosecutions for lighting offences during the Second World

War alone. This has much to do with the rather negative 'Put that bloody light out!' stereotyping of ARP wardens, and it should be pointed out that almost 7,000 civil defence workers were killed or seriously injured in the line of duty from 1939 to 1945.

Apart from damaging national morale in the manner described above, the blackout was also intrinsically dangerous. A striking feature of newspaper reporting, particularly during the Second War, is the large number of accidents that can be attributed largely or wholly to the lighting restrictions. During the first four months of the Second World War no fewer than 4,133 people were killed on Britain's roads. This seems a stunningly high figure, and to it can be added the many others who died as a result of walking into rivers, canals and lakes in the darkness, falling down steps or through glass roofs.

It would be very interesting to conduct a detailed investigation as to whether the severe blackout imposed in the Second World War actually had a net benefit. For all the damage it caused to morale and human life, there is no evidence that Luftwaffe crews found target location any more difficult than their counterparts 25 years earlier, when blackout restrictions were far less intense – even in London, for example, every fourth street lamp remained lit during the First World War.

Rumour and folk myth about bombing played its part in daily life in both wars. On a bicycle trip through Lincolnshire in 1915 one man heard tales of a devastating air raid on Hull, Cromer, Driffield, Beverley and Grimsby, with various rumours of great wreckage and loss of life. He later discovered the truth was that a total of two bombs had been dropped, one in an open field and the other in a garden. Similarly, in December 1940 Manchester's Town Clerk was forced to make a public statement about the extent of casualties following recent air raids, in order to check false rumours. In one case it was rumoured that several hundreds had been killed in a direct hit on a shelter, when in fact only a few were injured.

Rumours were not simply limited to exaggerated reports of damage and death. One of the most persistent and widespread folk myths of the 1914-18 war, the subject of various contemporary books and newspaper articles but never substantiated, involved a mysterious car that travelled the lanes of rural England by night, guiding Zeppelin raiders to their target by way of its headlamps.

A Second World War rumour circulated in the North West that East Enders had petitioned Churchill to end the war; this was more than matched by one about a pro-peace demonstration in Liverpool during its 'May Blitz' of 1941. Until the Clydeside Blitz of 1941, a sizeable proportion of Glasgow's population believed that they would be kept safe by a magnetic element in the Scottish mountains that dislocated aircraft engines!

It is difficult to be precise about the extent to which fear of bombing played a part in daily life; all we can be sure about is that it existed to some degree. Both wars began with a climate of considerable public apprehension about what the effects of bombing might be. In both cases, reality turned out to be somewhat different from the grim predictions of destruction and heavy casualties.

Prior to the First World War H. G. Wells's book *The War in the Air* (1907), in which a fleet of airships attacked and bombed New York, had helped lay the foundations for a general fear of the new German wonder-weapon – the Zeppelin.

In the press the Zeppelin was extolled as a symbol of the German spirit of invention, and its capabilities were graphically described in scenarios of mass bombardment, or grossly over-exaggerated, like the rumour that they could transport 350,000 troops from Calais to Dover in one night. Before the war, in both Britain and France, there had been 'Zeppelin scares' or outbreaks of 'Zeppelinitis' – frequent sightings of mysterious airships.

In a similar way, the atmosphere before the Second World War was full of even more apocalyptic visions of death and devastation. In 1937 British experts reckoned that Hitler's Germany could cause 600,000 casualties in the first 60 days of a major bombing campaign over Britain. Again, literature and the popular press fuelled a public feeling of apprehension, and this time they seemed to have hard facts to work with – the Condor Legion's bombing of the undefended town of Guernica during the Spanish Civil War:

> 'I always recall a large, front-page newspaper picture showing a mother, dishevelled and blood-spattered, sitting in the street with shattered buildings just behind her head, holding up her tear-stained face towards the cameraman … across her soiled lap lies the tiny body of her young child. I'm quite sure that particular shot brought home to all who saw it the realisation "My God, this could be my street, my family, any time" – it did me.'[13]

The atmosphere prior to both wars has been likened to a patient fearing a visit to the dentist – the British people suffered far worse agonies of anticipation than the realities of the treatment could possibly have produced. There was a common over-exaggeration of both the capabilities and numbers of aircraft employed by the enemy, and an under-estimation of defensive capabilities. Equally important was a fundamental ignorance of the hazards of aerial warfare – dirigibles and aeroplanes were never hampered by bad weather, never lost their way, always hit their targets, always caused widespread panic and demoralisation.

Despite the fact that events did not turn out as predicted, the psychological power of bombing persisted throughout both wars. There was often a particular fear of a particular kind of weapon. Take the Zeppelin – which at the start of the war was the German 'wonder-weapon'. Even today, in photographs, these airships have a particularly broody and menacing appearance; to many of those in Britain's towns and cities, as the Zeppelins approached for the first time, they were terrifying:

> 'Another man & myself were up in town, when the warning came that 5 hostile airships were over the London area. We rushed to the nearest taxi and told him to drive us back to Woolwich. He refused, being terrified of the Zeps. So I got the nearest policeman to come and talk to him. He still refused, so was arrested.'[14]

September and October 1916 was an important turning point in the war against the Zeppelin. Three times in four weeks a pilot of No 39 Squadron destroyed a German airship, twice in full view of the capital's population:

'On October 1st, we had the satisfaction of seeing a Zep brought down in flames, and a great cheer, which sounded like a dull roar in the dark night, rolled over London from millions of people. It was the most wonderful and queerest sound I shall ever hear.'[15]

Suddenly, the previously invincible Zeppelin was demystified – revealed to a euphoric population as vulnerable. Enormous crowds flocked to visit the Zeppelin crash sites and the successful pilots were feted as heroes.

One of the clearest similarities between the two British experiences of bombing is a definite public self-consciousness in the documentary evidence, a perception that both individuals and the nation were living through historic times. This final pair of extracts – the first from a nurse visiting the burned-out wreck of a downed Zeppelin, the second from a schoolboy in the Liverpool Blitz – illustrate one manifestation of this sense of history:

'The inhabitants of the village were smart enough to empty their dustbins and proceed to fill them with souvenirs which they offered for sale. It was certainly a great day for Cuffley and all supplies of beer etc in its one hotel (which is more like a barn than anything else) were soon sold out, and although more than a week has now elapsed a crowd still seems to go up and inspect the spot and dig and scratch for souvenirs.'[16]

'Going to school the next morning was a treasure hunt. Shrapnel could be dug out of the walls and the large wooden doors of Goodison Park football ground provided a rich harvest. Sometimes there were fewer kids in the class but I didn't really think about it. My mother promised Hell and Damnation if I played in the bombed houses. They had been known to collapse at odd times after a raid, but they were our equivalent of an adventure playground. There was a rumour that one of the kids had found a foot shortly after a raid – you never knew your luck.'[17]

The Scottish Museum of Flight contains dozens of souvenirs of bombing. There are paper knives, napkin rings, walking sticks and plaques fashioned from pieces of Zeppelin girder. There are fragments of bomb casing, bullets and even parts of V1 flying bomb and V2 rocket. The first German bomber to be brought down on British soil in the Second World War landed intact about 5 miles from where the Museum is now located. Now according to the historical record this aeroplane, a Heinkel 111 and obviously of considerable intelligence interest, was put under police guard and shipped off for a thorough inspection. However, at least 50 local people have authentic pieces of this aeroplane – and not all of them small! Like most war souvenirs they have little or no intrinsic value – by and large they would normally be considered worthless pieces of scrap metal. However, these souvenirs are permanent mementoes of a time, a place and an event perceived as important by their collectors, and have an immense cultural value. In the same way, probably the most jealously guarded souvenir in the world right now is any piece of the American stealth fighter that came down over Kosovo in 1999.

Souvenirs remind us of the central point about bombing in the First World War, the Second World War, or indeed any war – that bombing is about people. Bombs are dropped by people on people for human ends, and they have human consequences.

Recommended reading

Brown, Mike, *Put That Light Out! Britain's Civil Defence Services at War 1939-45* (Stroud: Sutton Publishing, 1999)

Calder, Angus, *The Myth of the Blitz* (London: Pimlico, 1992)

Cole, Christopher and Cheesman, E. F., *The Air Defence of Great Britain 1914-1918* (London: Putnam, 1984)

Gibbs-Smith, Charles, *Aviation: An Historical Survey from its Origins to the end of World War II* (London: HMSO, 1970)

Kennet, Lee, *The First Air War, 1914-18* (New York: The Free Press, 1991)

Steel, Nigel and Hart, Peter, *Tumult in the Clouds: The British Experience of the War in the Air 1914-18* (London: Hodder & Stoughton, 1987)

Notes

[1] Quoted in Charles Gibbs-Smith, *Aviation: An Historical Survey from its Origins to the end of World War II* (London: HMSO, 1970) p148

[2] Quoted in Trevor Wilson, *The Myriad Faces of War* (Cambridge: Polity Press, 1986) p510

[3] Manuscript recollections of Mr A. S. Hare about a raid on Southend, 12 August 1917, Liddle Collection, University of Leeds, 'Zeppelins' file

[4] Typescript recollections of Mike J. W. Rogers about a raid of 2 February 1944, Second World War Experience Centre, Leeds

[5] June MacDonald, letter dated 17 July 1917, Liddle Collection, University of Leeds

[6] Annie Sheelah Magan, letter dated 8 July 1917, Liddle Collection, University of Leeds

[7] Winifred Tower, quoted in Nigel Steel and Peter Hart, *Tumult in the Clouds: The British Experience of the War in the Air 1914-18* (London: Hodder & Stoughton, 1987) Chap 7

[8] W. Pritchett Diary, Liddle Collection, University of Leeds

[9] Trevor Wilson, op cit, p509

[10] Quoted in Angus Calder, *The Myth of the Blitz* (London: Pimlico, 1992) p33

[11] Recollections of Squadron Leader I. R. Dick (retd), Second World War Experience Centre, Leeds

[12] Letter written by Captain Ashby, dated 3 September 1916, Liddle Collection, University of Leeds, 'Zeppelins file', item number 34

[13] Mike Bree of Penzance, quoted in Mike Brown, *Put That Light Out!: Britain's Civil Defence Services at War 1939-45* (Stroud: Sutton Publishing, 1999) p3

[14] Sir Andrew Clark, 2nd/Lt Royal Field Artillery, Letters, Liddle Collection, University of Leeds

[15] Private W. Pritchett, recollections, Liddle Collection, University of Leeds

[16] From 'A F.A.N.Y.'s Experiences at Cuffley' by M. Moseley-Williams in the F.A.N.Y. newsletter, October 1916, Liddle Collection, University of Leeds

[17] Recollections of Brian H. Riley, Second World War Experience Centre, Leeds, accession number 99.233

Chapter 3

The experience of manipulation: propaganda in press and radio

Stephen Badsey and Philip M. Taylor

From the very outset, propaganda played an important, central and significant role in the conduct of both World Wars. In the First World War, largely unexpected nationally co-ordinated propaganda campaigns, together with the institutions to mount them, evolved only slowly as the conflict unfolded. From its very inception, however, the Second World War featured propaganda campaigns both larger and more sustained than anything ever seen before in wartime. This propaganda was expected to have a major impact not only in helping to sustain morale on the home front but also as an additional weapon that could help defeat the enemy. Ultimately, it was industrial and economic power, not to mention the sheer weight of armed force, that determined the outcome of the Second World War. Yet, as one British historian has recently written, we should not

'…underestimate the importance of propaganda, for the Second World War more than any other conflict since perhaps the seventeenth century, was a battle for men's minds. Entire peoples had to be convinced that the war was worth fighting and that ultimate victory was assured.'[1]

The idea of the home front or of a 'nation in arms' that emerged during the First World War, of mobilising entire populations for sustained conflict, affected all men, women, and even – or especially – children. By 1918, in the United States, children were being encouraged to collect peach stones for gas masks as part of the war effort. The best-selling Christmas toy for British children was a miniature tank. German children were subject to virtual 'brainwashing' through their schoolteachers as a propaganda arm of the state; and the French also attempted a conscious 'mobilisation of childhood' for the war.[2] These children would be the younger adults of the Second World War, and in one important sense that was the major difference between the two wars: civilians already had a very good idea of what the experience would be like, or at least believed that they did. Moreover, the perception that the next war would be even more 'total' in its impact upon civilians had been reinforced throughout the 1930s by a mounting fear of the bomber aircraft against which there was thought to be little defence. These fears and anxieties were reinforced in the new medium of sound cinema, most popular amongst younger people aged 16-34, with newsreel footage of the devastation of Guernica during the Spanish Civil War, and feature film depictions of mass bombing raids such as in Alexander Korda's *Things to Come* (1936).

At first, in Britain, the fear of an aerial apocalypse outweighed everything, so much so that on the outbreak of war all cinemas were closed in order to minimise bombing casualties. But as the population settled down for a long-drawn-out conflict, the recognition came that morale on the home front would require significant attention, including the distractions from war's realities offered up in the nation's 'picture palaces'. Within about a year, so all-pervasive was propaganda that the experience of being propagandised could almost be defined as the experience of having lived at the time. Few who experienced either World War could have stood back from the times they were living through and say 'that is just propaganda', except perhaps at specific moments or during specific campaigns. In other words, there was little sense of actually being manipulated. The challenge for the wartime British Coalition Government was how to unite the entire nation behind the war effort – to change the 'us and them' society epitomised by one of the earliest wartime posters that 'Your courage Your cheerfulness Your resolution will bring us victory'. Within a year, with Churchill as Prime Minister, the posters were imploring 'Let Us Go Forward Together'.

Propaganda was in fact everywhere, part of the fabric of wartime society. Although there was a widespread popular belief that propaganda was an activity that only the enemy conducted, whereas democratic governments largely told 'the truth', the manipulation of opinion to achieve desired thoughts and actions was a major wartime activity for every combatant government. It took the form of posters, picture postcards, china plates and ornaments, biscuit tins, cigarette cards, songs and music, and in some cases was capable of almost infinite applications, as with the British (and later also American) 'V for Victory' campaign of the Second World War. This was propaganda generated almost automatically by the home front for itself, and it is where the inevitable patriotism of a nation at war coincides with the propaganda employed to sustain popular support for its continuation.

The two most significant forms of mass media shared by both World Wars were print journalism and the cinema, which between them also played a major part in home front propaganda. The major difference was, of course, the existence in the Second World War of an entirely new form of mass communication in the form of the radio. This was used as a weapon against the British public in the form of German broadcasts led by William Joyce ('Lord Haw-Haw') and colleagues, and by the BBC in its broadcasts to occupied Europe. Its immediacy, together with its ability to communicate directly with the vast majority of homes that possessed a wireless receiver, regardless of class, education or wealth, brought news of distant events directly into the Second World War parlours, kitchens and living rooms. It was exploited in radio speeches, particularly by Winston Churchill, as well as in the famous 'Postscript' broadcasts by J. B. Priestley from the summer of 1940 onwards, credited by the BBC at the time with 'the biggest regular listening audience in the world'.[3] The importance of radio, in terms of both news and escapist entertainment for a population listening collectively as individuals, was what prompted Asa Briggs to refer to the Second World War as 'the war of words'.[4]

The mass media enabled populations, even outside the cities, to feel that they were all to some extent part of the conflict. Unlike radio, however, for which outside broadcasts were still in their infancy, both print journalism and film propaganda depended heavily on access to the fighting fronts. For the British, one thing that the two World Wars had in common was that in both instances it took more than a year for the military authorities to accept fully the need for war reporters and cameramen on the battlefield. The needs of military secrecy and operational security far outweighed the needs of civilian morale. In the First World War, after the initial war of movement, it was not until late 1915 that reporters and cameramen were allowed to visit the Western Front. Although reporters were allowed to follow after – but not accompany – the Field Force to France in 1939, the organisation and understanding for them to function properly did not really exist until 1941. This was because the Ministry of Information (MoI), which sprang into existence on war's outbreak (unlike in the First World War, when it took until 1918 for a full Ministry to emerge), was to a large extent still fighting the last war. Despite five years of pre-war planning, the MoI was ill-equipped initially to deal with the demands of this even more Total War – such as the boredom of the 'Phoney War' and the pressure of the Battle of Britain and the Blitz. The principal channel for communicating Government decisions and policy to the people as a whole thus became a source of media and public scepticism as it went through a series of ministerial and poorly thought-out organisational changes, until it finally settled down under the guidance of Brendan Bracken after 1941.[5] Thereafter, for those that cared to notice in their regular visits to the cinema that the film they were watching had been 'passed by the British Board of Film Censors', the MoI's influence was ever present and rarely noticed.

During the First World War, for countries such as Great Britain in which adult literacy and a mass popular press dated from less than a generation beforehand, newspapers were probably the single most important way in which the civilian population learned about the war. Even in small villages, pages from the local newspaper would be pinned up in the main square for passers-by to read. The extraordinary political power given to the 'Press Barons' of the time also reflected the insecurity felt by politicians towards the mass electorate. Political leaders and senior military officers deferred towards newspaper owners, and sought to control war reporters, in a way that was unique to that particular war.[6] But the rules (both official and unofficial) governing press censorship and the role of the war reporter were essentially the same in both conflicts. In Britain a draconian system of censorship and punishments existed, but was scarcely ever applied except in the case of outright press defiance of the Government, and the newspapers were largely left to be self-regulating. By the Second World War, the Press Baron had already begun to fade from the scene, and a number of factors ranging from the shortage of wood-pulp for paper to the emergence of alternative news sources all combined to lessen the importance of newspapers at the expense of the 'newer' media of film and radio. But a conflict of such a scale was bound to increase levels of public hunger for war news, and newspapers became part of the daily diet and variety of news that was now available.

For a relatively new mass democracy like Britain, the message for any government wishing to influence morale was simple: control the sources of information, and you could control the prevailing messages. For this reason, all sources of news from abroad coming into the country via the wire services, together with any film footage or radio copy were carefully scrutinised at source. Any material that was subsequently released for public consumption could then be packaged according to the editorial style of the medium concerned. And while the news was carefully controlled or censored, views were left alone. The result was the appearance of a free media functioning as if normally and with a variety of viewpoints, when in reality the spectrum of information on which such viewpoints could be formed was much narrower than it appeared.

Cinema-going was the most popular form of working-class recreation in Great Britain and many other countries, with two or three visits a week being not unusual, and this gave film a great significance for home front propaganda. The three main forms available were feature films, documentary films, and newsreels. In the First World War British official propaganda organisations made virtually no feature films. Having obtained permission to film on the fighting fronts they began in earnest with a pattern of full-length documentaries, starting in 1916 with *Battle of the Somme*, before changing over in late 1917 to a newsreel format. Quite a lot is now known about these films and public attitudes towards them. Generally, the civilian population welcomed what appeared as their realism, as giving them the belief that they shared in the experience of the fighting troops. But there is little to suggest a close connection between British official propaganda film policy and the fluctuations of British home front morale.[7]

The major change in film technology between the wars was the introduction of sound. Cinema-going remained an extremely popular form of entertainment, with children, women and younger couples making up a high proportion of cinema audiences, and factual newsreels remained a popular part of the programme, through to the start of the Second World War. Indeed, audience complaints against newsreels in 1940 were based chiefly on their lack of good news film, as they had been in 1915.[8] Whereas the development of actuality film propaganda in the First World War was from documentary to newsreel, in the Second World War both forms were used from the war's start. There were five main newsreel companies operating in Britain at the start of the war, which were all placed essentially under MoI control, as was the Crown Film Unit, which produced such effective early propaganda documentaries as *London Can Take It* (1940). With the exception of the RAF, the services were initially reluctant to venture into major documentaries until *Desert Victory* (1943) on the Second Battle of Alamein, followed by other major documentaries, culminating in the Anglo-American collaboration *The True Glory* (1945).[9]

Feature films also made much more of a showing in the Second World War, although as in the previous war this aspect of film making was largely left to Hollywood, especially once the United States entered the war as a British ally in December 1941. Through its control of celluloid nitrate (decreed an essential war material because of its use in munitions as well as in film-making), and through the certification and distribution system operated by the British Board of Film Censors, the Government could once again ensure that any audio-visual representation of what was actually happening in the war would comply with the official version. The difference between the start and end of the war is illustrated by the fact that there is very little footage of Dunkirk, whereas 450 reporters and cameramen were allowed to accompany the D-Day landings in June 1944.

Identifying the actual impact of propaganda on the civilians of the home front in any country of either war represents a major problem. For countries like Great Britain in the First World War, some anecdotal and statistical evidence has remained for historians to re-discover, but it has been easier to identify elite responses than those of the people as a mass. One French study of the home front and the Union Sacrée in the First World War, without citing any evidence, virtually discounts the impact of propaganda through the press in any war:

> 'In fact, the press, then as always, could not have played a crucial role in moulding public opinion because newspaper readers generally read into their papers what they want to read. That does not alter the fact that however small the influence of the French press may have been, it helped to cement French morale.'[10]

This lack of hard evidence for mass opinion has almost certainly distorted historical perceptions, since by definition domestic propaganda intended to gain mass support for the war was not aimed at elite groups, whose members tended to display a superior and rather condescending cynicism about the whole business. For them, manipulation was something that happened to other people. Robert Graves's poem 'The Persian Version', lampooning the style of First World War official communiqués, is a fine example from a temporary officer of that war. Agreeing with Graves's perspective, the American scholar Paul Fussell, a temporary officer in the Second World War, has loftily dismissed almost every aspect of wartime exposure to propaganda, with its 'attendant coarsening of responses' in comparison to the merits of real literature.[11]

By the Second World War the nature of information available on mass opinions had changed significantly. The extension of the franchise in both Great Britain and the United States had produced universal adult suffrage, and politicians were more comfortable with mass politics. The founding of the American Institute for Public Opinion by George Gallup in 1935, and its British equivalent a year later, provided statistical evidence for mass opinion in both countries in the Second World War, supplemented in Great Britain by the founding in 1936 of Mass-Observation. This at least offers some evidence for how people in the Second World War reacted to propaganda from their own side and from their enemies. However, Tom Harrisson, one of the three founders of Mass-Observation, was later equally dismissive of the extent to which propaganda actually manipulated civilians at war:

> 'Morale is not, in my view – and I spent years studying it in those days – affected by things like films. Pints of beer affect morale; being healthy and all

kinds of things affect morale. But official films never really came into it in people's own estimate of what affected them in the crunch... Looked at in the short term, on the spot, in the war, neither films nor posters nor leaflets, nor any other form of deliberate propaganda directed at the home front, really mattered at all. The war, morale and all that was going on at another level.'[12]

Some of Harrisson's own evidence accumulated for Mass-Observation suggests that this view is perhaps too extreme. But it is also an important caveat that responding to propaganda in support of the war might be only one aspect of the behaviour of civilians at war with a distinct agenda of their own. Small-town American cinema owners in 1917-18, by successfully displaying 'practical patriotism' in support of the war effort, lifted themselves and their industry from its 'flea-pit' reputation to reach local respectability by the 1920s. The Australian Government very consciously propagandised its own people with the military achievements of its armed forces in the First World War as an aspect of nation-building and national identity, including the provision of an official Australian war correspondent who later doubled as the official historian, Dr C. E. W. ('Anzac Charlie') Bean. The propaganda image and function of the British Royal Family during the Second World War was seen as essential not only to the preservation of their own role, but also closely related to the preservation of the British Imperial ideal.[13]

Despite racial segregation in the United States' armed forces, Hollywood films operating under Washington's guidelines frequently gave the impression of an integrated fighting service, while the new wartime labour role for women was tackled in such films as *Rosie the Riveter* (1944). Even the Disney Studios were recruited into the service of the nation at war, producing a range of films from short animated cartoons like *Donald Duck in Der Fuhrer's Face* (1943) to animated graphic inserts in documentaries like Frank Capra's *Why We Fight* films (1942-45), or even to full-length animated documentaries justifying the strategic bombing of enemy cities such as *Victory Through Air Power* (1943).

If audiences went to the cinema to escape the war for a few hours – and escapist feature-film entertainment remained more popular than war films throughout the Second World War – it was rare for them not to be exposed to some reference in the scripts that would resonate with their experience outside. Whether or not they noticed is to some extent irrelevant; as the MoI recognised from the outset, 'for the film to be good propaganda, it must be good entertainment'. The novelist George MacDonald Fraser, who experienced the Second World War as a Scottish schoolboy and later as a soldier in Burma, has commented on the image of the war portrayed by the feature film *The Way Ahead* (1944):

'We knew it was propaganda, and we were all for it; we would have felt neglected and let down if we hadn't been given it. It didn't convince us, or give us false illusions, nor did it mislead us... The British public were well aware of the score. They had a fair idea of what was true and what was false and what was glamorised and what was slanted; nobody ever sold them anything, except hope. The so-called propaganda of the wartime films was the equivalent of a pat on the back, and a reminder that what they were doing was worth while.'[14]

This has been a major discovery from both World Wars: people might be perfectly aware that they were being propagandised, but not actually care. The appeal of governmental propaganda was simply that, in wars of national survival, most people wished to believe the best of their own side, and the worst of the enemy. They obviously preferred good news to bad, but the conversion of Dunkirk into a national heroic legend revealed how bad news could be repackaged by emphasising the positive over the negative. The British military historian Sir John Keegan has described his own experience of being reassured by propaganda as a child evacuee in the Second World War:

> 'I also possessed an out-of-date edition of Jane's Fighting Ships (which I had read even more often than *Swallows and Amazons*), a complete set of Ministry of Information pamphlets on the war effort (Combined Operations, Bomber Command and the rest, now collectors' pieces and still a model of what sensible propaganda can achieve), and a file of articles on military subjects torn from Picture Post, including a particularly informative one on the Red Army.'[15]

Significantly, one Mass-Observation survey in January 1940 reported that:

> 'It would be as well for the newsreels to remember that the only class of the public that shows any marked opposition is the men under thirty of the middle classes. Of these 48 per cent dislike the newsreels, half of them giving as their reason that "there is too much propaganda".'[16]

In other words, civilians on the home front liked to be propagandised, but not too much. In a manner that defies simplistic explanation, the British home front propagandists of the Second World War even subjected themselves to self-knowing mockery. The Ministry of Information was satirised both by Tommy Handley's popular BBC radio show *ITMA* ('It's That Man Again') as the 'Ministry of Aggravation'[17], and by George Orwell as the 'Ministry of Truth' in his post-war novel *Nineteen Eighty Four*, despite the close association of the BBC with the Ministry, exemplified by Orwell's own wartime radio broadcasts and the value of Handley's show to national morale.

Many propagandists were themselves civilians, and thanks to memoirs and official records it is possible to reconstruct the attitudes of the time. If there is one image that is demonstrably false, it is of the cynical but all-knowing propagandist laughing behind his cloak as he deliberately manipulated facts or concocted lies to deceive his own people. It was not unknown for propagandists in either war to experience feelings of guilt and doubt about their work, either at the time or later.[18] This was especially true of those whose peacetime jobs depended on their credibility, such as reporters and political commentators. Even those who did not themselves hold such self-critical views have been subject to harsh criticism by some of their peers. Charles Lynch, a Canadian journalist of the Second World War, told fellow journalist Philip Knightley some decades later that:

'It's humiliating to look back at what we wrote during the war … and I don't exclude the Ernie Piles or the Alan Mooreheads. We were a propaganda arm of our governments. At the start the censors enforced that, but by the end we were our own censors. We were cheerleaders. I suppose there was no alternative at the time. It was total war. But for God's sake let's not glorify our role. It wasn't good journalism. It wasn't journalism at all.'[19]

Almost without exception, then, propagandists on all sides saw themselves as loyal members of the war effort, and they were no more in control of events than anyone else in wars of such gigantic scale and complexity. But in both World Wars the propaganda organisations of democratic countries sought to work with and through the existing institutions of mass media, which kept a notionally independent (or semi-independent) status. Although all the advantages were with the Government, this relationship between the 'wartime' and 'normal' functions of the media could easily have caused tension and disputes. But despite the celebrated and well-documented occasions when this did occur – the Powell and Pressburger film *The Life and Death of Colonel Blimp* (1943) being one example – what is remarkable, in six years of Total War, is just how few they were.

The words 'propaganda' and 'manipulation' carry considerable emotional and political baggage, which causes difficulty for historians trying to understand the phenomenon and how it was used as a weapon of war. Probably the first reasoned attempt to relate propaganda to warfare in the modern sense was the 1921 book *Die Propaganda als politisches Instrument*, published in Berlin by the German liberal intellectual Dr Edgar Stern-Rubarth.[20] The essential idea is that propaganda is a means of using the communications media in order to influence the behaviour of others to the advantage of the user. It is easy to see that this definition could equally be applied to advertising, or to ordinary political discourse; indeed, the United States' Government's chief propagandist for the First World War, George Creel, called his memoirs *How We Advertised America*. More recently, modern historiography has taken an extremely broad view of propaganda, taking almost any human activity from a novel to a football match to have some propaganda aspect.[21] Propaganda is now seen by most of its scholars as a value-neutral process of planned persuasion. Any moral judgement is more appropriately reserved for the motives of those doing the persuading; and through both World Wars democratic regimes were inclined more towards a 'Strategy of Truth' than 'The Big Lie'. This, of course, did not mean that they told the whole truth; it was their truth and they wanted their own people to believe it. It also needed one essential quality: credibility.

In the context of the two World Wars, however, propaganda took on much more sinister connotations than this. As a result of the experience of the First World War, there came to be implicit in the term the idea that propaganda – particularly enemy propaganda – could function as a form of spiritual virus, controlling the recipient in order to make him act against his own best interests. By the later stages of the First World War, and throughout the Second World War, the belief was strongly held on all sides that propaganda functioned chiefly as a means of attacking the enemy. If conventional weapons of warfare subjected the enemy to physical attack through violence, then propaganda could be used in conjunction with this to attack the enemy by persuasion – a simultaneous assault on the body and the mind.[22] A form of defensive propaganda aimed at a country's own people was therefore essential to counteract the effects of such an attack. Contemporary ideas distinguished between 'white propaganda' from an open and official source, which differed little from peacetime Government pronouncements; 'grey propaganda', which, although actually Government-funded and orchestrated, came apparently from non-partisan sources; and 'black propaganda', which purported to come from enemy sources for the purposes of deception (such as the famous 'black radio' stations run by the British in the Second World War). It was for these reasons that the Nazis had a Ministry of Popular Enlightenment and Propaganda, whereas Britain had a Ministry of Information and the United States had an Office of War Information.

In both World Wars the British in particular sought to preserve the credibility of their official organisations (and even the credibility of their 'grey propaganda') by stressing what Charles Masterman MP, who played a critical role in the First World War propaganda, called 'the propaganda of facts', based on the selection of information and force of argument rather than on deliberate falsehood. The British also consciously avoided the use of the term propaganda for their official organisations, preferring the more neutral 'Information', a device copied by the United States. The Germans had no such inhibitions, although in practice Goebbels's own position (if not the position of Hitler and the Nazi state) was often quite close to that of the British, namely that official media should not tell deliberate lies.

This position left the British vulnerable in both World Wars on the inevitable occasions that they failed to live up to their own standards. Early experience in the First World War demonstrated both how difficult obtaining the truth about the enemy could be in wartime, and also how the experience of one war might relate directly to the other. In the Franco-Prussian war of 1870-71, German troops encountered considerable difficulties with French irregular forces, known as *franc-tireurs* ('free-shooters'). Germany therefore planned for its invasion of Belgium in 1914 a deliberate policy of *Schrecklicheit* (translated by the British as 'frightfulness'), or terror-tactics, towards the Belgian civilian population in order to prevent any uprising of Belgian *franc-tireurs*.

Subsequently, German conduct in the invasion of Belgium was subject by the British to an enquiry under Lord Bryce, a respected professor of jurisprudence. The Bryce Report (or Report of the Committee on Alleged German Outrages) appeared in May 1915, describing German violations of the laws of war and humanity in Belgium in excessive terms, based on eyewitness accounts and other apparently solid evidence, although obviously its members could not visit occupied Belgium or question German witnesses. The report was widely used by British propagandists, particularly in the United States. But with hindsight it rapidly became apparent that Bryce had failed to distinguish genuine atrocities from fantasies or third-hand stories. Soon after the war it became fashionable to believe that all atrocity stories had been fraudulent. In 1928 the British MP Arthur Ponsonby in his influential book *Falsehood in War-Time* provided a collection of such imaginary tales from all sides in the war (although ironically even this book contained some of Ponsonby's own fictions). Tragically, this attitude – that accounts of deliberate and systematic atrocities must be exaggerated or fraudulent – played a part in the British and American reluctance to accept stories coming from occupied Europe in the Second World War, particularly regarding the fate of the Jews.[23] Hence, the distortions of one conflict helped to create scepticism about the realities of another, perhaps the most damning testimony to the effectiveness of falsehood propaganda.

In the First World War, propaganda organisations in Britain evolved together with the rest of the war effort, as initially a co-operative effort between the Government in London and local officials or businessmen, whose role in generating recruits helped produce the 'Pals' battalions of 1915.[24] At this early stage the links between these various propaganda organisations were informal and personal rather than institutional, and their ability to dictate propaganda themes for the home front was in practice quite limited. This 19th-century Liberal approach was replaced in the second half of the war by centralised government organisations run by newspaper-owners, increasingly challenging the direction of propaganda by civil service mandarins, whose focus was towards the persuasion of elites. This new policy of populist propaganda, very much in keeping with the ideas of Lloyd George as Prime Minister, culminated in his creation in the spring of 1918 of both the Ministry of Information and the Department of Propaganda in Enemy Countries (known from its headquarters as 'Crewe House'), under Lord Beaverbrook and Lord Northcliffe respectively, both prominent newspaper-owners.

The Second World War differed from the First World War in that it was preceded by peacetime propaganda, which was seen as an essential part of the prelude to war. For Nazi Germany, Fascist Italy and the young Union of Soviet Socialist Republics, propaganda was a way of life just as much as it was a way of war. Overt propaganda was not only expected to contribute to the solidarity of the state by motivating the population; it was also meant to support diplomacy by creating a false (and exaggerated) idea of military strength in the minds of potential enemies. The great military parades of the era had multifaceted meanings as exercises in propaganda, none more so than the Nazi annual Nuremberg Rallies, as exemplified by Leni Riefenstahl's film *Triumph of the Will* (1935).[25] By 1939, propaganda – whatever its label – was recognised just about everywhere as a necessary function of modern government.

Great Britain, France and particularly the United States (which had strong isolationist traits and hoped to avoid a European war altogether), had no comparable propaganda organisations between 1918 and 1938. But the British Government in particular worked through a series of informal arrangements and 'gentleman's agreements', both within Great Britain and outside it, which meant that some of its propaganda was quite well prepared when the Second World War finally broke out. This was especially true of film, where the existence of such

British inter-war propaganda organisations as the Empire Marketing Board provided an institutional base for the film-makers of the British documentary movement, and indirectly for the Crown Film Unit. The RAF also began its venture into film propaganda as early as 1935, culminating in *The Lion Has Wings* (1939) shortly after the war's outbreak.[26] More professional productions were to follow in what has been termed a 'golden age' for British cinema.

For the Second World War the British determined that a centralised Ministry of Information should exist from the start. There was no institutional continuity with the original MoI of the First World War, and those responsible for creating a new shadow MoI from 1935 onwards concluded that the old MoI papers had been destroyed or relocated to other parts of government soon after its closure in December 1918. The new MoI exercised a number of important co-ordinating functions, but never really achieved the importance of its First World War predecessor. Only Sir John Reith of the BBC earned himself notoriety during his own brief tenure as Minister of Information in the spring of 1940 by calling for the BBC to be placed under the Ministry in order to generate propaganda (a term he had no hesitation in using) and for the Cabinet to sanction a propaganda policy based on the idea of 'the nation's war'.[27] A Department of Propaganda in Enemy Countries was also created at Electra House under Sir Campbell Stuart in September 1938, and this organisation was responsible for ensuring that the first RAF raid of the war against Germany was a leaflet-dropping rather than a bombing mission. After a protracted Whitehall institutional fight, by August 1941 Electra House had evolved to become part of the Political Warfare Executive (PWE) under the Foreign Office. A further rationalisation in February 1942 provided British propaganda with its structure for the rest of the war, with the PWE broadly responsible for covert 'black' or 'grey' propaganda and for propaganda directed at enemy and occupied countries; while the MoI remained broadly responsible for 'white' propaganda and for the home front.[28]

The separation and sometimes duplication of functions of propaganda in Great Britain in both World Wars was in no way unusual. A similar rivalry existed in the United States in the Second World War between the Office of War Information and the Office of Strategic Services (originally the Office of the Co-ordinator of Information) on control of overseas and covert propaganda. Even in Nazi Germany, Goebbels's authority over propaganda was divided between three separate organisations, and also shared with the press and propaganda organisations of the German Armed Forces.[29] The point is that it would have been almost impossible for any government at war to have maintained a consistent propaganda line, had there not been already a great deal of solidarity of opinion within the country. While people did not take to the streets to celebrate in 1939, as they had in 1914, the relative degree of national unity and resignation to war's inevitability that greeted the Second World War belied the fears and anxieties of the 1930s.

It is important that for Great Britain in the first two years of both World Wars the principal target for propaganda, other than sustaining the home front, was the diplomatic one of bringing the United States into the war. In both World Wars Germany had the easier task in needing only to secure the preservation of United

States' neutrality; but on each occasion it was defeated by the British. In the First World War the chief target of British propaganda was the American civilian political elite (as defined by *Who's Who in America*), through a sustained series of 'grey propaganda' leaflets, newsletters and correspondence, the style of which was very much based on reasoned discussion. Who would describe a private letter from a member of the British political elite to an American friend-of-a-friend as propaganda? It was only after the war that the scale and organisation of the British effort became apparent, with a final mailing list of 260,000 United States' citizens. Compared to this, the enemy propaganda effort organised through the German Information Service in New York appeared clumsy and strident.[30] Indeed, on entry into the war in April 1917 the United States Government based its own propaganda organisation, the Committee on Public Information, on what it believed to be the British model, focusing chiefly on propagandising its own citizens to support the war effort.

Information about the scale and success of the British propaganda campaign began to appear in the United States in the inter-war years, with stories coming from British memoirs as much as from any other source. The chief architect of the British campaign, the Canadian-born novelist Sir Gilbert Parker, published his own account in Harpers in 1918. These revelations provoked a strong reaction among American elites at the belief that they had been manipulated into backing their country's entry into the war. By the 1930s the United States was on the alert for a second British attempt. In June 1938 Congress passed the Foreign Agents Registration Act, requiring all foreign agents to register with the State Department and the origin of their literature to be clearly marked, in a deliberate attempt to prevent another British 'grey propaganda' onslaught.

Once the Second World War began, American opinion became a regular target of conventional British diplomacy; but it was believed for some decades afterwards that the British continued to observe their 'no propaganda' policy in the United States. Only recently has it been shown that the British had instead simply been even more sophisticated in their manipulation. If an ostensibly private letter was a borderline case of propaganda, then what was a private dinner party? The British exploitation of contacts within the United States meant that they could run their propaganda campaign through American channels of communication, including the United States' own mass media. Rising support for Britain in the United States in turn contributed to President Franklin Roosevelt's more aggressive policy towards Germany and Japan, and so indirectly to Pearl Harbor.[31] That manipulation of the civilian population on this scale could happen twice without the United States being aware of it, the second time when it was specifically on the alert, is both a tribute to British skill and a warning that the 'experience' of being propagandised was sometimes so indirect as to be imperceptible. Against this remains the virtual impossibility of measuring the effectiveness of British propaganda in either war, and of assessing whether the behaviour of the United States would have been different had no such propaganda campaigns taken place.

Revelations about British propaganda in the First World War also had a dramatic effect on the style of propaganda in the Second World War. Just as the British closed down their propaganda organisations in 1918 in the belief that the war was won, so the new Weimar Government was making national and international moves to improve the image of Germany and its wartime conduct. Critical to this was the *Dolchstoßlegende*, the 'stab in the back myth' of German defeat. The myth, that the German Army had not been defeated in battle but betrayed by political collapse on the home front, was not simply a post-war political convenience for German politicians anxious to portray their country in the best possible light. It had been deliberately created in the last month of the First World War as a necessary part of the process of ending the war; and as such it represents one of the most successful examples of manipulation in either World War, practised by the German High Command on the German people.[32]

The belief that Great Britain was Germany's principal enemy in the First World War was also reflected in German propaganda, including the inspirational song for the German people, 'Hymn of Hate Against England' by Ernst Lissauer (which Field Marshal Wavell included in the Second World War in his own personal anthology of favourite war poetry).[33] The *Dolchstoßlegende*, in denying a German military defeat in favour of a collapse at home, attributed that collapse chiefly to a combination of two British strategies. One was the naval blockade of Germany, identified as a war crime by German interpretations of pre-war naval law. The other was a sustained British propaganda campaign against the German home front that had undermined civilian morale. This belief was reinforced by the claims of Lord Northcliffe's own men in the inter-war years. In fact, neither Crewe House nor the British as a whole ever mounted a large-scale propaganda campaign against the German home front, as distinct from an extensive leaflet campaign aimed at German front-line soldiers. In keeping with British foreign policy preoccupations, Crewe House's main target in 1918 was actually Austria-Hungary, although again directed at front-line troops as much as civilians.[34]

The belief that the deceitful lies of Crewe House had manipulated the minds of the German people was strongly promoted in the 1920s by one of the strangest alliances of convenience in history: a mixture of boastful British journalists and memoir-writers from Crewe House itself, critical British and European pacifists like Ponsonby, League of Nations supporters, American isolationists, and German proto-Nazis. German intellectuals such as Stern-Rubarth, who found a platform for his ideas in the United States in the 1930s, distinguished between 'positive' propaganda, advertising the strengths of one's own side, which he regarded as a legitimate function of government in wartime, and 'negative' propaganda, using lies to exploit enemy weaknesses, which he saw both as a war crime and as the characteristic Crewe House method.[35]

Adolf Hitler, who devoted considerable sections of his *Mein Kampf* to the issue of propaganda, took these ideas much further. Based largely on the *Dolchstoßlegende*, Hitler's position was that the mass of the people could be induced to believe any lie or falsehood that was given to them, providing that this was done at a simple and emotional level. So from the start of the Second World War, Nazi propaganda was heavily focused on the idea of doing to the French and British what they believed (wrongly) the British had done to them in 1918, by causing the collapse of the home front – hence the 'Lord Haw-Haw' broadcasts. In most countries, the view of intellectual and political elites on the vulnerability of 'the masses' to such propaganda lay somewhere between the snobbery of a Ponsonby and the utter conviction of a Hitler. The series of German military victories at the start of the war, and in particular the stunning collapse of France in six weeks in 1940, gave credence to the belief that there was at least something behind the idea of propaganda as an offensive weapon. After the fall of France, the Nazis devoted considerable time and skill to orchestrating the imagery of their victory, including the signing of the French surrender in the very same train carriage in the Forest of Compiègne that had been used in 1918. How better to send a message to the rest of the world that Germany had finally overcome the humiliation of defeat?

For civilian populations, the broad evidence from both World Wars is that elites and senior military commanders persistently under-rated their strength and resilience at war. In almost all cases there was no collapse of the home front unless there had also been an effective collapse of the armies first. In most cases this collapse also came only with the threat of physical occupation, or utter devastation by bombing. Even the marginal cases do not support the view of a home front collapse provoked by an enemy propaganda campaign. In both World Wars, in countries that had elections and parliamentary votes of confidence, there was little to support the view of widespread opposition to the war, and changes of government were always in the direction of a more effective prosecution of the war, not of ending it. The majority attitude in every belligerent country, including Great Britain, was that the war should be won; and the only widespread objection to propaganda was if it became blatant enough to be noticed, or so clumsy that it missed its target altogether.

In the final analysis, victory or defeat generated its own propaganda. Propaganda is most effective when it is credible, invisible or imperceptible. It works better with success than with defeat, despite the Nazis' ability to re-order perception about the events of 1918. Regardless of its effectiveness in the Second World War in getting people to 'Dig for Victory' or in any other specific campaign, words alone do not win wars. But they can affect the way they are conducted. Two words in particular had perhaps more impact on the conduct of both policy and propaganda in the Second World War than any others – 'Unconditional Surrender' – announced at the Casablanca Conference in January 1943. This is what differentiated one World War from another. There was to be no armistice this time, no treaty to provide defeated nations with excuses and opportunities for future conflicts, no points of negotiation or revision. This in turn denied the propagandists the line they had used in the First World War, namely the attempt to divide the German people from the German leadership. Those two words grouped all Germans together as war criminals, whether they supported Hitler or not. They ensured that Allied victory would be accompanied by a wholesale 're-education' of the German people who had elected Hitler to power.[36] They ensured the perception throughout the world of Nazi Germany as a criminal state for subsequent generations. But they also did something else, as Goebbels was quick to realise. By sending a message that Germany would have to fight to the very end, they gave credence to the Nazi propaganda slogan of 'Victory or Death'. By uniting the Allies in a 'People's War', they also united the people of the Axis powers behind their governments in a way that no previous domestic propaganda campaign had been able to do.

Recommended reading

Aldgate, Anthony and Richards, Jeffrey, *Britain Can Take It: The British Cinema in the Second World War* (Oxford: Basil Blackwell, 1986)

Cruickshank, Charles, *The Fourth Arm: Psychological Warfare 1938-1945* (Oxford: Oxford University Press, 1981)

Cull, Nicholas John, *Selling War: The British Propaganda Campaign Against American 'Neutrality' in World War II* (London: Oxford University Press, 1995)

McLaine, Ian, *Ministry of Morale: Home Front Morale and the Ministry of Information in World War II* (London: Allen & Unwin, 1979)

Messinger, Gary S., *British Propaganda and the State in the First World War* (Manchester: Manchester University Press, 1992)

Taylor, Philip M., *British Propaganda in the Twentieth Century: Selling Democracy* (Edinburgh: Edinburgh University Press, 1999)

Notes

[1] Brian Bond, *War and Society in Europe 1870-1970* (Thrupp: Sutton, 1998) p188

[2] John Toland, *No Man's Land: The Story of 1918* (London: Book Club Associates, 1980) p550; Gerard J. DeGroot, *Blighty: British Society in the Era of the Great War* (London: Longman, 1996) pxiii; Eberhard Demm, 'German Teachers at War', and Stephane Audoin-Rouzeau, 'French Children as a Target for Propaganda' in Hugh Cecil and Peter H. Liddle (eds), *Facing Armageddon: The First World War Experienced* (London: Leo Cooper, 1996) pp709-18, 767-79

[3] Quoted in Angus Calder, *The People's War: Britain 1929-1945* (London: Grenada, 1969) p160; Ernest K. Bramstead, *Goebbels and National Socialist Propaganda 1925-1945* (Michigan: The Cresset Press, 1965); Asa Briggs, *The War of Words: The History of Broadcasting in the United Kingdom*, Vol III (London: Oxford University Press, 1970)

[4] This was the title chosen by Lord Briggs for his multi-volume history of the BBC, *The History of Broadcasting in the United Kingdom* (1961 onwards). Subsequent scholarship has likened radio's role as providing an 'echo' of the war itself. See Sian Nicholas, *The Echo of War* (London: Oxford University Press, 1996)

[5] I. McLaine, *Ministry of Morale: Home Front Morale and the Ministry of Information in World War II* (London: Allen & Unwin, 1979)

[6] See Stephen Badsey, 'Haig and the Press', in Brian Bond and Nigel Cave (eds), *Haig: A Reappraisal 70 Years On* (London: Leo Cooper, 1999) pp176-95

[7] Nicholas Reeves, 'Through the Eye of the Camera: Contemporary Cinema Audiences and their Experience of War in the Film "Battle of the Somme"' in Cecil and Liddle, op cit, pp780-800; S. D. Badsey, 'Battle of the Somme: British War-Propaganda' in *The Historical Journal of Film, Radio and Television*, 3 (2) (1983), pp99-116; Nicholas Reeves, 'The Power of Film Propaganda – Myth or Reality?' in *The Historical Journal of Film, Radio and Television*, 13 (2) (1993), pp181-202

[8] Jeffrey Richards and Dorothy Sheridan (eds), *Mass-Observation at the Movies* (London: Routledge & Kegan Paul, 1987) p418; Nicholas Hiley, 'Audiences in the Newsreel Period' in Clyde Jeavons, Jane Mercer and Daniella Kirchner, *The Story of the Century!: An International Newsfilm Conference* (London: British Universities Film and Video Council, 1998) pp59-62

[9] See Philip M. Taylor, 'Film as a Weapon In the Second World War' in D. Dutton (ed), *Statecraft and Diplomacy in the Twentieth Century: Essays Presented to P. M. H. Bell* (Liverpool: Liverpool University Press, 1995) pp135-54

[10] Jean-Jacques Becker, *The Great War and the French People* (Leamington Spa: Berg, 1993) pp326-7

[11] Paul Fussell, *The Great War and Modern Memory* (Oxford: Oxford University Press, 1975) p85; Paul Fussell, *Wartime: Understanding and Behavior in the Second World War* (New York: Oxford University Press, 1989) p149

12 Quoted in Richards and Sheridan, op cit, p11

13 Leslie Midkiff DeBanche, *Reel Patriotism: The Movies and World War I* (Madison: University of Wisconsin Press, 1997) pp195-200; John F. Williams, *Anzacs, the Media and the Great War* (Sydney: University of New South Wales Press, 1999); John M. Mackenzie, *Propaganda and Empire: The Manipulation of British Public Opinion 1880-1960* (Manchester: Manchester University Press, 1986) pp248-9

14 George MacDonald Fraser, *The Hollywood History of the World: From One Million Years B.C. to Apocalypse Now* (New York: William Morrow, 1988) pp223-4

15 John Keegan, *Six Armies in Normandy* (London: Jonathan Cape, 1982) p5

16 Richards and Sheridan, op cit, p392

17 Angus Calder, op cit, pp75-6

18 See Keith Grieves, 'War Correspondents and Conducting Officers on the Western Front From 1915' in Cecil and Liddle, op cit, pp719-35

19 Quoted in Philip Knightley, *The First Casualty: The War Correspondent as Hero and Myth Maker From the Crimea to Kosovo* (London: Prion, 2000) p364

20 Cited in Harold D. Laswell, *Propaganda Technique in the World War* (New York: Alfred A. Knopf, 1927) p227

21 Oliver Thompson, *Easily Led: A History of Propaganda* (Thrupp: Sutton, 1999) pp1-5; Bertrand Taithe and Tim Thornton (eds), *Propaganda: Political Rhetoric and Identity 1300-2000* (Thrupp: Sutton, 1999)

22 Philip M. Taylor, *Munitions of the Mind* (Wellingborough: Patrick Stephens, 1990) p11

23 Gary S. Messinger, *British Propaganda and the State in the First World War* (Manchester: Manchester University Press, 1992) pp70-84; Arthur Ponsonby, *Falsehood in War-Time: Containing an Assortment of Lies Circulated Throughout the Nations During the Great War* (London: George Allen & Unwin, 1928)

24 Peter Simkins, *Kitchener's Army: The Raising of the New Armies 1914-1916* (Manchester: Manchester University Press, 1988) pp79-82

25 Ian Kershaw, *The Hitler Myth: Image and Reality in the Third Reich* (Oxford: Oxford University Press, 1987) pp69-70; Peter Vigor, *Soviet Blitzkrieg Theory* (London: Macmillan, 1983) pp76-9

26 Harry Watt, *Don't Look at the Camera* (London: Paul Elek, 1974) pp137-43; K. R. M. Short, *Screening the Propaganda of British Air Power: From RAF (1935) to The Lion Has Wings (1939)* (London: Flicks Books, 1997)

27 Asa Briggs, *The War of Words*, op cit, pp161-8

28 Charles Cruickshank, *The Fourth Arm: Psychological Warfare 1938-1945* (Oxford: Oxford University Press, 1981) pp9-24; Asa Briggs, op cit, pp417-86

29 Susan L. Carruthers, *The Media at War: Communication and Conflict in the Twentieth Century* (London: MacMillan, 2000) pp84-5

30 Gary S. Messinger, op cit, pp53-69; Philip M. Taylor, *British Propaganda in the Twentieth Century: Selling Democracy* (Edinburgh: Edinburgh University Press, 1999) pp35-48

31 Nicholas John Cull, *Selling War: The British Propaganda Campaign against American 'Neutrality' in World War II* (Oxford: Oxford University Press, 1995)

32 Laurence V. Moyer, *Victory Must Be Ours: Germany in the Great War 1914-1918* (London: Leo Cooper, 1995) pp329-30, 335; Holger H. Herwig, *The First World War: Germany and Austria-Hungary 1914-1918* (London: Arnold, 1997) p425

33 Robert B. Asprey, *The German High Command at War: Hindenburg and Ludendorff Conduct World War I* (New York: William Morrow, 1991) pp135-6; A. P. Wavell, *Other Men's Flowers: An Anthology of Poetry* (London: Penguin, 1960) pp329-30

34 Philip M. Taylor, *British Propaganda in the Twentieth Century*, op cit, pp49-62

35 Ernest K. Bramstead, op cit, ppxxi-xxii

36 N. Pronay and K. Wilson, *The Political Re-education of Germany and her Allies After The Second World War* (London: Croom-Helm, 1983)

Chapter 4

The home front in Germany

Heinz Hagenlücke

On 1 January 1956, a few months before his death, the distinguished German poet Gottfried Benn recalled his emotions on New Year's Eve 1899:

> 'For the happy world of the old days it was a sensation that a new century was about to begin. Everybody was awake, everybody cheered, the church bells were ringing on midnight, one expected something very special, a sort of paradise's dawning in- and outside. My father stepped out of the parsonage and embraced the Dorfschulze (mayor), a big rich farmer, all people were embracing themselves, it was a night without snow or rain; it was a huge event.'

Then he continued to describe the entirely different emotions he had felt on New Year's Eve 1914 and 1944 and came to the bitter conclusion: 'Three New Year's Eves, embracing two generations, two wounded generations, for whom everything had become doubtful, for whom there exist some luxuries [*Komfort*] again, but no more substance [*Inhalt*]'.[1] Indeed, while most Germans had greeted the beginning of the 20th century with a huge amount of optimism, sometimes even hoping it was going to be the 'German Century'[2], during the next 50 years the basic experience of the people consisted not of the heavenly conditions of which Benn had dreamed, but of the gruesome upheavals of war.

This chapter focuses on the different experiences of the home front (*Heimatfront*) in Germany during the two World Wars. As there are innumerable aspects of the civilian experience in wartime, the analysis will confine itself to the most important ramifications of the wars for German society. First, it will demonstrate how the population entered war in both 1914 and 1939. Then it will debate the problems of nutrition and food supply, which were extremely important for maintaining the morale of the *Heimat*, showing to what extent the Nazis had learned from the previous war. This will be followed by an analysis of gender relations and of the most striking difference between the First and the Second World Wars, namely the suffering of the civilian population from strategic bombing. Finally, it will examine the conclusions that the German people drew from losing two wars within just one generation.

One of the most lasting and far-reaching myths in German history is the alleged enthusiasm with which the outbreak of the Great War was greeted among most Germans.[3] According to the myth, the so-called 'August-Experience'

(*Augusterlebnis*) of these days came quite near to a second *Reichsgründung* (foundation of the Empire); the deeply divided German people had finally overcome all barriers, become aware of themselves as being Germans, found themselves united in being one strong nation and re-discovered the nation as the most important component of their personal lives. The rightist journal *Tägliche Rundschau*, for instance, wrote that 'what Germany has experienced in these days was a miracle, a renewal of oneself; it was a shaking off of everything small and foreign; it was a powerful recognition of one's own nature'.[4] Two days later, Chancellor Bethmann Hollweg said in the Reichstag: 'Whatever the future may have in store for us, the 4th of August 1914 will be to all eternity one of the greatest days for Germany.'[5] Twenty years after the war, Gertrud Bäumer, one of the leading figures of the German women's movement, wrote in her memoirs, 'Never will we, the generation living in 1914, forget these last days of July… Many may jumble what came after with those weeks … but the last days and nights, the emotional content of those hours which ripped through the torrent of the event are unforgettable.'[6]

But were the crowds on the Berlin boulevard Unter den Linden really eager to go to war? Is war-enthusiasm the correct term for the dramatic events that took place in July and August 1914? Did the throngs really represent all Germans and did they actually leave behind all political, social and denominational limits, as the Kaiser had proclaimed in his famous speech, uttering, 'I no longer recognise parties or confessions, today we are all German brothers, and only German brothers'.[7]

In recent years, scholars have drawn rather a different picture of the people's mood in the summer of 1914, sometimes going as far as denying any enthusiasm for the war at all. There is still much speculation on the matter, and generalisations are extremely difficult. What can be said, however, is that the phenomenon was basically an urban one. In the large cities of the Reich, like Hamburg, Munich and especially Berlin, undeniably large crowds of people gathered during these days and welcomed the outbreak of the war with great enthusiasm. However, these throngs chiefly consisted of the well-educated bourgeoisie (*Bürgertum*) rather than people from the working class, who were afraid of the things to come. On the contrary, virtually until the very last moment, German unity was shattered by huge anti-war demonstrations, organised by the Socialists and trade unions, which sometimes mobilised more than 100,000 people.[8] What is striking is the number of young men and women from the high schools and universities who went on the streets and cheered the war. Yet this euphoria did not reach all urban Germany. In the provincial town of Darmstadt, for instance, there was as much anxiety as jubilation.[9]

The reactions to the outbreak of the war in rural parts of the country were very different. In southern Bavaria there were serious war scares already after the Austrian ultimatum was handed over on 23 July; the bulk of the population was in a state of dismay and shock. After the German mobilisation, no signs of war-enthusiasm could be found; on the contrary, most of the Catholic people interpreted the outbreak of the war as a divine retribution (*Heimsuchung*). The late Fritz Fischer, at that time living in the small town of Ludwigsstadt near the border between Bavaria and Thuringia, recalled Sunday 2 August 1914 very well, since on that day 'many men, accompanied by the women and children, came from the villages nearby into our small town to the railway in order to go to their regiments. I still hear the women's crying and lamenting when they said goodbye. The excitement would not end and my father could hardly find any sleep.'[10]

It is interesting, however, to notice that young, single men in their 20s welcomed the war as something like a great adventure and an opportunity to leave their neighbourhood. Georg Eisenberger, the leading man in the Bavarian peasant movement after the war, heavily complained about the fact that his father had managed to prevent the authorities from drafting him: 'I did not like it at all that I was not drafted because I always had the desire to learn more and to see something of the world,' he later wrote in his memoirs.[11]

No matter how common war enthusiasm actually was in the summer of 1914, the 'August experience' and the 'spirit of 1914' played an important role in bolstering German nationalism, helping to keep morale and political mobilisation very strong. The universality of the war experience gave real shape to the ideal of the *Volksgemeinschaft* (people's community). The Nazi movement regarded itself as the true heir of the *Volksgemeinschaft* and skilfully exploited the 'spirit of 1914' for its own purposes.

When Adolf Hitler seized power on 30 January 1933, many voices from the left could be heard saying 'Hitler means war'. Just a cursory reading of his book *Mein Kampf* would have been sufficient to prove that the Führer indeed ultimately intended to go to war and fight for *Lebensraum*. And yet, although the regime virtually from the first days of its existence was planning for war, one must not underestimate the great impact of the Nazi peace propaganda in the early years – home and abroad alike. In his famous *Friedensrede* (speech on peace) on 17 May 1933, the new Chancellor uttered these very impressive words:

'It is, however, in the interest of all that present-day problems should be solved in a reasonable and final way. No new European war could improve the unsatisfactory conditions of the present day. On the contrary, the application of violence of any kind in Europe could have no favourable effect upon the political or economic positions that exist today. Even if a fresh European act of violence had a decisive result, the ultimate effect would be to increase the disturbance of European equilibrium and thus, in one manner or another, to sow the seed of further conflicts and complications. The result would be fresh wars, fresh uncertainty, and fresh economic distress. The outbreak of such infinite madness, however, would necessarily cause the collapse of the present social and political order... It is the earnest desire of the National government of the German Reich to prevent such a disturbing development by means of its honest and active co-operation... Speaking deliberately as a German National Socialist, I desire to declare in the name of the National Government, and of the whole movement of national regeneration, that we in this new Germany are filled with deep understanding for the same feelings and opinions and for the rightful claims to life of the other nations. The present generation of this new Germany, which, so far, has only known in its life the poverty, misery, and distress of its own people, has suffered too deeply from the madness of our time to be able to contemplate treating others in the same way.'[12]

The Führer never got tired of mentioning the fact the he had served as a simple *Frontsoldat* (front soldier) during the Great War and that this fact alone would prevent him from starting yet another war. Hitler was portrayed as a man of peace, a statesman, who realised his aims through political skill and not by force. The German people, most of them still suffering from the deprivations of the last war, were only too eager to believe him. Furthermore, the amazing, peaceful, successes of the regime in the realm of foreign affairs, combined with the ceaseless propaganda, which skilfully used such brand-new techniques as motion pictures and, above all, radio[13], convinced people of the regime's essentially peaceful character. The overwhelming majority of the German population backed the oft-proclaimed restoration of the Fatherland's power and honour, but was absolutely unwilling to risk a major war in order to attain that goal. This was impressively proved during the Sudeten crisis in 1938. While most people felt that the German assistance for the 'repressed' Sudeten population was justified, the longer the crisis went on, the more feelings of anxiety and a general war-scare could be detected, sometimes reaching almost panic levels. The *Sicherheitsdienst* (SD – the security service of the SS) stated that, throughout the year, there been a 'war psychosis' lasting until the Munich agreement, and described the mood of the population as 'serious and depressed'.[14] At the peak of the Czech crisis on 27 September 1938, the American foreign correspondent William Shirer made the following observations on the streets of Berlin:

'A motorised division rolled through the city's streets just at dusk this evening in the direction of the Czech frontier. I went out to the corner of the Linden where the column was turning down the Wilhelmstrasse, expecting to see a tremendous demonstration. I pictured the scenes I had read of in 1914 when the cheering throngs on this same street tossed flowers at the marching soldiers, and the girls ran up and kissed them. The hour was undoubtedly chosen today to catch the hundreds of thousands of Berliners pouring out of their offices at the end of the day's work. But they ducked into the subways, refused to look on, and the handful that did stood at the curb in utter silence unable to find a word of cheer for the flower of the youth going away to the glorious war. It has been the most striking demonstration against war I've ever seen.'[15]

As a consequence of the war scares that arose during the Sudeten crisis, Hitler decided to change the direction of propaganda:

'Circumstances have compelled me to speak for decades almost solely of peace. Only through continued emphasis on the German desire for peace and intentions of peace it was possible for me … to provide the German people with the armaments that were always necessary as the basis of the next step. It goes without saying that such a peace propaganda which has been cultivated for years also has a doubtful side; for it can only too easily lead to the view being formed in the minds of many people that the present regime identifies with the determination and the will to maintain peace under all circumstances.'[16]

In fact, in 1939 the propaganda abruptly ceased to stress the peaceful character of the regime and instead emphasised the newly created military strength of the Reich.

Around 1 August 1939 newspapers were full of articles commemorating the outbreak of the Great War 25 years earlier. Their *leitmotiv* was to demonstrate the parallels between now and then, concentrating on the alleged *Einkreisung* (encirclement) of the Reich, for which once again the British were held responsible. Although the papers confirmed that there was a 'steel axis of European order and peace'[17] ranging from Berlin to Rome, at the same time it was reassuringly asserted that the Great German Reich and its mighty Wehrmacht were ready to repulse any attack on the national honour.

To a certain degree, the Nazis had become the victims of their own peace propaganda. The psychological effects of the former peace propaganda could not be totally neutralised until September 1939.[18] Therefore, there were few signs of war euphoria in August and September. People were scared and anxious, resigned and apathetic.[19]

On 31 August 1939 William Shirer noticed a nearly defeatist mood among the Berliners and wondered: 'Everybody against the war. How can a country go into a major war with a population so dead against it?'[20] When the British ambassador Henderson left the capital, Helmut James Graf von Moltke, great-nephew of the Chief of Staff in the First World War and a prominent figure in the German resistance against Hitler, made the following observations, watching the crowd on the Wilhelmstrasse: 'Maybe three or four hundred people stood there, but no expressions of disapproval or whistles could be heard; one had the feeling that they would start to applaud any moment. Absolutely incomprehensible. People are apathetic.'[21]

Of course, the Nazis had crushed any organised opposition to the regime and police terror prevented people from showing any signs of disapproval. However, the Government had managed to create a certain feeling, among the uninformed population, that Germany was being threatened by other powers. All this helped the Nazis to create a fighting spirit, albeit strongly tinged with fatalism, which was sufficient to allow them to conduct the war.

German women's experiences of the wars were fundamentally different from those of the men. They were not eligible for drafting and thus not directly confronted with combat or death. Yet the *Heimatfront* was basically a female phenomenon; women contributed heavily to the war economy and were responsible for maintaining morale at home. It has long been argued that the Great War marked the beginning of female emancipation in Germany by providing millions of women with a rewarding role in the war effort, and led to a remarkable increase in female employment.[22] In fact, at the end of the war more than one-third of the industrial workforce was female; in the metal-processing plants in the west, the number of employed women rose from 19,000 in 1914 to 106,000 in 1918. Nationwide, the female industrial workforce rose by some 17 per cent during the war.

However, recent research has come to the conclusion that the growth of female occupation would have happened regardless of whether war had intervened.[23] The figures reveal that there was a notable movement among women who were already occupied, that they left their jobs in domestic service, or in the textile and food-processing industries, for employment in the factories producing war-related products, particularly the metal, engineering, electrical and chemical industries. But when the armament industry hired female workers, it did so by recruiting women who were already in employment, basically from service and other industries. Ute Daniel therefore correctly notes: 'Once and for all we should abandon the image of the hordes of women who supposedly appeared on the labour market for the first time between 1914 and 1918.'[24] At the outbreak of the war, with their men leaving for the front, many women, particularly from the working classes, found themselves at the head of the household. Public assistance became available, such as subsidies paid to the wives and dependants of the drafted men.[25] The legal basis for these subsidies was a law dating from 1888, which had to be revised during the session of the Reichstag on 4 August 1914. The allowances were actually very modest; during the winter months the minimum allowance was 12 marks a month, dropping to 9 in the summer for the wives and 6 marks for other entitled persons – illegitimate children were excluded until 1915. Until late 1915 an estimated 4 million families were supported in this way – ie more than 11 million people in the entire Reich – and the allowances were raised to some 20 marks for the wives and 10 for the children; the large cities often granted special financial aid for medical care, food and clothing. But even before the war, the cost of feeding a working-class family of four was 34 marks a month, and in 1917 it had increased to some 75 marks. It was perfectly clear that no woman in the Fatherland could live on this allowance alone.[26]

The war affected gender relations in more than just economic terms. First of all, it caused long-term separations of millions of men and women, which led to a remarkable decrease in marriage and birth rates. In 1917 a male author observed prophetically that 'the relationship between husband and wife has not become closer or happier as a result of the war, but is now more difficult, complicated and loose… It will take a lot of effort to clear this field of rubble and to build something new.'[27] Indeed, due to the men's long absence, the wives and children often became alienated from the father, causing a doubling of the divorce rate in the 1920s. Relationships between men and women were constantly accompanied by a widespread male fear of female infidelity. As the war progressed, an image emerged of the adulterous middle-class *Kriegerfrau* (soldier's wife), who was previously supposed to be sexually pure. Although there is no statistical data available for this, the German public was alarmed by the fact that in 1916, for the first time, more women than men were divorced because of adultery. Finally, a new and dark figure caused immense anxiety among many men – the *Schlafgänger*, a male lodger who paid for his bed and thus provided some additional money for the family, 'but then joined the family in other ways'.[28]

After the war, the important role women had played in the war economy, and more generally in sustaining morale on the home front, was forgotten exceptionally quickly. It took more than 20 years for women's role in defence of the Fatherland to be publicly acknowledged. In the late 1930s, as the Government was preparing for another war, several books appeared, praising the efforts of the women on the *Heimatfront*.[29] The Nazis often proclaimed that, in the next war, the *Heimatfront* would be at least as important as the battlefield. They consequently provided some social benefits, especially for the women, in order to secure their loyalty.

Allowances for the Kriegerfrauen in the Third Reich were much more generous than in Wilhelmine Germany. The wives of the drafted men obtained an average rate of 75-85 per cent of their husband's pre-war income. Furthermore, as the state paid the whole rent, school fees, medical care and so on, no women from the higher social strata were actually obliged to work for their living. On the other hand, women who were forced to work expressly for financial reasons, before the war, continued to work during the war. For them, the war meant an intensification of labour and hardship.

The Second World War witnessed no dramatic increase of female employment in Germany. Mostly due to the Nazi ideology, which confined the woman to her traditional role of mother and wife, the regime refrained from calling too many women to the factories. From 1939 to 1941 there was even a small decline in the female workforce, from 14.6 million to 14.1 million, slightly increasing to some 14.9 million in late 1944.[30] The proclamation of 'Total War' in February 1943 did not alter things at all.

The predominantly female *Heimatfront* did actually hold. There were no mass strikes and food riots, unlike in 1914-18. In 1939 more than 12 million women were organised in one or other Nazi organisation. All of these women were not necessarily convinced National Socialists, and the war did bring some hardship. However, the manifold services provided by the Nazi 'welfare state', particularly for women, combined with 12 years of exposure to the propaganda of the *Volksgemeinschaft*, produced a sort of mass loyalty towards the regime.[31]

In the agricultural sector, Germany entered the First World War totally unprepared.[32] But, as the dreadful 'turnip-winter' of 1916-17 painfully demonstrated, providing food was at least as essential to the war effort as the production of weapons, and played a decisive role in maintaining the popular morale of the *Heimatfront*. Before 1914 about 30 per cent of the whole German population was engaged in agriculture. Yet the country was far from being self-sufficient, contrary to what officials from the mighty peasant association Bund der Landwirte might have suggested. Not only did German agriculture need the support of several hundred thousands farmworkers from Russia (ie Russian Poland), who migrated every year over the border, but Germany also imported about 25 per cent of her food, particularly eggs, dairy products and meat. Most animal fodder came from Russia, Argentina or the United Sates – sources that dried up from the beginning of the war.[33] Moreover, the British blockade very soon led to a 25 per cent drop in German agricultural production.[34]

However, the Army maintained its pre-war supplies, as did the people, with approximately 25 per cent of the population continuing to work in the fields, where they had immediate access to a variety of foods. This meant that 75 per cent of the population had to compete for the remaining half of the pre-war farm production. Furthermore, during the course of the war 3.3 million men, formerly working in agriculture, were called to arms. Their work could not be replaced by the female labour force or by the 900,000 POWs working on the land.[35] The result was an ever-increasing shortage of food. During the first period of the war, lower-class families, who spent most of their money on food, were particularly affected by the shortages, while the well-off were able to maintain their pre-war standards. The Government tried to counter this by imposing price ceilings on bread, milk, potatoes and other staples. As the prices for these products were kept rather low, these goods disappeared completely from the market, or farmers started producing goods that were not regulated. When the price ceiling for milk was introduced, for instance, within a short time a milk shortage appeared, since the farmers either produced butter and cheese, whose prices were not yet regulated, or simply slaughtered their livestock for sale.

In the end, a general increase of food prices was the consequence. The Government reacted by introducing rationing and creating so-called Imperial Corporations, the first being the Imperial Grain Corporation (*Reichsgetreidestelle*) in January 1915, its task being the rationing and distribution of grain. The Grain Corporation became the role model for the administration of rationing in all sectors of agriculture; at the end of the war, there were more than 40 different Imperial Food Corporations. Yet the system failed. The corporations were not able to provide enough food for the population. While some goods like soaps, fabrics, clothing and footwear became almost unobtainable from 1916, what was even worse was the fact that the nutritional quality of food steadily declined. It is in this circumstance that the words *Ersatz* and *Strecken* (stretch) got a new meaning in the German language. The first true ersatz was the famous K-Bread, K indicating both Krieg (war) and Kartoffel (potato). Coffee, the most popular non-alcoholic beverage in Germany at the time, was made of chicory, grain, turnips and acorns; milk and beer were stretched with water. At the end of the war there existed 837 officially approved preparations for Wurst (sausage) ersatz, more than 1,000 for stock cube ersatz, and 511 for coffee ersatz.[36]

One important consequence of the daily fight for food was the ever-sharpening conflict between consumers on the one hand and producers on the other. The friction went back some 20 years and had a rich tradition in German history.[37] But now producers and consumers not only criticised the Government for being incapable of distributing the food, but also became increasingly critical of each other.[38] The conflict was surely one of the greatest threats to the *Burgfrieden* and grew in intensity as the war dragged on. It did not end in 1918, since that winter's shortages were worse than ever, but underlined the dividing lines between city and countryside and created an antagonism that was still vital in the first years of the Weimar Republic.

Until 1916 the authorities had managed to keep the general shortage somewhat under control; nobody in the Reich was at the edge of starvation. But the disastrous potato harvest of 1916, when nearly half of the winter potato crop was destroyed by a fungus, changed things radically. Before and especially during the war, the potato – a cheap, easy-to-grow and high-calorie vegetable – played a central role in the German diet, especially for the lower classes. The bad harvest of 1916 was responsible for a food crisis in Germany on a scale unheard of in the previous 100 years. The undernourishment of the urban population was particularly alarming; hunger (and cold) became the common features of the *Heimatfront*. Finally, an ersatz potato was found for humans and animals alike – the turnip (*Steckrübe*) – a bitter-tasting and execrable vegetable with low nutritional value. In the winter of 1916-17, the notorious 'turnip-winter', nearly everything was made of turnips – coffee, marmalade, bread and so on.

An Australian woman, Ethel Cooper, who spent the whole war in the city of Leipzig, described daily life in Germany during the winter of 1916-17 in a letter dated 4 February 1917:

'Coal has run out. The electric light is cut off in most houses (I have gas, thank Heaven!), the trams are not running, or only in the very early morning, all theatres, schools, the opera house, and cinemas are closed – neither potatoes nor turnips are to be had – they were our last resource – there is no fish – and Germany has at last ceased to trumpet the fact that it can't be starved out. Added to that the thermometer outside my kitchen windows says 24 deg. Fahr. below zero. I have never seen that before.'[39]

In a letter from the spring of 1917, she suspected that some sausages might contain rat. A friend answered, 'Oh, I don't mind rat … but I have a real horror of rat substitute!'[40] In Bonn, R. O. Neumann, a nutritionist, undertook to live solely on the official ration between November 1916 and May 1917. As a result he lost a quarter of his body weight in seven months, dropping from 76.5kg to 57.5kg.[41]

In the winter of 1916-17 public soup kitchens offering a hot meal for the poor became a common sight in German cities. Of course, there was always the alternative of the black market. Many products not available through the regular channels were offered there, but at exorbitant prices that the lower classes in particular could not afford.

In spite of the Treaty of Brest-Litovsk, the much-longed-for *Brotfrieden* (bread-peace), from May 1918 onwards there was, once again, a serious food crisis. Thereafter, both the population at home and the Army were forced to live from hand to mouth. In June 1918 the daily bread ration fell from 200 to 160 grams. During July and August influenza swept through Germany, causing many casualties among the exhausted population. The rations of meat from August to October had to be cut down to 100 grams a week; four weeks of these three months were *fleischlos* (meatless). It was perfectly clear: Germany was on her last legs.

In a meeting of the War Cabinet on 17 October 1918, the prospects of further German resistance were discussed between General Ludendorff and the Social Democrat, Scheidemann, who proclaimed the German Republic on 9 November 1918. Asked by the General if he – that is the SPD – might succeed in raising the morale of the people, Scheidemann answered:

'That is a question of potatoes. We have no more meat. Potatoes cannot be delivered because we are short four thousand cars every day. We have absolutely no fats left. The distress is so great that one stands before a perfect puzzle when one asks: How does North Berlin live and how does East Berlin live? As long as this puzzle cannot be solved, it is impossible to improve morale.'[42]

To be sure, Germany was primarily defeated on the battlegrounds of the Western Front – it was the Allies and their weapons, not hunger, that caused her downfall. However, the constant shortages, the craving for food and the frightening prospect of fighting yet another hard winter campaign, after the failure of the spring offensive in March 1918, united to smash the people's will to go on with the war. Moreover, the inefficiency with which the authorities handled the food problem, combined with its unequal distribution, had seriously undermined the legitimacy of the Wilhelmine regime itself. In the autumn of 1918, the fighting spirit and the will further to resist had definitely vanished. For most Germans, what was even more frightening than having lost the war was the fact that the end of fighting did not mean the end of hunger, since the Allied blockade continued until the summer of 1919.[43] It was precisely under these circumstances that the Germans signed the Versailles Peace Treaty.

During the inter-war period, there was much discussion about the organisation of food supply, and most observers agreed upon the fact that the permanent food shortage had played a considerable role in the outcome of the Great War. The Nazi movement and particularly Hitler himself shared this opinion; the Führer, for instance, had learned as a vital lesson from the Great War that under no circumstances should food prices be increased, and he clung to that principle until the bitter end. The regime, being well aware of the lack of enthusiasm for the war, feared nothing more than another November 1918, and was thus eager to spare the 'average German' as much hardship as possible.[44]

In his recent book about the economy in the Second World War, György Ranki correctly states that 'the fields in which the lessons of the First World War were constantly applied during the inter-war period were not armaments, but food and agriculture'.[45] A few months after the invasion of Poland, Reichsbauernführer Richard Darré wrote in a secret memorandum: 'Agrarian policy ever since the seizure of power was conducted in preparation for an eventual war…'[46] That may be somewhat exaggerated, yet in September 1939 Germany had a stockpile of some 6 million tons of bread grain and 2.4 million of fodder grain. Moreover, the country was self-sufficient in potatoes and sugar-beet. Fodder and fats, however, were lacking, and these deficiencies turned out to be virtually insoluble during the war.

Ration cards were introduced in August 1939, covering 14 different kinds of goods; adult consumers were placed in four categories, ranging from normal to heaviest workers. As mentioned above, a shortage of agrarian labour had turned out to be a crucial problem in the First World War. In 1939 no more than 18 per cent of the workforce was occupied in agriculture, so that even before the war agriculture relied heavily on foreign workers, most of them from Italy. Furthermore, approximately 2.5 million men from the countryside were called to arms in 1939. The regime managed to solve this shortage of labour by slightly increasing the female workforce and, above all, by forced labour. Particularly after the attack on the Soviet Union, the numbers of POWs and forced civilian labourers in agriculture rose constantly to some 2.7 million people by August 1944; all in all, about 6 million foreigners were employed in the German economy, more than a third of them from the Soviet Union.[47] Without this huge amount of forced labour, there would have been a situation very similar to that of the First World War and the German people would have been much more severely hit by problems of food and food supply. The ruthless plundering of the occupied European countries enabled the German population to at least maintain their standard of living until the very last months of the war. When 'Operation Barbarossa' was planned, it was the clear intention of the regime to let millions of Russians starve to death rather than to do without Soviet grain and food for Germany.

In June 1942 Secretary of Propaganda Goebbels publicly stated that the war against the USSR meant a war for 'grain and bread, for a laid table of breakfast, dinner and supper… It is time that we finally pocket (*einkassieren*)'.[48] On the other hand, one should not overestimate the impact of these food 'imports' from the occupied territories. The Wehrmacht consumed the biggest part of it and the civil population at home gained little. The Ukraine, for instance, helped to feed the troops that had been sent to occupy it.[49] Still, these additional sources of food helped to feed a certain part of the population at home.[50] In 1941 the normal consumer in Germany received 2,400 calories a day, slightly dropping to 2,200 in 1943 and some 2,000 at the beginning of 1945. Milk, bread and potato rations were constant until the last months of the war.

The supply of goods other than food was much better than in the First World War. Civilian production was given a higher priority; as late as 1944 43 per cent of those being employed were producing items for civilian consumption. The fixing of maximum prices, which had proved to be absolutely ineffective during the First World War, was replaced by an absolute freeze of prices, rents and wages.

Tales of soldiers on leave, bringing home huge packets of food and other products, were often told in Germany during the war. On 17 April 1942 Maranja Mellin wrote in her diary:

'Daddy came back from Paris. He brought with him a lot of cloths, stockings, writing paper, liverwurst, carrots in meat, gloves, belts, shoes, soap, washing powder, and so on. Four pears and almonds, cinnamon and pepper. The whole table was packed full. That has become the custom nowadays in Germany. Wherever the men are, they are buying, in Holland, Belgium, France, Greece, the Balkans and Norway.'[51]

In fact, the comparatively well-functioning food supply enjoyed by vast parts of the German population was vital for creating loyalty towards the regime.

Until 1914, there had been a sharp distinction between the theatre of war and the peaceful *Heimat*, between soldiers on the one hand and non-combatants on the other. The First World War gradually altered this perspective, since the civilian population became more and more directly involved in the war due to modern techniques. Unlike the Second World War, most of the German population did not experience occupation or witness the devastation of their own country by enemy soldiers. It was aeronautics and airpower that introduced new experiences of war to the *Heimatfront*. In this context it has to be noted that aeronautics, from the start, played a significant role in the war. On 3 August 1914 the Government announced that French aeroplanes had dropped bombs on the railway line between Karlsruhe and Nuremberg; Chancellor Bethmann Hollweg in his speech on the same day publicly justified the declaration of war against France with these alleged air-raids against German cities – a fact too many people took for granted.[52] The war also produced a formerly unheard of type of war hero – the *Fliegerasse* (flying aces). As in other countries, pilots like Manfred von Richthofen, Hermann Goering and, most of all, Oswald Boelcke fascinated the public with their alleged chivalrous and comparatively decent style of fighting. The pilots became role models for many young Germans and something like early media celebrities.

Yet it is less known that, even in the First World War, the German people suffered from Allied strategic bombing. According to the official figures approximately 16,000 bombs were dropped over Germany during the war, killing about 800 and wounding roughly 2,000 people.[53] Due to the limited range of the British and French aeroplanes of the time, only the west and south-west of Germany were threatened by Allied air raids. How did the people react to this new and deadly menace? First of all it has to be noted that from the early days of aeronautics, the German nation had been fascinated by airpower and aeroplanes, which was commonly seen as a *Wunderwerk* of a brand-new technique.[54] The General Staff, however, had not yet discovered the military value and the possible danger posed by aeroplanes, so that at the beginning of the war no more than four cities were provided with anti-aircraft protection.[55] Thus, the early French air attacks on unprotected cities like Freiburg shocked the people. The neurologist Alfred Hoche described as the most common symptoms during and after an air raid trembling and paleness, mechanical praying, hysterical laughter, acute diarrhoea, increased excretion of urine, expanded thirst, nervous vomiting, asthma and dizzy spells.[56]

And yet people were still fascinated by aeroplanes and displayed some very strange attitudes towards aerial bombing. Reactions of fear and terror were as common as curiosity and almost childish interest. Hoche also observed that even during breaks in the air raids, 'children and adults could be seen on the streets, looking for shell splinters as a souvenir'.[57] The first air raid on the town of Saarbrücken in August 1915 caused 13 deaths and a greater number of wounded, because most habitants had been curiously watching the raid instead of seeking shelter.[58] Allied air raids were meant seriously to depress the morale of the German people, but in the end did not attain their goal. Yet, for a small part of the population, they gave an impression of the horrors of a future war.

During the inter-war period many military experts and civilians alike expected the next war to become something like a total air war. Many were convinced that the aeroplane would be the decisive weapon in the struggle and that wars could be determined by air power alone. To a certain degree the Nazis shared this belief. In 1933 the Reichsluftschutzbund (Air Defence League) was founded, which periodically taught its more than 6 million members air defence measures. Still, during the first year or so of the war it seems that most Germans were not very upset about the prospect of a possible air war. Instead, behavioural patterns from the First World War reappeared – feelings of fascination and curiosity rather than fear or anxiety were predominant. Doris W. described her feelings, confronted with the first Allied raid on a small town near Berlin:

> 'Then there was air alarm, the sirens were wailing. I was tremendously interested – I never had seen this before – and stepped outside the house. And then, there was a huge tin roof inside the hospital – and I stood right beneath this tin roof and watched how the searchlights of the Flak had an aeroplane in their sights – then the Flak fired. And I thought to myself that it was raining – until someone tore on my shoulders and shouted: "Are you crazy, for goodness sake, these are splinters from the Flak, come in!" I did not understand at all.'[59]

However, this naiveté on being confronted with Allied air raids vanished the longer the war lasted. The devastating raids on Lübeck and Rostock in April 1942, and the 1,000-bomber raid on Cologne, marked an increase in intensity and accuracy of the RAF strategic bombing. Above all, the firestorm over Hamburg in July and August 1943 made people realise that the war had finally reached their homes. From now on, the streets of the cities were turned into a battlefield and the bombing became a decisive factor in daily life.

The regime reacted very quickly to this new situation. Victims of enemy air raids were referred to as 'fallen for the Fatherland', and decorations for wounds and injuries resulting from air raids were awarded to all German women, men and even children; obituaries appeared in the local press with the Iron Cross.[60]

One consequence of the bombing was the fact that from 1943-44 onwards, Germany involuntarily turned into a society of refugees, evacuees and *Bombengeschädigte*. Millions of people were forced to leave the blazing cities and were evacuated to safer areas of the country. Faced with the steady air raid warnings and the deteriorating military situation, many Germans fell into a mood that was a mixture of apathy and hedonism. The Berlin journalist Ursula von Kardorff described this strange disposition in a diary entry from 12 December 1943: 'Life is strange. Up and down, evil and good. But always colourful. Yesterday an evening in Zehlendorf, where everybody drank in an unrestrained, nearly dogged way. Everybody was flirting with everybody, and so did I. A sparkling quagmire.'[61] Half a year later, after the invasion of Normandy, she observed: 'Nobody is saving any more... Ordinary soldiers give tips amounting to half of their monthly pay. The waiter of a bar near Gendarmenmarkt has bought a small estate (Landgut) just from the tips he gets when he comes out with a bottle of Mosel. Money is flowing through hands just like water.'[62]

The air war over Germany cost more than 500,000 dead and 800,000 wounded; over 4 million houses were destroyed, 21 per cent of the whole stock existing in 1939. However, that was just the average rate; some cities witnessed much heavier destruction, like Cologne with 70 per cent, Dortmund 65 per cent and especially smaller towns like Düren (99.2 per cent), Paderborn (96.9) or Bocholt (89).

The collapse of morale as a result of area bombing, which the British in particular might have hoped for, did not happen. It seems that at least until late 1943, the aerial onslaughts stimulated and strengthened the popular will to resist rather than created an atmosphere of defeatism.[63] This was partly due to the quite effective measures with which the *Nationalsozialistische Volkswohlfahrt* (NSV – a welfare organisation of the NSDAP) helped the *Ausgebombten*. The NSV provided them with special ration cards and other supplies, provided them with furniture (mostly stolen from the houses of deported people, primarily Jews) and very generously gave financial assistance in every conceivable way.

Psychologically it was not the Nazi regime – which had after all started this war – that was held responsible for the air raids; rather the hate and anger of large parts of the population were turned against the Allies. Sometimes, however, people regarded the air raids as a kind of retaliatory measure for the German war crimes and particularly for the Holocaust. For instance, the famous scholar of Romantic language and literature, Victor Klemperer, wrote in his diary that people felt that the air raids on Berlin and the destruction of the city of Leipzig represented revenge for what the Germans had done to the Jews.[64] But despite that isolated view, one might argue that the Allies bombed the Germans into the *Volksgemeinschaft*, or at least did a good deal to create the *Volksgemeinschaft* that the Nazis had so often dreamed of.

In 1918 military defeat came as shock to most of the people. German troops were still deep into enemy country; vast regions of Russia were under German control – how could the war be lost? Too many people refused to accept defeat; instead the 'stab in the back' myth, particularly fostered by the rightist parties, grew very popular. After the downfall of the Hohenzollern monarchy, the country was shattered by a civil war. Yet, in spite of the defeat, there was still a functioning government and administration. Unlike great parts of Belgium and Northern France, the country was spared any serious damage. Most of all, Germany continued to be a great power, and it was foreseeable that in the near future the country would recover from the deprivations of the war.

The circumstances in the spring of 1945 were totally different. In contrast to 1918, the country was completely occupied by enemy troops – the fact that Germany was militarily defeated was only too clear. Furthermore, after the British had arrested the last head of state, Grand Admiral Dönitz, there was not even a responsible government, no parties, no trade unions, nothing. Vast tracts of the country were devastated either by strategic bombing or by the Allies advancing into German territory. Millions of people had lost their loved ones, their homes and – most of all – hope. Their view of the once mighty German Reich was now all too sober.

In November 1945 the philosopher Karl Jaspers wrote: 'We have lost nearly everything: the state, the economy, the safe conditions of our physical life, and much worse: the valid and connecting norms, the moral dignity, the unifying self-consciousness of being a Volk.'[65] Given these circumstances, the rapid recovery of the country and the integration of the Federal Republic into the Western community was something like a miracle. But that is another story.

Recommended reading

Boberach, Heinz (ed), *Meldungen aus dem Reich: Die geheimen Lageberichte des Sicherheitsdienstes der SS 1938-1945* (Berlin: 1984)

Broszat, Martin, Henke, Klaus-Dietmar and Woller, Hans (eds), *Von Stalingrad zur Währungsreform: Zur Sozialgeschichte des Umbruchs in Deutschland* (München, 1988)

Chickering, Roger, *Imperial Germany and the Great War, 1914-1918* (Cambridge: Cambridge University Press, 1998)

Fritzsche, Peter, *Germans into Nazis* (Cambridge, Mass: Harvard University Press, 1998)

Herwig, Holger, *The First World War: Germany and Austria-Hungary, 1914-1918* (London: Arnold, 1997)

Kardorff, Ursula von, *Berliner Aufzeichnungen 1942-1945* (München: Beck, 1976)

Kitchen, Martin, *Nazi Germany at War* (London: Longman, 1995)

Klemperer, Victor, *Ich will Zeugnis ablegen bis zum letzten: Tagebücher 1933-1945*, Herausgegeben von Walter Nowojski unter Mitarbeit von Hadwig Klemperer (Berlin: Aufbau-Verlag: 1996)

Kleßmann, Christoph (ed), *Nicht nur Hitlers Krieg: Der Zweite Weltkrieg und die Deutschen* (Düsseldorf: Droste, 1989)

Kundrus, Birthe, *Kriegerfrauen, Familienpolitik und Geschlechterverhältnisse im Ersten und Zweiten Weltkrieg* (Hamburg: Christians, 1995)

Mason, Tim, 'The legacy of 1918 for National Socialism' in Anthony Nicholls and Erich Matthias (eds), *German Democracy and the Triumph of Hitler: Essays in recent German history* (London: Allen & Unwin, 1971) pp215-39

Michalka, Wolfgang (ed), *Der Zweite Weltkrieg: Analysen, Grundzüge, Forschungsbilanz* (München and Zürich: Piper, 1990)
Der Erste Weltkrieg: Wirkung, Wahrnehmung, Analyse (München: Piper, 1994)

Niedhart, Gottfried and Riesenberger, Dieter (eds), *Lernen aus dem Krieg?: Deutsche Nachkriegszeiten 1918 und 1945: Beiträge zur historischen Friedensforschung* (München: Beck, 1992)

Rauh, Manfred, *Geschichte des Zweiten Weltkrieges* Vols 1-3 (Berlin: Duncker & Humblot, 1991)

Schäfer, Hans Dieter (ed), *Berlin im Zweiten Weltkrieg: Der Untergang der Reichshauptstadt in Augenzeugenberichten* (München and Zürich: Piper, 1991)

Verhey, Jeffrey, 'The spirit of 1914: The myth of Enthusiasm and the rhetoric of unity in World War I Germany' (dissertation, Berkeley, Ca: 1991)

Weinberg, Gerhard L., *Germany, Hitler and World War II* (Cambridge: Cambridge University Press, 1995)

Notes

[1] Gottfried Benn, 1956, in *Gottfried Benn, Autobiographische und vermischte Schriften, Gesammelte Werke in vier Bänden*, Herausgegeben von Dieter Wellershoff (Stuttgart: 8th ed 1995) Vol IV, pp175-6

[2] See Eberhard Jäckel, *Das deutsche Jahrhundert: Eine historische Bilanz* (Stuttgart: 1996) and Fritz Stern, 'Die zweite Chance? Deutschland am Anfang und am Ende des Jahrhunderts' in Fritz Stern, *Verspielte Größe: Essays zur deutschen Geschichte* (München: 1996) pp11-36

[3] Jeffrey Verhey, 'The Spirit of 1914: The myth of Enthusiasm and the rhetoric of unity in World War I Germany' (dissertation, Berkeley, Ca: 1991)

[4] *Tägliche Rundschau*, 2 August 1914

[5] Speech, 4 August 1914: Stenographische Berichte des Reichstages, Band 306, p5

[6] Gertrud Bäumer, *Lebensweg durch eine Zeitwende* (Tübingen: 1933) pp264-5

[7]   Peter Fritzsche, *Germans into Nazis* (Cambridge, Mass: 1998) p17

[8]   Between 26 and 31 July 1914 there were at least 288 anti-war demonstrations in 163 cities, with an estimated participation of 500,000 people. See Wolfgang Kruse, *Krieg und nationale Integration: Eine Neuinterpretation des sozialdemokratischen Burgfriedensschlusses 1914/15* (Essen: 1994) pp30-6

[9]   Michael Stöcker, *Das Augusterlebnis in Darmstadt: Legende und Wirklichkeit* (Darmstadt: 1994)

[10] Fritz Fischer, 'Sonnige Kindertage im nördlichsten Zipfel Frankens' in Rudolf Pörtner (ed), *Kindheit im Kaiserreich: Erinnerungen an vergangene Zeiten* (Düsseldorf, Vienna and New York: 1987) p276

[11] Quoted in Benjamin Ziemann, *Front und Heimat: Ländliche Kriegserfahrungen im südlichen Bayern 1914-1923* (Essen: 1997) p48

[12] Speech of 17 May 1933, reproduced in Max Domarus, *Hitler: Reden und Proklamationen 1932-1945* (München: 1965) Vol 1, pp270-9

[13] Until 1939 70 per cent of the German population was provided with a small radio receiver, the famous *Volksempfänger*, sometimes scornfully referred to as *Goebbels-Schnauze* ('Goebbels' snout').

[14] Heinz Boberach (ed), *Meldungen aus dem Reich: Die geheimen Lageberichte des Sicherheitsdienstes der SS 1938-1945* (Berlin: 1984) Vol 2, pp72-3

[15] William L. Shirer, *Berlin Diary: The journal of a foreign correspondent 1934-1941* (London: 1941) p179

[16] Secret speech of 10 November 1938, reproduced in Max Domarus, op cit, Vol 2, p974

[17] *Düsseldorfer Tageblatt*, 1 August 1939, No 203

[18] Wilhelm Deist, 'Überlegungen zur "widerwilligen Loyalität" der Deutschen bei Kriegsbeginn' in Wilhelm Deist, *Militär, Staat und Gesellschaft: Studien zur preußisch-deutschen Militärgeschichte* (München: 1991) pp355-69; and Wolfram Wette, 'Die schwierige Überredung zum Krieg: Zur psychologischen Mobilmachung der deutschen Bevölkerung 1933-1939' in *Aus Politik und Zeitgeschichte*, 1989, pp3-17

[19] Marlis G. Steinert, *Hitlers Krieg und die Deutschen: Stimmung und Haltung der deutschen Bevölkerung im Zweiten Weltkrieg* (Düsseldorf and Vienna: 1970) pp91-110

[20] William Shirer, op cit, p154

[21] Letter of 5 September 1939, reproduced in *Helmut James von Moltke: Briefe an Freya 1939-1945*, Herausgegeben von Beate Ruhm von Oppen (München: 1988) pp63-4

[22] Roger Chickering, *Imperial Germany and the Great War, 1914-1918* (Cambridge: 1998) p115

[23] See Ute Daniel, *Arbeiterfrauen in der Kriegsgesellschaft* (Göttingen, 1989) and the same author's 'Women's work in industry and family: Germany 1914-1918' in Richard Wall and Jay Winter (eds), *The Upheaval of War: Family, Work and Welfare in Europe, 1914-1918* (Cambridge: 1988) pp267-96

[24] Ute Daniel, *Arbeiterfrauen*, op cit, p269

[25] Officers' families were excluded from the allowances.

[26] Birthe Kundrus, *Kriegerfrauen, Familienpolitik und Geschlechterverhältnisse im Ersten und Zweiten Weltkrieg* (Hamburg: 1995) pp45-71

[27] Paul Göhre, 'Der Krieg und die Geschlechter' in *Die neue Generation* 13 (1917) No 12, pp536-7

[28] Roger Chickering, op cit, p120

[29] See, eg, Marie-Elisabeth Lüders, *Das unsichtbare Heer: Frauen kämpfen für Deutschland 1914-1918* (Berlin: 1936) or Margaretha Schickedanz, *Deutsche Frau und deutsche Not im Weltkrieg* (Leipzig and Berlin: 1938)

[30] Stefan Bajohr, *Die Hälfte der Fabrik: Geschichte der Frauenarbeit in Deutschland 1914 bis 1945* (Marburg: 1979) pp254-63

[31] Ute Frevert, 'Frauen an der "Heimatfront"' in Christoph Kleßmann (ed), *Nicht nur Hitlers Krieg: Der Zweite Weltkrieg und die Deutschen* (Düsseldorf: 1989) pp51-69

[32] August Skalweit, *Die deutsche Kriegsernährungwirtschaft* (Stuttgart, Berlin and Leipzig: 1927) p5

[33] Before 1914 Germany imported about 6 million tons of fodder, mostly grain, annually.

[34] For the impact of the British blockade on Germany, see C. Paul Vincent, *The politics of hunger: The Allied Blockade of Germany, 1915-1919* (Athens, Ohio: 1985) and Marion C. Siney, *The Allied Blockade of Germany, 1914-1916* (Ann Arbor, Mich: 1957)

[35] At the end of the war at least 2.5 million foreign workers were employed in the German economy, 1.5 million being POWs, 936,000 of them – chiefly Russians – working in the agricultural sector. See Jochen Oltmer, 'Arbeitszwang und Zwangsarbeit – Kriegsgefangene und ausländische Zivilarbeitskräfte im Ersten Weltkrieg' in Rolf Spilker and Bernd Ulrich (eds), *Der Tod als Maschinist: Der industrialisierte Krieg 1914-18* (Bramsche: 1998) pp97-107

36 August Skalweit, op cit, p61

37 Christoph Nonn, *Verbraucherprotest und Parteiensystem im Wilhelminischen Deutschland* (Düsseldorf: 1996)

38 Robert G. Moeller, 'Dimensions of Social Conflict in the Great War: The View from the German countryside' in *Central European History* 14 (1981) pp142-68

39 Ethel Cooper, *Behind the Lines: One Woman's War 1914-1918* (London: Denholm, 1982) p181

40 Ibid, letter of 25 March 1917, p189

41 Avner Offer, *The First World War: An Agrarian Interpretation* (Oxford: 1989) p33

42 Cabinet minutes from 17 October 1918, reproduced in *Die Regierung des Prinzen Max von Baden*, Bearbeitet von Erich Matthias und Rudolf Morsey (Düsseldorf: 1962) p229

43 N. P. Howard, 'The social and political consequences of the Allied blockade of Germany, 1918-1919' in *German History* 11 (1993) pp161-88

44 In private conversations, Hitler often 'gave to understand that after the experience of 1918, one could not be careful enough'. Albert Speer, *Erinnerungen* (Frankfurt am Main and Berlin: 1969) p229

45 György Ranki, *The Economics of the Second World War* (Vienna and Cologne: 1993) p247

46 Quoted in Gustavo Corni and Horst Gies, *Brot – Butter – Kanonen: Die Ernährungswirtschaft in Deutschland unter der Diktatur Hitlers* (Berlin: 1997) p404

47 There is no reliable data available for the last period of the war; ibid, p449

48 Quoted in R. D. Müller, 'Das "Unternehmen Barbarossa" als wirtschaftlicher Raubkrieg' in R. Gerd Ueberschär' and Wolfram Wette (eds), *Der deutsche Überfall auf die Sowjetunion* (Frankfurt am Main: 1991) p140

49 J. E. Farquharson, *The Plough and the Swastika: The NSDAP and Agriculture in Germany 1928-1945* (London: 1976) p241

50 For example, during 1943-44 41 per cent of the Russian harvest was confiscated by the German authorities.

51 Quoted in Margarete Dörr, *'Wer die Zeit nicht miterlebt hat': Frauenerfahrungen im Zweiten Weltkrieg und in den Jahren danach* (Frankfurt and New York: 1998) Vol 2, p20

52 In his memoirs, the young Ernst Toller described the effect this news had made upon him: he believed that the Fatherland had been attacked and that therefore Germany was fighting a defensive war. Ernst Toller, *Eine Jugend in Deutschland* (Amsterdam: 1933) p50

53 Christian Geinitz, *Kriegsfurcht und Kampfbereitschaft: Das Augusterlebnis in Freiburg* (Essen: 1998) p351

54 See Peter Fritzsche, *A Nation of Flyers: German Aviation and the Popular Imagination* (Cambridge: 1992)

55 Düsseldorf, Mannheim, Friedrichshafen (home of the Zeppelins) and Metz. The official term for an anti-aircraft weapon was 'Ballonabwehrkanone' (Anti-balloon gun); they were quite primitive weapons installed on trucks, and posed no danger whatsoever for enemy planes.

56 Alfred Hoche, 'Beobachtungen bei Fliegerangriffen' in *Medizinische Klinik* No 34 (26 August 1917) pp905-7

57 Ibid, p905

58 Hans Schwarz, 'Krieg an der Heimatfront: Zu den Auswirkungen des Luftkrieges auf den Großraum Saarbrücken' in *Als der Krieg über uns gekommen war: Die Saarregion und der Erste Weltkrieg* (Saarbrücken: 1993) pp45-73. See also Max Herrmannn, *Selbsterlebtes im Weltkriege 1914-1918* (Halle: 1925) p39

59 Quoted in Margarete Dörr, op cit, p249

60 Gerald Kirwin, 'Allied Bombing and Nazi Domestic Propaganda' in *European History Quarterly* 15 (1985) pp341-62

61 Ursula Kardorff, *Berliner Aufzeichnungen 1942-1945* (München: 1976) p94

62 Ibid, diary entry for 10 June 1944, p151

63 Marlis G. Steinert, op cit, p531

64 Diary entry for 29 January 1944, reproduced in Victor Klemperer, *Ich will Zeugnis ablegen bis zum letzten: Tagebücher 1933-1945*, Herausgegeben von Walter Nowojski unter Mitarbeit von Hadwig Klemperer (Berlin: 1999) p19

65 *Die Wandlung* 1 (1945) pp3-6

Chapter 5

'Frauen und Fraß': German women in wartime[1]

Ingrid Sharp

Both the First and the Second World Wars have been viewed as having advanced women's emancipation. Especially in 1918 it was obvious to even the most casual observer that the position of women had changed from pre-war times. Respectable women had left their homes and were present in public, had shed their constricting long skirts in favour of freer, more revealing fashions, and appeared if anything to have profited from the war more than the men who had fought it. In many, but not all, countries they had been granted the vote and had proved their capabilities in areas previously reserved for men.

However, more recent scholarship, especially by feminist historians, has gone a long way towards undermining the perception of either war as having been the father of women's emancipation, arguing that war did no more than accelerate or exaggerate tendencies already present in society. While the wars may have briefly catapulted women out of their familiar sphere, this was neither as widespread a phenomenon as previously assumed, nor did wartime employment have lasting or decisive effects on women's employment patterns in the post-war era.[2]

As far as political gains were concerned, although the vote was perceived as a reward for women's service during the war, closer examination reveals this view to be untenable. In the case of France, for example, Michelle Perrot argues that the impetus of a popular and energetic suffrage campaign was in fact interrupted by the Great War and the issue set back by decades, French women only achieving the vote in 1945.[3] The effect of both wars in the United Kingdom was in the direction of greater equality and democracy, both sexes benefiting from a general shift towards greater inclusiveness and equity. In Germany the vote was achieved not as a result of women's services during the war – the Kaiser rejected their petition as late as Easter 1918 – but as a result of a socialist revolution that included male and female suffrage in its revolutionary programme.[4]

If the social changes for women as a result of the wars are looked at in isolation, it is clear that these changes have been enormous. It is only when the relative position of men and women is examined that the significance of these changes can be assessed, and here it is clear that while women have indeed 'advanced', men have advanced even further and the pattern of male privilege and female subordination remains largely unchanged. This has been discussed by Higonnet and Higonnet, who argue that the true puzzle of gender relations and war is in fact the lack of change in the relative position of men and women in the wake of what appeared to be a major shift in the perception of women's role and capacities.[5] They use the image of a double helix, with its structure of two intertwined strands, to show the relationship of female to male experience. The position of women on their strand is subordinate to the position of men on the opposing male strand, so any advance up the female strand of the double helix is accompanied by a matching advance along the male strand, leaving the relative gender positions constant.

War has also been aptly described as a 'gendering activity', in that gender roles are most clearly marked during times of war and therefore tend to become cemented in public consciousness rather than challenged by temporary shifts in gender role, which are perceived as being 'just for the duration'. There is segregation of the sexes as men go to fight at the front, leaving women behind as guardians of hearth and home. Soldiers often view themselves as fighting to protect women and children who embody the core values of the nation. This makes women in some sense responsible for the war – the sacrifices made by the soldiers are for their sakes – and the only acceptable response is to conform to an idealised standard of femininity, pure, loving and eager to serve the men. This service might take a variety of forms, some of them an obvious extension of the female role, such as nursing the sick, caring for soldiers' families and sewing soldier 'comforts', others moving beyond what had previously been acceptable for women and into the sphere of male activity, such as mining, skilled factory work and hard agricultural labour. However, although women in wartime might engage in activities previously reserved for men, even considered 'unnatural' for women, these activities can be subsumed into their feminine role, so do not tend to challenge the fundamental gender polarity.

As Leila Rupp clearly demonstrates in her comparative study of German and American propaganda aimed at persuading women to undertake war work during the Second World War, this work is not intended to challenge the gender role division.[6] 'Rosie the Riveter' is clearly replacing the men, but only while they are otherwise engaged, and her work in war industry is seen as ancillary to the real business of war. In both countries, campaigns aimed at persuading women to replace the men stress the womanly virtue of sacrifice in times of national need as well as the temporary nature of the substitution. Traditionally female qualities such as motherliness, nurturing and love, together with the practical skills of housekeeping, are now to be extended to include the whole nation rather than restricted to a woman's own family. One German First World War propaganda poster depicted a happy working wife in an armaments factory with the slogan, 'Earlier I buttered bread for him, now I paint grenades and think, this is for him'.[7] This process of feminising women's wartime activities serves in some measure to explain why female gains in terms of employment, childcare, earnings and independence are swiftly eroded at the end of the war. Whatever women's wartime activities may be, those performed by men will always be assigned greater value – women's contribution will always be viewed as subordinate to that of the soldier males.

Another sense in which war tends to reinforce rather than undermine gender expectations is the relation of legislation to assumed wartime roles. In many Western societies men have been granted political rights in return for a readiness to lay down their lives in defence of their country. As this possibility is not open to women, they can be denied similar rights. The Germany unified in 1871 adopted Prussian laws and values and was a hierarchical, militarised society where privilege was based largely on birth, and where universal male suffrage was tempered by thresholds of class and wealth, which gave greater weight to the votes of the ruling classes. Until 1908 women were unable even to attend meetings where political subjects were discussed, a factor that made direct campaigning for female suffrage impossible.[8] Instead, middle-class women set out to earn political concessions by offering services to the nation, which, while reflecting women's special nature and destiny, would in some way be equivalent to the men's military role. There is no doubt that the leaders of the moderate women's movement saw the advent of war in 1914 as an opportunity to demonstrate women's capabilities as well as their loyalty and patriotism, both of which had been called into question in the years before the outbreak of war.

The umbrella organisation of the women's movement, the Bund Deutscher Frauenvereine (BDF) and its leader, Gertrud Bäumer, certainly felt that the war gave them an opportunity to prove their worth to society. From the moment war was declared women organised to support the war effort, and Bäumer saw her long-cherished plan for a national women's year of service put into practice. Women of the BDF took on welfare and voluntary work to alleviate the hardship of families whose men were at the front, acted as a labour exchange for women to release as many men for battle as possible, while knitting socks to keep the soldiers' feet warm. It was these women who exhorted the housewives to do their patriotic duty and make the best use of the dwindling resources available to them, teaching them to make jam out of turnips and substitute stewed fruit for butter.

In November 1916 Marie-Elizabeth Lüders was put in charge of female labour at the War Office. In the course of the war, women were drawn further and further into governmental policy implementation and performed a genuinely useful service; without their voluntary work the Government would have had to fund paid welfare workers, and without their efforts at the labour exchange the smooth running of war industry would have been disrupted. At last women saw their contribution recognised and supported. Indeed, Alice Salomon was moved to say, 'If these hadn't been times of war, the limitless power given to the women would have fulfilled our wildest ambitions.'[1] Women of the BDF saw the war as a unifying factor – a supreme challenge that drew together all members of society into a community. They dreamed of continuing their influence into peacetime, offering their 'organised motherliness' as a womanly contribution to the life of the state. However, contemporary male comment shows that this was open to interpretation. For one clergyman, the most important message of warfare was that men and women could never be equal and that women should not expect political rights:

'The war makes women so clearly aware of the natural and insurmountable limitations of their powers that the demand for full equality of the sexes is revealed as impossible.'[10]

And indeed, reading women's published comments about the war, we can see that they themselves valued the soldiers' heroism and sacrifice above anything they themselves could do; they saw their role as important, but purely ancillary to the real business of warfare:

> 'That is in fact the greatest experience for women of these terrible, cruelly great times. Man has once more become man and woman has once more become woman. She steps naturally and easily back into her old place.'[11]

Women's role in wartime is to preserve those feminine values that men have had to slough off in order to be able to kill and destroy. Women have to remain a well of goodness, love and humanity from which men can replenish themselves once the time for killing is over. Women are also needed to value life, mourn the dead and keep alight the flame of the nation's soul:

> 'If ever a cultural legacy has been particularly entrusted to women at any time, then it is the loving regard for life amidst the violent harvest of death.'[12]

After the war, men broken in battle need a woman's altruistic love to heal them and make them whole again. One woman wrote to her husband in 1914:

> 'Your soul is suffering something … that is so great and so heavy that surely only the simple, fervent, self-forgetting love of a woman can banish it.'[13]

It will be noted that most of the responses discussed above come from educated, middle-class women involved in the women's movement. There were, of course, other reactions. Radicals within the women's movement who had campaigned vigorously for women's rights before the outbreak of the war were appalled by their sisters' jingoistic response. Having always argued that exclusive male control over public life would lead to the moral bankruptcy of society, the radicals saw the war as a result and symptom of this moral collapse. They saw the war as a crime against humanity and vigorously opposed it at home and abroad. Not surprisingly, this response remained the province of a brave minority, and women campaigners for peace were silenced and marginalised as far as possible.[14]

The most important distinction to be drawn is, of course, one of class. While the middle-class women were happy to organise the labour of largely working-class women, claiming that German women would be 'only too willing' to do their duty for their country, working-class women were having a different experience that provoked a rather different response. Most of them only worked because they had to. On the one hand, economic necessity forced many poor women into the factories, but on the other, for some, the compulsion was more direct. Miners' wives had to replace their husbands down the mines or lose their tied housing. From January 1917 women were forbidden to switch from agricultural work into other (better-paid) branches of industry. Increasingly, women who worked from home were forced into the factories by cutting off their supplies of raw material for home production, and soldiers' wives could have their benefits cut if they refused to work outside the home.

At the same time, there were no support mechanisms in place to alleviate their double burden of household and childcare responsibilities alongside paid employment. As women moved into areas of industry previously dominated by men, their wages did increase enormously, but they still earned less (about 48-75 per cent) than male workers, leaving families replacing a male with a female breadwinner worse off than before. Although wages rose for both men and women during the war years, in real terms income fell significantly, until a hard day's work would not earn enough to cover even the most basic needs of the workers.

The conditions in the factories were appalling. Workers endured long working days in unhealthy conditions with no breaks, double shifts night after night, low wages and insanitary living conditions. Workers in factory accommodation often shared the same bed in shifts. Despite the fact that it became increasingly difficult to get time off for sickness, absence through illness increased during this period; tuberculosis, industrial poisoning and all the diseases of hunger and malnourishment were rife. The introduction of rationing encouraged the growth of the black market and speculation; fortunes were made by some while the poorest stayed hungry.

Women represented over 50 per cent of the workforce and suffered most from the shortages, as they were responsible for feeding the family. Women were a dominant presence in the bread riots, strikes and organised looting of middle-class shops, which increased as the war progressed and the conditions at home became worse. These women were not campaigning for political rights – what good was the vote during wartime? – but were concerned with the most basic human need, survival in an unjust society.

This sense of injustice is echoed in soldiers' experiences of the front. Just as class privileged certain women and caused resentment at home, so the different treatment of officers and soldiers caused class resentment at the front, even while this was being idealised as a community where class had no place. Walter Flex's *Der Wanderer zwischen beiden Welten*[15] perpetuates the myth of the community of the front as well as that of the beauty and meaning of the heroes' death in battle, while Lily Braun is sure that 'out there in the trenches Infantryman Schulze – who drives a beer wagon in civilian life – doesn't even know that good comrade Müller standing next to him is a senior civil servant!'[16] A more critical view of the 'front experience' was put forward after the event by works such as Ernst Friedrich's *Krieg dem Kriege!* of 1924 and Bruno Vogel's *Es lebe der Krieg*, which attempt to demythologise war and show class discrimination in all areas.[17] It is clear from these accounts and from the works of Otto Dix that those who had experienced the trenches bitterly resented civilians who pontificated about the glories of war and the 'hero's death'. Dix's works often show grotesquely disfigured war cripples begging on the streets while plump women and corrupt war profiteers with well-fed, intact bodies simply ignore them.[18]

A commonly drawn parallel, which highlighted the unfair distribution of scarce resources, brings us to the key area of sexuality. In his *Sittengeschichte des Weltkrieges*, Hirschfeld identifies the main concerns of soldiers as 'Frauen und Fraß' (Women and Food), the priorities shifting depending on the level of supplies at any given time. The common soldiers were forced to queue for prostitutes just as at home working-class women were forced to queue for food. There was class resentment inherent in both situations: officers were given far better conditions and far more privacy in terms of sex, while their wives were able to purchase scarce commodities on the black market.

Sexual attitudes during wartime are important because they both reflect and shape the sexual attitudes of peacetime. The approach to sexuality among the troops reflected the victory of the establishment view of the male sex drive as requiring satisfaction for the maintenance of health and morale. It was received wisdom that masturbation led to weakness and debility, not generally considered desirable qualities in the fighting man. On the other hand, venereal disease was another real threat to the soldier's fighting capacity, so prostitutes and clients alike were subject to strict controls to minimise the risks.

The regulation of the soldiers' sexuality during wartime constituted a massive invasion into the private sphere – Elizabeth Domansky argues that male sexuality was 'deprivatised and "nationalised", that is, subordinated to the needs of a nation at war'[19] – and conditions under which sexual intercourse was allowed encouraged a purely functional attitude to sexuality. Men write of their experience of routine inspection and injection before and after hurried, impersonal sex with overworked prostitutes, while army circulars on the subject make it clear that access to sex was planned and regulated as strictly as any other aspect of army life.[20] Field brothels enshrined the double moral standard, in that the strictest chastity was expected of women at home, while male adultery took place with the sanction of army and state.

Attitudes to women were affected both by the brutalising effects of the field brothels and by the illusion that regulation could prevent venereal disease. A new law for combating the disease was drafted and sent to the Reichstag for approval on 19 February 1918, and one of the first legislative acts of the new parliament was an emergency decree issued on 11 December 1918. This decree, which remained in force until 1927, adopted most of the measures proposed in the draft, including the forcible examination and treatment of suspected prostitutes and women with frequently changing sexual partners.[21]

Just like the men, German women had high expectations of the war, which was to be a public affirmation of German cultural values. Prior to the First World War Germany had been undefeated in battle for over a hundred years and it seemed that only good things for Germany could result from warfare. German unification had been achieved in 1871 in the wake of the Franco-Prussian war, but many within Germany expected the process to be completed in 1914; a new and truly German national identity was to be forged in the furnaces of war.

The war itself was seen as essential to national regeneration and was often described as a great storm, which would sweep away all that was moribund in German society:

'As the trees need the storm to strip them of their withered leaves in Autumn, cruelly breaking twigs and branches in order to pave the way for the coming Spring, so perhaps we, too, have need of such storms to shake off from us everything which is dead or stands in the way of life.'[22]

It seems that national vigour could only be restored through a blood sacrifice, and there is no doubt that this was an essentially masculine vigour; prosperity, urban decadence and the process of industrialisation had sapped the nation's strength and replaced men's backbone with effeminate weakness. Both would be restored by 'the great cleanser, war'.[23] Lily Braun writes:

> 'Those who set out across the borders in the same grey uniform were once again men, nothing but men bound together and glowing with an essential primitive sense of their sex.'[24]

This is matched by the women's response, as they experienced:

> '…the powerful re-emergence of that long-buried womanly feeling, which wants nothing but to help and to heal, of that primitive sense of their sex, which is expressed at its purest by one word: motherliness.'[25]

The women accepted the 'iron necessity' of the times and seem to welcome the imagined invigorating effects of warfare on their menfolk and on their culture, seeming at times to envy the men their sublime experience, even their death on the field of honour:

> 'Death on the battlefield is bound up in the great chain of human endeavour and struggle. With such a death, a generation ensures blessing and fulfilment for all those who come after them.'[26]

The idea of war as a theatre where masculinity could be honed and put to the test, with the possibility of a romantic 'hero's death', was so far from the slime and futility of the trenches, that many survivors lost their sense of what it meant to be a man. Instead of a vigorously masculine nation emerging from the 'steel bath' of war, trench warfare had emasculated the men. For some, the shame of not living up to internalised culturally imposed standards of bravery and 'manliness' led to hysterical or other pathological symptoms.[27] Even where men's bodies remained intact – and the injuries inflicted by the new technology were appalling – male gender identity was in tatters.[28]

Defeat in battle was doubly humiliating as it was completely unexpected and because Germany's sense of national identity was bound up with her military strength. Not just this, but the expected victory was seen as a sign of Germany's moral and cultural superiority over her enemies. With so much invested in victory, many were unable to cope with the reality of defeat. Myth-making was essential to give some meaning to the otherwise pointless sacrifices demanded of the fighting men, and the whole post-war period is characterised by an inability to face up to reality.

Ebert, the new Chancellor, greeted the returning soldiers as 'heroes undefeated on the field of battle'. This made them feel better, but as Germany had palpably been defeated somewhere along the line, if not on the battlefield, then where? Answer: the home front. In other words, civilians, profiteers and women. Not the war, but the revolution was blamed for the disastrous state of Germany after 1918.

Blame for the terms of the Versailles Treaty was unfairly apportioned through the *Dolchstoßlegende*. According to this theory, the brave troops had been close to victory when they were betrayed (stabbed in the back) by those at home. Variously blamed were international Jewry, feminists, intellectuals, pacifists, democrats and socialists, who had plunged the German nation into ignominious defeat – anyone but the brave fighting men at the front.

Women, as part of the home front, had failed to support the men, and worse, they had also failed to be worth fighting for. Even during the war men at the front had a suspicion that women were enjoying the sexual freedom of the war years as well as other freedoms. Soldiers' experiences in the brothels tormented them with fears of their own womenfolk's transgressions, and the stories of wives who presented their husbands with a bastard child on their return from the front were told in order to illustrate the moral failings of women.

Returning soldiers found a changed urban landscape; with the influx of women into factory and white-collar jobs it seemed as if women were everywhere. For some, the balance between the sexes had been destroyed by the circumstances of defeat, and women's empowerment was actually seen as causing male helplessness. This perception was not quite fair; after demobilisation in November 1918 women were dismissed in favour of returning soldiers at such a rate that by March 1919 the proportion of working women had returned to pre-war levels, but still women were seen as 'Kriegsgewinnlerinnen' (literally 'war winners'). While the harsh terms of the peace and the economic crash made even rudimentary provision for the 2.7 million war cripples impossible, it seemed that war and revolution had brought women jobs and political rights, not least the vote.

Having gained political rights so abruptly, the BDF seemed almost embarrassed to take full advantage of them, Gertrud Bäumer commenting:

'We feel ourselves to be too much bound up with our people to be able to look in isolation at the advances that have been made towards our own particular goals.[29]

The equality of the sexes may have been enshrined in the constitution, but there it remained. The wording of the equality clause in the constitution of the Weimar Republic admitted of exceptions – men and women were equal in principle, but there had been no legal reform, so the women were still bound by the restrictive family law of 1900. The institutions that had power in society remained bastions of male privilege: the Army, the Judiciary, the Civil Service and the Government.

Despite the much-vaunted shift in moral values, many sectors of society experienced a deep anxiety about the effects of female emancipation. Feminism was blamed for encouraging selfishness and career-mindedness in women, which caused the falling birth rate. Women were perceived as being out of control, the edges between masculinity and femininity dangerously blurred. The parties that gained by the women's votes were those that stressed the traditional role division between men and women, the primacy of the family and strong religious and moral values. In one aspect, the Weimar years could be viewed as the struggle for order against a rising tide of chaos. Anxiety about modernity and urban culture had been strongly present before the war, but was intensified by the growth of the city and the insecurity of the post-war years. At the heart of this anxiety were women.

For many, a moral regeneration of Germany would only be possible through a return to pre-war social certainties based on respect for the authority of the state and its institutions, which were represented in the family by the authoritarian father in control of both his wife and his children.[30] Gender hierarchies, in any case hardly challenged during the war years, were re-established and the ideology of hearth and home was revived. Regeneration was only possible through women returning to their traditional role as nurturing wives and mothers within a stable home. The altruistic love of women was seen as redemptive; a true woman could not only give returning soldiers a stake in society – something worth living and striving for – but by her classic femininity could give men back a sense of their gender identity as 'other' than woman. At the heart of the regenerative female identity was motherhood. Germany needed healthy children to replace the sick and the dead; a high birth rate was associated with a young and vigorous nation, a low one showed degeneration. And of course the emphasis on women's domestic, reproductive role had the effect of naturalising her position within the home at a time of increased job competition.

The antithesis to the true woman, and marked as an outsider by her lack of interest in motherhood, was the 'New Woman'. She is portrayed as highly urban, associated with the city as a site of crime, decadence and perversion. She is androgynous rather than womanly and, although highly sexual, she is sterile. In her extreme form she is presented as a degenerate who preys on men's sexual weakness and threatens bourgeois marriage.

These concerns were reflected in the political agenda of right-wing forces. Theweleit's powerful analysis of Freikorps and fascist literature reveals how Communists, the urban proletariat and sexualised women were seen as disgusting, contaminating filth that had to be eliminated, and how urban life was seen as a morass or swamp that had to be drained to restore the cleanliness and purity of the nation.[31] National Socialists insisted on standards of racial and moral purity that set them apart in their own minds from the verminous enemies of their race. The Nazi ideal of society represents the attempt by Hitler and those nostalgic for the 'steel bath' of war to impose the values of the front on to civilian society. They valued endurance, toughness and comradeship, despising any signs of weakness or softness, which might lead to defeat in the struggle against internal and external enemies:

> 'I want a violent, arrogant, fearless, cruel youth… There must be nothing weak or tender about it. The glorious, free predator must once again shine out of their eyes.'[32]

The German culture restored by the Nazis was explicitly masculine, in contrast to the womanish weakness of Weimar, as outlined by Auguste Reber-Gruber, official advisor on female education:

> 'If National Socialism has founded a state born out of the spirit of the front which demands all the masculine virtues from its citizens, embracing

German idealism and heroic attitudes in its new, all-encompassing world view, the severity of these standards has led some to call it a masculine state… We celebrate and affirm the masculine state because we had to do penance for the weakness of the past with bitter suffering and humiliating shame, we celebrate and affirm it because we want a free, strong Germany.'[33]

Gender and race were the twin pillars of Nazi ideology and their society was characterised by a strict gender hierarchy within the *Volksgemeinschaft* (racial community). The doctrine of the complementarity and essential polarity of the sexes was embraced and promulgated by the National Socialist Organisation of Women (NSF) whose major role was to educate all German women in their role of restoring and preserving German race and culture. Although the National Socialists spoke the language of conservative women's associations, what they meant by terms such as marriage, motherhood and love were subordinated to the racial, genetic and ideological concerns of the Nazi state, which, under the guise of greater autonomy for women within their domestic realm, infiltrated the most intimate spheres of human life. Even within the family, the Nazis expected mothers to conform to the National Socialist world view, while state youth organisations removed their children from their sphere of influence. All the Nazi policies were double-edged, their implementation depending on which side of the racial or ideological divide an individual woman found herself. For example, while abortion and birth control was prohibited for the women who were valuable as good breeding stock, sterilisation and abortion were encouraged, even imposed on, those women considered racially or genetically inferior.[34] The Nazis promised to honour women, especially mothers, and to return them to the dignity of their traditional domestic role, but this only applied to a highly circumscribed ideal. In the concentration camps, although the sexes were segregated, men and women were treated with equal inhumanity and the only recognition of women's special reproductive role was a privileged place in the extermination process: pregnant women or mothers with young children were almost always killed on arrival at Auschwitz.

War itself fitted into the Nazi programme as the means to fulfilment of Germany's historical destiny as the greatest nation, but this great nation did not include all those currently experiencing themselves as Germans. From the outset measures were introduced to rid the body politic of genetic and racial contaminants, and the long-term aim of breeding a master race of truly German citizens underlay all the Nazi policies. This stands in stark contrast to the approach of most nations entering into a period of conflict, which is to stress the common cause and foster a sense of social cohesion. In Germany war was waged on the home front as well as against external enemies. Citizenship was defined ever more narrowly to exclude Jews and other 'inferior' races: Slavs, gypsies, asocial groups, political or religious enemies of Nazi ideology and the mentally ill. These were the internal enemy, the 'November Criminals' who had betrayed Germany in 1918. The Nazi doctrine was one of limited sympathies:

'The SS man is to be guided by one principle alone: honesty, decency, loyalty, and friendship towards those of our blood, and to no one else… Whether other peoples live in plenty or starve to death interests me only insofar as we need them as slaves for our culture; for the rest it does not interest me. Whether 10,000 Russian women keel over from exhaustion in the construction of an anti-tank ditch interests me only insofar as the ditch for Germany gets finished.'[35]

Through the war, the Nazis were seeking to complete the affirmation of German culture that had been frustrated after the First World War. This time the outcome would be the acknowledged supremacy of Germany over all other nations.

The Nazis were very concerned to avoid the problems that had beset the home front during the First World War, especially food shortages and wage inflation caused by poor planning and a failure to anticipate a lengthy war. To this end they began preparing for war long before 1939, planning for a far longer conflict than they actually anticipated. To avoid wage inflation, a wage freeze was introduced in 1939, and to avoid poverty and want, they offered a generous system of state support for soldiers' families. Food distribution was controlled through strict rationing, while the goal of autarky was a cornerstone of Nazi policies from the outset, as they remembered the effects of the Allied blockade.[36] Women's domestic labour was also seen as significant in economic terms in that they were able to preserve scarce resources and turn unpromising rations into nourishing meals, and supplement food supplies by gathering wild nuts and berries as well as tending vegetable gardens. The women were encouraged to 'be comrades' and share scarce resources fairly, and help those members of the community who needed support. The Nazi organisation of women supported the war effort by collecting money and goods, such as warm winter clothes for the soldiers at the front.

The Nazis recognised the key role women played in fostering the right sort of fighting spirit, and contemporary publications aimed at women and girls provided clear guidelines as to how they were expected to behave in wartime. The magazine *Deutsche Frauen-Kultur* offered many inspiring role models throughout the duration of the war, among them the article 'Frau eines Soldaten' written by an army officer. The title refers to a conversation overheard among the enlisted men. One soldier was showing the others a photograph of himself and his eldest son in uniform. When asked, 'What does your wife have to say about that?' he replies simply, 'She is the wife of a soldier.' The German woman, we learn, has a key role to play in the success or failure of the German defence forces. She must bring up her children to value order, duty and racial hygiene, and instil in them a firm belief in victory, for if she gives way to defeatism, she undermines the fighting spirit of the entire nation. She must fulfil her duties at home as if she were a soldier facing the enemy in the trenches.[37]

Hitler saw the role of women in preserving the race as more stable and permanent than that of the men, and, even in wartime conditions, was loath to overturn the natural gender order for short-term advantage.[38] It is therefore not surprising that the effort to recruit women into the war economy was fraught with contradictions and ultimately unsuccessful in mobilising women for the war effort.

In contrast to other countries, such as the United Kingdom and the United States, which registered a rise in female employment at the outbreak of war, in Germany there was actually a sharp drop as 540,000 women left the workplace. This was partly a reflection of the regime's success in persuading women that their primary duties were in the home, and partly due to the generous support for soldiers' families. Women who married soldiers at the outbreak of war became eligible for up to 85 per cent of their husbands' peacetime wage, although the average was 73-75 per cent. This compares with figures of 38 per cent in Britain and 36 per cent in America.[39] With the most expensive and demanding family member absent, this was more than adequate and women were discouraged from working as the allowance was cut if women earned more than one-third of its value.

Although there had been legislation in place since 1935 that allowed the large-scale recruitment of women into the labour force in times of war, the regime proved remarkably loath to use its powers, instead relying heavily on persuasion. Racially valuable German women had to be courted and retained as mothers and homemakers, but even within this privileged group, distinctions were made and treatment was anything but uniform. Initially, only those women who were already in work were re-allocated jobs within the war industry, later targeting those women who had previously worked but who had left the work force, often to get married and raise families. This policy fuelled class resentment, as working-class women and their soldier husbands failed to see why they should shoulder the entire burden of the war effort alone.

Even from official correspondence, we can form a picture of the extent of that burden. A letter from the labour office in Niedersachsen describes the women, especially the married women, as at the limits of their capacities and unable to cope with 9-10 working hours and workplaces some distance on foot away from their homes. 'These women are out of the house for 11-12 hours and can't even rest in their free time, because they have their urgent household tasks to fulfil.'[40] Owing to the policy of freezing wages, these women were extremely poorly paid for their labour. It is further clear that the policy on women's recruitment was decided at the highest level in the Nazi hierarchy, and that officials often found it extremely difficult to muster convincing arguments to defend the official line.

The response of the husbands when their wives were enlisted was often extremely angry, as evidenced by this letter:

'Sir, I haven't slept in a bed for two years, apart from 28 days of leave during that time, but we are happy to do our duty out here in the filth and to risk our lives, because it's for Germany, but I do think we have the right to demand that our wives are left in peace. Why don't you make a bit of sacrifice and send your own wife to work?... In your place I would be ashamed to force a soldier's wife, with a six-month-old baby, out to work...'[41]

Another soldier writes that he has forbidden his wife to work in the munitions factory:

'Until the matter is dealt with fairly, and as long as it isn't an obligation for all women, regardless of social standing, in the spirit of true Volksgemeinschaft, to do their duty to the Fatherland for 6 to 8 weeks, then it is out of the question for my wife, too.'[42]

Another source of resentment among soldiers was the fact that their wives or mothers could not get time off from work while they were home on leave. Throughout the duration of the war, the inequity of treatment was bitterly resented, especially as middle-class women were not even expected to do without their domestic servants. In the United Kingdom there were 1.2 million household servants at the start of the war, and this dropped by 800,000 to 400,000 at the end of the war, while in Germany the number dropped by only 200,000 from 1.56 to 1.36 million.[43] The same outraged husband writes:

> 'There are probably women living in Niesky who don't know what to do with themselves for sheer boredom, but these women have to keep their maidservants, just so that they don't lose anything of their artificial beauty and natural laziness.'[44]

Advertisements placed by underemployed grass widows looking for 'female companions with lots of free time' could only increase the hostility.[45] Women worked in all areas of the economy, even within the Army itself, and were expected to cope cheerfully with the enormous demands placed on them, which became greater as the war progressed and the air raids became more frequent. One working-class woman, Frau Werner, describes how she lost everything in a single night in 1944:

> 'It was terrible. I had nothing but the clothes I wore. I could hang them up on one nail in the wall. That's all I owned... Nevertheless I had to go to work every day.'[46]

Hungry, homeless and completely exhausted, Frau Werner worked on the assembly line at Siemens:

> 'Do you know what a conveyor belt is? It's very hard on the line; the machines are running all the time, without interruption, and you have to move quickly... The assembly line ruined me. It was terrible. Nobody can bear it for a long time. I always said it made me kaputt. Nights we spent in the shelter, during the day we worked with nothing to eat. No human being is able to endure that.'[47]

Women who worked as nurses during the war were subject to the same long hours and inadequate food and rest as the factory workers, and often found themselves coping with levels of responsibility far in excess of their training under the most primitive circumstances. With an acute shortage of medicine and the constant interruption due to air raids, trainee nurse Waltraud G. describes how she and a midwife were left alone to care for 120 patients, while Elisabeth M. describes how she was on a work placement in a Swabian hospital shortly after the surrender:

> 'I was blood group O, and certainly didn't have that much blood to spare, but how often was blood group O needed? "Who's blood group O? Oh, come on, quick, quick!" We lay down on the stretcher, tube in here, blood out there. I always got a bottle of wine and a couple of eggs afterwards, but that's not why

I did it. There were hardly any blood supplies back then... Looking back, I just think that we must have had amazing strength in those days; no one ever gave up, neither the doctors nor the nurses.'[48]

Women continued to become pregnant and give birth under these circumstances, and could only hope that they would be able to have their babies in hospital rather than in an air raid shelter. In the later war years, when food, soap and clothing became very scarce, mothers were often too undernourished to breast-feed their babies. They had to cope with the care of their infants as best they could, washing cloth nappies in damp cellars, their nights interrupted by the needs of the baby as well as the frequent air raid sirens.

Even in 1939 the German economy lacked around 1 million workers, a situation that was bound to be exacerbated as more and more men were conscripted into the Wehrmacht – 4.3 million in the year from May 1939, 800,000 of these from industry.[49] As the war progressed the labour shortage became more acute, and the need for maximum production in the armaments sector increased as Germany became locked into battle on two fronts. At the same time, of course, more and more soldiers were needed to fight. By September 1941 there were 2.6 million vacancies, half of which were in agriculture, 50,000 in mining and 300,000 in the metal industries.[50] With the wage freeze in operation, workers could not be attracted into these areas by higher wages as in other countries, and the re-allocation of workers by other means proved slow and inefficient. In agriculture especially, the burden fell heavily on the women left behind to manage the farms. With the sole assistance of foreign workers, these women laboured like beasts of burden for 13-15 hours daily, often forced to involve their own children for heavy work that was beyond their strength and capacities. They were not safe from air raids and had only the compensation of easier access to food than women working in towns. The concept of leisure or family time was entirely alien under these circumstances.

Despite the gravity of the situation, no serious attempts were made to mobilise the reserve army of women until January 1943, when all women between the ages of 17 and 45 were required to report to the labour exchange. Within this group, pregnant women or women with one pre-school child or two children under the age of 14 were exempted automatically, and there were so many other loopholes that of the 3,048,000 who reported for work in June, only 500,000 remained at work by December 1943.[51] Although it made sense for women with young children to stay at home, there were still some 5.4 million married women without children as well as 1 million unmarried women who could have been drafted. Here, the inconsistency was even more apparent, as working-class mothers of very young children could be called upon to work long hours while their children were placed with relatives or into state nurseries. The number of working mothers can be gauged by the numbers of children in workplace crèches – by 1944, 32,000 crèches cared for 1,200,000 children, compared with 120,000 children cared for at the peak of US wartime provision.[52] A Mothers' Protection Law was introduced in 1942, which granted six weeks maternity leave before and after birth and insisted on the provision of workplace crèches and nursing facilities in firms employing large numbers of women. It appears, however, that these facilities were provided more for the benefit of the state than the welfare of the mothers, who had little choice about whether to remain at home with their children.

In sum, the burden of exhausting work with low wages and minimal training fell once again on the shoulders of poorer women, while middle-class women undertook pleasant voluntary work or whiled away the hours with tennis and tea-parties. Despite the strength of feeling about the obvious inequity and its negative effect on social cohesion, Hitler remained committed to his policy. After all, the best horse-breeders made distinctions between workhorses and thoroughbreds.[53] Instead, gaps were stopped with forced labour either from the occupied territories or by prisoners of war. Hitler considered it far more appropriate for 'sturdy' Russian women to perform factory work than 'slender, long-legged' Germans.[54]

As the war progressed, heavy industry and agriculture depended on foreign workers to an enormous extent; by 1944 some 7.6 million forced labourers were working in Germany, and although women did replace men in family businesses and agriculture, it was not until late 1944 that any systematic efforts were made to train women for work in the war industry itself.[55] In Britain and America women made up approximately 40 per cent of the munitions workforce.

The Nazi elite seemed to be aware of the regenerative function of family life and the part it played in reintegrating soldiers into peacetime society. The psychological effects of trench warfare on the soldiers had been well documented in the press and in the fiction of Remarque and Jünger, and the Nazis feared the brutalising effect on those who were charged with the killing of racial enemies in the East. Koonz quotes one of Himmler's officers who had witnessed the execution of 100 Jews:

> 'Look at the eyes of the men in this Kommando, how deeply shaken they are! These men are finished for the rest of their lives. What kind of followers are we training here? Either neurotics or savages!'[56]

Koonz argues that the perpetrators of dreadful crimes could refresh themselves in the cosiness of family life and preserve some sense of themselves as good men through their role as fathers and husbands:

> 'They relied on the sheltering family (or on its myth) to keep alive an ersatz sense of decency in the men who would work most closely with mass murder… They recreated the ideal of a family as refuge, as a place to renew contact with a private and more humane self. The SS man who excised "feminine" traits from his personality depended on a woman to salvage his sanity.'[57]

The reluctance of the Nazi elite to use legislation to mobilise women can be seen as an attempt to preserve the illusion of an intact social order, to which the soldier could return after the killing was over. This was important for morale – the men were fighting to preserve hearth and home, after all, and liked to picture their mothers, wives or sweethearts safe in a domestic setting. The illusion proved impossible to sustain, however, as aerial bombings caused huge civilian casualties and made it impossible to maintain an ordered home life. While a total of 51,509

British civilians were killed in bombing raids, 40,000 German civilians were killed in a single week in Hamburg during 1943, a year that saw an average of 7,000 casualties per month.[58] Unlike the Nazi elite, the bombs showed no respect for class distinctions and created a new social division that was to become especially relevant in the immediate post-war period between those who still had a home and some property, and those who had lost everything in the bombing. While the war continued, even those who had lost their homes attempted to maintain a semblance of order. Although the population was worn down and demoralised, workers still turned up for work and the social fabric did not completely disintegrate. In fact, the terrible conditions and the naked struggle for survival left little energy for political resistance to the regime.

The situation after the Second World War differed from 1918 in several respects. In 1945 the military defeat and total capitulation of the German nation left no room for a 'stab in the back' myth to develop. In contrast to the revolutionary disorder of 1918, there was no challenge to the authority of the occupying powers in East and West. The scale of the war guilt was vastly different, too. Although Germany had been seen as the aggressor in 1914, discovery of National Socialist racial policies and the liberated death camps horrified the entire world. With unconscious irony, disgust at Germany was often couched in national/racial terms, as if there were something inherent in the German national character that predisposed them to homicidal aggression towards other nations, which had at all costs to be kept under control; 'German' has meant at one moment a being so sentimental, so trusting, so pious, as to be too good for this world; and at another a being so brutal, so unprincipled, so degraded, as to be not fit to live.[59]

But these distinctions were primarily at a political and military level; at the level of the civilian population, things did not seem so clear cut. With 4 million men dead, and 11,700,000 prisoners of war, the majority of the civilian population in 1945 was women. After both wars, the cessation of hostilities did not mean an end to hardship – the influenza epidemic of 1918 killed 174,000 of the population weakened by hunger and privation. After the Second World War, the situation was arguably even worse, especially for those living in the eastern part of Germany under Soviet occupation or in territories no longer part of Germany. Bombing had stopped, but now the enemy was in the land, and there was cold and hunger as the extreme winter of 1945-6 had to be faced with an acute shortage of housing, fuel and food. Even in the American zone, rations were set at an average of 1,146 calories per day, but women classified as housewives counted as non-employed and received fewer calories. This meant that sick, enfeebled and undernourished women had to queue for meagre rations, travel long distances to attempt to supplement them by barter, and overcome shortages of clothing, soap and household utensils through ingenuity and hours of labour. As well as the task of rebuilding the broken men, reforging the family and regenerating society, the job of building up towns and cities after the destruction was largely left to women – in Berlin alone in 1945 40-50,000 Trümmerfrauen (literally 'rubble women') worked to clear the rubble left by the bombing and the battle for the capital at the end of the war.

With the re-allocation of territory after the Potsdam agreement of August 1945, approximately 12 million Germans, many of them women with responsibility for dependent relatives, the aged and infirm as well as young children, were uprooted from their homes and support networks. Whether those who survived the journey – and some 2 million did not – were able to survive in the hostile environment of post-war Germany depended largely on personal contacts and whether they had been able to salvage property that could be bartered for food and other necessities.

After both wars, the fact of defeat is psychologically significant, although even 'victorious' combatants often found it difficult to celebrate their victory and felt alienated from non-combatants who still saw the war in nationalistic terms. In 1918 as in 1945, the humiliation of the soldier male was underscored by his sexual humiliation at the hands of occupying forces. In 1918 there was the *Schwarze Schmach* ('black shame'), which saw German women in the occupied Rhineland ravished by black soldiers in the French Army, and after the Second World War the frequent rape of German women, most frequently but not exclusively by Russian and French soldiers. In both cases German women were violated by those whom they considered racially inferior, and, after 1918, the men were further emasculated by the taunt that the promiscuous German women were only too willing to mate with the potent black troops. 'German men resisted for five years,' they were told, 'German women only managed five minutes.'[60] In the period following both wars, German women used their sexuality to survive in times of need; in the time of hyperinflation in the early 1920s they were available to foreigners made rich by the exchange rate, just as they were available to the occupying forces in exchange for necessities after 1945. Both the rapes and the necessity for prostitution highlighted men's inability to fulfil their primary gender functions – to protect and to provide for their families.

The response to the women who 'fraternised' with the occupying troops after 1945 was ambivalent. While whole families could depend for their survival on one woman's friendship with an American soldier, these relationships were viewed with censure as well as envy. The American authorities did not encourage these relationships, referring to the women collectively as 'Veronica Dankeschöns' (ie VDs) to warn their boys of the dangers of foreign women, although the risk of infection was in fact greater for the women. At this most intimate human level, the 'Veronicas' mediated between the occupying troops and the German population, usually tending to replace the blanket picture of the evil Nazi with a more human one. At other levels, too, for example in the peace movement after both conflicts, women mediated between the Germans and their former enemies, helping to rehabilitate the German nation on the international stage.[61]

I have argued that war is a gendering activity, tending to cement rather than challenge existing gender roles, and that, despite apparent advances made by women in the field of employment, morals or politics, the relative positions of men and women remain static. The roles ascribed to men and women in the case of a hypothetical or actual war also have a major influence on gender roles in times of peace, as the role of protector, identified as exclusively male, is often used to justify male privilege in civil society. This is clearly demonstrated in West German legislation, which in 1957 enshrined the man's role as protector and provider, and confirmed his authority as head of the family on the basis of his role as defender of the German nation.[62] In his analysis of family law in post-war Germany, Robert Moeller comments:

> 'Strong patriarchs were back in uniform, strong patriarchs should also rule at home. In defense of the nation and in defense of the family, men had responsibilities that justified rights and privileges.'[63]

This legislation, however anachronistic, clearly shows the importance of war and the preservation of soldiering as a male activity in influencing gender relations. A year later, the response of Hildegard Krüger, a feminist legal expert, reminded German men that they had been signally unable to protect German women during the previous conflicts and would be even less able to do so in the nuclear age:

> 'How is it possible to speak at all about the protective function of the man who is subject to military service in light of the German women raped, frozen, trampled, and butchered on the streets of East and middle Germany, gassed in concentration camps, burned and wounded in Hamburg, Dresden, and in the cities of the Rhine and Ruhr?'[64]

Recommended reading

Bridenthal, Renate, Grossmann, Atina and Kaplan, Marion (eds), *When Biology Became Destiny* (New York: Monthly Review Press, 1984)

Crew, David F., *Nazism and German Society, 1933-1945* (London and New York: Routledge, 1994)

Daniel, Ute, *The War from Within: German Working Class Women in the First World War* (Oxford and New York: Berg, 1997)

Dörr, Margarete, *"Wer die Zeit nicht miterlebt hat…": Frauenerfahrungen im Zweiten Weltkrieg und in den Jahren danach* (Frankfurt and New York: Campus, 1998)

Higonnet, Margaret R. et al (eds), *Behind the Lines: Gender and the Two World Wars* (New Haven: Yale University Press, 1987)

Rupp, Leila J., *Mobilizing Women for War: German and American Propaganda, 1939-1945* (Princeton, NJ: Princeton University Press, 1978)

Notes

[1] 'Frauen und Fraß' (Women and Food). Funding by the AHRB under its Research Leave scheme enabled me to travel to Germany and research this article. The Archiv der Deutschen Frauenbewegung at Kassel also assisted me with material.

[2] See the Introduction and essays in Margaret R. Higonnet et al (eds), *Behind the Lines: Gender and the Two World Wars* (New Haven: Yale University Press, 1987)

[3] Michelle Perrot, 'The New Eve and the Old Adam: French Women's Condition at the Turn of the Century', ibid, pp51-60, p54

[4] For more detail on women's suffrage, see Ute Frevert, *Women in German History: From Bourgeois Emancipation to Sexual Liberation* (Oxford: Berg, 1989) and Richard Evans, *The Feminist Movement in Germany, 1894-1933* (Beverly Hills: Sage Publications, 1976)

5   Margaret R. Higonnet and Patrice L-R. Higonnet, 'The Double Helix' in *Behind the Lines*, op cit, pp31-47, p34

6   Leila J. Rupp, *Mobilizing Women for War: German and American Propaganda, 1939-1945* (Princeton, NJ: Princeton University Press, 1978)

7   Quoted in Claudia Koonz, *Mothers in the Fatherland* (London: Cape, 1987) p394

8   For a summary of women's rights in the 19th century see Ute Frevert, op cit

9   Quoted in Bärbel Clemens, *Menschenrechte haben kein Geschlecht: Zum Politikverständnis der bürgerlichen Frauenbewegung* (Pfaffenweiler: Centaurus Verlagsgesellschaft, 1988) p107

10 Prelate Planck, *Was lehrt der Krieg unsere Frauen und Töchter?* (Stuttgart: Verlag der Evangelischen Gesellschaft, 1916) p3

11 Anselma Heine, 'Der Strom der Kraft" in Karl Jünger (ed), *Deutschlands Frauen und Deutschlands Krieg: Ein Rat- Tat- und Trostbuch: Gesammelte Blätter aus Frauenhand* (Stuttgart: Verlag von Robert Lutz, 1916) pp33-4, p34

12 Gertrud Bäumer, *Der Krieg und die Frau* (Stuttgart and Berlin: Deutsche Verlagsanstalt, 1914) p9

13 'Aus Kriegsbriefen deutscher Frauen', *Deutsche Frauen-Kultur* (Leipzig: Verband Deutsche Frauen-Kultur, Verlag Otto Beyer) No 3 (1940) p5. Letter from Gertrud Niemeyer an Rittmeister Prof Dr Niemeyer, Stuttgart, 27 August 1914

14 For a collection of the most important pacifist writings, see Gisela Brinker-Gabler, *Frauen gegen den Krieg* (Frankfurt am Main: Fischer, 1980)

15 Walter Flex, *Der Wanderer zwischen beiden Welten* (Munich: Ch Becksche Verlagsbuchhandlung, 1937 [1917])

16 Lily Braun, *Die Frauen und der Krieg* (Leipzig: E. Hirzel, 1915) p33

17 Ernst Friedrich, *Krieg dem Kriege!* (Berlin: Freie Jugend, 1924); Bruno Vogel, *Es Lebe der Krieg!* (Leipzig: Verlag die Wölfe, 1925)

18 For more on the artistic portrayal of the war, see Mathias Eberle, *War I and the Weimar Artists Dix, Grosz, Beckmann, Schlemmer* (New Haven and London: Yale University Press, 1985)

19 Elizabeth Domansky, 'Militarisation and Reproduction in World War I Germany' in Geoff Eley (ed), *Society, Culture, and the State in Germany, 1870-1930* (Ann Arbor, Mich: University of Michigan Press, 1996) p449

20 There are many descriptions of the field brothels in the fiction and non-fiction of the period, including Ernst Friedrich and Bruno Vogel cited above (note 17). See also Max Hirschfeld and Andreas Gaspar (eds), *Sittengeschichte des Weltkrieges* (Hanau am Main: Verlag Karl Schustek, 1966 [1929]) Chap 10 'Organisation der Kriegsbordelle', pp231-54

21 'Verordnung zur Bekämpfung der Geschlechtskrankheiten December 11, 1918', Reichsgesetzblatt, 1918 1431, cited in Annette F. Timm, '"Dank seiner Manneszucht": The Military, Venereal Disease and the Post WWI Sexuality Crisis', a paper given at the Colloquium Geschlechter – 'Kriege: Militär, Krieg und Geschlechterverhältnisse 1914-1949', Berlin, 15-16 October 1999

22 Lily Braun, op cit, p10

23 Otto Binswanger, *Die Seelischen Auswirkungen des Krieges* (Stuttgart and Berlin: Deutsche Verlagsanstalt, 1914) p21

24 Lily Braun, op cit, p11

25 Ibid

26 Gertrud Bäumer, op cit, p10

27 See Binswanger, op cit, and Joachim Radkau, 'Das Stahlbad als Nervenkultur? Nervöse Ursprüng des Ersten Weltkrieges' in *Arbeitskreis Militärgeschichte e.V.* Newsletter 10, October 1999

28 Among the many works exploring the nature of masculinity in this context, see Erich J. Leed, *No Man's Land: Combat and Identity in World War I* (Cambridge: Cambridge University Press, 1979) and George L. Mosse, *The Image of Man: The Creation of Modern Masculinity* (New York and Oxford: Oxford University Press, 1996)

29 Gertrud Bäumer, quoted in Bärbel Clemens, op cit, p115

30 For a more detailed discussion of these issues, see especially Chap 8 of Richard Bessel, *Germany after the First World War* (Oxford: Clarendon Press, 1993)

31 Klaus Theweleit, *Männerphantasien* (Frankfurt am Main: Roterstern, 1978)

32 Adolf Hitler, quoted in Markus Fischer et al, *Der Nationalsozialismus: Eine Dokumentation über die zwölf dunklen Jahre deutscher Geschichte* (Bonn: Inter Nationes) pp270-1

33 Dr Auguste Reber-Gruber, 'Erziehung der Frau im neuen Deutschland', *Deutsche Frauen-Kultur*, No 9 (1934) pp1-3

34 Gisela Bock, 'Racism and Sexism in Nazi Germany: Motherhood, Compulsory Sterilisation, and the State' in Renate Bridenthal, Atina Grossmann and Marion Kaplan (eds), *When Biology became Destiny* (New York: Monthly Review Press, 1984) pp271-96

35 Himmler to his troops on 4 October 1943, quoted in Claudia Koonz, op cit, p411

36 Jill Stephenson, 'Propaganda, Autarky and the German Housewife' in David Welch (ed), *Nazi Propaganda* (Beckenham: Croom Helm, 1983)

37 'Frau eines Soldaten', *Deutsche Frauen-Kultur* No 3 (1940) p4

38 Hitler's speech to the NSF in September 1934, reproduced in Benz (ed), *Frauen im Nationalsozialismus*, pp43-4

39 Ibid, p42

40 Ursula von Gersdorff, *Frauen im Kriegsdienst 1914-1945* (Stuttgart: Deutsche Verlags-Anstalt, 1969) document 122, p300

41 Ibid, document 156, enclosed letter No 1, p345

42 Ibid, letter No 3, p346

43 Figures from Jeremy Noakes, 'Germany' in Jeremy Noakes (ed), *The Civilian in War* (Exeter Studies in History, No 32: University of Exeter Press, 1992) pp35-61, p44; and in Tim Kirk, *The Longman Companion to Nazi Germany* (Essex: Longman, 1995) p82

44 Ursula von Gersdorff, op cit, document 156, enclosed letter No 3, p346

45 Ibid, document 122, p302

46 Annemaire Tröger, 'German Women's Memories of World War II' in Higonnet, *Behind the Lines*, op cit, pp285-99, p291

47 Ibid, p292

48 Margarete Dörr, "*Wer die Zeit nicht miterlebt hat…*": *Frauenerfahrungen im Zweiten Weltkrieg und in den Jahren danach* (Frankfurt and New York: Campus 1998) p91

49 Jeremy Noakes, op cit, p38

50 Ibid, p39

51 Ibid, p43

52 Ibid, p46, and Ute Frevert, op cit, p224. NB: this legislation applied to domestic servants for the first time.

53 Hermann Goering, quoted in Martin Kitchen, *Nazi Germany at War* (London and New York: Longman, 1995) p139

54 Ibid, p44

55 Jeremy Noakes, op cit, p39

56 Raul Hilberg, *The Destruction of the European Jews* (Chicago: Quadrangle, 1961) p218, quoted in Claudia Koonz, op cit, p412

57 Ibid, p414

58 Jeremy Noakes, op cit, pp55-6

59 A. J. P. Taylor, *The Course of German History: A Survey of the Development of Germany since 1815* (London: Hamish Hamilton, 1945) p13

60 Christian Koller, 'Rasse und Geschlecht', conference paper given at the Colloquium Geschlechter-Kreige, Berlin 1999 (see note 21)

61 See Hermann-Josef Rupieper, 'Bringing Democracy to the Fräuleins: Frauen als Zielgruppe der amerikanischen Demokratisierungspolitik in Deutschland 1945-1952' in *Geschichte und Gesellschaft* (Göttingen: 1991) Vol 1, pp61-91

62 The fact of division and the Cold War had a major effect on the development of German society after the Second World War, but it is beyond the scope of this chapter to trace significant differences in the policies relating to women in East and West. For a summary, see Ingrid Sharp and Dagmar Flinspach, 'Women in Germany from Division to Unification' in Derek Lewis and John R. P. McKenzie (eds), *The New Germany: Social, Political and Cultural Challenges of Unification* (Exeter: University of Exeter Press, 1995) pp173-95

63 Robert G. Moeller, *Protecting Motherhood: Women and the Family in the Politics of Post-war West Germany* (Berkeley; Los Angeles and London: University of California Press, 1993) p222

64 Hildegard Krüger, 1958, quoted in ibid, p222

Chapter 6

The impact of war on Russian Society

Sergei Kudryashov

In both World Wars of the last century Russia was one of the principal combatants, and, moreover, bore the most casualties, with fatalities alone totalling around 45 million. The course of military action and its results had an enormous effect on the fate of the country and its development, and affected every generation growing up in Russia and the USSR in the 20th century. Contemporary society, however, perceives the two wars as being very different from each other. The war with Nazi Germany is known in Russia as the Great Patriotic War. Although Stalin (more by analogy with the First World War than the Patriotic War of 1812) thought up this name[1], most people today do not ascribe any propagandistic meaning to it. The public holiday on 9 May is widely observed each year, throughout the country thousands of memorials have been erected, and war heroes' names are known and respected. The same cannot be said of the First World War, with its Russian heroes being known in the main only to specialists and those with a keen interest in history.[2] For everyone else, this particular war has come to be seen as a dim and distant event, pushed into the background by the October Revolution and the civil war that ensued. Even after the great political changes of the 1990s, when those in power were looking for an appropriate ideology for their regime and threw themselves into the business of reviving the cult of Tsarist Russia[3], the country's participation in this war largely remains an object of academic interest. However, any aberrations in contemporary political awareness can in no way influence or change the significance of the historical events themselves.

In Western and Soviet literature, the history of Russia at the time of the First World War is treated in connection with the events of 1917. Such an approach is simple to explain and is perfectly correct. Of course it is true that in seeking 'objective causes' of what happened, there is a temptation to ascribe a similar level of importance to all the factors involved, treating the war as some kind of background to the other events. But if one is to agree with the many historians who are inclined towards the view that it was precisely the war that helped the Bolsheviks emerge victorious in the Revolution[4], the question 'Why?' nonetheless remains without an adequate answer, especially in light of the fact that the Second World War led to a previously unseen consolidation of the regime, and that *perestroika*, which was conducted peacefully, led to a disintegration of the country with consequences that can be compared to those of the 1917 Revolution.

Indeed, any war is an extreme situation in which the ability of the authorities to show their power is clearly put to the test. War can bring a nation together in the face of its enemies or destroy it. From Russia's point of view, the First World War began in far more favourable circumstances than the Soviet-German war, with time available to mobilise and deploy its forces. Tanks and military aircraft had yet to appear. From the very start the war was one of protracted manoeuvring, and this too was to the benefit of the vast Tsarist Army, which was 80 per cent comprised of peasants. The wave of patriotic fervour in the country, at least at the beginning, was extremely strong, and this undoubtedly influenced the spirit of the forces as well as strengthening their belief in the Tsar and their homeland. Another important fact was that the Eastern Front, despite the crucial nature of certain battles, was not the main front; the outcome of the war was decided in the West. Regardless of all this, the course of the war turned out unfavourably for Russia. Characteristic shortcomings in the Army and elsewhere began to make themselves felt: a certain sluggishness, a lack of speed in taking decisions and acting on them, a fear of taking the initiative, poor organisation of supplies to the Army, and a preference for hand-to-hand fighting, which resulted in large numbers of deaths, injuries and soldiers falling into the hands of the enemy. This situation repeated itself on an even more threatening scale in the early part of the Great Patriotic War, when the Germans succeeded in very quickly occupying significant territories that were home to almost a third of the country's population. Why did Stalin, unlike Nicholas II, succeed in turning events around, and did the nature of his regime play a part in this success?

In comparing the two situations, the most obvious difference is the flimsy ideological basis for the war in 1914. Regardless of the general understanding that they were fighting the Germans 'for the Faith, the Tsar and the Fatherland', the soldiers, who were overwhelmingly illiterate or semi-literate, had very little understanding of the causes of the war. General A. A. Brusilov wrote bitterly in his memoirs that in the Army they knew nothing of their brother Slavs, or of Serbia, which, for some reason, had caused the Germans to take it into their heads to wage a war. The less than comforting conclusion was that 'they were sending people off to slaughter for reasons unknown, that is, at the Tsar's whim.'[5] It is therefore unsurprising that, for the majority of those who took part, the war was largely something incomprehensible and 'alien'. The longer the war went on, the more indifferent the soldiers became, and consequently the more attractive became the idea of putting a stop to it.[6]

In the summer months of 1941 the illusion that 'German workers' would not fight against their 'class brothers' survived only a short time among the ranks. Reality made itself felt very quickly. The ideology of the war, its causes and its aims were clear to every soldier in the Red Army. At least, no documentary evidence has yet emerged to suggest that Red Army soldiers did not know against whom they were fighting or why. Political commissars (the main instrument of Party influence in the Army) played an undoubted role in achieving such a situation. It is no coincidence that the Reich had prepared ahead of time for their annihilation, and harsh Nazi terror campaigns were aimed precisely at them and the Jews. The Germans also treated the latter as 'Jewish-Bolsheviks'[7]. Using their experience of the First World War, the Soviet leadership also took preventative measures, removing all Germans and those bearing German surnames from the Army. Only a few were permitted to serve, and they found themselves under constant observation. The Tsarist Government, on the other hand, had ascribed little significance to this question, and as a result Russian society and the Army had been shot through with perpetual talk of treachery and sabotage, and it was a simple matter to put failures at the front down to the machinations of German agents. Such feelings gradually grew into opposition to the regime as a whole. After the February revolution in 1917, soldiers openly dealt with the 'traitors' (officers with 'German' surnames) in their own way. Several generals were required to publicly explain their Orthodox, 'non-German' provenance.[8]

The fight against anti-war agitation, defeatism and panic-rumouring was also regarded as being of prime importance. One can now say with certainty that the Tsarist administration lost this particular battle amazingly quickly, possibly even before it had time to organise itself for the task. The worst of all possible methods was conceived; the 'guilty parties' were recruited into the Army, and consequently demoralised it still further. These circumstances were exploited with no small success by the Social Democrats.[9] The rapidity with which the Romanov dynasty was discredited during the war is astonishing. Bawdy jokes at the Tsar's expense (invariably featuring Rasputin) were doing the rounds, and the Empress was said to be involved in plots and to be behaving in a depraved manner. Nicholas II was even despised by those in his immediate circle. The feeling that the authorities were incapable of dealing with matters was all-pervasive, and it was a feeling that was shared by people who held the most diverse political views.[10]

With regard to this issue, the Stalinist leadership applied itself with an unusual sharpness. Knowing how it had all ended in 1914-17, they came down hard on any anti-Government actions and strove to destroy any form of opposition at birth. A large number of personnel and special military detachments were set to work with this end in mind.[11] Moreover, not only direct action was punishable, but also relatively innocent or private acts, such as criticism of the local leadership, or simply the telling of a political anecdote. Nothing resembling anti-state activity was to be seen within the Army or on the home front. Agents of the NKVD and the Party apparatus kept a watchful eye on people's attitudes, and were especially on the lookout for any open expression of dissatisfaction. Reports of such cases may be found in the former archive of the Central Committee of the Communist Party of the Soviet Union in Moscow, though the main thing these materials have in common is the absence in the protests recorded of any kind of activity directed at the central authorities or Stalin in person, who held very great authority.

A striking quality, which is characteristic of Russian society throughout the 20th century, was making itself felt. In the understanding of the people, the 'Great Sovereign' (before the Revolution) and Soviet leaders (after 1917) have, strangely, been seen as having the country's best interests at heart, but having to struggle with an administrative class that often abuses its position. Either they 'don't know' what is going on in certain places, or they 'aren't being properly informed'. It is as if they are always somewhat remote from events, their lives shrouded in mystery.[12] Consequently there has always been the belief among the common people that one only has to let things be known 'at the highest level', and everything will change for the better. Stalin consciously used his understanding of this characteristic in his policies. During the war, even extremely experienced Western diplomats fell for it, the majority of them believing that a personal meeting with the General Secretary would solve any problem.

During the war years Stalin created the impression among many foreign officials that his power was severely limited in that he was dependent to a large extent on the Supreme Soviet, the Politburo and even the military. For example, the British Ambassador in Moscow, Stafford Cripps, seriously believed, in July 1941, that there was a serious struggle going on between the Party and the military for power in the Soviet Union[13], and a British delegation visiting the Soviet Union in August 1942 was not able to determine who actually held the reins of power in the country. Some suggested that Stalin was merely a tool of the Politburo, and Churchill attributed changes in Stalin's behaviour to pressure from the Soviet of People's Commissars (Sovnarkom). He told Anthony Eden, 'There are two Stalins. There is the true Stalin, who is well disposed toward Churchill, and there is Stalin and his circle, which both he and I have to take into account.'[14]

American historians make the observation that in discussions with the Americans, Stalin often talked about the Supreme Soviet as if it were a body with real power, and that everything depended on it. For example, Roosevelt asked Stalin to delay recognition of the Provisional Government of Poland, and Stalin mockingly answered:

> 'Of course, I understand what you are saying entirely, but there's something here that means I am powerless to help you. The fact is that the Presidium of the Supreme Soviet told the Poles on the 27th of December that they intend to recognise the Provisional Government of Poland as soon as it is formed. This means that I am powerless to carry out your request.'[15]

In March 1945, when Stalin needed to demonstrate his dissatisfaction with American policy, he once again made reference to the powers of the Supreme Soviet. A conference concerned with the setting up of the UN was scheduled for the end of April in San Francisco. Stalin decided not to send Molotov, and in a letter to Roosevelt gave the following reason:

> 'Things have worked out in such a way that Molotov, in actual fact, cannot take part in the conference. Both Molotov and myself regret this, but the deputies of the Supreme Soviet have called for a session in April, which Molotov absolutely must attend, and so he will be unable to take part in the first sitting of the conference.'[16]

The American diplomat Charles Bohlen calls these references to the Supreme Soviet 'Stalin's gambit'. The strange thing is that during the war, Bohlen himself believed that Stalin had to deal with opposition in the Politburo. When he wrote his memoirs, Bohlen went back over the reports he had made at the time, and was extremely surprised that he could have said anything of the sort.[17]

It is interesting to follow the development of relations towards the enemy in both wars. In the first war soldiers at the front had on several occasions refused to shoot at each other, and there had been large-scale fraternisation with the enemy. Feelings of enmity and hatred towards the Germans and Austrians were hardly universal, and, apart from certain excesses, tolerance was shown with regard to the enemy, and prisoners of war were treated with respect.[18] A quarter of a century later it was quite a different story. Creating the image of the enemy and kindling feelings of hatred and the desire for revenge was at the very core of propaganda and political activity in the Red Army. Formally, a distinction was made between 'Germans' and 'fascists', the essential point being that not all Germans were fascists, though the soldiers immersed in day-to-day life at the front hardly gave this a lot of thought. Nazi terror played a particular role here, with the cynical and systematic slaughter of civilians (in many places for racial reasons), the barbaric treatment of prisoners of war, plundering, and the senseless destruction of cultural objects all conspiring to turn the general mood against the Germans far more effectively than any propaganda leaflet.

The Army responded willingly to the well-known slogan 'Kill a German!' and the idea took hold in real life. This was to have repercussions for the Germans themselves when the Red Army pushed into German territory; the Soviet command was forced to take special measures to curb violent acts of revenge against prisoners of war and the civilian population. Declassified documents from Russian military archives give cause to believe that the mass organised killing of German civilians, which Nazi propaganda claimed to be taking place, did not actually occur. The majority of crimes were committed as the result of drunkenness and were of a sexual nature, and one can say with certainty that the Army command, including Stalin, made a stand against such acts.[19] Nonetheless, many of those who had been at the front retained their hostility toward Germans for many years. The author has met veterans who continued to avoid contact with Germans (including those from the German Democratic Republic) even in the 1970s and 1980s.

The nature of relations between ordinary soldiers and officers was another important aspect that affected the state of the Army as a whole to an extraordinary degree. We do find accounts of officers in the First World War treating their soldiers well, showing an interest in their general well-being or simply being able to relate to them on a common, human level, but more often than not these examples stick in the mind by virtue of their rarity.[20] There is far more evidence showing that the ordinary ranks and the officers found themselves separated from each other by a gulf of incomprehension and estrangement. It was not only such 'small details' as lifestyle, pay and mobility through the ranks that influenced these feelings, but also long-established tradition with which few officers showed any inclination to break. Their habit was to regard their soldiers as a silent, sullen, faceless mass, and of course the 'mass' responded to them in precisely that way. After the February Revolution, this mutual mistrust spilled over into terrifying bloody reprisals against the officers.[21]

The existence of officers as a distinct group was also a feature of the Great Patriotic War, but such enormous divisions between the ranks were not felt. Of course, Communist Party policy, focusing on social egalitarianism and internationalism, had a clear influence on this. One must not, however, reject the paradoxical role of Stalinist repression, which was aimed directly at the commanding officers, and severely undermined the ability of the Army to fight effectively, but, at the same time, in turning yesterday's Red Army soldiers themselves into commanding officers served to change the make-up of the Army, and in so doing served to level out the differences between those who did the ordering and those who received the orders. On the very eve of the war, the Red Army faced a catastrophic shortage of commanding officers, with ground forces alone requiring (in total) 66,900.[22] But even those who were already in place were to a large extent put out of action in the early days of the war, and a situation developed across the board in which new officers were effectively 'taught' and 'looked after' by their soldiers (this applied especially with the younger ones).

The nationality question deserves attention in its own right. In both 1914 and 1941 Russia was a country comprised of many nationalities and in both wars her adversaries tried to exploit this fact. In 1914 the Austrians and Germans financed the 'Union for a Free Ukraine' (Sojuz Vizvoleniya Ukrainy), whose aim was to see the Ukraine leave the Tsarist empire. In 1916, a little later than it might have, Germany set up the so-called 'League of Peoples in Russia' (Liga Narodov Rossii), which called for the defeat of Russia.[23] These organisations had little real political influence, though they did on many occasions manage to cause problems for Russian counter-intelligence.

Far more 'successful' in stimulating nationalist confrontation had been the Tsarist Government itself, which was responsible for a large-scale uprising in Turkestan (now Central Asia and Kazakhstan). Trying to have as many Russian soldiers at the front, the authorities decided to call up men of other nationalities (who had previously been exempt from conscription) to be deployed in the rear. A mixture of poor preparation, the lack of convincing propaganda, the introduction of the right to buy oneself out of the Army (which meant that for the most part recruitment was confined to the poor) and contemptuous relations between local officials and the indigenous population very quickly led to an uprising. Despite the fact that this uprising was brutally suppressed, the empire had, nonetheless, suffered a heavy blow, and some areas remained hotbeds of unrest even after the Tsar had abdicated from the throne.[24]

Twenty-five years later, in the very same place, the Soviet leadership succeeded in mobilisation on an even greater scale without bringing about any serious protest. Why was this? It would appear that the new administration had learned from the lessons of its predecessor. In the first place, the status of the indigenous peoples had been changed; they had been given equal rights, lived in their own republics and had their own administration. The campaign to eradicate illiteracy had also borne fruit, and had raised the cultural level of the local population. Second, the call-up was universal, and was conducted under a single system through the regional military commissariats. All potential conscripts were on a register. This had certainly not been the case in Tsarist Russia, where lists simply did not exist, and had to be compiled after the call-up had been announced. This is why during the uprising of 1916 it was precisely these lists that had been destroyed, thus depriving the authorities of information with regard to potential recruits. Also, in 1941 there was no legal possibility of buying oneself out of the Army. Finally, Moscow carried out a far more effective propaganda campaign, which depicted the war as a threat to all and sundry, which could only be won by the mobilisation of the whole country.

With the information available today, we can reasonably say that on the home front there were no substantial nationalist actions, with all known incidents of opposition towards the Soviet authorities (the nationalist underground in the Baltic states, the armed struggle of Ukrainian and Byelorussian nationalists) occurring either as a result of German occupation or its aftermath. In comparison with the Kaiser's Germany, the Nazis were more capable of exploiting the factor of nationality, and had trained foreign nationals and emigrants for work in the Army, in intelligence and occupying administration long before the attack on the Soviet Union. From the very moment that 'Operation Barbarossa' was put into action, prisoners of war and citizens were drawn into collaborating, and in all the occupied territories German propaganda presented this as fighting in the struggle against Bolshevism, fighting for freedom and independence. Later, former collaborators who had settled in the West would use a similar rhetoric when seeking to justify their links with the Nazis, the one difference being their assertion that they had been fighting not only against Stalin, but against Hitler as well. Some authors accept this propaganda as the truth.[25]

In fact, during the war years the Germans did not succeed in stirring up national conflicts within the USSR. 'The colossus with legs of clay' did not collapse, though the negative consequences of Nazi rule continued to be felt for a considerable time, and it would be wrong to disregard their influence even today. It is essential to point out that the German command deliberately stirred up antagonism between nationalities. For example, in Poland, Ukrainian and Russian mercenaries were used in punitive operations. In Belarus, Lithuanians, Latvians and Ukrainians were used, in Serbia, Cossacks and Russians, and so on. In all captured territories, anti-Semitic and anti-communist agitation was very visibly carried out, which nurtured all kinds of rumours and prejudices and stimulated ethnic mistrust among the local population. Millions of people lived under such conditions for several years, and there is no way that this could not have left its mark on society's consciousness. It is no coincidence that the Soviet authorities identified widespread anti-Semitism in the liberated regions of the Baltic States, Ukraine and Moldavia, as well as in Russia itself. The degree of ideological bitterness and open anti-Soviet propaganda served to turn citizens who had lived in the occupied territories into objects of particular interest as far as state security bodies and the Party were concerned. Although the authorities were well aware that one could not groundlessly accuse everyone of collaboration, it was nonetheless the case that being branded as having lived 'under the Germans' ruined the lives of many people. 'And what were you doing during the occupation?' became a standard question put to those who were seeking work or who wished to travel abroad in the post-war years.

Of course, the first to be subjected to persecution were those who had actively collaborated with the occupying forces. It is very difficult to determine precisely how many were punished for this, since partisans and the advanced divisions of the Red Army killed many collaborators. According to existing figures, between July 1941 and 1953 around 450,000-500,000 people were convicted by military tribunals, and in the courts, of treason or of working with the Germans. Sentences varied from a few years incarceration to death. The Soviet Union continued its pursuit and prosecution of war criminals until the early years of Gorbachev's *perestroika*. With the dissolution of the Soviet Union this was brought to a halt, and unbelievable things began to happen.

The new states (Ukraine, Latvia, Lithuania and Estonia), in search of an heroic past and a national idea, turned to the history of the war. Very soon, former members of the SS and the police, and Wehrmacht soldiers from the local population, as well as elderly nationalists who had fought against the Red Army, began to emerge as 'new heroes' and 'ardent fighters against totalitarianism'. The mass media gave them a platform, widely publishing their dubious views, and the Government treated them sympathetically, regarding them much as they regarded those who had fought against Nazism. Even the Government of the Federal Republic of Germany, which has still not resolved the question on the payment of compensation to war victims and former inmates of concentration camps, did not hesitate in starting to pay pensions to some veterans from the Baltic countries.

An astonishing turnaround had taken place. Now it was not the millions of murdered Byelorussians, Jews, Russians or gypsies, nor the tortured prisoners of war or the resistance fighters who were being presented as the tragic victims of the war, but those who had served the Germans and had been rewarded with rations, money and decorations. In the Baltic States and the Ukraine their activity is now called 'fighting against Bolshevism', which sounds suspiciously like the language of wartime propaganda with which we are familiar. At various international fora the leaders of these countries have on several occasions expressed their regrets, and have even gone so far as to apologise, but this has done nothing to alter the situation. By way of justification they tell one story or another of how most of those involved were forcibly called up into the German Army, where they were compelled to carry out orders. But if it really were that way, if they really were forcibly driven into the ranks of the SS, then why do they have their annual festivals and their parades, and why do society and local authorities treat them so sympathetically? After all, these are not former inmates of Dachau or Auschwitz getting together for festive dinners and parades to 'celebrate' their own imprisonment.[26]

Comparing the ways in which the Tsarist and Stalinist regimes conducted themselves during wartime one has to admit the success of the latter. In spite of monstrous miscalculations and mistakes, which cost the lives of millions of people, the Stalinist leadership was able to stabilise an almost hopeless situation and mobilise the people to achieve victory. In addition to this, it is obvious that the Soviet Government took past experience into account, and the benefits of this are obvious in many of the measures taken – the destruction of food warehouses and industrial installations before retreating, preventative measures with regard to the 'fifth column', the centralisation of administration, a strict censorship, capital punishment both at the front and in the rear, active propaganda, and so on. In other words, Stalin did what Nicholas II could well have done, or did inconsistently. Would it be possible to identify any of the qualities or characteristics of the regime, which show up in a positive light and played their part in achieving victory?

Soviet historiography usually pointed to the role of ideology, the Party, the socialist economy, discipline and heroism. It is doubtful that the official ideology, namely Marxism-Leninism, as revised by Stalin, played a very significant role. Many soldiers and officers had a very vague understanding of Marxism and of the particular nuances of Leninism, but fought well nonetheless. Heroism and discipline were equally characteristic of other armies, such as the American, British, German and Polish. The harshness of Stalinist discipline and harshness in general as a method of waging war, while assisting to a certain extent in seeing that orders are carried out, eventually takes on a negative quality. From the very first days of the war Red Army soldiers and officers were shot, and Stalin in actual fact made this legal with Decree No 227 in July 1942. It is the author's view that such decrees do more to demonstrate the weakness of a regime than its strength, since it is evident that it cannot lead by any other method. It is extremely doubtful that the sight of Red Army soldiers hanging from lampposts could have done anything to spur the Army on to greater exploits.

Regardless of the abundance of various kinds of documentation, as strange as it may seem, the role of the Communist Party demands more detailed analysis. Did Stalin hold Party meetings at General Headquarters? This is an interesting question, and one that still has not been answered. It is also not clear whether or not the All-Union Communist Party of Bolsheviks (not Stalin!) had any kind of influence on the activity of, for example, the General Staff or the NKVD. The Party certainly played no role in determining foreign policy during the war years. Stalin decided everything personally. There was not even any special department in the Central Committee that would have dealt with international affairs until May 1943 (after the dissolution of the Comintern). It begins to look as though the Party worked less as an ideological institution and more as an instrument for mobilisation and the carrying out of orders. Unfortunately for the Tsarist administration, there was no such instrument available to it in 1914.

Much effort has been put into understanding the Stalinist economy, but much remains unclear. For many years it was an object of pride in the Soviet Union that her economy had shown its 'superiority' and had 'won' the war. In the heat of all the arguments many authors failed to notice that the economies of the USA and Great Britain also won. It is impossible to say how Russia might have fared in 1941 if she had had a capitalist economy. Our business is with Stalin's system, where industry and agriculture were managed on the principle of orders and the fulfilment of orders, of punishment and encouragement, and victory in the war shows that such methods achieved material results. The experience of the USSR gives pause for thought. Who knows, it may be that the failure of *perestroika* and the dissolution of the USSR in 1991 could in part be ascribed to the overwhelming nature of the economic experience of the war, since the methods of Stalinist planning and management had actually remained unchanged since 1945.[27]

The hard-fought victory in the war conferred world-power status on the USSR, Stalin succeeded in achieving advantageous resolutions with regard to all territorial questions, and it is indisputable that never before had Russia held a position of such authority. Nonetheless, the contrast between the political results that had been achieved and the state of the economy, which was in ruin, was plain for all to see. The state of the economy was simply not appropriate to that of one of the world's leading powers, and one can hardly say that this was not understood. Economic revitalisation became the priority of the entire Party and state machine, but the maintenance of superpower status demanded considerable expenditure, from the need for a vast bureaucratic apparatus to having to keep considerable financial reserves in order to be able to provide aid and assistance to developing countries in the socialist camp. For many years it did indeed appear that the USSR had almost coped with these tasks, but the years 1988-91 proved that this was not the case.

We should turn our attention to one important fact that made it far easier for Stalin (among others) to carry out his plans. This concerns the peculiarities of the social situation of the population, which gave rise to a surprising ethical and psychological climate. Since 1914 people had lived more or less perpetually in a state of militarisation and mobilisation, and the prevailing atmosphere was one filled with all kinds of threats and dangers. This created a psychological climate that, on the one hand, united people in the face of the uncertainties ahead, and, on the other, forced them to learn to live with even the most barbaric acts on the part of the authorities. The expropriation of provisions and goods, the dispossession of the kulaks, the wave of repression in the 1930s and the deportation of whole peoples were explained by social expediency and the fact that there were enemies all around. Famine, which almost always followed war in Russia, had left an indelible impression on the people – 'If only it weren't for war and famine' was a mantra repeated countless times by mothers and grandmothers to their children and grandchildren. Consequently, there was the ever-present hope that the future would be better, if not for the parents, then at least for the children. Given such an atmosphere, even the slightest improvement in the availability of consumer goods was seen as being a sign that the authorities were taking care of the people. Even if the range of goods was limited, it was at least still something positive; after all, 'It was worse during the war'. One of the main reasons for Gorbachev's failure was that, at a time of relative stability and in peacetime, he made people remember war and famine.

The most terrible consequence of both wars was the number of victims. In the period from the beginning of the First World War to 1 March 1917, the number of those mobilised in the Russian Army reached 15.1 million, with total losses of personnel by 31 December 1917 of 7.4 million (1.7 million killed), and that does not include 3.4 million captured by the enemy.[28] Losses rose sharply as a result of the civil war and famine. Sadly, there are no accurate figures, but according to approximate calculations the population decreased in the period 1918 to 1922 by between 14 and 18 million. Of these, 5-6 million starved, 3 million died from illness, about 3 million from the 'red' and 'white' sides were killed, and approximately 2 million left the country.[29]

The USSR's human casualties in the Second World War have been a matter for political feuding for such a long time that it would appear that the precise figures will never be known. The only thing we can say with any degree of certainty is that these figures vary from 25 million to 32 million. It is a terrible fact that for every day of the war around 20,000 died. If we add to all this the tens of millions who were injured, crippled and maimed, and those left without relatives, then either directly or indirectly every Soviet family was touched by the war.[30] Material destruction was on a no less monstrous scale, with 1,710 towns, more than 70,000 villages and 6 million buildings (including 1,670 churches) being destroyed, ruined or burned. Around 25 million were made homeless. Losses during the war years were 20 times greater than the national revenue in 1940. In other words, the USSR lost around 30 per cent of her national wealth.[31]

The experience of both wars shows that each time it took around 10 to 15 years to rebuild the country and achieve a relatively normal kind of life. Paradoxically, Russia at the end of the 20th century found herself in something resembling a post-war situation. One can hardly predict the way Russia will develop, but the questions as to whether the people have enough patience, and whether the authorities have enough knowledge of history so as not to repeat the mistakes of the past, will in due course find their answers.

Recommended reading

Erickson, J., *Stalin's War with Germany* (London: Weidenfeld & Nicolson, 1975)

Frenkin, M., *Russkaya armiya i revolutsiya* (Munich: Logos, 1978)

Giatsintov, E., *Zapiski belogo ofitsera* (St Petersburg: Interpoligraftsentr, 1992)

Harrison, M., *Soviet Planning in Peace and War, 1938-1945* (Cambridge: Cambridge University Press, 1985)

Linz, S. J. (ed), *The Impact of World War II on the Soviet Union* (Totowa: Rowman & Allanheld, 1985)

Malia, M., *The Soviet Tragedy: A History of Socialism in Russia* (New York: Free Press, 1995)

Stone, N., *The Eastern Front, 1914-1917* (London: Penguin, 1998)

Wildman, A. K., *The End of the Russian Imperial Army* (Princeton: Princeton University Press, 1980)

Zetterberg, S., *Die Liga der Fremdfolker Russlands 1916-1918* (Helsinki: Finnische Historische Gesellschaft, 1978)

Notes

[1] Immediately after its beginning the First World War was formally proclaimed in Russia to be 'Great' and 'Patriotic'. In Western historiography some scholars still refer to the war as 'the Great War'.

[2] Daniel Orlovsky, 'Velikaya voina i rossiyskaya pamyat' in *Rossiya i pervaya mirovaya voina* (St Petersburg: 1999) pp49-57

[3] One can mention the re-creation of the Christ the Saviour Cathedral right in the city centre of Moscow, which cost millions of pounds.

[4] M. Malia, *The Soviet Tragedy: A History of Socialism in Russia* (New York: 1995) p16; V. Buldakov, *Krasnaya Smuta* (Moscow, 1997) pp17, 120-1

[5] A. Brusilov, *Moi vospominaniya* (Moscow: 1963) pp81-3

[6] E. S. Senyavskaya, *Psikhologiya voiny v XX veke* (Moscow: 1999) pp195-7

[7] For latest debates and documents see Peter Klein (ed) *Die Einsatzgruppen in der besetzten Sowjetunion 1941/42* (Berlin: 1997) and A. Mertsalov, *Stalinism i voina* (Moscow: 1998) pp320-36

[8] V. Buldakov, op cit, p122

[9] See D. P. Oskin, *Zapiski praporschika* (Moscow: 1931); M. Frenkin, *Russkaya armiya i revolutsiya* (Munich: 1978); A. K. Wildman, *The End of the Russian Imperial Army*, Vols I-II (Princeton: 1987)

[10] V. S. Diyakin, 'Nikolai, "Alexandra i Kamariliya"' in *Noviy Chasovoi* No 3 (1995) pp154-5; G. Z. Ioffe, *Velikiy Oktiabr i epilog tsarisma* (Moscow: 1987) p15

[11] The best-known in the West are the NKVD (internal secret police) and SMERSH (Soviet counter-intelligence body). The latter is an abbreviation of the Russian expression 'Death to the spies'.

[12] See V. G. Korolenko, 'Zemli! Zemli!' in *Novyi Mir* (1990) p169; V. Buldakov, op cit, pp22-21

[13] S. Miner, *Between Churchill and Stalin* (London: Chapel Hill, 1988, pp65-6; M. Kitchen, *British Policy towards the Soviet Union during the Second World War* (Basingstoke: Houndmills, 1986) pp66-7

[14] M. Kitchen, op cit, pp140, 148; M. Gilbert, *Winston S. Churchill*, Vol VII (London: 1986) pp189, 364

[15] R. Dallek, *Franklin Roosevelt and American Foreign Policy, 1932-1945* (New York: 1979) p504; W. Taubman, *Stalin's American Policy* (New York and London: 1982) p76; *Perepiska Predsedatelya Soveta Ministrov SSSR s presidentami SSHA i premier-ministrami Velikobritanii*, Vol 2 (Moscow: 1976) pp194-5

[16] *Perepiska*, op cit, Vol 2, p213; W. Taubman, op cit, p96

[17] C. Bohlen, *Witness to History 1929-1969* (New York: 1973) pp197, 217

[18] E. S. Senyavskaya, op cit, pp260-3

[19] *Velikaya Otechestvennaya voina, 1941-1945*, Kniga 4 (Vol 4) (Moscow: 1999) pp270-6

[20] See E. Giatsintov, *Zapiski belogo ofitsera* (St Petersburg: 1992)

[21] D. P. Oskin, *Zapiski soldata* (Moscow: 1929) pp45-6, 119-29; V. Buldakov, op cit, pp120-7

[22] *Kanun i nachalo voiny* (Leningrad: Dokumenty, 1991) p294

[23] *Krasniy Arkhiv* (Moscow: 1929) Vol 2, p10; S. Zetterberg, *Die Liga der Fremdfolker Russlands 1916-1918* (Helsinki: 1978)

[24] See *Vosstanie v Srednei Azii i Khazahstane* (Moscow: 1971)

[25] As an illustration of such literature see W. Alexeev and T. Stavrou, *The Great Revival: Russian Orthodox Church under German Occupation* (Minneapolis: 1976); C. Andreev, *Vlasov and Russian Liberation Movement* (Cambridge: 1987); J. Hoffmann, *Deutsche und Kalmyken 1942 bis 1945* (Freiburg: 1977); idem, *Die Ostlegionen 1941-1943* (Freiburg: 1981)

[26] Materials of the symposium on Holocaust and collaboration in the Baltic States, March 1999, United States Holocaust Memorial Museum, Washington, DC; Materials of the conference on Holocaust and Education, 26-28 January 2000, Stockholm (author's archive)

[27] For more details see Peter Gatrell and Mark Harrison, 'The Russian and Soviet Economy in Two World Wars' in *Economic History Review* Vol 46 (3) (1993) pp425-52; M. Harrison (ed), *The Economics of World War II: Six great powers in international comparison* (Cambridge: 1999)

[28] *Rossiya v mirovoi voine 1914-1918 goda* (Moscow: 1925) pp17, 30-1

[29] V. Buldakov, *Krasnaya smuta* (Moscow: 1997) p244

[30] See *Velikaya Otechestvennaya voina, 1941-1945*, Kniga 4 (Moscow: 1999) pp282-4

[31] Ibid, p294; *Narodnoye Khozyaistvo v Velikoi Otechestvennoi voine* (Moscow: 1990) pp52-3

Chapter 7

Italy: extreme crisis, resistance and recovery

Marco Pluviano and Irene Guerrini

The period between 1900 and 1950 saw a phase of forced modernisation for Italy that enabled her to overcome her relative backwardness. The two World Wars played a crucial part in this process, producing significant changes in daily life, and thus modifying centuries-old customs and habits.

To understand the impact of the two World Wars upon the Italian population it is important to note that, in the case of Italy, the concept of a 'Modern Thirty Years' War' is particularly relevant. The seizure of power by the Fascists and the ensuing violent repression of the opposition, the long and cruel war of reconquest in Libya, the war of aggression against Ethiopia, the participation in the Spanish Civil War, and the occupation of Albania were all examples of a continuum of acts of violence, mourning and militarist exaltation that reached a logical conclusion with the Italian intervention beside Nazi Germany in 1940. The progressive militarisation of the society by the Fascist regime, together with the 'campaign for autarchy' following the economic sanctions enforced by the League of Nations in 1935, contributed to a perpetual climate of 'latent war'. All of these elements combined to produce a degree of continuity in Italian society between the wars. In 1940, memories of the terrible impact of the First World War, and of the ensuing indelible cultural trauma, remained substantially intact, but nobody imagined that this time the impact on Italian society would be much worse.

By definition, soldiers are the first to face the impact of a conflict. With regard to the Italian soldiers, both wars discredited many myths nourished by the governments and the military authorities. The wars also brought soldiers face-to-face with the often unfamiliar realities of the modern world.

During the First World War, the vast majority of conscripts were peasants, snatched from their communities by the draft. Shifts in population were definitely not a new phenomenon in a country that had seen substantial numbers of its population emigrate overseas. This time, however, leaving home was not an individual choice; it was the State that used all its coercive powers to make men leave their families. The war brought the Italian peasants into unprecedented contact with the State, as it sought to provide them with weapons, training, uniforms, food and transport.

There was, in fact, little popular enthusiasm behind Italy's decision to enter the war. Very few people expected great advantages to result from the country's intervention; Italians either opposed the outbreak of the war or they accepted it supinely as a misfortune inflicted by destiny. Yet the war did help to forge a greater sense of national unity. For millions of Italians, the war provided their first opportunity to share their lives with people from other regions, with different customs and life experiences; most of the rural population, and even some urban dwellers, had not fully realised that they belonged to a single national community. The national language grew stronger. Those who normally spoke their own dialects began to speak Italian in order to communicate with comrades from other regions. The spreading of this sense of national belonging among those who were once excluded accompanied the diffusion of the concept of 'citizenship'; Italian soldiers increasingly thought of themselves as 'citizens' rather than as 'subjects'. This sense of national belonging was not therefore a factor that pre-dated Italy's participation in the war, but rather it was the outcome, resulting from coercion and the traumatic strains endured during the years of conflict.

An extraordinary change was produced in soldiers' lives by propaganda; only those citizens who had habitually read the pre-war press had previously been touched by it. The Army, with the support of civilian volunteers, began a campaign to create and organise public consent, which was combined with the coercion exercised by an inflexible and efficient Government apparatus. After the Caporetto retreat, propaganda leaflets flooded the trenches. This propaganda effort made use of the most recent means of communication, and included works by many famous artists. It was thus during the war that many ordinary soldiers had their first experiences of the cinema, the gramophone and the theatre. The war propaganda was extended to civilians, who were invited by every available means to join the common effort.

The war also brought a great change in the diet of most soldiers from rural and working-class backgrounds. In January 1916 the daily rations for soldiers consisted of 750gm of bread, 375gm of meat, 200gm of pasta and, in addition, sugar, coffee, cheese, wine and chocolate.[1] This involved for many northerners the replacement of polenta with pasta (which in the same period became the 'emblem dish' of the national cuisine), and for southerners the daily consumption of spirits. The men now had the chance to eat meat every day, instead of just a few times in the year. Most soldiers, during the conflict, improved their alimentary habits a great deal, with an average intake of 4,000 calories a day until November 1916 and 3,000 calories a day thereafter. These nutritional standards were much higher in comparison with those enjoyed, as an average, before the war, and they were never to be equalled during the Second World War. Soldiers in fact did not frequently complain about hunger in the period from 1915 to 1918, while the question of food shortages became a recurring complaint in the later conflict. In 1941 the Italian population consumed just 2,630 calories a day, falling to 2,125 calories in 1943 and only 1,800 calories in the period 1944-45. These amounts applied to soldiers and civilians alike, the former enjoying no special dietary privileges.[2]

During the First World War most soldiers fought bravely, bearing pain, facing danger and tremendous hardship, enduring tough discipline and completely modifying the habits and values that had guided their lives. Many of the soldiers were poorly educated, but the war gave a tremendous boost to literacy levels among the Italian population, with a vast number of letters and diaries being written. The need to maintain a relationship with their families and the so-called 'real world', in order to communicate their new and upsetting experiences in a written form, reached such an extent as to cause a sudden conversion from a mainly oral culture to a written one.

On the other hand, for the soldiers of the Second World War the situation was far more complicated. When the Fascist regime decided to take part in the war, the Italian population largely backed the Government, even though the first demonstrations of enthusiasm were restricted to sections close to the regime. The mobilisation of the Army was slower and less resolute in comparison with 1915, but it was carried on without the opposition registered 25 years before. Emilia Sasia's statement is representative of the attitude of most Italians:

> 'At first I was not against the war: the patriotic ideal, because it was being inculcated in our minds, was still there. Then after noting the disasters and realising that many were not coming back and, above all, when my landlord (a distinguished and very polite gentleman who was a Jew) was arrested, it's been as if I had opened my eyes, it's been almost a trauma. There was then a rebellion against Fascism, whose memory had not been so bad for me, since I was a teenager.'[3]

In the poorest regions of the country many people saw the war as a way to escape from unemployment. People had been convinced that the war would be short and victorious. There were consequently widespread expectations that the sacrifices required by the conflict would produce a great improvement in the standard of living in Italy, especially for the working classes.

Soldiers were actually to experience tremendous hardships very early on and were scattered in theatres characterised by harsh environmental conditions: the Greek-Albanian, the Russian and the African fronts. But poor organisation and a lack of adequate supplies exacerbated these difficult conditions. These latter deficiencies were especially striking when compared with the relative abundance in the previous conflict. In spite of all the militarist rhetoric of Fascism, the Italian Army entered the war poorly equipped and almost nothing was done to address its shortcomings. Italian soldiers had to get used to hunger, cold and disease. Margherita Giordana, sister of a soldier who disappeared in Russia, recollects:

> 'I know they were poorly equipped: my brother had just gone to the Russian front and my mother would already rush to the baker's, to send Francesco a bag of bread. And then she sent other bundles of socks and clothes and cognac and more bread. How can we win the war? In the hospitals in Karkov they did not even have bandages for our wounded, they used paper instead, and in the end even paper was missing. Russian population, poor people, were good and generous to our soldiers.'[4]

Francesco Tortone, another soldier who disappeared in Russia, wrote on 24 August 1942 from the Donetz basin: 'We have not seen bread since our departure from

Italy, just those ever-present hard biscuits, I dip them into the water.'[5] Problems were not only restricted to the issue of rations, or to poor equipment, but also to the lack of adequate transport, as Tortone noted on 21 September 1942: 'We have walked about six hundred kilometres to reach the front line and we have got there exhausted.'[6]

Such examples of disorganisation and inefficiency were not restricted to the Russian front. Giovanni Barroero wrote from Albania on 27 January 1941, in a letter to his parents: 'I wanted to ask you if you could send me something to eat and a pair of socks too with a sweater, besides a paper envelope, as I have run out of it. I want to add that I am here with half-frozen feet but I hope to recover my health without having to go to the hospital.'[7]

What did not change, in comparison with the First World War, was the use of propaganda. It was even more pervasive in the second conflict, permeating every aspect of military life. Discipline was, on the contrary, less hard. During the Second World War military justice sentenced to death 524 individuals (400 of whom were civilians), far fewer than the more than 4,028 such sentences that were pronounced (750 of which were executed) during the previous conflict. In the earlier conflict there were also 150 summary shootings.[8] Punishments were less severe. This was probably due both to the absence of political opposition, which had suffered from 20 years of repression by the police, and to the strong 'political' control exercised by officials and the State-Party's totalitarian apparatus. The repressive power of the State remained a factor until at least 1942.

During the Second World War soldiers experienced a new concern, unknown to those who had fought in the previous conflict: the fear of losing loved ones who remained at home. Since the start of the 19th century the 'home front' had not often experienced the horrors of war (except for those areas conquered by the Austro-German armies after Caporetto). However, after 1940, for the first time in 150 years, the entire civilian population of Italy was to suffer from armed conflict, from bombings and, after the summer of 1943, from invasion and civil war. To soldiers this constituted a real shock, which frightened them almost as much as the dangers they had to face in action.

A further element to take into consideration when examining the impact of the wars on Italian soldiers, is their attitude towards great defeats. After the tragedy of Caporetto, those who fought in the First World War found the energy to keep on fighting, even though the war remained far from popular. Indeed, the transition from an offensive war to the defence of the national territory actually helped to increase the soldiers' identification with their nation. Such feelings created greater support for Italy's war aims than had existed at the outset of the conflict.

The soldiers' reaction was completely different when faced with the most important event of the 1940-45 period, namely the moral dilemma of 1943. After the monarchical restoration, on 25 July, and the dissolution of the State structures following the armistice on 8 September, Italian soldiers faced a stark choice. They had to decide between loyalty to the monarchy, backed by those who sought to revive the democratic tradition, or support for the ties with a 20-year-old regime that had influenced a whole generation. For the first time soldiers had to make a decision of their own, without constriction and under no compulsion from hierarchies, and, paradoxically, even those who chose to follow the Fascist dictatorship did so freely. This was an opportunity to grow up – a coming of age for the overwhelming majority of Italians.

Most soldiers decided to abide by their promise of loyalty to the King and to support the forces that sought to restore freedom in Italy. This was not an easy choice: 600,000 of them were taken prisoner and interned in the German concentration camps, without being regarded and treated as war prisoners. The consequences were tragic: 80,000-100,000 prisoners died, victims of exhaustion, violence, starvation and disease, refusing the easy alternative of joining the Fascist forces. Hundreds of thousands took part in the Resistance in Italy, as well as in Albania, Yugoslavia and France. Those soldiers who chose to join the Neo-Fascist Social Republic were little more than 100,000. The others, either fighting against the Nazi-Fascist forces or refusing to contribute to the war effort of the Axis, made a choice of freedom during one of the most difficult moments in the national history, bravely redeeming themselves after 20 years of military submission to the Fascist regime.

We can conclude that in the period 1915-18 the response of individuals to the moral and material demands of war occurred in the context (and with the aid) of a strong and efficient socio-political system. By contrast, the later conflict was conducted in the context of the collapse of a socio-political system that had aspired to represent the essence and the totality of Italy.

Undoubtedly, the two World Wars' impact on soldiers' lives was deep, acute and often dramatic, but what the civilians underwent was not that different. The First World War involved, above all, a real haemorrhage of men, especially from the agricultural sector. In three and a half years more than 5 million men, out of a population of about 36.5 million, were mobilised. In the Second World War a slightly larger number was mobilised, but over a span of five years and with a population that had increased by almost 8 million people.[9]

Families had to cope with the sudden departure of the principal breadwinner. The cultural revolution provoked by the absence of men, the traditional decision-makers within a family, was equally profound. Women had to take upon themselves all the decisions, even though men often gave directions through their letters. Giovanni Viganò wrote in a letter to his wife, on 9 June 1916: 'Let me know if silkworms are according to plans, if the countryside is fine and what the pig's weight is ... all the money you earned is for the field workmen.'[10] Another example comes from Attilio Brandolini's letter to his wife, dated 14 May 1916: 'When you write to me, let me know how many pigs you've bought this year. I'd like also to learn how much we shall get from the veil's sale, the one that was born when I was at home. Let me know if you have made the hay-stacks and how things in the country are and how the season is going ... here, at the front, it's raining.'[11]

In the countryside women were helped by the old men but, nevertheless, they played an unprecedented role; in towns, where the pattern of an 'enlarged family' was less common, they had to take upon themselves much more fully the direction and management of the family. Not only did they have to take decisions, but they also had to contribute directly to the household income. As the allowance distributed to the soldiers' families was absolutely insufficient (and it was not assigned to the peasants' families that owned land, regardless of the quantity of land owned), families had to find whatever means they could to survive.

Women and young people entered the labour market in vast numbers. In the countryside women co-operated with the few males left, and did not limit themselves to the tasks that tradition had reserved for them. Two peasant women from the province of Cuneo recollect: 'My husband left on May 11, 1915. Well then, after I'd done my day's work; working night and day. I would close my children in the stable, to prevent them from going out, and for an hour I would carry on my back a pannier of dung up to the field, in order to manure it and to plant a couple of potatoes in spring…' And 'Both my brothers were at war … during those years I worked as a strong man, I had to replace them both.'[12]

In towns women and young people represented a labour reservoir from which industries drew to face the enormous increase of industrial production demanded by the war effort. Women were paid, on average, 50-70 per cent less than men doing the same jobs. The presence of this very large and cheap labour reservoir allowed industrialists and the military authorities, who supervised the Industrial Mobilisation, to restrain wage claims and control working regulations. Men were threatened with being sent immediately to the front if they violated the severe disciplinary rules. Initially it was women who lived in towns that thronged into industry and the public services, but by the middle of 1916 many women, both young and old, began to crowd into the factories from the rural hinterland around the big cities. This female workforce soon found work outside those sectors, such as textiles, that were reserved to them by tradition, entering what were considered to be the strongholds of the skilled male working class (iron and steel, engineering, chemicals). But women did not limit themselves to jobs as industrial workers; many middle-class women took advantage of the education they had been given, taking white-collar jobs, both in the industrial sector and in the state services. Even outside the labour market women reached an unprecedented level of public presence and social visibility.

For most middle-class women mobilisation amounted to involvement in welfare institutions, including work as hospital and Red Cross nurses. Working-class women, on the other hand, employed in industry, became involved in trade unions. Thus the expectations of employers and the authorities concerning the female labour force were not met. Far from displaying a moderate attitude in the factories, as had been anticipated, they became involved in controversy, promoting strikes and resisting attempts to increase their workload. They acted with a determination that reflected the State's inability to blackmail them – unlike their male counterparts, they could not be threatened with being sent to the front. The women who entered factories in that period, therefore, broke social conventions twice. On the one hand, they came out of the gender jobs entrusted to them by tradition, also experiencing night and Sunday shifts (a development that raised concern in conservative circles). On the other hand, they refused to comply with the traditional female non-involvement in the political world; instead, they promoted and participated in social conflict.

Among the effects of the war on Italian daily life was a worsening of working conditions: longer working shifts, with standard times raised from 60 to 70-75 hours per week, 12 hours a day. The purchasing power of salaries decreased, with an increase in the cost of living by 400 per cent in four years, alongside significantly lower average wage increases and an increase in workplace accidents.[13]

In spite of all this, the economic condition of working-class families did not get much worse; the massive demands for labour increased the number of employed, and each family could now rely on more than one salary. The application on a vast scale of piecework payment, albeit at the cost of heavy exploitation, meant that, on the whole, wages were maintained at sufficiently high levels. The food supplies of the urban populations were adequate, except for a few hard times in Turin and Milan. On the whole, urban populations suffered due to a considerably greater workload, an increased incidence of occupational and social diseases, a higher death rate and heavy social repression. They did, however, experience an increase in total consumption of 5 per cent in four years, and in 1918 their standard of living was higher than that recorded from 1942 until the end of the Second World War.

Farmers also experienced a situation of ups and downs. In some areas farmers sustained a limited improvement in their standard of living thanks to a rise in prices for foodstuffs and to the achievements of local trade unions. The automatic extensions of rents until the end of the conflict and the introduction of rent controls were particularly positive elements. The most disadvantaged were the farm labourers' families, who were not always supported by the trade unions.

The workers' experience was not entirely negative. From the beginning of 1917 the Government was persuaded to grant some advantages in favour of workers, in order to guarantee continuing high levels of productivity. Compulsory insurance against workplace accidents was introduced, and Conciliation Commissions were set up to tackle and settle disputes, thus undermining the authority of employers. Officials in charge of production control in the factories were often more disposed to grant salary increases, because that way productivity rates could be kept high. To all this it must be added that the State co-ordinated a large network of social centres, managed by private voluntary service and by local authorities. These initiatives certainly did not solve the basic causes of poverty, especially for those families that were unable to benefit from the increased employment opportunities, but they at least enabled the majority of these people to survive.

Those who witnessed the greatest deterioration in their standard of living were middle-class professional men and those who received fixed private incomes (revenues from land and house rents). The former, in fact, rarely had the chance to replace heads of families in their occupations. The latter suffered from the rent controls and the large increase in the cost of living. These classes, quite numerous at the time, provided the Army with a great number of reserve officers, and many of them did not return. At the end of the conflict they were among the social groups that suffered the greatest sense of economic hardship, and faced particular difficulties in recovering their financial position. These were the classes that most supported Fascism. In many cases they sold real estate, especially in the rural areas; in fact, the statistics show a considerable amount of smallholders and farmers in 1920, in comparison with ten years before.

The increased contact between the sexes at work, both in rural areas and the towns, alongside the increasing necessity for women to attend public places, deeply annoyed the most conservative parts of society, especially those that were most affected by church propaganda. But soldiers were also deeply upset by reports of sexual promiscuity, which were exaggerated by moralists who described the home front as a place of corruption and revelry, where 'shirkers' preyed on the virtue of soldiers' wives and girlfriends. This description of the situation was definitely exaggerated, but the war did change women's perception of their proper 'moral responsibilities'. Some among the younger generations began to attend the cinemas and dance halls. This was in part due to the possibility of keeping a part of their wages to spend on themselves. The chance of meeting young men at work favoured the development of love affairs outside their usual circles. The war had definitely been for most women an occasion for advancement, and for breaking away from the traditional hierarchies that had perpetrated female subordination. Moreover, for some of them this had also been a moment of sexual liberation, as they were able to conduct relationships without the knowledge or approval of male authority figures.

The families of Italian prisoners of war need to be considered separately. The very hard disciplinary system that ruled the Italian Army meant that the suspicion of being a deserter fell on those who were prisoners. The conditions under which they were captured had to be made extremely clear to avoid the risk of having charges brought, and to prevent punitive measures from being meted out towards their relatives (including suspension of the subsidy, or publication of their relative's name as a deserter).

The conditions of Italian prisoners of war in Austria-Hungary and Germany were very hard: hunger and disease raged through the camps and the only prisoners who could hope to enjoy better conditions were those assigned to agricultural work with local farmers. The Italian authorities did not assist prisoners' families with the dispatch of clothes and food parcels. Consequently, even though parcels were delivered regularly, they were generally insufficient, and many poor families were not able to send anything. Prisoners' letters contained constant requests for food and clothes, such as those made by Giuseppe Zonghi in a letter, sent from Ingolstad, dated 25 November 1917: 'Do not be astonished if I keep asking you to send as many parcels as you can, full of stuffing food such as beans, rice, dried chestnuts, etc, and bread especially.'[14] Annibale Calderale wrote in his diary: 'Germans have provided everyone with a handful of biscuits and a tin of meat for 25 people.'[15]

To make matters even worse, in contrast with the Allies, the Italian Government refused, for a long time, to organise its own shipment of aid to the prisoners. Italy expected, in fact, that the Austrian and German authorities should provide everything. This neglect of the prisoners, by their own Government, contributed to the deaths in prison of 100,000 Italians, suffering from cold, disease and malnutrition (about 1,000 calories were, on average, all that were granted to the prisoners). The experience of the prisoners' relatives in Italy was then a completely new one, both in terms of the scale and harshness of the phenomenon: about 600,000 men were imprisoned, leaving their relatives in a state of anguish, bitterness and economic hardship, and often facing the reprobation and suspicion of the authorities.

During the Second World War conditions for the civilian population deteriorated dramatically, in all respects. When the country entered the conflict, conditions were already poor; the previous wars had severely tried the economy, weighing heavily on the national budget. Public indebtedness had risen and the industrial and financial system had still to absorb the after-effects from the economic crisis of the early 1930s. Sanctions imposed by the League of Nations, as a consequence of the invasion of Ethiopia, had caused the Government to start the 'autarchy campaign'. At the end of the 1930s the working class was bearing a heavy burden, with a standard of living that had definitely deteriorated. Apart from the undeniable difficulties of the national economy, there was also the impossibility of the trade unions mounting even the slightest defence of working-class interests, as free trade unions had been banned in the 1920s. The middle class, on the contrary, had maintained a better standard of living, and therefore it felt even more deeply the impact of the war: devaluation, inflation, and the collapse in the value of shares, state bonds and other investments.

Consequently, poverty and malnutrition spread in social sectors that had historically been able to ignore such problems. In the spring of 1942 more than 40 per cent of the population was undernourished, and in 1943, in spite of a good harvest, 25 per cent were in the same condition. The situation deteriorated in 1944-45 in the regions that had not been occupied by the Allies. Thus it can be stated that the Second World War involved, for the average Italian, the rediscovery of hunger, and a shortage of the principal consumer goods and means of subsistence. The general impact of the conflict on Italy's inhabitants was to set living standards back by almost a century.

The reasons for the difficult situation were due to a combination of external and internal factors. The traditional dependence upon imports, due to limited agricultural production and a scarcity of industrial raw materials, became an almost insoluble problem because of the naval blockade imposed by the Allies. The latter's impact was only partially counterbalanced by some supplies from Germany, which were in any case paid for with agricultural and industrial products. Some of the harvests during the five years of war were poor, and, especially from 1943 onwards, heavy bombing caused serious disruption to both rail and road transport, making the supply of the big cities really difficult.

Many shortcomings of the Fascist Government exacerbated these difficulties. Arrangements for civil mobilisation were started late and worked badly, in contrast to the generally adequate measures adopted during the First World War. Factories and companies were slow to replace male employees with young female labourers, postponing this step until a point when they had to undergo this change suddenly, thus creating management difficulties and severely damaging productivity.

Rationing was also particularly inefficient. Even though complete self-sufficiency in corn production had not been established, bread (being with pasta the two main elements in the Italian diet) was not rationed until the beginning of October 1941. The rationing was not planned to cover all the fundamental needs of the population. The Government provided only a part of people's requirements (1,000 calories a day), leaving the rest to the 'free market'. The immediate consequence was the flourishing of the black market. Farmers did not deliver foodstuffs to the government pools, which, in their turn, were supposed to supply both the system of rationing and the free market. The farmers' reluctance resulted from a number of factors: distrust in the State and in the regime; inefficiency of the collection and distribution systems; and prospects of larger profits. From the end of 1942 foodstuffs began to reach cities along unofficial channels: the farmers who went to the cities and sold their products to middlemen or by retail; the inhabitants of towns who went to the areas of agricultural production to buy or exchange goods; or those who went to the country and bought agricultural products in large quantities to resell them to other customers in the cities.

The result was ruinous for the inhabitants of the urban centres. Citizens who wanted to obtain rationed products had to stand in long queues, which generally formed before dawn, and often many of them were left empty-handed. To buy products on the black market people were obliged to pay extortionately, thus exceeding the income of many. Consequently, for those belonging to the middle class, it became common practice to sell the family jewels and valuables such as pictures, furnishings, carpets, state bonds and shares. But those who did not own such items deprived themselves of their best clothes, bed linen and tablecloths. Giuliana Bizzarra from Rome recollects: 'My father went to exchange my mother's fine bed-linen for a handful of fruit and vegetables.'[16] The inhabitants of the Italian cities thus confronted not only hunger but also real impoverishment. They were forced to part with goods that had been handed down from generation to generation, and were reduced to bartering in order to survive.

Women especially fought this struggle for survival; men, even if they did not serve in the Army, were subjected to the discipline and heavy regulation of work, which did not leave them enough time to take care of provisions. It must be borne in mind that, from September 1943, when Italy was still under Fascist control, men ran the risk of being 'mopped up'. Anyone who was walking along a road, in the countryside or in a town, could be held hostage by Germans or Fascists, as an act of retaliation against the actions of the Resistance Movement, or captured and sent to hard labour in Italy or, more likely, in Germany. Besides all this it must be added that more than a million young people and servicemen refused to support the Italian Social Republic and were thus compelled to live illegally. This explains why women had to play a completely new role: no longer did they simply have to buy commodities but they had also to replace men in conditions of extreme difficulty. These difficult tasks contributed to a modification of women's traditional role, weakening the hierarchical subordination to which they were subjected, both within society and within the family.

The nightmares of hunger and cold haunted the lives of most Italians during the second half of the war. In the recollections of almost everyone both of these concerns constantly recur: life became for most a desperate search for food and fuel. This did not occur solely in the urban centres but also in the rural areas, which were less productive or were close to the front (from October 1943).

During the conflict another element that modified completely the life of the Italians was the Allied air raids on the cities. The people had been convinced by the regime's propaganda that their air forces and anti-aircraft artillery could defend them, but they were to discover the foolishness of this presumption from the earliest days of the war. In the summer of 1940, after the bombings against Turin and other cities in the south, the situation stabilised until the beginning of 1942. From that moment the Allies embarked on a heavy air offensive against the main Italian cities: the first two targets were the most important southern cities of Naples and Palermo, both of them ports and leading military and industrial centres. During the following months the industrial areas and the main centres of the road and railway network in central and northern Italy suffered several attacks.

Bombings were a new experience for Italians; even though during the First World War some cities had been attacked by Austrian and German planes, the destructive power developed in the years 1940-45 was incomparably more dreadful. The destruction of houses, factories, schools and monuments sowed dismay and terror. Families that had homes in the country, or had maintained social ties there, left the most damaged cities in haste. While men remained to work in the towns, women, children and old people were evacuated, following a direction given by Mussolini himself, which caused many people to recognise Italian impotence, leading to widespread perturbation and despair. Giovanna Spagarino Viglongo recalls, in an interview about the flight from the city of Turin, after the bombings between 18 and 21 November 1942: 'A thing I will never forget, it was a flight, the whole city going, on foot, by bicycle... To see the officers driving the tricycle, an open cart, with mattresses on it, driving them wearing their uniform and their hats. They were driving, carrying their families, one or two children on it and their wives on the bicycle and these mattresses, that's what struck me most.'[17]

For the city of Genoa 22-23 October 1942 were terrible days. On the 22nd there was a heavy air raid, with the dropping of incendiary bombs. There were 39 deaths and big fires all around the city. The day after there was a 'lighter' raid, but the people were terrified. At the gate of one air-raid shelter (Galleria delle Grazie) a panicking crowd trampled and killed 354 people. Lavinia Lapeschi remembers:

'The news of the tragedy ran through the city immediately. I was crazy, terrified. Early in the morning my mother took me to the railway station. There was a terrible chaos, everyone tried to take flight. We jumped on the first train; it was a goods train and we didn't know its destination. We arrived at Ovada [in lower Piedmont, 60km from Genoa]; we stayed there all the day. Only at night we came back home. Few days after we evacuated to Veneto.'[18]

Those families that could not evacuate, for economic or professional reasons, were compelled to live together in danger and terror. Almost all the adult witnesses agree that the air raids engendered a sense of transience and an awareness of the precariousness of life.

Life went on, however, and the social disruption that the Allied strategists expected to achieve proved to be quite limited. Industrial production continued and suffered more from difficulties of supply than it did from bombing. In Italy the response to bombing followed a pattern similar to that observed in other countries: public morale suffered most because of heavy raids on centres that were seldom bombed. Typical of this response was the case of Rome, which was substantially spared from major attacks until it suffered a heavy raid, on 19 July 1943, resulting in significant damage and substantial losses in the highly popular area of San Lorenzo. Disdain, fear and blame, directed at the military and organisational inadequacies of the regime, rapidly spread in all social sectors of the capital, and this played a critical part in the political crisis that led to the monarchical coup d'état on 25 July 1943.

Although life went on, conditions and habits changed radically. The nights were spent waiting for the whistle of the alarm sirens, with everything packed up, ready to rush into shelters. The few belongings that families still possessed were taken with them due to fears of plundering or destruction. As well as valued items there were also food supplies; witnesses often tell about hams, salami, whole cheeses or bottles of oil being carried into the shelters each time the alarm sounded. For example, Minnie Criscuolo Tonello remembers: 'One day mum succeeded, I do not know how, in buying a whole provolone at the black market … then a piece of dried stockfish was added to the provolone and we would always go down to the shelter with our valuables.'[19]

Life in the air raid shelters was difficult, but in these places social relationships developed, and solidarity networks were created. Indeed, the social fabric, which the war weakened on the surface, was actually reconstituted underground. It was not rare for whole families to establish themselves in the safest shelters. These shelters could be in the cellars of old buildings, they could be dug into the ground or hills, or they could be ad hoc structures, roomy, made from reinforced concrete. It was in just such environments, even though precarious and unhealthy, that families recreated substitute homes: pieces of cloth were hung to create a fictitious privacy, washing lines were put up to dry the poor (rarely washed) clothes, and beds were improvised.

Air raids were the principal cause of a deep change in the rhythms of life. The night became a time for vigilance – to listen for the air raid sirens, to watch over the last remaining valuables, to control children, who often viewed this tragic novelty as a game. During the day, when people were too engaged in looking for food, people seldom had time for each other. At night, however, the traditional time for family intimacy, social relations were re-established and barriers broken down. In this respect people adopted the habits of a more recently urbanised population; they reflected the meetings with neighbours that took place in the countryside, after sunset, in the yards or in the cowsheds.

Last but not least among the enormous changes produced by the Second World War, the tragic experience of mass persecution must be mentioned. Italy was certainly not new to repressive experiences. Even if we limit ourselves to the 80 years that had passed since unification, it is possible to cite the persecution by both the liberal and the Fascist State of political militants (socialists, anarchists, communists), of religious minorities (Jehovah's Witnesses, Pentecostals, Jews), of Masons by Fascism, and of groups marked by different behaviour or attitudes (homosexuals, conscientious objectors). The tragic novelty introduced into Italian society during the German occupation that followed the Armistice of 8 September 1943 was the planned extermination that motivated the repressive activities of those dreadful 20 months – the repression turned into a real manhunt.

The main targets were the Jews (there were fewer than 50,000 at the beginning of the war). To these it is necessary to add the active political opponents (partisans and their supporters), the Allied prisoners of war, who had escaped from the camps during the days of the Armistice, and the soldiers of the Italian Army who refused the recall to military service by the Social Republic. In particular there was a kind of mass effort to conceal those who refused to join the Army, resulting in a gigantic operation of disguise. Women especially produced suits to substitute for the soldiers' compromising uniforms, thus exposing themselves to danger. Chiara Serdi recalls the work carried out by her mother in Turin:

> 'She had asked for old clothes from everyone in the house then she had turned to the nuns of Via Assietta who always collected clothes to give to the poor, and had a good amount in stock in our cellar. Rumours spread and then these boys would always come and say: "Lady, I'm this size, don't you have anything for me?" and she answered: "Come with me." Oh! my mother was incredible, she had such a spirit of initiative … so she took them into the cellar, then saw them off at the station, she kissed and hugged, and she would say he is one of my relatives and she would find a place on the cattle wagon, because at that time there was nothing else.'[20]

These people were forced to live clandestinely, but all the precautionary measures would have been insufficient if there had not been such support on the part of the population. Jews, absentees and Allied soldiers were helped, healed and hidden by the inhabitants of the cities and, above all, by those in the country. This gigantic work of concealment of hundreds of thousands of people was an unprecedented experience both for those who benefited from it and for those who carried it out. Considering the popular consent and the small number of informers, it is clear that the operation did not only involve those who had made a conscious anti-Fascist stance. Many people risked the danger of very harsh Nazi-Fascist retaliation due to humanitarian rather than political motives. This popular participation was considerably affected by the attitude of the clergy who, in most cases, decided to protect both the persecuted and those wanted by the regime.

Another issue is the position of women. After 20 years in which Fascism had tried, successfully, to oppose the emancipation of women, the regime was compelled to accept their involvement in dealing with the war emergency. The restrictions on the employment of female labour were gradually lifted; women went back into the factories, public services and commerce in large numbers. Additionally, women had to take over, once again, responsibility for the management of family affairs, because their husbands had left for the front and often did not return until quite long after the war was over (especially those who were prisoners of war). Their absolutely essential contribution to the survival of the nation's civil networks, together with their active participation in the Resistance movement, helped to transform women's role in society. The results, however, were contradictory: on the one hand, as peace was re-established, the Catholic Church and conservative political forces restored the traditional gender roles; on the other hand, the formal equality between the sexes was sanctioned by the concession of voting rights for women, overcoming in a few months obstacles that had blocked this goal for half a century.

At the end of this brief analysis it is possible to conclude that while the two World Wars represented for Italians (as for all the Europeans) two very hard trials, full of sacrifices and sufferings, they simultaneously started processes of modernisation and rationalisation that proved decisive for the future of the country. In both wars living conditions got materially worse, and Italians had to expend much emotional and material energy in order to guarantee their survival and that of their dependants. Daily habits were significantly modified, in some cases marking a return to old customs, but in other cases anticipating the future shape of Italian society. Women experienced radical changes in status and moved forwards along the path to emancipation, even though in both post-war periods they lost some of their newly acquired influence.

Economic conditions and workers' living standards deteriorated in both periods, even though between 1915 and 1918 the welfare intervention by the State, and by privately owned firms, combined with the influence of the trade unions to minimise the pain. During the Second World War, however, there were no such ameliorating factors, and workers suffered the worst hunger and misery. On the whole, in spite of a death toll that was twice as high (almost 650,000 fallen against 325,000) the First World War had a far less negative impact on Italian society. In contrast, almost only ruins emerged from the Second World War. From so negative an assessment, just one positive aspect emerges: the definitive transformation of Italians from subjects into citizens. This process, already started during the previous war, then blocked by Fascism, suddenly matured. During the 20 months of armed struggle against Fascists and Germans, the Italian people proved themselves able to realise and support a complex military effort. They also developed an ability to question the traditional structures of power and authority. Most Italian people had lacked the capacity to question the legitimacy of a government that had betrayed its own promises. This capacity was acquired during the battle for liberation, and it produced not only the delegitimation of Fascism in the conscience of most Italians, but also brought condemnation for the monarchy's approval of Fascism. This represented a tremendous change for the population, at last bringing to fruition the hope expressed, 85 years earlier, by the great statesman of the Risorgimento, Camillo Benso di Cavour: 'After the making of Italy, Italians have to be made'.

Recommended reading

Amendola, Anna, *La mia guerra, 1940-45: Avventure, gioie e dolori degli italiani raccontati da loro stessi* (Milano: Leonardo, 1990)

Bravo, Anna and Bruzzone, Anna Maria, *In guerra senz'armi: Storie di donne 1940-1945* (Roma-Bari: Laterza, 1995)

Burgwyn, H. J., *The Legend of the Mutilated Victory* (London: Greenwood Press, 1993)

Cavallo, Pietro, *Italiani in guerra, Sentimenti e immagini dal 1940 al 1943* (Bologna: Il Mulino, 1997)

Fabi, Lucio (ed), *La gente e la guerra* (Udine: Il Campo, 1990)

Gibelli, Antonio, *La grande guerra degli italiani* (Milano: Sansoni, 1998)

Jones, S., *Domestic Factors in Italian Intervention in the First World War* (London: Garland, 1986)

Leoni, Diego and Zadra, Camillo (eds), *La grande guerra: Esperienza, memoria, immagini* (Bologna: Il Mulino, 1986)

Lepre, Aurelio, *L'occhio del Duce: Gli italiani e la censura di guerra, 1940-1945* (Milano: Mondadori, 1992)

Mafai, Miriam, *Pane nero: donne e vita quotidiana nella seconda guerra mondiale* (Milano: Mondadori, 1987)

Newby, W., *Peace and War: Growing up in Fascist Italy* (London: Picador, 1992)

Pave, Claudio, *Ulna guerra civil: Sago stork sully morality Della Resistenza* (Torino: Bollati-Boringhieri, 1991)

Procacci, Giuliana, *Soldati e prigionieri italiani nella grande guerra* (Roma: Editori riuniti, 1993)

Rasping, A., *The Italian War Economy, 1940-1943* (London: Garland, 1986)

Notes

[1]   Piero Melograni, *Storia politica della Grande Guerra* (Bari: Laterza, 1977) Vol 1, p121

[2]   Massimo Legnani, *Consumi di guerra, in Guerra vissuta, guerra subita* (Bologna: CLUEB, 1991) pp109-17

[3]   In Anna Bravo and Anna Maria Bruzzone, *In guerra senz'armi* (Roma-Bari: Laterza, 1995) p60

[4]   In Nuto Revelli, *L'ultimo fronte* (Torino: Einaudi, 1989) pxxxi

[5]   Ibid, p172

[6]   Ibid, p174

[7]   Ibid, pp25-6

[8]   Giovanni Sabbatucci and Vittorio Vidotto (eds), *Storia d'Italia* (Roma-Bari: Laterza, 1997) Vol 4 (Statistical appendix), p723

[9]   Ibid, pp721-3

[10] Contemporary History Archives at the Risorgimento Museum, Milan, 39/25150

[11] In Giovanni Bellosi, 'Lettere di soldati romagnoli dalle zone di guerra', in 'Rivista Italiana di Dialettologia', i (2) (1978) p280

[12] Interviews with Maria Galetto, born 1887, and Lucia Abello, born 1892, quoted in Nuto Revelli, *L'anello forte* (Torino: Einaudi, 1985) pp122, 209

[13] Giuliana Procacci, 'L'Italia nella Grande Guerra', in Sabbatucci and Vidotto, op cit, pp3-100

[14] In Antonio Gibelli, *La grande guerra degli italiani* (Milano: Sansoni, 1998) p129

[15] In Lucio Fabi (ed), *La gente e la guerra* (Udine: Il Campo, 1990) Vol 2, p162

[16] In Anna Amendola, *La mia guerra, 1940-45: Avventure, gioie e dolori degli italiani raccontati da loro stessi* (Milano: Leonardo, 1990) p27

[17] In Bravo and Bruzzone, op cit, p35

[18] Unpublished interview collected by the authors. At the time of the event, the witness was 14 years old.

[19] In Anna Amendola, op cit, p31

[20] In Bravo and Bruzzone, op cit, p68

Chapter 8

The Western Balkans

Peter Caddick-Adams

Making any study and comparison of Yugoslavia in the two World Wars is to focus on a region of Europe that until the 1990s had escaped the attention of most mainstream academics, journalists and military historians. Only since the break-up of Yugoslavia from 1991 do the place names, ethnic tensions and battles so familiar to the newspaper-reading public at the beginning of the 20th century have a resonance today. Attention once again has been drawn to this area, where no computer simulation could possibly anticipate the complex nature of shifting factional alliances and local ethnic conflict.

The region has a long tradition of ferocious independence, and Roman Emperors from Tiberius to Hadrian several times had cause to complain of unrest in Thrace and Dalmatia in the 1st and 2nd centuries AD.[1] From the 17th to the 19th centuries the Habsburgs recruited Orthodox Serb frontiersmen from the Ottoman-ruled Croatia-Bosnia border (the 'Krajina'), who were renowned for their agility and speed. Known as Croatian Light Forces, they fought in the Thirty Years War (1618-48), the Wars of the Spanish Succession (1701-14), the Wars of the Austrian Succession (1740-48), the Seven Years War (1756-63) and Austria's wars with Napoleon. The latter admired them enough to raise his own Croatian regiments in Dalmatia, by which time their fierce reputation had also inspired many monarchs to recruit them as palace guards.

Unlike the rest of Europe in 1914, the Balkan region had effectively just completed two dress rehearsals for the Great War in 1912-13, and was already an armed camp in a state of military tension. Although the First World War overshadows much of the region's military history, the First and Second Balkan Wars previewed the technology and tactics of 1914-15, and it may indeed be argued that the First World War began technically as a third Balkan War. The First Balkan War (9 October 1912-30 May 1913) was waged between the Balkan Alliance (Bulgaria, Greece, Serbia and Montenegro) and the Ottoman Empire. In the Second (29 June-10 August 1913) the belligerents altered sides, with Bulgaria ranged against Greece, Turkey, Serbia, Montenegro and Romania. Far from being obscure footnotes of military history, these two wars were notable for their concept of coalition warfare and for the use, by both sides, of the first, primitive armoured cars and aeroplanes. The conflicts also employed around 1,000 machine-guns and modern artillery. Both sides erected barbed wire barricades and dug trenches to protect their infantry and consolidate gains. In this sense, some observers argue that the experience of fighting the Great War began not in 1914, but in 1912.[2]

The scale of involvement was extensive, and involved an all-out national effort on the part of the belligerents. In August 1912, following an anti-Turkish revolt in the Ottoman provinces of Albania and Macedonia, those that bordered the area of the rebellion (Bulgaria, Serbia and Greece) insisted that Turkey grant autonomy to the rebels. Refusing to concede any form of independence, Turkey and the Balkan Alliance mobilised nearly 1 million men each, deploying about half of them, with over 1,000 guns apiece. On 9 October Montenegro attacked Turkey, followed by Bulgaria, Serbia and Greece on 18 October. Although the forces appeared fairly evenly matched, the Balkan Alliance had more modern equipment, particularly in artillery. Showing a remarkable degree of co-ordination, while Bulgarian forces moved south-east against Istanbul, Serbian armies attacked the Turks in Macedonia from the north, and Montenegro invaded from the west. As Tsar Ferdinand of Bulgaria was known to covet Istanbul and the restoration of the Byzantine Empire, Turkey deployed the bulk of its forces against its Bulgarian foes. The latter besieged Adrianople, using an aeroplane to drop bombs, which, it is claimed, was the first air raid in history. The Turks were beaten back in a series of battles, but the Bulgarian armies were unable to pursue, and the Turks dug in west of Istanbul.

These developments in the Balkans alarmed the Great Powers. While the Tsar of Russia supported his fellow Slavs of the Balkan Alliance, he did not want Bulgaria controlling access to the Black Sea. The Central Powers (Germany and Austria-Hungary), on the other hand, were concerned to prop up the Ottoman Empire, in danger of disintegration. Thus, owing to external pressures, an armistice was concluded in December 1912 between Bulgaria, Serbia and Turkey. However, in January 1913 hostilities recommenced and after more Turkish defeats, including the fall of Adrianople, peace was finally concluded in April, although Montenegro did not sign until the London Conference the following May.

As soon as the peace was signed, a series of disputes shattered the Balkan Alliance, as the victors fell out. Serbia felt cheated of access to the Adriatic, and demanded compensation with Macedonian territory, while Greece considered that Bulgaria, now its neighbour, had been awarded too much Ottoman territory. The result was the Second Balkan War, which began on 29 June when Bulgaria, encouraged by Germany and Austria, attacked Serb and Greek forces in Macedonia. The Serbs halted the Bulgars and counter-attacked, while on 10 July Romania attacked Bulgaria from the north. The Turks, smarting from the loss of their European territories, seized the chance to retake some of them, recapturing Adrianople. One month later, attacked from all sides and fearing complete defeat, Bulgaria surrendered. The Bucharest Peace Conference on 10 August was attended by Bulgaria, Serbia, Montenegro, Greece and Romania, and resulted in Bulgaria losing its gains from the First Balkan War. The lands given to Serbia included Macedonia and Kosovo. At the Istanbul conference on 29 November Turkey regained a strip of land including Adrianople.

These two sharp conflicts, fought across Europe's south-eastern religious fault-line, ended five centuries of Ottoman rule in the Balkans. While for the great powers the Great War of 1914 was the first major conflict between coalitions since

1815, for the Balkans this process had started earlier, in 1912. Influenced no doubt by romantic illustrations of empire-builders and heroic horsemen in school history books, those not conscripted flocked to recruitment offices in the towns and cities of Austria-Hungary, Russia, Germany, France and Great Britain to volunteer, fearing the war would be over by Christmas, and end without their contribution. In Britain, for example, 300,000 volunteered in August 1914, 450,000 in September, and an average of 100,000 each month from September 1914 to December 1915.[3] In the Balkans, mobilisation had already taken place over the preceding two years, and the civil populations had already experienced war, so the experience of July-August 1914 was altogether different.

Three of the states that were to make up post-First World War Yugoslavia – Slovenia, Croatia and Bosnia-Herzegovina – were part of the Austro-Hungarian Empire, and their citizens, who also included many tens of thousands of ethnic Serbs, were conscripted and scattered through the Imperial Army. Some Macedonians and ethnic Albanians from Kosovo found themselves fighting in the Ottoman Army. Of every hundred soldiers in the Austro-Hungarian Army in 1914, nine were of Serb or Croat origin, while two were Slovenians.[4] In overall terms, the Austro-Hungarian Army was approximately 44 per cent Slav, 28 per cent German, 18 per cent Hungarian, 8 per cent Romanian and 2 per cent Italian, and worked to three languages of command in war (German, Magyar and Serbo-Croat). One of its conscripts, the Czech novelist Jaroslav Hasek, has left us with a description of the confusion this caused, in *The Good Soldier Schweik*. Nevertheless, some conscripts flourished, such as Corporal Josip Broz (the future Tito) who was awarded a medal and promotion for gallantry in the Carpathian mountains serving with his Croat infantry regiment.[5] Despite the Slav majority, Serbian and Croat recruits were apparently treated as underdogs by their Austrian/Magyar officers throughout the Imperial Army, which suggests widespread disharmony.[6] This must have led to cultural confusion on the part of many 'Yugoslavs', and in the light of this disparate mix it is probably more informative to examine the 'Yugoslav' experience of the Great War in terms of Serbia, which had a keener sense of identity than most.

Before the Great War, Serbia was the only 'Yugoslav' land into which southern Slavs had consciously migrated during the 19th century, and Serbia had a relatively high standard of living compared to the surrounding areas controlled by the Austrians, or more particularly, by the Turks. Peasants from Montenegro, Bosnia, Macedonia and even southern Hungary, merchants and some professional classes were attracted to Serbia, contributing to its economic, political and cultural development before 1914.[7] The alternative was downward-spiralling hardship, or – for at least 6 per cent of the Croat and Slovene populations before 1910 – emigration, usually to the United States.[8] This cultural growth in Serbia was, however, a middle-class urban phenomenon, and most of the population remained in the countryside and illiterate.[9]

However, as John Gunther observed, 'The basic passion of most Balkan folk is nationalism. Their primitive and turbulent energies are directed to the preservation of their own political minority or country, rather than social revolution; nationalism is the pipe through which their energies are discharged.'[10]

This nationalism found expression in a very specific way in pre-war Serbia. Prior to the advent of Serbian independence in 1878, there was no concept of being a Serb among the young. With independence came the responsibility of organising an educational system and school curriculum. History, geography and grammar textbooks were rewritten and those that recounted the glories of past heroes and the hardships that past generations had endured under foreign rule proved to be the most popular with students and teachers alike. Gradually, a spark of nationalism was kindled, implicitly critical of neighbours and adversaries, in favour of the unification of the Serbian peoples.[11]

As most Serbians were educated only to elementary or secondary level (there were a mere 934 enrolments at the national university in Belgrade in 1910), and 85 per cent of the population lived in rural areas, such textbooks had a disproportionate influence in the education and indoctrination of a whole generation. There were simply no other means of acquiring information in early-20th-century rural Serbia, and these texts assumed the role of schoolbook and newspaper, fostering dreams of unification for a whole generation. Interestingly, the Serbs also claimed the Croat dialect and lands for their own in these books, undermining less vociferous calls for Croat unity within Austria-Hungary. Analysts of these school books conclude that until the eve of the First World War Serb students were taught nationalism – how to perceive their own nation – but were taught little about the other southern Slavs (Croats, Bosnians and Macedonians, for example) with whom they were to be united in 1918.[12]

It was no mere coincidence that a young Serb hothead succeeded in assassinating Archduke Franz Ferdinand of Austria in Sarajevo on St Vitus's Day, 28 June 1914. On that same day in 1389, Prince Lazar had chosen to lead his Serbs into battle against hopeless odds on the Field of Blackbirds in Kosovo, rather than submit to Ottoman aggression. The result was 500 years of Muslim rule, and, it is argued, the birth of Serb self-pity. Ever after, St Vitus's Day became the greatest Serbian annual festival (with Slobodan Milosovic using the 600th anniversary of the Kosovan battle in explosive fashion in 1989).[13] The assassination of a threatening foreigner on that particular day was a signal to a whole generation of Serbs with a new-found sense of history. This re-interpretation of their own past, mingled with national pride, ensured that Serbia would not back down in the face of Austrian threats.

One of the ten demands contained in Austria-Hungary's ultimatum to Serbia of 23 July 1914 was 'the elimination without delay from public instruction in Serbia … [of] all that serves or might serve to foment propaganda against Austria-Hungary'. This was a clear reference to these Serbian textbooks. By way of illustration, in 1907 Austria-Hungary complained about one 1905 schoolbook that stated, 'Austria persecutes and tortures both the Orthodox and Muslim [in Bosnia] and supports the Catholics; it builds Catholic schools, churches and monasteries everywhere and encourages the colonisation of these lands [Bosnia-Herzegovina] by Germans and Magyars. It does not allow the people to call themselves Serbs but Bosnians.'[14] Such passages indicate that Serbian nationalism was aimed as much at other Slavs as at the Austrian Empire. The books issue is relevant on two counts, in that it helped trigger the Great War, and that it inspired the Serbian troops serving in that war. Troops who had enlisted or volunteered in the earlier Balkan wars out of idealism, became officers in 1914, and kept alive a belief in a free, greater Serbia, during the dark days of 1915-18.

The plight of Serbia, as that of Belgium, evoked much sympathy in Great Britain, rather as Poland did in 1939 or Kuwait in 1990, and medical staff volunteered to tend to the Serbian Army, while money, medicine and clothing were forwarded from public collections. Serbia mobilised 11 infantry divisions in 1914[15], armed with 7mm Mauser rifles, and eventually an army of 650,000, which had all the hallmarks of one born from idealism, as Flora Sandes, then a British nurse attached to the Serb Army, described:

'They wore the rough, grey-brown, home-spun tweed uniforms of the Serbian Army: a short jacket buttoned at the neck, breeches and woollen stockings with a variety of flower patterns around the tops. These were embroidered ... by mothers or wives or girlfriends... Only a few possessed boots; most of them wore a sort of leather sandal fastened with thongs round their calves. All wore round sheepskin caps.'[16]

The first Austrian invasion of Serbia was brought to a halt by Serbian victories, under General Putnik, on the Cer Mountain and at Sabac in late August. In early September, however, a Serb offensive on the Sava River had to be broken off when the Austrians attacked again on the Drina River. A third Austrian offensive, culminating in their victory at Kolubara, forced the Serbs to evacuate Belgrade on 30 November; but by 15 December a counter-attack had retaken Belgrade and forced the Austrians to retreat. Poor weather and exhaustion hampered the Serb pursuit, but their triumph bought time for the Army to regroup. Serbia's initial success might be explained in terms of the superior motivation of her troops, intimate knowledge of the terrain, and perhaps a reluctance by some Austro-Hungarian troops to press home attacks on their fellow countrymen. Relying on superior numbers, Austria's three 1914 campaigns in Serbia, all very much issues of pride after Archduke Franz Ferdinand's assassination, thus resulted in failure, though at a high cost to the Serbs.

By the summer of 1915 the Central Powers concluded a treaty with Bulgaria, whom they lured to their side by offers of territory – in effect redressing Bulgaria's losses from the Second Balkan War – but the motivation was strategic. With Bulgaria in the fold, the Central Powers (Germany, Austria-Hungary and Turkey) were linked by land, and could rush troops and supplies by rail to any quarter they wished. Under General August von Mackensen's able direction, in co-ordinated offensives, Austria (stiffened by German reinforcements) attacked Serbia from the Danube on 6 October 1915, while the Bulgarian Army launched two strikes, first at eastern Serbia on 11 October and again against Macedonia three days later.[17] It is clear that these successes were due to German direction of the campaign, increased proportions of German officers and NCOs in the Austrian Army, and the ability to stretch Serbia between two fronts.

The Western Allies, warned of the prospect of a Bulgarian attack on Serbia, sent help through neutral Greece's Macedonian port of Salonika (Thessalonika), relying on the collusion of Greece's pro-entente Prime Minister, Venizélos. An Anglo-French Expeditionary Force from Gallipoli reached Salonika on 5 October, but on that day Venizélos fell from power. The Allies advanced northward up the Vardar into Macedonia but remained separated from the Serbs by the Bulgarian Army's advance west. Driven back over the Greek frontier, the Allies found themselves occupying little more than the hinterland around Salonika by mid-December, overlooked by Bulgar positions in the surrounding mountains. The Serbian Army and its followers, meanwhile, retreating before Mackensen, passed across the historic plain of Kosovo Polje and there split into four columns during 20-25 November. Each column (composed of civilians as well as soldiers) began an arduous winter retreat over the Albanian mountains on 23 November, reaching refuge on the island of Corfu in late February 1916, losing all but 150,000 men in the process. The columns included Austrian prisoners and Scottish nurses who had arrived in 1914, sponsored by the Women's Suffrage Federation, and cold, typhus and Albanian bandits all claimed a share of the unknown number of victims. As Alan Palmer suggests, 'this was the march of a nation, rather than the withdrawal of a fighting unit from battle'.[18]

Public sympathy was evoked once again in Britain, and a 1915 London 'Exhibition of Serbian War Pictures' included such romantic portraits as 'Serbia's Defender', a wounded Serbian boy-soldier of 14.[19] Ironically, while admiring such heroism abroad, one suspects that such a similar use of children in the BEF would have been frowned upon by the British public. The Serbian Relief Fund collected over £1 million, and employed over 700 voluntary workers in the region. Although armed with this goodwill, Serbian troops henceforth required outside help to achieve anything militarily, and were reclothed and re-equipped by their allies while on Corfu. As Flora Sandes, having by then abandoned her role as a nurse and now serving as a Sergeant Major in a front-line infantry regiment, noted in a romantic vein:

> '...no longer was it an army of peasant reservists who sang as they marched and gathered in the harvest between battles... Now their boots were British army issue, heavy and studded with nails; and they wore the horizon blue uniform of France ... and carried French army pattern steel helmets.'[20]

While their uniforms may have been borrowed, just as the Partisans and other free armies of the Second World War had to be clothed and equipped by their allies, there is no evidence that Serbian pride suffered. In the spring of 1916 the Allies at Salonika were reinforced by the revitalised Serbs from Corfu, as well as by more French, British and some Russian troops, and expanded their bridgehead east and west, but were confounded by Bulgar counter-attacks in May and August. An Allied counter-offensive, including Serb formations, took Monastir from the Bulgars in November 1916, but more ambitious operations, from March to May 1917, proved abortive; the Salonika front had reached stalemate and merely tied down some 500,000 Allied troops without troubling the Central Powers in any significant way. The experience of occupation for civilians left behind in Serbia was grim. They were subject to a brutal 'Bulgarisation' policy of all things Serbian.

Libraries, churches and schools suffered particularly, in a way that anticipated the excesses of the 1990s, in an effort to extinguish the Serb language and culture, and over 2,000 civilians were executed in a rebellion of March 1917.

In September 1918 General Franchet d'Espérey, the Allied C-in-C, launched a major offensive at Salonika with six Serbian and two French divisions against a 7-mile front held by only one Bulgarian division. The initial assault began early on 15 September, and a 5-mile penetration was achieved by nightfall the following day. The Royal Air Force supported the offensive by strafing and bombing enemy troops caught on mountain roads. By 21 September, with British and Italian troops also committed, the whole Bulgarian front had collapsed, and within a further five days the Bulgarian frontier had been reached. The Bulgars then sued for an armistice, which was concluded on 29 September at Salonika, accepting the Allies' terms unconditionally.

Another group of Serbs experienced war on an altogether different front during 1914-17. Given the widely disparate ethnic groups within the Austrian armed forces, it was inevitable that some lacked fighting spirit for the Austrian cause. This is reflected in the staggering 1.7 million Austro-Hungarians who were captured during the First World War: one suspects that many put up no fight at all. By comparison, 180,000 British and 500,000 French soldiers suffered the indignity of capture.[21] Among those taken while fighting under the double-headed eagle of Austria-Hungary were tens of thousands of Serbian troops, soldiering on the Eastern Front and captured by the Russians. Some, like Josip Broz, elected to stay and serve the cause of Communism in the Russian Revolution, but many were keen to return home. Several groups were repatriated by the Russians to Serbia, some 5,000 returning in this way in 1915.[22]

The majority of Serbs taken by the Russians, however, were encouraged to join one of General Mihailo Jivovic's two Serbian divisions, which fought under Russian command on the Eastern Front, and 80,000-90,000 eventually did so. Although motivated by a sense of Serb nationalism, felt all the more acutely when in captivity, they suffered from appalling Russian administration, including poor medical facilities (British volunteer nurses filled this gap) and 'at one stage some Serb units had to be kept indoors for weeks on end because they had no boots; and deficiency diseases due to malnutrition were rife. This was especially disillusioning for men who had earlier experienced the more satisfactory commissariat of the Austrian army.'[23] They later left Russia during the turmoil of revolution and returned to join their fellow countrymen fighting at Salonika in late 1917. The motivation of the original (mostly illiterate) volunteers must have been strong, when faced with a choice of POW camp or joining the firing line under foreign command, but latterly peer pressure would surely have swelled numbers.

In terms of cost, Serbia lost about 45,000 killed during the First World War, but 46.8 per cent of those 700,000 who were mobilised died, were wounded or were taken prisoner. The figure for Austria-Hungary, which included at least the 44 per cent of the army who were of Slavic origin, many of whom who might be considered 'Yugoslav', was a staggering 90 per cent killed, wounded or captured, demonstrating the inevitable collapse of the Habsburg Empire. By comparison, 35.8 per cent of British Empire and 73.3 per cent of French troops mobilised suffered death, wounding or capture in the Great War.[24] The experience of war in the Balkans had been characterised by a brutalisation of the civilian population, an enemy occupation of all the elements that were to comprise Yugoslavia, and a complete reliance on outside help to wage effective war. While the Serbian Army would have ceased to be an effective military force after 1915 without substantial British and French aid, Austria-Hungary was also heavily reliant on German leadership, doctrine and equipment to achieve anything of military value. Ironically, when motivated, Austro-Hungarian troops of poor quality turned into hard men when fighting under a Serb banner. By the war's end, the Serbian Army numbered just over 100,000, a fraction of its size in 1914, but demonstrably more effective.

With peace came the problem of forging a country out of six republics, five nations, four languages, three religions, and two alphabets. The Kingdom of the Serbs, Croats and Slovenes (Kraljevina Srba, Hrvata, I Slovenaca), founded on 1 December 1918, was dominated by Serbs in the inter-war period. In order to quell Croat unrest at Serb domination, King Alexander suspended the constitution and established a personal dictatorship with the aim of uniting his kingdom, growing daily more fractious, and on 3 October 1929, the kingdom's clumsy name was replaced by a term meaning 'land of the southern Slavs' – Yugoslavia. Following Alexander's assassination in Marseilles by a Macedonian in 1934, the kingdom was ruled by the weak Prince Paul, regent for the young King Peter II, Alexander's son. Despite proclaiming neutrality in September 1939, and although his sympathies lay with Britain, owing to the presence of Italian military forces in neighbouring Albania and Greece, Paul felt compelled to submit to an Axis Tripartite Pact with Italy and Germany on 25 March 1941. A popular uprising in Belgrade pushed out the Nazi puppets within three days, but on 6 April, in an operation named 'Strafgericht' ('Retribution'), Hitler invaded Yugoslavia.

The Royal Yugoslav Army of 1941 was a conscript force of 500,000 in which all males of 21-40 served for 18 months. In photographs they resemble their First World War ancestors, equipped with the French-style Adrian helmets issued to Serbian troops on Corfu, heavy greatcoats, with Mauser and Lebel rifles, but little modern equipment. Working to contingency plans, but mobilised for 'Strafgericht' in an extremely tight time-frame, the Wehrmacht invaded from Bulgaria and Austria with unanticipated speed, and in a series of lightning thrusts supported by the highly efficient Luftwaffe, linked up with Italian troops advancing from Albania. Bombers struck at Belgrade over four days causing 30,000 casualties, while fighters crushed the Yugoslav Air Force, which included a mixture of outdated British and French types as well as 60 Messerschmitt Me109Es, purchased in 1940. The main centres of population were occupied within two weeks, and some mobilised Yugoslav troops never managed to reach their units before being told to return home after the surrender.[25]

Seven panzer divisions clattered into the Balkans, and while General von Weichs' Second Army (11 divisions) occupied Yugoslavia, Field Marshal List's larger Twelfth Army invaded mainland Greece at the same time ('Operation Marita') and the two countries were subdued by 1 May, Yugoslavia having formally surrendered on 18 April.[26] In contrast to their antecedents' performance in 1914, the Royal Army simply ceased to exist within ten days, and was never thereafter able to concentrate, undermined by a lack of political will to resist. It lost about 300,000 prisoners, while German losses were around 500. In this respect the Yugoslav experience of blitzkrieg echoes that of France exactly a year before. The Army was defeated by the Wehrmacht's superior doctrine, their own inadequate anti-aircraft and anti-armour weapons systems, and by the paralysis or isolation of command centres by the Luftwaffe. A significant number of Volkdeutsche Yugoslav soldiers and civilians welcomed the Wehrmacht, inhabitants of the old Austrian provinces, who had found themselves part of the Slav state after 1918, but in view of the speed of the collapse there is little evidence of any fifth column activity.

At this juncture, some argue, the Germans erred in withdrawing too many of their combat units in preparation for 'Barbarossa', leaving a military vacuum and preventing an effective and systematic disbandment of all Yugoslav military formations, who destroyed their personnel archives, hid their weapons and melted into the countryside.[27] Post-war analysis by some commentators has sought to justify the Yugoslav Army's ten-day stand on the strategic grounds that it delayed 'Barbarossa' by several crucial weeks. But Martin van Creveld convincingly challenges this by arguing that it was the delay in assembling adequate transport from across occupied Europe, not the Yugoslavia-Greece campaign, that denied the Wehrmacht an earlier advance into Russia.[28]

Initially, the Yugoslav communists led by Tito co-operated with the occupiers, or at least did not hinder them, as the Non-Aggression Pact between Tito's political master, Stalin, and Hitler was still in force. 'Operation Barbarossa', the invasion of Russia, on 22 June 1941 was Tito's signal to open hostilities with Berlin. His forces numbered fewer than 10,000 and competed with Colonel Draza Mihailovic's royalist all-Serb Chetnik guerrillas, whom he eventually fought as viciously as the Germans. Chetniks (from Cheta – an armed band) traced their origins to the guerrilla units that operated behind enemy lines in the Balkan wars of 1912-3. This 6 April-22 June 1941 period is acutely embarrassing for the Partisans, and must lead us to question Tito's political judgement, the more so in view of his later truce with the Nazis. Tito's first operation was not until 7 July, but Mihailovic's guerrillas had been active since 3 May.

Although it seems that the need to conduct guerrilla warfare against the Germans may have come as a shock to Tito, it is worth remembering that he was already used to the cloak-and-dagger world of secret printing presses, hidden weapons and safe houses, as his communists had been an illegal organisation under the pre-war Yugoslav monarchy. The jury remains out on whether Tito's goal was the defeat and expulsion of the Nazis, or the eventual Communist domination of Yugoslavia. Perhaps one developed into the other, but at times his patriotism is, at best, suspect. Less suspect were the motives of his rival résistant, the Francophile ex-defence attaché in Prague, Colonel Mihailovic. He had led the unofficial anti-Nazi wing of the Royal Yugoslav Army and had written pamphlets that anticipated a German invasion and urged training for guerrilla warfare. Fortunately for both, most Yugoslavs serving in the formations of Mihailovic and Tito in the early days were pre-war conscripts with basic military knowledge. Later on, youngsters and women also served, and had to be taught their military skills.

The experience of 1941-45 for a Yugoslav Partisan is characterised by a special brutality that seems to be a hallmark of war in the Balkans, whether 1914-18, 1941-45 or 1991-95. Even the name of Tito's men – the Partisans – suggests this. Although first adopted by the Russians, the label comes from the French, 'one who takes sides'; Tito certainly forced the Yugoslav people to choose sides in 1941-45. There was no room for neutrality or ambivalence. In the memoirs of another close associate, Milovan Djilas, there is a tendency to lump together all Yugoslav enemies of the Partisans as Chetniks, which is a gross over-simplification. Besides the other ethnic groups, not all Serbs joined the Chetnik bands; neither did the rest collaborate with the Nedic regime. Many chose to do neither, but were thus still considered enemies. Tito's deputy, Edvard Kardelj, stated, 'We must at all costs push the Croatian as well as the Serb villages into the struggle. Some comrades are afraid of reprisals, and that fear prevents the mobilisation of Croat villages… In war, we must not be frightened of the destruction of whole villages. Terror will bring about armed action.'[29] Tito triumphed because he adopted this long-term strategy of terror, ignoring all the suffering and casualties along the way. In a Machiavellian sense, the end did indeed justify the means. The gratuitous violence experienced in the Partisan war is captured well in Djilas's memoirs, which wallow in the gore of slitting the throats of German and Italian prisoners, of Ustashe and Chetnik alike:

> 'I unslung my rifle. Since I didn't dare fire, because the Germans were some forty yards above – we could hear them shouting – I hit the German over the head. The rifle butt broke and the German fell on his back. I pulled out my knife and with one motion slit his throat. I then handed the knife to Raja Nedelijkovic, a political worker whom I had known before the war, and whose village had been massacred in 1941. Nedelijkovic stabbed the second German, who writhed but was soon still.'[30]

Such brutality was extended to captured hospitals and ambulance convoys, while the dead and living were routinely mutilated; this brutality would today be labelled 'war crimes'.[31]

Tito sought to indoctrinate his followers with communism, a conveniently anti-royalist creed, and one that (to a degree) successfully overcame the ethnic and religious divisions that had traditionally dogged Yugoslav politics and would do so after his death. His forces were regarded initially with suspicion by the right-wing monarchists under Mihailovic, and were unwelcomed by much of the population on whom the Croat Ustashe, Italians and Germans heaped brutal reprisals. After a series of guerrilla-inspired uprisings in Serbia and Croatia that caused a violent German reaction, in December 1941 Tito and his men were hounded out of Croatia. In a trek that recalled the Serbian retreat through Albania of the winter of 1915-16, they moved into the Bosnian countryside, and were restructured into Partisan brigades, in imitation of Stalin's bands of resistance fighters operating behind German lines in Russia. In the end there were 53 Partisan divisions, containing 175 brigades, but care is needed when discussing military formations in Yugoslavia (as in the 1991-95 war), for the number of personnel in Partisan 'brigades', 'divisions' and 'corps' fluctuated wildly, and they did not necessarily correspond to units of similar designation operated by regular armies. Partisan 'brigades' frequently contained 200-300 men, a tenth of the numbers in a regular formation. Tito began with about 10,000 supporters, but by December 1941, after casualties, this had slid to about 2,000. In January 1943 he had 45,000 under his command, and 60,000 six months later. By mid-1944 he could claim 300,000 and perhaps 800,000 by the war's end.[32] By late 1944, though, with such numbers, clothed and equipped to a common standard, Tito could hardly claim to lead a resistance movement. His Partisans had already become the Yugoslav Army.

Résistants of all political and ethnic shades initially took to the hills with their Royal Yugoslav Army uniforms and kit, or rugged civilian garb. As these wore out, they clad themselves in odd items of captured German, Italian or Bulgarian military clothing, or cast-off civilian items, a bizarre range of headgear and an enormous selection of weaponry, from shot-guns to captured Schmeissers and parachuted British Sten guns. This author in 1996 witnessed the discovery of a cache of ex-Partisan weapons by NATO troops in Bosnia, which included 36 different weapon types and ten different calibres of ammunition, of vintages between 1898 and 1943. By 1944, however, British and US aid had included a simple one-piece uniform for all, and boots. In assessing what motivated them to fight, it is worth turning to the Italian novelist Italo Calvino, whose observations (made in 1947), although about Italian Partisans, are as relevant to Yugoslav guerrillas in this period. He lists the different categories caught up in the fighting:

'First, the peasants who live in these mountains, it's easier for them. The Germans burn their villages, take away their cattle. Theirs is a basic human war, one to defend their own country, for the peasants really have a country. So they join up with us, young and old, with their old shot-guns and corduroy hunting jackets; whole villages of them … they sacrifice even their homes, even their cattle to go on fighting. Then there are other peasants for whom "country" remains something selfish; their cattle, their home, their crops. And to keep all that they become spies, Fascists … there are whole villages that are our enemies. Then there are the workers. The workers have a background of their own, of wages and strikes, of work and struggle, elbow to elbow… They know there's something better in life and they fight for that something better. They have a "country", too, a "country" still to be conquered, and they're fighting here to conquer it. Down in the town there are factories which will be theirs; they can already see the red writing on the factory walls and the banners flying on the factory chimneys… Then there is an intellectual, or a student, or two. Very few of them though, here and there, with ideas in their heads that are often vague… Their "country" consists of words… Who else is there? Foreign prisoners who've escaped from concentration camps and joined us; they're fighting for a real proper country, a distant country which they want to get back to … then take Dritto's detachment; petty thieves, carabinieri, ex-soldiers, black marketeers, down-and-outs; men on the fringes of society, who got along somehow despite all the chaos around them, with nothing to defend and nothing to lose…'[33]

The experience of Yugoslavia during the Second World War through British eyes is interesting. By August 1943 Britain had dispatched military missions to both Mihailovic and Tito to ascertain which was the better bet in defeating the Germans, and thus worthy of military aid. The reports of the senior British officer at Tito's HQ, Brigadier Fitzroy Maclean (as outlined in his immensely readable memoir *Eastern Approaches*), and accusations reaching London that Mihailovic was collaborating with the Germans, caused the British to divert all support to Tito, and increase the quantity of aid substantially, a decision confirmed by Roosevelt, Churchill and Stalin at the Tehran Conference that November. The accusations against Mihailovic need to be treated carefully, for at least two commentators have found difficulty in proving anything more than local Chetnik factions taking temporary advantage of the military situation to attack their Partisan foes.[34]

There is a hint, for those party to conspiracy theories, that left-wing and Communist members within the Special Operations Executive (SOE), the Office of Strategic Services (OSS) and the British Broadcasting Corporation (BBC) spread these falsehoods to boost the credibility of their fellow Communist, Tito.[35] Accusations of Mihailovic's treachery also need to be treated with caution because there is firm evidence that in March-May 1943 Tito himself actually concluded a temporary truce with the Germans in order to finish off Mihailovic's Chetniks (an understandable lure for the Germans who were keen to see the elimination of at least one guerrilla band), and exchange prisoners.[36] This followed earlier, informal and localised truces in the summer of 1942, where prisoners had been exchanged. German-Partisan hostilities were soon resumed, but Tito had established his force in the meantime as the dominant resistance movement. Interestingly, as late as February 1943 German military intelligence had assessed Mihailovic's Chetniks as being the dominant resistance force, which may explain why a deal was struck the next month for Tito to eliminate them.[37]

By 1943 Tito was portraying himself as general of a national liberation army, rather than leader of a communist resistance group, and had initiated a Pan-Yugoslav Council of Unity in Bihac (November 1942) as a means of appealing for more support, with the slogan 'bratstva i jedinstva' ('brotherhood and unity'). This was also an advertisement to the outside world that he was assembling a government-in-waiting.[38] In September 1943 Italy concluded an armistice with the Allies, which brought almost four divisions' worth of men with their equipment over to the Partisans, and gave the British a base across the Adriatic from which to supply them more directly. The decision in 1943 to divert all support to Tito, at the behest of Fitzroy Maclean, and confirmed by the Big Three at Tehran, enhanced the Partisan leader's status considerably. He now held the rank of Marshal, bestowed at Jajce, when it was also agreed that the post-war future lay not with a monarchy, but with Communism.

The extent to which Tito was reliant on British (and US) aid is debatable. SOE historians such as Basil Davidson and M. R. D. Foot, and Maclean himself, understandably tend to stress the British contribution, which was important – it included 100,000 rifles, 50,000 machine-guns and 97 million rounds of ammunition as well as boots and clothing – both in fact and in terms of morale, of 'hands across the sea'.[39] There are echoes here of Britain's re-clothing and re-equipping the Serbian Army on Corfu in 1916. Arguably, the significant quantities of Italian war booty and manpower that arrived after September 1943 may have dwarfed Britain's contribution. Many Serbs would also have recalled (or served in) the Salonika expedition of another World War, and Churchill certainly used the carrot of another commitment by British ground forces as an incentive to Tito to kill more Germans. From mid-1944, with victory within his grasp, the situation was reversed; Tito turned down all plans for Allied landings along the Yugoslav coast, and goodwill rapidly deteriorated. This was noted by the irascible Evelyn Waugh in his memoirs, and admitted by Maclean himself. Hitler, too, was haunted by Salonika, and kept troops needed elsewhere in the region to deter an assault, after the success of 'Operation Torch' (November 1942) in French North Africa.

The experience of Yugoslavs under occupation during the Second World War was as grim as it had been for Serbians in 1915-18. In Macedonia, the Bulgarians returned and took up where they had left off in 1918, with a brutal 'Bulgarisation' policy, not merely policing occupied territory, but eradicating all traces of local culture. Such brutality fluctuated widely, as policy for the occupation was confused, due to the speed with which the invasion had been launched. Partly rewarding the territorial ambitions of his neighbouring allies – Hungary, Italy and Bulgaria – Hitler carved up the sovereign state of Yugoslavia, which simply ceased to exist. Croatia was divided into Italian and German zones of occupation, under poglavnik (Prime Minister) Ante Pavelic, whose authority rested on bands of Ustashe, the Croatian ultra-nationalist organisation founded in Zagreb, a direct response to the establishment of King Alexander's royal dictatorship of January 1929. Pavelic was a brutal character, and the Italian journalist Curzio Malaparte famously recalled seeing a wicker basket of Dalmatian oysters on the poglavnik's desk in the summer of 1941. Malaparte recoiled on being told by Pavelic that the 'oysters' were in fact '…a present from my loyal ustashis. Forty pounds of human eyes'.[40] The veracity of this tale has been challenged, but it captures well the experience of naked terror in wartime Yugoslavia.

A Pétain-like figure ruled the state of Serbia – General Nedic, a former Chief of Staff of the Royal Yugoslav Army, which maintained uneasy relations with the Chetniks. Albania, under Italian military rule, was expanded to include Montenegro and part of Serbia; northern Slovenia, with its Volkdeutsche, was absorbed into the Third Reich proper, while east and south-east Yugoslavia was occupied by Hungary and Bulgaria. Thus, Hitler unwittingly discovered one of the easiest ways to control the area – divide Yugoslavia into several opposing groups, motivated by politics or ethnicity, and rule. The German military structure for the Yugoslav states was exceedingly complex, and apart from the Wehrmacht's South East Command in Athens, the police, SD-Gestapo, Luftwaffe and Foreign Ministry all had their own separate chains of command to Berlin.[41] This had bizarre consequences, for example when in October 1941 at Kragujevac and Kraljevo German troops trying to meet reprisal quotas (100 civilians executed for every dead German, 50 deaths for a wounded German) shot over 4,000 Serbs, including two classes of a high school, executed with their teachers, and the entire workforce of an aeroplane factory, working for the German war effort.[42]

Comprehensive SD reports exist detailing guerrilla activity in Slovenia (which had been absorbed into Greater Germany), where the first recorded use of the term 'Partisan' was recorded on 8 September 1941, in a note left on the body of a pro-German Slovene farmer. It read: 'Death to the traitors of the Slovene nation. Partizani'. Slovene guerrillas were really an extension of mainstream Yugoslav resistance, though they provided the only organised anti-Nazi activity within the borders of GroßDeutschland. Their activities included the distribution of leaflets urging local workers to destroy mines, ignore call-up papers and join the liberation army. Acts of sabotage increased, particularly after 20 July 1944 (the attempt on Hitler's life), and there was widespread forced recruitment, as the following report of June 1943 details:

> '...At 9.45pm a large force of partisans entered the village... The partisans were very systematic, surrounded individual houses with ten or twelve men, searched them and took the men ... they were wearing spotless grey green uniforms, and carrying arms, revolvers and hand grenades. On their caps they wore both the Yugoslav tricolour and the Soviet star...'[43]

Just as many future Yugoslavs experienced army life under the double-headed eagle of Austria-Hungary during 1914-18, so many joined the Axis armies and militias in 1941-45. Apart from gaining an easier life under occupation, this was also a crude vehicle for removing personal enemies. For the occupied people of Europe in 1941-43, the Germans were masters for the foreseeable future, perhaps decades if not centuries, and working for the occupation authorities was therefore a logical step to take. Many Bosnians had converted to Islam during five centuries of Turkish rule for exactly the same reason, so the enormous expansion of militias (particularly Croatian) should be seen in this light. Many Croats served in Wehrmacht formations, some perishing at Stalingrad with the 100th Jäger (Light) Division. There were three other all-Croat infantry divisions, the 369th, 373rd and 392nd, but they served only within the Balkans.

At least four Waffen-SS mountain divisions were raised from ethnic Yugoslavs; the 7th 'Prinz Eugen' recruited Serbs, the 13th 'Handschar' attracted Bosnian Muslims, the 21st 'Skanderbeg' was formed from Albanians and ethnic Albanians from Kosovo, while the 23rd 'Kama' contained anti-communist Croatians. By the war's end 16,000 Albanians, 18,000 Bosnians, 8,000 Croats, 6,000 Slovenes and 4,000 Serbs were serving within the ranks of the SS, but it should be observed that the Waffen-SS and the Wehrmacht fought for the same recruits, and that the first volunteers joined foreign legions of the Army, only later being forcibly transferred to the SS. Perhaps 10,000 Serbs, and a similar number of Slovenes, served in state Home Guard-type formations, under nominal Axis control, while more than 250,000 Croats wore uniform and carried arms under Fascist banners. Just as with the Austro-Hungarian Army of 1914-18, the Germans regarded these local units as unreliable and desertion rates were high.[44] That these local militias, and all the organs of the Third Reich represented in Yugoslavia, acted with extreme brutality is beyond question – this chapter has not examined the concentration camps set up within Yugoslavia, for example. As in Russia, Hitler encouraged the concept of a *Vernichtungskrieg* (war of annihilation) against the Slavs, in which most Germans felt able to play a part. Mark Mazower has concluded that quite ordinary non-Nazi Wehrmacht units took part in executions and massacres in the region, whilst Philip Blood has uncovered evidence of Luftwaffe and even Kriegsmarine participation in what we would today term 'war crimes'.[45]

There is a common belief that Tito and Mihailovic held down substantial numbers of German troops throughout the war, badly needed elsewhere. Figures of 35-40 divisions of Axis troops fighting guerrillas are common currency, and exaggerate the Partisans' achievement. These arguments surfaced again in 1994-95, prior to the NATO peacekeeping deployments to Bosnia. The reality was different. In fact, there were often the equivalent of 30 divisions stationed in the Yugoslav area, perhaps 300,000 men, but less than one-third of these were regular Wehrmacht formations. The majority of the Axis garrison comprised locally raised militias, of poor morale and with high desertion rates, as noted earlier. Bulgarian divisions under Wehrmacht control were ignorant of modern war fighting, while most Wehrmacht 'divisions' in the Balkans were static formations, containing just one (or occasionally two) infantry regiments, little transport and no artillery. Their soldiers were the old, lame or sick, and they were supplemented by auxiliary Hilfswillige (Hiwi) battalions of Italians (post-September 1943), Russians, Ukrainians and Poles, whose reliability became increasingly suspect the nearer the Allies advanced. The picture was exactly the same in Normandy, where some static divisions and Hiwi battalions collapsed within 24 hours of the June 1944 invasion.

By mid-1944 the war was a long way from being decided in Yugoslavia, a fact underlined on 25 May by the German parachute and glider assault on Tito's new HQ in Drvar ('Operation Knight's Move' – *Rösselspring*). This attack was part of a German offensive that cost the Partisans 6,000 casualties, but Tito escaped (though losing most of his personal staff) and was brought by the British to Vis, one of the islands off the Croatian coast, and defended by the Royal Navy. A German plan to capture Vis was allegedly cancelled in the confusion following 20 July. Thereafter Tito commanded from the Adriatic, but was aided considerably by the RAF in the form of the Balkan Air Force, which engaged in a systematic campaign of aerial interdiction against German ground and sea forces, and supply of the Partisan columns.

Interpretations of the experience of liberation vary. The traditional view that Tito's Partisans liberated their own country without the major intervention of external foreign ground forces, and were the only resistance movement so to do, is effectively challenged by several military historians, including Stevan Pavlowitch and Sir Michael Howard. They argue that it was Allied pressure in Italy, Russian pressure in eastern Yugoslavia, along the Hungarian and Romanian borders, and the consequent withdrawal of Army Groups E and F under Field Marshal von Weichs, creating a military vacuum, that enabled the Partisans to control so much of their own country by 1945.[46] When Belgrade fell on 20 October 1944 it surrendered to Marshal Tolbukhin's Third Ukrainian Army with only a token force of I Partisan Corps, by which time the Russians controlled fully one-third of Yugoslav territory.

The final Yugoslav experience of the Second World War leaves no glory for Britain or Tito. Operations in the north Balkans, aimed at the annexation of Austrian and Italian territory, brought Partisan forces into confrontation with British and New Zealand troops over the occupation of Trieste in April-May 1945, which many Yugoslavs believed had been unfairly restored to Italy in 1918. Although the Partisans withdrew, Allied forces watched with distaste as 6,000 locals were arrested and more than 1,000 executed. Many of these proved not to be collaborators, but bourgeois 'class enemies'. By late May 1945 large numbers of ethnic Yugoslav troops and auxiliaries who had sided with the Germans were attempting to cross the Drava River into Austria near Bleiburg, but were consistently turned over to the Partisans by British troops. These various groups, including civilians associated with the occupation regimes, totalled perhaps 120,000 Croats, 11,000 Slovenes, 10,000 Chetniks and a similar number of Serbs. Machine-gun fire in the distance confirmed to the British (generally unhappy in their role of border guards) the grizzly fate awaiting the refugees, and by the year's end two-thirds of these waifs and strays from the 1941-45 Yugoslav conflict had simply 'vanished' on death marches and in Yugoslav detention camps.[47]

The oft-quoted cost of the Second World War in Yugoslavia was a staggering 1.7 million lives, nearly 11 per cent of the 1939 population of 15.5 million. This toll was more the result of brutal ethnic fratricide than anti-German resistance, and Partisan casualties are estimated at 300,000 dead and 425,000 wounded.[48] These figures may be too low, for calculations based on the pre- and post-war censuses show a negative balance of 2.2 million people; however, this figure includes deaths, expulsions, emigration and deportation, as well as losses sustained by the wartime drop in birthrates.[49]

A direct comparison of the Yugoslav experience in the two World Wars is challenging. It is important to remember that the concept of the Yugoslav state only came into being after the First World War, the area being previously divided between the Austro-Hungarian and Ottoman Empires, with Montenegro and Serbia as independent entities. Following the Axis occupation of 1941, the region was sub-divided again in almost Roman style, into Fascist client states under German-Italian military rule, supported by local turncoats. With this ever-shifting network of frontiers, it is arguable that for western Europeans there has been a certain amount of diplomatic safety in referring to the region merely as 'the Balkans'. Deriving from a Turkish word for 'wooded mountain', the Balkans encompass present-day Romania, Bulgaria, Greece, Albania, the former Yugoslavian states and sometimes, erroneously, Hungary. Thus, it is as vague a description as its Hollywood celluloid counterpart, the fictional eastern European country of 'Ruritania'. The very adjective 'Balkan' has descended during the 20th century from a descriptive term for a geographic region to the pejorative, implying an area where terror and slaughter reigns unchecked.[50] Sinister implications apart, the 'Balkan' label is arguably helpful if studying the experience of past generations of Yugoslavs in the two World Wars, for it makes allowance for the continual re-drawing of the map, for which the region is notorious.

John Gunther's influential *Inside Europe* (1936) summed up a typical western view of the Balkans, which still has a resonance today:

'Beyond ... lie the deep Balkans. They are, it has been said, a sort of hell paved with the bad intentions of the powers ... it is an intolerable affront to human and political nature that these wretched and unhappy little countries in the Balkan peninsula can, and do, have quarrels that cause world wars...'[51]

This sinister generalisation had been as current before the First World War as it was in the 1990s. Even at the time of writing, it can be suggested that the region is perhaps seen as the 'darker side of western civilisation', particularly when viewed from across the Atlantic. Back in 1936 Gunther wrote with both inaccuracy and barely concealed prejudice that, 'Some hundred and fifty thousand young Americans died because of an event in 1914 in a mud-caked primitive village, Sarajevo. Loathsome and almost obscene snarls in Balkan politics, hardly intelligible to a Western reader, [therefore] are still vital to the peace of Europe...'[52] Any visitor to Sarajevo will realise that the city was anything but primitive or mud-caked, even in 1914.

There is also a tendency to identify Yugoslavia with Serbia, perhaps not least because the Yugoslav Karadjordevic royal dynasty were Serbs (descended from a bandit chieftain who freed Serbia from the Turks in 1810), the capital, Belgrade, is also the Serbian principal city, and the antics of later Yugoslav politicians (notably the Serbian President Slobodan Milosovic and the leader of the Bosnian Serbs, Radovan Karadzic). This was as true in the past; the entry in *Chambers Encyclopaedia* (1936 edition) for Yugoslavia reads simply 'see under Serbia'. Such confusion was perpetuated deliberately by the Nazis. As far as Berlin was concerned, during the occupation of 1941-45 Yugoslavia did not exist, and the whole Balkan region (Greece, Yugoslavia, Albania and the eastern Mediterranean islands) was collectively the responsibility of Field Marshal Wilhelm List's South East Armed Forces Command. His area was treated administratively as a single super-state, sub-divided into Army and Corps zones of responsibility, the natives merely possessing different regional dialects or cultures. Perhaps the arrogance of re-drawing international borders in such fashion can be seen in the context of the Third Reich being designed to last a thousand years.

With confidence, we can sum up the Yugoslav experience of two World Wars as one of undiluted terror. While partly a reaction to repression and hardship, there is also, as Mark Almond suggests, a long tradition of violent resistance originating in five centuries of harsh Turkish rule, and ruthless banditry in a hard, mountainous country, perhaps a tradition still evident in parts of Albania today.[52] The 1991-95 war taught the world that this tradition still lurks within the Balkans.

Recommended reading

Banac, Ivo, *The National Question in Yugoslavia: Origins, History, Politics* (Ithaca: Cornell University Press, 1984)

Djilas, Milovan, *Wartime: With Tito and the Partisans* (London: Secker & Warburg, 1977)

Djordjevic, Dimitrije (ed), *The Creation of Yugoslavia, 1914-1918* (Santa Barbara: Clio Books, 1980)

Krippner, Monica, *The Quality of Mercy: Women at War, Serbia, 1915-18* (Newton Abbot: David & Charles, 1980)

Lampe, John R., *Yugoslavia as History: Twice there was a country* (Cambridge: Cambridge University Press, 2nd ed, 2000)

Lederer, Ivo J., *Yugoslavia at the Paris Peace Conference: A Study in Frontier-Making* (New Haven: Yale University Press, 1963)

Roberts, Walter R., *Tito, Mihaijlovic and the Allies, 1941-1945* (New Brunswick: Rutgers University Press, 1973)

Tomasevich, Jozo, *War and Revolution in Yugoslavia: 1941-1945*, Vol 1 'The Chetniks' (Stanford: Stanford University Press, 1975)

Wheeler, Mark, 'Pariahs to Partisans to Power: The Communist Party of Yugoslavia', in Tony Judt (ed), *Resistance and Revolution in Mediterranean Europe, 1938-1948* (London: Routledge, 1989)

Zhivojinovich, Dragan, 'Serbia and Montenegro: The Home Front, 1914-1918', in Bela K. Kiraly and Nandor F. Dreisziger (eds), *East Central European Society in World War I* (Boulder, CO: Social Science Monographs, 1985) pp239-59

Notes

1   Albino Garzetti, *From Tiberius to the Antonines* (London: Methuen, 1976)
2   Ibid, Chap 27
3   Ian F. W. Beckett and Keith Simpson (eds), *A Nation in Arms* (Manchester: Manchester University Press, 1985) p8
4   Margot Lawrence, 'The Serbian Divisions in Russia, 1916-7', in *Journal of Contemporary History* 6 (4) (1971), pp183-92
5   Nora Beloff, *Tito's Flawed Legacy* (London: Victor Gollancz, 1985) pp37-8
6   Geoffrey Wawro, 'Morale in the Austro-Hungarian Army: The Evidence of Habsburg Army Campaign Reports and Allied Intelligence Officers', in Hugh Cecil and Peter H. Liddle (eds), *Facing Armageddon: The First World War Experienced* (London: Pen & Sword, 1996) p400
7   Mirjana Gross, 'Social Structure and National Movements among the Yugoslav Peoples on the Eve of the First World War', in *Slavic Review* 36 (3) (1977) p632
8   Ibid, p631
9   Ibid, p640
10 John Gunther, *Inside Europe* (London: Hamish Hamilton, 1936) p384
11 Charles Jelavich, 'Serbian Textbooks: Toward Greater Serbia or Yugoslavia?', in *Slavic Review* 42 (4) (1983)
12 Ibid
13 'Nations and Their Past: The Uses and Abuses of History', in *The Economist*, 21 December 1996, pp53-6
14 Quoted in Charles Jelavich, 'The Issue of Serbian Textbooks in the Origins of World War I', in *Slavic Review* 48 (2) (1989) p217
15 Norman Stone, *The Eastern Front, 1914-1917* (London: Hodder & Stoughton, 1976) p221
16 Alan Burgess, *The Lovely Sergeant* (London: Odhams Press, 1963) p90
17 Norman Stone, op cit, p243
18 Alan Palmer, in A. J. P. Taylor (ed), *A History of World War One* (London: Phoebus Publishing, 1974) p85
19 Ibid, p86
20 Alan Burgess, op cit, pp129-30
21 Geoffrey Wawro, op cit, p404
22 Margot Lawrence, op cit, p184
23 Ibid, p188

24 *Encyclopaedia Britannica* (1953 ed), Vol 23, World War One Casualties

25 See, eg, the experience of Flora Sandes in Alan Burgess, op cit, pp204-7

26 François de Lannoy, *La Guerre dans les Balkans: Operation Marita: Yugoslavie-Grèce* (Bayeux: Editions Heimdal, 1999)

27 Vern Liebl, 'A Non-Partisan View of World War II Yugoslavia', in *Command Magazine* 22 (May-June 1993) pp32-45

28 Martin van Creveld, *The Balkan Clue: Hitler's Strategy 1940-41* (Cambridge: Cambridge University Press, 1973)

29 Nora Beloff, op cit, pp75-6

30 Milovan Djilas, trans Michael B. Petrovitch, *Wartime: With Tito and the Partisans* (London: Secker & Warburg, 1977) p283; also quoted in John Keegan, *A History of Warfare* (London: Hutchinson, 1993) p54

31 'German AntiGuerrilla Operations in the Balkans (1941-1944)', Department of the Army Pamphlet No 20-243 (Washington DC: August 1954) p34.

32 Vern Liebl, op cit, p44

33 Italo Calvino, trans Archibald Colquhoun, *The Path to the Spiders' Nests* (London: William Collins, 1956)

34 David Martin, *Patriot or Traitor? The Case of General Mihaijlovic* (Stanford: Stanford University Press, 1977) and Walter R. Roberts, *Tito, Mihaijlovic and the Allies 1941-1945* (New Brunswick: Rutgers University Press, 1973)

35 Accusations supported by Nora Beloff (*Tito's Flawed Legacy*) and Sir Duncan Wilson, in *Tito's Yugoslavia* (Cambridge: Cambridge University Press, 1980)

36 Nora Beloff, op cit, and Walter R. Roberts, 'Wartime in Yugoslavia', in *Slavic Review* 37 (2) (1978) pp491-4

37 Nora Beloff, op cit, p79

38 Basil Davidson, 'Makers of the Twentieth Century: Tito', in *History Today* (October 1980) pp25-9

39 Major d'Arcy Ryan, *The Guerrilla Campaign in Yugoslavia*, Strategic & Combat Studies Institute, Camberley, Occasional Paper No 6 (1994), p33

40 Curzio Malaparte, trans Cesare Foligno, *Kaputt* (London: Panther, 1967) p233

41 Christopher R. Browning, *Fateful Months: Essays on the Emergence of the Final Solution* (New York: Holmes & Meier, 1991) pp39-40

42 Mark Mazower, 'Military Violence and National Socialist Values: The Wehrmacht in Greece 1941-44', in *Past and Present* 143 (1994) pp129-58, and Nora Beloff, op cit, p72

43 Tim Kirk, 'Limits of Germandom: Resistance to the Nazi Annexation of Slovenia', in *South East Europe Review* 69 (4) (October 1991) pp646-67

44 Vern Liebl, op cit

45 Mark Mazower, op cit, and Philip Blood, ongoing PhD thesis, Cranfield University (2000)

46 Stevan K. Pavlowitch, 'The Second World War in Yugoslavia: An Imaginary Debate', in *European Studies Review* 11 (1981), pp543-53, and Sir Michael Howard, *The Times*, 7 June 1983

47 Vern Liebl, op cit, pp44-5

48 Major d'Arcy Ryan, op cit, p15

49 J. Wüscht, 'Population Losses in Yugoslavia in World War Two', in *Forum* (1963), quoted in Nora Beloff, op cit, p74

50 Maria Todorova, 'The Balkans: From Discovery to Invention', in *Slavic Review*, 53 (4) (1994)

51 John Gunther, op cit, p437

52 Ibid

53 Mark Almond, *Europe's Backyard War: The War in the Balkans* (London: William Heinemann, 1994)

Chapter 9

The experience of middle-class Japanese women[1]

Naoko Shimazu

I t is often tempting to present war as a picture of extremes. In the case of Japan in the Second World War, one could posit the fanatical militarists on the one hand, and the oppressed masses on the other. What this picture neglects to reveal, however, is that there were sections in society that were neither fanatical nor suffering, and did not fit into the neat pattern. Moreover, wars often induced incremental rather than sudden social and economic changes. In order to have a meaningful comparison, how can we deal with the huge gap in the degree of Japanese participation in the two World Wars? If we divert our attention from the usual male-centred depiction of war, we can arrive at an 'alternative' female-centred perspective that presents a view of a more normalised, mundane life of society at war. For this purpose, I have chosen to analyse a journal called *Fujin Kôron* (*Women's Review*), which occupied the position of opinion leader since its inception in 1916. There are two main justifications for using this particular journal. First, it was one of the most influential women's journals in pre-war Japan, setting trends in opinions on political and social issues. Second, being categorised as a women's journal, it escaped, to some extent, the scrutiny of censors to which other influential mainstream opinion journals were subjected, and hence managed to sustain a surprising degree of freedom of expression until 1943. This study will illuminate the existence of a surprising level of plurality of views in Japan, even during the Second World War.

In terms of the structure of this study, the two World Wars will be dealt with separately because Japan's involvement in them was so markedly different. However, wherever appropriate, comparative remarks will be incorporated.

In 1916, when *Fujin Kôron* was first launched, Japanese liberals dominated public opinion, expounding their views on liberal democracy and its applicability to Japan. This reflected the general political movement of the time, known as the 'Taishô democracy'.[2] *Fujin Kôron* was launched with a clear mission. It was intended not only to 'awaken' women from their life of servitude and inertia, but also to 'awaken' Japanese society, imbued with patriarchal, feudalistic attitudes towards women. The journal was elitist, addressing that section of society that it regarded as providing the most likely vehicle for social change and progress. During the period of the First World War, which covered the first three years of its publication, the articles in *Fujin Kôron* tended to be idealistic, progressive, and prescriptive. In other words, it sought to change the way women thought and lived their lives. Although *Fujin Kôron* is generally considered to belong to the genre of women's journals, its readership initially was not gender specific, as more than one-third of subscribers were male, reflecting its disproportionately political content.[3] Most noteworthy with regard to the period of the First World War was that the journal made very little reference to the war itself. This underlined the generally detached Japanese attitude towards the war, which was seen as 'the European war', the only incident to whip up public fervour being the Siberian troop deployment in 1918.[4] Within the discussion of the journal in the First World War, three particularly prominent themes will be examined. They are the 'new women', 'free love' and marriage, and the pro-Western attitude.

Without doubt, *Fujin Kôron* was much preoccupied with disseminating the concept of 'new women' to 'awaken' Japanese women from their 'unfree' condition.[5] The opening article of the founding issue of January 1916 started with an article entitled 'The Path which Contemporary Women Must Take', written by Abe Isoo, in which he spearheaded the attack on the pitiful state of women's rights in Japan:

> '[In] political issues, our country has finally abandoned the barbaric system by establishing constitutional foundation, but as regards women's issues, women are still obeying the tyrannical power of men.'[6]

Accordingly, men should 'respect women's individuality', while women should stand up for their rights, like the heroine, Nora, in Ibsen's *A Doll's House*. In fact, Ibsen's Nora became a metaphor for the oppressed 'unfree' condition of the Japanese female. One female activist, Itô Noe, wrote that what women were asking for was 'to be able to move according to their own wishes, rather than like soul-less dolls which were manipulated by other people's wishes'.[7] However, she did not forget to add that in order to produce the 'new women', we need to create the 'new men'.

Many prominent male authors wrote instructing women to stand up for their rights. In the first three years after publication, men dominated authorship; only 25 per cent of the contributions were from women.[8] Yoshino Sakuzô, the most famous proponent of liberal democracy in the Taishô period (1912-25) wrote that women should participate in constitutional politics through 'moral power', without explaining what he meant by it.[9] Ishikawa Hanzan advocated educating women in politics and diplomacy so that Japanese democracy would become a better democracy.[10] Seemingly progressive, he fell into the trap of praising women not for their intrinsic ability to undertake political responsibility but as a civilising influence on men who participate in politics.[11] In its first year of publication, *Fujin Kôron* ran an interesting series of essays in which prominent male intellectuals were asked to comment on their images of the 'new women'.[12] Evidently, there was widespread recognition that women's status needed to be improved in order to be compatible with the new age of liberalism. However, Ukita Kazutami struck the cord of the enlightened male when he concluded in his article that 'at the end of the day, a woman's happiness lies with being a man's wife, and a good mother', and thus, perpetuating the Meiji ideal of 'good wife, wise mother' (*ryôsai kenbo*).[13]

Indeed, most fell short of being able to take the stance of the truly enlightened male such as Anesaki Masaharu, who stated that the time had come to end the subjugation of women to the traditional virtue of the 'Three Obediences' to parents, husbands and sons.[14] He expressed great concern that the present condition of 'keeping women as slaves' would imply halving Japan's human resources. Undoubtedly, the liberal, progressive 'new men' wanted to improve women's status. However, they were not willing to concede absolute equality to women on the basis of the biological difference. Instead, these 'new men' wanted the best of both worlds – to have more educated, intelligent, but nonetheless deferential housewives who would make more suitable partners for themselves, who were the forerunners of modern liberal society.

Women's perspectives on the issue of political rights remained divided. Notwithstanding the enthusiasm expressed by the 'new men', some women expressed caution about the radical nature of the proposals for social change aimed at improving women's status. Kawada Yoshi, for one, criticised these 'new men' for their tendency to beautify women's issues by making them into abstract ideals, which unfortunately had the effect of exaggerating values attached to such changes. Instead, she believed that women should seek more modest goals given that they had designated roles in society.[15] Kawada's article represented the backlash against the aggressively progressive attitude taken by many contributors, whose messages on women's rights appeared unrealistic and even undesirable by more conservative women. This points to the gap between what the journal was demanding rhetorically and the reality for many women, who, given the conditions they were in, must have felt unable to keep up with the lofty idealistic figure of the 'new woman' created for them by the 'new men'.

Not surprisingly, the harshest criticisms of existing conditions came from women. Yosano Akiko, the famous female poet, accused Japanese democracy of 'barbarism' because it refused votes to women, who constituted one half of the nation.[16] Evidently she was much affected by the general international environment of the time, which presented Wilsonian liberal idealism as the new alternative to the old order, since she heralded the end of the age of male supremacy as being commensurate with the end of the First World War. Yosano contended that Japan could not be a true democracy until it gave universal suffrage to both men and women over 25 years of age.[17] Yosano's fiery, uncompromising statements were refreshing as, ironically, most other contributors writing on women's rights were men.

Another dominant theme in *Fujin Kôron* during the period of the First World War was that of 'free love' and marriage. Here, the majority of writers were women. On the question of the sexual morality of the sexes, there was severe criticism of the hypocrisy existing in Japan concerning male and female sexual morality. The most representative view was that advocated by Hiratsuka Raichô, one of the most notable women's rights activists in pre-war Japan. In October 1916, in 'Debates on Male and Female Morality', she underlined the existence of an unimaginable gap between female and male sexual morality. Indeed, it was more accurate to say that sexual morality did not apply to men.[18]

Even the term 'morality' was heavily gendered as, when applied to women, it automatically implied 'sexual morality' as opposed to any other morality. Hiratsuka reiterated that in all stages of life, women were judged by sexual morality: women should be virgins, whereas men should be sexually experienced before marriage; married women should not commit adultery whereas men practise effectively what amounted to polygamy by having mistresses; and widows should never remarry whereas widowers always remarried. Therefore, women were sexual possessions of men and, effectively, sexual slaves. Men worried about women's chastity not usually because of true love, but because they were concerned about the social implications of not being able to control their sexual possessions. Hiratsuka contended that all these sexist notions of marriage had to be abandoned in favour of the new concept of 'free love', which should lie at the heart of the new morality for 'new women'. Only with 'free love' could there be equal relationships between men and women. Hiratsuka's notion of 'free love' partly implied 'romantic love', in which women should be allowed to fall in love with and marry men of their own choice, as opposed to men chosen by their parents. Most importantly, 'free love' became symbolic of women's need to make their own choice in life. Therefore, it had an indirect political implication by making women aware of their rights.

Many writers were critical of women's submissive and inert attitudes, which made them susceptible to male domination. Often the picture they painted of Japanese women was not a flattering one. Apparently, Japanese women were vain, passive, insincere, and 'blood-sucking'.[19] To compound the problem, they did not have an ounce of self-reflection nor self-criticism.[20] These negative characteristics were applied generally to middle-class women from economically well-off backgrounds. According to Yamada Waka, what the women's movement was aiming to do was to change fundamentally the characteristics of both men and women by making men more understanding and humane, while making women more independent and sincere.[21] Hiratsuka also proposed her solution to this general problem of female inertia, by adopting a 'new morality' based on women's pursuit of knowledge, entrepreneurship, and social activism.[22] Such attitudes of inertia held by some middle-class women continued unabated and posed serious problems of motivation during the Second World War.

In 1918 Yosano Akiko and Hiratsuka Raichô clashed over the debate on the compatibility of motherhood and work. Yosano argued that women should be able to raise children and work; hence those women who could not should not be given state assistance. On the other hand, Hiratsuka argued that women had the right to demand state assistance, because motherhood should be compensated financially as a form of labour.[23] In fact, Hiratsuka criticised Yosano's elitist bourgeois attitude, which applied her high personal standard to the rest of the female population.[24] A third-party observer, Yamakawa Kikue, commented that Yosano's position was akin to that of Mary Wollstonecraft, while Hiratsuka's was closer to Ellen Key.[25] Yamakawa, instead, advocated fundamental changes in economic relations between the sexes. Although a few writers such as Hiratsuka did attempt to highlight the plight of female factory workers, the journal did not feature many articles dealing with the problems associated with the socio-economically disadvantaged women.[26]

Another salient feature of *Fujin Kôron* during the First World War was its pro-Western attitude. In general, the journal catered to the progressive liberals, which meant that there existed a strong respect for Western liberalism. This was reflected in its highly positive coverage of the West as a source of inspiration for Japanese women.

The journal was impressed with the commitment shown by Western women to the war. One such representative article described the major wartime activities undertaken by women of the belligerent states.[27] Both French and German women were praised for taking over responsibilities for primary education during the war. In particular, there was great respect shown towards German women's war effort as they became the force behind keeping alive agriculture, which expanded in wartime due to their ingenious use of prisoners of war as a source of farm labour. One amusing example was the so-called 'Hindenburg of the Kitchen' who pioneered wartime recipes and wrote *Wartime Cookery*, for which she received a medal from the German Government. Even more surprisingly, Russian women reportedly formed female suicide squads! The author concluded that these women would undoubtedly demand political and social changes once the war was over, as it had made them aware of their capabilities.

Of course, all of these pro-Western articles had a prescriptive element to them, which was to 'awaken' Japanese women to endless possibilities demonstrated by Western women. In 1917 Uchigasaki Sakusaburô stated that war provided a great opportunity for the advancement of women.[28] He pointed out that the war had made European women economically integrated through work from driving tractors to running banks, which made them feel that they could ask for equal rights with men. This would change the idea of marriage, as women would demand a more equitable partnership after the war. Uchigasaki called on Japanese women similarly to seize the opportunity provided by war to change their socio-economic status. Another stated that a great gap existed between Western and Oriental civilisations in terms of political rights. On the one hand, British women were promised the right to vote as soon as the war was over. On the other hand, not all Japanese men had this entitlement.[29] Needless to say, British women obtained the voting right only after demonstrating their enormous contribution to the war effort. Similarly, it was noted that women had voting rights in the Scandinavian countries and in some of the states in the United States.

Overall, the pro-Western attitude is hardly surprising in the light of the strength of the Taishô democratic movement, which was much influenced by Wilsonian liberalism. Most notably, the Japanese did not choose to make any distinction between the women of the West, regardless of whether or not they were enemy nations. Instead, all Western women were put on a pedestal and presented as models from which Japanese women must learn. Intriguingly, this tendency to give special regard to all Western states continued to be prevalent well into the Second World War.

As Japan launched into the Second World War effectively from the Marco Polo Bridge Incident of July 1937, the term 'Second World War' in this chapter is used to denote the period 1937-45. Until *Fujin Kôron* faced a publishing crisis in March 1944, when it was forced to close down, it continued to provide a fascinating insight into Japanese society at war, the picture not being the one with which we are familiar. We witness the existence of a plurality of views in Japanese society about the war and about priorities in everyday life. However, the editorial's notion of the 'ideal' woman did not sit comfortably with that of its readers, who became more conservative, favouring the Meiji model of 'good wife, wise mother'.[30] In this section we shall focus on the following topics: the middle class 'ennui'; war as an opportunity; marriage; work, education and motherhood; women and the empire; and attitudes towards the West.

In analysing *Fujin Kôron* in the period 1937-44, the most striking revelation is the general attitude of ennui held implicitly towards the war by the readership. Although this observation is somewhat speculative, it is difficult to ignore the underlying sentiment that can be gleaned from the tone of writing adopted by contributors and from their choice of topics. This observation questions the received knowledge of Japanese society during the Second World War, which is that of an oppressive totalitarian state that governed its citizens through highly organised social units. Intriguingly, this clearly did not prevent some city women, who were socially and economically better off, from remaining uninterested in the war. The middle class concentrated in urban centres, occupying around 21.5 per cent of the population in Tokyo as early as 1920.[31] Consequently, the acute sense of national crisis one would expect in wartime only became evident in the pages of the journal in 1943, when one begins to notice a tense, alarmist tone.[32]

The ennui that seeps through the pages of the journal reflects the dominant social class of the readership. By the 1930s the readers were mostly women who belonged to the educated, well-off middle class. What is particularly interesting is that these women did not seem to want to be bothered by the war, and carried on with their daily routine as long as they could, until around 1943. Some of them came from the 'Ladies who lunch' crowd or its Japanese equivalent, 'Mitsukoshi Department Store today, the Imperial Theatre tomorrow'. One activist lamented that the hottest topic among the Tokyoite women was whether or not to have a perm.[33] Some Japanese women, who had just returned from abroad in 1940, expressed their surprise to see how easy-going Japan was in wartime.[34] They even heard some Japanese women vowing that they would rather die than not eat white rice. As late as September 1942, the editorial of *Fujin Kôron* talks about the difficulty of motivating young women 'to think about the war and about the state'.[35] After all, why should they be patriotic and warmongering, when they had been left out of the political process and moulded to be submissive women by the cultural ideal? Without being anti-war, these women continued to resist unconsciously being drawn into war on the terms set out by the state.

Was the journal responsible for generating this attitude of indifference? Continuation of the editorial policy of adopting a measured, liberal approach on the selection of published materials did, to some extent, have the effect of protecting the readership from war propaganda. This is not to say that the journal did not include articles on the war. On the contrary, it had to publish the increasingly frequent 'bureaucratic contributions' sent from the military, and from the Ministries of Education and Interior, in order to evade the tightened censorship. Examples of this censorship are the regulations instituted by the

Ministry of Interior in 1938, which clamped down on women's magazines. However, the fact that the contents pages of the journal often looked like a mixed bag of disparate articles indicated that the editorial department was determined to continue its policy of publishing whatever it wanted. In any one issue, the reader would likely find a xenophobic 'bureaucratic contribution', next to a serious article on topics such as female labour and education, a panel discussion on 'wifely love', reports on theatre trips, and an 'agony aunt' column on the infidelity of husbands. As we shall see, indifference towards the war on the part of middle-class women contradicted the editorial position.

During the Second World War *Fujin Kôron* continued to hold the belief, as it did in the First World War, that wars presented an important opportunity for women in terms of advancement of their rights. Although the journal avoided being drawn into the state propaganda machinery, its position was essentially supportive of the war. Reflecting the editorial's pro-war position, Yamakawa Kikue made an attempt to 'awaken' women in 1938:

'Contemporary wars change women. That is from passive to active, from love object to living human being. This is the phenomenon of contemporary wars, simply an extension of military warfare to economic warfare, needing men and women regardless of sex to continue to fight in peacetime and wartime economically, and hence, it is possible to maximise national labour, and as a result, women need to be educated and can elevate their level socially. Women will have a lot to learn from this trying period.'[36]

In the opening editorial of the January 1939 issue, the journal takes the similarly prescriptive stance, mirroring Yamakawa's views above.[37] It argued that the state had an important task of educating women in order to meet the needs of war. Moreover, Yamakawa added that not only did women need to be better educated, but better fed since they had the highest death rate from tuberculosis in the civilised world.[38] In fact, there was quite a concern about the poor condition of women's health generally, due to a lack of adequate nutrition.[39]

On the whole, it was clear that the editorial department was not willing to be as political as it had been in the early days of its operation. Most likely, it reflected the widening gap between the liberal, progressive attitude of the editorial staff and the more conservatively inclined readership. This was a salient characteristic of the journal throughout the Second World War, as its normative messages of wanting to change women's status did not manage to strike a cord with many of its readers.

In comparison to the advocacy of 'free love' in the First World War, the notion of marriage in the 1937-44 period was conservative. Anxious mothers continued to worry about the eligibility of their daughters even in the deepest throes of the war. In one discussion, parents worried that daughters were incapable of finding suitable partners for themselves, and moreover it was 'dangerous' if they did so.[40] They were most concerned about daughters having the 'ideal' image of husbands formed from films and novels. Most parents believed that 'marital love' as opposed to 'romantic love' would develop after marriage: 'Even if there was no romantic love to begin with, the different sort of love will "spring out" with the husband, and one can gain satisfaction and happiness from it.'[41]

The question of marriage extended to the issue of marrying injured soldiers. On the one hand, some thought it unwise that young women of impressionable age should sympathise with these soldiers and plunge into marriage by 'sacrificing themselves'. On the other hand, the prevailing view was that these soldiers made good marriage partners since they possessed good genes in spite of their external injuries, and also that they received good war pensions.[42]

More pressingly, the view remained divided about the remarriage of war widows. Conservatives believed that widows should refrain from remarriage and remain chaste to the dead husbands who had sacrificed their lives for the state.[43] One patriotic war widow from the Association of the Yasukuni Widows argued that women must feel joy from the death of their husbands who died for family honour and the emperor.[44] However, one female writer complained that so much fuss was being made about the stoic heroism of wives of professional soldiers that the majority of war widows, who were wives of ordinary conscripted soldiers and did not have the same sense of ethics and moral rectitude, were being neglected.[45]

Very infrequently, the more progressive contributors attacked such status quo views about marriage. In one discussion session, the central debate was that women should rethink the idea of marriage in the light of the New Order being established by the Government as the new basis of Japanese polity. This was a great opportunity for women to 'rationalise' marriage and reorganise their position in society. They should no longer expect their husbands to support them but be financially responsible, and even married women should be required to work to support the war effort.[46]

Interestingly, many discussions on women's work and education were tied to the issue of motherhood. Evidently the majority of Japanese men and women did not want women to leave home even in wartime. This implied that the enthusiasm expressed in the days of the Taishô liberalism about the 'new women', and their elevated role in society, did not manage to change social attitudes towards women. As a result, the Meiji model of 'good wife, wise mother' was still just as valid some 60 years later.

During the Second World War many articles were published concerning women's 'work'. In most cases, however, this effectively meant 'housework'. Much practical advice was given to readers on how to rationalise housework in wartime.[47] In addition, there was a widespread call for improving women's education so that they could be of more use to the war effort. However, most people believed that the ultimate objective of improved education for women was to produce more efficient homemakers, so that they could more ably assist men.[48] People often talked about 'the way of women' (*fudô*), the female version of 'the way of the samurai' (*bushidô*), in an attempt to give more cachet to the art of educating women to become better homemakers.

In this social climate, the question of female labour was a sensitive question. According to Oku Mumeo, a female activist, there were contradictory attitudes in society that hindered women from joining in the productive labour force.[49] Problems were two-pronged: one resulted from the physical condition of female-unfriendly workplaces, and the other reflected attitudes that condemned working women for neglecting housework. As a result, Oku argued that the state did not have a clear policy on female labour, causing women to be sandwiched between two contradictory pressures. Oku's solution was to institute a more 'rationalised' family life, which allowed both partners to work and establish a 'new order' in family life.[50]

Notwithstanding all the discussions about the importance of mobilising women, female mobilisation often consisted of 'ideological' mobilisation, which meant fostering pro-war sentiment, living an economical daily life, efficient use of foodstuff, and, rarely, female labour.[51] Clearly, the most pressing issue, the mobilisation of female labour, was not condoned by society, which was not willing to let women leave home to assist the war effort. In practical terms, the biggest obstacle to persuading women to work in factories was their safety away from the home, or more precisely, how to preserve their virginity and chastity.[52] Women were further burdened by the perception that working outside of home somehow stripped them of their femininity.[53] Later in 1942, in line with the national slogan of 'devotion by hard work', city women were sent out to the countryside to help with farming. However, the scheme backfired, as city women could not be usefully employed to undertake farm labour.[54] The editorial voiced its concern in 1943 that if the state wanted women to work, then it should take over responsibility for childcare facilities and social benefits.[55]

Women's associations presented one of the few socially acceptable ways of being involved in war effort. In the late 1930s there were women in white aprons standing on street corners asking for *senbonbari* (1,000 stitches on a cloth as a sign of good luck), displaying 'selfless patriotism'.[56] Needless to say, there was a great rivalry between the white aprons of the National Defence Association for Women (*Kokubô fujinkai*), and the Patriotic Women's Association (*Aikoku fujinkai*), whose members wore a khaki-coloured top with white sash. Ironically, as men ultimately controlled these associations established to assist the war effort, their public showdowns revealed the extent of rivalry between the military (controlling the National Defence Association for Women) and the Ministry of Interior (Patriotic Women's Association) in vying for domestic influence.[57] The most commendable example of female mobilisation was the women of Kitakari Village, in Shizuoka Prefecture, where an extremely active women's association aimed at improving their working conditions. It ran efficient and well-organised programmes that included organised military training given by the local reservist association.[58]

It was the military that remained most conservative in its attitude towards women and women's role in war. When General Ugaki offered his wisdom on the subject, he stated categorically that women's identity was with the home, and this was particularly important during wartime.[59] Even Prime Minister Tôjô Hideki wrote a piece dedicated to war widows, in the November issue of 1941, which commended the enormous inner strength of wives who dedicated their husbands to the state.[60] Tôjô stated that women were the bearers of the future of Japan, which meant that they and their children should lead a life of moral rectitude in order not to embarrass the dead spirit of their husbands, who had sacrificed their lives for the state. In December 1942, to commemorate the first anniversary of Pearl Harbor, Tôjô reiterated the message about the nobility of motherhood:

'In truth, the love of Japanese mothers is the basis of Japanese bushidô, and in order to nurture strong soldiers and great Japanese citizens, it is the women's input that we need.'[61]

Another military official preached that women had an extremely important role to play in national defence, that of increasing the population, by marrying to breed.[62] By October 1943 there was increasing pressure for war widows to remarry in order to produce more children and so to demonstrate their patriotism.[63]

Evidently there was strong resistance to mobilising women. Even as late as August 1943 it was considered to be a positive sign that Japan had the lowest rate of mobilisation of women among the belligerent states, because it meant that the traditional virtues of Japanese women, as bearers of children, were being protected.[64]

Corresponding to the expansion of the Japanese Empire in 1942, there was an increased concern about women's role in the Greater East Asia Co-Prosperity Sphere. In practice, women needed to be persuaded to play a larger role in developing the empire by emigrating to populate the colonies. Satô Toshiko preached that, 'If Japan needs to lead Asia in the future, then Japanese women must lead the women of Asia'.[65] She contended, however, that the position of Japanese women would be undermined in the eyes of the others by the fact that they did not possess voting rights. Hirade Hideo wrote that Japanese women, like Chinese women, should be prepared to go and live in the colonies in order to turn them Japanese.[66] He underlined that the 'natives' were polite and respectful towards the Japanese. Interestingly, Chinese women were often regarded as being more active, harder working and more willing to take the initiative than their Japanese counterparts.[67] In October 1943 another contributor wrote that Japanese women needed to be better trained to enable them to offer 'leadership with dignity' in a multi-racial environment like Manchukuo.[68]

The need to send 'educated good-quality' women as 'continental brides' was increasingly perceived as being a priority in the light of the fact that many women pioneers in the colonies tended to come from the 'water trade' (prostitution).[69] All in all, these articles reveal two things: on the one hand, the increasing pressure to populate the colonies by sending middle-class women; on the other hand, the reluctance of these women to be drawn into an unappealing life in the colonies.

Possibly the most surprising revelation was the continued pro-Western attitude shown by the journal, even during the Second World War. What stood true in the First World War – the refusal to distinguish enemy Western nations from Allied Western nations – still held true in 1937-44.

Reports and descriptions of what went on in Western countries continued to attract editorial interest. For instance, there was an amusing piece on the family life of the great Western leaders, namely Mussolini, Roosevelt, Franco and Hitler.[70] An important contribution was made by the chairwoman of the Nazi Women's Association in Germany, in which she described the prominent role of German women in war, dating back to the First World War.[71] Accordingly, the Nazis recognised the importance of the family as the basic unit of the state, which made women indispensable through their roles as mothers and housewives. In order to train 'perfect mothers', the Nazis established the prototype 'Mothers School' in Berlin, which now had 430 branches across the country. Japanese women were now facing a similar predicament to that of Nazi women, and hence they should take up the challenge in order to strengthen their position in society through their role as mothers. In 1943 there was an increased effort to persuade women to mobilise by providing comparisons of women mobilised in the West. One such article, written by a Navy official, described the important role played by women in the United States, where women in the US Navy were given military ranks, and formed their own units.[72] In another piece, women of France and Britain were cited as examples for Japanese women to emulate even as late as March 1943.[73]

Evidently there existed an underlying desire by the editors not to demonise the Anglo-Saxon countries, which continued to command respect amongst die-hard liberals as the birthplace of liberalism. This indicates that even in totalitarian wartime Japan, there remained some pockets of intellectual freedom where pro-Western and pro-Anglo-American views continued to be expressed.

What sort of images do we gain of Japanese society at war from an analysis of the issues of *Fujin Kôron* that were published during the two World Wars? *Fujin Kôron* was consistent in two respects. First, it believed in the dictum that women needed to take advantage of wars in order to improve their status. Although Japan did not play a large role in the First World War, the journal was able to take advantage of Taishô liberalism to be as progressive and as prescriptive as possible in its advocacy of women's rights. Hence, 'new women' became the byword for the new age, though the 'new men' turned out not to be as reconstructed as they appeared to be. Clearly the journal had not lost its sense of mission as, after 1937, it continued to reiterate its message. However, it was the readership that had changed, as society in the late 1930s had become more conservative since the heyday of liberalism in the second decade of the century. Whatever happened to the 'new women' and the 'new morality'? They disappeared under the resurgence of the traditional role model of 'good wife, wise mother'. In reality, the traditional role model never disappeared from the scene, continuing to serve the vested interests of the patriarchal society. During the Second World War the state made motherhood sacrosanct because of the need to reproduce the population to meet the demands of an expanding empire. With or without state endorsement, however, issues such as marriage remained central to women's lives and continued to preoccupy the readers.

The second point of consistency was in the journal's pro-Western attitude. Because the general image of mutual racial hatred between the Japanese and the Allied Forces during the Second World War remains so strong, it was surprising to discover that there was not a hint of animosity shown towards Anglo-Saxon powers during the war in *Fujin Kôron*. This is a clear testimony that the editorial department had managed to maintain a reasonable degree of independence from state censorship, in order to remain true to their belief that Japan needed to learn from the West, especially from the Anglo-Saxon West, where women's equal status was secured through political rights. However, the editorial decision not to demonise the enemy nations meant that it was difficult for readers to ascertain what Japan was fighting for in the war.

Hence, the task set out by the progressively minded editors to motivate middle-class women to stand up for their rights, by taking the initiative in support of the war effort, was not easily accomplished. Middle-class women resisted in quiet ways by remaining uninterested in the war. Even the state through the Imperial Rule Assistance Association noted, in April 1943, the difficulty of persuading women to take the idea of total war seriously.[73] What this study has revealed is that Japanese society was not as monolithic as it appeared, because there were agents within the society, *Fujin Kôron* being one of them, that continued to disseminate ideas and information, albeit in small ways, to offer plurality in society at least until 1943. Of course, the war became all-encompassing in 1944, when all activities became subsumed in the final stages of the struggle to survive.

Recommended reading

Berstein, Gail Lee (ed), *Recreating Japanese Women, 1600-1945* (Berkeley: University of California Press, 1991)

Cook, Haruko Taya and Cook, Theodore F. (eds), *Japan at War: An Oral History* (New York: The New Press, 1992)

Dower, John, *Japan in War and Peace: Essays on History, Culture and Race* (London: Fontana Press, 1993)

Sievers, Sharon L., *Flowers in Salt: The Beginnings of Feminist Consciousness in Modern Japan* (Stanford: Stanford University Press, 1983)

Tsurumi, Shunsuke, *An Intellectual History of Wartime Japan 1931-1945* (London: Kegan Paul International, 1986)

Notes

[1] I would like to express my gratitude to Emeritus Professor Banno Junji, University of Tokyo, for the highly stimulating discussions I had with him on this topic. Special thanks are also due to the Birkbeck College Appeal Fund for part-funding my trip to Japan from July to December 1999, which enabled me to write this chapter.

[2] Generally speaking, the Taishô period (1912-25) is considered to be the 'democratic' interlude between the oligarchic politics of the Meiji period (1868-1912) and the militarism of the 1930s.

[3] Hanzawa Seiji, *Taishôki no zasshi kisha: Ichi fujin kôron kisha no kaisô* (Tokyo: Chûô kôronsha, 1986) p67

[4] Naoko Shimazu, 'Detached and Indifferent: The Japanese Response', in Hugh Cecil and Peter H. Liddle (eds), *At the Eleventh Hour: Reflections, Hopes and Anxieties at the Closing of the Great War, 1918* (London: Leo Cooper, 1998) pp224-34

[5] For a general discussion of 'new women', see Laurel Rasplica Rodd, 'Yosano Akiko and the Taishô debate over the "New Women"', in Gail Lee Berstein (ed), *Recreating Japanese Women, 1600-1945* (Berkeley: University of California Press, 1991) pp175-98

[6] Abe Isoo, 'Gendai fujin no ikubeki michi', *Fujin Kôron* Vol 1, No 1 (January 1916) pp1-8

[7] Itô Noe, 'Dansei ni taisuru shuchô to yôkyû', ibid, Vol 1, No 2 (February 1916) pp27-34

[8] 'Fujin kôron no hakkô jôkyô ni kansuru ichi kôsatsu', Kindai josei bunkashi kenkyûkai (ed), *Fujin zasshi ni miru taishôki: Fujin kôron o chûshin ni* (Tokyo: Kindai josei bunkashi kenkyûkai, 1995) p39

[9] Yoshino Sakuzô, 'Rikken seiji no igi', *Fujin Kôron*, Vol 2, No 6 (June 1917) pp1-11

[10] Ishikawa Hanzan, 'Jisei o shire', ibid, Vol 2, No 2 (February 1917) pp6-12, and 'Sôsenkyo to fujin', ibid, Vol 2, No 3 (March 1917) pp8-15

[11] Ishikawa Hanzan, 'Fujin to seiji', ibid, Vol 1, No 11 (November 1916) pp10-15, and 'Fujin to teikoku gikai', ibid, Vol 1, No 12 (December 1916) pp17-24

[12] See 'Taishô shin onna daigaku' in ibid, Vol 1 Nos 1-9 (January to September 1916). For an analysis of this series, see 'Taishô shin onna daigaku o yomu', in *Fujin zasshi ni miru taishôki*, op cit, pp94-101

[13] Ukita Kazutami, 'Taishô shin onna daigaku 3', *Fujin Kôron*, Vol 1, No 3 (March 1916) pp44-50

[14] Anesaki Masaharu, 'Fujin no seishinteki dokuritsu', ibid, Vol 1, No 4 (April 1916) pp17-22

[15] Kawada Yoshi, 'Josei no fujin mondai ni taisuru taido', ibid, Vol 1, No 3 (March 1916) pp26-9

[16] Yosano Akiko, 'Fujin to seiji undô', ibid, Vol 2, No 3 (March 1917) pp16-20

[17] Yosano Akiko, 'Fujin mo senkyoken o yôkyûsu', ibid, Vol 4, No 3 (March 1919) pp7-12

[18] Hiratsuka Raichô, 'Danjo seiteki dôtokuron', ibid, Vol 1, No 10 (October 1916) pp1-10

[19] Yamada Waka, 'Fujin undô no kichakuten', ibid, Vol 3, No 2 (February 1918) pp31-42

[20] Hiratsuka Raichô, 'Fujin no jiyû kaihô to kojinteki shûyô', ibid, Vol 2, No 8 (August 1917) pp18-27

[21] Yamada Waka, op cit, pp31-42

[22] Hiratsuka Raichô, op cit, pp18-27

[23] Yamakawa Kikue, 'Yosano, Hiratsuka nishi no ronsô', ibid, Vol 3, No 9 (September 1918) pp22-34. Later, Hiratsuka Raichô expands on this view in 'Gendai katei fujin o nayami', ibid, Vol 4, No 1 (January 1919) pp30-5

[24] Hiratsuka Raichô, 'Yosano, Kaetsu ni shi e', ibid, Vol 3, No 5 (May 1918) pp18-25

[25] Yamakawa Kikue, op cit, pp22-34

[26] Hiratsuka Raichô, 'Nihon ni okeru jokô mondai', ibid, Vol 4, No 6 (June 1919) pp19-34

[27] Morishita Iwatarô, 'Kôsenkoku fujin no mezamashii katsudô', ibid, Vol 2, No 11 (November 1917) pp50-8

[28] Uchigasaki Sakusaburô, 'Oshu sengo no fujin mondai', ibid, Vol 2, No 1 (January 1917) pp50-7

[29] Universal male suffrage did not arrive in Japan till 1925, with the first election taking place in 1928. Ishikawa Hanzan, 'Fujin no sanseiken mondai', ibid, Vol 2, No 8 (August 1917) pp1-10

[30] 'Fujin kôron ni miru josei kaizôron to kôdokusha', *Fujin zasshi ni miru taishôki*, op cit, pp102-3

[31] Margit Nagy, 'Middle-Class Women During the Interwar Years', in Gail Lee Berstein, op cit, p201

[32] Ishizuki Shizue, 'Senjika minshû josei no sensô kyôryoku', *Rekishi hyôron* No 552 (April 1996) pp63, 65

[33] Yamakawa Kikue, 'Josei jiron', *Fujin Kôron*, Vol 23, No 5 (May 1938) pp329-30

[34] 'Sekai no josei o kataru kai', ibid, Vol 25, No 3 (March 1940) pp196-8

[35] Editorial, ibid, Vol 27, No 9 (September 1942) p21

[36] Yamakawa Kikue, 'Sensô wa fujin o dô kaeru', ibid, Vol 23, No 8 (August 1938) p361

[37] Editorial, 'kensetsu to seichô', ibid, Vol 24, No 1 (January 1939) p57

[38] Yamakawa Kikue, '"Otoko wa tatakai, onna wa hataraku"', ibid, Vol 22, No 12 (December 1937) pp71-5

[39] Nozu Yuzuru, 'Fujin to taiku', ibid, Vol 23, No 6 (June 1938) pp490-5

[40] 'Senjika no kekkon zadankai', ibid, Vol 23, No 10 (October 1938) pp166-91

[41] Ibid, p173

[42] Ibid, pp186-7

[43] Sakurai Tadayoshi, 'Senshisha no mibôjin ni yosete', ibid, Vol 24, No 12 (December 1939) pp212-8

[44] 'Senbotsusha no tsuma ni kiku', ibid, Vol 24, No 2 (February 1939) p205

[45] Satô Toshiko, 'Mibôjin to jûgo fujin no kyôdô', ibid, Vol 24, No 1 (January 1939) pp222-5

[46] 'Jikyoku to wakaki josei no seikatsu', ibid, Vol 25, No 9 (September 1940) pp224-37

[47] Ueno Yôichi, 'Kono kikai ni kaji rôdô no gôrika o', ibid, Vol 22, No 11 (November 1937) pp116-9

[48] Round table discussion, 'Atarashii joshi kyôiku no hôkô', ibid, Vol 27, No 7 (July 1942) pp52-63

[49] Oku Mumeo, 'Katei no shakaika to kyôdô no shinseikatsu e', ibid, Vol 25, No 11 (November 1940) pp60-4

[50] 'Seikatsu shidô ni tsuite', ibid, pp144-51

[51] Miyamoto Takenosuke, 'Kokka sôryokusen to josei dôin', ibid, Vol 26, No 9 (September 1941) pp80-4, and Mizuno Seiji, 'Seikatsu no naka no shisôsen', ibid, Vol 28, No 12 (December 1943) pp28-9

52 Ikeda Kimie, 'Shokuba to katei seikatsu', ibid, Vol 28, No 5 (May 1943) pp20-4

53 Ibid, p23, and round table discussion, 'Kinrô haichi ni tsukuhito no tame', Vol 28, No 12 (December 1943) p40

54 Editorial, ibid, Vol 27, No 5 (May 1942), no page number, and 'Kinrô hôshi to jogakusei', ibid, Vol 27, No 11 (November 1942) pp104-9

55 Editorial, ibid, Vol 28, No 2 (February 1943) p21

56 Rôyama Masamichi, 'Nihon no josei ni atauru sho', ibid, Vol 23, No 1 (January 1938), pp62-8

57 Ichikawa Fusae, 'Fujin dantai no genjô to sono tôsei mondai', ibid, pp572-4, and 'Aifu to kokufu wa gôdô seyo!', ibid, Vol 23, No 9 (September 1938) pp344-8

58 Ikaejima Shigenobu, 'Busô suru fujingun', ibid, Vol 28, No 8 (August 1943) pp28-34

59 Ugaki Kazushige, 'Sensô to josei', ibid, Vol 25, No 6 (June 1940) pp96-9

60 Tôjô Hideki, 'Yasukuni no tsuma ni yosu', ibid, Vol 26, No 11 (November 1941) pp46-8

61 Tôjô Hideki, 'Dai tôa sensô isshûnen o mukaete', ibid, Vol 27, No 12 (December 1942) p24

62 'Shina jihen kinenbi ni nippon josei ni yosu', ibid, Vol 27, No 7 (July 1942) pp36-9

63 Kaneko Takanosuke, 'Kaerimi wa seji no seishin', ibid, Vol 28, No 10 (October 1943) p18

64 Kameyama Kôichi, 'Senryoku zôkyô to joshi dôin: Rômu dôin no imi to hôsaku', ibid, Vol 28, No 8 (August 1943) pp57-60

65 Satô Toshiko, 'Kokumin saisoshiki to fujin no mondai', ibid, Vol 24, No 4 (April 1939) pp266-9

66 Hirade Hideo, 'Nanpô shisatsu no tabi yori kaerite', ibid, Vol 27, No 7 (July 1942) pp46-51

67 Editorial, ibid, Vol 25, No 6 (June 1940) p55

68 Mutô Tomio, 'Korekara no josei', ibid, Vol 28, No 10 (October 1943) pp6-10

69 'Senjika no kekkon zadankai', ibid, Vol 23, No 10 (October 1938), p189, and 'Nanpô kensetsu to josei', ibid, Vol 27, No 4 (April 1942) pp28-38

70 Inoue Matsuko, 'Mussorini, ruuzuberuto, furanko, hittoraa no katei seikatsu', ibid, Vol 23, No 7 (July 1938), pp322-8

71 G. Shoruttsukuringu, 'Nachisu fujin jigyô no gaikan', ibid, Vol 25, No 9 (September 1940) pp93-107

72 Takado Akitaka, 'Amerika josei wa kaku tatakau', ibid, Vol 28, No 8 (August 1943) pp18-22

73 Miyamoto Takenosuke, 'Sensô to josei chôyô', ibid, Vol 27, No 2 (February 1942) pp60-9, and Ikeda Kimie, 'Shokuba to katei seikatsu', ibid, Vol 28, No 5 (May 1943) p20

74 Ishizuki Shizue, op cit, p58

Chapter 10

America

James J. Cooke

In the autumn of 1907 President Theodore Roosevelt stood on the deck of the USS *Mayflower* anchored off Hampton Roads, Virginia. He was obviously excited at what he was seeing – a parade of American warships preparing to sail around the world. Roosevelt was a true hero of the 1898 war with Spain, leaving the United States with a far-flung empire from Cuba and Puerto Rico in the Caribbean to the Philippines in the Pacific. Under his predecessor, the assassinated William McKinley, America raised the Stars and Stripes over Hawaii. Although the Spanish-American War was not an example of how wars should be fought, ignorance won out over incompetence, and Roosevelt and many of his contemporaries felt that the United States had entered on to the world stage. The nation was young and clumsy but had the potential to be a world power. She was protected by two great oceans, and had what appeared to be unlimited natural resources and a vast reservoir of manpower. Roosevelt loved the word 'Bully' to describe good things with enthusiasm, and as he looked at the Great Fleet he really felt that it was 'Bully' to be an American in this century that was only seven years old.

Ten years after Roosevelt viewed his pride and joy at Hampton Roads, the United States entered the Great War on the side of the Western Allies. Much to Roosevelt's distress the nation went to war under Woodrow Wilson, a progressive member of the Democratic Party, who was first elected in 1912 and campaigned in 1916 for re-election on the theme 'He Kept Us Out of War'. One of the most popular songs in 1916 was 'I Didn't Raise My Boy To Be A Soldier', which reflected Wilson's and America's isolationism; one year later Americans were singing 'Over There'. The American soldier – the 'doughboy' – and his commander General John J. Pershing were the darlings of the public and the press. French Premier Georges Clemenceau described Wilson as a 'kind of clergyman', and, in many ways, Wilson had to preach the crusade to the America people. He had to because there were large segments of the very diverse American population, which were not too sure that they needed to be 'Over There' in the trenches of the Western Front.

In 1917 America was a vast country stretching 3,000-plus miles from the Atlantic to the Pacific. It was, despite all of the self-congratulatory tales of the 'melting pot', a country of very diverse elements, languages and cultures. The United States was the Tower of Babel named New York City, but also the homogeneous towns of the South, the hamlets of the Midwest, the farm fields of Kansas, Iowa and Nebraska, and the hot, arid lands of the Southwest, where one heard as much Spanish as English. A little over half a century before, a blink of the eye in European history, the country had torn itself apart in a terrible four-year civil war, the scars of which had not healed. The city of Milwaukee was decidedly German in nature, French was spoken across the width of Southern Louisiana, Norwegian could be heard in rural Minnesota, and Italian filled the air in New York City, blending with Yiddish and Russian.

The great majority of Americans lived in small hamlets and towns and would spend their lives without ever seeing New York City, Chicago, or their nation's capital for that matter. Most Americans went to church in families, congregations equally divided between male and female, young and old, but there were divisions – Protestant and Catholic, Jew and Christian. All were immigrants or children of immigrants, first coming before the Revolution against England, then the influx of 1848 into the 1870s, and finally the tidal wave — the Irish, the Italians, the Jews, the Lebanese, the huddled masses of the late 19th, early 20th century. Then there were the Orientals such as the Chinese, who contributed so much to the building of the railroads, and the Japanese. There were rumblings of discontent over such a large number of 'non-Europeans' coming to America, especially in California, where whites – Anglo-Americans, Hispanic-Americans – tried to stem the flow by legislation that soured American-Japanese diplomatic relations. Could this variegated tapestry of very different peoples be taken into a great conflict?

Woodrow Wilson had a great problem in that his party, the Democratic Party, had a very heavy ethnic base. The Irish of New York and the Germans of Wisconsin and the Midwest were factors that had to be considered if indeed the United States went to war in 1917. In the hard-fought presidential campaign of 1916, the popular song 'We Take Our Hats Off To You, Mr Wilson' praised Wilson's pacifist stand. Wilson talked about a nation too proud to fight, but conditions had changed. Early in 1917 the Imperial German Government announced an end to its self-imposed halt in unrestricted submarine warfare, and by late March Wilson decided that the United States was indeed not too proud to enter the conflict. On 2 April he went before a very divided Congress to ask for a Declaration of War, and that was by no means certain. It was a political risk because his own party was deeply rent over the war issue. For five days the bitter debate raged, and finally, on 7 April 1917, the United States went to war. No civilian really knew just how unprepared the American Army was, nor did they realise that it would take a frustratingly long time for the industrial sector of the country to make the transition from peace-time to war-time production. Even in the War Department there were those officers who found it incredible that America would even consider sending troops to serve in Europe.

It surprised the politicians – but not the old fighter ex-Colonel, former President Theodore Roosevelt – that the Declaration of War electrified the people. The American Civil War was now just memories. In 1913, on the 50th anniversary of the great battle of Gettysburg, tottering old soldiers met again on that field so eloquently dedicated by Abraham Lincoln. Except for the Indian Wars and the short Spanish-American War, the American people had not been called to send sons to fight. The American youth of the new century had yet to try their own wings, and this crusade 'to make the world safe for democracy', to repay Lafayette, to defeat the 'Hated Hun', was the chance to be a part of a great movement. The Regular Army was small, the National Guard would be called, but from the start it was clear that the fighting army would have to be a National Army, a force of conscripts. The last time there was a national draft it was filled with inequities, and in 1863 there had been riots in New York and in Richmond, Virginia. What would happen now? On 5 June almost 10 million men registered for the draft, and on 20 July the Secretary of War, Newton Baker, selected the first soldier to be called to the colours in this 'great national lottery'.[1] Many would go 'Over There', but what about those who remained 'Over Here'?

The most obvious manifestations of the war were the volunteering and drafting of men. National Guard units were called to the nation's defence, and some units, normally at regimental strength, had served from 1916 into 1917 along the Mexican Border. Men were quickly being summoned to their armouries or camps to begin training for war. 'During 1917, the War Department was only half at war,' wrote one scholar. 'Propelled by the exigencies, the United States moved in several directions, all at the same time. Mobilisation resulted more from panic than from procedures.'[2] What was clear to civilians was that camps were springing up all over the United States, and, in fits and starts, erstwhile soldiers were on trains going to those camps. Where once there were great tracts of land there were camps, named usually after war heroes. Whole forests in the great American Northwest were being levelled to provide wood for barracks, mess halls, supply rooms, headquarters buildings and the like. Men arrived before the timber could be fashioned into buildings, and they rested in huge tent cities. There were no uniforms for the troops, no weapons, no gas masks, no machine-guns, no artillery pieces.

While men in key industries were sensibly exempt from the draft of 1917-18, the vast majority of the male population, except for a small number of conscientious objectors and enemy aliens, registered and waited for their number to be called. The outburst of patriotism and eagerness for war, which followed the 6 April declaration, was based on total ignorance of war and of all its horrors. Not to be involved was something shameful – one woman wrote to her soldier son, who left early for France:

> 'Roy S… is some place in Texas taking oficers [sic] training and his mother said he was agoing [sic] to take aviators training when he finished this, anything to keep from going across. And I just told her that I did not think he was anything but a slacker just from one thing to another to keep out of it.'[3]

University students who in 1916 looked forward to the academic demands of college life and the thrills of football games on a crisp Saturday afternoon found themselves in the Student Army Training Corps (SATC). Herbert R. Hamm of the University of Maine wrote to his mother, 'You tell Dad those gloves he gave me come in pretty handy these cool mornings at drill. We have to turn out for drill at 7 o'clock so you see it is quite cool.'[4] The new patriotism of the Great War allowed for no slackers.

One of the first things American soldiers noticed in France was the fact that almost every woman wore black, having lost one or more loved ones in the fighting, but that brutal fact of war had not yet reached America. During the first six months of war few troops moved out of their camps, rationing of food and other commodities was slow in coming, and the Government did not regulate the railroads until December 1917. Throughout the war the United States never really went on a total war footing and relied heavily on a spirit of voluntarism among the public.[5] To be sure there were meatless, wheatless, heatless days, but all were encouraged by the Wilson administration and by the agencies founded by wartime legislation. During the winter of 1917-18 civilians were encouraged not to buy new woollen coats for winter so that wool could be used for uniforms, which were in very short supply in the American Expeditionary Forces (AEF). Stationery provided for soldiers and civilians by various civic and church groups urged the writers to 'Save by writing on both sides of the paper', and 'To the folks at home: save food, buy liberty bonds and war savings stamps'.

One way the public could become involved in the war effort was through the purchase of a 'Liberty Bond', which was the brainchild of Secretary of the Treasury William Gibbs McAdoo. McAdoo went before Congress in April 1917 and received authorisation to issue bonds amounting to 2 billion dollars. McAdoo, a mildly progressive Southern Democrat, labelled these bonds as a 'Liberty Loan', and, much to his delight and the relief of President Wilson, the issue was oversubscribed. There would be many such issues and bond drives throughout the war.[6] Popular entertainers volunteered to appear at bond rallies, and every civic and church group was enlisted to promote public participation in the war in a very tangible way. Even the Boy Scouts of America became bond salesmen, with a motto 'Every Scout to Save a Soldier'.[7] To make a bond participant visible, little celluloid buttons were produced for each Liberty Loan drive; the Third Loan, for example, had a picture of the Liberty Bell. Celluloid buttons became all the rage as the public became more and more involved. The United War Work Campaign had a button with the slogan 'For the Boys Over There'.[8]

While the soundness of the financial policy is still debated, the reasoning behind the loans drives was based on the idea that wars were successfully prosecuted when people, government and armed services were united in the effort. To make sure that patriotic bond-buying did not languish, Osage County, Oklahoma, assessed everyone for the Fourth Liberty Loan in the fall of 1918. One old Confederate veteran, who had a successful general store, was marked down for $500. Before the old soldier left for a Confederate Veterans' reunion in Tulsa, Oklahoma, that man who had fought against the United States doubled his pledge to show his unfailing support for the war effort.[9]

In August 1917, after a month-long, bitter debate in Congress, the Lever Food and Fuel Act was passed. The law led to the establishment of a Government-funded Grain Corporation, which set the price for wheat. It was critical that both military and civilian demands for bread and grain be met without seriously dislocating the markets. In addition to the Grain Corporation, the Lever Act allowed President Wilson to control fuel prices and to assure the flow of fuels, particularly coal, for civilian industrial purposes and for military needs. During the very cold winter of 1917-18, the Fuel Administration did not handle the distribution of coal very well. There were disturbances as the snows of winter set in, but by and large most citizens accepted some shortages. One mother wrote to her son, 'We are all right and in a land of plenty can get anything we want and thank God have the money to get it.'[10] To no one's surprise there was a constant struggle to keep food prices down for both civilians and for the military. This was complicated by a dual authority of food purchase by the Army, but by December 1917 a Food Purchase Board was established by the military to assure a flow of food to the camps in the United States and to the AEF in France. When there were shortages on the grocery store shelves, the priority was to the troops.[11] In France, however, the standard doughboy fare was a stew made of corned beef (called Slum, for Slumgullion Stew), bread and coffee. Most often, when combat allowed, breakfasts were slabs of bread, bacon, molasses and coffee. Unfortunately, because of popular misconceptions caused by strict censorship in the AEF, many Americans believed that the AEF dined on fine French fare washed down with wines.

It should have come as no surprise that, with the many measures taken by the Government and by civilian groups to rally the nation to accept shortages and control prices, the issue of loyalty should have come into play. There was a hunt for the disloyal, the unpatriotic, during the war. At the silly end of the scale was the renaming of sauerkraut as liberty cabbage and the Frankfurter sausage, the mainstay of any visit to the baseball park, as a hot dog. German names were suspect, but in a nation where German immigrants abounded it was difficult to tell who was what. The Army constantly searched for enemy aliens in the ranks.[12] The search for the disloyal reached into every aspect of American life; one woman wrote, 'The government took our priest as an enemy alian [sic] and I think he was… I never had any faith in him he was so bitter against America. He was not naturalized and he would not register … you know all Germans had to register the first week of this month [February 1918]… Aunt Maggie thinks it was just pregadice [sic].'[13]

What about the Irish-Americans who manifested no love for the British? This was a grave problem in that a number of American infantry regiments were composed of the Irish. The 165th Infantry Regiment of the 42nd Division (National Guard) was formally the 69th New York Regiment, which earned fame as part of the Irish Brigade of the American Civil War. There were many fathers and mothers in New York who prayed for the safe return of their sons and also that their soldiers did not have to serve with the British. With such national paranoia civil liberties were bound to suffer, and with the Russian Revolution, and eventual Red victory, conditions became even worse as more possible enemies were added to a growing list.

The Great War unleashed forces in America that no one could have foreseen in April 1917. With so many men, including black Americans, being recruited or conscripted, women had to adjust to the wartime situation. As in previous wars, women had to cope with shortages of food and fuel and having loved ones far from home in harm's way. The armed forces had women in their ranks, many serving in France as telephone operators, nurses and secretaries. Women volunteered for various religious and charitable organisations that worked with soldiers, often near the front, under fire. Of course, the vast majority of women were 'Over Here', and many found ways to do war work in the factories or in service organisations. The Young Women's Christian Association (YWCA) of America's National War Work Council organised Hostess Houses to give soldiers a place to write letters, have a respite from barracks life, have a home-cooked meal and enjoy entertainment. At Kelly Field, Texas, for example, between November 1917 and the end of the year over 25,000 meals were served at the House. The Kelly Field Hostess House made Christmas celebrations a major part of its service work.[14] The ladies of the Hempstead Garden Club of Hempstead, New York, devoted a great deal of time working with the YMCA at Camp Mills, New York. Thousands of women worked for organisations like the Salvation Army, meeting troop trains at camps throughout the United States with hot coffee, hot chocolate, cookies, and cigarettes for the soldiers.

Not all women were satisfied with being 'Doughnut Dollies' in the camps or at the train stations. A good case in point was Caroline Stoddard Mitchell, wife of the US Air Service's controversial General William 'Billy' Mitchell. Born into wealth and society in Rochester, New York, she attended Vassar College. When her aviator husband left for the AEF in 1917, she returned from Washington to Rochester, and began teaching French to soldiers departing for France. Not happy with this role, she volunteered for a Red Cross course in automotive mechanics and driving, then drove an ambulance, freeing male drivers for service in France. After her time as a driver, she took a course that qualified her as a surgical nurse's assistant and worked in the local hospitals.[15] Numerous women, especially those who were well educated, sought out this type of volunteer work, and many even went to France to continue their war work.[16] These were roles that women had not assumed before in such numbers, and the impact in the years after the war, and on the part women played in the next great global conflict, would be immense.

While many American women were finding a niche in the war effort, other groups did not fare as well. Racial tensions were high in the United States due to a number of factors such as competition for jobs, being in camps in large numbers, the use of many black workers as strike-breakers, and a massive migration from the rural, agricultural South to the industrialised Northern states.[17] There were outbreaks of sporadic violence against blacks in a number of Northern cities, while in the South the idea of blacks being conscripted into the Army and sent to France, where it was thought society was much more tolerant, brought on reprisals and increased discrimination. But the Army was not a very hospitable place for blacks either, and remained racially segregated. When the first conscript law was passed in 1917 blacks were excluded from the draft, but subsequent additions to the law made them eligible for a call-up. Once in the service, blacks usually found themselves in support units, which included working as construction engineers or stevedore work for the Quartermaster Corps. The one combat division, the 92nd, saw limited action and was not as well supplied with arms and equipment as were the white divisions. A few black units served well with the French, but by and large Pershing and the hierarchy of the Army were content with a segregated system. This would not change until several years after the next World War.

The United States was in the war for one year and seven months, but the AEF did not begin large-scale combat operations until after July 1918. The strict censorship imposed by the AEF on letters, journalists' stories and the like ensured that very few civilians on the home front had any concept of the cost of the Great War. After July, however, the number of telegrams from the War Department informing next of kin of a soldier's death became more frequent. To help ease the grief of the families the American Red Cross took charge of sending information about the burial of remains whenever possible. The Red Cross acted in concert with the United States Army's Graves Registration in France. The family would receive three photographs of the grave with the number and location of the site. A letter from the Army accompanied the photographs and said as gently as possible that it was impossible, during time of combat, to bring the body home. The families were asked not to try to send flowers or extra markers for the grave site since the remains would be shipped home after the war.[18] After the armistice of November 1918, most families would be advised to allow the remains to be buried in special American military cemeteries in France.

When word finally reached the United States about the Armistice, 11 November 1918, there was great rejoicing and celebration. The Great War had indeed been the United States' first foray into world combat, and, despite the sorry state of preparedness and the slowness of getting doughboys into the fighting in 1918, the nation had every reason to be proud of its fighting men and its women who served 'Over There' and 'Over Here'. Like any first step it was halting, and there were severe problems for the nation during and after the war. Several million men served in the armed forces, and the majority of them went to Europe to serve in the AEF, but when they returned home they found an uncertain future. The Wilson administration had not secured their re-employment, and many former draftees found themselves with no work. As far as families were concerned the soldiers of the Great War spent on average only a year in uniform, and re-integration into a family unit was not as difficult as it would be for the GIs of the Second War.

The failure of Wilson to secure the ratification of the Versailles Treaty left a bad taste in the mouths of the veterans, but how many of them were convinced that the United States really had an expanded world role to play? Unlike the next war, this one did not see women pour into the factories, and the dislocation caused by their replacement by veterans would not be as severe as in 1945 and 1946. The Government really had no plan for the veterans, as it would with the educational and housing benefits that were presented to the veterans of the next war. Altogether, the Great War was a step forward and a three-quarter step backwards, and the war left more questions than there were answers. 'As the old order thus settled heavily back into place, it crushed many of the aspirations that the war had so giddily lifted,' wrote historian David M. Kennedy.[19]

It would take another war – this time four years in duration and truly global in combat – to lift the old aspirations. In some cases soldiers served for five years, and the impact on the home front would be much more dramatic than that of the First War. Twenty-three years had elapsed between 1918 and 7 December 1941, when the Japanese attacked American forces at Pearl Harbor in the Hawaiian Islands. Two years short of a quarter-century is not a long time, but for the United States those years saw tremendous change that would make the home front experience of the Second War so very different from that of the first. The cinema was now in colour and could talk, the radio brought national and world events into everyone's living room, and towns and cities were bound together by ribbons of concrete and asphalt over which comfortable automobiles travelled at will. Width or depth did not bind the Americans of the Second World War as aeroplanes flew from coast to coast. The 1920s and 1930s saw great national debates, commissions and legislation that made the American aircraft industry one of the most formidable in the world.

The sexes were no longer constrained by late Victorian-Edwardian restrictions. In the 1920s skirts went above the knee and the 'flapper' was all the rage. More young women went into college, and 'Betty Coed' was becoming an accepted fixture in American society. Dancing couples did the frenetic 'Charleston' in the 1920s and the 'Jitterbug' in the 1930s and 1940s. Jazz and the 'Big Band Sound' were the rage. The girls of the Second War would be the leggy, kittenish, perhaps even seductive pin-ups – Betty Grable, Veronica Lake, Dorothy Lamour – a challenge for the girl next door. But of more importance to the war effort was 'Rosie the Riveter', who made the planes and tanks, the muscle of battle.

Those who served overseas or on the home front during the Second World War were deeply affected by the Depression and Franklin Roosevelt's 'New Deal' policies. A radical departure from traditional American methods of conducting business, industry, and even society, the New Deal effort at recovery paved the way for those who had to fight the next war. Unlike the outburst of unbridled patriotism of 1917, which was based on a total ignorance of modern war, the generation of the Second War faced tasks with a 'get the job done' mentality. To be sure, the home front had its patriotic pins, celluloid buttons, posters and mass-produced knick-knacks, but the thrust was different because society had changed. President Roosevelt, unlike President Wilson, favoured preparing for war, and his chief advisor, General George C. Marshall, expertly guided pre-war efforts to enlarge the armed services. Roosevelt, Marshall and their American political allies faced a serious problem in 1939 when war broke out in Europe. There was a sizeable body of public opinion that did not favour intervention in this second European war because the view was clouded by the less-than-satisfactory outcome of the first. There were those who still held that America was safe behind the Atlantic and Pacific Oceans.

On the other hand, the cinema and the radio played a great role in altering public opinion toward measures to prepare America for possible war. The cinema newsreels did not paint a sympathetic view of Hitler and the revival of German militarism. During the Battle of Britain, pro-Allied reporters like Edward R. Morrow broadcast from London during the most terrible moments of the Blitz. In the spring of 1940 Roosevelt and Marshall asked for a number of measures that in 1917 terms would have been unthinkable. In April 1941 Roosevelt created the Office of Price Administration and Civilian Supply (OPACS) to make certain that the pressures of the war in Europe and the demands on the American economy did not create inflation or make for severe competition between the civilian sector and the growing needs of an expanded military, and to ensure that industry could make the transition from civilian to war-time production. This was one of the first of the so-called 'alphabet soup' agencies that would mushroom when America became involved in the war. Marshall asked for an expansion of the military, including the call-up of nearly 100,000 National Guard troops for a year. Once that was done (and it should have been a lesson for future American wars, especially Vietnam) the local communities could see a tangible expression of preparedness and their role in it. George C. Marshall handled the call-up with tact and with an eye toward making the citizen-soldier better able to assume a major role if war did indeed come.[20]

War did come, on 7 December 1941, when naval air forces of the Japanese Empire launched an early-Sunday-morning attack against American installations in the Hawaiian Islands. Nothing could have galvanised the American people more than what they saw as a 'sneak attack', and Roosevelt's speech to Congress was a masterpiece, explaining in stark terms the task before the nation and the belief in eventual victory. The 8 December speech set the tone for hard work and sacrifice, which motivated the home front through four years of involvement in global combat. The draft law, which had been in place for over a year, went into full throttle as men were called to serve. Eager volunteers overwhelmed recruiting offices, and National Guard units were quickly mobilised. Everyone had a role to play in this new war, and even grade-school children devoted time to gathering used newspapers and scrap metal, and spent part of the school day packing small Red Cross boxes for wounded soldiers.

Rationing went into effect very quickly under the Office of Price Administration (OPA). Americans received small ration books with little stamps (usually with pictures of guns, tanks and the like), which could be used when purchasing items. Black marketeering was harshly dealt with, and the public, through posters, radio and movie announcements, was told that hoarding of food was unpatriotic and deprived the armed forces of needed items. This was a radical departure for Americans who were used to an unending supply of food and creature comforts. Food producers and the Department of Agriculture issued recipe books on how to cook dishes without critically rationed items. Sugar and butter were always in short supply during the war, and oleomargarine in a pale white block could be purchased with a package of yellow food colour, which when mixed with the oleo at least had the colour of butter. Silk and nylon disappeared from the stores, and American ladies had to do with 'leg make-up', which when applied gave the appearance of dusky-coloured stockings. Gasoline and tyres were also impossible to obtain, save for a few rationed gallons for the public. Americans, many of them urban dwellers, tried their hand at growing a Victory Garden to alleviate the strain on farms producing for the troops. Seed producers sold packages of Victory Seeds with smaller amounts of seeds for the small gardeners. Sometimes the shortages became irritating for the folks back home. One mother from Cannelton, Indiana, wrote to her son who was serving in Sicily:

'I read in the paper where you could buy silk hose in Sicily, if you ever run across any would be delighted to have a few pair of light tan ones … you can't buy any in the states, and these old rayon ones are terrible.'[21]

Americans, now faced with the staggering prospect of global war, found their lives radically changed. Regulatory agencies had to be put in place to cope with the massive task of winning a war. In January 1942 Roosevelt established the War Production Board (WPB) to co-ordinate efforts and to try to bring a seriously fragmented economy into line with the war effort. Other such 'alphabet' agencies were created, and while it is beyond the scope of this chapter to describe each one, suffice to say that the regulation was unprecedented, and that American society would never be the same again, even after victory over Germany and Japan in 1945. The Controlled Materials Plan (CMP) allocated critical materials such as steel, aluminium and copper to industries. Never had American industry been so regulated by a central government, and there was grumbling, but winning the war was the first priority. While many of the strict regulations and regulatory agencies would be disbanded after the war, the precedent was set for a post-war expansion of central government powers.

Small pleasures once taken for granted before 1941 were curtailed by wartime needs. One Massachusetts man wrote to a soldier friend, 'We had planned all winter to go deep sea fishing as two of the boys bought a 26 foot motor boat but we found that fishing parties for pleasure are banned as gasoline is to be used for other than outboard motors.'[22] Saving and scrimping became the order of the day for those on the home front. Those who remained at home, and those in the service, were encouraged to invest in Savings Bonds and Stamps. One thrifty wife told her soldier husband that, 'Your little wife got another bond today. That makes 17 x 25.00 = 425.00 which isn't bad – is it? I buy one $25.00 one every monthly pay, but of course I can't get the $25.00 out of them until 1950.'[23] It was possible for a woman working in one of the defence-related industries to do that. The same wife wrote that she was making $50 a week (which was more than he made as a Private in the Army), and would get a raise of $2 per week the following month.[24]

Everywhere Americans looked they saw the letter V for Victory, and nowhere was this symbol of the home front effort more visible than in the defence plants where countless thousands of women now worked at jobs formally held by males. The Office of War Information carried on a massive campaign to recruit women into the armed services and into industry, and the female workforce increased by 32 per cent between 1942 and 1945, making a very great contribution to the overall war effort.[25] The popular figure of 'Rosie the Riveter' was that of a white, attractive, middle-class housewife working in the plant during the day and managing a home at night. The reality was that women of all races, classes and marital status seized the opportunity to go into defence work and earn their own living, which often well exceeded the male soldiers' pay. The problem for the thousands of 'Rosies' was one of permanence. What would happen to their gains once the war was over and the men were demobilised? Unlike the period of the Great War, the United States Government had taken steps to ensure servicemen's re-employment rights once the conflict ended.

Two other questions bothered the home front: the disloyal citizen and the ever-present problem of race. The authorities quickly detained members of pro-Nazi and pro-Fascist organisations. The German-American Bund and a varied host of coloured shirts, from black to brown to silver, had been in evidence in the 1930s, and their membership was easily identified. The attack on Pearl Harbor made most of their members realise very quickly that loyalty to another country or anti-democratic ideology was simply not going to be tolerated. Enemy agents were another matter, and posters quickly appeared warning Americans against loose talk about defence work, troop movements and the like. One man, writing to an old friend in the Army, said, 'I seldom write anything about our work [in the defence plant] as one can not be too careful what is said or implied.'[26] As one can imagine, civil liberties were often trampled upon in a climate of distrust and extreme caution. Nowhere was this more evident than in dealing with Japanese-Americans in the wake of the Pearl Harbor attack and during the early days of the war in the Pacific.

It is difficult to view the plight of Japanese-Americans after 60-plus years, but the Pearl Harbor disaster was indeed a national embarrassment, which was very hard to explain to the American public. The Army and Navy commanders in the Hawaiian Islands were harshly dealt with in hearings held by Congress. Scapegoats were sought to explain how the great battleships of the Pacific fleet were so easily attacked and destroyed by Imperial Japanese naval aviation. Panic swept the West Coast of America, especially in California, where there had been a long history of antagonism toward Japanese immigration. Innocent and loyal Japanese-Americans were incarcerated in camps on the West Coast and throughout America in a terrible miscarriage of American justice. Where one might suspect bitterness (and there certainly was) and resistance (there was none), there was an eagerness on the part of many young Japanese-American males to show their loyalty. The famed 442nd Regimental Combat Team and the 100th (Military Intelligence) Battalion were formed and sent to Camp Shelby in the southern part of the state of Mississippi. At that time the state practised strict racial segregation, and it seemed a strange place to send thousands of Japanese-Americans.

But Mississippi was not California, and the colour-line in the state was black and white. Many veterans of the Regimental Combat Team remembered their acceptance by the local population, and a few returned to marry local girls and to reside in the area. These units went on to render exemplary service in the European Theatre of Operations, some went to the Pacific to work with hard-pressed American intelligence, and, in fact, the 442nd became one of the United States' most decorated units of the war.[27] The 442nd was an example of successful race relations during the war, but it was one of the few. Blacks continued to serve in segregated units, trained at their own camps. One all-black parachute unit was to see only fire-fighting duties in the Pacific Northwest during the war. Blacks were barred from the various service organisation canteens or had their own special nights, when they would not come into contact with whites; this was the rule in the whole of the United States, not just in the Southern part of the nation. This problem, so evident during the Great War, remained a festering sore that would not be dealt with until years after the end of the Second World War.

For America of the war era it did not seem unfair or unjust to segregate troops by colour. Black leaders questioned it, but only a few whites did. During the war it was a question of what could be done for those soldiers who would soon be on the battlefields from Europe to North Africa to Burma to the Pacific. By late 1942 into

1943 it was painfully clear that many would never return to the United States. One of the great manifestations of war support was the 'canteen', staffed by United Services Organisation (USO) with an aim to give a meal, some cheer, and at times a pretty dancing partner for the departing GIs. Every major city had several, the largest ones being near the Ports of Embarkation, but the most spectacular one of all was the Hollywood Canteen, where lads from the farms of the South and Midwest, the small towns and the cities, could meet with and dance with the most beautiful actresses of American cinema. Famous radio and screen actors served coffee, soft drinks and sandwiches to the soldiers. So spectacular a success for the home front war effort was the Hollywood Canteen that Warner Brothers Studio made a movie about it starring some of the great names of the entertainment industry — the Andrews Sisters, Jack Benny, Eddie Cantor, Bette Davis, Jimmy Dorsey and his band, and many others.[28]

To co-ordinate efforts throughout the country the United Service Organisation oversaw the opening of canteens and directed the efforts of thousands of volunteers. The USO also provided services to troops overseas and brought well-known American entertainers to every theatre where troops were deployed. During the Great War, service organisations such as the YMCA, the Jewish Welfare Board, the Knights of Columbus and the Salvation Army operated separate programmes for the troops. To better direct the efforts of these groups to provide the best 'home away from home', the USO was formed in 1941 as a private organisation with very little Government support. The Hollywood Canteen and other such places of 'wholesome social contact' came under the USO, which was cited as one of the great success stories of the war, due in large part to the volunteer spirit of the home front.

Another area of volunteering was in Civil Defence: men and women who donned white-painted Great War-styled helmets and patrolled the streets making sure that black-out restrictions were observed, and who stood ready to assist in emergency situations. In plain terms, American society was mobilised for war, and, if one was not in military training or deployed overseas, there was a myriad of ways in which a person from schoolchild to retiree could contribute something. Factories, schools, stores and most private homes displayed a banner with a red border and white field, which had upon it blue stars representing the number of friends or family members who were in service. When an employee or loved one was killed the blue star was replaced with a gold one. Reminders of service and sacrifice were everywhere, and support often took the form of military-styled jewellery, celluloid buttons with mottoes of support, and the like. One enterprising company manufactured chamber pots with the face of Adolf Hitler or Tôjô Hideki painted on the bottom.[29]

The American cinema turned out movies and cartoons to support the war effort. Some were first-rate, such as the 1943 film *So Proudly We Hailed*, the patriotic story of brave nurses at Bataan; but there were also children's cartoons, which carried a racist picture of Japanese soldiers and airmen as nasty monkeys or Mussolini as a disagreeable pig. Throughout the war Chesterfield Cigarettes sponsored a series of posters aimed at convincing women to volunteer for everything from Army Nursing to Civil Defence work.[30] The Government fostered the volunteer spirit very early in the war when the Secretary of the Treasury, Henry Morgenthau Jr, commissioned Irving Berlin to write a song supporting the buying of bonds and stamps, now termed the Defence Savings Program. His song, 'Any Bonds Today', appeared in 1941, and the sheet music was distributed free to those who participated in the programme.[31]

The V-sign symbolised the belief that America would get the job done, but it was at a terrible price in human life and suffering. The home front had been mobilised as never before, and the war effort permeated every aspect of American life. Rationing, the constant flow of Hollywood films about the war, the picture of 'Rosie the Riveter' going off to the defence plant, the changing of a blue star to gold, were constant reminders of a nation at war. In comparing Europe to the United States, one must say that the great difference was that America never experienced the actual horrors of modern war. There was no Blitz, no bombing raids, no Coventry on American soil. The only real enemy Americans saw 'Over Here' was on the newsreels in the cinema or when German prisoners of war were brought to the United States. So secure were the Americans that selected German prisoners were brought into towns every so often to buy small luxuries. There were precious few escapes from the German POW camps in the United States, for that matter. But through government and private efforts the home front came to feel part of a World War that was being fought thousands of miles from the soil of the United States.

There are similarities between the Great War and the Second World War, as far as the home front was concerned. The spirit of patriotism was manifested in the bonds, the Liberty Loans, the opening of places of food and recreation for the soldiers, and the like. But there were vast differences in the America of 1917 and of 1941. After the attack on Pearl Harbor there could be little question that the United States was at war, for the right reasons. It was Adolf Hitler who declared war on the United States, not the other way around. There was no question that the United States would send troops to fight in many parts of the world. American industry was much better situated to make the transition from peace to war. Then there was Franklin Roosevelt and the New Deal, and while many Americans disliked the programmes of the New Deal, they were at least in tune with a new regulation of American life, a regulation that made the demands and sacrifices of war more palatable. There was chaos and confusion as men poured into the camps simply because the nation was mobilising millions of men and women for the services, but in less than a year after Pearl Harbor Americans were in combat in North Africa.

Of equal importance for the home front of the Second War was the advance of technology, including transportation, which bound the nation together through roads, the radio, the cinema and such like. The citizens of 1941 were much more aware of the country and the world around them than were their parents in 1917. The voice of Edward R. Morrow saying 'This is London' during the darkest hours of the Blitz brought London into an American home. The participation of America in the Great War was a little over 18 months, while some soldiers of the Second World War, who were in the call-up of 1940, were in uniform for five years. While the home front experience of 1940-45 was successful, critical problems remained unresolved, especially in the area of race relations. The Great War was seen as a crusade, a way, as President Wilson said, 'To make the world safe for democracy.' In the long run that failed, but Franklin D. Roosevelt, through the maintenance of the alliances and the establishment of the United Nations, was determined that after the war America would not retreat behind her ocean walls. There were many of the same strains present in both wars as far as the home front was concerned. On the other hand, the home front experience of the Second World War helped to bring the United States into the world scene as a major, if not dominant, player.

Recommended reading

Freidel, Frank, *Over There: The Story of America's First Great Overseas Crusade* (New York: McGraw-Hill, 1990)

Hartmann, S. M., *The Home Front and Beyond: American Women in the 1940s* (Boston: Twayne Publishers, 1982)

Higonnet, Margaret Randolph (et al), *Behind the Lines: Gender and the Two World Wars* (New Haven: Yale, 1987)

Kennedy, David M., *Over Here: The First World War and American Society* (New York: Oxford University Press, 1980)

The Home Front and War in the Twentieth Century (Colorado Springs, CO: US Air Force Academy, 1984)

Polenberg, R., *America at War: the Home Front, 1941-1945* (Engelwood Cliffs, NJ: Prentice Hill, 1968)

Notes

[1] Frank Freidel, *Over There: The Story of America's First Great Overseas Crusade* (New York: McGraw-Hill, 1990) pp5-6

[2] Phyllis A. Zimmerman, *The Neck of the Bottle: College Station, Texas* (Texas: A&M University Press, 1992) p21

[3] Mrs Susan Cosby to Pte Elijah Cosby, Tupelo, Miss, 19 February 1918, in the Cosby Family Papers, author's personal collection

[4] Hamm to Mother, 6 October 1918, Orono, Maine, in the Herbert A. Hamm Letters, author's personal collection

[5] David M. Kennedy, 'Rallying Americans for War, 1917-1918', in *The Home Front and War in the Twentieth Century* (Colorado Springs, CO: US Air Force Academy, 1984) pp50-1

[6] David M. Kennedy, *Over Here: The First World War and American Society* (New York: Oxford University Press, 1980) pp98-9

[7] Ibid, p105

[8] From the author's personal archives and collection

[9] Joseph Strauss to Pte Elijah Cosby, Pawhuska, OK, 18 October 1918, Cosby Papers

[10] Susan Cosby to Son, 19 February 1918, ibid

[11] Phyllis A. Zimmerman, op cit, pp50-1

[12] For a study of one unit with severe immigrant problems, see James J. Cooke, *The All-Americans at War: The 82nd Division in the Great War* (Westport, CT: Praeger Publishing, 1999)

[13] Susan Cosby to Son, 19 February 1918, Cosby Papers

[14] H. D. Kroll (ed), *Kelly Field in the Great World War* (San Antonio: San Antonio Printing, 1919) pp28-33

15 Information pertaining to Caroline Stoddard Mitchell's war work provided by the Alumnae and Alumni Association of Vassar College, Poughkeepsie, New York

16 Arlen J. Hansen, *Gentlemen Volunteers* (New York: Arcade, 1996) pp140-4

17 David M. Kennedy, op cit, pp281-3

18 Taken from the Richardson Family Papers, author's personal collection

19 David M. Kennedy, op cit, p287

20 Forrest C. Pogue, *George C. Marshall: Ordeal and Hope, 1939-1942* (New York: Viking, 1966) pp58-9, 99-101

21 Mrs. E. Franzaman to Son, Cannelton, Indiana, 8 November 1943, in the Franzaman Family Papers, author's personal collection

22 Donald Baker to Pte Julian Wilson, Rockland, Massachusetts, 8 May 1943, in the Wilson Family Papers, author's personal collection

23 Margaret Wilson to Husband, 24 April 1944, ibid

24 Margaret Wilson to Husband, 18 January 1944, ibid

25 Leila J. Rupp, 'War is Not Healthy for Children and Other Living Things', in David M. Kennedy, op cit, p159. See also Margaret Randolph Higonnet (et al), *Behind the Lines: Gender and the Two World Wars* (New Haven: Yale, 1987)

26 Donald Baker to Pte Julian Wilson, 8 May 1943, Wilson Family Papers

27 Camp Shelby, Mississippi, WWII Commemorative Open House, Reunion and Homecoming, 442nd RCT and 100th Battalion, 16-18 June 1995. At that time I was serving at Camp Shelby as a Colonel on the staff of the Adjutant General of the state, and I took notes of conversations with the Japanese-American veterans.

28 The Remick Music Corporation of New York issued the sheet music from 'Hollywood Canteen' in 1944.

29 Author's personal archives and collection

30 Liggett & Myers Tobacco Company Posters, 1942-45, author's personal archives and collection

31 Irving Berlin, 'Any Bonds Today' (Washington: US Government Printing Office, 1941)

Chapter 11

China

Diana Lary

'Dianpei liupei' ('Wandering, made homeless by war')

'Liuli shisuo' ('Homeless, displaced by war')

The first of these two Chinese proverbs (*chengyu*) about the horrors of war comes from the Analects of Confucius, written in the 5th century BC. The second, by one of China's greatest poets, Bo Juyi, was written in the 9th century AD. They are part of a constant lament in Chinese literature about the suffering that warfare inflicts on civilians.

The Chinese Empire was born in war, in the conquest of the remaining autonomous states by the hideously brutal first emperor of unified China, Qinshihuang.[1] His legacy was a unified state, the hauntingly beautiful terracotta warriors of Xian and a folk memory of savagery. His dynasty, and most of the dynasties that followed, was brought down in the flames of war by peasant rebellions or foreign conquest. Each new dynasty was brought into being by military conquest. All of China's capitals before Beijing (capital since the 14th century) were razed to the ground. The pattern was broken with the end of the last dynasty, the Qing, in 1911, which was brought down by military-backed revolutionaries, but without violence.

The long record of civilian suffering in warfare explains why China's civil bureaucrats recoiled from warfare and glorified the rule of the brush, the scholar's weapon, over the sword. The tradition of elevating the civil and the literary over the military explains the weakness of the martial tradition in China. Warfare in Chinese history is not associated with glory and sacrifice, with feats of courage and boldness, but with the suffering and cruelty that soldiers inflict on civilian society. Japan celebrated the way of the warrior (*bushidô*), China despised it. The Chinese people traditionally thought very little of their armed forces. They thought even less of them in the early years of the Republic, when warlordism wracked the country. Warlordism meant the de facto fragmentation of China into a whole range of small and large satraps under the command of men who rose to power as the central state disintegrated. These warlords armed their men with surplus arms from the First World War, making China, in the eyes of many civilians, an indirect victim of that conflict. The status of the military rose under the new (after 1928) Guomindang Government of China, but the underlying mentality did not change. This was summed up in the traditional Chinese saying 'You do not use good iron to make nails, or good men to make soldiers'.

China had supported Britain and France in the First World War, but took little active part in the conflict. Her major contribution was to send the famous Coolie Corps, whose job was to provide labour support for the British and French, including digging trenches. The men were recruited in Shandong and shipped to France via Canada. Most of them returned to China at the end of the war, though some died of illness, and are buried in separate cemeteries in France, the *cimetières chinoises*.

For China the real importance of the First World War was not the fighting but the peace negotiations that followed it, at Versailles. There the Chinese negotiators were horrified to see the former German concessions in China (especially Tsingtao) handed over to the Japanese, who had played no part in the European War at all, but had used the absence of the European colonial powers from Asia greatly to expand their own position, at the cost of China. Thus the sense that China was an indirect victim of the 1914-18 war increased when it became apparent that Japan was the conflict's real winner in Asia. What the Chinese saw as the betrayal at Versailles led directly to the birth of the Chinese nationalist movement, to a complete lack of trust in the British and to a gradual edging towards the infant Soviet Union.

Even before the First World War, China had been reeling from Japanese aggression. The first part of China occupied by Japan, the island of Taiwan, was taken in 1895, at the end of the first Sino-Japanese War. Japanese pressure on China intensified during the 1920s and 1930s. In 1931 Manchuria was seized from China, and some Chinese accounts actually date the start of the second Sino-Japanese War from that year. In late 1932 Shanghai became the first major city in the world to be bombed, as Japan made an abortive attempt to gain control of the Shanghai region. Throughout the mid-1930s bits of Northern China fell into Japanese hands. When full-scale war finally broke out, this was not the result of new hostilities but another stage in the irreversible advance of Imperial Japan.

The outbreak of war, in 1937, effectively marked, for China, the beginnings of the Second World War, which is also known as the Eight-Year Anti-Japanese War. It brought popular feelings of revulsion and anguish concerning warfare to a new pitch. To China the war was completely unprovoked, and the Chinese saw themselves as the innocent victims of Japanese aggression. The war caught China at a huge disadvantage in terms of military strength; her armies were not well armed and were insufficiently trained to resist Japan's might. The early defeats of the Chinese armies only enhanced the sense of victimhood. The people saw courageous but ill-trained and poorly equipped men going up against an exceptionally well-armed enemy.

After 1937 the war came to involve almost every part of the country. This was war on a scale that even China had not known before. The Japanese brought new weapons of mass destruction for their invasion of China, such as bombs and incendiaries, and continued the practice they had started in 1932, at Shanghai, of bombing civilians. They had complete superiority in the air and nothing to fear either from fighters or from anti-aircraft fire. At the same time they waged a war against civilians that was almost medieval, and involved putting civilians to the sword. The war was so ferocious in some parts of China that it seemed to many Chinese that the Japanese were waging a race war against a people whom they despised as weak and decadent.

The scale of the war was immense. Huge campaigns, involving hundreds of thousands of soldiers, were fought over northern and central China. Enormous numbers of civilians died or were displaced in each of these campaigns. The scale of the casualties was beyond what can be grasped; estimates of civilian deaths are between 20 and 30 million for the eight years of the war. Many died as an incidental result of warfare, from hunger, neglect or suicide. But many were killed, either by bombing or in massacres. Some 300,000 were killed by Japanese troops in one incident alone, the Nanjing Massacre, in December 1937, when the Guomindang capital fell to the Japanese. There are two recent accounts of what happened in Nanjing, Iris Chang's *The Rape of Nanjing*, and the diary of John Rabe, *The Good Man of Nanking*. The latter tells the extraordinary story of a German businessman who saved thousands of civilians by setting up an international protection zone in the middle of Nanjing.[2] But Rabe's good deeds stand in stark contrast to the horror that was going on all around him.

The Nanjing Massacre was only one of hundreds of civilian massacres perpetrated by the Japanese armies. An authoritative account by a leading Taiwan scholar, Lee En-han, lists 439 separate atrocities committed by Japanese troops in China between 18 August 1931 and 25 August 1945.[3] These involved the killings, in single incidents, of several hundreds to tens of thousands of people. Almost any one of them would be an infamous atrocity in the context of the Second World War in Europe, but most are still unknown in China. The entries in Lee's book are terse in the extreme:

'30.1.1938: Two hundred Japanese soldiers surrounded the village of Hedong in Zizhou, Shandong. On the day they entered the village they killed 276 people. The next day in the villages of Luojia, Maojia and Xingjia they killed 33 people.

1.1.1939: In Ziguzhen, Lingshou, Hebei, more than a thousand Japanese troops massacred 74 people, and burned down a large number of houses.

22.5.1940: In Yangcheng, Shanxi, Japanese troops gathered 220 refugees who were living in the town under the pretext of holding a meeting and killed 200 of them.'[4]

These are dates chosen at random from page after page of two- to three-line descriptions of massacres. The total number of casualties is impossible to state accurately – a fact noted by some Japanese historians who use this imprecision as the foundation for arguments that deny the scale of the killings, a version of Holocaust Denial. The Japanese did not have the same obsessive interest in recording their actions that the Germans did, and have very limited records of casualties. The Chinese local officials fled before the Japanese arrived, while the local survivors of atrocities were seldom able to write down the details; many of them were illiterate, and those who were not were too terrified of reprisals to make written records. The people did, however, know who in their communities had died; the casualty figures recorded by Lee and in almost identical PRC sources are usually quite precise. The figures that are missing are for those who died away from home, as refugees, and those who died in instances when whole communities were wiped out.

The reasons for the degree and extent of Japanese brutality are hard to fathom. There have been attempts to understand Japanese behaviour. The best is Ian Buruma's recent book *The Wages of Guilt*, which looks at a range of German and Japanese attitudes to the war.[5] Yang Daqing has analysed the different accounts of the Nanjing Massacre, including the many Japanese attempts to deny it.[6] Here there is no effort to take these studies any further, but instead an attempt is made to view these events through Chinese eyes. The Chinese victims of Japanese brutality were so shocked and stunned by what happened to them that they came to associate the savagery more with inhuman, devilish cruelty than with deliberate policy, or even a comprehensible pattern of behaviour.

Not all civilians died at Japanese hands. The largest single number of casualties were the more than 800,000 peasants in the provinces of Henan, Anhui and Jiangsu who were drowned when the Yellow River dykes were opened by Chinese forces in June 1938, in a futile attempt to halt the Japanese advance on Wuhan – 'using water to replace troops' as the strategy was known. None of the figures given for casualties in this disaster are reliable, because of the nature of the disaster and the destruction of whole communities by flood waters. Those cited here are from a recent Shanghai publication, and fall within the middle range of available figures – there are others that give higher and lower figures.[7]

Province	Deaths	Refugees
Henan	325,589	1,172,639
Anhui	407,514	2,536,315
Jiangsu	160,200	202,400
Total	893,303	3,731,354

These figures are for the three provinces through which the waters of the Yellow River passed on their way from the breach in the dyke at Huayuankou (Henan) to the Yellow Sea.[8]

With casualties on this kind of scale, and an experience of such prolonged horror, it becomes possible to understand why many Chinese civilians have tried to blank out the memories of the war; it was something they survived, not something they gloried in. At the official level the 'memory' of the war has necessarily been partial and imprecise.

The official Chinese telling of the war has been highly politicised, because this was the conflict that indirectly brought the Chinese Communist Party (CCP) to power, by destroying Guomindang (GMD) military strength and morale. The war led almost immediately to the three-year Civil War, in which the CCP, which came out of the war vastly strengthened, triumphed.

In the GMD reconstruction, the war is cast in terms of China's dogged courage and endurance, as one stage of China's ancient struggle for survival, with the eventual victory (yet to come) guaranteed. In the CCP reconstruction, the war is a people's war, led by the CCP, an epic of guerrilla warfare in which the people of China were the water in which the fish (the guerrillas) swam. The war is marked by heroic feats of resistance, in which Mao Zedong's brilliance at creating a mood of stark, courageous optimism is given highest credit. His article, 'In Memory of Norman Bethune', written in 1939, encapsulated this mood by holding up to the Chinese the example of a doctor who came from distant Canada to help the Chinese and died for their cause.[9]

Neither of these accounts bears much relationship to what the people of China actually experienced and endured. Most of the war was passed in states of ignorance and anxiety. There were no functioning radio networks or cinema newsreels to bring knowledge of what was going on (or propaganda) to the majority of the Chinese people. Many families were separated by the war, and when this happened they had very little idea of what had happened to each other. The postal service, the most efficient of all Chinese systems, never collapsed, and even carried mail between zones occupied by different forces, but it was still very difficult to get news of family members. People were often out of touch for years on end, not sure whether their relatives were alive or dead.

The story of the war has yet to be told in detail, in history, in film or in fiction. Its pain is still there, but in China the pain is masked and overlaid by closer events, which were equally agonising. The war was only one stage in a much longer calvary, whose stages included the Civil War (1946-49), the Great Leap Forward (1957-59) and the Cultural Revolution (1966-67), each of which left behind oceans of suffering and deaths. The famine that followed the Great Leap may alone have accounted for 30 million premature deaths.[10] The agony of civilians that started with the Anti-Japanese War was prolonged for four decades, for many so painful that their experiences are impossible to describe in writing. It is not an accident that the first popular novel about the war should have been written by a Chinese-American writer, Amy Tan, trying to understand her own parents – *The Joy Luck Club*.[11]

The impact of the war on civilians varied enormously, depending on what part of China they were in. The common feature was a long, draining experience of fear and loss that took many forms: a terrible, acute fear of the Japanese; a chronic fear of generalised chaos and a loss of any sense of a secure future; the loss of contact with family and friends, and a normal social life; the loss of property; and the loss of income, status and the possibility of education and a future career. None of these losses was resolved by the Japanese defeat. The general confusion continued, through the Civil War and the first three turbulent decades of CCP rule. The Japanese invasion created a chain of chaos from which Chinese people have not recovered until very recently, unless they left the mainland and settled in Taiwan, Hong Kong or North America.

Civilians in the longest-occupied area of China, Taiwan, ceded until 1985, probably suffered less than any other part of China during the war itself. A stable government was in place there, whose general lines had been established by the progressive Japanese reformer Goto Shimpei. The economy was closely integrated with that of Japan and did not disintegrate until quite close to the end of the war. The island saw no actual fighting. The Japanese administration was harsh but comprehensible; people could make reasonable accommodations to it. The worst days for the people of Taiwan came, in fact, after the end of the war, when the GMD took over. In a short while relations between the GMD and the people soured to the point that, on 28 February 1947, the Government turned on the people in a massacre that became the touchstone for Taiwanese calls for independence.

The three north-eastern provinces of Manchuria, occupied in 1931, were less fortunate. By then the pace of Japanese expansionism had accelerated. Many extreme Japanese nationalists were stationed in Manchuria; though there was lip service to the creation of a new world, the puppet state of Manzhouguo, the region was in fact ruled under harsh military law. The Depression ensured that the economy was weak; instead of flourishing with Manchuria's wonder crop, the soya bean, it stagnated throughout the 1930s. Conditions for Chinese workers got harder and harder. In the 1920s and 1930s they were still paid for their work; as the war dragged on, more and more industrial workers and miners were treated as slave labour. The worst treatment of all was meted out to those who were subjected to medical experiments in camps near the new capital, Xinjing (Changchun).

In areas occupied after 1937, the impact of the Japanese forces on the civilian population varied. In the northern cities that fell into Japanese hands without fighting, Japanese behaviour was severe but not brutal. The Japanese were careful to show a civilised face in Beiping (formerly Beijing), the old capital and the cultural centre of China, which they saw as the base for their 'transformation' of the old Chinese culture into a Pan-Asian culture centred on Tokyo. Life continued there quite normally – though 'normal' meant a state of decline and ossification, which had set in when the capital of China was moved to Nanjing in 1929. Many people, especially students and intellectuals, fled rather than live under Japanese rule.

In the Yangzi region, on the North China Plain and in South China, the Japanese occupation was a story of terror and desolation. The Nanjing Massacre was one of the most savage events of the entire Second World War, but it was only the largest of many massacres, mainly in North China. After the initial occupation the surviving civilians passed through a period of abject terror, then gradually subsided into resignation. The establishment of a puppet government in Nanjing in 1940 did little to mitigate the iron-fisted administration, nor to revive the badly damaged economy. The occupied population lived through a long dark night from which no release seemed possible.

Not everyone stayed on. Those who could, fled, either to the GMD areas of Free China in the west and south-west, or to the CCP-controlled areas in the north-west. Virtually all the middle class and the intelligentsia fled. Industry moved from Shanghai and Wuhan into the interior, just ahead of the invading Japanese. The machinery and workers from over 300 factories were moved; those factories that could not be moved were destroyed. This trans-shipment did not lead to the re-establishment of industrial production in the interior, but it did reduce the amount of industrial plant available to the Japanese.[12] The economy of the cities of China along the eastern seaboard stagnated, leaving the Japanese with a costly problem of maintaining the population.

By the time the Japanese took Hong Kong, at the very end of 1941, they were intent on divesting themselves of the urban population; people who had not fled before they arrived came under great pressure to leave. Much of the Chinese population fled to the mainland, and the population shrank to a fraction of its former size.

The Japanese occupied the major cities and the transport lines of northern, eastern and central China, and all the coastal cities. But they did not hold many of the rural areas. Some remained under the control of the GMD or CCP; local forces, made up of former militiamen, bandits and patriotic guerrillas, controlled others. Much of the successful guerrilla warfare was later 'claimed' by the CCP, though at the time leadership was localised and independent. The most famous example of this is the guerrilla organisation in Manchuria, described in Xiao Jun's novel *Village in August*.[13]

The population in these areas suffered a general decline in standards of living and in personal security. The war caused enormous damage and disruption to the market economy, reducing peasants to a subsistence and barter economy. They might not have starved, but they suffered considerable privation. The decline in personal security was even more severe. Many of the unoccupied areas behind the lines saw a collapse of civil order; the previous local government leaders and the gentry had fled into Free China, leaving the civilian populations at the mercy of often predatory local armed men. The flight of the elite left a well of bitterness behind among peasants who felt that they had been abandoned to their fates. These areas, especially in northern China, in the last few years of the war, turned out to be fertile ground for the Communist Party to win converts and to set up bases. By the end of the war they had almost 100 million people directly under their control in the base areas.[14]

The worst horrors that the people in these areas experienced from the Japanese were mopping-up campaigns, intense at the beginning of the war and again in the early 1940s, as the Japanese launched hit-and-run attacks into areas of guerrilla activity. The Japanese called these attacks 'draining the water', in response to the saying attributed to Mao Zedong that the people were the water and the guerrillas the fish that swam in it. To get the fish the water had to be drained – the people had to be killed.[15]

The peasants of northern China were dealt even more severe blows by nature, in the form of the great famine, which ravaged Northern China, especially Henan, from 1942 to 1943. There was no relief from this disaster, because of the disruption of civilian government, and because of the corruption and incompetence of the remainder of the GMD Government authorities. As many as 3 million people may have died in that famine.[16]

There was a vast area of western and south-western China that remained under GMD control for much of the war – though the Japanese made substantial advances into the south-west in the last years of the conflict. This area, already very populous, was overcrowded during the war with refugees from the occupied areas, and with the armies of the GMD that withdrew there. The first wave of refugees took hundreds of thousands of people from northern China down into Sichuan and Yunnan in the autumn of 1937. Shortly afterwards millions of people fled west up the Yangzi into Sichuan in late 1937 and early 1938. Others escaped from Guangzhou into the unoccupied parts of Guangdong and Guangxi. After the Japanese took Hong Kong in late 1941, another wave fled into Guangxi.

Some of the provinces into which people fled were rich agricultural lands, but they were unable to meet the needs of the swollen population. Other provinces were very poor, incapable of feeding themselves well, let alone millions of incomers. Shortages of food were common throughout the war. There was no industrial base in Free China, and there was an almost complete shortage of manufactured goods.

In the cities of Free China the war was far away but always present, in the form of Japanese bombers that the GMD had no air force to repel. The wartime capital Chongqing came under bombardment on any day clear enough for the Japanese planes to fly; the population welcomed any cloudy day. The cliffs on which the city was built were honeycombed with giant bomb shelters. In the beautiful south-western city of Guilin the famous peaks and caves provided protection for the civilians, locals and refugees alike.

Early in the war the mood in the cities of Free China was defiant and positive. The refugee population brought a new sophistication to previously conservative areas, which became quite cosmopolitan as foreigners from the Allied countries moved in. The courage and the stoicism of the Chinese under attack were reported to the world, especially in the years before the outbreak of the Second World War in Europe and in Asia. But as the war dragged on, and victory seemed impossibly far away, the mood soured and there was a gradual erosion of morale. Shortages, which bore particularly heavily on the poor and the refugees, fuelled corruption, which seemed to benefit only the GMD and its close associates. Rising inflation, as the GMD financed its war effort by printing money, hit salary earners and refugees particularly hard. By the end of the war the inflation had already crippled the monetary economy – though this was only a foretaste of things to come.[17] The peasant population was little affected by the inflation, since they could move to a barter economy, but the middle classes were wiped out financially.

The war brought some unexpected cultural flowerings. One of the greatest universities of all time was created in Kunming (Yunnan), the Southwest United University, the faculty and students of all the great northern universities combined together; they had travelled there from the north, some by train, others by truck and some on foot. Students and professors were all virtually destitute, hungry and homeless, but classes were held throughout the war, and students could study with any of the great scholars of China. In Guilin (Guangxi) there was a great flowering of southern culture, the product of the arrival of refugee actors, writers and poets from Hong Kong and Guangzhou.

Some of the most dismal problems for the civilians of Free China were long-term ones, the gradual erosion of morale as the war stagnated, the debilitating effects of insecurity and the anxiety of inflation. Behind these problems was the nagging fear that the conflict might never end. The Chinese armies were inactive against the Japanese for much of the last five years of the war, apparently waiting for the other

Allies to defeat the Axis Powers. The sense of futility, of time dragging, of hopelessness, weighed heavily on the civilians.

The Chinese Communist Party seemed at first sight to be in even worse circumstances than the Guomindang. It held only a small, mountainous, arid area of northern China, in Shaanxi. Its capital was a small town, Yanan, which saw the emergence of a great vitality, the Yanan spirit, celebrating the 'poor and blank' spirit, the simplicity of life, and an espousal of peasant songs and dances. Foreign journalists who went to Yanan were entranced by the asceticism of life there, and came back with happy tales of Mao Zedong growing his own tobacco plants and rolling his own cigarettes. The reality was grimmer; the CCP was already exerting tough control over its supporters.

Yanan collected its share of refugees from the north and from Shanghai, including the starlet, Blue Apple, who became Mao Zedong's fourth wife, Jiang Qing. These refugees replenished the Communist movement and brought in new intellectual blood. They were active in the many mass movements that the Communists set up along Soviet models.[18]

The CCP armed forces embraced the strategy and tactics of guerrilla warfare, harking back to the ancient strategist Sunzi. They used the mountainous topography of the region to harry Japanese outposts, cut communication lines and stage lightning attacks on Japanese troops. These acts of boldness and daring gave the impression that the CCP, unlike the GMD, was really fighting the Japanese, and not just waiting until the Japanese were defeated by the Americans. This impression ignored the fact that guerrilla warfare could incur huge costs for the civilian population, in the form of Japanese reprisals.

The war may have been worse for some parts of China's population than for others, but it was only a matter of degree. Virtually no one had a 'good war'. It is hard to find anyone who enjoyed even a small part of the war, who shows any kind of nostalgia for a time that seemed, in retrospect, like a prolonged nightmare.

Among the population the suffering of war was not even-handed. There were several special categories of civilians who suffered most acutely during the war, and whose suffering has not really, even today, been recognised or compensated.

The families of dead soldiers and civilians were usually condemned to a life of great hardship. There was no compensation, no insurance, and no pensions to look after those who lost their main support. Within the traditional Chinese social system the family rather than the state was supposed to care for those who could not look after themselves. But in the context of war many families were too overburdened to care for their disabled members; the latter were forced to become beggars.

One highly visible group of victims were those who were physically damaged by fighting. There was no medical care for civilians or soldiers injured in warfare, for those who were crippled, maimed or blinded, either in fighting or in Japanese attacks on cities, towns and villages. Their fate was grim. Until Deng Xiaoping's son Deng Pufang, whose back was broken in the Cultural Revolution, became prominent in the 1980s, there was little allowance for the war-wounded in China. There was none of the special treatment given to the *mutilés de guerre* or the *Kriegsbeschadigte* in Europe, and no allowance given at all for civilian victims.

Another group to suffer particular grief were the families of soldiers. The several million men under arms in China had an even greater number of dependants, very few of whom were cared for by the military authorities. Many were dependants of soldiers in the GMD armies, who were left behind in Occupied China when the armies withdrew into the west. These families were left for eight years without the financial support of male breadwinners, and teetered on the verge of destitution for most of that time. For some the experience lasted much longer. Those women whose husbands fought in the Civil War, then left the mainland for Taiwan in 1949, were only reunited in the 1980s, when it finally became possible for by now elderly men to visit China again for the first time since the 1930s. The situation of abandoned families was only slightly better than that of the families whose men were killed; there were no pensions for the widows and orphans of dead soldiers, who were left destitute in a society where there were few charitable institutions beyond the family. After 1949 these families shared with the abandoned families the fate of being labelled as families of counter-revolutionaries.

The dependants of Communist troops fell into two categories. Those who had been left behind when the Communists withdrew from Southern China were in chronic distress, if they survived at all. Many women were never reunited with their husbands. The families of soldiers recruited after the Long March were slightly better off, since many of them were close to their men, in the hills of the north-west; the Red Army had replenished its forces locally after the Long March. But these families still had to survive with very little help from their men, either financially or in terms of labour.

Women suffered especial horrors in Occupied China. There was first of all the constant fear of rape, especially when a place was being taken over. The accounts of the fall of Nanjing, and of countless other small places, are full of references to rape. Often the victims of rape were killed; if they survived they could never talk about what had happened to them. Nor could the comfort women whom the Japanese Army conscripted to gratify the carnal needs of their men. These women suffered an especially grim fate, as yet unrecognised and unmentioned in China. Wherever it went the Japanese Army set up brothels, and forcibly recruited Chinese girls and women. They also imported many Korean women into Occupied China.[19] These women, if they survived, kept their pasts secret. They had to live in a sexually conservative society, in which there was no place for the victims of rape and sexual abuse. They buried the story of what had happened to them as deeply as possible.

Women were not the only victims of Japanese entrapment. Huge numbers of men were conscripted as forced labour, especially in northern China, to work in Manchuria and in Japan. Since the 19th century men had migrated to Manchuria to work as contract labourers, going north in the spring and returning to the south in the winter. Their pay was very low, but at least they earned some money. By the early 1940s the Japanese had decided to stop paying for labour – or to put it another way, the Japanese Army supplied labour to Japanese companies. Labourers were essentially kidnapped in northern China, transported to Manchuria or Japan and forced to work as slave labour in atrocious conditions. Hundreds of thousands did not survive the war. Young men in the unoccupied areas also ran the constant danger of being press-ganged, either to serve in the Army or to work as coolie labour.

Less obvious victims of the war, in the short run, were members of the generation that came of age in the late 1930s. These people were denied a proper education, had little chance of making normal careers, and saw their lives blighted by the war – whether or not they took part in it directly. The opportunities denied to them affected not only individuals, but also China as a whole when, later on, there was an acute shortage of capable people.

One inglorious aspect of the war was the widespread collaboration with the Japanese, which occurred in Occupied China. The first people to collaborate were members of the old Manchu and Qing imperial elite, out of power for only 20 years when the Japanese took Manchuria in 1931. They rallied to the Japanese, who set up the former emperor, Pu Yi, as a puppet in 1933, as head of the 'state' of Manzhouguo. Manchu collaboration was followed several years later by the collaboration of one of Sun Yat-sen's closest followers, Wang Jingwei, who headed a puppet government set up in 1940. In every part of occupied China, the people worked for the Japanese, with different levels of enthusiasm.

Some of the collaborators worked for the Japanese out of self-interest and optimism, others out of necessity, some perhaps because they thought they could mitigate the harshness of the Japanese. Many people assumed that the Japanese occupation would last for ever – and indeed until well into 1945 it seemed that this expectation was entirely justified. Whatever the reason, and whatever the degree of collaboration, the fact of collaboration left a bitter taste after the war. There were immediate recriminations when the occupied areas were liberated – but rather than systematic punishment of collaborators, this took the form of confiscation of property from people who had lived under Japanese rule, a form of carpet-bagging that swept in far more innocent people, who had lived under Japanese occupation, than guilty ones, who had actively collaborated.[20] Very few Chinese were tried for collaboration. Wang Jingwei escaped punishment by conveniently dying before the end of the war. Some were punished; many more disguised their actions during the war and tried to pretend that they had always been patriotic. There were many people in China in the decades after the war who had much to forget.

The story of the people's experience of war in China is a sad and depressing one. There is almost no sense of elation, of pride in resistance. Instead there is the shame of occupation, the humiliation, for a proud nation, of not being able to kick the Japanese out without help from outside. Added to these negative feelings is the galling knowledge that Japan has yet to make a formal apology for the sufferings of the Chinese, or to pay reparations. The problem here is that because this was not done immediately after the war, the Japanese see no reason to re-open the issue; they also know that China needs good economic relations with Japan.

These complex feelings have made it difficult for discussion of the war to take place, except in highly coloured terms. In the minds of many people the war is not finished, the scars are still there. They have been masked to some extent by the awful things that have happened since, but there is a sense that the war was what started the descent into chaos and brutality.

The idea of the war as the start of a prolonged period of chaos is equally applicable to China's economy. The Japanese invasion suspended economic development; the nascent industry and the fledgling modern economy of coastal China were stopped in their tracks. After 1946 the Civil War prevented any further development, while Maoist economic policies damaged the economy even further. Not until the early 1980s did real economic growth start again; this long delay is part of the explanation of why China's growth since the early 1980s has been so phenomenally rapid. Thus, from China's perspective, the war was the start of several decades of economic privation.

The Chinese historical tradition is that the history of a period cannot be written until after it has come to an end. Usually this means a dynasty. In the modern period it seems to mean a lifetime. As the generations that experienced the war and its long aftermath pass from the scene, we may find a greater interest in talking and writing about it. Younger scholars, writers and artists are beginning to try and make sense of the tragedy of a war that probably affected China more cruelly than any other country involved in the conflict. It is only now that the pain has begun to ease enough for the Chinese to talk about the war.

Recommended reading

Buruma, Ian, *The Wages of Guilt* (London: Cape, 1994)

Chang, Iris, *The Rape of Nanking: The Forgotten Massacre* (New York: Basic Books, 1997)

Johnson, Chalmers *Peasant Nationalism and the Rise of Communist Power* (Stanford: Stanford University Press, 1962)

Lary, Diana, *Warlord Soldiers* (Cambridge: Cambridge University Press, 1985)

Liu, F. F., *A Military History of Modern China* (Princeton: Princeton University Press, 1956)

McCord, Edward, *The Power of the Gun* (Berkeley: University of California Press, 1993)

Rabe, John, *The Good Man of Nanking* (New York: Knopf, 1998)

Waldron, Arthur, *From War to Nationalism* (Cambridge: Cambridge University Press, 1995)

Notes

[1] Chen Kaige's recent film *The Emperor and the Assassin* captures Qinshihuang's megalomania brilliantly.

[2] Iris Chang, *The Rape of Nanjing: The Forgotten Massacre* (New York: Basic Books, 1997) and John Rabe, ed Erwin Wickert, trans John Woods, *The Good Man of Nanking* (New York: Knopf, 1998)

[3] Lee En-han, *Ribenjun zhanzheng baoxing zhi yanjiu* (*The Violent Behaviour of the Japanese Army in War*) (Taipei: Shangwu yinshudian, 1994) pp332-88

[4] Ibid, pp344, 354, 359

[5] Ian Buruma, *The Wages of Guilt* (London: Cape, 1994)

[6] Yang Daqing, 'Convergence or Divergence: Recent historical debate on the Rape of Nanjing', in *American Historical Review* 104 (3 June 1999) pp842-65

[7] Li Wenzhi, *Zhongguo jindaishi da zaihuang* (*Great Disasters in Modern Chinese History*) (Shanghai: Renmin chubanshe, 1993) pp254-5

8 Diana Lary, 'Drowned earth: the breaching of the Yellow River dyke in 1938', in *War and History* (forthcoming)

9 Mao Zedong, 'Jinian Baiqiuen' ('In memory of Norman Bethune'), in *Selected Works*, II (Beijing: Renminchubanshe, 1964) pp653-4

10 Jasper Becker, *Hungry Ghosts* (London: John Murray, 1996)

11 Amy Tan, *The Joy Luck Club* (New York: Putnam, 1989)

12 F. F. Liu, *Military History of Modern China* (Princeton: Princeton University Press, 1956) pp155-6

13 Hsiao Chun (Xiao Jun), *Village in August* (New York: Smith & Durrell, 1942)

14 Wu Yuexing, *Zhongguo Kangri zhanzheng shidi tuji 1931-1945* (*Collection of Maps from the Anti-Japanese War 1931-1945*) (Beijing: Zhongguo ditu chubanshe, 1995) p254

15 Chalmers Johnson, *Peasant Nationalism and the Rise of Communist Power* (Stanford: Stanford University Press, 1963) pp55-6

16 Theodore White and Annaly Jacoby, *Thunder out of China* (New York: William Sloan, 1946)

17 Chiang Kia-gnau, *The Inflationary Spiral in China 1939-1950* (Cambridge: MIT Press, 1958)

18 Chalmers Johnson, op cit, pp89-90

19 George Hicks, *The Comfort Women: Sex Slaves of the Japanese Imperial Army* (London: Souvenir, 1995)

20 Suzanne Pepper, *Civil War in China* (Berkeley: University of California Press, 1978) pp20-4

Chapter 12

Colonial India: Conflict, shortage and discontent

Sanjoy Bhattacharya

The two World Wars effected marked social and political changes in India. This was inevitable as the sub-continental economy was very closely tied to that of Britain, and South Asia remained a vital contributor of manpower and material to the Allied war efforts during both conflicts. The results of this participation were complex. Whereas some sectors of the economy – and the sections of the population that controlled them – did particularly well from wartime contracts, other groups fell prey to the serious economic, social and political dislocation engendered by the official mobilisation strategies. And, unsurprisingly, the political uses made of the resultant civilian discontent ensured significant doses of constitutional advance in India.

The First World War created, and sharpened, numerous contradictions between British and Indian interests in colonial South Asia. It, of course, kindled tensions within Indian society as well.[1] The pressures of war on the Indian economy were undeniable: there was a 300 per cent increase in the defence expenditure, which not only heralded the imposition of war loans but also caused a sharp rise in taxes and a modification of the entire financial structure. Military recruitment increased dramatically and the size of the wartime Army rose to 1.2 million men, of whom the province of Punjab contributed 355,000 soldiers.[2] While this recruitment drive injected money into selected localities, the outfitting of the wartime Army caused severe difficulties in other parts of the country. For instance, the export of grains and other raw materials for the military's use often caused local shortages. One report, dated as late as January 1919, from Sir George Lloyd, the Governor of Bombay, to Edwin Montagu, the Secretary of State for India, stated that, 'Large quantities of valuable fodder are being exported from here to Mesopotamia by the Army… Luckily the Horniman Press [a reference to B. G. Horniman, the editor of the nationalist *Bombay Chronicle*] have not tumbled to the fact that fodder is being exported while the Deccan starves.'[3]

Moreover, the wartime transport bottlenecks and disruption, primarily in the form of a sharp fall in shipping space available for non-military needs, caused a sharp fall in imports, and contributed to the general inflationary trends.[4] At the same time, the export prices of Indian agricultural goods did not go up in the same proportion due to the dislocation in world economic relations. The consequent shift in conditions of trade against agriculture adversely affected all grades of cultivators producing for the market. Poorer peasants and landless labourers were also affected in another way: the price of coarse foodgrains, which constituted their staple food, went up dramatically. The increase in the price of foodstuffs affected other occupational groups as well. Artisan labour in particular was badly hit, and ironically even the industrial workers attached to businesses benefiting from wartime demands suffered. Although employment in organised industries and plantations went up from 2,105,824 in 1911 to 2,681,125, wages remained low in a period of high prices and super-profits for employers. For example, in the C. N. Wadia Century Mills – an Indian-owned concern – an 80 to 100 per cent increase in foodgrain prices was counterbalanced by only a 15 per cent increase in wages between 1914 and 1918, even though the industry made a 100 per cent profit on its capital investment of 1918.[5]

Indeed, some select businesses – many Indian-owned – benefited greatly from wartime demands, the decline in foreign competition, the price differential between agricultural raw materials and industrial goods, and the stagnation or decline in real wages. In eastern India, for instance, mill magnates gained from the boost in the price of jute manufactures (like sandbags and canvas), and the cotton textile industry of Ahmedabad, Bombay and Sholapur went through a period of decisive growth at the expense of the Lancashire mills.[6] In fact, two Indian businessmen – G. D. Birla and S. Hukumchand – would utilise the windfall profits gained from speculation in jute and other commodities to start the first Indian-owned jute mills soon after the war.

As the First World War affected different groups in substantially distinct ways, it was perhaps inevitable that it would evoke starkly distinct indigenous responses. The Indian industrial magnates and commodity speculators, the main beneficiaries of the unsettled wartime economy, remained solidly supportive of the Allied war effort. In fact, the wartime alliances, informal or otherwise, between state and Indian capital were strengthened in a post-war scenario marked by a wave of industrial action. Valuable new research on the Sholapur cotton industry explains how:

'...mills ... were profit-making concerns despite unfavourable conditions during the war. Years of scarcity were turned to their advantage by the millowners who recruited cheap labour from the city and its surrounding district. The location at Sholapur of the largest criminal tribes settlement in India facilitated the industry which was facing acute labour shortages on account of the plague and influenza epidemics. The criminal tribes settlement acted as a penal colony making available a cheap, captive and loyalist workforce for the mills. The government claimed that it was on a civilising mission trying to reform the tribals. In reality, they were saved the expenditure of maintaining the settlement due to the employment of settlement workers in the mills and also the expense of starting relief works in Sholapur, a district in the Deccan Famine Zone. This informal contract between colonial and capitalist interests ensured speedy suppression of industrial strikes in the immediate post-war period.'[7]

Needless to say, these alliances were by no means limited to Sholapur, and this was powerfully underlined by the whole-hearted support provided by the Indian industrialists to the official Armistice celebrations.[8]

Industrial labour suffered, but the wartime experience forced workers to move towards the organisation of a trade union movement.[9] The Madras Labour Union was, for example, started in April 1918 by G. Ramanajulu Naidu and G. Chelvapathi Chetti, and this was the first organisation with regular membership lists and subscriptions.[10] Agriculturists of all grades were scarred by the wartime economic trends and began to display a greater willingness to be involved in both organised politics and episodes of rioting intended to release food hoards, so much so that new leaders thrown up from the localities began to challenge the Indian National Congress central leadership's directives.[11] To the great concern of the British authorities, such disturbed political trends also became visible in the province of Punjab, the main source of manpower for the British Indian Army. Even though the political upsurge in the Punjab was a primarily urban phenomenon, stray, but significant, episodes of demobilised troops being involved in rural agitation rattled the authorities at both the provincial and central level of colonial government. A notable result of these trends was the complete and effective re-organisation of the provincial military recruitment and training schemes through the development of a system based on District Soldiers' Boards.[12]

Economic factors might also explain the sudden upsurge of middle-class interest in nationalist politics. This increasingly vocal group was hit by the rise in the price of foodstuffs and other essential goods, as their fixed salaries lagged far behind the rapid rise in the cost of living. Moreover, the official tendency to stifle press references to their complaints by the regular use of special censorship regulations, without taking sufficiently effective measures to improve their lot, angered them further and became a focal issue in their increased participation in new nationalist agitation like the anti-Rowlatt [Sedition] Act movement organised by Gandhi from 1919 onwards. That these trends were politically significant cannot be denied. Indeed, historians like Milton Israel have pointed out, quite justifiably, that a 'priority for the immediate post-war years was the establishment of an information system that would allow it to compete with other users, particularly with the developing communications network of the nationalist movement... Public opinion, whatever its perceived quality, had become important to the Government of India and it was determined to influence it.'[13]

While the Indian experience during the First and Second World Wars was similar in some respects (for instance, most industrial concerns began to enjoy super-profits once again), there were extremely significant differences as well. All the major Indian political parties opposed Britain's unilateral decision to involve India in the Second World War. The conflict ultimately reached India's borders, converting the sub-continent into a major military base, and the wartime shortages of food, cloth and medicines were completely unprecedented in scope. All these factors shaped indigenous attitudes towards the official efforts to mobilise for the Second World War, particularly after the Japanese entry into the conflict in December 1941.

The situation in India remained relatively settled during the first two years of the war, to the undisguised relief of the administrative authorities.[14] Indeed, the marginality of the European war to the Indian situation was highlighted by the fact that the economic fluctuations remained rather unspectacular, political opposition was easily contained in the face of the Congress's inability to mobilise significant levels of support for its agitation, and military recruitment was kept up to the desired levels. Indigenous responses to these trends remained equally undramatic. Apart from a few spurts of panic withdrawals of personal savings from banks and post offices, usually corresponding with the news of specific Allied defeats in Europe and Africa, the war seemed a very distant event to most Indians, except perhaps families of soldiers sent off on overseas duty.[15] Describing the settled situation in the spring of 1941, a senior Civil Servant based in the United Provinces declared that, 'Congress were now campaigning openly against the British regime. They held meetings advocating opposition to the war effort, an offence under the Defence of India Act. The effect on recruitment to the armed forces was slight but, if only to maintain self-respect, the authorities were bound to prosecute.'[16]

The strategic, economic and political situation changed quite dramatically after December 1941. The Japanese entry into the war and the succession of major Allied defeats in South East Asia, especially the fall of the 'fortress' of Singapore and British Burma, set the alarm bells ringing in both official and civilian circles in India. Eastern and southern India, regions faced with a probable Japanese invasion, were palpably unprepared for war. The armed forces were pathetically under-equipped, and in the first half of 1942 there was no air defence worth speaking of. There were virtually no anti-aircraft guns, air-raid searchlights or radar sets, and the Royal Indian Air Force could only deploy eight 'serviceable Mohawks' to defend Calcutta, which, being the hub of the British war effort in eastern India, was open to attacks from carrier-based Japanese planes.[17]

These weaknesses were also mirrored in other areas. No airfield in India was suitable for use by modern heavy aircraft in 1941, and even as late as mid-1942 Calcutta was the only urban centre in the eastern provinces with an airport capable of serving military aircraft. The Japanese threat and the need to facilitate the arrival of the American Air Force in India resulted in an 'urgent demand' for 200 airfields.[18] The result, inevitably, was the launching of a great range of defence works. By November 1942, for instance, there were five aerodromes 'complete in all respects', 83 aerodromes containing one all-weather runway, and 60 with 'fair weather strips'.[19]

Similarly, an expansion of the road communication networks in southern and eastern India, which did not receive much attention till the outbreak of the war in the Far East, was also begun. Road building was given tremendous significance for a variety of reasons. First, the Japanese mastery over the Bay of Bengal forced the closure of the ports on India's eastern seaboard, which impeded the transfer of both men and material.[20] Second, an extension of the rail network, which could have compensated for the loss of shipping routes, could not be pushed through due to a shortage of rolling-stock, which was imported from Britain. The construction of a new road was, therefore, started in October 1942 with a view to linking Dumri, Deogarh, Hansdina, Purnea, Siliguri, Cooch-Behar and Dhubri, while

improvements were begun on two other important highways in the region, the
Raipur-Vizagapatnam road and the Assam access road.[21] These activities involved
a considerable mobilisation of resources (the enormity of the task undertaken is
reflected in the central Engineering Department's burgeoning budget between
1941 and 1944, which is indicated in Table 1) and forced the requisitioning of vast
amounts of land and other private property for military use.[22]

Table 1
The progressive rise in the budget of the Engineering Department, Government of India, 1939-1944

Years	Amount (millions of rupees)
1939-40	40
1940-41	200
1941-42	450
1942-43	1,000
1943-44	1,000

Source: 'War Department History – Engineer Matters (September 1939-August 1945), p3, L/R/5/282, Oriental and India Office Collections, British Library, London

These official strategies, often enforced by strategic necessity, proved very
disruptive to local economies and societies, as the creation of the new military
installations forced the regular evacuation of entire villages.[23] The fact that the
compensation offered for requisitioned property was usually considered insufficient
in a period of rapid inflation did not help matters and engendered much
dissatisfaction in the localities.[24] Moreover, the problems were exacerbated by the
fact that the local inhabitants, many of whom were dispossessed cultivators, were
not engaged in military construction sites, where use was made instead of
specialised 'labour battalions' that were composed primarily of the members of the
'aboriginal tribes' of Bengal, Bihar and Orissa.[25] Activists attached to the Congress,
and even parties ostensibly loyal to the British war effort, like the Communist Party
of India, would regularly tap into such discontent. Congress members based in the
affected localities were, for example, encouraged to report on all 'negative
reactions' to requisitioning policies and, whenever possible, busy themselves in
organising protests around them. This was, of course, not very difficult considering
the level of social dislocation caused by the mobilisation for the war effort.[26]

Other defensive measures began also to have an adverse impact on the quality
of indigenous civilian life. The application of a 'partial denial policy' in the
provinces of eastern India (the whole region was now being treated as a single
administrative unit by the military for the sake of effective defence
administration[27]), through which the colonial authorities sought to dispossess any
invading Japanese forces of resources, damaged transport and food-supply
networks.[28] In May 1942, for instance, about 50,000 maunds of rice were
transported from Orissa to Bihar 'mainly to assist the Denial Policy scheme under

which large surpluses of rice [we]re to be removed from the coastal areas.'[29] While bureaucrats in the localities recognised the unpopularity of the 'denial policy', their enduring fear of a Japanese invasion and the existence of considerable pressure from the local military authorities, ensured that measures were carried through.[30] However, the matter became a potent symbol in the hands of those challenging the authorities, and one official report from Bengal complained that:

> 'Measures for the denial of transport continue in certain coastal areas but difficulties are reported from most districts... In Contai and Tamluk the Congress, whose collaboration in implementing Government's policy was promised when the Minister for Civil Defence Co-ordination recently visited the area, is now reported to be misrepresenting the denial policy and causing difficulties...'[31]

Similarly, the CPI cadres based in the affected localities of Eastern Bengal were found to be organising rallies and spreading 'strong propaganda' against the denial measures, even though the party's politburo had acknowledged the necessity of the policy. The Government of Bengal dealt with this particular problem by arming its district administrators with comprehensive powers to ban their activities.[32]

Apart from contending with criticism about the 'denial policy', the colonial authorities also had to deal with problems arising from the presence of an enormous Allied army in the sub-continent. The number of British troops in India had risen to 1,689,988 by October 1943[33], and they were supported in turn by a large number of African[34], American[35] and Chinese military personnel[36]. Even though the central and provincial governments tried to limit the friction between the army detachments and civilians by making the task of requisitioning goods needed by the sub-continental military formations solely a civilian government function, clashes between troops and the general populace remained common and very often serious in nature.[37] The misdemeanours on the part of the military personnel ranged from murder, rape, arson and robbery to petty theft, and caused additional administrative burdens to be placed on the already overworked provincial and district bureaucracies.[38] However, the settling of criminal cases in which American forces were involved proved particularly difficult, as the provisions of the Allied Forces (United States of America) Ordinance of 1942 precluded colonial officials from prosecuting the guilty personnel, who could only be tried by American courts.[39] One analysis prepared by the Government of India's Home Department, on the basis of reports received from the provinces, declared that:

> 'While the relations between the American forces and civilians are reported to be satisfactory by most of the Provinces, the reports of Bengal and Assam are far from positive in this respect. The reason is twofold: Some of the serious offences were concerning women and trespass into private homes for immoral purposes. This form of crime, of course, arouses widespread public indignation. Secondly, the results of some of the trials gave the impression that the American Courts Martial had not done justice in those cases. The fact remains that in parts of Bengal and Assam the relations between the

civilian population and American troops have not been entirely satisfactory owing to the behaviour of those troops.'[40]

Not surprisingly, such tales, real or contrived, of Allied troops misbehaving with Indians, especially women, were utilised by political activists opposing the war effort.[41] Public protests, albeit usually temporary due to the swift implementation of government restrictions aimed at reducing civilian criticism of the armed forces[42], were organised throughout 1943 to 1945 in the localities of Bengal to condemn incidents arising from the 'sexual enthusiasm' of Allied troops[43], and the local vernacular press would sometimes level criticisms against 'immoral white soldiers'[44]. Military intelligence noted in 1943 that leaflets were being disseminated with the purpose of 'exacerbating Hindu feelings' against civilian and army authorities by accusing them of slaughtering 30,000 cattle daily, including 'even pregnant cows and cows with milk', for feeding foreign soldiers.[45]

Accusations about the misbehaviour of troops fitted in well with economic worries, and the authorities were also consistently attacked for the wide range of wartime shortages. The Allied reverses throughout South East Asia – and Burma in particular – during 1942, and the defensive measures initiated in eastern India, had an almost immediate negative impact on the region's supply of food items (especially rice, oils and salt), cooking and lighting fuels (coal and kerosene), cloth and medicines.[46] The severity of food shortages kept increasing till there was an outbreak of famine conditions in eastern and southern India in 1943, with the Bengal famine claiming millions of lives through starvation and disease.[47] While belated official interventions, in the form of temporary provisioning and medical measures in the worst affected localities, stabilised the situation somewhat, the food shortfall in 1944 continued to be so serious that the military authorities volunteered to forgo 10 per cent of the wheat allocated to them by the central government's Food Department.[48] The distress arising from the famine conditions proved to be very politically damaging to the colonial wartime administration. Activists ranged against the authorities now found it politically expedient to dwell upon graphic, and sometimes exaggerated, descriptions of starvation deaths in the countryside, the break-up of families during the exodus from the affected localities and the British responsibility for all these problems.[49] Once again, these themes proved to be effective means of mobilising protest meetings and agitation, most commonly in the form of 'hunger marches', in the localities.[50]

Indeed, the quite dramatic rise in negative political activism against wartime state policy, at all levels of administration, was directly linked to the great civilian discontent about contemporary economic and social trends. The colonial state was, however, unable to respond adequately to these crises due to a persistent shortage of resources, both material and manpower; a situation much exacerbated by the decision of the Government of India and the General Headquarters (India) to accord absolute primacy to the needs of wartime mobilisation. This, in turn, caused colonial officials to adopt a range of novel measures to tackle the situation, notably the administrative tendency to prioritise Indian social groups in terms of their strategic 'worth', which divided them into 'priority' and 'non-priority' classes. The increasing paucity of administrative resources meant that the former, which included army and bureaucratic personnel and their families, industrial and military labour, and urban populations generally, became the primary target of the various special official distributive and welfare measures between 1942 and 1945.[51]

But the amount of time, effort and resources spent by the authorities on targeting the 'priority' groups necessarily meant that very little time could be spared to deal with the 'general' civilian population. Officials had been aware that such an eventuality might arise and Theodore Gregory, the Permanent Economic Adviser to the Government of India, noted in January 1943 that it was even going to be impossible to arrange comprehensive rationing schemes for entire urban populations.[52] Gregory's insights were not far off the mark – the state's wartime priorities resulted in a situation where general distributive schemes could not be regularised despite the persistence of continued economic difficulties, with officials only managing to attend to severe local problems and, even then, very often in a sketchy manner. Of course, this meant that the levels of distress amongst the 'non-priority' segments of the civilian population, especially in the rural areas, grew very noticeably between 1942 and 1945.[53] Indeed, rural areas in India, with the exception of districts providing military recruits or housing military formations, were systematically denuded of resources by officials (British and Indian) and private traders (mostly Indian) in order to provision the Army based in the sub-continent and the bigger urban centres, where some of the most politically visible – and thus 'troublesome' – sections of Indian society resided.[54] The weaknesses of official policy, and of its results, were cruelly exposed as the famine conditions progressed in Bengal.[55] During this period, resources could only be arranged for the poor based, or arriving, in the cities and selected district towns of eastern India, and the Final Report of the Famine Enquiry Commission pointed out that the prominence given to the needs of the industrial workers caused a delay in the initiation of rationing measures for the poorer sections of the 'non-productive' civilian population.[56]

Indigenous reactions to such strategies were understandably varied. Political parties, without exception, seemed to find it expedient to link up their struggles with the various local demonstrations that tended to be organised to protest against the abiding shortages. Even parties ostensibly allied to the war effort found it expedient – if not necessary – to look the other way as their local activists joined, or organised, agitation aimed at making the wartime administration more responsive to local problems.[57] In fact, the difficulties faced by the state in responding to the problems experienced by the 'non-priority' sections of the civilian population caused the authorities to allow 'legal' political parties to take part in relief measures. However, this often led to the provision of aid to be carried out along party lines, causing, in turn, religious affiliations to be given great significance, as members of the Hindu Mahasabha and the right-wing sections of the Muslim League and the Congress began to target primarily their own co-religionists. Such relief distribution patterns, whose organisers also continually highlighted the British responsibility for the troubles between 1942 and 1945, seem to have had the dual effect of weakening the standing of the state and communalising Indian politics.[58]

Interestingly, the colonial authorities remained aware that the measures deployed amongst the 'priority classes' were only going to be effective in the short term. Indeed, the policy of offering special privileges, without ever hiding the threat of their removal during extremely difficult economic times, was bound to encourage a very transient loyalty to the official war effort. This was particularly true with regard to the industrial labour operating in the war industries in India; while the factory workers received frequent increases in cost allowances and state-subsidised issues of free food, cloth and domestic fuels, they were also continually reminded that these benefits could be withdrawn if they participated in protracted strikes.[59] However, these official strategies, designed to manage wartime labour relations, also had the effect of stoking tensions between the state and other groups in Indian society. For example, while the factory managers remained happy to receive official financial assistance towards distributive schemes, they remained much less enamoured about the other facets of state policy. Central government's efforts at skimming off some of the profits being made by the industrialists through special insurance schemes and Defence of India Regulations, its strategy of trying to use communist assistance amongst workers, and its insistence that a greater proportion of the profits be used for improvement measures, remained very unpopular, and this further weakened official attempts to develop a wartime consensus.[60]

At the same time, the travails of war in India, the selectivity of the state policies designed to tackle these problems, the visibility of the civilian opposition to these measures, and the increasing ability of the nationalist parties to stoke violent protests had a deeper impact on the structure of the colonial state itself.[61] Indian elements of the colonial administration, both military and civilian, began to question the ability of the British to retain India much beyond the war. Ironically, these fears tended to be stoked, especially after 1942, by the state's own public relations campaigns regarding the inevitability of independence among these audiences.[62] The result was an unmistakable move towards political re-negotiation on the part of Indian officials, and this was noticeable at all levels of the civilian administration. Some Indian bureaucrats within the Central Government were considered unreliable enough to be removed from bodies involved in managing public relations campaigns intended to attack the Congress Working Committee[63]; other Indian officials in charge of provincial and district administration would try to keep up links with locally prominent nationalist leaders[64], and military intelligence from the rural areas began to report that village administrators, including subordinate policemen, had begun to leak information to nationalist activists, thereby allowing them to escape custody.[65] Worryingly for the colonial authorities, South Asian soldiers serving in the sub-continent, who would ordinarily represent their first line of defence during a serious uprising, had also begun to air doubts about their future in an independent India, possibly dominated by a Congress-led government.[66] There can be little doubt that these trends – and their ability to accentuate British nervousness about their position in India – proved a significant determinant in the timing of the dissolution of the Raj.[67]

To conclude, the First and Second World Wars represent extremely important episodes in Indian history that managed to significantly re-shape the political and social trends in the sub-continent; both conflicts forced adaptations within the structure of the colonial state, societal formations and the forms of nationalism. And yet there were distinct differences in the degree of change wrought by the two wars. The Second World War presented by far the greater challenges, and these came to pass at a time when the devolution of power in colonial India was well advanced. Therefore it was perhaps inevitable that the developments wrought between 1942 and 1945 were dramatic enough to ensure the inevitability of South Asian independence. By redefining collaborative alliances between state and society, by noticeably radicalising Indian society, and by re-orienting the focus of nationalist politics to a primarily agitational mode, the Second World War was able to set into motion trends that could not be ignored or rolled back; so much so that new political alliances and agreements that might have seemed unthinkable a decade before were formed between the British, the Congress and the Muslim League in anticipation of Indian independence.

Recommended reading

Bhattacharya, S., '*A Necessary Weapon of War*': *State Policies towards Propaganda and Information in Eastern India, 1939-1945* (Richmond: Curzon Press, 2000)
'British Military Information Management Techniques and the South Asian Soldier: Eastern India during the Second World War', in *Modern Asian Studies* 34 (2)
'An Official Policy that went Awry: The British Colonial State's propaganda against the Indian National Congress during the Second World War', in B. Pati (ed), *Issues in Modern Indian History: For Sumit Sarkar* (Mumbai: Popular Prakashan, 2000)
'Anxious Celebrations: British India and the Armistice', in Cecil, H. and Liddle, P. (eds), *At the Eleventh Hour: Reflections, Hopes and Anxieties at the Closing of the Great War, 1918* (London: Leo Cooper, 1998)
Bhattacharya, S. and Zachariah, B., '"A Great Destiny": The British Colonial State and the advertisement of post-war reconstruction in India, 1942-45', in *South Asia Research* 19 (1) (1999)
Bose, S., 'Starvation Amidst Plenty: The making of famine in Bengal, Honan and Tonkin, 1943-46', in *Modern Asian Studies* 24 (4) (1990)
Brown, J., *Modern India: The Origins of an Asian Democracy* (Delhi: Oxford University Press, 1984)
Israel, M., *Communications and Power: Propaganda and the press in the Indian nationalist struggle, 1920-1947* (Cambridge: Cambridge University Press, 1994)
Kamat, M. N., 'The War Years and the Sholapur Cotton Textile Industry', in *Social Scientist* 26 (11-12) (1998)
Low, D. A. (ed), *Congress and the Raj* (London: Heinemann, 1977)
Pandey, G. (ed), *The Indian Nation in 1942* (Calcutta: K. P. Bagchi, 1989)
Pati, B. (ed), *Turbulent Times: India, 1940-44* (Mumbai: Popular Prakashan, 1998)
Sarkar, S., *Modern India, 1885-1947* (Delhi: Macmillan, 1983)
Siddiqi, M., *Agrarian Unrest in North India: United Provinces, 1918-1922* (New Delhi: Vikas, 1978)
Voigt, J. H., *India in the Second World War* (New Delhi: Vikas, 1987)

Notes

1   S. Sarkar, *Modern India, 1885-1947* (Delhi: 1983) pp168-9
2   The Government of India made a 'gift' of £100 million to the British war effort at the outbreak of the conflict, followed by a further £45 million in 1918. See A. L. Levkovsky, *Capitalism in India: Basic Trends in its Development* (Bombay: 1966) p96
3   Quoted in A. D. D. Gordon, *Businessmen and Politics: Rising Nationalism and a Modernising Economy in Bombay, 1918-1933* (Delhi: 1978) pp33-4
4   Indeed, an official statistical abstract on prices supplied the following all-India index numbers (1873=100):

1913	143	1919	276
1914	147	1920	281
1915	152	1921	236
1916	152	1922	232
1917	196	1923	215
1918	225		

From J. Brown, *Gandhi's Rise to Power: Indian Politics, 1915-1922* (Cambridge: 1972) p125
5   S. Sarkar, op cit, p175
6   A. Bagchi, *Private Investment in India, 1900-1939* (Cambridge: 1972) and B. Chatterji, *Trade, Tariffs and Empire: Lancashire and British Policy in India 1919-1939* (Delhi: 1992). See also P. J. Mead, 'Industrial Expansion in Bombay Presidency', Industrial Handbook, 1919 (Calcutta: 1919) p33
7   M. Kamat, 'The War Years and the Sholapur Cotton Textile Industry', in *Social Scientist* 26 (11-12) (1998) p77. See also M. Kamat, 'Labour, Ethnicity and Violence: The Dynamics of Industrial Unrest in Sholapur, 1920-30' (unpublished MPhil dissertation, University of Cambridge, 1991)
8   S. Bhattacharya, 'Anxious Celebrations: British India and the Armistice', in H. Cecil and P. H. Liddle (eds), *At The Eleventh Hour: Reflections, Hopes and Anxieties at the Closing of the Great War, 1918* (London: Leo Cooper, 1998) pp190-2
9   See, eg, 'Report of an Enquiry into Family Budgets of Cotton Mill Workers in Sholapur City' (Bombay: 1928)
10 The Madras Labour Union was presided over by B. P. Wadia, a close confidant of Annie Besant. However, the most dramatic increase in the number of trade unions came in 1920 when some 125 were formed. The first All-India Trade Union Congress also met at Bombay in November that of year. S. Sarkar, op cit, p175
11 There was an increase in the incidence of food riots, involving especially the looting of grain shops and small town markets and the seizure of debt bonds, from 1918 onwards. In Bengal, for example, 38 market looting cases with 859 convictions were reported from Noakhali, Chittagong, Rangpur, Dinajpur, Khulna, 24 Parganas and Jessore districts in 1919-20. According to Sumit Sarkar, 'Such outbursts could take on varying significance depending on local political conditions: contributing to anti-Marwari rioting by Muslims in central Calcutta in September 1918, but also playing a significant part in the very widespread anti-Rowlatt Act upsurge in many Indian cities in April 1919.' S. Sarkar, op cit, p176
12 An excellent description of the development of the system based on District Soldiers' Boards in the Punjab is provided in the work of Tan Tai Yong. See T. Y. Tan, 'The Military and the State in Colonial India, 1900-1939' (unpublished PhD dissertation, University of Cambridge, 1992). See also T. Y. Tan, 'Maintaining the Military Districts: Civil-Military Integration and District Soldiers' Boards in the Punjab, 1919-1939', in *Modern Asian Studies* 28 (4) (1994)
13 M. Israel, *Communications and Power: Propaganda and the press in the Indian nationalist struggle, 1920-1947* (Cambridge: 1994) pp29-30
14 Reports on the political situation in India by the Central Intelligence Officers touring the provinces, c1941, Home Political Files (Internal) [hereafter 'HPF (I)'] 241/41, National Archives of India, New Delhi, India [hereafter 'NAI']
15 R. Hunt and J. Harrison, *The District Officer in India, 1930-1947* (London: 1980) p206
16 Recollections of E. A. Midgley, Indian Civil Service, MSS EUR F. 180/78, Oriental and India Office Collections, British Library, London [hereafter 'OIOC']

[17] A massive effort was made to modernise and enlarge the Royal Indian Air Force from April-May 1942, and by December of that year there were 29 fully operational squadrons based in India. 'War Department History – Modernisation and Mechanisation of the Armed Forces of India (September 1939 to February 1944)', pp23-70, L/R/5/275, OIOC. For more information on the growth of the Royal India Air Force, see 'Secret War Department History – Expansion of the Armed Forces in India', p66, L/R/5/273, OIOC

[18] 'Secret War Department History – The Defence of India, 6 May 1944', pp35-6, L/R/5/274, OIOC

[19] 'War Department History – Modernisation and Mechanisation of the Armed Forces of India (September 1939 to February 1944)', pp65-66, L/R/5/275, OIOC

[20] In March 1942, the Ministry of War Transport and the Admiralty instructed their representatives in Calcutta to reduce the tonnage proceeding north of Vizagapatnam to the 'absolute minimum'. On 6 April 1942 all sailings from Calcutta were discontinued. Note on shipping losses in the Bay of Bengal, c1942, L/WS/1/1287, OIOC

[21] 'History of the War Transport Department, July 1942 to October 1945' (New Delhi: 1946) p50, L/R/5/297, OIOC

[22] Memorandum on steps taken to facilitate and expedite the execution of increased demand for public works for the duration of the war, no date, 'War History of the Department of Works, Mines and Power', L/R/5/298, OIOC

[23] See, eg, recollections of G. M. Ray, Indian Civil Service, p6, MSS EUR F. 180/23, OIOC

[24] 'Reports on the "grievances" which were subject of the [Congress] Working Committee's resolution of 10 July 1942', c1942, L/PJ/8/596, OIOC

[25] 'Report on the Revenue Administration of the United Provinces for the year ended 30th September 1942' (Allahabad: 1944) pp2-3, V/24/2445, OIOC

[26] Secret express letter from R. Tottenham, Additional Secretary, Government of India [hereafter 'GOI'] to the Chief Secretaries, Governments of Assam, Bengal and Bihar, 5 June 1942, HPF (I) 4/4/42, NAI. See also File Number G-31 on refugees and evacuees, 1942, All India Congress Committee Collections, Nehru Memorial Museum and Library, New Delhi

[27] The decision to avoid the implementation of a Soviet-style 'scorched earth' policy was taken due to a variety of practical reasons: the enormity of the threatened areas; the lack of skilled and reliable personnel for supervising a comprehensive policy of denying resources to the enemy; the realisation that any large-scale measures could not be kept 'entirely secret' from the civilian population; and a fear that it would create 'millions' of refugees in eastern India (a situation that the provincial governments were not equipped to handle). Secret telegram from the Defence Department, GOI, to L. Amery, Secretary of State for India, Government of Britain, 31 March 1942, L/WS/1/1242, OIOC

[28] P. D. Martyn, an officer serving in Bengal, mentions how he was responsible for 'the movement to North Bengal of elephants from the Chittagong area and the sinking, or trans-shipment, out of the danger area, of much of the riverine craft of the Sunderbans.' Recollections of P. D. Martyn, Indian Civil Service, p21, MSS EUR F. 180/13, OIOC

[29] Confidential memorandum from J. W. Houlton, Secretary, Government of Bihar, to the Headquarters, Eastern Army Command, 17 May 1942, War Series File [hereafter 'WSF'] 50(iv)/1942, Bihar State Archives, Patna [hereafter 'BSA']. Grain was also removed from the coastal delta region of East Bengal. See recollections of W. H. J. Christie, Indian Civil Service, p14, MSS EUR F. 180/96, OIOC

[30] See recollections of F. O. Bell, Indian Civil Service, MSS EUR F. 180/8, OIOC, and the memoirs of O. M. Martin, Indian Civil Service, p233, Martin papers, Centre of South Asian Studies Archives, Cambridge

[31] Extract from the Bengal [Chief Secretary's] fortnightly report for the second half of May 1942, HPF (I) 164/42, NAI

[32] Letter of J. A. Herbert, Governor, Bengal, to Lord Linlithgow, the Viceroy of India, 7 July 1942, MSS EUR F. 125/42, OIOC

[33] 'Secret War Department History – Expansion of the Armed Forces in India', p42, L/R/5/273, OIOC

[34] African troops were considered invaluable for operations in Burma. Most secret telegram from A. Wavell, Commander-in-Chief, India, to the War Office, Government of Britain, 9 December 1942, L/WS/1/963, OIOC

35 The American Army was divided into three separate groups in India, each with its own headquarters and Commanding General. Most secret note titled 'Order of Battle: US Forces in India', enclosure to most secret letter from R. C. McCay, India Office, Government of Britain, 8 July 1942, L/WS/1/1292, OIOC

36 Confidential note by General Staff Branch (Intelligence Section), General Headquarters (India), on the training of Chinese troops by Americans in India, c1943, L/WS/1/1292, OIOC. By mid-1944 the number of Chinese troops in India had almost doubled to 102,000, a figure that remained largely constant till the end of the war. See secret telegram from the War Department, GOI, to the Secretary of State for India, Government of Britain, 24 May 1944, L/WS/1/1362, OIOC

37 Recollections of A. H. Kemp, Indian Civil Service, p13, MSS EUR F. 180/18, OIOC

38 Like scores of other district officials, H. F. G. Burbridge recalled how his district was stricken with troubles after he was forced to comply with 'endless demands' for buildings, land and vehicles by the military authorities. Note entitled 'The war in Assam 1939-45, from the view of a district police officer', no date, by H. F. G. Burbridge, Indian Police Service, MSS EUR F. 161/32, OIOC. Cases of troops entering markets and assaulting shopkeepers remained quite common. See, eg, Police File 196/43, NAI

39 See 'List of cases involving assaults [by American personnel] upon Indian civilians between 1 January 1944 and 30 August 1944', Police File 7/9/45, NAI. For the provisions of the Allied Forces (United States of America) Ordinance of 1942 see M/3/1197, OIOC

40 Departmental note, Home Department, GOI, c1945, Police File 7/11/45, NAI

41 'Monthly Intelligence Summary (GHQ and AHQ)', No 4, 4 April 1942 (Simla: 1942), p1, L/WS/1/317, OIOC

42 S. Bhattacharya, 'Wartime policies of state censorship and the civilian population: Eastern India, 1939-45', in South Asia Research 17 (2) (1997)

43 Recollections of G. P. Woodford, Indian Civil Service, p18, MSS EUR F. 180/16, OIOC

44 See, eg, Chief Secretary's Fortnightly Report, Bihar, for the second half of January 1942, HPF (I) 18/1/42, NAI

45 Most secret Weekly Intelligence Summary (India Internal), 12 February 1943, L/WS/1/1433, OIOC

46 See, eg, letter from J. A. Herbert, Governor, Bengal, to Lord Linlithgow, Viceroy of India, 19 June 1942, MSS EUR F. 125/42, OIOC

47 See A. K. Sen, Poverty and Famines: An essay on Entitlement and Deprivation (Oxford: 1981) and P. R. Greenough, Prosperity and Misery in Modern Bengal: The Famine of 1943-44 (New York: 1982)

48 Secret telegram from A. Wavell, Viceroy of India, to L. Amery, Secretary of State for India, Government of Britain, 4 March 1944, L/I/1/1110, OIOC

49 See, eg, Hindustan Times, 5 July 1943, and an article entitled 'A Second and Worse Famine Threatens Bengal: Causes of Last Catastrophe Coming Again' in Amrita Bazar Patrika, 18 January 1944. Officials bemoaned the tone of such pieces and a report complained that 'one calculator ha[d] killed a quarter of Bengal's population'. Secret telegram from the External Affairs Department, GOI, to L. Amery, Secretary of State for India, Government of Britain, L/WS/1/1247, Part 1, OIOC

50 See, eg, extracts from secret reports by District Magistrates in Bihar, Eastern United Provinces and Assam, c1943, WSF 63/iii/43, BSA. In fact, communist participation in these agitations annoyed colonial officials greatly, as the Communist Party of India was supposed to be supportive of the war effort after the Government of India legalised the organisation in order to encourage its 'People's War' line. Thus, such hostile communist activism provided the context in which local alliances ignored the 'alliance' between the Government of India and the CPI politburo, and cracked down on the local party units. For further details see S. Bhattacharya, 'The Colonial State and the Communist Party of India, 1942-45: A Reappraisal', in South Asia Research 15 (1) (1995)

51 S. Bhattacharya and B. Zachariah, '"A Great Destiny": The British Colonial State and the advertisement of post-war reconstruction in India, 1942-45', in South Asia Research 19 (1) (1999)

52 Gregory represented those who believed that the wartime administration could only cater to the needs of a few select groups. Gregory collection, ff14-15, MSS EUR D. 1163/6, OIOC

53 In October 1943 the official agencies were providing relief to almost a million destitutes in Calcutta and the districts. However, a vast majority of the aid recipients were based in the city: 840,000 were based in Calcutta, while only 118,000 were located in Mofussils. Letter from T. Rutherford,

Governor, Bengal, to A. Wavell, Viceroy of India, 2 October 1943, R/3/2/49, File 2, Coll IX, OIOC. During the famine, military and civil reports from eastern India constantly identified the 'small village cultivator', the 'village labourer' and the 'labouring classes in towns' as being the worst hit by the crisis. Most secret Weekly Intelligence Summary (India Internal), 27 August 1943, L/WS/1/1433, OIOC

54 See, eg, extracts from secret reports by District Magistrates in Bihar, Eastern United Provinces and Assam, c1943, WSF 63/iii/43, BSA

55 For some excellent new research on the topic, see Srimanjari, 'Denial, Dissent and Hunger: Wartime Bengal, 1942-44', in B. Pati (ed), *Turbulent Times: India, 1940-44* (Mumbai: 1998)

56 'The Famine Enquiry Commission Final Report' (Madras: 1945) V/26/830/11, OIOC

57 Military intelligence was reporting an increase in 'hunger marches' inspired by Communist and Congress groups active in rural areas by mid-1943. These demonstrations were, of course, directed at a number of targets – the local administration, landed notables and grain merchants – all of whom were blamed for the food crisis. In keeping with the scale of the shortages and starvation, many of these demonstrations were aggressive in tone, and one military report declared that the 'character of some is reported as such that only a very little propaganda will be required to incite the demonstrators to acts of violence'. Most secret Weekly Intelligence Summary (India Internal), 4 June 1943, L/WS/1/1433, OIOC. See also extracts from secret reports by District Magistrates in Bihar, Eastern United Provinces and Assam, c1943, WSF 63/iii/43, BSA

58 See secret report on the activities of the various relief committees and legal aid committees organised by Congressmen, c1943, HPF (I) 4/1/1944, NAI. See also correspondence between the district magistracy and local military commands, Bihar, United Provinces and Bengal, c1943, WSF 65/1(1)/43, BSA

59 Discussions of the 'effectiveness' of this strategy would frequently crop up in the discussion between the civilian and military authorities. See, eg, correspondence between the district magistracy and local military commands, Bihar, United Provinces and Bengal, c1943, WSF 65/1(1)/43, BSA

60 The growing tensions between the Government of India and the industrialists was revealed in the official complaints that industries with 'Congress leanings' preferred to pay out 'excessive bonuses' and dearness allowances to staff rather than pay money to the authorities in the form of Excess Profits Tax. See Appendix A in Most secret Weekly Intelligence Summary (India Internal), 25 July 1943, L/WS/1/1433, OIOC. The military contractors' ability to draw away labour, not least from the mines, with promises of higher pay proved to be a major irritant between state and industry. Indeed, the popularity of employment in military projects led ultimately to a crisis in coal production. Most secret Weekly Intelligence Summary (India Internal), 24 December 1943, L/WS/1/1433, OIOC. Initially the Government of India sought to counter the labour problem by reversing an earlier decision about not letting women work in the mines. This, however, proved insufficient to tackle the coal production crisis, the reversal of which was declared to be a 'war priority' by the end of 1943 as the shortages had begun to affect industrial output in other strategic industries like the jute and cotton mills. Yet this did not signal an improvement in relations between the industrialists and the authorities, as the other official tactics to make workers more 'productive and stable', that is the initiation of welfare and health schemes, were made the responsibility of the industrialists. The Government of India's role was limited essentially to supervising the implementation of these special projects, and, in the context of difficult strategic situations, central government officials proved extremely eager taskmasters. This caused the mine-owners to express much unhappiness at such 'official arm-twisting'. See, eg, extracts from secret reports by District Magistrates in Bihar, Eastern United Provinces and Assam, c1943, WSF 63/iii/43, BSA

61 See S. Bhattacharya, '*A Necessary Weapon of War*': *State Policies towards Propaganda and Information in Eastern India, 1939-45* (Richmond: 2000)

62 S. Bhattacharya, 'An Official Policy that went Awry: The British Colonial State's Propaganda Campaign Against the Indian National Congress', in Pati, B. (ed), *Issues in Modern Indian History: For Sumit Sarkar* (Mumbai: 2000)

63 See, eg, transcript of taped interview with V. Sahay, Indian Civil Service, MSS EUR T. 122, OIOC. The Government of India's Home Department was forced to control the anti-Congress propaganda onslaught throughout 1942-44 as the Information and Broadcasting Department, which was dominated by Indian civil servants, was reported to be uncomfortable with it. Departmental

memorandum by S. J. L. Olver, Under Secretary, Home Department, GOI, 21 December 1943, KW to HPF (I) 48/4/44, NAI

[64] See, eg, letter from R. P. N. Sahi, Deputy Commissioner, Chota Nagpur Division, Government of Bihar, to E. O. Lee, Commissioner, Chota Nagpur Division, Government of Bihar, 15 May 1942, WSF 17 (xix)/1942, BSA

[65] For instance, an intelligence report (dated 3 September 1942) from Bihar mentioned how a military party that had gone to the village Dariagawan to arrest Jagannath Singh, the local Congress leader who also happened to be the son of the local rural magnate, found that he had escaped the previous night, since the news of his forthcoming capture had been 'leaked out' by officials. Similar incidents were also reported from the villages of Chatran and Barnia. Secret (daily) intelligence summaries, 27 August 1942 to 8 September 1942, Stanton-Ife papers, Centre of South Asian Studies Archives, Cambridge

[66] Most secret Army in India Morale Report for August-September 1943, L/WS/2/72, OIOC. See also Secret Weekly Intelligence Summary (India Internal), 6 October 1944, L/WS/1/1433, OIOC

[67] For a more detailed discussion of this topic, see S. Bhattacharya, 'British Military Information Management Techniques and the South Asian Soldier: Eastern India during the Second World War', in *Modern Asian Studies* 34 (2) (2000). The question of the disloyalty of the South Asian soldier began to worry senior British officials after the violent 'Quit India' movement of August-September 1942. One communication declared, for instance, that 'it is fair to say that as the war draws to its close … the general IS [internal security] position is bound to deteriorate, as interested parties begin to prepare (as they are now preparing) for the eventual struggle for power. In addition, the severe inflationary process that is going on in the country today is bound to cause serious trouble.' Extract from Most secret letter from GHQ (India) to the Military Secretary, India Office, Government of Britain, 20 December 1942, L/WS/1/1337, OIOC

Chapter 13

Australia

Joan Beaumont

Despite the fact that Australia is essentially a non-militaristic society, the two World Wars played a central role in shaping the national sense of identity in the 20th century. Paradoxically, given the global scale of the conflict of 1939-45, it is the First World War that has dominated Australian memory of war, at least at the collective level. The Gallipoli campaign of 1915 spawned the legend of Anzac, a celebration of the supposedly unique qualities of the Australian soldier that has proved remarkably resilient in the past 85 years. Even as Australian society has changed over the century from being almost exclusively Anglo-Celtic in its ethnic composition to being broadly multicultural – and as its rigorously masculine culture has been challenged by feminism – the mythology of the First World War has continued to act as a powerful national focus. So much so that knowledge of the Second World War remains relatively limited among Australia's younger population. Almost every schoolchild knows of Gallipoli (thanks, in part, to Peter Weir's film of that name, which continues to socialise younger Australians into the mythology of Anzac); but few can name even one campaign of the Second World War. Whereas for Britain the Second World War produced epics such as the Battle of Britain and Dunkirk to rival the Somme and Passchendaele in national memory, for Australia possibly only Kokoda, in 1942, plays this role. The campaigns of the Mediterranean and the Middle East in 1940-42, the loss of the 6th Division in Greece and Crete in April-May 1941, the role of Australians in Bomber Command's offensive over Germany, and the New Guinea campaigns of 1943-44 are all, in contrast, relatively unknown. If there is any mythology from 1939-45 to rival that of 1914-18 it is the story of the prisoners of the Japanese, one third of whom died in captivity – though even this has itself been interpreted within the broader framework of Anzac.

There are many reasons for the relative eclipsing of the Second World War experience in Australian national memory. Some of these concern the nature of Australia's role in the two World Wars; the fact, for example, that Australia's role in the war of 1939-45 was, in some troubling sense, anticlimactic. In the Pacific War of 1941-45 – the war that 'mattered' in the sense that Australia's national sovereignty was at stake in a way that it was not in Europe and the Middle East – Australia found herself progressively marginalised in the offensive against Japan by her dominant ally, the United States. The island campaigns of 1945 – to which Australian troops were consigned, as General Douglas MacArthur monopolised the glory for his own troops in the spearhead campaigns of the South West Pacific

– were acknowledged, even at the time, to be 'unnecessary wars'. They were strategically irrelevant to the outcome of the war. They stood in stark contrast to Australia's role in the final campaigns of 1918, which, even if we set aside the more chauvinistic claims of some Australian historians, can be reasonably claimed to have been instrumental in Allied victory.

A second reason for the dominance of the First World War in Australian memory has been the Anzac legend itself. Though the growth of the legend was not entirely spontaneous – it was appropriated by successive Australian governments as a means of encouraging recruitment for the 1st Australian Imperial Force (AIF) and, later, of imposing an orthodoxy of imperial 'loyalty' – it struck such a responsive chord in a nation traumatised by grief that by 1939 it effortlessly subsumed the experience of the 2nd AIF. On the declaration of war in 1939 the Australian press typically represented the relationship between the 1st and 2nd AIFs as that of father and son. In many instances this was literally so, but there was a clear sense in which the model of what it meant to be an Australian soldier was fixed, and simply being transmitted from one generation to another. So far as we can tell from such oral history as has been conducted with Second World War veterans[1], many saw Anzac as the ideal to which they had to aspire. Nothing in the war of 1939-45 had the power to challenge this model. On the contrary, even Australians who suffered defeat and were taken prisoner often strove in their memoirs to demonstrate that the celebrated qualities of the Anzac – resourcefulness, laconic humour and, above all, mateship – had typified the experience of captivity. In the post-1945 years, therefore, the dates on which Australians have commemorated their losses in war have remained the anniversaries of the First World War: Armistice Day and, pre-eminently, the day of the landing at Gallipoli, 25 April. Anzac Day has in many ways become the national day, which may eventually supplant Australia Day, 26 January; the latter, given that it celebrates the beginning of white settlement, is now tainted with the oppression of the indigenous population.

There is a third reason for the dominance of the First World War: the scars it left, physically and socially, on Australia were greater. In 1914 the population of Australia was fewer than 5 million. Of these some 330,000 men served overseas in the next four years; more than 58,000 died, while over 156,000 were gassed, wounded or taken prisoner of war. In 1939-45, in contrast, the death toll was lower; from a population of over 7 million, some 27,000 servicemen were killed and wounded.[2] The mobilisation of civilian Australian society in the Second World War was much greater, as we shall see, but the number of families bereaved and anguished as a result of the conflict was simply fewer. Moreover, the more developed state of medical technology meant that the Second World War did not leave such an appalling and ever-present legacy of wounds and injuries as had the earlier conflict. The memoirs of George Johnston, *My Brother Jack*[3], opens with an unforgettable description of life in an inter-war Australian home that was a refuge for men whose faces and bodies had been ruined on the Western Front. The only comparable presence in post-1945 society was that of the prisoners of war of the Japanese, for whom the physical and emotional legacy of captivity was to prove profound. But their disabilities were in some senses less immediately visible and it took some decades before the impact of captivity on former prisoners' morbidity and life expectancy was fully recognised and acknowledged by reluctant public authorities.[4]

The scars of the First World War were also greater in the sense of the damage done to the Australian social and political fabric. It has now become a cliché among Australian historians to speak of Australia as a 'divided society' in the First World War, but it is indisputable that the experience of war in 1914-18 tore Australian society apart. The Second World War, in contrast, had a more generally unifying impact. Again it is a cliché, but the slogan used to mobilise community effort during the Second World War – 'All in!' – did have some resonance with reality.[5]

From the earliest days of war, in 1914-15, there were signs of a corrosive division of opinion within Australian society.[6] On the one hand, there was an enormous enthusiasm for the war effort, represented by the rush of volunteers for the 1st AIF in the first months of war, and the almost universal endorsement of the Government decision to commit Australian naval and land forces to the war in Europe. In fact, the constitutional relationship with the United Kingdom in 1914 meant that Australia had no choice but to follow Britain into war, but this position was not the subject of any criticism in the public domain. The vast majority of Australians felt their personal and national identity and security to be so extricably linked to that of Britain that there was no opposition to the war. Indeed, for all the tension that did develop in Australia in 1914-18, the anti-war movement – as opposed to the anti-conscription movement – never represented more than a very small minority.

On the other hand, there was a much larger group of Australians who quickly formed the conclusion that the burden of the war was being inequitably shared. This resentment, which was fuelled by disrupted employment and trade, rising prices, and the failure of the Government to address these concerns effectively, generated an atmosphere of ever more strident confrontation and distrust between the trade union movement and governments, at both the federal and state levels. In many ways this confrontation was class-based, though there was an overlay of sectarianism, attributable to the fact that many of Australia's Irish-Catholics (who made up 21 per cent of the population) were working class.

Industrial disputation was not unique to the First World War; the refusal of the trade unions to surrender their right to strike in the Second World War was a source of constant frustration to the conservative press, as it was to Australia's American ally.[7] But what made the situation in 1915-16 so explosive was the nature of military recruitment for the war. The 1st AIF was entirely a volunteer force. At first this was because of the constraints of the Defence Act of 1903, which limited the permanent Army to administrative, instructional and support staff and artillery and engineer forces, and which prevented the deployment of the regular military forces outside Australia and its territories. Hence the military tradition in Australia before 1914 – and indeed until the post-1945 era – was one of volunteer citizen soldiery.

In the first 18 months of the First World War this voluntary tradition proved adequate to meet the demands of the war. A decline in enlistments in early 1915 was redressed when the news of Gallipoli generated a mood of nationalistic euphoria, and major recruitment campaigns were conducted in mid-1915. But by mid-1916, with the commitment of the AIF to the Western Front, its expansion from two to five divisions, and the much greater casualty rates that resulted from the Somme campaign, the Government of W. H. (Billy) Hughes concluded that voluntarism was inadequate and that compulsion would be necessary. In 45 days on the Somme, the AIF's casualties were only 2,000 fewer than those from the whole Gallipoli campaign of nearly eight months.

There is not the space here to describe in full the battles associated with the issue of conscription in 1916-17. Suffice to say that Hughes, the leader of a Labour Government, concluded that a policy as radical as conscription for overseas service – a policy that he himself had opposed earlier in his political life – could not be introduced without the legitimisation of a popular vote. On two occasions, in October 1916 and December 1917, he sought unsuccessfully to gain this mandate through referenda. The campaigns preceding each of these referenda released a torrent of vitriol, mutual accusation and recrimination that has never been rivalled in Australian political history. Even the profoundly divisive national debate about Australia's commitment to Vietnam in the 1960s could not match 1916-17 for raw bitterness. The conscription referendum of 1916 split the Labour Party – Hughes staying in power at the head of a reconstituted government incorporating his former non-Labour opponents – and polarised Australian society into politically, and often physically, warring camps. In Queensland the violence was such that the State teetered on the edge of civil anarchy.[8] Both here and elsewhere in Australia the situation was inflamed by the heavy-handedness of the Hughes Government, which used the wartime censorship and civil liberties powers unashamedly for domestic political advantage. The Irish nationalist cause also added fuel to the sectarian divide after the Easter uprising of 1916. But beyond all this was the sheer hysteria of a society traumatised by grief. The two conscription referenda were held against the backdrop of the Somme and Third Ypres campaigns on the Western Front, the latter campaign causing 38,000 Australian casualties. The conscription referenda were therefore almost 'ballots of death'. A vote in favour of conscription, as the 'no' case argued, was a vote quite possibly to send a man to his death.

The impact of the conscription debates at the level of the local community in Australia was profound. Whereas in other societies, such as Britain and New Zealand, the option of personal choice was removed by the Government decision to impose conscription in 1916, in Australia, whether a man chose to serve or not remained a bitterly contentious issue throughout war. The moral coercion of 'shirkers' – the singling out of men for stigmatising and shame – was a corrosive element in interpersonal relations. Imagine, for example, a society in which one of the leading women's organisations, the National Council of Women, passed a resolution to the effect that women and girls should refuse to play tennis, golf or any kind of sport with eligible men; where food contained slips of cooked paper instructing the eater that he ought to enlist; and where a 'one woman, one recruit' movement arose in mid-1917. The organiser of this movement 'urged the female sex [to] fix upon one man, even if he were the poor, unfortunate but eligible tradesman who knocked at the back door each day … [one woman] converted her baker after two years of unremitting effort. The baker had finally enlisted and rushed back from his rounds to tell her.'[9]

It is symptomatic of the value attached to voluntary recruitment in Australia that many Australian memorials to the war of 1914-18 list everyone who served overseas, not just the dead. The very fact that a man volunteered made him one of a revered elite.

The contrast with the Second World War is dramatic. In September 1939 the response to the outbreak of war at the government and personal level was muted in comparison to 1914. With the Government of Robert Menzies prevaricating as to whether it should dispatch Australian troops overseas while Japan's intentions in the region remained uncertain, there was no great rush to volunteer for service in the armed forces. The Government evoked the power that the Defence Act had always granted it, to conscript men of military age for home defence, but it made no effort to compel men to serve in what became known as the 2nd AIF. Australian forces in the North African, Mediterranean, Greek, Crete and Syrian campaigns were all volunteers, as were the men of the 8th Division who were captured by the Japanese in Malaya, Singapore, the Dutch East Indies and the islands to Australia's north in early 1942.

The issue of conscription for overseas service only became a serious concern later that year. The Australian militia that was conscripted for home defence was able to be deployed in Papua and north-eastern New Guinea in 1942 – the Defence Act's prohibition on conscripted forces being sent overseas notwithstanding – since Papua was an Australian-administered colony, and New Guinea a League of Nations mandate for which Australia had gained responsibility in the 1919 peace settlement. But the militia could not be used in the immediately adjacent territory of west New Guinea (now Irian Jaya); nor in other Pacific islands of obvious strategic importance to Australia in 1942. This anomalous situation was increasingly criticised within the United States – why should US GIs be sent where Australian conscripts would not go? – and MacArthur, ever the politically conscious animal, pressured Prime Minister John Curtin to amend Australian policy. In January 1943, therefore, the Australian Government introduced legislation that allowed the conscripted militia to be used in 'such other territories of the South West Pacific Area as the Governor-General proclaims as being territories associated with the defence of Australia'. This, in effect, included the Solomon Islands, Timor, most of Java, the Celebes and Borneo.

As it happened, no Australian conscripted troops were ever sent to these areas, but what is remarkable is that Curtin introduced this policy when he had himself been jailed in the First World War for opposing conscription for overseas service; and that the opposition within Australia to the change in policy was so limited. There were still within the Australian Labour Party some passionate opponents to conscription for overseas service, but more widely the issue that had divided Australia 25 years earlier provoked little controversy.

Why? Much of the answer must lie in the different perceptions of the national security issues at stake. Although in the First World War it was assumed, justifiably, that a British defeat would have exposed Australia to German economic and political pressure, nothing in 1914-18 matched the threat to national sovereignty of 1942. The Japanese, in fact, decided against invading Australia, as US intelligence knew by mid-1942; but the Australian public was not informed of this. Moreover, Australian towns were bombed by the Japanese in 1942, and although the civilian casualties were slight compared to those of Britain, Germany, Japan and the Soviet Union, they were of sufficient scale to generate a sense of panic in Australia.[10] Air raid precautions were anxiously undertaken, even in such unlikely target areas as the Otway Mountains of southern Victoria! In such a climate there was a moral logic to conscription that it had never possessed in 1914-18 when the war was so remote from Australian territory.

Beyond this, however, the issue of conscription was simply better managed by the Australian Government in 1943 than in 1916-17. Curtin's leadership style was a profound contrast to that of Hughes[11] and his success in introducing conscription can only be understood within the context of the Labour Government's wider achievement of creating a consensus about the need for national wartime mobilisation. In the first two years of the war Australian domestic politics had been marked by in-fighting within the governing United Australia Party and the often lack-lustre leadership of Menzies. There was a lack of urgency in economic mobilisation for the war effort. Restrictions on domestic consumption, for example petrol rationing, were resented and became political footballs in the general election of 1940.[12] The crisis of the Japanese victories of early 1942 gave Curtin, in power only since October 1941, the opportunity to impose a regime of governmental and bureaucratic controls over domestic life and employment that would have been unacceptable in the climate of 1940 – and unthinkable in 1917.

It is unwise to overstrain the image of 'consensus' in Australia's response to the Second World War. There were major elements of resistance to, and non-compliance with, many of the wartime regulations after 1942, and the level of industrial disputes remained high. In late 1944 Australian politics took time out from the war to fight a bitter referendum – not about conscription but about the powers of the federal government.[13] This campaign gave the resurrected Menzies a chance to scaremonger effectively about the threat of domestic socialism, a tactic he continued to exploit with even greater effect after the war. In the early years of the war there was also harassment and internment of radical movements and civilians of enemy extraction, as there had been in 1914-18.[14] But for all this, Australian society was far less fractured by the experience of war in 1939-45 than it had been in 1914-18.

Hence, it could also be more extensively mobilised for war production. The Curtin Government introduced manpower policies regulating the mobility of civilian labour, took on responsibility for the construction of projects in Australia and overseas, prohibited the manufacture of unnecessary commodities, issued identity cards for civilians, brought in tightened restrictions on consumption, trade and traffic, and sharply increased taxation. Some of these changes persisted after the war, with the result that the Second World War witnessed a more permanent shift in government powers from the States to the Federal government than did the First World War.

With mobilisation came far greater social changes than had occurred in the First

World War, particularly in the lives of women and the Australian indigenous populations. In the First World War women had played a major (and often overlooked) role in the war effort through voluntary organisations. They raised a prodigious amount of funds – some £14 million when the total Government expenditure on defence in the war years was about £188.5 million. These were used to provide comforts for the troops overseas and to support the families of active, wounded and killed servicemen at home. In many ways this voluntary effort provided an essential social support system, while the Government's efforts at developing a welfare system were embryonic. The Red Cross, of which women were the mainstay, also sent 400,000 parcels from Australia to Germany, Holland, Austria and Switzerland, the equivalent to more than 14,000 parcels for each month that Australian troops were engaged on the Western Front.[15] Through this voluntary work middle-class women had the opportunity to develop new public profiles and new organisational skills, skills that almost certainly were translated into a surge of new activism in women's organisations in the 1920s and 1930s.

Yet all this wartime activity was carried on within traditional models of women's public activism. Even those women who were active in the campaigns for and against conscription generally worked behind the scenes rather than in the public domain. The more conservative women prided themselves on what their counterparts in the United States and Britain called their 'patriotic feminism'[16] – that is, a new claim on citizenship earned through women's war work – but whatever the changes in women's own perceptions of their status, in general it is agreed that in Australia the war reinforced rather than challenged the gendered status of women. As the feminist historian Carmel Shute showed in the two major articles that she published in 1975-76[17], official propaganda during the war defined masculinity in terms of heroism and violent aggression, while femininity was constructed as synonymous with motherhood, maternity and sacrifice. Men were the warriors and defenders of the home front and family; women were the nurturers, the bearers of the children of the race, the ones whose primary function in war was to be stoical and wait at home.[18] The only women who were permitted to break with this model and to serve overseas with the forces were those in a traditional feminine nurturing occupation, nursing.[19]

Within Australia itself there was little change in women's employment patterns. In contrast to the situation in Britain, where formal employment of women rose by almost a million, in Australia the increase in the number of women in paid employment was only in the order of 2,000-3,000.[20] Women's wages did not improve relative to men's. The lack of any major munitions industry in Australia and the failure of the war to effect structural changes in the Australian economy were the major reasons for this lack of change, but it was also attributable to the fact that the war reinforced deeply entrenched prejudices about gender roles.

The Second World War brought far more obvious changes in women's employment and status, though these did not occur until at least two years into the war.[21] Initially, everyone assumed that the war would be a repeat of that of 1914-18 in terms of gender roles. The voluntary associations, knitting circles and fund-raising activities were all re-activated as women slipped into the well-worn roles of voluntary activity. However, by mid-1941, with the commitment of almost four

AIF divisions overseas and the mobilisation of the civilian militia for home defence, the demands on manpower were such that even the Conservative Government of Menzies had to introduce the kind of innovations that had been resisted in the war of 1914-18. Auxiliary women's forces for all three services were created in 1941, though women were assigned to support roles rather than combat.

In the civilian economy women were progressively mobilised to fill the gaps left in industry by the recruitment of men. Most dramatic was the shift of women out of domestic service into better-paid industrial work; the percentage of the female workforce employed as domestic servants dropped from 18 per cent in 1939 to 4 per cent in 1943, and never recovered its former levels after the war.[22] Significant also was the entry into the paid workforce of many middle-class women, freed by the wartime emergency from the former taboos on their working outside the home. Women also crossed what had previously been a deeply entrenched sexual division of labour in Australia, which classified some occupations as 'male' and some as 'female'. By 1942 women were employed as tram conductors, agricultural labourers, and clerical workers in the public service, banks and offices.

In some ways these changes were not as dramatic as many commentators at the time believed them to be. The increase in the proportion of all women working, for example, was only in the order of 5 per cent: in 1939 almost 644,000 women, most of them working class, were already in paid employment; by 1944, the peak year, the number was 855,000. This was about one-quarter of the total workforce and about one in three women between 15 and 65 years of age.[23] Moreover, the patriarchal structure of many industries remained unchallenged, with overseers and managers continuing to be mostly male. And women's wages remained at lower levels than did men's, even in key industries such as munitions, where women were awarded 90 per cent of the male wage. While trade unions reluctantly concluded that women should earn the same wages as men, for fear that if they did not they would undercut male wages after the war, the employers' concern to ensure a ready supply of cheap labour generally won the day.

Nonetheless, for all these qualifications the Second World War did see major changes in the patterns of women's employment in Australia, although many were constructed at the time as being temporary – an expedient resorted to 'for the duration' of the war only. Indeed, there was a decline in women's employment immediately after the war, but this decline was itself temporary, and within a few years of 1945 women's employment levels had returned to their wartime peak. Admittedly, women were forced out of the men's jobs they had been occupying during the war, but within traditional female occupations, such as textiles and food production, the wartime shortage of labour had resulted in increased wages.[24] Moreover, if we move beyond the quantifiable measures of wage levels and employment statistics, it is clear that the war was the agent of attitudinal change. In particular, if we seek to understand what the feminist historian Marilyn Lake has called women's subjectivities, or women's sense of their own experience, then the impact of the Second World War on Australian women can be seen to be more complex.

The demand for women in the labour force generated a whole range of social issues not encountered in the First World War, issues that provoked an ongoing debate about the role of women within society and the family: for example, how to provide child care when married women were returning to paid work, and how to avoid absenteeism resulting from the conflicting demands of family and work. Given that many of the changes in women's employment were viewed by the Government and employers as temporary, solutions to these problems were only partial. In the absence of adequate formal childcare arrangements provided by a range of philanthropic and educational organisations, many women were forced to rely on family, friends and neighbours to care for their children. With the end of the war many childcare centres actually closed.

The handling of the issue of childcare was indicative of the broad unease, sometimes verging on a 'moral panic', on the part of public authorities during the Second World War about the changing roles and expectations of women. While women were desperately needed in the workforce, their absence from the home was seen as deeply threatening to family structures and the social order. The traditional family was already eroded by the absence of the male from many households (for Australians, military service overseas often meant years away from home); many children were, in effect, fatherless. Marriage rates were high, but so too were divorce rates, particularly after the war. Though only a few Australian children were subjected to the forcible change of home that British children experienced during the Blitz, there was still a troubling disturbance and anxiety associated with their childhood. Increased rates of juvenile crime were seized upon, by anxious social commentators, as 'evidence' of the disintegration of the family under wartime pressures.

All of these concerns, however, were eclipsed by the anxieties engendered by the presence, from 1941, of up to a million US servicemen in Australia.[25] The changing economic roles for women, the separation of married couples for prolonged periods, and the wartime compulsion to live for the day were enough in themselves to generate some panic about the possibilities of a new sexual licence; but whereas in the First World War Australian troops were posted overseas and took their leave in France or Britain, from 1941 there was a ready source of foreign soldiers within Australia to test the morals of Australian women. The fact that these men were better paid, better dressed, more sophisticated in courtship and glamorised by their national association with Hollywood only added to the danger. So too did the fact that a proportion of the US troops were black, an uncomfortable challenge to the racial exclusiveness of the White Australia Policy that since 1901 had formally barred almost any but Anglo-Celtic immigrants. After initially trying, without success, to oppose the stationing of black US forces in Australia, the authorities responded by confining blacks to remote rural locations, or to designated 'coloured' zones in urban areas. Racially differentiated patterns of recreation and leisure were also enforced, with black American troops having minimal access to white Australian women, and being allocated black Aboriginal prostitutes.[26]

Many of the relationships formed between Australian women and US GIs posed no threat to the traditional moral or racial order – some 7,000 war brides travelled to the US at the end of the war – but the public authorities became fixated with the threat posed to public health by promiscuity, especially on the part of women who were inexperienced sexually. In an effort to control the rising incidence of sexually transmitted diseases the Government at federal and state levels responded with regulations including enforced examination and detention of those suspected to be infected. Although this was in some senses a necessary response to a health issue that had the capacity to debilitate an army, the manner in which the policies were enforced – and the public debate surrounding them – indicated that a far broader issue of controlling women's sexuality was at stake.[27]

The impact of all these changes on women's sense of themselves has been the subject of considerable study by feminist historians. It is commonly argued that the wartime changes in employment and social behaviour bestowed on Australian women a new sense of independence, autonomy and self-reliance, the qualities that British women supposedly gained from new employment opportunities during the First World War. But it is also commonly assumed that these gains for women's self-perception were eroded after the war when Australian women retreated into the home and resumed the traditional role of wife and mother. An alternative view is that the wartime experience had a lasting impact on women's perceptions of what it meant to be feminine; that it contributed to an ongoing process of the reconceptualisation of femininity that revolved around sexuality, sexual attractiveness and youthfulness. To quote Marilyn Lake:

> '…the stationing of foreign troops in a country has the effect of sexualising the local female population. Just as Australian servicemen rendered Egyptian, French and English women during World War I as the objects of their desire, so too did the Americans based in Australian cities during World War II … women's interest in and right to sexual pleasure has been established.'[28]

Another interpretation of the impact of the Americans on Australian society is that it accelerated a shift in gender relationships from courtship to dating. The 19th-century style of courtship took place in the home, with an established set of rituals and social expectations; dating, in contrast, involved the woman accompanying the man into the outside world with her company bought, as a commodity, by a man willing to invest money in the social experience. With their considerable disposable income – their much-noted capacity to shower girls with chocolates, flowers, nylons, and so on – the American GIs accelerated the adoption of these dating practices, and the 'commodification of romance and sexual relations', within Australia society.[29]

On balance, then, the Second World War had a more wide-ranging impact on the position and attitudes of Australian women than did the First World War, for all the individual trauma and grief that the latter conflict involved. The same can be said of the impact of the two wars on the status of Australia's indigenous population. In the First World War about 400-500 Aborigines enlisted in the armed forces, but despite their military service neither they nor their fellow Aborigines were entitled to citizenship rights after the war. They lacked the vote in State and Federal elections, and a regime of deeply paternalistic and racially prejudicial laws controlled almost every aspect of Aboriginal life in the inter-war years. The Second World War, in contrast, saw many more Aborigines and Torres Strait Islanders drawn into the war effort. As was the case with women, in the initial years of the war Aborigines were generally excluded from military service, other than in the Royal Australian Air Force, the authorities fearing that racially mixed units would be militarily ineffective. But as the demands of the war for manpower became inexorable, with the emergence of the Japanese threat in mid-1941, Aborigines began to be admitted to the armed forces in larger numbers. Moreover, as the vast northern and western regions of Australia became exposed to enemy attack, Aborigines in the Northern Territory, Queensland and Western Australia were formed into irregular forces, which were intended to capitalise on their bushcraft skills and knowledge of the environment for purposes of reconnaissance, surveillance and, should invasion occur, guerrilla war. Some 3,000 Aborigines were also recruited into labour units, which performed a wide variety of roles in developing infrastructure in the isolated north and centre of Australia.

These varied roles provided Aborigines with unprecedented opportunities for economic and self advancement. In the military, for example, where over 3,000 Aborigines and Torres Strait Islanders served, many became non-commissioned officers, confounding the pre-war prejudice that blacks were incapable of commanding whites. Others acquired new skills, new knowledge of the world and greater economic independence. How much this translated into a new sense of indigenous empowerment and self-confidence is difficult to quantify. As with women, many of the wartime opportunities closed after the war when the armed forces re-introduced their bans on the service of non-Europeans. Under public pressure the Australian Army removed the bar on voluntary enlistment of non-Europeans in 1949, but the Defence Act continued to bar the conscription of Aborigines and Islanders until 1992. Moreover, although those Aborigines and Torres Strait Islanders who served in the Second World War were allowed to vote in Federal and State elections, full citizenship rights were not granted to Aborigines until the 1960s. Nonetheless, the war did leave some legacy in changed attitudes and expectations on the part of both whites and Aborigines, while the experience of better accommodation and higher living standards in the labour units 'had a considerable but indirect influence on the future of Aboriginal relations' in central Australia, to quote the leading scholar of 'black diggers'.[30]

From this short overview of changes in Australia during the Second World War it is clear that this conflict had a greater impact on the Australian people than the First World War, if one uses participation of previously marginalised groups in the war effort as a measure of social change.[31] But the limitations of this as a means of assessing the full impact of war on a nation's psyche are also clear. This chapter opened by exploring the paradox in Australian memory of war: namely, that the Second World War, which globally was by far the greater conflict, has been assigned a secondary place in Australian national memory. The changes that occurred in women's and indigenous people's status during the Second World War only reinforce this paradox for contemporary historians, for whom ideologically many of these changes were overdue.

The conclusion is inescapable that recent developments in the study of war, which emphasise the importance of exploring the interface between history and memory, are critical if we are to fully comprehend the legacy of war. Obviously, professional history, written with access to archival records and informed by increasingly sophisticated theoretical paradigms, provides an essential interpretation of events, but it does not necessarily accord with the way in which communities, at the individual and collective level, recall the experience of war. In Australia, for example, for many years the dominant public memory of the experience of captivity under the Japanese was the Burma-Thailand railway. Other memories of captivity – in Manchuria, Borneo, Japan, Ambon, Hainan and New Britain – were preserved largely within the communities affected by them, such as the battalion associations. At some point, and as part of a process that we do not fully understand, such local memories are translated into national memories, commemorated in public ritual and incorporated into the national iconography of war. In Australia the process whereby the many diverse memories of the Second World War have been thus translated into the national domain remains incomplete. The First World War, for which this translation occurred with dramatic speed, continues, for the moment, to dominate the public memory of war.

Recommended reading

Beaumont, Joan (ed), *Australia's War, 1918-18* (Sydney: Allen & Unwin, 1995)
  Australia's War, 1939-45 (Sydney: Allen & Unwin, 1996)
Damousi, Joy and Lake, Marilyn (eds), *Gender and War: Australians at War in the Twentieth Century* (Melbourne: Cambridge University Press, 1995)
Darian-Smith, Kate, *On the Home Front: Melbourne in Wartime, 1939-1945* (Melbourne: Oxford University Press, 1990)
McKernan, Michael, *The Australian People and the Great War* (Melbourne: Nelson, 1980)
  All In!: Australia during the Second World War (Melbourne: Nelson, 1983)
Saunders, Kay, *War on the Homefront: State intervention in Queensland, 1938-1948* (St Lucia: University of Queensland Press, 1993)

Notes

[1] See, eg, John Barrett, *We Were There: Australian Soldiers of World War II Tell their Stories* (Ringwood, Victoria: Viking, 1987)
[2] There is, as always, considerable debate about the accuracy of casualty figures. The figures quoted here are taken, for the First World War, from Alan D. Gilbert, John Robertson and Roslyn Russell, 'Computing Military History: A Research Report on the First AIF Project', in *War & Society* 7 (1) (1989), and Jeffrey Grey, *A Military History of Australia* (Melbourne: Cambridge University Press, 1990); and, for the Second World War, from the Australian official history, Gavin Long, *The Six Years War: Australia in the War of 1939-45* (Canberra: Australian War Memorial, 1973) p474
[3] Sydney: Collins, 1964
[4] See Stephen Garton, *The Cost of War: Australian Return* (Melbourne: Oxford University Press, 1996) pp219-27
[5] Michael McKernan uses this as the title of his study of the Second World War: *All In!: Australia during the Second World War* (Melbourne: Nelson, 1983)

[6] For an overview of the domestic political situation, see Joan Beaumont (ed), *Australia's War, 1914-18* (Sydney: Allen & Unwin, 1995) Chap 2

[7] For a brilliant account of this, see Raymond Evans, *Loyalty and Disloyalty: Social Conflict on the Queensland Homefront, 1914-18* (Sydney: Allen & Unwin, 1987)

[8] See Mamie Haig-Muir and Roy Hay, 'The Economy at War', in Joan Beaumont (ed), *Australia's War, 1939-45* (Sydney: Allen & Unwin, 1996) pp122-3

[9] L. L. Robson, *The First AIF: A Study of its Recruitment* (Melbourne: Melbourne University Press, 1982, 1st ed 1970) p144

[10] At least 243 civilians were killed in the bombing raid on Darwin in the Northern Territory on 19 February 1942. The best account is to be found in Alan Powell, *The Shadow's Edge: Australia's Northern War* (Melbourne, Melbourne University Press, 1988)

[11] For Hughes see L. F. Fitzhardinge, *The Little Digger: William Morris Hughes: A Political Biography* Vol II (Sydney: Angus & Robertson, 1979); for David Day Curtin see *John Curtin: a Life* (Sydney: HarperCollins, 1999)

[12] Although Menzies wished to follow the British model of a national government, the Australian Labour Party rejected this. Australia therefore continued to hold Federal elections, in 1940 and 1943. For a short account of Australian politics during the war, see David Lee, 'Politics and Government', in Jean Beaumont (ed), *Australia's War, 1939-45*, op cit. The fullest account is the two-volume official history by Paul Hasluck, *The Government and the People* (Canberra: Australian War Memorial, 1952, 1970)

[13] See David Lee, 'Politics and Government', op cit, pp98-9

[14] For the First World War, see Gerhard Fischer, *Enemy Aliens: Internment and the Homefront Experience in Australia, 1914-1920* (St Lucia: University of Queensland Press, 1989); for the Second World War, see Margaret Bevege, *Behind Barbed Wire: Internment in Australia during World War II* (St Lucia: University of Queensland Press, 1993)

[15] Joan Beaumont, 'Whatever Happened to Patriotic Women?', in *Australian Historical Studies* (forthcoming 2001). This article provides an overview of the Australian historiography of women during the First World War.

[16] See John F. Hutchinson, *Champions of Charity: War and the Rise of the Red Cross* (Boulder, CO: Westview Press, 1996) p352, for the use of this term

[17] 'Heroines and Heroes: Sexual mythology in Australia, 1914-18', in *Hecate* 1 (1) (1975), reprinted in Joy Damousi and Marilyn Lake (eds), *Gender and War: Australians at War in the Twentieth Century* (Melbourne: Cambridge University Press, 1995) pp23-42; and '"Blood Votes" and the "Bestial Boche": A case Study in Propaganda', in *Hecate* 11 (2) (1976) pp6-22

[18] The chapter on the patriotic funds in the official history of the Australian home front, by Ernest Scott (Sydney: Angus & Robertson, 1936) begins with the quotation from Milton's sonnet that 'they also serve who only stand and wait'.

[19] See Jan Bassett, *Guns and Brooches* (Melbourne: Oxford University Press, 1992) and '"Ready to Serve": Australian women and the Great War', in *Journal of the Australian War Memorial* 2 (1983) pp8-16

[20] Jennifer Crew, 'Women's Wages in Britain and Australia during the First World War', in *Labour History* 57 (1989) p31

[21] For a good overview of women during the Second World War, on which the following paragraphs draw, see Kate Darian-Smith, 'War and Australian Society', in Joan Beaumont (ed), *Australia's War 1939-45*, op cit, pp54ff. Darian-Smith's more detailed study of Melbourne is *On the Home Front: Melbourne in Wartime, 1939-1945* (Melbourne: Oxford University Press, 1990). For women in voluntary work see Michael McKernan's *All In!*, op cit

[22] Robin Kramar, 'Female Employment during the Second World War', Third Women and Labour Conference Paper (Adelaide: 1982) p451

[23] Richard White, 'War and Australian Society', in M. McKernan and M. Browne (eds), *Australia: Two Centuries of War and Peace* (Canberra: Australian War Memorial and Allen & Unwin, 1988) pp410-2

[24] See Lynn Beaton, 'The importance of women's paid labour: Women at work in World War II', in Margaret Bevege et al (eds), *Worth her Salt: Women at Work in Australia* (Sydney: Hale & Iremonger, 1982) pp84-98

25 There are several studies on the impact of the US servicemen on Australian society: E. Daniel Potts and Annette Potts, *Yanks Down Under 1941-1945: The American Impact on Australia* (Melbourne: Oxford University Press, 1985); Anthony J. Barker, *Fleeting Attraction: A social history of American servicemen in Western Australia during the Second World War* (Nedlands: University of Western Australia Press, 1996); and Rosemary Campbell, *Heroes and Lovers: A question of national identity* (Sydney: Allen & Unwin, 1989)

26 See Kay Saunders and Helen Taylor, 'The Management of Segregation: Black American Servicemen in Queensland, 1941-45', in Kay Saunders, *War on the Homefront: State Intervention in Queensland 1938-1948* (St Lucia: University of Queensland Press, 1993) pp59-80

27 See Kay Saunders and Helen Taylor, 'The Policing of Morals: State Intervention into Public Health 1937-45' in Kay Saunders, op cit, pp81-105

28 'Female Desires: The meaning of World War II', in Damousi and Lake, op cit, pp67, 75. Lake's important article was originally published in *Australian Historical Studies* in October 1990.

29 See Lyn Finch, 'Consuming Passions: Romance and consumerism during World War II', in Damousi and Lake, op cit, pp105-16

30 Robert A. Hall, in Peter Dennis, et al, *The Oxford Companion to Australian Military History* (Melbourne: Oxford University Press, 1995). Hall's *The Black Diggers: Aborigines and Torres Strait Islanders in the Second World War* (Sydney: Allen & Unwin, 1989) is the standard text on the subject.

31 This was one of the key measurements in Arthur Marwick's now rather dated model of war and social change – *War and Social Change in the Twentieth Century: A Comparative Study of Britain, France, Germany and Russia and the United States* (London: Macmillan, 1974)

Chapter 14

New Zealand: 'From the uttermost ends of the earth'

Christopher Pugsley

'Leaving home finally was a dreadful experience. Dad was okay but Mum and the girls were very upset. Mum had a brother in the 1914-1918 war, and although he returned, she did not expect me to be so lucky. She was distraught and very fearful for my safety. The mail-coach driver tooted the horn. "Get on the bloody bus and go, lad," said Dad. "Mum will recover."'[1]

New Zealand had gone enthusiastically to war in August 1914. Britain had declared war on its behalf, with New Zealand having no say in the matter nor wanting one. Throughout the country young men flocked to the drill-halls to enlist, worried that the war would be over before the ships from New Zealand could reach Europe. There was no such enthusiasm on 3 September 1939 when, at the same time as the United Kingdom, New Zealand declared war on Germany (9.30pm New Zealand standard time, 11am. British summer time). The war clouds that had been gathering over Europe, fuelled by Hitler's ambition, had at last arrived. New Zealanders listened anxiously to the radio broadcasts. On 6 September the Prime Minister, Michael Joseph Savage, spoke to the nation:

'Both with gratitude for the past, and with confidence in the future, we range ourselves without fear beside Britain. Where she goes, we go. Where she stands, we stand.'[2]

This was a decision made by a small country of one and a half million people, loyal to the Empire, but also by a Labour Government, many of whom had been imprisoned for their opposition to conscription in the First World War. New Zealand's declaration of war was an admission that its Government's peace and disarmament initiatives through the League of Nations had failed, and it began the Second World War with no coherent view on how New Zealand's contribution should be made.[3]

There was a sombre realisation of war's realities from an older generation who had seen their men so joyously march to war 25 years before, and had lived with the shattered dreams of those who returned. Shorty Lovegrove's mother's anguish was mirrored in many New Zealand homes:

'When it did happen there was almost a sense of deja vu. The Germans were still the enemy; again it seemed it would all take four years… Those marches through the streets of Wellington of those early Echelons as they headed to embark on the troop ships, the faces different, the uniforms a bit more modern, but strangely familiar to those photos we had grown up with of the figures crowding the rails, clambering over the lifeboats, smiling, waving to the more sombre figures left behind on the wharves.'[4]

As this same woman also wrote, 'War was the process by which the abnormal became the normal.'[5] Only the young thought of it in terms of 1914; bitter experience would show that this war would commit everything that New Zealand had, and more. Pat Cozens was 14 in 1939, living in Taihape, where her father was a drover:

'I was standing in the kitchen and we had the radio on and they broadcast Chamberlain's announcement. I remember it distinctly. Well, we knew it was coming but it was still a bit of a shock. I can remember sitting in the class room and looking around at the boys, and thinking [that] none of them will see action in this war because everybody thought it would be over so quickly. But they did. Over half the class ended up in the forces. Taihape lost a lot of good people in that war.'[6]

At first there was a sense of unreality; the Territorial Force was called up and the coastal artillery batteries manned. Fred Mosley was one of the gunners manning the 6-inch guns at North Head at the entrance to Auckland's Waitemata Harbour. 'All parades and turnouts were controlled by bugle call and there were complaints made by nearby residents that the bugles were used too often at night and early morning.'[7] While thousands of Territorials were 'called up for the duration', a major construction programme began to build barracks for troop accommodation. Coastal batteries were improved and added to, coast watch stations established, and wire entanglements erected on likely landing beaches.

Public Safety Emergency regulations were passed introducing petrol rationing and censorship regulations. This was followed by price stabilisation measures aimed at forestalling the rapid increase in prices and cost of living that had been a feature of the First World War. The Labour Government moved swiftly to suppress anti-war propaganda, and prominent anti-war campaigners such as the Methodist minister Ormond Burton, a decorated soldier in the First World War, were arrested each time they tried to speak in public. Burton was first arrested outside Parliament Buildings the day after war was declared. He found himself in Mount Crawford Prison overlooking the entrance to Wellington Harbour, on the first term of what would total two years and eight months in jail during the war, 'with the ships coming in and out at your very feet… When the Second Echelon went out I gave them a general salute with my shovel – it was so like the movement when the transports commenced to steam out of Mudros Harbour to the blue waters of the Aegean, and towards the slopes of Chunuk Bair gleaming yellow in the sunlight of a quarter of a century ago.' An old soldier, who now fought for peace as vigorously as he fought for his country on Gallipoli and the Western Front, was still moved by the 'the spectacle of brave youth moving out to battle'.[8]

New Zealand was far less prepared in 1939 than it had been in 1914. In August 1914 New Zealand was in a position where under the capable direction of Major-General Sir Alexander Godley, GOC New Zealand Forces, mobilisation plans had been drawn up and a Territorial Force was in being specifically aimed at producing an expeditionary force for overseas service. On 7 August 1914, on receipt of an already anticipated request from London, a force of 1,413 all ranks was mobilised to seize German Samoa. Drawn from Auckland and Wellington units of the Territorial Force, it paraded fully equipped on the Wellington wharves ready to embark on 11 August. It was a further three days before transports and escorts were ready, but on 29 August this force rowed ashore at Apia and seized German Samoa, the first German territory to surrender to the Allies in the First World War.

Mobilisation of the Main Body of the New Zealand Expeditionary Force (NZEF) was equally swift, and the Force was complete by 28 August. Its dispatch was delayed because of New Zealand's reluctance for it to sail without sufficient escorts, given the threat of the German Pacific Squadron. It finally sailed on 16 October 1914, numbering 8,574 men and 3,818 horses. It consisted of an infantry brigade of four battalions, a mounted rifles brigade of three regiments plus an independent mounted rifles regiment, a field artillery brigade of three four-gun batteries together with signal, medical and supply units, 10 million rounds of small arms ammunition, and 6,000 rounds of artillery ammunition.[9] It was the anticipated climax to the most intense and sustained period of defence preparation in the dominion's history. With the exception of the mobilisation of the British Expeditionary Force to France, New Zealand was the only member of the Empire to mobilise her forces on the basis of pre-war planning, with both Australia and Canada making ad hoc arrangements on the outbreak of war, and also considerably increasing the size of their contributions.[10]

During the First World War the Dominion of New Zealand was a junior partner of the Empire. The size of the force that its population of 1 million could raise for war would never be of sufficient magnitude to have a decisive influence on world events. It could not influence the strategy nor the tactics employed, but it could ensure that once committed its expeditionary force would be maintained at full strength, and reinforced with trained and equipped soldiers for the duration of the war. By November 1918 New Zealand had sent 100,660 men to war and 550 nurses, at a cost of 59,483 casualties, including 18,166 dead – 2,721 in Gallipoli, 12,483 in France and Belgium, and 381 in Sinai and Palestine. It had required 20,000 men a year to maintain a 20,000-strong expeditionary force on active service. Both the New Zealand Division in France and the New Zealand Mounted Rifle Brigade in Palestine were maintained at full strength, and at the Armistice the 17,434-strong division had 10,000 trained reinforcements available to it in France and the United Kingdom, and a further 10,000 under training in New Zealand. It was the only Empire force that could guarantee to maintain its contribution at full strength into 1920. This was no small achievement, but one achieved at enormous cost. Eight per cent of the men of military age (19-42) were dead, and in 1920 34,571 people were receiving war pensions and allowances.[11]

It was very different in 1939. The Territorial Forces had been run down to almost nothing, and there was a total lack of modern arms and equipment. Belated steps were taken from 1935 onwards to increase defence preparedness. The Royal New Zealand Air Force was established as a separate service in 1936, and an increase in defence expenditure was mostly directed to this service. An interdepartmental Organisation for National Security was established, with its secretariat based in the Prime Minister's Office. This was to play a crucial role in harnessing the national effort in the years ahead; however, Savage's Government was reluctant to contemplate the contribution of an expeditionary force, and given Labour's vehement opposition in 1916-17, even more reluctant to consider one based on conscription.[12]

On 6 September 1939 Cabinet authorised the mobilisation of a Special Force of 6,600 volunteers between the ages of 21 and 35 for active service within and beyond New Zealand, but were still undecided on how it should be employed. Within a week 12,000 men had volunteered, and the Government, gripping both the urgency of the situation and the public mood, offered a complete infantry division to be raised in three echelons for service overseas.[13] New Zealand had raised 17 battalions of infantry in the First World War, which had taken their designation from the province that raised them, Auckland, Wellington, Canterbury and Otago. Now the battalions were numbered, starting with number 18 for drafts raised from Auckland, Wellington forming 19 Battalion, and Canterbury and Otago combining to produce 20 Battalion, and so on.[14]

In the First World War the single focus of the country's war effort had been on the NZEF with its naval and air effort, which, while important in the public mind, was relatively insignificant in terms of numbers. That would change in the Second World War; it would be 12 months before the first elements of the Second New Zealand Expeditionary Force (2NZEF) were committed to operations as part of O'Connor's Western Desert offensive in November 1940. Before that it was the exploits of the Navy and New Zealand personnel serving with the RAF that provided proof of New Zealanders playing their part.

In 1914 New Zealand's naval forces consisted of the single training cruiser, HMS *Philomel*, its first naval unit; this escorted the Advance Party to Samoa, and, after escorting the Main Body convoy to Albany in Western Australia, was then deployed on operations in the Red Sea for the next two years. In February 1916 Able Seaman Knowles RNR became the first New Zealander belonging to a New Zealand ship to be killed on active service when a landing party was fired on by Turkish soldiers near Alexandretta. *Philomel* returned to New Zealand in March 1917, and was paid off to finish her career as a training depot and floating accommodation hulk alongside the wharf at Devonport Naval Base.[15] In addition hundreds of New Zealand seamen crewed merchant ships and served as naval reservists. Some, like Lieutenant Commanders William Sanders VC DSO and Frank Worsley DSO and Bar, earned distinction as commanders of Q-ships operating against German U-boats.[16]

The most visible contribution was HMS *New Zealand*, the 'Indefatigable' Class battlecruiser that New Zealand presented to the Royal Navy in 1912. During the war only three of its officer complement were New Zealanders, but she symbolised the country's willing contribution to the Empire. Regarded by its crew as a lucky ship, because of the Maori face painted on its central top, she was the only capital ship to take part in all three major clashes between the British and German battle fleets in the North Sea, and was also present at the surrender of the German High Seas Fleet. Although only 10 years old, but already obsolete, she was dismantled and scrapped at Rosyth under the provisions of the Washington Naval Treaty of 1922.[17]

In 1939 the New Zealand Division of the Royal Navy, renamed the Royal New Zealand Navy in 1941, possessed two modern 6-inch 'Leander' Class cruisers, HMS *Achilles* and *Leander*, and the minesweeping trawler *Wakakura*. Even before the outbreak of war, *Achilles* was released to its war station in the Atlantic, and *Leander* sailed for the cable station on Fanning Island with a platoon-size garrison, drawn from a 593-strong Regular Force.[18] *Achilles* won fame in the defeat of the *Admiral Graf Spee* off the River Plate on 13 December 1939, and, as the official historian recorded:

'When the alarm rattlers sounded in the Achilles, a signalman with a flag under his arm ran aft shouting: "Make way for the Digger Flag!" and proceeded to hoist a New Zealand ensign to the mainmast head to the accompaniment of loud cheers from the 4-inch gun crews. For the first time a New Zealand cruiser was about to engage the enemy.'[19]

Achilles's role in the River Plate victory also galvanised public opinion, being the first tangible proof that New Zealand was playing its part. It also brought home the inevitable cost. Patricia Connew was 19 when the war broke out, and was living with her parents in Te Awamutu. Two of her six brothers were in the Navy, one on *Achilles* being severely wounded at the River Plate. 'After my brother ... was wounded we got this terrible telegram. Each day you'd see the postman come down the road and you'd think, "Oh, another telegram today."'[20] Another telegram arrived when Connew's fiancé, who sailed in the First Echelon, was killed. For her and many New Zealand families, these were the start of the 'distressing days'.[21] *Leander* was equally successful, in the Red Sea and Indian Ocean, sinking the Italian auxiliary cruiser *Ramb I* in February 1941 and seizing the Vichy-French motor vessel *Charles L D* the following month, before returning to New Zealand in September 1941.

Control of New Zealand merchant shipping was taken over by the Government on the outbreak of war, and for the defence of home waters three trawlers were fitted out as minesweepers, and small craft were used for port duties. The fast passenger liner *Monowai* was requisitioned and fitted out as an armed merchant cruiser, and six merchant ships were armed with a single 4-inch gun. The German merchant raiders *Orion* and *Komet* brought the war to New Zealand waters in 1940, laying mines and attacking shipping, which led to the loss of the *Niagara*, *Turakina* and *Rangitane*. Always the forgotten heroes, merchant seamen on New Zealand-registered ships numbered 2,990 in 1940, and by 1945 110 were known to have died and 123 interned.

Until the outbreak of war in the Pacific, New Zealand's primary role was providing manpower to the Royal Navy. Naval personnel were enlisted into the Royal Navy Volunteer Reserve (NZ), later the RNZVR. On the outbreak of war with Japan, part-time volunteers were employed on coastal patrols in the NZ Auxiliary Patrol Service, and, as the demands for manpower increased, the Women's Royal New Zealand Naval Service – 'Wrens' – was formed for home service in 1942, and reached a maximum strength of 512. Some 7,000 New Zealanders served with the Royal Navy during the Second World War, on every type of craft from battleship to midget submarine, and in every ocean. New Zealand naval strength peaked at 10,635 in September 1944, 4,901 of whom were serving in the Royal Navy. More than 1,000 New Zealanders also joined the Fleet Air Arm of the Royal Navy, particularly when the growing number of surplus pilots from 1944 onwards left little prospect of flying with the RAF; New Zealanders made up 10 per cent of Fleet Air Arm officers.[22]

In 1914 New Zealand had one trained military pilot, Lieutenant Wallace Burn of the New Zealand Staff Corps, who became New Zealand's contribution to the Australian 'Half Flight' that served in Mesopotamia. Burn died in 1915 when the plane in which he was observer force-landed while returning from a reconnaissance mission over Basra, and he and the pilot were attacked and killed by Arabs. By 1918 some 1,000 New Zealanders had served in either the Royal Flying Corps, Royal Naval Air Service or the RAF, after its formation on 1 April 1918; at least 70 were killed and some 17 became prisoners. In addition, 203 pilots graduated from two private flying schools set up in New Zealand under contract to the British Government to provide pilot training, only 68 of whom arrived in time to see action. This wartime contribution included men such as Arthur 'Mary' Coningham and Keith Park, who both remained in the RAF and became Air Marshal and Air Chief Marshal respectively in the Second World War.[23]

New Zealand played a much greater part in the air war during the Second World War. Initially the role of the RNZAF was to provide trained aircrew to the RAF under the Empire Air Training Scheme; its own operations were limited to coastal surveillance, and reconnaissance with obsolete aircraft. In all, 880 pilots were to be trained in New Zealand, and in addition partly trained personnel (520 pilots, 546 observers and 936 air gunners) were sent to Canada to complete their training before posting to the RAF. By 1941 these quotas had been exceeded, with New Zealand providing 1,480 fully trained and 850 partly trained pilots a year. This was part of a Commonwealth contribution that allowed the RAF to expand its first-line combat strength from 332 squadrons in September 1942 to 635 squadrons by the end of 1944.

As part of the pre-war expansion of the RNZAF, New Zealand had ordered 30 twin-engine Wellington bombers; the first six, together with their New Zealand crews, were training in England when war was declared. These became the basis of No 75 (New Zealand) Squadron RAF, the first of seven designated New Zealand squadrons in the RAF. There were already a large number of New Zealanders in the RAF, with Flying Officer E. J. 'Cobber' Kain becoming the first British air ace of the war, with 14 aircraft to his credit, before being killed in an aircraft crash in June 1940. Four New Zealanders commanded fighter squadrons during the Battle of Britain, and 95 fought as fighter pilots, with Hurricane and Spitfire pilots such as

Des Scott, Al Deere, Johnny Checketts and others capturing public attention. However, New Zealand was equally well-represented in both Bomber and Coastal Commands. The casualty figures reflect New Zealand's contribution. In October 1944 New Zealanders with the RAF peaked at 6,127 out of a total of 10,950 New Zealanders who are known to have served with the RAF during the war. Of these, 3,285 were killed, at least 138 seriously wounded, and 568 became prisoners of war.[24] The battle of attrition fought in the skies over Europe, which saw 30 per cent killed of all New Zealanders who served with the RAF, was New Zealand's equivalent of the Somme and Passchendaele during the Second World War. As one New Zealand Mosquito fighter bomber pilot reflected, 'We had four years away from home growing up from callow youths to seasoned old men, seeing death in all its guises.'[25]

However, as in the First World War the major effort facing New Zealand, in the first months of the war, was in raising 2NZEF. It was achieved by voluntary enlistments, with a total of 60,000 enlisting in the services in the first nine months of the war. Egypt was decided upon as the logical training base, and, as in 1914, Peter Fraser, acting Prime Minister for the terminally ill Savage, refused to let the New Zealand convoy sail until, over the protests of the Admiralty, he got an increase in the size of the naval escort. Japan, whose black-hulled cruiser *Ibuki* had escorted the Main Body convoy in 1914, was now a potential foe. New Zealand's contribution of an expeditionary force was confirmed only when Britain reassured New Zealand that Japan was unlikely to direct its attentions southwards in the immediate future, and if the unlikely did happen, Britain's 'duty to our kith and kin would prevail' over all other obligations.[26] The three Echelons, totalling almost 20,000 men, lacking equipment and only partially trained, sailed in January, May and August 1940.

It was a small group of regular officers and warrant officers in their 40s who bore the brunt of resurrecting this military force for overseas service. Balding citizen soldiers, who had reputations as sound platoon and company commanders in the First World War, found themselves leading hastily raised untrained battalions. Unlike 1914, there was no obvious choice to command 2NZEF; Major-General John Duigan, the GOC New Zealand Forces, was close to retirement and did not have the confidence of his Government or his subordinates. In November 1939, after careful deliberation and consultation, Fraser accepted Major-General Bernard Freyberg's offer to command 2NZEF.

A New Zealander who had won legendary fame with the British forces in the First World War, Freyberg, like Godley before him, proved the ideal choice to command the NZEF, but, unlike Godley, he would combine the appointments of GOC 2NZEF with that of GOC New Zealand Division for most of the war.[27] Also, unlike Godley, Freyberg proved an adept tactician who, despite the bitter aftertaste of the failures on Greece and Crete, won the grudging admiration and respect of his men, and the trust of Fraser, who, after the death of his predecessor, became Prime Minister on 1 April 1940. After discussions with Godley in Britain, Freyberg flew to New Zealand via Australia where he consulted with Australian military authorities on command relationships. In New Zealand he had further discussions with Sir Andrew Russell, who commanded the New Zealand Division throughout its existence from 1916 to 1919. With this background Freyberg and Fraser drew up guidelines in the form of a 'Charter' on the relationship to exist between 2NZEF and its Government.[28]

Both Freyberg and Fraser understood that 2NZEF was the national army of New Zealand, and were determined that it had to be recognised as such; it was not to be absorbed and dispersed into the mass of the British Army. To achieve this, Freyberg had to walk the fine line between being a loyal subordinate to his British superior commanders and also meeting his responsibilities as an agent of the Government of New Zealand. It was a relationship that was tested in defeat on Greece and Crete in 1941, and again in adversity during the worst of the Libyan and Egyptian campaign of 1941-42.[29] He had to educate Middle East Command that 2NZEF was 'the Expeditionary Force of a Sovereign State, a partner in the British Commonwealth of Nations ... an ally, and a very close one it is true, but we are not part of the British Army... All major decisions, such as the employment of the force, are made by the New Zealand War Cabinet, and the force only comes under the command of an Allied Commander in Chief for operational purposes.'[30] This relationship would be tested again under the Allied command structure during the Italian Campaign.

This was very different from the relationship that existed in the First World War. Even during 1917, the worst year in New Zealand's experience on the Western Front, there was little or no questioning on New Zealand's part concerning how its expeditionary force was to be used. Strategic employment was an Imperial matter and tactical employment a matter for the theatre commander. However, the fate of New Zealanders overseas reflected back on the political fortunes of the Government at home. Both wars saw the establishment of uneasy wartime national governments. In 1914, William Massey's Reform Party had a narrow majority over its Liberal and Labour opponents. Neither of the two major parties, Reform or Liberal, under its respective leaders, Massey and Sir Joseph Ward, was anxious to combine into a national government, but was forced into an alliance by public opinion and media pressure. The small Labour Party remained determinedly outside the arrangement. Ward became Minister of Finance with a powerful voice in the conduct of government. Known as the 'Siamese twins', Massey and Ward jointly attended the Imperial Conferences in 1917 and 1918, and both also insisted on being New Zealand's representatives at the Versailles Peace Conference. In 1939 the Labour Government was in a much more powerful position and governed alone. In 1942 Fraser invited the Leader of the National Party opposition and two other senior members to be part of the War Cabinet, but the arrangement broke down after only three months. Under Fraser's capable and often inspired leadership, Labour won the 1943 election, and continued in office until 1949.[31]

During the First World War the Minister of Defence, James Allen, was acting Prime Minister during the absence of the 'Siamese twins', and was the driving force and master of detail in Massey's national wartime administration.[32] He was the architect of the Military Service Act of 1916, which introduced perhaps the most effective system of conscription employed by any country during the war. Allen was also an effective foil in imposing brakes on Massey's enthusiasm for offering additional manpower resources to the War Office, over and above what the country could sustain.[33]

Allen had an uneasy relationship with Godley; he respected Godley's undoubted administrative strengths, but was less certain of his willingness to subordinate his personal ambitions to the needs of the NZEF.[34] Balanced against this, from 1916 onwards, was the undoubted ability of the GOC New Zealand Division, Major-General Sir Andrew Russell, who, with Godley's concurrence, corresponded with Allen and provided a detailed and honest commentary on the strengths and weaknesses of his New Zealanders.[35] Russell, like Allen, abhorred waste and considered the division's trained manpower his most important asset. He was also a masterly tactician who, even within the restricted scope of a divisional commander on the Western Front, achieved a surprising degree of latitude in his operational planning, particularly at Messines in June 1917, again during the German March 1918 offensive, and in the final 100 days of 1918.[36] He was Freyberg's equal in this regard, but unlike him was not shackled by a lack of reinforcement manpower, which crippled Freyberg's employment of his division during critical stages of the Italian Campaign.[37]

Pre-1914 mobilisation planning assumed a joint Australasian divisional force on the basis of two-thirds Australian, one-third New Zealand.[38] This became the foundation of the Australian and New Zealand Army Corps (ANZAC) of 1914, of which the hybrid New Zealand and Australian Division formed a part. This grew into the two Anzac corps, numbering five Australian divisions and the single New Zealand division, that fought on the Western Front in 1916-17. It was always a second-best option with Australia battling for its own Australian Corps, which was finally achieved in late 1917. Only in Sinai and Palestine was the word 'Anzac' a working reality, in the shape of the Anzac Mounted Division, made up of the New Zealand Mounted Rifles Brigade and brigades of the Australian Light Horse.[39]

On the Western Front I Anzac Corps under Lieutenant-General Sir William Birdwood was always the de facto Australian Corps. Godley's II Anzac Corps, consisting throughout 1917 of Major-General John Monash's 3rd Australian Division and Russell's New Zealand Division, was more like a typical British Army corps picking up divisions, both British and Australian, for operations and detaching them once completed. Mythologised at Gallipoli, 'Anzac' was an important symbol for both Australian and New Zealand servicemen to aspire to, and served as a powerful motivating force throughout the Second World War. Clarence Moss, a machine-gunner in 27 (Machine Gun) Battalion, expressed this, on 25 April 1940, his first Anzac Day in Egypt: 'Have read and reread [sic] of the Anzacs but never thought that one day I would be one myself. Let's hope I and everyone else measures up to their standard.'[40] However, in 1939 Freyberg was lukewarm on an Anzac corps grouping, believing, as did Fraser, that New Zealand had outgrown such a need. Both considered that such a buffer would only dilute the New Zealand Division's identity, and weaken Freyberg's line of communication with his higher command.[41] An Anzac Corps came briefly into existence during the Greek campaign of 1941, but it did not survive the evacuation.[42] Later attempts to revive an Anzac Corps foundered when Japan entered the war.

Split by the diversion of the Second Echelon to the United Kingdom after the fall of France, it took 18 months before Freyberg eventually assembled his division in Egypt. With Europe overrun and Italian forces in Libya threatening Egypt, keeping it together was a constant battle. When Italy entered the war, Freyberg had to strike a balance between essential training and meeting urgent manpower requests from O'Connor's Western Desert Force. He provided signals and transport and reluctantly allowed members of his Divisional Cavalry and 27 (Machine Gun) Battalion to be temporarily detached to the Long Range Patrol, later better known as the Long Range Desert Group. They remained temporarily detached until 1943. Freyberg's division was not complete until March 1941 when the Second Echelon joined it in Egypt. Three days later on 6 March 1941 the first elements of the division sailed for Greece.

The Greece and Crete campaigns were New Zealand's equivalent of the ill-fated Gallipoli campaign. However, while initially at least Gallipoli held promise of success and important strategic gains, Greece was a doomed enterprise from the start. As 19-year-old Vincent Salmon recorded, 'We did what we went there for and saw some fighting... Certainly saw plenty of his air force however ... the dive-bombers and fighters gave us a deuce of a time.'[43] The German invasion on 6 April 1941 broke through the weak Greek Army and threatened to outflank 'W' Force, made up of the New Zealand Division, 6 Australian Division and 1 British Armoured Brigade. Under constant air attack from the Luftwaffe, the force withdrew through potentially strong positions that it lacked the resources to defend. Like Gallipoli, enthusiasm and individual enterprise could not compensate for command inexperience and poor staff work. Of the 16,720 New Zealanders who served in Greece, 291 were killed, 599 wounded and 1,614 taken prisoner.

The hasty evacuation from Greece saw two of the Division's three infantry brigades dumped on Crete and involved in its defence under Freyberg's overall command. They numbered some 7,000 of the 35,000 mixed garrison of British, Australian, New Zealand and Greek forces, which lacked all the essentials for an effective defence, such as vehicles, heavy weapons, radios, equipment and, most critically of all, air support. Aided by Ultra intelligence, which provided details of the German air and sea landing plans, Freyberg's defensive plan was sound. However, many of his subordinate commanders were exhausted. Dispirited by the failure on Greece, they lacked Freyberg's confidence. Despite the initial successful repulse of the German parachute and glider landings on 20 May 1941, Lieutenant-Colonel L. W. Andrews VC, commanding 22 Battalion, lost his nerve and withdrew his battalion from Point 107, the vital heights controlling Maleme airfield. This allowed critically needed German reinforcements to be flown in the next day. After an unsuccessful New Zealand counter-attack the fate of the campaign was sealed, and evacuation the inevitable consequence. New Zealand casualties on Crete numbered 671 dead, 967 wounded and 2,180 captured (including 488 wounded), a total of 3,818 out of the 7,702 New Zealanders on the island.

It was the highest proportion of losses suffered by New Zealand in any ground campaign during the Second World War and came closest to mirroring the casualty lists of Gallipoli and the Western Front. Fraser was in Egypt en route to London, and insisted that every effort be made to evacuate the garrison, which was done at great loss in both ships and lives:

'I stated that while the United Kingdom, with its 45 million people, could sustain a heavy loss of men without very disastrous effects, and that even Australia could sustain a large loss much better than New Zealand, it would be a crushing disaster for our country and its war effort if such a large number of men fell into the enemy's hands without every effort being made to rescue them.'[44]

It was the first time that a New Zealand Prime Minister had directly involved himself in tactical decisions concerning the NZEF, but the interests of New Zealand demanded nothing less.

What made Greece and Crete, and indeed the campaigns in North Africa, different for New Zealand from those of the First World War was the high percentage of prisoners of war who featured in the casualty statistics. Fewer than 500 New Zealanders were taken prisoner during the First World War, compared to 7,876 in 2NZEF alone in the Second.[45] Some, like Ray Riddell, were captured a number of times, first on Crete, then in Libya when, in November 1941, 'I was taken prisoner by Rommel at Sidi Aziz with about 800 others and marched into the "Pen" at Bardia where I had to cool my heels for seven weeks before the South Africans released us.'[46] It provided a different dimension for the families at home, with the anguish of the telegram reporting their loved one missing, then weeks or months later the notification of his captivity. Personal effects were returned as if he was dead, and family life revolved around the routine of packing POW Red Cross parcels, and the receipt of a letter about every six months. '[It] was like a perfect stranger writing to a perfect stranger. He had permission to let me know he was in the best of health and doing fine.'[47]

Crete was the graveyard of a number of New Zealand reputations, and shook Fraser's faith in Freyberg. The Prime Minister made clear to his Commander 2NZEF that in future he expected to be reassured before each major operation to which New Zealanders were committed, that adequate resources, particularly in the form of air and tank support, were available. The resources were certainly available in November 1941 when, after a period of rest and retraining, the full-strength New Zealand Division, 20,000 strong and with 2,800 vehicles, took part in 'Operation Crusader', the 8th Army offensive to relieve the besieged port of Tobruk. However, Freyberg grew increasingly unhappy as to how British armoured resources were employed, particularly as it was his infantry that bore the brunt of the fighting to open the corridor into Tobruk, then had to withstand Rommel's counter-attack without adequate tank support. This was some of the hardest fighting involving the Division during the war, at a cost of 982 dead, 1,699 wounded, and 1,939 taken prisoner. After Tobruk's relief the exhausted division was withdrawn to Syria for rest and retraining.

It was during this battle that the New Zealanders heard that Japan had entered the war and that New Zealand itself was threatened. Instead of being at the 'uttermost ends of the earth' from the conflict, New Zealand faced a war on its very doorstep. The Japanese attack on Pearl Harbor brought the United States into the war. In February 1942 the fall of Singapore proved how illusory the 'fortress' was as a bulwark against Japanese ambitions in Asia. Four days later Darwin was bombed. The effect on 2NZEF was immediate; reinforcements dried up as all trained men were retained in New Zealand. Morale was also affected, as there was a general feeling in the Division that it was more important to go back and fight the Japanese in the Pacific. The withdrawal of the first two Australian divisions increased this belief.[48] However, the situation facing the 8th Army in Egypt prevented any immediate return.

In June 1942 Rommel's offensive and advance into Egypt saw the New Zealanders rushed back in action, taking part in a series of savage encounters in defence of Egypt on the Alamein line in the summer of 1942. By the time the line had stabilised in August 1942 the soldiers had lost faith in Army command, hated British armour and held Rommel in high regard. Distrust of British armour and a lack of infantry reinforcements led 2NZEF to withdraw the badly mauled and understrength 4 Brigade and form it into an armoured formation. The New Zealanders played a critical role at Alam Halfa, where the newly appointed 8th Army Commander, Lieutenant-General B. L. Montgomery, stopped Rommel's attempt to break through. Freyberg's Division was his infantry spearhead during the Battle of El Alamein in October 1942, opening a corridor for British armour to pass through. The New Zealanders led the advance on Tripoli, fighting in turn at Sollum, Halfaya Pass, the left hooks at El Agheila and Nofilia, Medinine, and the third left hook at Tebaga Gap. It ended with hard and costly fighting at Enfidaville, before Freyberg took the surrender of the Italian First Army, including the German 90th Light Division, and the fighting in North Africa ended on 13 May 1943. Between November 1941 and May 1943, New Zealand lost 2,755 dead, 5,036 wounded, and 3,622 taken prisoner in North Africa. At the end of the campaign the division was understrength and exhausted. It desperately wanted to go home.

At home in New Zealand it was a distant war. However, all this changed in June 1940. The public certainties of victory, which had been a feature of the First World War, even during the darkest months of 1917 and early 1918, were shattered after the fall of France, and darkened again with the entry of Japan in December 1941. Even more than with the manufactured hatred of the 'bestial Hun' in 1914-18, this Second World War was a crusade against an evil that threatened the survival of the British Empire and of New Zealand's way of life. Any outspoken opposition to the war earned public disapproval, and 'aliens' of German, Italian and Japanese origin, who might be disloyal, were interned for the duration as they had been in the First World War. Appropriately enough it was in May 1940 that 'God Defend New Zealand' was made the national hymn.[49]

At the beginning of the war, volunteer home guard units modelled on the British system were set up to protect 'hearth and home'. The fall of France led to their formal recognition by the Government as a semi-military organisation that would provide pickets and coastal patrols, guard vital points, and co-operate with the Army in the event of an emergency. All privately owned rifles were impressed to equip the Home Guard, and by May 1941 its strength reached 100,000. This was formalised on 30 July 1941 when the Home Guard became an integral part of the military forces. The National Military Reserve, formerly a Territorial Reserve, was also incorporated and mobilised. In response to the deteriorating war situation the Emergency Reserve Corps Regulations were gazetted in August 1940. These linked the Emergency Precautions Scheme (EPS), the Women's War Service Auxiliary (WWSA) and the Home Guard under the National Service Department.

Emergency Precautions Schemes became compulsory for all local authorities, and at the end of six months recruiting they numbered 80,000 people. In each municipality the local mayor became chief warden, and suburbs and towns were divided into blocks and sections led by wardens and sub-wardens, who headed local committees. They were responsible for 'air-raid shelters, anti-gas precautions, lighting controls, evacuation procedures, auxiliary fire brigade, emergency communications, demolition work, water supply and the protection of vital points.'[50] It was a total community effort modelled on the British experience. Slit trenches were dug, air raid shelters built, and air raid drills were carried out on a regular basis. Jenny Jones was a school girl in the small town of Waimate in South Canterbury:

'Every so many months they'd have a big day when everyone was involved in an air raid practice. We all had our part to play. Mother had to go to her first aid station. Pop went off with the Home Guard. My oldest brother had to bike to the corner of Queen Street and Mill Road and pretend he had his buttocks blown off. He had to lie there and wait for the ambulance... I had the glorious task of lighting a bonfire in the section next door to our house which the fire brigade put out. It was an absolute hoot and we had a lot of fun.'[51]

It was more real for adults. An intense effort was made to increase food and raw material production, as well as establish the local production of munitions and other secondary goods whose supply had been cut off by the war. Walter Nash, as Minister of Finance, managed to finance the war without overseas borrowing, which had proved such a crippling cost to New Zealand after the First World War. Price stabilisation measures were introduced to avoid inflation, and war loans and war bonds absorbed the high wages that the population was earning. In this way New Zealand managed to finance war expenditure from current revenue and by borrowing on the domestic market. 'Farm exports were taken over by the Government for bulk sale to the United Kingdom at prices lower than the prevailing world level, but still high. A share of the farmers' earnings was held back in reserve accounts as an anti-inflationary measure.'[52] By judicious financial management 'the increase in the cost of living in New Zealand in wartime was considerably less than with most Allied powers.'[53] New Zealand matched its contribution in manpower overseas with home production, shipping to the United Kingdom 1,800,000 tons of meat, 685,000 tons of butter, and 625,000 tons of cheese. In addition, 5,400,000 bales of wool were collected for shipment to the United Kingdom, much of which remained in storage in New Zealand. When Japan entered the war, New Zealand supplied United States forces in the Central

Pacific, producing 190,000 tons of meat, 23,000 tons of butter, and 137,000 tons of vegetables. In addition, New Zealand industry produced war equipment and munitions to the value of £42 million.

Labour established a national register of all persons over 16 to be directed into industry and other essential work. In January 1941 married men without children were called up for home service, and by July all married men were called up. With over 80,000 men and some 1,000 women conscripted into the services, critical shortages emerged in the labour force. 'Manpowering' became the term to describe industrial conscription whereby both men and women were directed into essential industries, and by March 1944 these employed over 40 per cent of the labour force. Already in late 1941 a Land Corps, later the Women's Land Service, was set up to provide female labour to farms. Pat Cozens left school at 18 in 1942:

'I was going to teachers training college but my father was running the farm ... and the boy he had with him was called up ... so I had to stay at home on the farm. I had to join the land army otherwise I would have been manpowered to a factory in the cities. I got issued with a uniform and working clothes. I had boots, and riding pants, because everything was done on horses in those days. We just worked on the farm. My father and I would have our breakfast in the dark and we'd be out in the paddock with the drill loaded ready to start sowing as soon as we could see where we were going. I often think that he died at 46 because he worked too hard. But it had to be done, because we had a war effort and we were supplying meat and butter to Britain.'[54]

The volunteer work, which had absorbed so much of the women's war effort in the First World War, continued with fundraising, packing parcels for the troops, and the knitting of socks and balaclavas, all carried out under the auspices of the National Patriotic Fund Board. The Women's War Service Auxiliary (WWSA) was set up in 1940 to co-ordinate women's war work through the provision of drivers, cooking, home nursing and first aid. Their hard-fought battle to have the right to wear uniform became an important symbol of the women's war effort. This was followed in 1941 by all three services, in turn, enlisting women, and by 1943 more than 8,000 women were in the forces.

In addition, women were in increasing demand to replace men in essential industry. Already appeals had been made to attract more women into factory work, and in June 1940 labour legislation was suspended to allow women to work night-shifts in industry if satisfactory arrangements could be made to transport them home after their shift. In 1939 there had been 180,000 women in the workforce; by 1943 this had risen to 228,000, with another 8,000 in the armed services. Pay rates also rose from 47 per cent of men's pay in the mid-1930s to 60 per cent in 1945. Estelle Rolfe worked in a bank after leaving school, replacing men who went away to war:

'This was the first time they took women in the banks... I got a notice from the Manpower Board to say I was going to be manpowered ... into essential work… But the bank managed to hang on to me and said I was essential because I had a man's job. Most of my friends went to Watties Canneries… I had such poor pay [£91 a year] that I did work at Watties Canneries on Saturday afternoons. That was the only way you could exist on the bank money.'[55]

The war saw certain occupations such as herd-testing and Auckland women tram conductors receive equal pay. The Public Service Association began a campaign for equal pay for civil servants in 1943 as the percentage of women employed in the Public Service rose from 5 per cent in 1939 to 25 per cent by 1946.[56]

The austerity and unemployment of the depression years gave way to labour shortages and good wages for those who remained at home. In many ways it was a time of freedom and opportunity for single women, but for families it was back to the rationing of scarce resources and making do:

'War was blackouts, power cuts, rationing, shortages, but life had often been austere, and these were not too unusual. There was usually enough to eat; babies hardly used their rations of tea or sugar; if they woke in the night when the power was off, then one could always find a torch or candle. "Appliances" dominated our lives much less in the days when refrigerators and washing-machines, for instance, had hardly appeared on the scene. And as for petrol, who had a car in those days?'[57]

During the First World War the existing Territorial Force structure provided the recruiting framework for the NZEF, and recruits flowed in. By 1915 the Gallipoli losses led to a national register being established for all males between the ages of 17 and 60. The Military Service Act of 1916 established an Expeditionary Force Reserve, which consisted of all males between the ages of 20 and 46. The Act divided the eligible male population into two divisions. The First Division consisted of all single men, including those with dependants; the Second Division was married men, who were placed in priority according to the number of dependants, those with the least being called up first. If there were insufficient volunteers, the balance of the monthly reinforcement requirement could be balloted from the Reserve. It was a very clever way of introducing gradual conscription for overseas service. The first ballot under the Act to make up the shortfall in volunteers for the 23rd Reinforcements was held on 16 November 1916. This ensured 'equality of sacrifice' and was generally accepted by the New Zealand public. The first ballots for married men were held in October 1917, and they marched into camp in January 1918. At the end of the war married men with two children were being called up for service.[58]

Conscription was opposed by the New Zealand Labour Party and also by individuals on both religious and philosophical grounds. Military Service Boards made up of prominent citizens could hear appeals against call-up. 'Shirkers' who refused to come into camp when balloted were arrested, and, in some cases, forcibly sent overseas to join the NZEF. Initially conscription did not apply to Maori, who offered a Maori Contingent, which became the Pioneer Battalion of the New

Zealand Division. This was kept up to strength with volunteers. However, the Waikato-Maniapoto tribes of the central North Island refused to supply any recruits until the injustices they had suffered from the land confiscations, after the Crown's invasion of the Waikato in 1863, were corrected. This led to the application of selective conscription of the Waikato tribes, but although some were sent into camp for training, the war ended before any were sent to the front.[59] Again in the Second World War a Maori unit, 28 (Maori) Battalion, was raised and served with 2NZEF. Unlike the Pioneer Battalion of the First World War, it had a combat role, maintaining its strength through voluntary enlistments. Its outstanding war record was a source of pride to the Maori race, but the high casualty figures were to impact on Maori leadership for the rest of the century.

Labour adopted a far more pragmatic approach in the Second World War. The National Service Emergency Regulations of 1940 introduced conscription, and a General Reserve was established, made up of all males between the ages of 16 and 46. Voluntary enlistment ended on 22 July 1940 when all males between 18 and 46 became liable for ballot. This was amended in 1942, making any member of the armed services liable for service wherever required, whether in New Zealand or overseas. However, as a matter of policy no soldier under the age of 21 was permitted to serve outside New Zealand. Conscription was administered by the National Service Department, which was the civilian agency responsible for recruiting and training men for service overseas for each of the three services. By the end of 1941 there were 109,000 men, including Territorials, in the three services. Appeal Boards were set up to deal with appeals, and those excused were sent to labour camps. Of the 7,000 appeals, 600 were upheld, and a further 800, mainly conscientious objectors, refused to accept the finding of the Board, became military defaulters and were sent to detention camps 'for the duration'.

As in the First World War, New Zealand was far more draconian in its percentage of dismissed appeals and in the severity of the sentences than either Australia or the United Kingdom. Camp conditions were spartan and the rules harsh. After release the defaulters still faced a loss of civil liberties, being banned from employment in the Public Service, not eligible to vote until the 1951 elections, and barred from the teaching profession until the 1960s.[60] It was perhaps even more difficult for the defaulter's family. Walter Lawry was one of those detained for the duration of the war:

> 'When my mother died the authorities were attacked for giving me leave to attend her funeral, and the Returned Services Association demanded that the city council sack my wife from her job in the Electricity and Gas Showroom because she was the wife of a detainee.'[61]

Japan's entry into the war saw an increase in military and industrial mobilisation for home defence. By July 1942 the strength of the three services totalled 154,549, or 43 per cent of the eligible population, with 58,200 serving overseas. American victories at Coral Sea, Midway and in the battle for Guadalcanal led to more personnel being released for overseas service. By 1944 a crisis in manpower led to the withdrawal of 3 Division from the Pacific in order to maintain reinforcements of 2 Division in Italy and sustain production of food and supplies. By November 1944 340,846 men, including volunteers, had been called up for military service, with 80,959 serving overseas.[62]

The Pacific War saw New Zealand face the dilemma of either defending her homeland or deferring to Allied grand strategy and continuing her presence in Egypt. The deciding factor was the decision by the United States to position forces in New Zealand as a base for operations. In late 1942 both Churchill and Roosevelt persuaded Fraser that the return of 2NZEF would disrupt essential shipping, and that the Allied cause would be better served by it remaining in North Africa. Roosevelt undertook to send a United States division to New Zealand on condition that the New Zealanders remained in Egypt, and Fraser agreed.[63] The issue was again raised at the end of the campaign in North Africa, when the Allied High Command requested that the Division take part in the Sicily landings. Fraser could not guarantee this, having promised that the future of the Division would be decided by Parliament, and this uncertainty ruled the New Zealanders out of the Sicily campaign. Once again it was the combined recommendations of both Churchill and Roosevelt that persuaded a reluctant New Zealand Government to retain its forces in Europe, while Curtin, the Australian Prime Minister, did not disguise his anger at New Zealand's decision.[64]

During 1942 New Zealand embarked on a major construction programme of airfields, camps and coastal defences to protect itself against Japanese attack. During this time it was invaded by those Roosevelt sent to protect it. The 'American invasion' began at the end of May 1942 with the arrival in Auckland of the convoy carrying 145 Regiment of the 37 Division, and the setting up of Vice-Admiral Ghormley's Headquarters South Pacific in Auckland. The North Island soon resembled one vast military establishment with camps for American servicemen centred on Auckland (29,500 personnel) and Wellington (21,000).

The new arrivals made an enormous impression on New Zealand society. Estelle Rolfe did voluntary work in the American Service Club canteen in Wellington: 'They had tons of money and they used to give flowers and chocolates and cigarettes and everything.'[65] It was a generosity not reserved for females alone. Spencer Jones was at school in Havelock North when the Americans arrived: 'We used to hang around with them and they'd shout us ice creams ... they seemed to have tons of money, and they used to spend it ... they were just tops.'[66] It was a natural response by often lonely young soldiers away from home for the first time in their lives.

From New Zealand the Americans embarked for operations in the Central Pacific, and, in turn, hospitals in New Zealand received back American wounded. In all some 100,000 United States servicemen passed through New Zealand en route to war. Some 1,400 New Zealand women married US servicemen, many of whom settled in the United States.[67] There were inevitable tensions, particularly with the New Zealand soldiers returning on furlough leave from the Middle East, but as Clarence Moss wryly noted, 'Yanks not to blame it's the way of soldiers the world over.'[68]

New Zealand had already deployed a brigade-strength garrison to Fiji and smaller garrisons to other South Pacific islands, including a number of coastwatchers. The Fiji garrison became the nucleus of a second New Zealand division, 3 Division, which after training in New Zealand deployed to New Caledonia in November 1942 as a two-infantry-brigade-strength formation. Commanded by Major-General H. E. Barrowclough, who had commanded 6 NZ Brigade with distinction in the battle to relieve Tobruk, 3 Division deployed to Guadalcanal in August 1943. In September its two brigades took part in two separate amphibious landings on Vella Lavella and Mono islands as a prelude to a major landing by United States Marines on Bougainville. In February 1943 the division mounted an amphibious landing and secured the Nissan or Green Islands. Their capture marked the end of the Solomons Campaign, and effectively the end of 3 Division's operational role. In March 1944 it was withdrawn to New Caledonia and gradually reduced to cadre strength as its personnel were sent as reinforcements to Italy or returned to essential industries in New Zealand. It was disbanded on 19 October 1944, and it was the RNZN and RNZAF that continued New Zealand's contribution to the Pacific War.[69]

Both *Achilles* and *Leander* and the armed merchant cruiser *Monowai* were involved in escorting convoys in the months following the Japanese attack on Pearl Harbor, and both cruisers took part in the battle for control of the sea lanes around Guadalcanal. *Achilles* was badly damaged by Japanese aircraft, returning to service in time for the final operations off Okinawa and in the Sea of Japan as part of the British Pacific Fleet. *Leander* was torpedoed in a night action between ships of the American Task Force and the Japanese Navy off Kolombangara in the Solomons in July 1943. It was only the superb seamanship of her captain, Commander S. W. Roskill RN, that prevented the ship from sinking. HMNZS *Gambia*, a light 'Fiji' Class cruiser, was lent to New Zealand to replace *Leander*. With *Achilles*, it took part in operations in the Sea of Japan, and was struck by a Kamikaze aircraft while the 'Cease hostilities against Japan' signal was flying, announcing the end of the war. A large number of small ships and motor launches of the RNZN also served in the Pacific, with two minesweepers, HMNZS *Kiwi* and *Moa*, sinking the Japanese submarine *I-1* off Guadalcanal in late January 1943.[70]

The Pacific War changed the RNZAF from a training organisation providing aircrew for the RAF into a truly independent air force with its focus on operations in the Pacific. At its peak in February 1945 the RNZAF numbered 7,929 personnel in the Pacific, with a total of 24 squadrons serving at some time in the theatre. At the war's end the New Zealand Air Task Force was supporting Australian ground operations to clear Bougainville, New Ireland, and other by-passed Japanese garrisons, while the United States forces advanced on the Japanese mainland.[71]

In Italy the New Zealanders of 'Freyberg's Circus' landed at Taranto in October 1943 and spent 19 months slogging their way up the Italian Peninsula before reaching Trieste in May 1945. It was a very different war from North Africa, and the Division, consisting of two infantry and one armoured brigade, while ideally balanced with its mix of armour and infantry to conduct a desert campaign, lacked the infantry numbers to perform effectively in Italy. The Division's initial success, in crossing the Sangro, ended at Orsogna, where four unsuccessful attacks, in November/December 1943, led to heavy casualties and a realisation by the New Zealanders that they had much to learn on the co-ordination of infantry and armour in the hills of Italy. The Division was again unsuccessful in hard, difficult fighting at Monte Cassino between February and May 1944. This was followed by the advance to Florence in July to August 1944, Rimini in October/November 1944, and the battle for Faenza in December 1944.

By Christmas 1944 it was a tired, weary division that was losing its fighting edge and suffering from a critical shortage of infantrymen. Freyberg recognised the dangers and re-organised the Division, forming an additional infantry brigade. The release of veterans back to New Zealand on furlough saw them replaced by reinforcements drawn from 3 Division in the Pacific. After hard training it was this revitalised Division that led the 8th Army in the crossing of the Senio and the pursuit to Trieste in April/May 1945. At the end of the war in Italy, 2 Division was the longest-serving division in the 8th Army. Its losses over six years of war totalled 6,581 dead, 16,237 wounded and 6,637 prisoners of war. New Zealand's decision to keep it in Europe allowed it to play a significant role in a major theatre of war, an opportunity it would not have had if it had returned to the Pacific in 1943.[72]

The war ended after the dropping of the atom bombs on Hiroshima and Nagasaki and the surrender of Japan on 15 August 1945. Its suddenness took New Zealanders by surprise, with many anticipating a hard-fought invasion of Japan involving further New Zealand casualties. New Zealand was a different country in 1945. On the Home Front it saw the creation of a welfare state and the central role of Government in the affairs of its people. What had seemed radical in 1939 had become the norm by 1945. It had been a World War of such scale that it forced New Zealand to constantly assess where its national interests lay, and what its priority of effort should be. This often put it at odds with its allies. Australia resented New Zealand's failure to return 2NZEF to the Pacific in 1943, and both Britain and the United States were angry at the temerity of the Anzac Pact between Australia and New Zealand in 1944, when both countries sought to assert some say over post-war security issues in the Pacific. Under Fraser's careful and pragmatic ministership, New Zealand generally accepted the role it was asked to play, but also sought to influence the outcomes in the best interests of the nation. He ensured that New Zealand had a voice, and worked hard to make the United Nations, which was established in the closing months of the war, the forum where it could be heard to effect. Unlike 1914-18, there was no conviction that this was a war that would end all wars. New Zealand faced the post-war world with the knowledge that with maturity also comes uncertainty, in which it would have to play a minor but active part.

Recommended reading

Crawford, J. A. B. (ed), *Kia Kaha: New Zealand in the Second World War* (Auckland: Oxford University Press, 2000)

Edmond, Lauris (ed), *Women in Wartime* (Wellington: Government Printer, 1986)

Kay, Robin, *Chronology: New Zealand in the War 1939-1946* (Wellington: Government Printer, 1968)

Pugsley, Christopher (ed), *Ordinary People: New Zealanders Remember the Second World War* (Wellington: Department of Internal Affairs, 1995)

Te Hokowhitu A Tu: The New Zealand Maori Pioneer Battalion in the First World War (Auckland: Reed, 1995)

Pugsley, Christopher et al, *Scars on the Heart: Two Centuries of New Zealand at War* (Wellington: David Bateman, 1996)

Wood, F. L. W., *The New Zealand People at War* (Wellington: War History Branch, Department of Internal Affairs, 1958)

Notes

[1] Sgt L. H. (Shorty) Lovegrove, *Cavalry! You Mean Horses?* (Glendorran, 1994) p15, quoted in Chris Pugsley et al, *Scars on the Heart: Two Centuries of New Zealand at War* (David Bateman, 1996) p167

[2] Robin Kay, *Chronology: New Zealand in the War 1939-1946* (Wellington: Government Printer, 1968) p1

[3] F. L. W. Wood, *The New Zealand People at War* (Wellington: War History Branch, Department of Internal Affairs, 1958) pp42-71

[4] 'Extraordinary Times', in Lauris Edmond (ed), *Women in Wartime* (Wellington: Government Printer, 1986) p253

[5] Ibid

[6] Pat Cozens in 'Our Stories', in Defence Partners (Christopher Pugsley, ed) *Ordinary People: New Zealanders Remember the Second World War* (Wellington: Department of Internal Affairs, 1995)

[7] F. G. Mosley, 'This May be of Interest!', Auckland War Memorial Museum (AIM) MS89/237

[8] Ormond Burton, *In Prison* (Wellington: A. H. & A. W. Reed, 1945) pp10, 57

[9] Christopher Pugsley, *Gallipoli: The New Zealand Story* (Auckland: Reed, 1998) p63. See also Christopher Pugsley, 'At The Empire's Call: New Zealand Expeditionary Force Planning 1901-1918', in John Moses and Christopher Pugsley (eds), *The German Empire and Britain's Pacific Dominions 1871-1919: Essays on the Role of Australia and New Zealand in World Politics in the Age of Imperialism* (Claremont, USA: Regina Books, 2000)

[10] Christopher Pugsley, 'At The Empire's Call', op cit

[11] Lieutenant Colonel John Studholme, *Record of Personal Services during the War* (Wellington: Government Printer, 1928) p383; G. J. B., 'War Pensions', in A. H. McLintock (ed), *An Encyclopaedia of New Zealand*, Vol 3 (Wellington: Government Printer, 1966) p557; Malcolm McKinnon (ed), *New Zealand Historical Atlas* (Wellington: David Bateman in association with Historical Branch, Department of Internal Affairs, 1997) plates 77-8

[12] F. L. W. Wood, op cit, pp72-89

[13] Robin Kay, op cit, p3

[14] Major-General Sir Howard Kippenberger, *Infantry Brigadier* (London: Oxford University Press, 1949) pp1-7

[15] Captain Hall-Thompson, 'The Work of the "Philomel", in H. T. B. Drew (ed), *The War Effort of New Zealand* (Wellington: Whitcombe & Tombs, 1923) pp63-86

[16] Chris Pugsley et al, *Scars on the Heart*, op cit, pp144-57

[17] Chris Pugsley, 'HMS *New Zealand*, New Zealand's Gift to the Empire', in *New Zealand Defence Quarterly Magazine* 7 (Summer 1994)

[18] R. A. B., 'Defence – Army', in A. H. McLintock (ed), *An Encyclopaedia of New Zealand*, Vol 1 (Wellington: Government Printer, 1966) pp461-7

[19] S. D. Waters, *Royal New Zealand Navy* (Wellington: War History Branch, Department of Internal Affairs, 1956) p44

[20] Christopher Pugsley, *Gallipoli*, op cit, p63. See also Christopher Pugsley, 'At The Empire's Call', op cit

[21] Patricia Connew in 'Our Stories', op cit

[22] W. E. Murphy, 'Wars', in A. H. McLintock (ed), *An Encyclopaedia of New Zealand*, Vol 3, op cit, pp568-9

[23] Vincent Orange, *Sir Keith Park* (London: Methuen, 1984) and *Coningham* (London: Methuen, 1990)

24 W. E. Murphy, 'The Air Force', in A. H. McLintock (ed), *An Encyclopaedia of New Zealand*, Vol 3, op cit, p575

25 Author's notes from conversations with Bill Simpson, 109 Squadron RAF, quoted in Chris Pugsley et al, *Scars on the Heart*, op cit, p185

26 F. L. W. Wood, op cit, p99

27 The title '2 New Zealand Division' was not officially adopted until 29 June 1942; Robin Kay, op cit, p3

28 For full text, see *Documents relating to New Zealand's participation in the Second World War, 1939-45* (3 Vols) (Wellington: War History Branch, Department of Internal Affairs, 1949) Vol I, No 39

29 For an example of Freyberg's employment of these powers, see J. L. Scoular, *Battle For Egypt* (Wellington: War History Branch, Department of Internal Affairs, 1955) pp1-6

30 *Army Quarterly*, October 1944, p33, quoted in F. L. W. Wood, op cit, p102

31 'History', in A. H. McLintock (ed), *An Encyclopaedia of New Zealand*, Vol 2 (Wellington: Government Printer, 1966) pp57-65

32 J. O. W., 'Sir James Allen, GCMG, KCB, (1855-1942)', in A. H. McLintock (ed), *An Encyclopaedia of New Zealand*, Vol 1, op cit, pp35-6

33 See Paul Baker, *King and Country Call* (Auckland: Auckland University Press, 1988) and Christopher Pugsley, *On The Fringe of Hell* (Auckland: Hodder & Stoughton, 1991)

34 Christopher Pugsley, 'At The Empire's Call', op cit

35 Godley-Allen correspondence, General Sir Alexander Godley, WA 252/1-6, and also in Hon Sir James Allen Papers, M1/15, National Archives, and Russell-Allen correspondence in Allen Papers, M1/32

36 Christopher Pugsley, *On The Fringe of Hell*, op cit. See also Christopher Pugsley, 'Andrew Hamilton Russell', in Claudia Orange (ed), *The Dictionary of New Zealand Biography*, Vol Three, 1901-1920 (Wellington: Auckland University Press, Department of Internal Affairs, 1995; 'The New Zealanders at Passchendaele', in P. H. Liddle and H. P. Cecil (eds), *Passchendaele in Perspective* (London: Leo Cooper/Pen & Sword, 1997); and 'New Zealand: "The Heroes Lie in France"', in Hugh Cecil and Peter Liddle, *At The Eleventh Hour* (London: Leo Cooper/Pen & Sword, 1998) pp200-12

37 Christopher Pugsley, 'The Second New Zealand Division of 1945: A comparison with its 1918 predecessor', in J. A. B. Crawford (ed), *Kia Kaha: New Zealand in the Second World War* (Auckland: Oxford University Press, 2000)

38 Christopher Pugsley, 'At The Empire's Call', op cit

39 For the best summary of the operations of the Anzac Mounted Division, see A. J. Hill, *Chauvel of the Light Horse* (Melbourne: Melbourne University Press, 1978)

40 Clarence J. Moss, 'Circus Days', War Diaries, MS 93/134, AIM, quoted in Chris Pugsley et al, *Scars on the Heart*, op cit, p168

41 *Documents relating to New Zealand's participation in the Second World War, 1939-45*, op cit, Vol II, pp1-16

42 The Anzac Corps was formed under General Blamey's command on 12/13 April 1941; W. G. McClymont, *To Greece* (Wellington: War History Branch, Department of Internal Affairs, 1959) p223

43 Private Vincent J. Salmon, 19 Battalion, 2 NZEF, letter dated 11 June 1941, AIM MS927, quoted in Chris Pugsley et al, *Scars on the Heart*, op cit, p186

44 James Thorn, *Peter Fraser* (London, 1952) p195, quoted in Chris Pugsley et al, *Scars on the Heart*, op cit, p192

45 W. G. Stevens, *Problems of 2NZEF* (Wellington: War History Branch, Department of Internal Affairs, 1958) p292

46 R. E. Riddell, 'War Experiences in Crete, 1941', MS1537, AIM, quoted in Chris Pugsley et al, *Scars on the Heart*, op cit, p192

47 'Tui interview', in Lauris Edmond (ed), *Women in Wartime*, op cit, pp118-22

48 Clarence J Moss, op cit, quoted in Chris Pugsley et al, *Scars on the Heart*, op cit, p202

49 'Chronology of Events', in Lauris Edmond (ed), *Women in Wartime*, op cit, p265

50 Rose Young, 'The Home Front', in Chris Pugsley et al, *Scars on the Heart*, op cit, pp204-17

51 Jenny Jones in 'Our Stories', op cit

52 'History', in A. H. McLintock (ed), *An Encyclopaedia of New Zealand*, Vol 2, op cit, p63

53 Ibid

54 Pat Cozens in 'Our Stories', op cit

55 Estelle Rolfe, ibid

56 Rose Young, 'The Home Front', op cit, pp204-17

57 'Extraordinary Times', in Lauris Edmond (ed), *Women in Wartime*, op cit, p253

58 Chris Pugsley et al, *Scars on the Heart*, op cit, pp97-9. See also Paul Baker, op cit, and Christopher Pugsley, *On the Fringe of Hell*, op cit

59 Christopher Pugsley, *Te Hokowhitu A Tu: The New Zealand Maori Pioneer Battalion in the First World War* (Auckland: Reed, 1995)

60 Rose Young, 'The Home Front', op cit, pp204-17

61 Walter Lawry in 'Our Stories', op cit

62 R. A. B., 'Compulsory Military Service', in A. H. McLintock (ed), *An Encyclopaedia of New Zealand*, Vol 1, op cit, pp384-6

63 *Documents relating to New Zealand's participation in the Second World War, 1939-45*, op cit, Vol II, pp141-55

64 Ibid, pp182-221

65 Estelle Rolfe in 'Our Stories', op cit

66 Spencer Jones, ibid

67 Rose Young, 'The Home Front', op cit, pp204-17. See also Nancy M. Taylor, *The Home Front* (Wellington: Historical Publications Branch, Department of Internal Affairs, 1986) Vol 1, pp621-61

68 Clarence J. Moss, op cit, p203

69 O. A. Gillespie, *The Pacific* (Wellington: War History Branch, Department of Internal Affairs, 1952)

70 S. D. Waters, op cit

71 J. M. S. Ross, *Royal New Zealand Air Force* (Wellington: War History Branch, Department of Internal Affairs, 1955). See also John Crawford, *New Zealand's Pacific Frontline* (Wellington: HQ NZ Defence Forces, 1992)

72 N. C. Phillips, *Italy*, Vol 1 'The Sangro to Cassino'; Robin Kay, *Italy*, Vol 2 'From Cassino to Trieste' (Wellington: War History Branch, Department of Internal Affairs, 1957, 1967)

Chapter 15

Canada: fact and fancy

Dean Oliver

The history of Canada's wars and military excursions in the 20th century is in many ways a curiosity. From the populist, subservient imperialism that drove a reluctant Prime Minister, Sir Wilfrid Laurier, to permit the raising of a volunteer contingent for service in Britain's South African War in 1899, through London's legally binding declaration of war in 1914, to the carefully cultivated humanitarianism of Canada's post-Cold War foreign policy mandarins, a casual reader of Canada's historical record might be forgiven for assuming that with national maturation has come Delphic wisdom. Unlike their stiff-necked, stiff-lipped Anglophile precursors, one might assume, contemporary Canadian decision-makers are, after more than 130 years of national gestation, free to exercise the courage of their convictions. Shorn of imperial obligation, with the deep scars of past conscription crises faded from the modern memory, they act nationally to tailor from whole cloth foreign policies in response to global events whose effects on the collective psyche are not predetermined by linguistic or legal ties to Europe or, more accurately perhaps, by the vibrant, derivative politics of the Old Country's transplanted progeny. It is a common enough tale, self-evident in many respects, whose implications are nevertheless as contradictory as they are engaging.

The Second World War is a defining moment for this strain of proto-nationalist assessment, the necessary, cataclysmic waypoint on the more or less linear road 'from colony to nation'. In delaying by a week (to 10 September) its declaration of war on Germany, the government of W. L. M. King demonstrated dramatically the effect of the Statute of Westminster on Britain's former colonies. Parliament's 'right to decide' was in large part a sop to a domestic politics riven with sectional, class, and linguistic division, and hence marginally impervious to far-off imperial concerns in any case, but it was symbolically critical, as King understood – a break with the past and a bold thrust into the future.

And it was not just symbolic. In as much as Ottawa had attempted studiously to avoid having any foreign policy at all in the inter-war years, or at least one that might risk overseas military entanglements, successive governments, Conservative and Liberal, had always acted in the certainty that foreign affairs threatened domestic equilibrium in a most direct and dangerous way. The lesson of Flanders, in short, was to avoid Flanders again, at nearly all costs. If, as King – though not all members of his Cabinet – acknowledged, fighting for the Empire in some future war could not be avoided, as public opinion would undoubtedly insist upon Canada's involvement, shrewd politicians could at least act early on to set the parameters and preconditions for the bartering of Canadian lives for global peace. Guns – Canadian-produced, of course – and money, with limited and manpower-light forms of military assistance, seemed in 1939 an ideal, and beneficial, approach to the new European crisis. The forces of history, driven in this case by the brilliance of Hitler's panzer generals, would soon dictate otherwise, but the motivations behind Canada's initial approach to the second, 'good' war were rooted deeply in its experience of the first, 'bad' one.

This transformation, the replacement of King's vision of a limited liability war with a total war against global fascism, ultimately served Canada – and its allies – well, even if, during the bitter conscription crisis in late 1944, the principals involved might have been forgiven for musing otherwise. The senior dominion emerged from the struggle in similar circumstances to the United States, physically unscathed and pregnant with possibilities; its large military, massive industrial capacity, and incipient financial strength made it a ranking member of the wartime alliance and a principal player in the post-war world. Indeed, while post-war fears had informed strongly the policies of all parties in the 1945 federal election, won – with a reduced majority – by King's incumbent Liberals, they dissipated quickly and, for the most part, the months to come were uneventful. As in 1919, post-war Ottawa displayed a palpable reluctance to rattle anew its victorious sabre, cutting its defence budget and armed forces with almost indecent haste, but each denouement had its peculiar characteristics.

After 1945, a confident internationalism, forged by the wartime alliance and the apparent lessons of pre-war appeasement, fired the imaginations of many senior diplomats, military officers, and policy professionals. Spared the economic ravages of a post-war recession that never occurred, Canada memorialised Hitler's defeat by not retreating entirely to the isolationist bulwarks of the 1920s and early 1930s. Leftists, then and now, cried lamely over the opportunities missed by the state to ensure full employment and income redistribution in a peacetime socialist paradise, but for most of those Canadians who had won the war, its aftermath was marginally better than they had assumed and far better than history might have led them to expect. Self-assured, prosperous, and surprisingly worldly, by 1948 Canadian officials led the North American side in discussions of a North Atlantic alliance, a historic break with nearly a century of cautious peacetime diplomacy; nearly a decade later, during the Suez Crisis in 1956, they led in the development of international peacekeeping as well.

These were neither the acts of a middle power predisposed to a low-maintenance foreign policy nor the hallmarks of activism born of unconditional independence – the Liberal Government, after all, was criticised fiercely by Opposition Progressive Conservatives for having allegedly abandoned Britain during Suez – but they did flow directly from the experience of the Second War. They were the lessons of war and, by broad consensus, the price of peace. Indeed, the entire history of Canada's military and foreign policies might well be divided into distinct epochs drawing directly from the country's wartime exploits in 1914-18 and 1939-45. The turning points would track loosely those of other nations, like Britain or Australia or the United States, but would also evince a distinctly

Canadian face. The first may be said to have ended in April 1917 with the triumph of the Canadian Corps at Vimy Ridge and, in a phrase that has been both weakened and ennobled by its repetition, Canada's 'coming of age'. Canadian participation at Versailles was the fruit of this labour, but, not least in the minds of the troops, independence had already been established at Vimy. Inter-war malaise, in some ways inexplicable given Canada's battlefield accomplishments and international notoriety during the war, constitutes a second age ending only in 1939, or perhaps mid-1940 for those who ascribe prognostic qualities to defence budgets and troop strengths rather than political declarations. The international obligations confidently assumed in the post-1945 period continue to the present day, unless one assumes that a new world order after 1989 replaced, more or less definitively, the broad features of the Cold War system.

The boundaries for these three periods are hardly as precise (or as sacrosanct) as any arbitrary division might assume. The 1930s was not a homogeneous decade in a foreign policy sense; peacekeeping has undergone several dramatic spasms in Canadian practice, and the period from roughly 1945 to 1956 is widely considered to have been a 'golden age' in Canadian diplomacy, meaning that the rest fares badly by comparison. But the historiography does permit of some generalisation. And to the extent that it does so, such generalisation is based on Canada's experiences – or rather, the historians' understanding of Canada's experiences – in the two World Wars. This is neither an indictment of three-quarters of a century of scholarship, the progress of which has been well analysed and well catalogued elsewhere, nor an endorsement of it. Undermining the chronological benchmarks routinely employed to delineate Canada's 20th-century military history is a labour worthy of Sisyphus and unnecessary to a current project that, while revisionist to some small degree, is really more speculative than destructive. That the wars as written might depart slightly from the wars as experienced is a tangential (and not entirely original) departure from an otherwise perpendicular script. Moreover, to the extent that it is true, the sins may be more of omission than commission, lying blameless in the blank pages of books not written and theses not completed. That the Canadian Corps' first war adventures may have overshadowed, inevitably but unjustly, the Second War's more ambiguous accomplishments is likewise perhaps a minor contention.

And yet at the confluence of such conclusions lie intriguing possibilities. Short-changing, even inadvertently, both the experience of war and, especially, the experiences of Second World War veterans, may have harnessed both popular and scholarly perceptions of Canada's crusades to a panorama of interpretative vignettes of great breadth but questionable depth. A few have already been called into question by recent scholarship; others await judgement with remarkable staying power. The cumulative effects of such optical imprecision have been both dramatic and ironic. Thus, the sordid and brutalising First World War is said to have witnessed the flowering of Canadian military talent, and this with solid biographies of only one Canadian general, Sir Arthur Currie; the moral clarity deriving from the struggle against Hitler, on the other hand, was waged allegedly by a caste conspicuous only by its mediocrity, but this conclusion too comes without biographies, solid or otherwise, of most of the senior military figures. Such ironies cry out for emphasis: Canada's First War generals, even the British ones, escaped for the most part Alan Clark-like denunciations of their military professionalism. Their Second War successors, who incurred roughly 25 per cent fewer fatal casualties in a far longer struggle, are derided, often explicitly, as uninspired and incapable, with one or two notable exceptions; in general, they are deemed unworthy of Currie's successful mantra.

The Canadian Corps, in helping to defeat the Kaiser's powerful but arguably unexceptional military, is likewise held up as a paragon of military excellence, the shock army of the British Army according to one recent account, while the First Canadian Army and its counterparts at sea and in the air during the Second War, despite helping to defeat, in Hitler's military machine, possibly the finest European military force of the 20th century, have been found wanting by two generations of armchair strategists. Myths attaching to the generals and their national military establishments likewise gravitate, inevitably, towards the men and women under their command. Was the First Canadian Army in Normandy an unworthy successor of the Canadian Corps? Were sons inferior warriors to their fathers?

The grounds for comparison between the sea and air wars in the two struggles are less firm than for land operations, if only because of Canada's comparatively small First World War naval service and the fact that most Canadian fliers served in British formations after 1914. But even here lurk indiscreet questions. The Royal Canadian Navy fought a losing struggle against Germany's submarines for most of the Second War, the poorly equipped, inadequately trained junior partner of larger and better-armed British and, later, American fleets. Number 6 Bomber Group, the Royal Canadian Air Force's largest strike formation in the air war against occupied Europe, likewise fared badly for many months after its formation, incurring catastrophic casualties while its fliers, ground crew and commanders learned the rudiments of strategic bombing technique. This muted praise, and occasional disdain, proffered by academic scholarship on the efforts of Canada's Second World War commanders is slightly at odds with the favourable treatment usually accorded the country's political leadership, and with the praise frequently reserved for the military's rank and file. Canada's fighting forces, it seems, avoided the leadership of donkeys in the First War, only to follow tragically an entire herd in the Second.

Similar disparities emerge on the home front where the broad comparisons are so firmly established as to be almost articles of faith. The First War was followed by dislocation and, according to the labour historians, near revolution; the Second ushered in a period of unheralded wealth and social stability, despite the bold imperfections of a male-dominated, conservative, consumerist, racially intolerant status quo. The First War generated social cleavage and regional squabbling that resulted very nearly in the country's sundering in the decade to come; the Second spawned its share of internecine sniping too, especially over manpower policy, but sagacious leadership and the different circumstances of 1939 piloted the country to a far different and more stable outcome six years later. King's political common sense, his seemingly innate ability to snatch victory from the jaws of defeat, stands in marked contrast to the single-mindedness, perhaps even simple-mindedness, of his Tory predecessor in the First War, Sir Robert Borden. The economy ran more smoothly in the Second War and with better, more effective direction. Central Government worked under King and led directly to the foundations of the modern welfare state, whereas it had not been fully tried, save in quixotic and ham-fisted convulsions, under Borden. The First War left Canada victorious but bled white, astonished at its own successes and appalled at their cost, human, financial and political; the Second left the country successful but urbane, imbued with the quiet confidence of a nation that has faced its demons and stared them down. The First War may have forged the conditions for the fulfilment of constitutional independence afterwards, but its benefits were dearly bought; the Second confirmed sovereignty's permanence, but this time with righteous certainty.

None of this is uncontested. On King's leadership travails alone a small library has been authored. But broad brushstrokes notwithstanding, there is a marvellous juxtaposition that attends most comparisons of Canada's wars under Borden and King, at home and abroad. There is no need to rehabilitate Borden's tattered image to appreciate the incongruity of it – a successful and skilled war leader whose sins in the name of peace helped lay the foundations for Canadian political independence and military victory, whose failings are at least as attributable to the period's vituperative politics, and to the views of their latter-day expositors, as to any objective assessment of his admittedly flawed character, tagged by scholarly convention as one of Canada's least able prime ministers. On the other hand, a paunchy spiritualist reviled by the troops and by their generals, whose opportunism and occasional ruthlessness were the objects of fear and loathing even among Liberals, is held up to posterity as the quintessence of Canadian political acumen.

This caricatures crudely their differences, to be sure, but it highlights too the oddities in a scholarship that has lionised the First War's soldiers but the Second War's politicians. Borden's political cronies and the vast majority of those generals and admirals who fought Hitler are remembered, where they are remembered at all, with rancid indifference. It also highlights the difficulties in untangling fact from fancy, opinion from event, in the tangled interpretative skein that now appears – with deceptive consensus – in high school and university texts, mass-market publications, and popular television documentaries. It is hardly to assume that historiography has got the First World War wrong, or pronounced prematurely on the bloody price of nationhood. Borden's Government presided over some of the most reprehensible legislation in Canadian history and, as socially conscious college lecturers never forget to remind their charges, no amount of context can excuse satisfactorily the disenfranchising of entire categories of recent immigrants or the blanket incarceration of enemy aliens. His long suffering of the irascible, irreverent, and possibly insane Minister of Militia and Defence, Sam Hughes, would rank as a black mark against any war leader. Economic half-measures, profiteering scandals, a confused overseas command structure, and, above all, the 1917 conscription election and its associated misdemeanours are further indication of a ship of state steered awkwardly, and sometimes maliciously.

What makes Borden's historiographical fate intriguing is not the case for his defence. Rather, it is the manner in which the broader First World War literature exudes ambiguity and contention in ways distinct, more or less, from its Second World War counterpart, and how such contentions now appear before the interested public. This is not in itself surprising, given the literature that followed the First War and the social and labour troubles that plagued the post-war years. But the contest over the appropriate voice in which to tell Canada's war stories speaks both to the secondary literature's load-bearing capacity and to the manner in which current punditry embraces, or conveniently rejects, the contemporary record. Perhaps this is the inevitable concomitant of history's increasing commercialisation and the fashionable espousal of the sensational over the mundane, but it reflects too a splintering of the historical profession and a lingering unease in some quarters with the self-professed motivations of the war's most central actors, its soldiers.

Robert Fulford, commenting in the *National Post* on 8 February 2000 in response to Niall Ferguson's *The Pity of War*, called the First World War 'Our darkest hour' and claimed that most Canadians had been too traumatised to admit of the possibility that it may have been 'wrong-headed and foolish'. His comment was poorly informed – numerous anti-war tracts had appeared in the inter-war years, in Canada as elsewhere – but it evoked a spirited exchange with two of the country's leading historians, David Bercuson and Jonathan Vance (*National Post*, 11 and 14 February). Vance was especially eloquent in reply, noting that the persistence of Canada's 'colony to nation' myth was explained not by the mysterious failings of historical practitioners or traumatised veterans, but simply by the fact that it was largely true. The war 'was the catalyst that transformed Canada into a nation,' Vance argued. 'It was the seminal event in the lives of countless Canadians, an experience that, perhaps for the first time, made them feel distinct from Britain. To suggest otherwise simply because it also produced discord is to employ a crude reductionism.' The counter-factual flirtations of Ferguson and Fulford, Vance suggested, were badly misguided. The period's decision-makers should not be assessed 'by standing, as many of us tend to do, on the lofty heights of the present and sadly shaking our heads at the small-minded and blinkered generations that came before us. Instead, we must judge their world on their terms – we must see with their eyes, think with their minds, feel with their hearts.'

Fulford's reply was intriguing. Claiming that Vance's rebuttal was 'more royalist than the king,' he proceeded to assert, especially in reference to his 'cynical and literally battle-scarred uncle,' that veterans, in his experience, 'would have snorted with disgust at the idea that the calamity in which they took part was an act of nation-building.' They may indeed have done so, but memoirs, interviews, and other forms of contemporary testimony support strongly, though far from unanimously, Vance's position. *In Flanders Fields*, for example, a series of interviews conducted with some 600 veterans by the Canadian Broadcasting Corporation for a multi-episode radio history in 1964, contains numerous explications of the war's effect on Canadians' self-perceptions, most of them echoing Vance's conclusions. Indeed, they suggest, in their number and clarity, a simple method by which disputes over the war's contemporary meaning and implications might be resolved: by resort to the opinions and pronouncements of the contemporaries themselves.

This too is a crude reductionism: personal experience, as Fulford's familial allusions demonstrate, can prove all things most of the time. But in suggesting, as Vance (and Bercuson) did, that the consensus Fulford so reviled in fact rested on a combination of contemporary testimonial and subsequent scholarship, his respondents pegged accurately the relationship that ought to exist between experience and interpretation in the divination of the national past. This is no more than an injunction, and perhaps an unsophisticated one, to best practices in the historical craft. But it speaks directly nevertheless to the hollowness of a literature imbued with either weakness: inattention to the complexities of contemporary voice, however disturbing in hindsight it might appear, and indifference to the quality of interpretations that emerge, in part, in consequence. Vance's award-winning 1997 book, *Death So Noble: Memory, Meaning, and the First World War*, makes precisely this point: a history of the war's social and cultural impact based on a broad sampling of primary records, and not just those produced by well-known literati, overturns much of the historical canon. Popular novels, church records, and the papers of veterans' organisations, for example, help explain the manner in which Canadian society sought to memorialise the war in ways that made sense of their sacrifice. This was not, Vance insists, to bolster the social order, but 'because it filled needs… The war had to be recalled in such a way that positive outcomes, beyond the defeat of German aggression, were clear. In short, the mythic version existed to fashion a useable past out of the Great War.'

Canada's Second World War literature likewise is replete with substantial gaps. There is no history of the home front, no study of rehabilitation or reconstruction, no detailed accounting of the wartime economy, no biography of defence minister J. L. Ralston, and no published biographies of senior officers like H. D. G. Crerar, Chris Vokes, Bert Hoffmeister, or Ken Stuart. Indeed, there has been no comprehensive study of wartime politics since J. L. Granatstein's 1975 volume, *Canada's War*. But it is not in these areas that the historiography has been most pointedly challenged. Instead, in a way strangely similar to Vance's return to more populist records, veterans and several military historians have returned 'to the documents' to rewrite the wartime record.

George Blackburn was an FOO, a Forward Observation Officer, in a Canadian artillery regiment during Canada's second great crusade. He fought through North West Europe and into Germany, was decorated for bravery, and wrote an award-winning three-volume memoir of his experiences in uniform. It is a fascinating study, not least by virtue of the fact that, chronologically, it is written oddly, the first volume dealing mainly with the Normandy campaign, the second with the final campaigns of the war, and the third with his early wartime experiences. It is erudite and passionate in ways that compare favourably with the best wartime memoirs. He writes impersonally of himself, in the second person, describing in graphic detail the sights and smells of death, the thunder of a mortar barrage, the fear of battle. Indeed, much of Blackburn's memoir is about fear, of death, of the enemy, of losing friends and comrades, of performing creditably impossible tasks in impossible times. The memoir also begins with anger.[1]

In a few raw passages that riddled the professional historical community like shrapnel, Blackburn claimed that Canadians' understanding of the Second World

War, especially the battlefield experiences of the troops, was fatally flawed. He began by dismissing, matter-of-factly, the official historians, whether of countries, armies, or regiments. Having wanted to write of the human misery, drama and sense of battle, he was quickly disillusioned by the paucity of such information in existing official accounts. The official record-keepers 'seem to have been entirely disinterested in recording such matters'. None 'make any serious attempt to describe what was entailed in simply staying alive during those terrible days and nights.' Such deficiencies 'led to inaccurate, irresponsible conclusions bordering on outright dishonesty – even in the works of our own official historians – regarding the training and fighting qualities of Canadian officers and men in World War II.' This was 'insulting to the memory of all those Canadians who died facing the enemy while the official record-keepers sheltered miles to the rear.'

Those base-wallahs who since the war have dared to criticise the Canadians for not closing the Falaise Gap sooner – inferring from what seems to have been slow daily progress a general lack of aggressiveness – were obviously not around at the time to see and experience what it was like for the troops at the cutting edge of the Canadian Army. And while lack of first-hand experience in a writer may be forgiven, no such tolerance can be extended to those pretending to be historians who purposely ignore the evidence provided by the awful casualty rate among the Canadian divisions, which on the road to Falaise and beyond rose to twice the American rate and two and a half times the British rate...

The historians, Blackburn thundered, were 'sickeningly arrogant'. Their 'coldblooded analyses' were 'particularly obscene'.

He was not alone in making these criticisms. Denis and Shelagh Whitaker, in their account of the Dieppe raid, made a similar charge, lambasting as foolish and inaccurate the views of post-war scholars that Canadian troops in the United Kingdom had clamoured for action as an antidote to boredom and low morale.[2] This amounted merely to a repetition of contemporary propaganda, they argued, a justification for a bungled operation that too many historians had since accepted as established fact. Denis Whitaker, an officer and decorated veteran of the raid, addressed the question in one of many first-person segments in the narrative, calling it 'nonsense'.

It is not just aggrieved veterans who have expressed dismay at the literature's tendency to downplay qualitatively Canada's Second World War efforts. Historian Terry Copp, arguably the country's leading expert on the Normandy campaign, has made the rehabilitation of Canada's fighting reputation a central theme of his extensive writings.[3] Echoing the views of Blackburn and others, including naval historian Marc Milner, Copp has attempted to place Canadian performance, especially in the weeks leading up to Falaise, in a broader tactical context. Focusing his analysis on the performance of Canadian units at brigade level and below, his work emphasises the problems posed by terrain, communications, the quality and quantity of German resistance, the weather, training, and other factors in reassessing the consensus view of Canadian tactical performance. Rejecting out of hand what he has called the pro-German bias of many Western scholars, Copp has established himself as a champion of Second World War veterans, weaving their recollections carefully into his own work but bolstering them also with after-action reports, operational analyses, and tactical message logs. The result has been an eloquent rebuttal to critics of Canadian combat proficiency.

Nothing in this debate subverts the other essential components of Canada's Second World War canon. The brilliance of King, the effects of the war on the Canadian State, and the selective morality displayed by most citizens towards Japanese-Canadians or women in uniform remain untouched by such ministrations. But it does place in relief the need for fresh approaches to broad components of the literature. Moreover, it encapsulates neatly the critical, but yet more expansive, question of the role of veterans in interpreting the events in which they participated. The latter, clearly, have no special claim to history's receptivity to their cause and service but, as the debate over *The Valour and the Horror*, a television programme that veterans claimed misrepresented history, demonstrated, they do have the right to be heard. In a public dispute that filled the airwaves and editorial columns for months in early 1992, veterans (supported by historians like Copp and Bercuson) charged that the producers of the series had, in effect, demeaned their past service. In attempting to be fair to Canada's German and Japanese foes, the veterans contended, the films permitted moral relativism to eclipse historical accuracy. The producers, and the journalistic community generally, responded that any proprietary defence of historical 'truth' was itself a breech of faith with the ideals for which the wars were fought. As Bercuson and S. F. Wise wrote in their edited collection on the controversy, which sided closely with the veterans, 'it does not matter so much *who* writes history; what matters is *how* history is written.'[4]

The Valour and the Horror dispute highlighted, in many ways, the curiosity with which this chapter began: the confident, progressive quality that has attached to the sweep of Canadian military history despite the broad scholarly gaps, due occasionally to inattention to certain categories of evidence, that continue to persist. The vigour with which most undergraduates are taught the follies of their First World War leaders, the successes of the Canadian Corps to the contrary notwithstanding, is countered by the laudatory bent of modern scholarship on Mackenzie King and the faint praise accorded his senior officers. Enhanced understanding hardly requires that the consensus on either war be internally consistent, much less that each very different war be assessed by similar criteria across time and place. But the challenges posed by Vance, Copp, Blackburn and others address more fundamental questions than views on a particular individual, battle or political platform. Instead, they re-introduce forcefully essential questions of evidence, argument and interpretation that have already delivered important correctives to the historical canon of which they now form part. They may yet result in the gradual congruence of two otherwise fruitful but disparate literatures, at least in the realm of battlefield performance, though that too is an unnecessary concomitant. The modern fragmentation of the Canadian historical community, epitomised by a polarisation of national historical associations, will militate against it in any case. What such efforts really demonstrate, especially in their belated attentiveness to the concerns of the veteran as actor, author and interpreter, is the pivotal relationship between experience and scholarship in the construction of historical memory. In this, demography has already conceded the First War's terrain to the historians and journalists, but the Second War's battles, figuratively speaking, can yet be contested.

Recommended reading

Bercuson, David J. and Wise, S. F., *The Valour and the Horror Revisited* (Montreal and Kingston: McGill-Queen's University Press, 1992)

Craig, Grace Morris, *But this is our War* (Toronto: University of Toronto Press, 1981)

Douglas, W. A. B. and Greenhous, Brereton, *Out of the Shadows: Canada in the Second World War* (Oxford: Oxford University Press, 1977)

Granatstein, J. L. and Morton, Desmond, *Marching to Armageddon: Canadians and the Great War, 1914-1919* (Toronto: Lester & Orpen Dennys, 1989)

Morton, Desmond, *Canada and War: A military and political history* (Toronto: Butterworths, 1981)

When Canada Won the War (Ottawa: Canadian Historical Association, 1995)

Notes

[1]   The following quotations all come from the introduction to the first volume. George G. Blackburn, *The Guns of Normandy: A Soldier's Eye View, France 1944* (Toronto: McClelland & Stewart, 1995)

[2]   Denis and Shelagh Whitaker, *Dieppe: Tragedy to Triumph* (Toronto: McGraw-Hill Ryerson, 1992) pp75-7

[3]   See, eg, Terry Copp, *The Brigade: The Fifth Canadian Infantry Brigade, 1939-1945* (Stoney Creek, Ont: Fortress Publications, 1992)

[4]   David J. Bercuson and S. F. Wise, *The Valour and the Horror Revisited* (Montreal and Kingston: McGill-Queen's University Press, 1992) p10. Emphasis in original.

Chapter 16

South Africa

Bill Nasson

'In 1939 South Africa was a British Dominion, comprising the provinces of the Cape of Good Hope, Natal, the Orange Free State, and the Transvaal, with the additional mandated territory of South West Africa. Rich in gold and diamonds, as well as coal and iron ore, and other strategic raw materials, South Africa possessed an industrial base capable of ready expansion. Yet compared to Australia, Canada, and New Zealand, its contribution was limited. The reasons for this are not hard to find. South Africa entered the war against Germany deeply divided.'[1] One could easily push back the date to 1914, and Ian Phimister's recent crisp overview of the Union of South Africa at war would read as accurately for the First World War as for the Second, with the sole exception that in 1914 the colony of German South West Africa was not yet a mandated possession. Even here, though, this was about to fall into the lap of Louis Botha and Jan Smuts as the opening stroke of the South African war effort. In terms of national experience, then, the World Wars represented an extraordinary level of continuity for South Africa: not merely a comparatively lower level of mobilisation than other British Dominions, despite its considerable strategic resources and solid industrial base, but in distance from the main theatres of warfare, in remoteness from the harsh experience of indiscriminate total war, and in sustaining only a fairly patchy kind of war-willingness. So, at this fairly summary level, the picture does not really change. Whether 1914-18 or 1939-45, South Africa seemed to have fought essentially the same war.

As elements of national history, these intersecting World War realities have long been reflected in both scholarly and more popular literature.[2] And it is not hard to provide a thumbnail sketch of the common factors, which tell roughly the same tale, or at least provide the basic assumptions about warring South African society. Briefly, what were these conditions? Most Afrikaners, the larger segment of the ruling white minority, were vehemently opposed to participation in the World Wars, or at least to South African involvement on the Allied side. In 1914, still smarting from British imperial victory in the Anglo-Boer or South African War of 1899-1902, Afrikaner republicans and nationalists had no wish to wage what was seen as a British war; over half of this disaffected population turned their backs on patriotic calls from the Empire-loyalist, Anglo-Afrikaner governing elite for a collective effort on behalf of the Empire.[3] Again, in 1939, with the Afrikaner National Party all for neutrality, and with mass Afrikaner hostility to war even more vocal and organised than before, the Smuts coalition only just managed to squeak through a parliamentary declaration of hostilities, obliging it to take the country to war without a popular mandate from the white electorate.

It followed that in neither war could the authorities risk the touchy consequences of forcing through conscription. In any event, both wars had other inflammatory domestic repercussions, as a radical Afrikaner nationalist constituency swung towards non-constitutional, extra-parliamentary action against pro-Empire and pro-war administrations. The years 1914-15 saw an armed Afrikaner rebellion, and by 1940 some far-right movements were well on the way to becoming pro-Nazi paramilitary bodies, bent on making trouble for the home front and committed to the violent overthrow of the state.[4] An unambiguous will to war and a sense of cause and direction, that the fights were to defend Britain and its imperial system against German expansion, existed only among English-speaking whites, 'actually a minority of a minority'[5], and a dusting of Anglo-Afrikaner loyalists. In the end, for the enfranchised political community, there was probably never a point at which Union leadership could have counted on a national commitment to hold the line against a British enemy. Had South Africa not been quite so far south, the British economic and strategic stake in the Union might well have ended up on the brink of disaster.

If white society were brittle, what of the World War attitudes of the black South African majority? Here, too, sentiment was mixed. On the one hand, the educated black elite and their political organisations were loyally supportive of the war effort, immediately and enthusiastically in the First World War, if slower and more cautious in the Second. Moderate, middle-class, African, Coloured and Indian leadership clung to a wispy belief in the liberal and moral capacity of British imperialism, trusting that patriotic service would bring some kind of political dividend through London finally using its humanitarian persuasion to get Pretoria to grant improved rights.[6]

Even though African leadership resented the indignity of the 1912 Union Defence Act, which barred Africans from any armed service, in both wars they vigorously encouraged men to enlist for non-combatant roles, and joined hands with the authorities in raising money from black rural and urban communities for war funds. If African nationalism were understandably less wide-eyed about the democratic pretensions of South Africa's war in 1939, as in 1914 there was definite acceptance of the basic circumstances, namely, 'that the government's decision to declare war on the side of Britain was correct'[7]. This was a judgement shared by Coloured political leaders, who did their bit and more to fan volunteering for a Coloured infantry Cape Corps and non-combatant auxiliary service. Whatever their grievances over segregation, and by the end of the 1930s these were obviously weighty, a sense of necessary war duty and responsibility permeated the language and ideology of black political leadership.

On the other hand, such consciousness could hardly be said to have been the outlook of the majority of black South Africans. In both wars many were simply puzzled isolationists, for whom a far-away struggle meant nothing, and represented a concern only when shortages and rising inflation began to chafe. Many others in rural areas adroitly dodged or stiffly resisted the doubtful promises or pressures of recruiting campaigns, slipping off into the bush until these passed; if they were to be drawn into the wars, they would have to be winkled out.[8] If there was apathy and inertia in the countryside, popular war resistance was less passive and often edgy in urban areas. African mine and other industrial workers were more inclined to associate English masters with reducing wages than upholding human rights and freedoms, and were not slow to denounce the Union war effort. Among some, there was even satisfaction at German military accomplishments in the First World War, and at German and Japanese advances in the Second.[9] Within the ranks of such grumpy labourers, there were even those who looked to some heady social emancipation should South Africa's enemies sweep aside Pretoria's power.

Lastly, and alongside such sentiment, the wars also encouraged the crackling growth of millenarian strains within rural communities, some of which became gripped by transcendent peasant visions of war as a second coming to bring deliverance from white colonial domination, either through Westphalian cavalry thundering down through Africa to lift the Xhosa, or the Japanese fleet taking up station off the Natal coast to unbolt the Zulu so that they could reclaim their lost land.[10] Given the existence of such deep fissures and levels of incoherence within the consciousness of both white and black society, on neither occasion was South Africa ready or able to fight a war on anything approaching total terms.

Finally, at this overview level, there were several other fundamental areas where the South African experience of 1939-45 was strikingly similar to that of 1914-18. On the home front, what kept the wars at arm's length for so many inhabitants, whites in particular, was their relatively limited direct impact on consumption. While there was wartime distress in impoverished rural areas, in popular memory neither war represented a phase of extreme deprivation or hunger for most people. In the First World War, disruption of shipping routes and the subordination of British industry to the needs of military production led to shortages of imported consumer goods, an irritation fairly quickly soothed by the growth of local import-substitution enterprise. Wartime agricultural demand was an opportunity to boost production of fruit, grain and other foodstuffs to supply domestic as well as export markets. While there were intermittent stock shortages, these never amounted to a crisis needing the imposition of statutory food control and rationing systems. As to the Second World War, it was only after the impact of Japanese entry into the conflict, in 1941, that the Government had to turn to the national rationing of fuel and some foodstuffs, and the introduction of price and import controls. In other words, for the first three years of the war suburban voters faced little more than the hell of queuing for rice, having to restrict their use of white flour, and nodding at Government entreaties to tighten their belts a little more, through households being requested not to employ more servants than were absolutely necessary.[11] Whatever sacrifice was being made, it was not something to seriously lighten the table.

On the combat side of affairs, there are perhaps four defining South African service characteristics worthy of note. One was the distinctly qualified or conditional conception of service in the Union Defence Force. In the First World War men volunteered for duties in a specified campaign, such as German South West Africa or East Africa, rather than being asked to commit their bodies for the duration of the war. Authorities opted for a short-service, defence of Union borders deployment as likely to encounter least recruiting resistance. This meant that with the wrapping up of the South West Africa operation, all Active Citizen Force units were demobilised, released completely from any further active service obligations. Any soldiers committed to staying in the war against Germany then had to re-attest for the German East Africa theatre or for France.

This provisional style of war was there again in 1939-45, despite the suggestion from some writers that what distinguished the Second from the First World War was that Union Defence Force recruits 'volunteered for the duration of the war'.[12] Although at commencement men volunteered for the long haul, the envisaged service term was that of home-based defence of the Union of South Africa. From the early months of 1940 all new white volunteer soldiers were inducted by oath, which obliged them to serve anywhere in Africa; for men already enlisted, this was optional rather than binding. Those who took the continental service oath displayed a familiarising orange 'Red Tab' strip on their khaki issue, signifying a blunt distinction between groups of troops with differing levels of commitment and ways of thinking about the war.

In 1943, as the scale of hostilities continued to grow, South Africa introduced a new oath for recruits willing to serve anywhere on the Allied front. This further variation in the direction of the South African war effort produced a spurt of uncertainty and vacillation not unlike that of 1915, when recruiters began to nudge wary individual German South West African and East African campaign veterans towards re-enlisting for the Western Front. Now, some volunteers who had declined to take the 1940 oath obviously again declined to sign an expanded re-commitment, and other prickly servicemen refused to renew their initial oath when its scope changed. Underlying these blockages and frustrations for the Union Defence Force high command was a testing reality. In both wars South Africa was fated to remain critically short of a respectable complement of white combatants for its forces, while at the same time refusing to allow black South African volunteers to enlist freely for armed service.[13]

As a second element in the shaping of fighting ability, the imbalance and strain caused by this political equation can be readily illustrated. South Africa supplied just over 145,700 white soldiers in the First World War, 67,300 of these serving in the first-wave conquest of German South West Africa, with some 47,500 going on to plunge into German East Africa and also Central Africa. Only around 30,800 men re-volunteered for France. Of the approximately 51,500 African and Coloured soldiers committed to the African campaigns, fewer than 7,000 were permitted to bear arms as infantrymen in the Cape Corps, others being restricted to auxiliary work as members of various Labour Battalions and Labour Corps. Around 5,800 of these non-combatant troops opted subsequently for service in France, where they joined 21,000 auxiliaries of the South African Native Labour Corps in support tasks behind the lines.[14]

In terms of the level of contribution and the line of role demarcation between white and black servicemen, the Second World War was almost a mirror of the First. In all, some 334,200 South Africans volunteered for full-term service, just over 132,000 of these being white infantry (fewer than in 1914-18), with a further 54,000 white regulars spread between the South African air and naval forces.

African and Coloured volunteers, numbering approximately 132,000, were assembled in the Union's Non-European Army Services division. Almost without exception, these men were confined to unarmed logistical or other support service to ground forces.[15] The obligations of a segregationist order ensured that in the World Wars it was always going to be tricky to muster front-line fighting capability on a scale proportionate to that of more cohesive Dominions like Australia and New Zealand; and recruiting ceilings were already cramped by domestic English-Afrikaner nationalist enmities.

The most fervently patriotic of South Africa's middle-class English, Anglo-Afrikaner and Scots-Afrikaner citizens were all too aware of how difficult it was to get a full and uncompromising Union commitment to armed service against Britain's enemies abroad. So, a third response at the outset of both wars was set by those vaulting individuals who were determined not to see out hostilities in a country that seemed to be a marginal belligerent, or for whom war appeared to be a national side-show. This meant embracing war overseas directly in British ranks, for well-educated, skilled and professional men like the Afrikaner loyalist, Deneys Reitz, who by 1918 was commanding a Battalion of the Scots Fusiliers, or Bob Gaunt, who by 1942 was a seasoned motor torpedo-boat officer in the Royal Navy. There was, of course, nothing unusual about Empire and Commonwealth volunteers paying their own way to join British ground, air or sea forces, or using adjunct service connections to lever themselves into British units, as Christopher Somerville's fine study, *Our War*, has recently underlined in the case of the Second World War.[16]

But, at the same time, there was something particular or perhaps paradoxical about an assertively South African or 'Springbok' identity within British ranks during the World Wars. The essential point is that to many enthusiastic metropolitan observers on the one hand, it signified the courage and unstinting patriotic commitment of a hardy breed of white colonial supermen, whether as the sacrifice of the 1st South African Infantry Brigade at Delville Wood in 1916, or as the exhilarating combat flying accomplishments of 'Sailor' Malan in the Battle of Britain.[17] On the other hand, the early presence of such pushy South Africans in Europe represented a brisk and impatient break from the restraints and frustrations of national soldiering in politically fractured domestic circumstances. It is not for nothing that the cultural historian, Samuel Hynes, has generally concluded, 'irony is the inescapable tone of modern war'.[18]

Another sense of paradox is at the core of a fourth characteristic of South African World War experience. During the 1939-45 conflict, the performance of the Union's armed forces peaked in African and Middle Eastern theatres, and in the taking of the Indian Ocean island of Madagascar. Areas like East Africa and Egypt saw the most concentrated efforts, with ground forces sustaining their most severe losses of the war in the Middle East. It was not until April 1944 that a South African Division crossed the Mediterranean to be fed into the Italian campaign, in which it fought until the end of the war. Likewise, in the air, the South African Air Force ran the lion's share of its missions over the Western Desert and East Africa, achieving air superiority as hunters in an African continental war. The earlier momentum of 1914-18 was little different. A South African Expeditionary

Force rolled up German South West Africa at little cost, while other Union troops went off to trail across the deserts of North Africa, or to play cat-and-mouse with the enemy in East Africa through to the very end of hostilities. Only towards the end of 1915 was a modest volunteer Infantry Brigade mobilised to see out the rest of the war along the Western Front and in Flanders. Yet, in the popular imagination of white South Africa, it was the rolling heroic accomplishments of Springboks in the European war that counted more as a kind of campaigning epic, with the significance of the Union's wars being marked as mighty battles on European soil, whether Delville Wood in 1916, or Monte Cassino in 1944, reported as stupendous clashes in which South African patriots contributed their large share to the maintenance of Western democratic civilisation.[19] The indigenous African wars of great arid desert spaces and a maze of bush and rocky outcrops, those sites of South Africa's deepest war effort, seemed too tatty and colonial to lodge very sharply in the wartime collective consciousness. This led to the anachronism of South Africa being seen in its pro-war press as having somehow made its most telling contribution to the World Wars through its fairly modest European interventions.

These generalised perspectives on national responses to the World Wars, and to aspects of wartime conduct and experience, provide one indication of how South African people reacted to the sweep of external total war. But while synthesis may tell one 'national' story, the individual realm of personal experience can provide another peephole altogether into how an ordinary South African may have felt and responded to the pressures of war in particularly South African ways. Naturally, no single personal memoir can be representative of South Africanness: a British-hating Afrikaner republican rebel of 1915 or a 1940 home front Zulu gunner in a South African Artillery field regiment would have had hugely different national experiences and understandings of their respective war involvement. But there is value to the meaning of war experience for 'this soldier, at this place, feeling this', in the useful Hynes formulation.[20]

On that basis, let us turn to consider the rare service memories, through oral testimony, of Joe Samuels, a South African veteran of both World Wars. Born into a poor Jewish working-class family, Samuels slipped the leash of elementary schooling at a young age, hoping to pick up work around the mineral fields of Johannesburg and Kimberley; there, he found that the pavements were more likely to scrape his skin than to be covered with gold or diamonds. At the itchy age of about 13, he ended up drifting as a labour migrant between Leopoldville in the Belgian Congo and Johannesburg, running casual office errand jobs interspersed with warehouse and logging work. The responsibilities of a sinewy boyhood were few, leaving him 'free to go whenever I wanted to'.[21]

Aged 16, the unskilled Samuels was doing minor jobs on the Witwatersrand when he first learned of the outbreak of a European war. The news was picked up 'on the streets, a big surprise… I never took any notice of what was going on in the world … never looked at a newspaper'. Acting on a whim, he swiftly massaged his age and enlisted for infantry service in the Rand Rifles. His was a solitary kind of joining, drifting into the war on impulse rather than being driven by any sense of patriotism or masculine bravado. 'Well, I was thin and small, and not exactly a fighting man,' he recalls, but the Rand Rifles promised 'something different', as well as the attraction that 'regular pay for a steady period wasn't to be sneezed at'. His few friends thought his action 'quite mad', asking him what 'this war had to do with living here in Johannesburg ... other people like Afrikaners were saying this sort of thing, of course, and they were saying it very strongly'. Unlike the broad band of mainly middle-class English-speaking combat volunteers, Samuels had no immersion in the military cadet traditions of South African collegiate school life, no 19th-century family history of service in colonial warfare, and no awareness of the convictions of local Empire patriotism. Having heard 'of some problems with the Kaiser' was his closest touch with ideology.

While Samuels may not have volunteered to fight for a personally felt cause, he expected his war to be confined to a familiar world. Like many other South Africans, he expected his war service to be geographically limited. This meant not being 'despatched to some far place to make war with the Germans, lots of us couldn't see the point of going off ... as we saw it, it wasn't as if England didn't have enough men of their own'. Good soldiering meant 'defending our borders' against any possible hostility from neighbouring German South West Africa.

Before Christmas 1914, the Rand Rifles was mobilised as part of a seaborne Expeditionary Force to invade the nearby German protectorate, something to which Samuels resigned himself as 'having to be done, although I preferred to stick to patrolling our own ground to keep out trouble'. His experience of the South West Africa invasion was of a very low-key, small-scale and slightly muddling sort of do, fixed by the clear light and immense emptiness of an African terrain in which the enemy seemed to hold no visible position. Encountering no armed resistance in overrunning the capital of Windhuk, Samuels exulted in roaming over 'sand as fine as flour' and 'white as pearls'. Guarding railway lines and slithering in and out of dugout posts, he found a war not of death, wounds and destruction, but of formidable natural elements, a continuous battle with searing desert heat and running sand, making it 'a job just to keep your rifle working', and 'starting any lorry just a joke'. Conditions were taxing, but tolerable.

Assigned to the interior prong of the Expeditionary Force, Samuels anticipated going into the desert to meet the enemy, and feeling 'very nervous about this strange place', but confrontation eluded him. 'We never saw them ... a few prisoners were the only enemy I remember seeing, if they were the enemy. I suppose they must have been, even if we weren't fighting them.' Just before his mid-1915 release, Samuels again ran into Germans, a rather soft encounter, which left him with distinctly mellow feelings. Posted to guard a clump of 'German political prisoners, they were civilians, mostly businessmen', he regarded them as looking 'far too miserable to be real spies ... difficult to think of them as our enemy'. For the Rand Rifleman, the South West Africa war experience was something of a puzzle, in which none of his personal 'pals' met death or injury, and in which victory felt flat, something gained in passing. 'So few Germans,' recalls Samuels, 'I couldn't feel what the threat was ... they just didn't seem to be any sort of real enemy ... how could they be, if all you did was feel sorry for them?'

The South West Africa operation also brought him face to face with the racially segregated and discriminatory terms of service in the Union Army. With Samuels

battling to handle pack animals properly, his despairing unit commander sent him
off to a Cape Corps Labour Battalion to be coached in mule-riding by its skilled
Coloured drivers, 'experienced men who made it look cushy, so easy for them'. His
attitudes towards 'a tough lot' of 'remount types' were ambivalent, one part
admiration for Cape Corps strength and proficiency, another part cool recognition
of social difference: 'Well, I suppose we'd share a bit of rations, sugar or coffee, stuff
like that, now and again, but it wasn't as if we'd all get into the same tent to play
cards.' The muleteers were 'rough soldiers whose lot seemed to be more work for
less pay … they were common Coloureds, their position was lower than us, so we
never thought of them as pals'.

Now integrated into a band of volunteers from mostly late-19th-century British
immigrant families, Samuels linked up with several others who, after their 1915
demobilisation, opted to re-enlist in a South African Infantry Brigade, which was
being raised for service on the Western Front. 'It was our duty as veterans to step
forward and continue to serve South Africa, that was what officers were saying,' he
remembers. 'Veterans of what, quite a few of the boys were asking, and to have to
go out to another hole of a place. After South West, lots had already had enough.'
As for Samuels himself, 'for my own part, I stayed on, not having much to go back
to.'

A pay reduction in 1916, when the Union Government cut the earnings of its
infantry to the level of the British Army, ignited smouldering resentment in the
ranks of men who now found themselves worse off than other Dominion troops
like Canadians and New Zealanders. Among white miners, mechanics and
craftsmen, there was a feeling of being turned into 'more like beggars than
anything, man … you could hardly afford smokes'. Until allowances were raised
'there was almost a rebellion, real trouble'. Still, once in Europe there was national
affirmation as well as economic discontent. With others, Samuels exulted in white
colonial 'tribal' singing, raucously recycling war songs inherited from later 19th-
century Southern African settler folk-memory. The stock chorus 'Hold him down,
you Zulu warrior, Hold him down, you Zulu chief' was a popular chant to the
essential 'warrior spirit' of the Zulu, earlier subdued but now glamorised by a
dominant white society. For Samuels, periodically indulging in 'Zulu' burlesque
was not only an invented masculine ritual; it was also a cultural reinforcement of
white South Africans' sense of a distinctive African colonial camaraderie and
identity. 'Well, we did a fair bit of prancing about, I suppose,' reflects Samuels,
'what with our native war cries and shaking rifles above our heads like spears. That
was our sort of emblem, you could say, or our mark, coming as we did from South
Africa.'

Immersed in the trench lines of the Western Front, he was struck by the extreme
contrast between the neatly parcelled, arable countryside of northern France to his
rear, and his experience of the sweeping openness of scrubby African landscapes.
The Rand Rifleman was struck, too, by the industrial or 'machine' feel to the
European war, 'all that big artillery, wire, aeroplanes around, that really was a quite
different business from the bush'. Also very different was his experience of the
general remoteness of the British High Command, 'not much interested in who we
were, certainly not us privates'; Samuels's earlier South West African campaign

experience had been both small-scale and run on exceptionally personalised generalship, with every Rand Riflemen having been introduced to and been spoken to personally by Louis Botha, the South African Commander-in-Chief.[22]

Yet, in another way, France at first seemed an extension of the African war experience, 'again never knowing what the hell was going on, certainly down where we were, we were mostly just stuck out there in the open, hoping we would eventually see what was going on'. Exasperated, groping around in a blinkered world, and still with no sense of a cause for which he was fighting, Samuels found his battalion moving on a night-march in mid-July 1916, 'stumbling around in the dark, none of us knowing where the hell we were, or where we would be going ... it was mad, with the chaps blackening up with candle soot to look less visible ... anyway, almost black enough to do a Zulu charge'. He had no inkling of the carnage that now awaited the South African Infantry Brigade. On 15 July Samuels was moved towards a 'a big forest, thick and green ... it looked a lovely spot'. Although a little disconcerted by the sight of 'quite a lot of dead bodies', which had 'turned dark blue, gassed, that was why', the thickly oaked woodland ahead still appeared 'a handy place for a rest, and to have a cup of coffee, or whatever'. What loomed was not exactly a recreational spot: this was Delville Wood, which South African Brigade command had been ordered to take 'at all costs'.

A heavy price was carried by Joe Samuels and some 3,000-odd fellow Springbok infantrymen, as Delville Wood became the key national engagement of the Union's First World War involvement, a South African Gallipoli that bestowed the myth of white nationhood through fire, and the sacrifice of what the *Rand Daily Mail* called a 'pasture of heroic khaki gazelles'[23]. For Samuels, it was being sucked into 'hell ... what we found ourselves in is still unspeakable, in every minute of our situation then it was kill or die'. The Somme was not only a far cry from the Southern and Central Africa he knew, it was also another war, more intense and more horrendous. There was its unexpected heat, 'boiling, hotter than the Congo'; there was the enveloping stench of unburied corpses, 'it was everywhere, that smell, just of rotting away around you'; there was an overall feeling of having been hit by a shock-wave, of disorientation, being 'almost in a trance' and feeling numb about running at the enemy, 'no feelings then, at all, really, all I knew was utter self-preservation, perhaps that was what the Germans knew, too'; there was, finally, coping with the deaths of close companions, most of them men whose African war had inflicted little more than sunburn. 'All I can say is that the whole thing was terrible,' Samuels reveals. 'I know what happened to people, but it's too painful, it's too bad just to think about.' Samuels himself emerged with shrapnel in his skull, but his luck had been with him, for 'no one else in my section came out at all, dead, all of them dead'.

For this South African, the rest of the war was deceleration, following recovery from injuries and fitness training in Rouen, 'one of those bull rings of the French', in which 'sergeants made sure you were made fit again, ready to be slaughtered'. The war had worked on his mind, leaving him more mocking and bitter about his circumstances. A mordant chorus, 'Springboks duck, Springboks pluck, Springboks fly, Springboks die', now seemed to carry a truer meaning than the chirpy assertions of a Zulu warrior. The last months of the war saw Samuels posted to a Folkestone supply base, a position from which front-line service life in France 'felt unreal', and yet he felt 'no nearer to getting back to things which were familiar'. It was

> '…hard to believe that we and the Germans were just going on and on, killing each other, and all this only a few miles away. I felt myself longing for South Africa's sun. Being away from it all, I seem to have lived a hundred lives. And when I thought about those Somme battles, it all seemed like some terrible dream. I remember once, joking, that what we needed with us was a native witchdoctor, you know, with their divining bones and bits of skin. In that existence, those heathens were probably the best bet to tell you your fate.'

His fate was to survive not one war, but two. Leaving his business as a rural trader, Samuels enlisted at the beginning of 1940. This time, he recalls, his opinions and motives were clear:

> 'The news was another war overseas between the English and the Germans, and I knew it was bad. Even after what I'd gone through, I didn't think all that much about the risk, or about fighting, or whether I'd get through. Certainly, there was enough about there being a lot of discrimination against Jews, with that Hitler. Anybody of the Jewish faith, like me, couldn't not be worried … the country, of course, was in a real state. You had these bad types among Afrikaner people who were strongly for the Germans. Me, I was South African English, and Jewish, so I knew I had to stand with my side.'

Samuels was also more knowing in other ways. He 'knew how to handle guns and to look after equipment', knew the distinction between base area and front line, and knew 'where places generally were, if it was the Middle East or up in the North, how it would be in the desert again'. After his horror on the Somme, he worried about a posting to Europe; 'there, anything could happen, you could be shoved into line to face the worst'. Now, too, he saw the enemy differently – not an unknown presence beyond some territorial boundary, but palpably close, men who could disrupt and damage the peace of life at home. 'You always felt on standby, even in your mind, wherever you were,' he records, 'because a problem was that the country had all these Germans in places like Johannesburg. They and their sympathisers were a threat to the railway system and various depots and the like … sabotage and all sorts of other crimes, that was always around.'

As an artillery NCO in the motorised 1st South African Brigade Group, Samuels arrived in Kenya in July 1940, finding 'the sort of bush warfare training we had to do a real drudge, it was like preparing for Windhuk all over again'. The irony of the sight of South African Air Force Junkers Ju86 bombers departing on raids against Italian positions in Abyssinia did not escape him; 'there they were, bought before the war rather than British planes, going off to strike at the German side'. Meanwhile on the ground, Samuels's Brigade launched a series of lunges at targets in southern Abyssinia and Italian Somaliland, inflicting heavy losses at negligible cost.

In these actions, South African combatants were augmented by the strength of a Gold Coast Brigade Group, making operational co-ordination a mixed kind of African Commonwealth experience. Predictably, within South African high and middle command the racial control anxieties of the First World War were reproduced ever more forcefully in the Second; for maintaining the proper hierarchy, it would not do for black South African soldiers to be placed on a footing of armed equality with their white counterparts. So, while the Union's East African units contained Native Military Corps soldiers, such men were confined to auxiliary service as drivers, bearers and construction workers. It is thus not surprising that South Africans like Samuels found their proximity to regular Gold Coast troops so novel an experience. Whereas he had found himself unable to converse meaningfully with Tswana truck drivers because of their limited English, Samuels found 'a more educated outlook from some of these West African blacks with the British, chaps of fighting rank – we talked about all kinds of things, mainly war news, but also about our families, and the future'. Although too much should not be made of such threads of social interaction, finding themselves on a roughly common footing with Gold Coast soldiers undoubtedly had some effect on South African troops, with Samuels recognising 'that we got on all right, we were all in it together'. In these ways, it was possible for some more liberally inclined white South African servicemen to insert themselves into 'the cordial relations that often existed between Africans and Britons'[23] in particular British regiments during the war.

Equally, in their own way, it was almost inevitable that sooner or later some South African commanders in the field would wink at segregationist imperatives from Pretoria. Shifted from artillery to an advanced mechanised column for an invasion of southern Abyssinia at the end of 1940, Samuels recalls the aftermath of a string of storming engagements, in which South African armour easily overran light Italian garrisons, which mostly fled to slip being captured.

> 'We had with us at least a couple of hundred of experienced Cape Corps lorry drivers and mechanics, as well as a bunch of tough Native miners, from the gold mines, who were doing the engineering work, clearing the tracks so supplies could be brought up … they were tireless, and doing as much as any man to sort out the Italians.'

In taking flight, opposing forces had left behind not only large fuel stocks but 'hundreds of rifles and boxes of ammunition, tossed down all over the bush'. A Natal Carbineers officer 'had the weapons collected and checked to see which ones were all right', and then astonished everyone by going over to the Cape Corps and Native Military Corps auxiliaries. 'He praised them for their hard work and the spirit in which they were sticking to things, and then told them that each man should collect one of the Italians' guns, and go off to practise … it was right that they should have weapons to look after themselves if they got into a tight spot.'

As Samuels recollects it, this story is an ironic testimony to the general drift of South African wartime experience. In key respects, Union society was more firmly segregationist in 1940 than in 1915, yet for certain individual white South

Africans, like a mature Second World War Joe Samuels, there was a greater sense of regard and 'close quarters' affection for fellow black soldiers than in the First World War. Why was that? Part of the answer, perhaps, lay in the seriousness of motivation among these 'minority of a minority' volunteers; theirs was a sense of moral cause, that it was 'right to sign the General Oath or any other oath', to carry arms wherever they were needed to maintain British South African 'freedom' against an inhumane Nazi threat. This did not mean that Samuels necessarily questioned the discriminatory segregationist order maintained by his own Government, let alone the differential pay scales of the Union's armed forces, which tailed off rather sharply for black servicemen. But it did mean a close, if paternalistic, fair share acknowledgement of the humanity of black fellow soldiers, 'steady, reliable, decent, Non-Europeans, who went at it with their transports and their back-up jobs'.

Another part of a possible explanation is that against a background of stiff Afrikaner nationalist opposition to the war effort – louder, more violent and more destabilising in the Second than in the First World War – a good number of white volunteer soldiers were acutely aware of how their own side was being helped by the loyalty of such bodies as the Cape Corps or Native Military Corps. 'Back there in Johannesburg and Pretoria,' remarks Samuels, 'there were types who would actually betray the whole country's position ... very dangerous. Every Non-European we had along with us made things stronger for our side and made the enemy's prospects weaker.'

This time, his personal World War did not lap beyond the Egyptian coastline. Samuels's war dragged on wearily through North Africa, an experience of being buffeted by 'sandstorms which made South West look a picnic', and pounded by the Afrika Corps, until June 1942. Then, hemmed into a 1st SA Division defensive line at El Alamein, he became one of a large number of casualties, and was shipped back to South Africa, where he served out the remainder of the war in an artillery training centre, at Potchefstroom in the Orange Free State. For this last lap

'...feelings were mixed, I think. I certainly didn't need anyone in the war to tell me that at the end of the day, the Germans would have to be settled with back in Europe again, lots of us knew that, well enough. Still, I'd seen enough in France before not to give too much of a damn to have missed overseas ... up in the North, we were something, we Springboks, even Egyptian sellers remembered that name, from the first war.'

That, then, is one fragmentary South African experience of two great and terrible wars. It represents a kind of singularity, but can also be viewed as a reference point for the rocky, uncertain world that made up South African consciousness during this time. Whether encapsulated in aggregate terms, or as individual experience, it is hard to escape the conclusion that there was something about South Africans' extremely divided war attitudes and choices that made going to war a striking act. For this prodigal part of the Commonwealth, there was no ideal time to fight in a World War.

Recommended reading

Byl, Pieter van der, *Playgrounds to Battlefields* (Cape Town: Maskew Miller, 1971)

Cryws-Williams, Jennifer, *A Country at War, 1939-1945: The Mood of a Nation* (Johannesburg: Ashanti, 1992)

Digby, Peter K. A., *Pyramids and Poppies: The 1st SA Infantry Brigade in France and Flanders, 1915-1919* (Johannesburg: Ashanti, 1993)

Gleeson, Ian, *The Unknown Force: Black, Indian and Coloured Soldiers Through Two World Wars* (Johannesburg: Ashanti, 1994)

Grundlingh, Albert, *Fighting Their Own War: South African Blacks and The First World War* (Johannesburg: Ravan, 1987)

Keene, John (ed), *South Africa in World War II: A Pictorial History* (Johannesburg: Human & Rousseau, 1995)

L'Ange, Gerald, *Urgent Imperial Service: South African Forces in German South West Africa, 1914-1915* (Johannesburg: Ashanti, 1991)

Reitz, Deneys, *Trekking On* (London: Faber, 1937)

Notes

[1]   Ian Phimister, 'South Africa', in I. C. B. Dear and M. R. D. Foot (eds), *The Oxford Companion to the Second World War* (Oxford: Oxford University Press, 1995) p1024

[2]   See, eg, John Keene (ed), *South Africa in World War II* (Cape Town: Human & Rousseau, 1995); Jennifer Crwys-Williams, *A Country at War, 1939-1945: The Mood of a Nation* (Johannesburg: Ashanti, 1992); S. Katzenellenbogen, 'Southern Africa and the War of 1914-1918', in M. R. D. Foot (ed), *War and Society* (London: Hurst, 1973) pp107-21; Marian Lacey, 'Platskiet Politiek: The Union Defence Force (UDF) 1910-1924', in Jacklyn Cock and Laurie Nathan (eds), *War and Society: The Militarisation of South Africa* (Cape Town: David Philip, 1989) pp32-6

[3]   N. G. Garson, 'South Africa and World War 1', in *Journal of Imperial and Commonwealth History* 8 (1) (1979), p76; Bill Nasson, 'War Opinion in South Africa, 1914', ibid 23 (2) (1995), p261

[4]   Patrick J. Furlong, *Between Crown and Swastika: The Impact of the Radical Right on the Afrikaner Nationalist Movement in the Fascist Era* (Johannesburg: Witwatersrand University Press, 1991) pp138-60

[5]   Ian Phimister, op cit, p1024

[6]   Albert Grundlingh, *Fighting Their Own War: South African Blacks and the First World War* (Johannesburg: Ravan, 1987) p14; Thomas Karis and Gwendolyn M. Carter (eds), *From Protest to Challenge: A Documentary History of African Politics in South Africa, 1882-1984* (Stanford: Hoover Institution, 1972) Vol 1, p38

[7]   John Pampallis, *Foundations of the New South Africa* (London: Zed, 1991) p157

[8]   *Diamond Fields Advertiser* 12 January 1916; *Natal Mercury*, 4 December 1941

[9]   Union of South Africa, House of Assembly Debates, 10 November 1915, col 36; *Rand Daily Mail*, 22 April 1922

[10] Albert Grundlingh, op cit, pp130-1 – *East London Daily Dispatch*, 15 October 1942

[11] *Cape Times*, 12 January 1941; *Rand Daily Mail*, 18 January 1941

[12] Peter K. A. Digby, *Pyramids and Poppies: The 1st SA Infantry Brigade in Libya, France and Flanders, 1915-1919* (Johannesburg: Ashanti, 1993) pp5-6

[13] Ian Phimister, op cit, p1026

[14] Consolidated figures from Peter Digby, Jennifer Crwys-Williams, John Keene, Albert Grundlingh, and Ian Phimister, all op cit, and Union Government, Official History, *Union of South Africa and the Great War* (Pretoria: 1924)

[15] Ian Gleeson, *The Unknown Force: Black. Indian and Coloured Soldiers Through Two World Wars* (Johannesburg: Ashanti, 1994)

16 Christopher Somerville, *Our War: How The British Commonwealth Fought The Second World War* (London: Weidenfeld & Nicolson, 1998) pp96-7

17 *Natal Witness*, 9 September 1916; *Cape Times*, 12 September 1916; *The Star*, 17 July 1940; *Rand Daily Mail*, 3 August 1940

18 Samuel Hynes, *The Soldiers' Tale: Bearing Witness to Modern War* (London: Pimlico, 1998) p114

19 Bill Nasson, 'A Great Divide: Popular Responses to the Great War in South Africa', in *War & Society* 12 (1) (1994) p48; M. Bisset, 'South Africa's D-Day Veterans', in *Militaria* 24 (2) (1994) pp9-12

20 Samuel Hynes, op cit, p284

21 Joseph Samuels, b 19 November 1897, d 4 September 1998, interviewed in Cape Town, May 1997. For a version of his First World War life history, see Bill Nasson, 'A Springbok on the Somme: Joe Samuels, A South African Veteran of the Great War', in *Oral History* 25 (2) (1997), pp31-8

22 *Rand Daily Mail*, 26 January 1915

23 Ibid, 30 August 1916

24 Ashley Jackson, *Botswana 1939-1945: An African Country at War* (Oxford: Clarendon Press, 1999) p93

Chapter 17

Black men in white men's wars

Bernard Waites

Imperial co-belligerency was Britain's 'secret weapon' in the two World Wars of the 20th century. In 1914 the British Empire's colonial subjects wholeheartedly committed themselves to a European war in which they had no obvious interest. What they offered – in terms of manpower and money – was more than Britain would have dared demand. In 1939, though there was far more opposition in India and South Africa to imperial co-belligerency, the commitment of the Empire-Commonwealth to Britain's war effort was still a triumph of sentiment over self-interest. Assurances of loyal support came from all quarters of the colonial Empire.[1] This chapter is concerned with the military service of a particular category of colonial subjects: men of African race from the West Indies and colonial Africa. Their total numbers cannot be accurately computed and depend partly on how we define 'military service'. About 34,000 troops were raised in British East Africa and about 25,000 in British West Africa during the First World War, while 15,204 West Indians were recruited to the British West Indies Regiment.[2] In the Second World War, the military forces in colonial Africa were vastly expanded: between September 1939 and May 1945 the number of East Africans on the military strength rose from 11,000 to 228,000, and of West Africans from 8,000 to 146,000. Probably half a million men, drawn from all parts of Africa, passed through the ranks.[3] The expansion of the military forces in the Caribbean colonies (from 4,000 to 10,000) was comparatively modest, but significant numbers of West Indians enlisted in the British 'home' services: from 1943 the RAF recruited 5,500 men for ground duties, and over 800 air crew.

Military recruitment returns give only a partial indication of the contribution of black manpower to the imperial war effort in either 1914-18 or 1939-45. Most blacks served in non-combatant roles in both wars, and the line between a civilian auxiliary and a labouring serviceman was not always clear-cut. By far the largest category of black participants in the First World War was the million or more carriers recruited for the East Africa campaign.[4] Though they were not engaged as fighting men, it would be churlish to deny the 'military' character of their service; they laboured under military discipline, were often exposed to danger, and about 10 per cent died from disease, malnutrition and exposure. In the Second World War many of the Africans in uniform formed the core of the huge labour reserve required by the British Empire forces in the Middle East. They loaded and transported supplies and undertook guard duties, but were not intended for combat. Their contribution to the war effort was basically no different in kind from that of the civilian labourers (many of them conscripted) who constructed the great chain of airfields and logistical installations in West Africa. Even amongst the 56,000 African troops sent to Burma, the distinction between soldier and labourer was blurred; large numbers were unarmed soldiers employed as carriers. Nor should we forget, in this reckoning of black participants, those who served and died in the Merchant Navy; 5,000 colonial seamen (mostly from the Caribbean) lost their lives.

It almost goes without saying that men with whom we are concerned were extraordinarily diverse in language, ethnicity, and religious and social traditions. In 1914 the West Indies was a Creole society in which the light-skinned monopolised political and economic power but where black and mixed-race people had long internalised the intersecting ideologies of race and imperialism. The monarchy was seen as a symbol of emancipation, and the concept of liberation had been incongruously annexed to the idea of Empire. Those clamouring to serve the 'King and Empire' included Marcus Garvey, founder of the Universal Negro Improvement Association, and a progenitor of black consciousness.[5] Northern Nigeria had been incorporated in the Empire as recently as the turn of the century and was still a slave-holding society. In pledging their loyalty to the King-Emperor, its Emirs and native chiefs were consciously following the example of the Indian princes.[6] They imposed a virtual feudal levy on pagan and Muslim tribesmen to satisfy British demands for recruits to the West African Frontier Force.

Such gross differences in political and cultural traditions were slightly less evident in 1939, yet Britain still had an uncanny knack of rallying to its cause Caribbean nationalists and labour leaders, as well as African chiefs and traditional rulers. The Governor of Jamaica reported that reaction to the outbreak of war has been 'unanimously loyal'. 'A wave of patriotism is passing over the country ... [it] is fully understood that the fight is for liberty.' Norman Manley – who had known violent colour prejudice during his service in the Field Artillery between 1915 and 1918 – instructed his National Party to call off all meetings and political agitation, and publicly declared that this was no time for domestic strife. William Bustamente placed the services of the labour unions unreservedly at the Governor's disposal. Nevertheless, Whitehall was warned that Jamaicans had 'many bitter memories' of the way their willingness to serve in the last war had been spurned.[7]

Blacks became acquainted with the myriad faces of war like any other men, and their experiences were just as variegated. What framed and (to a degree) homogenised those experiences was the institutional racism of the imperial state they served. I am not denying that white officers often treated their black troops with respect and affection, and that these feelings were frequently reciprocated. But racist regulations and assumptions set limits to how black troops were trained and deployed, the rank they could achieve, and how and with whom they socialised behind the lines. In short, their experience of the two World Wars was a segregated experience in which a racial hierarchy was taken for granted.

Up to 1939 men of African race were discriminated against by a colour bar on their recruitment to the 'home' forces; by a ban on their holding King's Commissions in any of the colonial armies; and by a prohibition on their being put in any position of command over white servicemen.[8] The *Manual of Military Law* operative in 1914 explicitly allowed for the enlistment of 'men of colour' in the British Army, but recruiting depots practised a semi-official racial exclusiveness. Whether a man of mixed race was accepted depended partly on his degree of colour, partly on the vagaries of individual recruiting officers. In November, black West Indian volunteers arriving in Britain at their own expense were rejected by the Army, though 'lighter coloured' men were accepted.[9]

Black doctors who had qualified in Britain were turned down by the RAMC because of the ruling that commissioned officers had to be 'of pure European descent'. A Dr Jenner Wright of Sierra Leone offering his services was told to go home where he was enlisted as a 'Native Medical Officer'.[10] The War Office did not relent on the colour bar in the 'home' army until June 1918; but it was a response to the manpower shortage, not an acknowledgement of the injustice of discriminating against a man because of his race. The institutional racism of the armed forces was, if anything, more explicit after the war than it had been before. The Air Force Act, for example, stated that enlistment was open only to men of pure European descent, though aliens were admitted to the service. In October 1938, after a black Briton had attempted to enlist, the Army Act was amended to regularise the colour bar, on the putative grounds that it had been impossible to integrate this coloured recruit into the ranks.

With the outbreak of war in 1939, blacks in Britain wanting to enlist encountered much the same prejudice that had been evident in 1914. A Jamaican-born dentist was rejected by the RAF because he was not of pure European descent. The Tank Corps refused Arundel Mood, a public schoolboy. Black university students who had tried to enlist in the OTC complained they had been barred on racial grounds. Nevertheless, history did not simply repeat itself. Racial discrimination in the armed services was politically embarrassing to the Colonial Office, which lobbied hard – and successfully – for the removal of the colour bar. In October the Colonial Secretary was able to announce in the House of Commons that colonial subjects, whatever their race, were to be on the same footing as those of pure European descent as regards voluntary enlistment and eligibility for emergency Commissions. The first black Briton to become an officer in a home regiment was commissioned in 1940; the first African was commissioned in the West African Division in 1942. Of the 'home' services, the RAF proved the most open to advancement by black and brown servicemen: over 70 men of non-European descent from the colonial territories had gained RAF commissions by the end of the war.[11] Though the last cannot be dismissed as 'tokenism', there was a large dose of hypocrisy in British official attitudes. The principle announced in October 1939 was persistently thwarted by various administrative measures, and a Colonial Office official is supposed to have said 'we must keep up the fiction of there being no colour bar'.[12]

For the hundreds of thousands of blacks serving the British Empire in the Middle East and Africa, the fact that Britain was officially 'colour blind' made scarcely any difference. Segregation was a fact of military life. D. H. Barber, who commanded a company of Ugandans in Egypt and later became a Public Relations Officer attached to GHQ in the Middle East, observed that 'he was a bold African indeed who entered a NAAFI meant for British troops. In some cases he would be welcomed, but in others he would be cold-shouldered.' Until African Clubs were formed, there were few places that off-duty black soldiers could frequent. The British NCOs seconded to African units were always considered 'senior' to African NCOs, and invariably messed separately. African padres visiting a company would mess with the African Warrant Officers while the British padres would mess with the British officers.[13] Not all the racial discrimination black servicemen encountered was of military origin; some was specific to the colonial situation in which they were stationed. It was made clear to West Africans shipped to Kenya in 1940-41 that they were 'in a white man's country'. Nairobi's cinemas were closed to them, along with the canteens and hospitals for troops. Kenya's petty apartheid was especially humiliating to educated West African patriots who strongly objected to being treated like primitive tribal warriors. One wrote in May 1941:

> 'Many [of us] have voluntarily enlisted to service [sic] the Empire Overseas, leaving very good appointments, out of sheer loyalty and eagerness to play a part in winning the war. European troops are receiving much hospitality from friends in Kenya, whereas we are always judged and assessed by the standards of the local askari.'[14]

In 1914 Britain's military leaders had no wish to deploy black troops in a European theatre of war or in any conflict in which whites fought whites. Blacks were considered ill-adapted to the rigours of a northern winter, and the spectacle of European internecine war would – it was thought – lower the whites' prestige in black eyes. Furthermore, the Colonial Office regarded itself as the trustee of black Africans' welfare and had humanitarian scruples about using them as soldiers or military labour outside Africa. Later in the war it successfully opposed the War Office's proposals for West African supply and tunnelling companies on the Western Front, and for West African labour units in Mesopotamia.[15] Unlike their French allies – whose public ideology in matters of race was, in any case, more egalitarian – the British were never compelled to forego their prejudices and scruples. Africans served only within Africa, and their participation was much less problematic for British institutional racism than that of the black West Indians drafted to the Western Front in 1916.

Black troops were used to overrun the tiny German territory of Togo in August 1914, in the much longer campaign in Kamerun (where the last German garrison did not capitulate until February 1916) and in East Africa. The Kamerun campaign (in which the French had the larger role) proved tougher than anticipated, but was tactically no different from other 'small wars' in tropical Africa. Disease, climate and ecology were the overriding determinants of military operations. The advancing columns suffered grievously in the south because of dense bush, malaria and tsetse-fly infestation, and incessant rain that washed out the few motorable roads. Out of 7,000 British African soldiers engaged, there were 4,600 casualties, nearly all from disease, (and 1,668 deaths).[16] Carrier casualties are unknown.

The vast majority of West African recruits in 1914-18 were illiterate non-Christians from the northern territories of the Gold Coast and Nigeria, with little knowledge of the outside world and no inkling of why the war was fought. In peacetime, sufficient recruits could be obtained voluntarily but, as the wartime demand for soldiers and carriers rose, men were coerced into service, usually by the tribal satraps of 'indirect rule'. Conscription was not officially introduced – as it was in French West Africa – but, as Governor Clifford admitted, very few recruits were in any real sense voluntary.[17] Young men fled across international borders to escape recruitment and many conscripts absconded en route to training centres. Well over 10 per cent of the Gold Coast Regiment's soldiers deserted during the war, most of them while in the Gold Coast. In Nigeria the situation was much the same.[18] Desertion rates were particularly high when units were about to proceed overseas, because ocean-voyaging was believed to disorganise or destroy fetishes.

The break-down of Nigeria's manpower effort reveals just how much military force in tropical Africa depended for its mobility on human muscle power; roughly 17,000 combatant rankers were recruited, 1,800 gun carriers, 35,000 transport carriers, 350 motor transport drivers, 800 inland water transport men and under 500 railwaymen, postmen, policemen and artisans.[19] Enlisted carriers on the regimental strength were trained for special tasks; the Gold Coast expeditionary force, for example, included 381 battery and ammunition carriers together with 980 African rank and file. The Regiment's 2.95mm Hotchkiss quick-firing mountain guns would each be dismounted into ten loads on the march, and the speed with which they were remounted for action was obviously vital.[20] But the typical carrier was unskilled, and often unfit to bear his load because chiefs pressed into service the most physically vulnerable men. In West Africa the norm was about three carriers to every two fighting men; in East Africa, where lines of communication stretched to unimagined lengths, the ratio was much higher.

West African troops went barefoot and came cheap: a private was paid 3d a day in 1914, out of which he provided his own rations or 'chop'.[21] If they did not already speak it, soldiers had to learn Hausa, the WAFF's language of command, though some also acquired pidgin. Even Christians were usually polygamous, which had considerable consequences for the social organisation of garrisoned units. (It also led to domestic strife where a man sent his son by one wife for enlistment, but 'spared' the son of another wife.[22]) White officers had an unfeigned admiration for the African's good-humoured stoicism, but looked down on the native ranks with a bemused paternalism. They invented facile stereotypes the easier to understand the ethnic patchwork under their command. The comments of the West African Regiment's commandant are fairly representative. It was, he wrote,

'... a fine body of disciplined black troops. Intellectually nothing to write home about, [the men's] brain boxes might be divided into two compartments, the first containing wool, the second cunning... [M]en enlisted from pagan tribes (Memdis and Temnis) though possessing many soldierly qualities, were prone to excitability, and difficult to handle and control under sustained fire... Muslim soldiers were excellent fighting material and considered themselves superior to their pagan comrades, whose throats, with little encouragement, they might be disposed to slit in the name of Allah.'

The same informant noted that Afro-Caribbeans from the West India Regiment stationed in Sierra Leone were 'endowed with a higher intellect than the West Africans ... many of them were well-educated and intelligent, making first class signallers and telephone operators.'[23]

In East Africa, Britain anticipated another 'small' imperial war fought principally by Indian troops, with Africans providing carrier labour but having no military role. Unfortunately, the German commander, von Lettow-Vorbeck, proved a master of guerrilla warfare, and dragged the British Empire into 'the largest, longest and most determined' of the colonial satellite campaigns.[24] Though forced on to the defensive in early 1916, he conducted a fighting retreat over thousands of miles of bush. Retaining the loyalty of his askaris was, perhaps, the most remarkable aspect of von Lettow's campaign, since the Germans had pacified their East African colony with exemplary brutality. For both sides, the most formidable adversary was disease, but the German askaris had the inestimable advantage over Indian and white troops of greater immunity to local pathogens, and could withstand the climate better.

It was because the toughest battle was against Africa that Britain was compelled to Africanise the war. In March 1916 blacks numbered only 5,000 amongst 45,000 British Empire troops in East Africa. White South Africans constituted the largest contingent, but so many fell sick that they had to be withdrawn. The burden of the campaign fell increasingly on the greatly expanded King's African Rifles, who were recruited in Kenya and Uganda, and (despite the reluctance of the Colonial Office) on West Africans who were shipped via the Cape to Mombasa. In all, the British used over 50,000 African troops. Conditions, particularly in low-lying regions during the rainy months, were ghastly. Early 1917 was the wettest season known in East Africa for many years and the valley of the Rufiji, where the Nigerians were encamped, became a vast lake. Motor vehicles were useless, pack animals died, human carriers were scarce, rations ran short, and malaria was rife.[25]

No units had trained above the company level before the war, and they had to adapt to operations on an altogether greater scale. Although the actual engagements were tiny compared with the gigantic battles in Europe, they involved forced marching over tyrannous distances and made huge demands on combatants and their logistical support. The attrition rate was high. In the six weeks ending 11 November 1917, when the Nigerian Brigade was in constant pursuit of von Lettow's columns, it suffered 35 per cent casualties among the African rank and file, and 44 per cent among the European officers. Over 6,000 African combatants died in the campaign and, according to official statistics, 95,000 non-combatant followers.[26] The latter figure probably underestimates carrier losses since it does not include war-related deaths among discharged carriers who returned home diseased and emaciated. Throughout a vast area, most young men were either coerced into porterage or fled into the bush, and their experiences left a deep imprint on the social psyche. East Africans' responses to the outbreak of a new war in 1939 were profoundly affected by their memory of the last.

From Liwale, in Tanganyika, it was reported: 'No natives in the Territory have a greater dread of war than those of this district ... [t]he horrors of decimation by disease in the last great war, are living memories for many.' Similarly, in Bagamayo, the local population 'still retain[ed] vivid recollections of the methods employed in collecting slaves and of the more recent 1914-1918 war when all and sundry were impressed as porters.'[27]

Black soldiers in the East African campaign left no first-hand testimony, and it is difficult to get an 'inner' sense of their experience. The glowing European accounts of the men's dogged resolution and courage under fire – though perfectly credible as to particular engagements – have a sanitised feel overall.[28] A harsh disciplinary regime and the corporal punishment liberally administered by African NCOs were 'airbrushed' from the historical record. The Gold Coast Regiment, especially, won plaudits for its services in East Africa; four men were awarded the Military Medal for outstanding conduct during a fierce engagement in November 1916, and Brigadier Edwards placed on record his high appreciation for its distinguished and gallant services. The less palatable fact that nine men were sentenced to death by courts martial between September 1916 and October 1918 (three for cowardice, two for sleeping on duty, two for murder, one for casting away his arms in the face of the enemy, and one for desertion) was glossed over.[29] The total Gold Coast rank and file dispatched to East Africa was 3,582 and, though nine capital sentences may not seem an exceptional number, it was significantly greater than that incurred by the Nigerian Regiment. Only two death sentences were passed on Nigerians, though 6,500 served in East Africa. We can only speculate about the reasons behind this discrepancy. Was discipline in one regiment that much more draconian than in the other?

While Africans were coerced into the ranks, West Indian loyalists embarrassed the imperial Government with their offers of service. In 1914 the West India Regiment was the only local regular force, and it could not act as the focus for black military aspirations. It had never served in Europe and one battalion was always stationed in Sierra Leone (whence small detachments took part in the Kamerun and East African campaigns). Black loyalty was channelled into the demand that West Indian contingents be raised for the war in Europe. Military participation was seen as the entitlement of men aspiring to be equal citizens of a great empire. According to *The Federalist* newspaper:

> '[C]oloured people ... will be fighting ... to prove to Great Britain that we are not so vastly inferior to the whites that we should not be put on a level, at least, of political equality with them. We will be fighting to prove that the distinction between God-made creatures of one empire because of skin, colour or complexion differences, should no longer exist... We will be fighting to prove that we are no longer merely subjects, but citizens – citizens of a world empire whose watch-word should be Liberty, Equality and Brotherhood.'[30]

To the growing anger of West Indians, British officialdom procrastinated until late May 1915, when the War Office relented its opposition and authority was given to raise contingents. Turkey's entry into the war deflected some of the racial prejudice against black participation in a white men's conflict; senior Colonial Office officials, aware of the political importance of satisfying black aspirations, had argued that West Indian soldiers could be deployed in Egypt. But George V's intervention was the main reason for the War Office's change of heart. Manpower considerations were irrelevant at a time when Britain had more 'Kitchener' volunteers than it could equip.

The British West Indies Regiment (BWIR) was constituted in October 1915, but its funding was the responsibility of a private body, the West Indies Contingent Committee. The troops did not become a public charge until March 1916 when the Jamaica Legislative Council voted to assume the cost of the island's contingent (accounting for about two-thirds of the Regiment's strength). But, since the island's public finances were in a poor state, annual payments had to be deferred until the war's end, so the War Office agreed to pay all immediate costs. Men served at British Army rates of pay, while separation allowances were similar to those paid in the West India Regiment. White West Indians refused to serve in the ranks and the rule that the King's Commission could be granted only to men of 'wholly European parentage' was, at first, strictly observed. In September 1917 the Army Council conceded that governor's commissions might be granted to 'slightly coloured persons'. In the awarding of pensions, there was discrimination in favour of white married men, whose widows were entitled to a larger gratuity. Black and coloured recruits came from all ranks of life; they included agricultural workers, day labourers, carpenters, clerks, schoolmasters, small businessmen, shoemakers, smiths, masons and printers.[31]

The recruitment, transport to Britain and training of the West Indians exhibited more than the usual incompetence on the part of the military authorities. The first two contingents were safely dispatched, but their winter quarters at North Camp, Seaford, Sussex, were lethally cold and damp. Many died from pneumonia, and an epidemic of mumps paralysed the battalions. Although warmly – evenly ecstatically – received by British civilians, socialising with the locals was forbidden, so boredom magnified the general despondency. In March 1916 the third contingent was caught in a freezing gale off Halifax in a poorly heated ship and without winter clothing. Amputations had to be performed on 106 frost-bitten men, and hundreds of others were less severely affected. Between May and September 1916 nearly a fifth of those who had left Jamaica the previous year were invalided home, without seeing any active service.[32] The consequences for local morale and recruitment were very damaging. There were numerous cases of shirking and insubordination among recruits still in Jamaica, and several serious confrontations between unruly volunteers, civilians and the police.[33]

The military hierarchy was unsure what to do with its inconveniently patriotic blacks once they were trained. In a secret Cabinet memorandum of October 1915, Bonar Law, now Colonial Secretary, had warned that the appearance of black soldiers on the Western Front would create difficulties for white supremacy after the war was over.[34] Senior officers, convinced that black nerves would fail in modern combat, readily endorsed this. Consequently, none of the Regiment's battalions were deployed in fighting units in Europe. From January 1916, the 1st and part of the 2nd Battalion were assigned to garrison duties with the Egyptian Expeditionary Force, which seemed the West Indians' destiny as far as the War Office was concerned. From the summer of 1916, however, the growing scale of Britain's military commitment on the Western Front led to a growing demand for military labour at the ports, on lines of communication and in the Armies' rear areas, and the War Office developed a coherent policy of using non-white colonial and Chinese labour for logistical operations.[35] In July it ordered the transfer of the BWIR's 3rd and 4th Battalions from Egypt to work as ammunition carriers in France. They also built trenches and roads, unloaded ships and acted as stretcher bearers.

As regular troops enlisted for the 'duration', the 8,000 West Indians were something of an anomaly among the colonial helots. In the South African Native Labour Contingent – the largest black labour unit – workers were contracted for a year and, at the South African Government's insistence, could only be used at ports and near the coast. They were tightly segregated in 'compounds' and had their own 'native' hospitals.[36] West Indians were technically combatant forces enrolled in the British Army under the same rubric as contingents from the self-governing white dominions. Though exposed to the pervasive racism of the British ranks, they did not suffer the grotesque abuse meted out to Chinese, Indian and Egyptian labourers. They were seen as more 'British' and 'civilised' than other blacks, and usually treated in the same hospitals as white soldiers.[37] In 1917 Haig publicly commended them for 'very arduous work … carried out almost continuously under shell-fire'. Their discipline was, he wrote,

> '…excellent and their morale high. They have rendered valuable services at times of great pressure and have been of the utmost assistance to the Siege Artillery of the Armies… [U]nits have been employed in all the main operations that have taken place, including the battles of the Somme, Arras, Messines, and the operations near Ypres this year.'[38]

One artillery officer stated that where a white man could handle 3 tons of shell in a day, the West Indian could move 5. The private judgements of officers in the Labour Department were sometimes more sceptical. Colonel Wetherell noted that 'the BWIR is of considerable value in handling ammunition in warm weather, but practically useless in wet and cold weather. On the whole however this labour was not a success.'[39]

West Indians who remained with the Egyptian Expeditionary Force were kept out of front-line service until late in the Palestine campaign. Allenby took over his new command in the summer of 1917 with all the racist prejudices of his class and generation. He opposed the use of coloured troops anywhere in the Middle East, and asked for Europeans to replace the West Indians 'owing to the prestige attached to the white man' by Egyptians and Arabs. Blacks were also morally suspect; whether their infection rate from venereal disease was higher than of white units is difficult to establish, but they had a reputation for succumbing more easily to the sexual temptations of Cairo.[40] West Indian units were not given an opportunity to show their fighting qualities until August-September 1918, when the 1st and 2nd Battalions held the trenches for some six weeks opposite the Turks on the western side of the Jordan. They were several thousand feet below sea level and conditions were very debilitating. Nevertheless, they showed exemplary valour during the battle of Megiddo when the 1st Battalion had to advance 1,600 yards under very heavy shell-fire. General Chaytor commended their discipline in the trenches, their great enterprise on patrol, their steadiness under fire and dash in attack.[41]

As was the case with all units, West Indian morale deteriorated the longer the war dragged on. Like any other men they were worn down by boredom, absence from home, and sickness. The number who died from disease (1,071) was about six times greater than the number killed or dying from wounds (185). In addition to the normal stresses of service overseas, they regularly confronted racist harassment. According to a sergeant stationed in Egypt, relations with other troops were 'just as strained as those between black and white in the USA'; men were treated 'neither as Christians nor British Citizens but as West Indian "Niggers"... Instead of being drawn closer to the Church and Empire we are driven away from it.'[42]

There is suggestive evidence that the disciplinary regime for black troops was more severe than for whites; eight West Indians (all privates) were sentenced to death by courts martial between September 1916 and December 1918 (though four were reprieved). Three were convicted of striking superiors, two of murder, and one apiece of sleeping on duty, desertion and mutiny. Not too much can be read into such small figures, but the proportion of executions was high compared with cases involving white soldiers.[43]

The War Office caused enormous disgruntlement when it declared West Indians 'definitely ineligible' for the pay award made to British soldiers under Army Order No 1 of 1918.[44] Serious insubordination broke out when the battalions were congregated at Taranto in November-December 1918 preparatory to embarkation. Some working and fatigue parties were assigned to duties considered demeaning – including cleaning latrines used by the Italian labour corps – and 'mutinously refused' to perform them.[45] Members of the 9th Battalion assaulted their officers and for several days men refused to work. One hundred and eighty black sergeants petitioned the Colonial Secretary to protest against the denial of the pay award under Order No 1 and the ban on their promotion to higher rank. Between 50 and 60 men were charged with mutiny, and the Regiment was disarmed and speedily repatriated.

West Indian military service in 1914-18 left an ambiguous legacy on both sides of the imperial divide. An enquiry into the riots among demobilised blacks in Belize revealed deep resentment against racist discrimination and abuse while in the Army. For some, military service had been a politicising experience. A group of sergeant petitioners at Taranto formed the Caribbean League, a forerunner of the black nationalist movement.[46] Many ex-servicemen nursed grievances about pay and pensions throughout the 1920s and 1930s. Whitehall consistently denied that they had any cause for complaint, and Colonial Office mandarins became very disparaging about the ex-servicemen's lobby:

'The trouble with West Indian ex-servicemen [one observed] has been that "having fought for King and Country" (most of them, in fact, never saw a shot fired) they expected to be maintained in comfort for the rest of their lives. In British Honduras they rioted soon after their return from Europe, and … in other colonies the ex-servicemen gave a great deal of trouble. Probably as a result of this, they have been treated with a marked lack of sympathy, which has led to their being still more troublesome.'[47]

Nevertheless, the Governor of Barbados reported in May 1940 that there was no evidence of disgruntled feeling among ex-servicemen discouraging West Indians from coming forward to offer their services: 'Rather it is the case that grousing arises from our inability to offer [them] any avenue for war service.' There was great disappointment 'at the failure of the Home Country to call for the services of a West Indian contingent'. The reason for this 'failure' is plain. The men running Britain's war effort in the 1940s had a jaundiced view of how West Indian soldiers had performed two decades or so earlier. In February 1941 the Army Council decided, in the light of experience of the last war, not to recruit coloured West Indians either as combatant troops or as labour units. Sir John Grigg, Secretary of State for War, told the Colonial Secretary in December 1943 that it should be 'remembered that in the last war West Indians were employed in a combatant role in Palestine where they proved quite unsuitable and caused considerable trouble'.[48] This was a slur, but the fact that Grigg believed it was significant, and surely not unrelated to the War Office's foot-dragging with respect to the implementation of the Order of October 1939.

In recruiting African soldiers after 1939, the British encountered many of the problems of the First World War but on a greater scale. Enlistment in the Army was ostensibly voluntary, but in fact large numbers were 'conscripted volunteers', arbitrarily sent by their chiefs.[49] The King's African Rifles were an exception – they enjoyed an elite reputation and were paid well above East African wages. The military authorities only sought recruits among the 'martial tribes', such as the Luo and the Ngoni. The East African Military Labour Service, on the other hand, could fulfil its military quotas only by resorting to conscription, which provoked bitter opposition and flight into the bush. In West Africa, when recruiting parties were announced, fit young men emigrated in droves. When recruiting officers arrived in a district, they often had to conscript men in poor physical condition. About half the so-called able-bodied men enlisted in rural Nigeria were unfit for heavy manual labour.[50] Desertion rates were high, especially when troops were due to move overseas; over 15 per cent of the total Gold Coast Regiment were posted as deserters in late 1943. Among Asante recruits, the figure was over 42 per cent.[51]

The main changes in the character of West African forces were their greater ethnic and religious diversity by comparison with 1914-18, and a higher proportion of men with technical skills. Because of wartime expansion, and the need for clerks, storemen, medical auxiliaries and the like, recruiting was extended to the southern, more educated and Christianised parts of Nigeria and the Gold Coast. By 1945 Christians made up 47 per cent of West African forces, Muslims were one-third, and the rest pagan. Ethnic rivalries often threatened to subvert military discipline, and the Army avoided the formation of platoons and sections out of single tribes for fear of inter-ethnic conflicts. Major Carfrae, who served with the Nigerians, found his African NCOs could keep some measure of control over ethnically mixed units while under the European eye, 'but off duty the niceties of the military hierarchy were forgotten. Platoons would then gather into tribal groups and it was the senior tribal member who held the greatest influence, whatever his rank.'[52]

From 1940 West Africa supplied about 200,000 soldiers and labourers (mostly Nigerians) for military service in the Abyssinian campaign, North Africa, and, after 1943, in Asia. Thanks to a remarkable memoir written some time after the war by Private Isaac Fadoyebo, we can follow the processes of recruiting, training and deploying these men through the experiences of an African ranker. The account was written at the prompting of a white official in the Lagos Department of Labour (for which Isaac worked after the war) and may, for this reason, rather flatter the British. But it gives an authentic sense of the war as seen through an African soldier's eyes.[53]

A Yoruba, Fadoyebo was born in 1925 in the Owo Local Government Area of Ondo State into a polygamous household, though his father was professedly a Christian. The eldest son, he was given a primary education at Anglican schools and his father wanted the boy to become a pupil teacher. Instead, the 16-year-old enlisted at Abeokuta in January 1942. He represented the more educated southerners needed for military jobs requiring literacy and technical skills, and was trained as a hospital orderly. Later he became a medical auxiliary with a casualty clearing station. Drill and discipline were instilled into raw recruits by 'indigenous non-commissioned Officers who were rough in mind and in some cases callous to the extreme… They would shout at us as if we were no human beings and generally developed hatred for those who had a bit of education.' African NCOs routinely beat their men – Major Poore had a Sergeant Rigg known as 'sergeant bend down' for this reason – who were not allowed direct access to white commissioned officers.

At the training centre, Isaac and other tradesmen formed E Company, which had a fair share of literate personnel – men who found it rather painful to learn that 'the army was not the type of organisation where an individual or set of people could claim any right'. Other companies consisted mostly of illiterates. The troops underwent basic training in drill kit utterly inappropriate to the Tropics: heavy-duty pants that stopped half-way between the knee and ankle and a woollen jersey that had to be worn for six days before it could be washed. When laundered, it shrank and could hardly cover the upper part of Isaac's stomach. Meals mostly comprised gari (cassava meal), rice and beans served in sufficient quantities, and jero, which southerners did not like but northerners loved. Like his European officers, Isaac had to learn Hausa; after his first year of service he was able to speak a little.

The Army introduced Isaac to organised sport, such as boxing and track events, and he enjoyed singing with Yoruba comrades. He is reticent as to any off-duty sexual relationships and, as a young Christian, may well have been chaste. If so, he was exceptional. This is a matter a white historian touches on at his peril, but there is much evidence to suggest that the West African soldiers were open and unashamed about satisfying their sexual appetites. It was not that their sex drives were any more compelling than white servicemen's, but Africans were less culturally encumbered by sexual puritanism. Major Carfrae bluntly asserted:

'Women were important to the Africans … sexual relations were to them as essential and matter-of-fact as food and drink. To be a week without a woman was hardship; any longer was inconceivable. All the Nigerians were promiscuous to a greater or less degree and the Kaduna harlots … took plenty of money from wifeless young recruits.'[54]

The military strove to limit the incidence of venereal infection by various means; officers in Egypt were known to lecture Africans on the dangers of VD, and ET centres were established in some camps. When tens of thousands of Africans were stationed near Madras in 1945, a private brothel was set up, on which the MO kept a close check.[55] Changes in the Army's social organisation after 1939 may have contributed to the 'normalisation' of promiscuous sex. In the peacetime Army, soldiers' wives had lived with them in barracks and cooked their food. The senior wife of the African Sergeant-Major had usually ruled the roost with an iron hand. The Army's wartime expansion and the formation of the West African Army Service Corps to cater for the troops shattered these domestic arrangements. Soldiers' wives were given notice to quit.

After basic training, Isaac's unit was shipped from Lagos to Freetown, though soldiers were given no prior information as to their destination. On board ship, many became acquainted with flush lavatories for the first time. Isaac recalls:

'…we felt we were being discriminated against in the use of the toilet and bathroom. The complaint against us was that we blacks often soiled sanitary conveniences to the annoyance of the crew… Usually, we were free to make use of them only after the captain had completed his daily inspection of the boat. As an alternative, a crate was constructed and attached to the tail end of the ship for those who might wish to ease themselves while the toilet was locked up… Frankly speaking, there was some justification for the action taken by the staff of the ship. Several times I did observe that some of the WCs were badly used and on one occasion, I saw an empty sardine tin floating in one of them.'[56]

At the hospital at Port Loko, Isaac encountered a westernised African, such as he had rarely met before. The pharmacist, Sergeant Taylor, was 'a real creole boy', fond of European food, who 'practised all the norms that belonged to members of the establishment'. Isaac 'really envied his class and exalted position'. Though a small incident, it typified the way wartime service took African soldiers out of their familiar social enclaves, and made them aware of other social roles and mores. In this respect, meeting blacks from different cultural milieus almost certainly made a deeper impression than meeting whites.

Isaac returned to Nigeria with many Sierra Leoneons as part of the 29th

Casualty Clearing Station, under the command of Major Moynagh, whom the men 'all loved and respected'. This affection was not unconnected with the major's having no aptitude for military service. He was a mild and gentle Anglican, with a fondness for morning prayers that other officers found irksome, and whose orderly room judgements were always merciful. When Moynagh was transferred, discipline in the unit broke down because of a bewildering series of promotions and demotions among the African NCOs. The delicate ethnic balance was upset when a demoted NCO from one group felt he was being jeered at by another. 'There was a riot within the unit: we threw off all discipline and engaged ourselves in a fracas.'[57]

Around October 1943, prior to being shipped to Asia, Isaac went on four weeks home leave for the first time since enlistment. His people were astonished to see him alive – since it was generally thought that anybody who joined the Army would eventually be killed – and his father urged him to desert. The Army had introduced a system of deferred pay to discourage desertion, but it was the prospect of disgrace, rather than pecuniary loss, that persuaded Isaac to return to duty. On the day he left, 'my father was so down he could not see me off'.

His unit sailed to Bombay by the Cape, then went by train to Calcutta. There the men were given a taste of big city life by being 'taken to some expensive restaurants for first class meals, and also cinema theatres'. They also experienced their first air raid.

In early 1944 the 29th Casualty Clearing Station took part in the first ill-fated Kalladan campaign, in support of the 81st (West African) Division. Unlike in the First World War there were no inhibitions on deploying African troops outside Africa, and the decision to send them to Burma was influenced by a variety of factors. The clearing of Axis forces from North Africa had released African troops from defensive duties in the Middle East, and they were not wanted for the invasion of Europe. They had a propensity for bushcraft, and the tropical forest zone of West Africa provided a suitable training ground for jungle warfare. The Kalladan terrain and the shortage of motorable roads dictated 'a carrier's war' for which African formations were considered highly suited. Additionally, their sickness rate in tropical conditions was remarkably low. Whether this was a calculation in their deployment in Burma I cannot say, but Major Poore, who served with the Gold Coast Regiment, recalled, 'For every man we had sick the next best Division had sixty… The Africans were not seriously inconvenienced by malaria.'[58]

Isaac was one of a considerable number of African soldiers who embarked on the re-conquest of Burma unarmed. He recalls: 'Only CSM Duke and Motor Drivers of all ranks were allowed to bear arms…' It is understandable that medical auxiliaries such as Isaac were not issued with weapons, but too many of his comrades were human substitutes for lorries or mules. Allowing large numbers of unarmed carriers from Auxiliary Group into close contact with the Japanese was military folly. They required constant protection by riflemen and in times of stress were parasitic on their comrades.

Isaac's unit advanced in small groups each led by at least a British NCO. They went down river using bamboo rafts, and sometimes hired wooden canoes from

Indian settlers, which their owners would paddle. The Burmese struck Isaac as wretchedly impoverished and unfriendly. Though instructed to behave well towards the local people, the troops had little compunction about raiding native plots for water melons and cucumbers: 'We needed food to keep going.' As they moved further from base, meals became irregular and scarce, and some supplies were dropped by parachute drops. Until they reached the fighting zone, they received mail periodically. As with any other servicemen abroad, letters from home were enormously important to Africans. Many could read but not write, and on mail day literate soldiers were kept very busy, not only answering their own letters, but the letters of their friends.[59] Isaac recalls receiving three letters on one night. They were the last that reached him before coming under fire, and he had neither the time nor the material to answer them.

Shortly after, Isaac's right knee was shattered in a surprise Japanese attack during the battle of Nyron. He and Sergeant David Kagbo, who was less seriously wounded, were stranded in enemy-occupied territory for nine months, and they owed their survival to Bengali settlers loyal to the British. Though his account is engagingly modest, it is clear that both men showed extraordinary initiative and fortitude in staying alive and at liberty. They passed themselves off as Muslims to ingratiate themselves with the Bengalis, and acquired sufficient of their language to communicate competently. Gurkhas rescued them on 10 December 1944.

Isaac's kneecap was subsequently removed by Lt-Col Neil ('a kind and dedicated officer') and his disability was assessed at 60 per cent. During the sojourn in the jungle, he had been posted killed in action, and he returned home something of a celebrity. He was feted in the local African press, but also in a weekly journal owned and managed by the Nigerian Government's Public Relations Department. Nationalist journalists depicted him as a young man maimed for life in a Europeans' war, the Government publicists as a loyal war hero. He was discharged in June 1945, with an L18 gratuity and an 18 shillings per month pension, and awarded the Loyal Service Badge. When he finally arrived at Enure-Ile in early August, there was a tumultuous crowd to greet him:

> 'It was as if a man was back to life – resurrection of a sort. I had difficulty in wading through the multitude before I could finally get to the door of our house… I was hugged by my parents and other relations after they had splashed sand on me. The belief was that anybody who reappeared alive after his death had been mourned, should have his body sprayed with dust.'[60]

The participation of black servicemen in Britain's 20th-century wars is part of a common imperial history. To see it in terms of awakening national consciousness among colonial peoples and as a prelude to decolonisation is, on the whole, a mistake. This argument has some validity for the West Indies, but even in that context the dominant feeling was resentment at the clumsy and grudging attitude of the British state towards the genuinely popular desire to serve the Empire. In Africa, men who soldiered away from home in the 1940s were probably less politicised than groups caught up in the economic mobilisation of the colonies such as cocoa farmers and civilian labourers. Some educated African NCOs resented their automatic subordination to white NCOs, but otherwise there is little evidence of military service engendering anti-European feeling. Most insubordination had 'normal' causes, such as the denial of leave to men too long away from home; signs of racial hostility towards white superiors and resentment of discriminatory treatment are rare.

Major Carfrae observed that, 'Africans did not seem to look on us, their leaders, as usurpers; there was no hostility nor lack of trust; indeed they plainly admired us, were touchingly loyal and sometimes devoted.'[61] Isaac's account, albeit only one African's recollections, confirms this. Though he was crippled for life, his memoir is touchingly free of rancour. The colonial African forces were, certainly, racist institutions, but the British officers seconded to them were rarely bigots. They knew that loyalty would not be won by showing dislike for Africans or bored indifference. They had to work with the grain of the troops' temperament. Former officers paid many tributes to their men, but none is more quietly eloquent than that of Captain Cookson, who commanded a Gambian company during fierce fighting in Arakan:

'During the long noisy week that followed the first attack, I acquired a new respect for the Africans as soldiers. They lived at their firing positions in a state of perpetual discomfort and watchfulness, and yet they never failed to greet me with a joke and a laugh. Without a murmur of complaint they defended a country whose inhabitants they despised in a quarrel whose implications they did not understand. They had volunteered to fight for the British, and if the British brought them to a wilderness that was a sufficient reason. They squatted down in their trenches, polished the leather charms next to their skin, prayed to Allah for his protection and good-humouredly got on with the job.'

When Punjabis relieved them after eight days and nine attacks, he found himself 'regretting something that had been lost, some inner circle of friendship and confidence that had grown in the Company out of the common task and common risk.'[62]

Recommended reading

Farwell, B., *The Great War in Africa* (Harmondsworth: Viking, 1987)

Haywood, A. and Clarke, F. A. S., *The History of the Royal West African Frontier Force* (Aldershot: Gale & Polden, 1964)

Joseph, C. L., 'The British West Indies Regiment', in *Journal of Caribbean History* 12 (May 1971)

Killingray, D., 'If I fight for them, maybe then I can go back to the village: African soldiers in the Mediterranean and European campaigns', in Addison, P. and Calder, A. (eds), *Time to Kill: the Soldier's Experience of the War in the West* (London: Pimlico, 1997)

'Military and Labour Policies in the Gold Coast during the First World War', in Page, M. E. (ed), *Africa and the First World War* (London: Macmillan, 1987)

'Military and Labour Recruitment in the Gold Coast during the Second World
War', in *Journal of African History* 23 (1982) pp83-95

Killingray, D. and Clayton, A., *Khaki and Blue: Military and police in British colonial
Africa* (Athens, Ohio: Ohio University Press, 1989)

Moyse-Bartlett, H., *The King's African Rifles* (Aldershot: Gale & Polden, 1956)

Notes

[1]   *The Colonial Empire (1939-1947)*, pp1946-47, x, Cmd 7167, p1

[2]   The basic source for recruitment figures in 1914-18 is *Statistics of the Military Effort of the British
     Empire during the Great War*, pp382-3; see also C. E. Carrington, 'The Empire at War, 1914-1918',
     in E. A. Benians et al (eds), *The Cambridge History of the British Empire* (Cambridge University Press,
     1959) Vol 3, p642

[3]   Cmd 7176, Appendix II; see also D. Killingray, 'Labour Mobilisation in British Colonial Africa for
     the War Effort', in D. Killingray and R. Rathbone (eds), *Africa and the Second World War*
     (Macmillan, 1986)

[4]   See G. Hodges, 'Military Labour in East Africa and its Impact on Kenya', in M. E. Page (ed), *Africa
     and the First World War* (Macmillan, 1987) p148

[5]   See G. D. Howe, 'West Indians and World War One: A Social History of the British West Indies
     Regiment' (PhD, University of London, 1994) p38. For the political and social context I have drawn
     on H. Johnson, 'The British Caribbean from Demobilization to Constitutional Decolonisation', in
     J. M. Brown and W. R. Louis (eds), *The Oxford History of the British Empire*, Vol 5 (Oxford University
     Press, 1999)

[6]   See 'Nigeria and the Cameroons', in C. Lucas (ed), *The Empire at War*, Vol 4 (Oxford University
     Press, 1923) p59

[7]   PRO, CO 318/441/4, 'Reactions of West Indian Labour to the War', Governor of Jamaica to
     Secretary of State, 6 September 1939

[8]   The Indianisation of the Indian Army Officer Corps had begun at the end of the First World War.

[9]   See C. L. Joseph, 'The British West Indies Regiment', in *Journal of Caribbean History* 12 (May 1971)
     p96

[10] See D. Killingray, 'All the King's Men? Blacks in the British Army in the First World War', in R. Lotz
     and I. Pegg (eds), *Under the Imperial Carpet: Essays in Black History (1780-1850)* (Crawley: Rabbit
     Press) p179

[11] See D. Killingray, 'Race and rank in the British Army in the Twentieth century', in *Ethnic and Racial
     Studies* 10 (3) (1987) p281. A useful of account of racial discrimination in the forces is M. Sherwood,
     Many Struggles: West Indian Workers and Service Personnel in Britain (1939-45) (Karia Press, 1982)

[12] M. Sherwood, op cit, p15; no reference is given for this remark in Sherwood.

[13] D. H. Barber, *Africans in Khaki* (Livingstone Press, 1948) pp91-2

[14] Quoted in A. G. Russell, *Colour, Race and Empire* (Gollancz, 1944) p80

[15] D. Killingray, 'Military and Labour Policies in the Gold Coast during the First World War', in M. E.
     Page (ed), op cit, p155; the objections of British trade unions to black labour were another factor in
     the shelving of these proposals.

[16] See 'Nigeria and the Cameroons', in C. Lucas (ed), op cit, Vol 4, p69

[17] For a detailed account, see R. Thomas, 'Military Recruitment in the Gold Coast during the First
     World War', in *Cahiers d'Etudes Africaines* 57, 15-1, pp57-83

[18] See D. Killingray, 'Military and Labour Policies in the Gold Coast...', op cit, p162, and J. K.
     Matthews, 'Reluctant Allies: Nigerian Responses to Military Recruitment 1914-18', ibid, p103

[19] Figures in C. Lucas (ed), op cit, Vol 4, p130

[20] See E. Gorges, *The Great War in West Africa* (Hutchinson, 1930) p42

[21] Ibid, p32

[22] See R. Thomas, op cit, p65

[23] E. Gorges, op cit, pp32, 43

[24] H. Moyse-Bartlett, *The King's African Rifles* (Aldershot, 1956) p259

25 See 'Nigeria and the Cameroons', in C. Lucas (ed), op cit, Vol 4, p141

26 G. Hodges, op cit, p148

27 See N. J. Westcott, 'The Impact of the Second World War on Tanganyika, 1939-1949' (PhD, University of Cambridge, 1982) p46

28 The quasi-official accounts are H. Clifford, *The Gold Coast Regiment in the East African Campaign* (Murray, 1920) and W. D. Downes, *With the Nigerians in German East Africa* (Murray, 1920)

29 I am indebted for information on military executions to Gerard Oram, who is completing a doctoral thesis on this topic.

30 *The Federalist*, 27 October 1915, cited in G. D. Howe, op cit, p60

31 See F. Cundall, *Jamaica's Part in the Great War* (West India Committee, 1920) p26

32 Ibid, pp24, 28

33 The fullest account on the BWIR is now Dr Howe's, to which I am much indebted.

34 Cabinet memorandum, 'Question of Raising Native Troops for Imperial Service', 18 October 1915, PRO CAB 37/136/19

35 See R. Kilson, 'Calling Up the Empire: The British Military Use of Non-white Labour in France, 1916-1920' (unpublished PhD, Harvard, 1990) p186 and passim

36 See A. Grundlingh, *Fighting their Own War: South African Blacks and the First World War* (Johannesburg: 1987)

37 G. D. Howe, op cit, p214

38 Quoted in A. Aspinall, 'The War Effort of the British West Indies', in C. Lucas, (ed), op cit, Vol 2, p339

39 WO 106/33 AG 12 (Col Wetherell's appended notes), quoted in R. Kilson, op cit, p187

40 See L. James, *Imperial Warrior: The Life and Times of Field-Marshal Viscount Allenby 1861-1936* (Weidenfeld & Nicolson, 1993) p123. G. D. Howe, op cit, pp267-8, raises some doubts about the official statistics for black infection rates.

41 Chaytor is quoted in A. Aspinall, loc cit, pp337-8

42 See W. F. Elkins, 'A Source of Black Nationalism in the Caribbean: The Revolt of the British West Indies Regiment at Taranto, Italy', in *Science and Society* 34 (2) (1970) p100

43 See G. Oram, *Worthless Men: Race, eugenics and the death penalty in the British Army during the First World War* (Francis Boutle, 1998) p106

44 C. L. Joseph, loc cit, p101. The increase was later passed to the Regiment after strong protests.

45 Ibid, p119

46 W. F. Elkins, loc cit, p103; C. L. Joseph, loc cit, p119

47 PRO, CO 318/445/6, confidential circular of 16 March 1940 in a file entitled 'Royal Commission on West India, Grievances of ex-Servicemen'. The signature is indecipherable, but from the context it is clear that the writer was a former Governor of British Honduras.

48 Grigg to Oliver Stanley, CO 968/17/15, 17 December 1943

49 See D. Killingray, 'Military and Labour Recruitment in the Gold Coast during the Second World War', in *Journal of African History* 23 (1982) p89

50 See M. Hailey, *An African Survey* (Oxford University Press, revised 1956) p1283

51 See D. Killingray, loc cit, p94 (note 52)

52 C. Carfrae, 'Dark Company: An account of four years' sojourn with West African soldiers in Nigeria, India and Burma', typescript ms, Imperial War Museum (IWM), p14

53 I. Fadoyebo, 'A Stroke of Unbelievable Luck', typescript memoir, copy in the IWM

54 C. Carfrae, op cit, p14

55 D. H. Barber, op cit, p89. The Madras brothel is mentioned in the P. Poore papers, 'The First Kaladan Campaign', IWM, p12

56 I. Fadoyebo, op cit, p28

57 Ibid, p31

58 P. Poore, op cit, pp83, 90

59 See D. H. Barber, op cit, p57

60 I. Fadoyebo, op cit, p56

61 C. Carfrae, op cit, p15

62 D. M. Cookson, typescript ms, 'With Africans in Arakan', IWM, pp78, 80

Chapter 18

The French Empire

Philip Dine

In the early hours of 4 August 1914, the German battle-cruisers *Breslau* and *Goeben* attacked the French North African ports of Bône and Philippeville. The short but intense shelling resulted in some understandable panic among the local Algerian population, and left 17 dead. There was little if any defensive riposte, and the two vessels steamed away unhindered. In military terms, this isolated and unrepeated action had no significant impact.[1] However, at a symbolic level this first show of strength by extra-colonial 'Others' would hint at their longer-term role – specifically, their radical disruption of the imperial status quo, together with the assumptions upon which it was founded, and the identities to which it gave rise. This process of destabilisation and interrogation would intensify throughout the First World War, and would carry over into the inter-war years, before reaching its apotheosis with the Second World War.

The psychological and political importance of the latter conflict's transformation of the French Empire from a peripheral to a central theatre of operations is nicely captured by Mohamed Dib in *Le Métier à tisser* (*The Loom*), an autobiographical novel published in 1957, at the height of his homeland's armed struggle for independence from colonial rule. Dib's young protagonist, the apprentice weaver Omar, lives in Algiers, which in November 1942 is dominated, on the one hand, by the echoes of the European war, and on the other, by the abiding verities of colonial oppression. In the final pages of the novel, Omar is amazed when he comes face to face with the first of many newly landed American troops: a young, smiling, blue-eyed boy, handing out bars of chocolate and miniature stars-and-stripes flags. To the amazed Algerian adolescent, the scarcely older GI appears as strange as a being from another planet. Crucially, however, he is perceived instantly in positive terms:

> 'There could be no doubt about it: he was a foreigner; there was only the slightest resemblance between him and the Europeans from here…
> THE A-ME-RI-CANS!
> Omar's heart leapt in his chest as he was overwhelmed by an insane feeling of joy. An impossible hope seized him, his throat tightened, and he thought that he was going to cry.'[2]

As the novel closes, Omar strides off – 'with a serious, almost fierce, expression on his face'[3] – into a future permanently altered by this fleeting personal contact with the forces of communal liberation and national self-determination. Three decades after the Kaiser's Navy had revealed to indigenous Algerians that their colonised homeland was part of a much bigger political equation, the Anglo-American 'Torch' landings thus encouraged the radicalisation of local responses to the continued presence of the French occupier. As the remainder of this chapter will attempt to show, similar forces were at work throughout the French Empire in the periods 1914-18 and 1939-45.

At the most basic level, the two World Wars were temporarily to make and durably to break *la France d'outre-mer* (overseas France). For 'it was in the years when the First World War was imminent that the colonial system was finally established'[4], and in the immediate aftermath of the conflict the French Empire would achieve its greatest territorial and demographic expansion. Moreover, the Empire's contribution to the French war effort had, for the first time, demonstrated its value to a hitherto sceptical metropolitan public, thus allowing the colonial lobby to market the colonies in new and more effective ways. This concerted campaign of imperial propaganda would reach its climax with the spectacular international colonial exhibition staged in Paris in 1931. To France's established territories in North, West and Equatorial Africa and Indo-China had now been added her share of the spoils from the dismembered German Empire, Togo and Cameroon, together with mandates from the League of Nations in Syria and the Lebanon. The French Empire was thus at its apogee and official and popular enthusiasm for *la plus grande France* (Greater France) at its height, just as Europe began its slide into the next generalised conflict, this time with genuinely global consequences.

Following the fall of France and its occupation by the Germans in the summer of 1940, the Empire would magically be transformed into France herself, both in the rhetoric of the collaborationist administration of Maréchal Philippe Pétain – the hero of Verdun in 1916 – and in that of *la France combattante*, the 'fighting French' forces, now commanded by one of Pétain's junior officers in the earlier war, General Charles de Gaulle. The regular use of slogans such as 'Ici la France!' ('This is France calling!') and 'La France, capitale Alger!' ('France, capital Algiers!') by the Free French, once the 1942 Allied landings had allowed the establishment of de Gaulle's Provisional Government of the French Republic in the city, was part of a mobilisation of the Empire that, in common with the activities of the internal resistance movement, would enable France to contribute to her own liberation, and thus to re-establish her national pride. However, this strategy was to prove something of a double-edged sword, for the unprecedented colonial consensus that resulted would make the French determined to cling on to their overseas Empire in an era of decolonisation. It would take two savage wars of national liberation – in Indo-China and Algeria – to make the French see the error of their ways.

For the peoples of the French Empire, the two World Wars would have disruptive and galvanising effects that in some ways were the negative image of those experienced by metropolitan France. Where the First World War effectively brought the Empire – its strategic, economic and, above all, human potential – to the *métropole*, the Second World War would take 'mainland' France, and especially the spectacle of its weaknesses and divisions, to the Empire. In both cases, international conflict would allow cracks to appear in the imperial edifice, through which powerfully subversive, and ultimately fatal, new ideas would be transmitted, in spite of the best efforts of the colonial authorities. Informed by developments in the emerging superpowers of the United States and the Soviet Union, both under Wilson and Lenin, and Roosevelt and Stalin, such ideas would encourage the rise of colonial nationalism in the wake of the First World War, and its ever greater militancy during the Second World War. This process would lead inexorably to the independence of France's principal overseas territories, and thus to the end of her Empire. To understand the complexities of that profound transformation it is now necessary to focus in turn on the very diverse experiences of individuals and communities in each of the two global conflicts. The continuities and changes, revelations and ambiguities that characterised the broader process will be discussed by way of a conclusion.

In terms of direct military impacts, the Great War's effect on the French Empire would prove negligible. However, the colonies were undoubtedly of broad economic significance, primarily as suppliers of food and raw materials, but also through the levying of war taxes and other forms of fund-raising. Yet the Empire's industrial role was inevitably limited by the general lack of established infrastructures that could be geared to military production. Instead, its main attraction was as an apparently limitless reserve of manpower, both in the form of soldiers for the Western Front and other theatres, and as replacement workers for French factories and mines, where mobilisation had had a significant impact on production levels in spite of a variety of attempts to replace those workers who had volunteered or been conscripted, including the first large-scale employment of women. Although France, in common with the other European empires, had made extensive use of indigenous troops and workers before 1914, their deployment had essentially been restricted to the colonies. The dramatically changed circumstances of the European conflict were thus to bring about a major departure from established colonial practice: 'The huge and unprecedented manpower requirements of the First World War gave rise to the first large-scale mobilisation of colonial or non-European forces into the metropolitan heartland.'[5]

Recruitment took many forms, from genuine appeals for volunteers, to myriad forms of conscription, both official and unofficial, and not infrequently involving threatened or actual violence. Local responses were similarly mixed, with some significant examples of resistance being recorded. As far as the raising of troops was concerned, the French territories in North and West Africa were the most readily accessible, and thus the most called upon, with the bulk of the imperial contingent being made up of *tirailleurs* (colonial infantrymen) from Algeria and Senegal.[6] In the early months of the war, the great majority of existing colonial regiments were quickly sent to the Western Front, with consequent heavy losses among both those experienced men who had joined up in the pre-war period and the new volunteers who had signed up for the duration of the hostilities. Although such recruits were relatively numerous in 1914, they would become much harder to find as the war continued and intensified.[7] French recruitment procedures would be toughened up in consequence, and so would the resistance of the colonised to this latest imposition, which was often compounded by longer-term economic and administrative problems, as well as more immediate local crises.[8] As Alice Conklin has pointed out with regard to West Africa, hostility to recruitment for military service frequently went beyond the native populations to the territory's colonial administrators:

'African reaction to recruitment in 1914 and 1915 was the same everywhere, although most pronounced where European representation was thinnest: despair and even hysteria of the families, who were convinced their sons would never return, and who often resorted to force to release conscripts rounded up by the local authorities before these new recruits left their region of origin; passive, spontaneous, and individualised resistance in the form of flight to neighbouring foreign colonies or into the bush and forests, or self-mutilation; presentation of physically unfit men, who would automatically be rejected by the army agents. This last tactic hardly qualified as a form of resistance. What the decision to recruit in West Africa revealed was the deplorable state of the population after a recent famine in the Sahel, and the endemic diseases upon which French medical care had had so little impact. Given these conditions, the request for all able-bodied men three times in the same year, disrupting the cultivation and harvesting of their crops when supplies were at their lowest, antagonised not only Africans but many lieutenant governors, who feared for French authority if recruitment continued unabated.'[9]

Such fears were to prove well founded, with armed uprisings reported in several of France's West African territories.[10] Similar responses were also experienced in North Africa, the most serious of which occurred in September 1916 in the Constantine region of Algeria, and was prompted in this case by resistance to the conscription of workers. This major revolt would last until the end of the year, and would commit between 14,000 and 16,000 French troops to a guerrilla campaign in the Aurès mountains that genuinely prefigured the events of the Algerian war of independence, which would itself erupt in the same location in 1954; all this for 1,366 conscripted workers, the majority of whom had already presented themselves to the colonial authorities before the repression began.[11] However, such outbreaks remained the exception, and French colonial authority was not, on the whole, called into question as a result of the recruitment drive.

In West Africa, the recruitment effort would be considerably assisted by the efforts of Blaise Diagne, the first black African to be elected to the French Parliament as a Deputy for his native Senegal. He personally toured the relevant territories in 1918 encouraging military service in France's hour of need in return for a new vision of the Africans' relationship with the colonial 'mother country'. His initiative met with considerable success: no fewer than 63,000 *tirailleurs* enlisted, with no further disruptions being recorded in the territories concerned.[12] As the war went on, the colonial authorities also became more sophisticated in terms of the ideological investment that they made in native recruits: 'It was during the war that psychological action aimed at the colonised made its first appearance', in the form of films, photographs, pamphlets, newspapers and the like aimed at encouraging colonial support for French war aims.[13]

In total, the Empire was to provide somewhere in the region of 556,000 troops for the French Army, and 184,000 civilian workers for French industry. Fatalities were of the order of 78,000 men, the great majority of whom were Algerian or Senegalese, with many more wounded. Together with the small number of mobilised French citizens resident in the colonies proper (some 4,000) and the much larger number of French Algerian recruits (73,000, from the three départements of a territory that had, since 1848, been administratively and politically incorporated as an integral part of France), the Empire was thus able to provide between 7 and 8 per cent of the available French forces.[14] Given the vast potential of the French Empire's human resources, this figure may appear relatively modest. However, the impact on colonial societies was enormous, and time spent at the front or in the factory was to be of the greatest significance for subsequent developments in the various territories. The respective experiences of soldiers and workers were, inevitably, very different, but both would share in the abiding experience that, for the first time, and albeit only briefly, the seemingly unstoppable advance of French colonialism had, against all expectations, been halted, and a widespread 'decompression, and even a sense of liberation' had been felt throughout the Empire in consequence.[15]

While the experiences of metropolitan French troops in 1914-18 have given rise – as elsewhere in Europe – to a large body of personal testimonies, and subsequent academic discussion, those of colonial soldiers have been less well served by posterity. The widespread literary '*prise de parole*' ('speaking out') noted by Stéphane Audoin-Rouzeau, and documented in monumental fashion in the French context by Jean-Norton Cru[16], would not appear to have extended to colonial troops, who were, of course, often illiterate. Myron Echenberg's pioneering attempt to give a voice to the *tirailleurs sénégalais* is all the more important against the background of this general silence. Yet even the single Senegalese testimony identified by Echenberg – 'the memoirs of Bakary Diallo, one of the few first-hand African accounts we have of the "face of battle"'[17] – actually tells us very little about colonial service in the trenches. The principal interest of Diallo's testimony is to be found rather in his glowing depiction of the welcome given to colonial troops by French civilians, and in his more nuanced account of his convalescence following his serious wounding at the battle of the Marne in 1914, and of the complications attached to his eventual demobilisation and repatriation. We must therefore look elsewhere for accounts of the wartime experiences of France's colonial conscripts.

The testimony of a French sergeant in the 3rd Algerian *tirailleurs*, recorded by Gilbert Meynier, hints at the genuine comradeship in adversity that would seem to have been experienced at a personal level by colonial troops:

'The French soldiers got on well with the Arabs. They were just like us: poor blokes. We were all in the same bloody mess [la même merde].'[18]

That relations between men at the front would seem to have been as good as the terrible circumstances allowed would also seem to be borne out by the linguistic exchanges that, as the same witness confirms, took place between Algerian Arabic and colloquial French, in both directions, at this time. Similarly, French veteran Paul Tuffrau, in his own war journal, speaks well of the valour, military effectiveness and self-sacrifice of Moroccan troops fighting alongside him, also on the Marne.[19] However, the stance adopted by the military authorities meant that service in the French Army would remain a deeply ambivalent experience for the majority of colonial troops. So, on the one hand, a genuine – if often clumsily paternalistic – attempt was made to integrate them, while on the other, they were subject to constant surveillance. For if colonial recruits were to find themselves better treated in the Army than they had become used to in the colonies, they were never, for all that, regarded as the equals of French troops.

On the positive side, efforts were made to respect the eating habits and religious beliefs of the *tirailleurs*, while racial humiliation of the kind that could be expected at home was generally avoided. However, there was clear discrimination in leave and convalescence arrangements, both for practical reasons and also for moral and political ones. The fear of contamination by French mischief-makers, particularly on the Left, was one such reason for surveillance, while the possibility of romantic liaisons with French nurses or other women whose husbands were away at the front was another cause for concern on the part of the authorities. For the minority of *évolués* (the élite group of 'evolved', or assimilated, colonial subjects) who aspired to officer status, the most difficult discrimination to bear was that which limited them to the rank of lieutenant in all but the rarest cases, with, at all levels, colonial troops obliged to obey the orders of a French colleague of similar standing. This situation has been linked to what was a rare defection from the French side, that of Lieutenant Rabah Boukaboya, an Algerian former schoolteacher who deserted on the Oise in April 1915 and was taken to Berlin, where he contributed to the production of German propaganda aimed at North African troops.[20]

While seasoned colonial units would seem to have fought as well as any in the early carnage of the 'race for the sea', the heavy losses sustained led to the rapid incorporation of young, and inadequately trained, *tirailleurs*, who did not always respond as effectively to the demands placed upon them as their French commanders expected. The new arrivals' sense of geographical and cultural dislocation was undoubtedly compounded by the rigours of the northern European climate, while related pulmonary diseases and an epidemic of scarlet fever also took a disproportionately heavy toll among colonial troops. In a number of cases inexperienced men panicked, leading to refusals to comply with orders, and thus to summary executions. The most dramatic of these occurred on 15 December 1914, when a genuine decimation of a Tunisian company was ordered and carried out, with the express authority of General Foch himself. When General d'Urbal, the commander of the French Eighth Army, was informed of this unit's refusal to move forward, he instructed that one *tirailleur* in every ten should be selected by the drawing of lots, paraded before the troops at the front wearing a notice bearing the single word 'coward' in French and Arabic, then executed. This order was carried out at 5 o'clock in the evening of the day in question, by a firing squad made up of French Algerian zouaves.[21]

Whether as a result or in spite of such harsh treatment, France's colonial troops became better adapted to the qualitatively new conditions of modern warfare as the conflict continued, and may even have proved decisive in some cases; one French historian has thus identified the contribution made by West African troops to the defence of Verdun in 1916, and in the Ardennes in 1918, as of particular significance, while another has pointed to the fact that the *tirailleurs algériens* ended the war as renowned fighters and the French Army's second most decorated corps.[22] For both the French and German propaganda machines, the *tirailleurs* were shock troops and the terrors of the enemy, although where the French saw them as natural soldiers (and instinctive killers), legitimately used against a barbaric enemy, the Germans depicted them as savages only too liable to commit atrocities. The latter theme would reach its climax with *die schwarze Schande* (the black shame), as the Germans described the role played by Senegalese troops in the post-Armistice occupation of the Rhineland. Central to the German case were the allegations – strenuously denied – of numerous sexual assaults on German women.[23] On the French side, not surprisingly, more favourable images of the mobilised *indigènes* (natives) predominated, and the beaming smile of the *tirailleur sénégalais* became indissolubly associated in the public imagination with a popular children's breakfast drink, through its 'Y'a bon Banania!' advertising campaign, with the soldier's grinning black face and red tarboosh being retained as the company's logo to this day.

Whatever the real or imagined effectiveness of these troops, their loyalty under the most extreme of hardships was beyond doubt. It is remarkable that no Algerian troops were involved in the widespread French mutinies of 1917 – in which as many as half of all French units were implicated – while only a single Senegalese battalion was drawn into the movement. Indeed, 'the black contingents of Tirailleurs sénégalais showed a readiness to fight in the second half of 1917 that native white Frenchmen had, at least temporarily, lost'.[24] Moreover, confidence in the loyalty of the colonial troops was such that they would actually be used at this time to put down revolts by metropolitan troops. Nor were they greatly affected by Germano-Turkish propaganda, which tried vainly to play the Islamic card both on men at the front and on prisoners of war. As one French historian has put it:

'...in the midst of the slaughter which men had to endure, all normal discrimination seemed to have been suspended. The military order seemed to most colonial soldiers much more egalitarian than the colonial order. Their stay in France in the most appalling of conditions served paradoxically and durably to nurture an image of a welcoming French nation with which a certain solidarity in the face of suffering could be achieved.'[25]

Thus it was that Bakary Diallo, in spite of what, from this distance at least, looks like decidedly shoddy treatment by the French military authorities following his demobilisation, could still conclude his account of his wartime experiences with the following tribute to the French and their assimilationist model of colonial development: 'You have changed me, I swear to you, in my head, my heart, my spirit, and my soul.'[26] As we shall see as we turn now to consider the role played by mobilised colonial workers, such rosy impressions of metropolitan France were by no means the rule, and even genuinely positive experiences like Diallo's did not preclude criticism of the colonial situation – indeed, they were often to encourage it.

While the *tirailleurs* had principally been recruited in Algeria and Senegal, colonial workers tended to be drawn from Algeria, once again, and Indo-China. Algeria's double contribution to the war effort meant that 'in all about 300,000 Algerians crossed to France during 1914-1918. This represented about one-third of all Algerian males of working age, a massive recruitment in relation to the size of the total population'.[27] Although there was considerable recruitment of 'free' colonial labour by major private employers – such as the Renault car plant at Boulogne-Billancourt in the Paris suburbs[28] – most imported workers were organised by the military authorities. Although they were in theory housed, fed and otherwise *encadrés* (supervised), this part of the French war machine was less well provided for than the Army itself. Some woeful accommodation and hygiene standards were thus experienced, with a significant number of deaths resulting from epidemics of meningitis and typhoid. There were also problems with alcoholism, and some tensions both between the various ethnic groups represented, and with the local labour force, who, with some justice, perceived the low-paid immigrants as a threat to their own positions.[29] Colonial workers were generally given little in the way of training and specialist skills, most often being restricted to basic labouring duties, with a consequent impact on their rates of pay and possibilities for promotion.

Yet, on the positive side, in spite of the strenuous official efforts made to prevent fraternisation, there was inevitably some movement and mixing, including in particular a first exposure to trade unions and political parties that would have a profound impact on many colonial workers. Patterns of migration and settlement were also established at this time that would be maintained and intensified in later years; the first immigrant *quartiers* would thus be created in the major French cities, on the model of the celebrated Goutte d'Or district in Paris. In such places, the squalor and overcrowding that characterised the daily lives of a mass of homesick single men were offset to some extent by the opening of traditional shops, cafés and restaurants to service the needs of the transplanted community. Moreover, this first encounter with paid work, industrial rhythms, and previously unencountered modes of consumption would have a dynamic impact on colonial attitudes and aspirations in the post-war period.[30] For the most politically aware of this first wave of colonial migrants, contact with the French Empire's industrial centre would encourage a new militancy that would lead them to seek the outright independence of their respective nations; the founding of the revolutionary Etoile Nord-Africaine movement by Messali Hadj in Algeria can thus be traced to this experience, as can the conversion to socialism (and later communism) of the young Indo-Chinese nationalist Hô Chi Minh. In a stinging critique of French imperialism entitled 'Le Procès de la colonisation française' ('The Trial of French Colonisation'), which he published in the early 1920s, the future President of independent Vietnam drew attention to the fate that awaited those colonial *poilus* (veterans of the First World War), and their civilian counterparts, when the hostilities finally came to an end:

'As soon as the guns have eaten their fill of black and yellow flesh, then the loving declarations of those who govern us are silenced as if by magic, and Africans and Indo-Chinese are immediately transformed into a "dirty race".'

…And the former poilus – or what's left of them – after valiantly defending human rights [le droit] and justice, return empty-handed to their "native" status, in which human rights and justice are unknown.'[31]

The experience of having been courted by France when times were hard and manpower was urgently required, whether as cannon-fodder or as cogs in the industrial machine, would leave many of those who returned to the colonies with an abiding awareness of new social possibilities. In particular, the enlistment of colonial troops – the representatives of races themselves so recently described as 'savages' – in what was claimed to be a defence of civilisation against the alleged barbarism of the 'Boches' would have long-term psychological and political implications of the greatest importance. By the same token, while the hierarchy and comradeship of the French Army may have served as a substitute for the traditional structures of clan or tribe that had been left behind, the war's legitimation of lethal violence against Europeans may also have served to liberate long-repressed forms of colonial aggression that would not easily be forgotten.[32]

The Bolshevik revolution of 1917 (and the publication of Lenin's theses on national and colonial questions in July 1920) would inevitably contribute to this process of destabilisation, as would the anticolonial principles stated by US President Woodrow Wilson in January 1918. The repatriation of colonial troops thus gave rise throughout the French Empire to a 'crisis of authority', with a variety of challenges to the established order being recorded. However, hopes for a genuine reform of the colonial regime – a 'New Deal' on the American model – would prove short-lived as repression once again became the norm. Yet the rise of colonial nationalism, for which the experience of the First World War had been the catalyst, could not be denied indefinitely.

Whatever the strength of nationalist sentiment and consequent demands for widespread reform, if not full independence, in the inter-war years, such was the French authorities' determination to keep firm control of the colonies that their future was not seriously questioned. However, France's catastrophic defeat in 1940 and the country's subsequent division into an occupied northern zone and a 'free' southern zone, with a collaborationist administration based in Vichy, would forever transform the French Empire. As in the First World War, the *tirailleurs* were called upon to serve in the front lines during the débâcle of 1940 – 'there were seven African divisions and three other colonial divisions out of the eighty French divisions defending the borders of France in 1919'[33] – and would thus suffer the consequences of Hitler's Blitzkrieg, including particularly incarceration for large numbers of them in POW camps. Such was the rapidity and the decisiveness of the German victory, in fact, that French soldiers and politicians alike were presented with a stark choice: make peace with the invaders, or flee the country and attempt to continue the war outside France. Pétain, the Great War hero, was to follow the first path; de Gaulle, his erstwhile subordinate, would opt for exile in London, where he began to organise the fledgling Free French forces from those few troops who rallied to his historic call of 18 June 1940.

For both the Vichy regime and the Gaullists, the Empire now took on an altogether greater significance. Pétain, and the followers of his fascistic 'National Revolution', looked to the colonies as an important bargaining-counter in their attempted preservation of national interests through collaboration with the Germans. The settler populations of North Africa – the only extensively settled area of the Empire – were generally attracted to the variously reactionary and racist policies of Vichy, and in particular its repeal in October 1940 of the Crémieux decree of 1870, which had extended full citizenship to Algeria's Jewish population. The destruction of the French fleet by the Royal Navy at its North African base of Mers-el-Kébir on 7 July 1940, with the loss of 1,300 lives, in order to prevent it falling into German hands, significantly added to pro-Vichy and anti-Gaullist sentiment among French civilians and military personnel in North and West Africa, as well as in Indo-China. However, in other parts of the French Empire, support for Vichy was not as clear-cut, as Andrew Shennan explains:

'The initial coincidence, which triggered the anti-vichyites' interest in [the Empire], occurred in the summer of 1940. In the first months after the armistice, the New Hebrides, French Oceania, the five cities of French India, New Caledonia, and much of French Equatorial Africa rallied to the London dissidents. From this founding period, in which the support of a fraction of the empire provided Free France with its strongest claim to legitimacy, the movement retained a mystique of empire at the heart of its ideology.'[34]

This symbolic linkage would have significant practical implications as the Gaullists attempted to continue the war in and through the French colonies. As early as December 1940 Moroccan *spahis* (mixed European and indigenous cavalry units) were attached to British Indian Army forces fighting the Italians in Eritrea.[35] However, the failure of de Gaulle's Dakar expedition of September 1941, in spite of significant support from the Royal Navy, meant that it was only with the Allied landings in North Africa in November 1942 that the large-scale involvement of colonial troops in the Free French war effort could begin in earnest. The landings would see the local Vichy administrators deposed and the Gaullists established – under Anglo-American hegemony – as the legitimate authority, while the Allies prepared for the invasion of Hitler's 'Fortress Europe'. Reservists were mobilised in North Africa in 1943, and would subsequently see service in various European theatres.

One such *tirailleur* was the future nationalist leader, Ahmed Ben Bella, who fought in Italy in 1944, including at the battle of Monte Cassino. Cited four times for gallantry during the campaign, he was awarded the Médaille Militaire shortly after the taking of Rome. He would be decorated by de Gaulle himself, who was, as always, determined to play a prominent role in the celebration of the Free French contribution to the Allied war effort:

'As he pinned the medal on my chest and gave me the traditional embrace, the great statesman can little have suspected that the man who stood before him would, eighteen years later, preside over the destiny of the independent Algerian Republic.'[36]

While Ben Bella and many like him remained notably loyal to France for the duration of the war, the indigenous populations of North Africa and the other French colonies would increasingly turn against a colonial regime that everywhere promised reform but produced only more repression in response to the changed circumstances of the conflict.[37]

In North Africa, the Allied landings and the sweeping away of Vichy were perceived by the indigenous populations not as a victory for the Free French, but rather as a second humiliation for the colonisers as a whole.[38] Comprehensively defeated by the Germans, France was now revealed to be powerless to stop the invasion of its territory by the Allies, whose forces included in particular significant numbers of black American troops. Yet, whether under Vichy or the Gaullists, the coercive apparatuses of French colonialism remained strong enough to prevent significant displays of nationalist sentiment in North Africa until very late on in the conflict.

The subsequent rallying of the greater part of the French African territories to the Free French cause, together with renewed anti-colonial pressure from the United States, would encourage de Gaulle to envisage a reformed colonial order in the latter stages of the conflict. The conference held at Brazzaville in the French Congo in January 1944 offered a new version of colonial paternalism – or at least a new rhetoric of 'association' rather than that of 'assimilation' – through the re-organisation of the Empire into a 'French Union'. With limited autonomy promised for the constituent territories, it was hoped that this initiative would offset the increasingly vocal demands of the colonial nationalists. In Algeria, an important moment had occurred with the publication on 10 September 1943 of the 'Manifesto of the Algerian People', signed by 43 elected Algerian representatives, including the leading nationalist figure, Ferhat Abbas. Opening with a reference to the Allied landings of November 1942, and the resulting spectacle of the French faction-fighting for positions of influence with the Allies, the Manifesto went on to link the Algerian people's current predicament to its sacrifices in an earlier conflict:

'For the second time in the 20th century, the whole world is fighting for the triumph of justice and human rights, and for the freedom of peoples.

But for the second time the world is witnessing this distressing and tragic spectacle, behind the soldier who gives his life for human freedoms and the well-being of humanity, diplomatic conferences and international agreements come into play. What role will be granted, in these discussions, to the rights of peoples?

The Peace of 1918 was achieved at great cost. The sacrifice of combatants of all nationalities and all religions was in vain. The greed of the rich peoples and the injustice which it engenders have survived the supreme sacrifice of the dead.'[39]

More spontaneous demonstrations against the conditions of life in Algeria in the later years of the war would include demonstrations by Muslim boy scouts, large-scale protests by native women demanding bread for their families, disturbances at sporting fixtures, the painting of seditious slogans, and various attacks on the representatives of the colonial order. These would culminate in nationalist riots in the Sétif region on VE Day, 8 May 1945, which led to about a hundred deaths on the European side, with many more fatalities (numbered in thousands) among the local Algerian population as a result of the particularly harsh repression that followed.[40]

Another example, and perhaps the most poignant, of the French colonial administration's reversion to repressive type as the tide of war turned occurred at Thiaroye barracks, near Dakar in Senegal, in December 1944. There it was that the most serious in a series of clashes between alienated *tirailleurs* and the military authorities occurred. Having failed to receive the back pay and the demobilisation premiums that were their due, 1,280 repatriated former POWs refused to obey orders, going so far as to take the commander of the French forces in West Africa hostage. Although some of the protesters were still armed, the uprising did little damage itself, but was put down with exemplary force by the colonial authorities:

'The official report written soon after the bloody event states that thirty-five Africans were killed, an equal number seriously wounded, and hundreds more or less seriously injured. ...On the colonial side, no lives were lost; one African policeman was wounded and three French officers suffered lacerations.'[41]

Another five of the 34 former POWs sentenced to long jail terms for their part in the Thiaroye mutiny were to die in prison before an amnesty was eventually granted in June 1947. Like Sétif for the Algerian nationalists, this event would become a potent symbol of French colonialism at its most brutally oppressive.

However, France was faced with its most serious challenge in Indo-China, which had effectively come under Japanese control following the fall of France in June 1940. Following the signing of the Franco-Japanese agreement on 30 August 1940, a modus vivendi existed that inevitably, given the relative strengths of the two sides, favoured the Japanese. Nevertheless, the French still had their colonial authority intact, as well as an army at their disposal, which concentrated now on combating nationalist agitation by Communist-backed groups in northern Vietnam. With the Vichyite administration unwilling or unable to challenge the Japanese, and with the Free French limited to making a purely symbolic declaration of war, the only effective resistance was that offered by a new and broad-based nationalist grouping, established in 1941, the Viet Minh. Headed by Hô Chi Minh, and his brilliant guerrilla commander, General Giap, the Viet Minh would, with clandestine American support, make a substantial contribution to the liberation of the country from the Japanese, who formally surrendered on 2 September 1945. On that same day, the 'Declaration of Independence of the Republic of Vietnam' was proclaimed. Opening with a quotation from the American Declaration of Independence of 1776, the document went on to cite the

French Revolutionary Declaration of the Rights of Man and of the Citizen of 1791, before commenting on the colonisers themselves:

'...for more than eighty years, the French have abused their liberté, égalité, fraternité by violating the land of our ancestors and oppressing our compatriots. Their actions are contrary to all ideas of humanity and justice.

...In the autumn of 1940, when the Japanese fascists invaded Indo-China ... the French imperialists went down on their knees and delivered our country to them.

...In fact, in the autumn of 1940, our country ceased to be a French colony and became a Japanese possession instead.

...The truth is that we took our independence back from the Japanese, not from the French.'[42]

This was, indeed, the truth. However, such was the political consensus in France at the end of the Second World War regarding the necessity of retaining the Empire, in order to re-establish the nation's great power status, that France would vainly attempt to reassert its authority in Indo-China by means of military force. The resulting war would rage from 1945 until 1954, when the French Army was catastrophically defeated at Dien-Bien-Phu in a battle that became known as 'a tropical Verdun'. Yet even this experience would not prevent the French from engaging in a new military campaign in Algeria from 1954 to 1962, any more than it would prevent the United States from waging its own disastrous war against the particularly sorely tried peoples of this part of the former French Empire.

The French Empire's experience of two World Wars may be characterised as one of colonial continuities and nationalist changes; thus the Empire twice confirmed its attraction to the colonial power, while the colonised populations became conscious first of their own national identities, then of the need for revolutionary political change. The tragedy for the indigenous peoples of the Empire was that the colonial mind-set permanently lagged behind such developments on the ground, leading politicians and administrators to promise future reforms while never trusting in the present to anything other than repression. From this point of view, the colonial vision of assimilation through blood sacrifice may be regarded as a monstrous lie told to those Africans and Asians called upon to suffer and, all too often, to die '*pour la France*' in 1914-18 and 1939-45. By the same token, the celebrated cases of Ahmed Ben Bella and Hô Chi Minh may be seen as typical of a broader colonial experience in the two World Wars: a process of awakening to alternative possibilities, by soldiers and workers alike, which would lead inexorably to revolt against the colonial order. However, this was by no means the only possible personal itinerary, and it is therefore necessary to recognise the reality, as well as the mythology, of the French model of assimilation, and particularly its contribution to the ultimate sacrifice knowingly and even willingly made by a select band of ideologically committed colonial troops. This phenomenon is epitomised by the case of Charles N'Tchoréré, from Gabon in French Equatorial Africa. Myron Echenberg takes up his poignant tale:

'Captain Charles N'Tchoréré was one of the rare African officers to have served in the Tirailleurs Sénégalais in both World Wars. By one of the terrible ironies of war, he led a company ... in defence of Airaines, a village on the Somme not far from Amiens, and was killed on 7 June, the very day his son, Corporal Jean-Baptiste N'Tchoréré, fell, also on the lower Somme. ...N'Tchoréré's honour as a proud French officer was to cost him his life. Whereas his son was killed in combat, Captain Charles N'Tchoréré was taken prisoner. With French officers as eyewitnesses, N'Tchoréré was ordered by a young Panzer officer to place his hands over his head and to stand with the African rank-and-file troops. When N'Tchoréré refused, insisting on his right to be treated equally with the other French officers, his German captor shot him on the spot.'

Lightning may, indeed, strike twice.

Recommended reading

Conklin, Alice L., *A Mission to Civilize: The Republican Idea of Empire in France and West Africa, 1895-1930* (Stanford: Stanford University Press, 1997)

Dalloz, Jacques, *The War in Indo-China, 1945-54* (Dublin: Gill & MacMillan, 1990; translation by Josephine Bacon of *La Guerre d'Indochine, 1945-1954* (Paris: Seuil, 1987)

Echenberg, Myron, *Colonial Conscripts: The Tirailleurs Sénégalais in French West Africa, 1857-1960* (Portsmouth, NH: Heinemann; London: James Currey, 1991)

Friedenson, Patrick, 'The impact of the First World War on French workers', in Wall, Richard and Winter, Jay (eds), *The Upheaval of War: Family, Work and Welfare in Europe, 1914-1918* (Cambridge: Cambridge University Press, 1988) pp235-48

Suret-Canale, Jean, *French Colonialism in Tropical Africa, 1900-1945* (New York: Pica Press, 1971); translation by Till Gottheiner of *Afrique Noire*, Vol II 'L'Ère coloniale, 1900-1945' (Paris: Éditions Sociales, 1964)

Thobie, Jacques, Meynier, Gilbert, Coquery-Vidrovitch, Catherine, and Ageron, Charles-Robert, *Histoire de la France coloniale*, Vol II '1914-1990' (Paris: Armand Colin, 1990)

Notes

[1] Gilbert Meynier, *L'Algérie révélée: La guerre de 1914-1918 et le premier quart du XXe siècle* (Geneva: Droz, 1981) pp263-4

[2] Mohamed Dib, *Le Métier à tisser* (Paris: Seuil, 1957) p204. All translations from French sources are my own unless otherwise stated.

[3] Ibid, p205

[4] Jean Suret-Canale, *French Colonialism in Tropical Africa, 1900-1945* (New York: Pica Press, 1971); translation by Till Gottheiner of *Afrique Noire*, Vol II 'L'Ère coloniale, 1900-1945' (Paris: Éditions Sociales, 1964) p129

[5] Neil MacMaster, *Colonial Migrants and Racism: Algerians in France, 1900-62* (London: Macmillan, 1997) p58

Iain Leggatt, aged 3½, in May 1942. 'I clearly had the urge to see the enemy off – from the safety of my Uncle Jim's back garden in Arbroath.' *Iain Leggatt, SWWEC, Leeds*

Below Babies of Leeds factory girls, Burley Park Nursery, Leeds. M. Oldham, SWWEC, Leeds

Above left British soldier Joe Kitchen with two Italian workers, No 5 War Graves Registration Unit, Cassino. *Joe Kitchen, SWWEC, Leeds*

Above Elizabetta Di Biasio as an Italian partisan, soon to be Joe Kitchen's fiancée. *Joe Kitchen, SWWEC, Leeds*

Left Napoleon Zervas, Greek guerrilla leader of an EDES unit, inspects newly taken German prisoners, November 1944. *G. A. W. Heppell, SWWEC, Leeds*

'Let's glorify our banners with new victories.' A Soviet war poster painted by V. Koretskiy. *per Sergei Kudryashov*

Left Midday lunch break for Chinese workers making an airfield for their American allies, Chengtu Valley. *H. J. Cavigli, SWWEC, Leeds*

Right 'I don't think I could ever go back to housework after this.' The fragility of some of the changes in Australian women's roles during the Second World War is reflected in this *Bulletin* cartoon of 6 January 1943.

Below Typical of the hysteria generated by the conscription referenda in Australia during the First World War is this cartoon by David Low, depicting a vote for No as essentially a vote for the enemy.

THE VOICE OF THE TEMPTER

Cyril Bassett, a New Zealander who earned a VC on the heights above Anzac, Gallipoli, August 1915. *C. Bassett, Liddle Collection, University of Leeds*

POPULAR SOUVENIRS

CAPTURED
Jardiniere (8" Howitzer)

GERMAN CARTRIDGE CASES
TRANSFORMED INTO ATTRACTIVE UTILITIES.

Pedestal
(5.9" Gun & 8" Howitzer)

COLLECTED on the Western Front during the war, they are unique and useful, and are the most popular of War Souvenirs. Strongly constructed of the best brass, they are practically everlasting. Having most of their weight in the base, they are not easily overbalanced, and are therefore ideal for the display of large bunches of flowers or gum tips. They are specially lacquered and retain indefinitely the highly-polished finish in which they are delivered.

For prices and particulars apply to—

AUSTRALIAN WAR MEMORIAL MUSEUM.
Exhibition Building,
SYDNEY.

An advertisement for 'Trench Art' artillery shell case souvenirs on sale at the Australian War Memorial Museum, Sydney, Australia, during the 1920s. *N. J. Saunders*

Above left Cover page of the journal *Fujin Kôron*, Vol 27, No 12, December 1942. *Courtesy of* Fujin Kôron, *Chuokoronsha, Tokyo*

Above George Millar, the novelist described by Anthony Powell as the best young British writer on the literary scene. He won the DSO and MC during the Second World War.

Left Colin MacDougall, novelist, who served in Italy with the Princess Patricia Canadian Light Infantry. *per Hugh Cecil*

1941-42 Free French Poster, printed in Manchester. *Jacques Mantoux, SWWEC, Leeds*

Popular music and wartime comfort – with surely many a tear. *Liddle Collection, University of Leeds*

Servicemen and sweethearts united in music. *Alistair Stead, SWWEC, Leeds*

6   While Senegalese units were made up entirely of African troops, North African *tirailleurs* generally included a proportion (up to as much as 30 per cent) of Europeans drawn from the territory's French population.

7   Jacques Thobie, Gilbert Meynier, Catherine Coquery-Vidrovitch and Charles-Robert Ageron, *Histoire de la France coloniale*, Vol II '1914-1990' (Paris: Armand Colin, 1990) p76

8   Ibid, pp76-7

9   Alice L. Conklin, *A Mission to Civilize: The Republican Idea of Empire in France and West Africa, 1895-1930* (Stanford: Stanford University Press, 1997) p147

10 Ibid, pp147-9

11 Gilbert Meynier, op cit, pp591-8

12 Alice L. Conklin, op cit, pp150-1. The linking of military service and French citizenship (as opposed to colonial subject status) was a staple of colonial thinking. See, eg, Charles Mangin, *La Force noire* (Paris: Hachette, 1910) and Paul Azan, *L'Armée indigène nord-africaine* (Paris: Charles Lavauzelle, 1925)

13 Jacques Thobie et al, op cit, p79

14 Figures taken from Guy Pervillé, *De l'Empire français à la décolonisation* (Paris: Hachette, 1991) pp56, 81; cf Jacques Thobie et al, op cit, pp76-9, and Neil MacMaster, op cit, pp58-9

15 Jacques Thobie et al, op cit, p96

16 Stéphane Audoin-Rouzeau, Preface to Paul Tuffrau, *1914-1918, Quatre années sur le front: Carnets d'un combattant* (Paris: Éditions Imago, 1998) p11; Jean-Norton Cru, *Témoins: Essai d'analyse et de critique des souvenirs de combattants édités en Français de 1915 à 1928* (Paris: Éditions Les Etincelles, 1929; Nancy: Presses Universitaires de Nancy, 1993)

17 Myron Echenberg, *Colonial Conscripts: The Tirailleurs Sénégalais in French West Africa, 1857-1960* (Portsmouth, NH: Heinemann; London: James Currey, 1991) p38; Bakary Diallo, *Force-Bonté* (Paris: Les Nouvelles Éditions Africaines & Agence de Coopération Culturelle et Technique, 1985; first published in 1926)

18 Gilbert Meynier, op cit, p442

19 Paul Tuffrau, op cit, p55

20 Jacques Thobie et al, op cit, pp86, 101

21 Gilbert Meynier, op cit, p275

22 Marc Michel, *L'Appel à l'Afrique: Contributions et réactions à l'effort de guerre en AOF (1914-1919)* (Paris: Publications de la Sorbonne, 1982) p472; Gilbert Meynier in Jacques Thobie et al, op cit, p103

23 Myron Echenberg, op cit, p35

24 John Keegan, *The First World War* (London: Pimlico, 1999) p403

25 Gilbert Meynier in Jacques Thobie et al, op cit, pp104-5

26 Bakary Diallo, op cit, p168

27 Neil MacMaster, op cit, p58

28 See Gilbert Hatry, *Renault, usine de guerre: 1914-1918* (Paris: Éditions Lafourcade, 1978)

29 Neil MacMaster, op cit, pp64-5. Cf Patrick Friedenson, 'The impact of the First World War on French workers', in Richard Wall and Jay Winter (eds), *The Upheaval of War: Family, Work and Welfare in Europe, 1914-1918* (Cambridge: Cambridge University Press, 1988) pp235-48

30 Jacques Thobie et al, op cit, pp107-12

31 Hô Chi Minh, *Action et Révolution, 1920-1967* (Paris: Union Générale d'Éditions, 1968) pp47-8

32 Jacques Thobie et al, op cit, pp105-6

33 Myron Echenberg, op cit, pp87-8. The same author, p19, discusses in this context the 'remarkable publication' in French West Africa from 1 January to 1 June 1940 of 'the most consistent vehicle for communicating war aims to semiliterate and nonliterate African soldiers [which] was a comic strip entitled *Mamadou s'en va-t'en guerre*'.

34 Andrew Shennan, *Rethinking France: Plans for Renewal, 1940-1946* (Oxford: Clarendon, 1989) p142. The black Governor of Chad, Félix Éboué, played a central role in this first recognition by the Empire of the Gaullists' legitimacy.

35 Jean-Noël Vincent, *Les Forces françaises dans la lutte contre l'axe en Afrique: Les Forces françaises libres en Afrique, 1940-1943* (Vincennes: SHAT, 1983) pp67-8

36 Robert Merle, *Ahmed Ben Bella* (Paris: Gallimard & NRF, 1965) p59

37 Wartime colonial repression was at least as severe elsewhere. See Catherine Akpo-Vaché, *L'AOF et la Seconde Guerre mondiale (septembre 1939-octobre 1945)* (Paris: Éditions Karthala & CNRS, 1996) pp64-5, on the 'concentration camps' organised by the Vichyite administration in Dakar to hold Gaullists, foreigners, and, above all, suspect Africans. See the same author, pp124-5, regarding African participation on both the Vichy and Resistance sides in French West Africa.

38 Jacques Thobie et al, op cit, p334

39 Service Historique de l'Armée de Terre, *La Guerre d'Algérie par les documents*, Vol 1 'L'avertissement, 1943-1946' (Vincennes: SHAT, 1990) p31

40 The exact figures remain a matter of considerable dispute, as do those for the deaths that occurred as a result of the repression of the uprising in Madagascar in 1947. See Charles-Robert Ageron, *La Décolonisation française* (Paris: Armand Colin, 1991) pp57, 69

41 Myron Echenberg, op cit, p101. This incident was commemorated by the poet and future Senegalese president, Léopold Sédar Senghor, himself a former POW, in his *Hosties Noires* volume (1938). The relevant poem is reproduced in Marc Michel, op cit, p1

42 Jacques Dalloz, *The War in Indo-China, 1945-54* (Dublin: Gill & MacMillan, 1990); translation by Josephine Bacon of *La Guerre d'Indochine, 1945-1954* (Paris: Seuil, 1987) pp210-2

43 Myron Echenberg, op cit, pp166-7

Chapter 19

The Arab world

Tarif Khalidi

The sources utilised here to recreate the atmosphere of daily life in the Arab world during the First World War are overwhelmingly autobiographical in character. These autobiographies have their own problems. Some are written by politicians anxious to demonstrate the accuracy of their predictions regarding the course of events and only more rarely concerned to tell us about ordinary lives and experiences. Since many of these politicians belonged to old-established families of wealth or prestige, the depth of their social focus is limited. Memoirs of 'ordinary' people on the other hand are less common – they tend to be composed by literary figures with ties to the ruling elites. The majority are urban in perspective; I have consulted two rural autobiographies and they are all the more valuable for being so. The few novels we have were written decades after the war and are of some help in evoking psychological moods, but they tend towards the melodramatic in plot and the theme of love doomed by war.[1]

What of other sources? The press is of diverse value. Where it operated in relative freedom, as in Egypt, it was by necessity not well informed on daily life in other Arab regions, like Greater Syria, which had become, as it were, enemy territory.[2] The Syrian press in turn was totally muzzled by the Ottoman military administration, thus strident in its propagandistic tone; little of real worth can be found in it where daily life is concerned. Nor does poetry fare much better than the press. The bulk of it seems to have consisted of ceremonial odes in praise of various Ottoman dignitaries or the occasional imperial war success.[3] Something can be learned from private interviews, but time dictates that most informants alive today are already at one generation distant from adult eyewitnesses. There are finally the memoirs or reports of Western diplomats, soldiers, residents or relief workers. These are not utilised here since they are quite well known and well tapped by modern scholarship.[4] Here then are the bibliographical limits, material and conceptual, of the observations that follow. Their principal merit, if they have any, is that they draw attention to some autobiographical sources not yet widely known to workers in this field.

The Arab world that concerns me directly is limited to the Arab lands of western Asia: roughly Iraq, Arabia, Egypt and, especially, Greater Syria (excluded is the Maghrib, ie Arab North Africa). Within this region, which was more or less part of the Ottoman Empire, war had an atomising effect. Under its impact the whole region seemed to turn into a chequer-work of sub-regions where very ancient division boundaries were often re-assumed. As the war progressed, this meant among other things that people were immobilised within the confines of their sub-regions as travel became both dangerous and pointless, albeit with occasional massive movements of refugees.[5] Regional self-sufficiency was soon to be the norm. If one were to survey this territory from some height, one would be struck by how like a mosaic it must have appeared. For it is quite evident that regions often contiguous fared very differently. Some suffered grievously from famine while others were barely affected. Thus, in Greater Syria, the sub-region of Mount Lebanon experienced a famine of epic severity, while a few kilometres to the south the sub-region of South Lebanon was on the whole relatively prosperous.[6] In Iraq, Baghdad appears to have escaped the worst, but the Mosul countryside was severely affected.[7] By and large the commercial coastal cities of Greater Syria (Latakiya, Tripoli, Beirut, Jaffa) appear to have suffered more than the string of agricultural cities of the Syrian hinterland (Aleppo, Hims, Damascus).[8] Breadbasket zones like the central Syrian plains, the Hawran in Syria, the Biqa` valley and South Lebanon suffered less from famine because peasants could often substitute grain for cash for tax purposes and in the process benefited from the inefficiency that accompanies any military-bureaucratic attempt to collect crops in wartime.[9]

But none of these preliminary soundings of wartime conditions is to be seen as in any way to underestimate the frightful hardships of a region that, some modern scholars argue, suffered, relative to population, one of the highest civilian death rates in the world.[10] The global character of the upheaval was vividly felt by contemporaries, while for modern Arabic, and indeed Western, historiography the Great War still looms large as the baptism by fire of the 20th century. It is widely regarded in the contemporary Arab world as a period of historic acts of injustice, of betrayal, of great expectations followed by massive let-downs. For the generation of Arabs who were adults during both World Wars there was simply no comparison between the two conflicts. The second could almost be described as a comic rerun of the first. In the First War the Arab world paid the heavy price of imperial collapse and military defeat; in the Second it sat largely on the side-lines and watched.

Given the autobiographical focus of this chapter, it seemed best to proceed by allowing as many voices as could be gathered to speak of their experiences, periodised and arranged under a few dominant themes. As an essay about memories and perceptions, it is more than usually at the mercy of its informants. Some were children or young adults at the time and separated from the events recollected by years of tranquillity, making the process of recollection even more selective and stereotyped than it normally is. The scenes of famine, for instance, are recalled in very similar images of human skeletons piled up on street corners begging for their very lives. So too are the perceived acts of betrayal, by the Turks, the French or the British. For our rich or well-fed informants, these stock scenes of famine or political betrayal alternate with glimpses of daily lives that flowed slightly above, sometimes far above the surrounding misery.[11] A pall of doom and impotence hangs over these memoirs. An empire is collapsing around them. As it does so, it is seen to be committing a number of unforgivable mistakes, most notably the public hangings of nationalist leaders in 1915-16. With the Ottoman

Empire collapsing, Ottomanism also collapsed.[12] Identity needed redefinition. What are we to be reborn as: Lebanese? Syrians? Palestinians? Iraqis? Arabs? Muslims? This questioning became particularly acute after the hangings: 'Anyone to govern us, even apes, but not this tyranny!' was one cry heard in Beirut.[13] And yet, here and there in these memoirs one finds a residue of nostalgia for the empire that had passed away, not a surprising sentiment when one considers the ancient ties that linked urban Arab grandees to their imperial capital, or the sense of pride associated with working for the imperial Ottoman civil or military service.[14]

If one were to periodise the ebb and flow of daily lives during the war, those at least that felt its miseries most painfully, one might propose the following partitions: the period from early 1914 to about April 1915; the two years 1915 and 1916; the period from 1917 to about April 1918; and the collapse and final Ottoman retreat from Syria, completed in late October 1918. Given the mixed fortunes of the various regions of the Arab world, this periodisation does not have pan-Arab applicability. Nor do I intend in the following remarks to follow this periodisation strictly, although I think it may have some use if one wants to retain a notion of the rhythms of wartime existence.

The war was prefaced with a series of shocks, each of which, like seismic waves, widened the circles of rumour and panic. In Aleppo, Ottoman military detachments were seen in the early summer of 1914 roaming the markets and warehouses, registering the quantities of grain or textiles and ordering some merchants to withhold sale, others to sell.[15] Such activity was judged unprecedented and ill-omened. Among the first ripples on the surface in Lebanon was the 'fire-storm', which gripped the wealthy Egyptian and Syrian families spending their summers in Lebanese mountain resorts. July and August are the height of the resort season, but no sooner did the news from Sarajevo reach them than they were seen to pack their belongings and rush to crowd the boats or carriages that carried them home.[16] Their hasty departure was a confirmation of the worst fears of less mobile onlookers.

In the coastal cities of Beirut, Latakiya and Jaffa, those who could afford it sent their families away, perhaps as a result of some collective historical reflex, to the Syrian interior or to Cyprus, not unlike the rich Londoners who headed for the countryside in September 1939.[17] General mobilisation, another stage in the plunge to war, was then followed in quick succession by a war-tax, the issuance of new identity papers, censorship of the press and the mail service, a 'war' between pro-French and pro-German newspapers, and a marked increase in the activities of spies and informants.[18] It was the mobilisation of 21 July, however, that filled people with the greatest dread. It was widely seen as unjust since it made no exceptions for the weak, the only child or the sole breadwinner. Some regarded it as a measure that the ruling Committee of Union and Progress adopted in imitation of German mobilisation regulations and their subordination of civilian to military requirements.[19] An attempt was made at legitimising the general mobilisation by coupling it with Jihad through a fatwa issued by the Shaykh al-Islam, the highest religious dignitary of the Empire, in Istanbul in November, shortly after the outbreak of hostilities. In traditional cities like Aleppo or Baghdad, this call was at first well received.[20] But many Muslims were later to question the legitimacy of a call to Jihad against some Christian powers (Russia, France and Britain) while allied to others (Austria and Germany). Meanwhile, an Arab nationalist man of letters in Jerusalem, a Christian, recorded in his diary that the call to Jihad was a throw-back to the dark ages of bigotry.[21] It was clearly not an empire whose citizens, in any significant proportion, had any deep or sincere or even jingoistic desire to die in its defence.[22]

How did the war begin to distort 'the way in which ordinary people went about their normal lives'?[23] Among the earliest impressions one gathers from a city like Jerusalem are those of the same man of letters cited above:

'Wednesday, September 30, 1914. This general war has taught us to economise, indeed to be thrifty. Since it broke out two months ago and until today, our daily expenses have not exceeded 2 or 3 qurush. Days have passed when we ate nothing but bread, grapes and salads. Meat did not enter our house… My debts amount to only a few francs. If crises have any value, economy and good management are among their greatest benefits. People have given up pleasures and entertainments and have grown simpler in dress and living. Indeed, they've grown used to straitened circumstances. After being frightened of the least thing, they now care for nothing. It is as if these crises and the dangers that they themselves have witnessed have created in them new hearts, rendering them closer to manliness and courage than ever before.'

In the passage immediately following, our diarist speaks in ironic mode of how war distorts language:

'People today read nothing but telegrams, since most local newspapers have ceased publication, and Egyptian newspapers have been forbidden. Hence, people will inevitably grow accustomed to telegramese. The virtue of conciseness will become a habit. When speaking or writing, they will incline to express their thoughts in the most succinct manner and with minimum verbiage. Who knows but that this too may be one of the benefits of these days.'[24]

Echoes of this disenchantment with officialese are heard in Damascus, where the scion of a prominent pro-Ottoman family describes how he and his 13-year-old friends, despite their general Ottoman sympathies, grew so cynical of military proclamations announcing victories that it was easy for them to parrot their unchanging phraseology, which they came to know often masked heavy defeats. These repetitive proclamations, we are told, had the effect of convincing most people that the war would eventually be lost.[25]

Southern Iraq was the first Arab region of the Ottoman Empire to fall to the Allies. In the city of Basra, its former Deputy in the Ottoman Parliament (Mab`uthan) records with some revulsion how quick people were to change allegiance:

'The transfer of power from the Ottomans to the English led to a number of substantive changes in people's lives and in the social and political values of individuals. In other words, the English occupation of Basra represented a decisive upheaval in the various aspects of the city's life. When I returned to the city [18 December 1914], many of its distinctive features had changed. A new class of merchants, contractors and notables had made its appearance on the scene. This class extended an exaggerated welcome to the new occupiers, linking their interests to those of the occupiers. For their part, the imperialists banished all who refused to wallow at their door-step or were too dignified to vie in gaining their favours.'[26]

In rural or outlying regions of the Empire, different voices are heard. There, the rhythms of daily life seem far less affected by the overwhelming military presence observable in the autobiographies from major cities. In distant Yemen, whose very name signified exile to Near Eastern Arabs, a historian writing in traditional annalistic staccato mode records the following under the year 1333 AH (commenced November 1914):

'The Great War grew in intensity. All routes of commerce by land or sea were blocked. People suffered great harm as a result… In Yemen during this period [of the war] agriculture and fruit farming improved. The only commodities which were unavailable were kerosene and sugar. In all other types of agricultural products and food-stuffs, the Yemen became self-sufficient, with plenty of fruits and much honey.'[27]

Likewise, two village boys, destined later to become distinguished scholars of Arabic and university colleagues, the one from Mount Lebanon and the other from the border of the Syrian desert, recapture their war memories in terms that often conjure up an idyll. First the Syrian village boy:

'My village suffered hardly any hunger or famine throughout the war years, because … it was a village rich in farms and fountains. At the same time, it was far from the eyes of the authorities so that its harvests remained in it and only a little of its crops were ever requisitioned. There is a plain that lies between my village and Tadmur [Palmyra] into which drained floodwaters from surrounding hills. These flooded lands the peasants of the village cultivated intensively, and the land produced crops greater in quantity than what was produced by the best agricultural lands… And so passed the years of the First World War. We, however, living at the edge of the desert, knew little of its news other than what reached us in some newspapers that came from Hims or via some government officials or merchants.'[28]

The Lebanese boy adopts a more sarcastic tone. In his mountain village, it was a villager who had made good, gone to Beirut and established a stationery shop who broke the news of the outbreak of war to the assembled elders. The boy recalls the following village dialogue:

"'Is it true that war has broken out? Between whom and whom?'

"Yes, war has broken out, and may God protect us from its evils.'

"I say, is Russia involved? And what about our Sublime State?'

"Of course. It is on the side of Germany.'

"Would that it had entered on the side of Russia! God give victory to Russia! Without its help, we would never have hung up the bell in the tower on the Church of Our Lady.'"

He adds:

'As for us youngsters, we paid scant attention to the war and its news. In the summer of 1914, we were happy to return to our friends and playgrounds. We felt the sweetness of freedom following our harsh prison of a boarding-school, and left the news of the war to our elders. Each Friday they would await the arrival of the stationery shop owner to tell them news of the war. A strong-willed woman of our village would comment, "Why for heaven's sake are you all so concerned? I hope they slaughter each other."'[29]

These memories of a Lebanese mountain village in wartime are unusual in that their author intends to portray in detail what he calls a 'narrative of a village family life which may be regarded as typical of what other Lebanese mountain village families suffered by way of hunger, disease and repression'. He proceeds to describe a rhythm of life in which constant and resourceful adaptation to the environment ensured that the village escaped the worst effects of locusts, famine and blockade. Every available plot of the family's land was intensely cultivated producing onions, potatoes and beans. The father of our author resumed his long-abandoned craft as tanner and was suddenly back in great demand. The locust invasion of April 1915 was met with a determined, village-wide campaign of building ditches into which the locusts were driven then burned. The wheat blockade was circumvented by hardy village muleteers who carried grain back from Syria through secret mountain passes.[30] Caught between a naval blockade of the Eastern Mediterranean by the Allies and a blockade of wheat, which normally came from Syria, the villages in Mount Lebanon had to fend for themselves as best they could.[31] In this particular village, as the war bit ever more deeply into daily lives, one gathers that severe hardship rather than famine was experienced. Other villages were not so lucky. This is made plain when the boy comes face to face with real starvation:

'One night I returned home to encounter a sight which astounded me. It was the skeleton of a child wrapped in a woollen blanket. Its head was shaved. I was quite terrified and asked, trembling: Who is this child? The answer came back: a child picked up on point of death from a neighbouring village lane to be cared for by our family until the orphanage is made ready. My mother, I remember, was instructed to feed him nothing but water and milk because his intestines had adhered to each other.'[32]

The invasion of locusts in April 1915 heralds in some accounts the advent of new horrors. From his relatively elevated station as Secretary to the last Ottoman Governor of Mount Lebanon, one informant tells us that the locusts blocked the rays of the sun, causing immense panic. Locusts were an omen of famine in the best of times. In wartime, this omen was sinister indeed. 'When summer arrived, it resembled autumn. Trees had shed their leaves and not a green twig could be seen anywhere.'[33] This infestation came only a few months after an edict from the Damascus Governorate forbidding the export of wheat to Lebanon and Palestine. In the following year, in June 1916, the harvest was largely destroyed by excessively hot winds.[34] The result was a famine that, by forcing regions to become self-sufficient, fell hardest upon refugees from less fortunate districts who desperately made their way to the big cities only to collapse on the roads or die in city streets.[35] Some of these refugees travelled long distances; from distant Mecca a group arrived in Aleppo in 1915, fleeing the famine, while a few more fortunate were able to make their way to Egypt.[36] Among the more poignant descriptions of the famine in Beirut is an account by a woman informant, then aged 17:

'Death opened its jaws, gulping down the crowds of hungry people sprawled in the streets. As we heard the cry: "I am hungry … I am hungry" we would rush to the windows and balconies and call out to whoever amongst them could walk to approach and would hand out food to them or send food to those who could not move. I recall that my mother always carried with her when she left our house some bread or dry food to distribute to the hungry, rather than a few qurush which would have done them little good… Once, as we were leaving a shop on Burj Square, a banana seller approached us and we bought some bananas from him. No sooner had we begun to peel the bananas than we were surrounded by a large crowd of children who scrambled to pick up the peels and wolf them down. We could not eat any more and gave them what was left.'[37]

Another informant, then aged 16, tells the following story:

'Among the scenes of famine which I can never forget is when I once met on a Beirut street a former school friend of mine. He had been a rich student, indeed a spendthrift. I failed at first to recognise him, so thin he was and tattered. As soon as he saw me, he rushed forward to ask: "Are you not so and so? Do you not recognise me? I am so and so." Leaving me no time to recover from my surprise and pain, he eagerly asked, "What is in that bag of yours, food?" In a few seconds my friend was gone, wolfing down the sandwich I carried in my bag as he disappeared from view.'[38]

Frightful as these scenes must have appeared to contemporaries, even more heartless were the attempts made by officialdom to hide those dying in the streets from the eyes of visiting dignitaries.[39] One theme that runs quite strongly through these recollections is the theme of greed and indifference versus compassion. In Damascus, a literary man recollects at some length instances of both patterns of behaviour. There are first the war profiteers, a few of whom he names, with their boundless appetites and their cynical attitude to the suffering around them. But there are also the shining examples, those who transcended sectarian divisions in their charity or else undertook, though not rich, to play an active role in famine relief.[40] Famine was interspersed with epidemics, chiefly typhus, one of which seems to have struck with particular force in Aleppo and Damascus in the winter of 1915.[41]

Compounding these miseries were the prominent families sent into exile, to Anatolia by the Ottomans and to India and Malta by the British in Iraq and Egypt.[42] But perhaps no single political event of the war could compare with the impact of the public hangings of prominent nationalists in 1915-16, in Beirut and Damascus. The shock waves were felt throughout Greater Syria and all the way to Baghdad and Arabia.[43] Anger, horror, sullen resentment, were directed at Jamal Pasha, Commander of the Fourth Ottoman Army and Ottoman supremo in Greater Syria. Many of the 'martyrs' were personally known to our autobiographers. But these widespread feelings of grief were soon to transmute into the glum realisation that the days of the Empire were numbered. It may be that our sources reproduce in this respect a judgement formed after the events, a sort of retrojected wisdom, but these sources do nevertheless reflect a sense of a nationalist rupture between Turks and Arabs, of an empire that could no longer stand firmly on all its ethnic pillars.

How can one explain the general apathy of the population, their silent suffering, and even their reluctance to attack the granaries and warehouses in order to satisfy their hunger?[44] One powerful evocation of this apathy attributes it to physical weakness:

'It became plain that the weakness of their bodies through starvation resulted in feebleness of will and of thinking among the poor, who refrained from burglary and theft, and surrendered instead to their fate. You could see the hungry people who had come to Beirut from Mount Lebanon in search of food lying in the streets awaiting death. But all around them there were stores replete with food-stuffs and the houses of the rich and mighty littered with tables heaped full of delicacies. The poor however did not dare to attack them or at least help themselves to some of the food to stave off their hunger.'[45]

Other informants attribute this to the fact that the location of government granaries became a tightly guarded secret.[46] In Damascus, however, bread riots were not unheard of and there is one memory of bakery boys scampering over roof-tops to make their deliveries for fear of being attacked on the streets.[47] One writer muses about a general decline of religious belief, leading to total reliance on divine miracles and submission to fate. Another writer, a religious reformer, comments on how the calamities of war made the rich more corrupt and cruel and the poor more ready to reject their Maker.[48] In many memoirs, the theme of an ignorant populace is to the fore.[49] In Iraq, for instance, and three years after the end of the war, there were barely 8,000 students in all the primary and secondary schools of the country.[50] In Egypt, a major political figure occasionally deplores the low level of education and 'good manners' among the 'commoners'.[51]

More telling are his comments on his countrymen in an Egypt under occupation but where physical hardships were far lighter than elsewhere in the Arab East:

'Woe to a people whose affairs are managed by foreigners! Virtue is nowhere to be found among them. Their hearts grow sick. None amongst them ever rises to prominence. If by chance a decent man is found, misery is his inevitable fate. His people do not understand him nor he them. They do him harm although he does them good. There is nothing more hurtful to a person with a free spirit than to be let down by his countrymen, nor anything more painful to his soul than to be abandoned by family and friends.'[52]

A parallel may be drawn between the widely observed apathy of the Syrian populace and the 'sick hearts' of wartime Egyptians. Another parallel is the feeling of constriction of horizons, a shrinkage of imaginative space especially experienced in the large cities, a growing preoccupation with the immediate and the nearby. It is odd, for instance, that one of Egypt's most prominent political personalities has nothing whatever to say in his daily memoirs about the public hangings in Syria. It is odder still when one recalls that Egypt during the war acted as a haven for a large number of Syrian refugees, many of whom were a highly politicised intelligentsia. It may be that the public mood in Egypt was overshadowed by the British occupation, whose noose was to tighten visibly as the war progressed. Echoes of this are found in Iraqi poetry, which, probably under Ottoman inspiration, called the new British-imposed Khedive of Egypt a 'traitor to Islam'.[53] For their part, however, the Egyptians are repeatedly described as pro-Ottoman in sentiment; so great, it seems, was their discontent with the abrupt ending by the British of their rising political expectations and so deep-seated their sense of pan-Islamic solidarity.[54]

Sectarianism is considerably to the fore in many of our memoirs. But given the complexity of Ottoman alliances, ie with some Christian powers and against others, it was not at all obvious to many ordinary people how religion could be used as a criterion of political allegiance.[55] It was in Iraq, after all, where a mutiny broke out among Indian Muslim soldiers of the British Army who refused to fight against Muslim co-religionists.[56] The brutal suppression of the mutiny was an indication of how seriously the British had always regarded this eventuality.[57] Some writers adopt a hostile attitude towards the sentiments of the 'commoners', Christian or Muslim, whose religious instincts caused them to welcome British, French, German or Ottoman victories purely out of sectarian prejudice and without due heed to consequences.[58] In Syria, the Patriarch Gregorius Haddad comes in for special praise for his anti-sectarian sentiments and his willingness to distribute food to the needy of all sects.[59] On the other hand, the dreaded Jamal Pasha, described as not in the least religious in personal life, was nevertheless sufficiently aware of the strength of Muslim sentiment to exploit it without hesitation in furthering his control in Syria.[60] A number of Christian and Muslim religious leaders are subjected in some memoirs to severe criticism for dereliction of duty and corruption.[61] But there are two passages where writers speak in broad terms about sectarian relations. In the first, a Muslim Syrian religious reformer who fled to Egypt observes:

'I gathered, from news of my Syrian homeland related to me by those who fled
to Egypt during wartime and from items published in European and Egyptian
newspapers that the calamities of war erased all enmity and rancour between
religions and sects, making hearts more compassionate. Whoever owned a
loaf of bread would divide it with friend or neighbour… But as the war
progressed, and people observed the immorality of tyrannical commanders,
unjust officials and the rich and affluent, their bad example was catching.
Hearts grew harder, feelings petrified, greed grew stronger.'[62]

In the second, a Damascene man of letters writing in the 1940s looks back half a
century to a different era of sectarian relations:

'I believe that fifty years ago relations between Christians and their Muslim
brethren were closer to amity and harmony than they are today. If some
among them falsely imagine that they have acquired power and support, this
provokes in them certain instincts that had not been manifest before… And
if some dhimmis care to remember some violations of their rights in the
Ottoman period, it must be pointed out that neither Islamic law nor the
native Muslims are responsible for this. It was rather the doing of those who
then ruled absolutely. It was they who urged the rabble on occasion to
humiliate certain sects and tempted some of their lackeys to work to sow
discord among sons of the same nation. My own experience is that in the
villages, Christians and Muslims loved and supported one another as if they
belonged to the same family more than is the case today.'[63]

It is possible that our first informant adopts a view of history too simplistic in its
moral parameters while the second is perhaps a little nostalgic. Both accounts,
however, affirm the moral responsibility of the Ottoman Government, a favourite
target of almost all autobiographical accounts.

The mid to late period of the war witnessed a severe inflation made worse by the
issuance of paper money in 1915-16. There are some references to the inflated
prices of specific commodities: a ratl of rice cost 1 gold lira in Damascus, a ton of
wheat cost 2,000 Syrian lira or more, a canister of kerosene 1 Ottoman gold lira, a
ratl of bread 45 qurush. A hotel owner in Aleppo in early 1918 was happy to accept
two cans of ghee as payment for a stay of ten days by a group of five people.[64] These
figures do not mean much since we are not told what the normal prices of these
commodities were, but soaring prices are widely reported.[65] We hear of changes in
eating habits and the substitution of sugar by molasses, of rice by cracked wheat, of
coffee by roasted barley and of tea by camomile, and also of the large-scale
adulteration of wheat with darnel, vetch and earth.[66] But wealthy families seem to
have been barely affected where their food and ordinary celebrations were
concerned.[67] Senior government officials also seemingly suffered less hardship
than others, being recipients of government food subsidies.[68]

Paper money was at first welcomed in a city like Aleppo where people found it
easier to handle than silver and gold coinage.[69] But although bills first circulated
at par against gold, their market value was soon to drop to one-fifth and lower,

causing havoc in debt settlements and creating instant and unlawful wealth. Many peasants, for instance, simply refused to accept paper money.[70] A government measure intended to stabilise the economy had created the opposite effect and, like the catastrophic decision to forbid the export of wheat to Lebanon and Palestine, compounded the perception of a bungling, corrupt and brutal Empire no longer able to provide even a minimum level of service to its citizens.

In 1917 a slow change seems to have come over Ottoman Government policy in Syria, accompanied by an apparent change of heart in Jamal Pasha himself. In a city like Beirut, Jamal had reportedly made wide use of the qabadays, the strongmen of city quarters, who were used to intimidate the streets and to act as spy-catchers. He had also disbursed large sums of money in secret to a number of Muslim clerics, allegedly to further his own personal ambitions to become Khedive of Syria.[71] The popular impression was of a Government that was either indifferent to the suffering or else incapable of alleviating it. But by 1917 active government encouragement began to be given to the formation of native relief committees, orphanages and the like, and Jamal himself seemed more favourably disposed towards Mount Lebanon, allowing quantities of wheat to be shipped to its poor and needy.[72]

These measures, however, came too late. It was becoming clear that the Ottoman military front in the Near East was experiencing very serious shortages of food and supplies. One participant describes that front as being as plagued by hunger as the civilian population, and speaks of massive desertion rates from the ranks.[73] Another witness of the collapsing Jerusalem front in late November 1917 speaks of a 'heart-rending scene' of wounded Ottoman soldiers transported on horses with nothing to cover them from the harsh winter weather. The next entry in his diary is as follows:

'Wednesday, November 21, 1917. It rained steadily all night. I went to sleep thinking of the soldiers fighting each other on mountain-tops or perched behind their guns in the valleys. I compared in my mind the Ottoman army with the English, imagining the state of each. I pictured the British soldier covered from head to foot in woollens, with a sturdy tent nearby and all his food and drink provided in plenty, full of life and health. I then pictured the Ottoman soldier, hungry, his uniform in tatters, his boots in shreds, with nothing to protect him from the rain and cold, standing in the open behind his gun, shivering from the cold, doubled up with hunger, and finding nothing to eat but scraps of dried bread. And there I was sleeping comfortably and securely in my bed, despising myself and my lack of zeal.'[74]

To a reader of these memoirs, it appears as if the war chugged slowly to its end like some locomotive that had run out of steam. In a country like the Sudan, which had been under British rule throughout, the war had been a distant event, and its end was celebrated by rulers and ruled alike.[75] In Egypt, on the other hand, we hear of a glum populace refusal to participate in the celebrations.[76] In Iraq, Baghdad fell to the British in March 1917, but a famous poet refused to believe that this was indeed the end, and wrote a poem , 'The Wailing Tigris', in which the river calls upon the retreating Ottomans to turn back and leap like a lion upon the enemy.[77] In Mount Lebanon, the village boy quoted earlier and now aged 16, was transporting his sick uncle on a mule over a mountain track:

'When we reached the village of Ba`abdat, we saw Indian soldiers! Where were the Turks? We heard it whispered about that the Turkish army had fled and that the English army had liberated the country. In our village, we had not been aware of what was going on in the rest of the world. All we cared about was hunger and disease. Reaching the town of Brummana, we met soldiers whose faces indicated that they were of north European stock. Where were the Turks? They had fled and the English had liberated the land… On the way back to our village, we heard people speaking of the "signing of the armistice". I had not heard the word before. Our joy at home was great, not because of the signing of the armistice but because my dying uncle had miraculously recovered.'[78]

A sense of relief is found in other memoirs, but mixed with nagging uncertainty about the future and about the true intentions of the victorious Allies. For some, the end of the war was a moment of comic surreality.[79] For others, the 'baleful and defeated' sight of the last Ottoman Governor of Beirut leaving the city in a small procession of cars that carried him, his family and staff and their belongings, was cause for intense joy.[80] But perhaps the strangest of all the narratives about the war's end comes in the memoirs of a remarkable nationalist and intellectual, destined thereafter for political prominence in Iraq as one of King Faisal I's closest advisers. His memoirs begin in the final days of the war when he and other nationalists stole out of Damascus in secret on 10 August 1918 and travelled through Southern Syria to join up with the advancing Arab forces of their idol, Faisal.[81] Remarkably, this journey of 20 days reads in large part like an anthropologist's field-notes. He records long and dispassionate observations on the habits and customs of the Druses and the Bedouins, through whose territory he needed to pass. According to his nationalist ideology, these were fellow Arabs. And yet to read him one might imagine that he was describing some alien tribes whose rituals were foreign to him, almost exotic, and worthy of scientific record. This was a journey of discovery. For the nationalists of his generation, Istanbul had been the real capital of Arab nationalism. When the war came, the Arab world fragmented even further, as we saw above, and its regions increasingly became cut off from one another. Now, however, with the war coming to an end, the various parts of that world were slowly coming together again. It is this image of a world constricting, then slowly recirculating that may be considered dominant in these memoirs.

The following brief observations on the Arab world during the Second World War are even more selective as a record of rhythms of daily life than were the previous observations on the First War. The majority are based on personal communications from a small number of living informants who remember the war well. But my purpose in this section is strictly comparative. I will attempt to highlight those features of daily life during the Second War that stand in greatest contrast with those during the First. The literature on the Second War is quite vast in comparison with the First. My remarks therefore are little more than preliminary soundings. But coming as they do from witnesses, all of whom were very ready to share their memories, their vividness might compensate for their limited range and character.[82]

Beginning with the feeling of constriction very much to the fore in the First War, Second World War memories range far more widely in space and reflect an Arab world whose various regions live in much greater intimacy and interdependence. Egyptian intellectuals visit Palestine, Lebanese students go off to study in wartime Cairo, Palestinian teachers are attracted to work in Iraq, Iraqi students gravitate to Lebanon, Syrian businessmen in Egypt negotiate imports of rice. The impression is of an Arab world opening out to itself, rediscovering its ancient links, sharing its aspirations and trading vigorously; it was, for example, an era of pan-Arab conferences of various kinds. It seems too that this world was far more sensitive to news from the various theatres of war. A declaration by Winston Churchill, in February 1944, that the war was not about to end soon sent prices soaring in Damascus.[83] Huge open-air cinema screens were erected in Syria to display to the public the military might of the Allies.

But it was quite clearly the radio that was the novel and truly revolutionary medium and facilitator of communications and of propaganda. All my informants speak of the radio as having been central to their everyday lives; listening to either Berlin or the BBC was a daily family or cafe ritual. For the Arab world, the undoubted radio personality of the war was Yunus al-Bahri, an Iraqi from Mosul, who began each of his short nightly news bulletins from Berlin with the same sonorous phrase: 'Salute to the Arabs! ... This is Berlin!' The BBC was never able to match him with one of its own and British attempts at jamming were not very effective since the Berlin bulletins could still be heard through the crackle.

The radio was the prime example of the 'virtual reality' that the war was soon to become for most Arabs. The competing broadcasts filled their ears and helped to shape their reactions to events. But while the war dominated everyday life, it brought no unbearable hardships to the vast majority of Arabs and was thus in large part a spectacle, an 'amusement arcade' where warring was largely a game followed on a screen. The war electrified the Arab world but in the process politicised it to a very high degree. Where the First War had passed in sullen and starved silence, the Second was a tumultuous affair where the political domain was active and very noisy. For some informants the war is indeed remembered as the happiest, or at least the most edifying, period of their lives. Every day revealed a new corner of the globe, introduced a new technology or advertised new commercial products. And unlike the First War, the Second teemed with magazines and newspapers that carried pictures of the Egyptian royal court to peasants in Greater Syria, brought Arab intellectuals together in two or three leading literary journals, or provided up-to-date news of the world-wide theatres of war. There is simply no comparison in the quantity of news available to the Arab world as between the two wars.

Unlike the First War, when the few schools that existed, at least in Greater Syria and Iraq, suspended classes, most Arab schools during the Second War remained open. The inter-war period was also something of a 'golden age' for Arab universities. Thus, when the Second War began, secondary and university students were often to the fore in political activism. In Egypt and Syria, for example, university student strikes and demonstrations would last for months.[84] In Iraq, schoolboys received regular military training as part of their curriculum. The reputation of some Lebanese schools and universities attracted students from all over the Arab world and political parties of various ideologies found many young and enthusiastic recruits. Young Arab kings like Faruq of Egypt and Ghazi of Iraq were at least for a while icons of Arab youth and prefigured a brighter and more dignified and independent Arab future. The war largely bypassed the Arab world and therefore did not inspire the sort of terror that hangs like a fog over First World War memories. Wealth was thus flaunted on a large scale and Parisian fashions could be admired in those same Lebanese mountain resorts that had emptied so quickly in the First War. A European-style cafe life came to flourish in cities like Cairo and Beirut where the privileged and wealthy classes openly expressed their political discontent.

It is therefore not surprising that none of my informants speaks of any severe shortages of food or other basic commodities. Right at the beginning of the Second War there was a brief period of panic in a city like Mosul, which had experienced famine in the First War, and the names of certain merchants were mentioned as war profiteers. In Jerusalem, too, some people stocked up on a few essentials like sugar and rice. But white sugar was soon replaced by brown or Egyptian sugar. Rice, interestingly enough, was replaced by cracked wheat, as was the case in the earlier war, but seems not to have completely disappeared from the markets. Meat became expensive but remained quite plentiful, and there are no reports of shortages of fruits or vegetables. The items most frequently remembered as being in short supply are gasoline, tyres, medicines, clothing and all imported goods. Inflation was rampant throughout the war but wages rose as well, so the hardship was lessened.

As regards grain, the major difference between the two wars was the tight control of production by the Mandatory powers, introduced by Britain and the Vichy (later Free French) regime, in Palestine, Syria and Lebanon. The so-called Miri Bureau in Syria and Lebanon established a veritable monopoly over grains, buying from producers at prices set by itself and selling to bakeries according to capacity. A Damascus diarist, while constantly bemoaning the escalating prices of all commodities, nevertheless informs us that bread was very cheap.[85] War profiteers were mocked in Egyptian magazine cartoons and the inability of governments to control them was frequently condemned, but the criminality that attached to them in the First War is not present in the memories of the Second. This is partly because, following the British campaign against the Vichy regime in Syria and Lebanon in 1941, the British Army became a vast employer, supplier and consumer, creating an economic boom whose benefits reached large sectors of the population. In addition, a huge black market came into existence in a country like Iraq, but although this increased the hardship of the poorer classes, it did not result in famine. In Palestine, Syria and Lebanon food coupons were issued but seem to have largely disappeared by 1944.

In all, the massive presence of Allied troops in the Arab Near East created what was in effect a huge market: 'You could buy anything you wanted from army surplus stores' is how one informant remembered it. Canned food, jams, bottled drinks and even ammunition and rifles could be had, often for very little. Many Arab industries and service companies that still exist today began their life by buying surplus stocks from Allied armies at the end of the war. True, in Syria and Lebanon, the Free French employed Senegalese and Maghribi troops to put fear into student demonstrators, but on the other hand the Australians and New Zealanders are still widely remembered with what one might describe as affectionate contempt.

We most often remember the past in black and white. We see it in black and white and we interpret it likewise. Days are short, nights are long. Heroism is bright, villainy is dark. And the memories of the First War are a limpid example. This quirk of memory makes it difficult for the historian to reconstruct the colours of history. Memories of the Second War, however, are an exception to the rule: they are in Technicolor. Additionally, First War memories seem imprisoned by their world and are often plaintive and repetitive, while Second War memories flow forth with ease, freely exploring self and surroundings. But the full story of the Arab world during the two World Wars has yet to be told. The remarks above attempt to tap some memories of personal experience and are offered here largely in the hope that they may echo other memories in other regions of the world.

Recommended reading

Antonius, George, *The Arab Awakening* (London: Hamish Hamilton, 1938)

Cleveland, William, *A History of the Modern Middle East* (Oxford: Westview Press, 1994)

Hourani, Albert, *A History of the Arab Peoples* (London: Faber, 1991)
    The Emergence of the Modern Middle East (London: Macmillan, 1981)

Marsot, Afaf L., *A Short History of Modern Egypt*)Cambridge: Cambridge University Press, 1985)

Khoury, Philip, *Syria and the French Mandate* (London: Tauris, 1987)

Sanders, Liman von, *Five Years in Turkey* (Annapolis, MD: United States Naval Institute, 1927)

Notes

[1] The best-known war novel in Greater Syria is probably Tawfiq Yusuf `Awwad, *Al-Raghif* (*The Loaf of Bread*) (Beirut: Maktabat Lubnan, 1998; first published 1939)

[2] See, eg, Muhammad Rashid Rida, Rihlat al-Imam Muhammad Rashid Rida (ed), *Yusuf Ibish* (Beirut: al-Mu'assasa al-`Arabiyya, 1971) pp227-8, 232; Sa`d Zaghlul, `Abd al-`Azim Ramadan (ed), *Mudhakkarat Sa`d Zaghlul* (Cairo: Al-Hay`a al-Misriyya al-`Amma, 1992) Vol 5, p76 and Vol 6, p111

[3] See, eg, the poems of Ma`ruf al-Rusafi in `Abd al-Karim `Allaf, *Baghdad al-Qadima* (Baghdad: Matba`at al-Ma`arif, 1960) pp233, 241

[4] The following are particularly relevant and well-documented articles: Nicholas Z. Ajay, 'Political intrigue and suppression in Lebanon during World War I', in *International Journal of Middle East Studies* Vol 5 (1974), pp140-60; L. Schatkowski Schilcher, 'The Famine of 1915-1918 in Greater Syria', in 'Problems of the Modern Middle East' in John P. Spagnolo (ed), *Historical Perspective: Essays in Honour of Albert Hourani* (Reading: Ithaca Press, 1992) pp229-58; Rahid Khalidi, 'The Arab experience of the War' in Hugh Cecil and Peter Liddle (eds), *Facing Armageddon: The First World War Experienced* (London: Leo Cooper, 1996) pp642-55

5   Shakib Arslan, *Sira Dhatiyya* (Beirut: Dar al-Tali`a, 1969) p166; Yusuf Al-Hakim, *Bayrut wa Lubnan fi `Ahd Al-`Uthman* (Beirut: Imprimerie Catholique, 1964) p245

6   See Tarif Khalidi, 'Shaykh Ahmad `Arif al-Zayn and Al-`Irfan', in Marwan Buheiry (ed), *Intellectual Life in the Arab East: 1890-1939* (Beirut: American University of Beirut, 1981). See also note 32, below, where it appears that even within Mount Lebanon contiguous villages suffered diverse fates.

7   Fawzi Qawuqji, *Mudhakkarat Fawzi al-Qawuqji: 1912-1932* (Beirut: Dar al-Quds, 1975) Vol 1, p42. There is no mention of famine in either Baghdad or Basra in `Abd al-Karim `Allaf, op cit, or in Sulayman Faydi, *Mudhakkarat* (London: Saqi Books, 1998)

8   Muhammad Rashid Rida, op cit, p227; Shakib Arslan, op cit, p234. L. Schatkowski Schilcher, op cit, p230, disputes this, at least for the last two years of the war.

9   See Tarif Khalidi, note 6 above. See also Jibra`il Jabbur, *Min Ayyam al-`Umr* (Beirut: Jam`iyyat Asdiqa` al-Katib, 1991) p48; Aziz Bey, *Suriya wa Lubnan fi al-Harb al-`Alamiyya* (Beirut: np, 1933) p288

10 L. Schatkowski Schilcher, op cit, pp229-31 and notes 3 and 13, where she cites George Antonius for the death rate estimate. Muhammad Rashid Rida, op cit, p219, calculates that two-thirds of the population of his home town, Qalamun in North Lebanon, died of famine.

11 See, eg, Khalid Al-`Azm, *Mudhakkarat* (Beirut: Al-Dar al-Muttahida, 1973) and `Anbara Salam al-Khalidi, *Jawla fi al-Dhikrayat bayna Lubnan wa Filastin* (Beirut: Dar al-Nahar, 1978)

12 There are vivid accounts of this identity crisis in Fawzi Qawuqji, op cit, p12 and in Khalid Al-`Azm, op cit, p67

13 `Anbara Salam al-Khalidi, op cit, p107

14 See, eg, Khalid Al-`Azm, op cit, p39; Bishara Khalil al-Khuri, *Haqa`iq Lubnaniyya* (Beirut: Manshurat Awraq Lubnaniyya, 1960) Vol 1, p30; Sulayman Faydi, op cit, p231

15 Muhammad Fu`ad `Ayntabi, *Halab fi Ma`at `Am* (Aleppo: Manshurat Jami`at Halab, 1993) Vol 2, p141

16 Yusuf Al-Hakim, op cit, p131; the expression 'fire-storm' comes from Hakim.

17 Ibid, p132; Khalil Sakakini, *Kadha Ana Ya Dunya* (Beirut: Al-Ittihad al-`Amm li`l Kuttab wa`l Sahafiyyin al-Filastiniyyin, 1982) p80; `Anbara Salam al-Khalidi, op cit, p93; cf Angus Calder, *The People's War: Britain 1939-1945* (London: Pimlico, 1997) p36

18 Yusuf Al-Hakim, op cit, pp133, 139

19 Muhammad Fu`ad `Ayntabi, op cit, p141; Khalil Sakakini, op cit, pp80, 85; Muhammad Rashid Rida, op cit, p231; cf Jay Winter and Jean-Louis Robert (eds), *Capital Cities at War: Paris, London, Berlin 1914-1919* (Cambridge: Cambridge University Press, 1999) pp10-11, for the subordination of civilian to military priorities in the German war effort.

20 Muhammad Fu`ad `Ayntabi, op cit, p142; `Abd al-Karim `Allaf, op cit, pp233-4, for a poem on that occasion

21 Khalil Sakakini, op cit, p80

22 Khalid Al-`Azm, op cit, p75

23 The question comes from Winter and Robert, op cit, p11

24 Khalil Sakakini, op cit, pp79-80, 88; cf Sa`d Zaghlul, op cit, Vol 5, p76 and Vol 6, p111; see also *The Times Literary Supplement*, No 5053 (4 February 2000), p7, for a discussion of a quote from Robert Graves about 'newspaper language' in wartime.

25 Khalid Al-`Azm, op cit, pp64, 67

26 Sulayman Faydi, op cit, pp207-8; cf Yusuf Al-Hakim, op cit, p167

27 `Abd al-Wasi` ibn Yahya al-Wasi`i, *Tarikh al-Yaman* (Cairo: al-Matba`a al-Salafiyya, 1926) p258

28 Jibra`il Jabbur, op cit, pp44-5

29 Anis Frayha, *Qabla an Ansa* (Tripoli, Lebanon: Gross Press, nd (1980)) p50

30 Ibid, pp53-59

31 For roadblocks see Yusuf Al-Hakim, op cit, p260

32 Anis Frayha, op cit, p56

33 Yusuf Al-Hakim, op cit, p249. See also Aziz Bey, op cit, p60

34 Aziz Bey, op cit, p60

35 Muhammad Rashid Rida, op cit, p227

36 Muhammad Fu`ad `Ayntabi, op cit, p153; Muhammad Rashid Rida, op cit, p232

37 `Anbara Salam al-Khalidi, op cit, p106

38 `Ajjaj Nuwayhid, *Sittuna `Aman ma`a al-Qafila al-`Arabiyya: Mudhakkarat `Ajjaj Nuwayhid* (Beirut: Dar al-Istiqlal, 1993) pp21-2

39 See, eg, Muhammad Rashid Rida, op cit, p228, and Yusuf Al-Hakim, op cit, p236. L. Schatkowski Schilcher, op cit, p255, alludes to individual acts of generosity and adds: 'In time, further archival work will ... reveal the identities of other isolated individuals who played a noble role.' A few references are cited in notes 40 and 59, below.

40 Muhammad Kurd `Ali, *Mudhakkarat* (Damascus: Matba`at al-Taraqqi, 1948) pp825-9, 956; Aziz Bey, op cit, p106; Yusuf Al-Hakim, op cit, pp251-4; cf the images of the profiteer in Winter and Robert, op cit, pp104-32

41 Muhammad Fu`ad `Ayntabi, op cit, p153; Khalid Al-`Azm, op cit, p58

42 Yusuf Al-Hakim, op cit, pp167-8; Shakib Arslan, op cit, pp185-6; Sulayman Faydi, op cit, pp202-7; al-Rafi`i, `Abd al-Rahman, *Mudhakkarati* (Cairo: Dar al-Hilal, 1952) p27

43 Musa, Sulayman, *al-Haraka al-`Arabiyya: Sirat al-Marhala al-Ula li`l Nahda al-`Arabiyya al-Haditha 1908-1924* (Beirut: Dar al-Nahar, 1970) pp107-23; Sulayman Faydi, op cit, pp244-5; `Abd al-Karim `Allaf, op cit, pp183-4. In Egypt the reaction seems to have been muted.

44 This question is raised by L. Schatkowski Schilcher, op cit, p257. Her explanation is that the network of 'clientage' was responsible. The causes of this apathy, however, appear to have been more complex.

45 Yusuf Al-Hakim, op cit, p251

46 Fawzi Qawuqji, op cit, p42

47 For bread riots, see L. Schatkowski Schilcher, op cit, p230. The story of the bakery boys delivering from roof-tops I owe to Mme M. T. Moussallem (December 1999); it is corroborated by Khalil Sakakini, op cit, p138

48 For reliance on miracles, see Khalil Sakakini, op cit, p139. For the effect of calamities, see Muhammad Rashid Rida, op cit, pp228-9

49 Khalid Al-`Azm, op cit, p70; Rustum Haydar, *Mudhakkarat Rustum Haydar*, ed Najdat Fathi Safwat (Beirut: al-Dar al-`Arabiyya li`l Mawsu`at, 1988) p137; cf Sa`d Zaghlul, op cit, Vol 5, p101

50 `Ali Jawdat, *Dhikrayat :1900-1958* (Beirut: np, 1967) p349

51 Sa`d Zaghlul, op cit, Vol 6, p348

52 Ibid, Vol 7, p67; see also Khalil al-Khuri, op cit, p86, an exile from Lebanon, who describes Egypt as prosperous, having been 'spared the horrors of war'.

53 `Abd al-Karim `Allaf, op cit, p234

54 Sa`d Zaghlul, op cit, Vol 5, pp187, 201; see also Vol 4, p231; Vol 5, p77; Vol 6, p24

55 There is an interesting discussion of this theme in al-Maqdisi, Anis al-Khuri, *Ma`a al-Zaman* (Beirut: np, nd (1976)) pp35-40

56 There are fascinating echoes of this mutiny in David Omissi, *Indian Voices of the Great War: Soldiers' Letters, 1914-1918* (London: Macmillan, 1999) p199, Letter no 340 and note 1. See also p202, Letter no 346, for the ambivalence in mood regarding the revolt of the Sharif Husayn of Mecca

57 Sa`d Zaghlul, op cit, Vol 5, pp187, 201

58 Khalil Sakakini, op cit, p90; Khalid Al-`Azm, op cit, p76

59 Muhammad Kurd `Ali, op cit, pp137-9; Yusuf Al-Hakim, op cit, pp253-4; Aziz Bey, op cit, p105

60 `Anbara Salam al-Khalidi, op cit, p113; Aziz Bey, op cit, p105

61 Aziz Bey, op cit, pp105-6; Muhammad Kurd `Ali, op cit, p205

62 Muhammad Rashid Rida, op cit, p232

63 Muhammad Kurd `Ali, op cit, p204

64 Khalid Al-`Azm, op cit, pp74-5, 82; Khalil Sakakini, op cit, p138

65 Aziz Bey, op cit, p113; Yusuf Al-Hakim, op cit, p245

66 Khalid Al-`Azm, op cit, pp74-5; Yusuf Al-Hakim, op cit, p251

67 Khalid Al-`Azm, op cit, pp76-7, who feels some guilt about his life of luxury in the midst of famine

68 Yusuf Al-Hakim, op cit, p255

69 Muhammad Fu`ad `Ayntabi, op cit, p152; see also Sevket Pamuk, *A Monetary History of the Ottoman Empire* (Cambridge: Cambridge University Press, 2000) p223

70 Yusuf Al-Hakim, op cit, p254; Aziz Bey, op cit, pp287-89; Anis Frayha, op cit, p59

71 Aziz Bey, op cit, pp104-5, 152

72 `Anbara Salam al-Khalidi, op cit, pp106-17; Yusuf Al-Hakim, op cit, pp252, 257-8

73 Fawzi Qawuqji, op cit, p43
74 Khalil Sakakini, op cit, pp91-2
75 Babakr Badri, *Tarikh Hayati* (Omdurman: np, 1959) p137. These memoirs, otherwise fascinating, contain only one other reference to the war: pp121-2
76 Sa`d Zaghlul, op cit, Vol 7, p190
77 `Abd al-Karim `Allaf, op cit, pp245-6
78 Anis Frayha, op cit, p61
79 Khalid Al-`Azm, op cit, pp87-8
80 `Anbara Salam al-Khalidi, op cit, p119
81 Rustum Haydar, op cit, pp119-60. See also Khalil Sakakini, op cit, pp154-6
82 My affectionate thanks to the following informants: Mrs Rasha Salam al-Khalidi, Mr Hani al-Hindi, Prof Assem Salaam, Prof Usamah al-Khalidi, and Prof Yusuf Ibish. I have not attempted to ascribe their information individually.
83 Khalil Mardam Bey, *Yawmiyyat al-Khalil* (Beirut: Mu`assasat al-Risala, 1980) p126
84 Ibid, p80
85 Ibid, p41

Chapter 20

The Netherlands and Sweden: the experience of neutrality

Bob Moore, Susanne Wolf and Paul M. Binding

The Dutch experience in the First World War

As the diplomatic crisis in the summer of 1914 became more acute, the Dutch Government was forced to contemplate what it would do in the event of a general European war. In reality, the choices were extremely limited. Traditionally isolated from mainstream European affairs and concerned primarily with her Empire, the odds were undoubtedly stacked against this small nation holding out against its much larger and more powerful belligerent neighbours for any length of time. The country was geographically sandwiched between Britain and Germany, and dependent on them both as trading partners and for free passage for the shipping on which that trade, and the overall economic viability of the Netherlands, relied.

The Dutch never considered themselves to be a warlike nation. In his chronicle of the war years, Ritter notes that 'our people were – what they still are – a peaceful people. We do not have the ability to hate another people, and "militarism" is not only unpopular but also rare.'[1] The partial mobilisation of Dutch troops ordered on 30 July 1914, followed by a general mobilisation one day later, were therefore not steps taken lightly. Tentative last-minute efforts to form a defence union with Belgium had floundered when the German forces crossed the Belgian border on 4 August. The Dutch Government was placed in the unenviable position of having to choose between joining one of the two belligerent alliances or attempting to maintain its neutrality for as long as the war lasted.[2]

Writing to justify neutrality in September 1914, the art historian and critic Just Havelaar argued that it should be seen not as 'colourless' or a 'monotone middle-way' but as 'heroic' in the face of a war that was

> '…not only the greatest and most horrific, but undoubtedly also the stupidest ever waged. Who in the world can feel enthusiasm for this miserable slaughter, which was inevitable, which had been prepared for years but which no one wanted.'[3]

Whether the Dutch themselves preserved their neutrality by affirmative political action or whether the belligerents merely allowed them to retain their neutral status, because that best suited their plans, is a question that has not yet been fully addressed by Dutch scholars, or by international historians, and one that lies outside of the scope of this study. What can be said with some certainty, however, is that although the Dutch managed to preserve their neutrality and avoided direct involvement in the war, they were by no means unaffected by it. While the Netherlands did not have to endure the horrific loss of life experienced by those nations who sent their sons to fight on the front line, the years 1914 to 1918 were in many other respects just as difficult for the Netherlands as they were for the belligerent European powers.

Although the Dutch Army in 1914 was a reasonable size relative to the population it served, it was nevertheless tiny compared to the armies of Germany, Britain and France. Thanks to the foresight of the then Chief of the General Staff, Luitenant-Generaal C. J. Snijders, it had spent much of 1913 exercising against a possible attack on its borders. However, it relied heavily on conscripts and reservists to boost its numbers. In the light of the gathering storm clouds over Europe, many of those who would have completed their military service in mid-1914 were kept in uniform indefinitely, making some 200,000 troops available to be sent to guard the Dutch frontiers against a possible attack.[4] How effective these troops would have been against a concerted German attack is debatable. Snijders, who was appointed as Commander-in-Chief of the Dutch Army and Navy on 31 July 1914, then promoted to Generaal the following week, clearly recognised the inadequacies of the situation. By the end of the war he had succeeded in persuading the Government to more than double the number of men under arms to a total of over 450,000 and invest heavily in new equipment.

The status of the Army was strengthened shortly after the mobilisation when areas of strategic importance, such as the border areas and districts that housed internment camps or other sites of military significance, were declared to be in a *staat van beleg* (state of siege) or *staat van oorlog* (state of war), which gave the military authority over the civilian population and institutions. Snijders was constantly at odds with the Cabinet over plans for a possible attack. Politically he favoured an alliance with Germany over one with the Entente Powers, a view strengthened by his military experience, which led him to believe that in the event of an attack the only way to ensure that the Netherlands was on the winning side was to make an alliance with Germany – the only power that he believed could realistically win a battle for Dutch land. This was in direct opposition to the Cabinet's view, which held that an attack by one side would not necessarily mean that the Netherlands immediately joined forces with the opposing side. The prospect of an independent Netherlands fighting both Germany and Great Britain at the same time was one that Snijders, perhaps understandably, found to be totally unrealistic, but this was the only option for which the Dutch Government were prepared to plan.[5]

Mobilisation had an immediate effect on Dutch domestic life. Ritter writes of women and children weeping as they waved goodbye to husbands and fathers who were transported to the border on one of the many specially chartered trains. He also speaks of the young men who were clearly excited at the thought of military action.[6] Life also changed for the inhabitants of the border regions, who suddenly found soldiers billeted on them or a tented army camp appearing overnight next to their village:

'All at once, around two o'clock, we heard music. We rushed outside and yes, there came the third regiment, out of the Molenstraat marching in time with the music towards Bergen op Zoom with standard unfurled. It was a perfect sight – the men were extremely well turned out. At the back of the column, the essential ambulances and other encumbrances. The locals were overjoyed; many had never seen anything like this before.'[7]

For the inhabitants of Limburg in the south of the country, the presence of the war was particularly evident as they could hear the guns. From the high ground, near Maastricht, it was even possible to observe the battles between the German invaders and the retreating Belgians. However, the sounds of battle could also be heard much further north. Queen Wilhelmina noted that the great explosion that rocked Antwerp had been clearly audible in many parts of the Netherlands, and that:

'On a short holiday at Het Loo during the war we could hear the front in Flanders. Afterwards in our house near the North Sea coast we could hear the same sounds in the dips but not on top of the dunes. My ADCs taught me to distinguish between drumfire and ordinary fire.'[8]

In spite of the general abhorrence of war, the immediate threat to the Netherlands and its neutrality initially united the Dutch population behind the Government and its decision to mobilise. As the war progressed, however, and the contingencies introduced began to bite, this support began to wane. The problems created by removing a large section of the working male population soon became obvious. Military pay, averaging Dfl1.50 a day, was a good deal less than the pre-war income most families had enjoyed.[9] Many small businesses were left without their management or workforce and farms had no one left to bring in the harvest. The Government was not unsympathetic and, excepting times when the threat to Dutch borders was perceived to be particularly high, allowed its servicemen long periods of leave for a variety of reasons including business, study and domestic problems. It would not, however, accede to the demands from some politicians and sections of the public who called for demobilisation once, in their opinion, the immediate danger to the Netherlands had passed. For all its trust in the Dutch ability to remain neutral throughout the war, the Cabinet also clearly believed that the deterrent of a well-guarded border was also essential.

For the men mobilised into the Dutch Army, boredom became a way of life. One described the routine of his fellow soldiers:

'The two guards sat good-naturedly behind the barricade and tried to drive away the monotone dullness with a pipe of tobacco. In serene resignation they killed time by blowing beautiful smoke rings… As far as the eye could see, the fields lay spread out under a blaze of sunshine. To the right of the barricade lay heavily wooded, hilly terrain. In the distance, they could hear the bark of a guard-dog at one of the Belgian farms. The two sentries felt that they had lost all contact with the inhabited world. For city-dwellers, life at the frontier is alarming for its audible stillness.'[10]

Yet the peculiarity of their position was not lost on these Dutch servicemen:

> 'In this situation it was impossible to imagine that in other parts of this country only a short distance away, towns and villages were being consumed in fire and flames and the murderous lead did its inhumane work.'[11]

Although the Dutch forces were not called upon to fight, there were still some Dutch casualties, most of them civilians. The largest group to suffer was fishermen. Many lost their livelihoods or even their lives through encountering mines laid in the seas around Holland. The merchant marine was similarly affected and the commencement of the unrestricted submarine war in early 1915 swiftly claimed two major casualties, the SS *Medes*, on 25 March 1915, followed by the SS *Katwijk*, on 14 April, both sunk by a German U-boat. This loss of shipping was a feature that lasted until the end of the war. In February 1916 the SS *Rijdam* limped back to port with a large hole in its bow, having lost two crewmen.[12] Less than a month later the newly commissioned passenger ship SS *Tubantia*, from the Koninklijken Hollandschen Lloyd, was sunk by a torpedo just off the Nord-Hinder lightship. The public outcry was enormous, especially when the Germans refused to accept responsibility for the sinking despite the presence of German submarines in the vicinity.[13] Only later, when fragments of a German torpedo were found among the ship's wreckage did they agree to pay compensation. Estimates suggest that some 147 merchant ships and 151 fishing vessels were sunk during the war at the cost of some 1,169 lives, some by mines and others by the 'raging fury' of German U-boats.[14] It was estimated that the fishing village of Scheveningen alone lost 300 of its seafarers.[15] The *Eindhovensch Dagblad* echoed the thoughts of many in 1917 when it responded to the latest attack on a Dutch fishing boat with this editorial:

> 'How long still will Germany treat us this way? How long still will the conflict for the free sea impose on our rights and cramp our freedom? Hundreds of German children are lovingly saved from starvation every week by the Netherlands and still her Navy vents its anger on poor, simple fisher folk.'[16]

Nor were the families of these sailors safe on land either, as stray British and German torpedoes damaged Dutch coastal villages on more than one occasion. Threats to Dutch civilians came not only from the sea but also from the air, as lost or damaged aircraft from both sides dropped explosives on to property or caused damage by crash-landing inside Dutch territory. For example, a lost German airship dropped two firebombs over Gorkem on 22 October 1916, startling but not injuring the inhabitants. Casualties from these incidents were rare, but on the night of 29/30 April 1917, bombs dropped from a British aircraft on Zierikzee killed three civilians.[17] Eventually the Cabinet ordered the Army to open fire on any non-Dutch aircraft crossing the border, resulting in several aircraft being brought down.

The Dutch economy felt the effects of war even before the first shots had been fired. Uncertainty over the future led to such volatility on the stock market that the Amsterdam exchange was closed on 29 July 1914. This financial nervousness soon spread and there was a general run on the banks. Public confidence in paper money was lost and traders insisted in being paid in coins, accepting notes only for considerably less than their face value. The number of coins, especially silver coins, in circulation proved hopelessly inadequate as people began to hoard them. Eventually the Government stepped in and issued statements in all leading newspapers to the effect that paper money would be honoured in full. This proved sufficient to restore public confidence in the currency and a degree of normality returned, although the exchange remained closed far longer than initially anticipated, and did not fully re-open until 1916.

Despite assurances to the Dutch public that all was well with the Dutch banks, precautions were taken to preserve the financial institutions. On 3 August 1914, at the instigation of the Minister for Agriculture, Commerce and Industry, M. W. F. Treub, a law was passed prohibiting the export of key items such as grain, horses, coal and gold. The law was aimed at preserving stocks of essential products for domestic consumption, but the attempts by the belligerent powers to control goods moving in and out of the Netherlands was to prove one of the biggest headaches for the Dutch authorities as they tried to negotiate their way through the diplomatic minefield created by the outbreak of war. The problem with trade was twofold. First, there were the suspicions in both Britain and Germany that the Netherlands was trading more favourably with their enemies than with themselves, which caused them to restrict exports to the Netherlands. Second, there was the more basic problem of shipping being unable to negotiate seas that were mined and patrolled by belligerent warships and submarines. The result of these two problems was that, as the war progressed, the Dutch found it increasingly difficult to import sufficient essential supplies for domestic consumption. The Allied attempts to impose a blockade on Germany resulted in the formation of the Nederlandsche Overzee Trustmaatschappij (NOT), an organisation designed to oversee Dutch external trade and demonstrate that all goods imported into the Netherlands were for home consumption and not for re-export to Germany. The NOT soon became very powerful and to a large extent it achieved its aim.[18] Unfortunately, the price Germany was prepared to pay for supplies meant that, despite the best efforts of the Dutch authorities, smuggling was rife. Once the Germans closed the Dutch/Belgian border in 1916, smuggling became more difficult and lives were lost on the electric fence erected by the Germans along the entire length of the border.

Food, fuel and other goods were soon in short supply and their market prices inevitably increased. To counteract this, the Government brought in the *distributiewet* (distribution law), a policy designed to provide a basic supply of food for all at an affordable price. Local councils were responsible for buying in supplies, often at very high prices, then organising the redistribution of rations at a fixed price. Central government met 90 per cent of the shortfall and local government the remaining 10 per cent. This distribution system, although sound in theory, did not work well in practice and was subject to a barrage of public criticism. First, it was expensive.[19] Not only were goods bought in at a loss, but there was also an increase in the number of civil servants needed to administer the system. Many of these hastily recruited staff were either incapable of performing their duties or were open to corruption. In addition, this huge bureaucratic enterprise was cumbersome and very slow; food sometimes rotted before it could be distributed.

As in Germany, the winter of 1916/17 was very hard. Gas and electricity were both rationed, which gave added emphasis to the food crisis, and a growing housing shortage meant that overcrowding, with all its inherent health risks, compounded the problems of many ordinary Netherlanders. The increased submarine activity in the North Sea meant that very little food was getting through, and in early February 1917 the bread ration was set at 400gm per day. A form of bread rationing had been in place since 1915, but this was now tightened. On 24 March 1917 the ration was reduced to 300gm, and by April this was only available for seven in every nine days.[20] With the entry of the United States into the war, all hopes of further grain supplies disappeared and such potatoes as were available had to be exported to Germany in exchange for coal – essential for domestic fuel and industrial use. This proved too much for the Dutch population and riots broke out in many of the larger towns with protests about the food shortages in general and the lack of potatoes in particular. These riots were led by women, the unfortunate Dutch housewives who were unable to find food to feed their families. By 1918 even the first-class Hotel Krasnapolsky in Amsterdam had a 'fat-catcher' on its staff to reclaim used or discarded fats for resale to the soap or oil industries.[21]

One of the most significant aspects of the war for the Netherlands, especially in 1914, was the mass movement of people that it engendered. This involved not only the internal movement of men from civilian to military roles and their mobilisation to take up defensive positions along the border, but also a colossal number of refugees who entered or passed through the Netherlands as they tried to escape the advancing German forces. As a neutral nation, the Netherlands had an obligation to intern any soldiers from belligerent forces who crossed its border in order to prevent them from re-entering the war. This was a new area of international law, as the regulations concerning internment in a neutral country were, as yet, largely untested in 1914, and the legislation incorporated into the post-war settlements owes much to the Dutch experience. As early as the first week of the war, the Dutch found themselves dealing with Belgian and German troops that had, for a variety of reasons, strayed over the border.

Disarming belligerents was not always a straightforward process, or free from danger:

> 'A detachment of soldiers ... came out of the firing line. Wild-eyed. One had a wound here, another there. They had had to leave fallen comrades behind. Disarming 150 took time. Unfortunately all too soon it became apparent that the Belgians were still intoxicated by the war. Suddenly Germans arrived to check that the border was secure. The Belgians stood less then fifty metres from German occupied territory, but safe on neutral soil. They had nothing more to fear... The appearance of the Germans made such a strong impression on two of the Belgians that they produced hand grenades and threw them at the Germans, screaming "come over here if you dare".'[22]

The Belgians had to be led away, by the Dutch commander, at gunpoint.

Internment camps were established at Gaasterland for the Belgians and at Bergen for the Germans. By the end of October these had become completely inadequate as the Dutch found themselves having to intern 1,500 members of the British Naval Brigade and around 35,000 Belgian troops. The arrival of some of the latter was reported in the Dutch press:

> 'Laboriously, the men trudged along the road, some in clogs, some in slippers, some clad in old hats or a cap, some bareheaded. Nearly all of them carried something: a bundle in a coloured cloth, a small bag. Many had a blanket hung over the shoulder as a bandolier. It was a sad sight, these unshaven, unwashed faces.'[23]

These soldiers were not the only people fleeing the German advance. During a few short days in October 1914 around 1 million Belgian refugees also entered the Netherlands. Many of these were in considerable distress, hungry, injured and very tired. Families had been separated and large numbers of children were wandering alone. On 6 October a resident of Roosendaal, a town close to the Belgian border, recorded in his diary:

> 'The number of refugees becomes ever greater. It is impossible to describe what is happening here. Refugee Belgians, fleeing Germans, soldiers, you would not know the town any more.'

The following day:

> 'I have no idea what is going to happen. Thousands, without a word of a lie, thousands of refugees from Antwerp and surrounding districts come by train, by cart and on foot to Roosendaal. Rich and poor, they all flee to the Netherlands... Ten thousand refugees fill the streets; everywhere is full of unlucky people; everyone – with no exceptions – has refugees in their house, and still there are hundreds begging just for a place to sit, just to be able to rest for a while.'[24]

The response of the Dutch authorities was immediate and generous. Any and all buildings in the border areas were pressed into service. Blankets and food were gathered as quickly as possible and distributed amongst the cold and hungry. Help also came from charitable organisations and institutions as well as many private individuals who simply opened their homes to those in need.

When the numbers became so great that the border regions could no longer cope, refugees were then sent in special trains to other areas of Holland. Some continued their journey still further by embarking on ships at Vlissingen and reaching Great Britain, but many stayed in Holland. Understandably this huge influx of refugees placed a great strain on Dutch resources, which although not so limited as they would become later in the war, had already been stretched by the recent mobilisation.

To alleviate the situation, the Dutch Government began negotiations with the German military commanders at Antwerp to allow for the safe return of those who wished to go home. While initially uncertain that the new German rulers in Belgium could be trusted, many refugees did take advantage of the special trains laid on by the Dutch Government for their repatriation. Despite efforts to try and persuade the remainder to go home, some 100,000 refugees chose to stay in the Netherlands for the duration of the war. Many of these were the families of Belgian soldiers already interned in Holland, some simply had nowhere else to go. A great deal of support was given to those remaining, much of it initially funded by the Government. Special refugee camps were erected, schools established, workshops started. Charitable committees in every part of Holland found in the Belgian refugees an outlet for all their philanthropic impulses.[25] The presence of these refugees, frequently featured in the Dutch press, also provided a constant reminder to the Dutch people of what their near neighbours had suffered and what they had, so far, managed to escape.

The internees presented different problems. The Dutch Government's decision to place the many Belgian soldiers in guarded camps rather than allowing them to remain with their families in the refugee camps brought much criticism, not only from the Belgian Government based in Le Havre, but also from liberal Dutch opinion, which thought that their Government was being unduly harsh. As the war progressed, and especially after the German closure of the Dutch/Belgian border reduced the chances of Belgian soldiers wanting to escape home, many of the internees were allowed out of the camps to take up employment. Priority was given to those who had families to support, especially if those families were also in Holland. As a result many thousands of internees were able to spend more than half the war living with their families and leading a more or less normal existence. The plight of the internees is a good example of the Dutch Government's attempts to maintain a humanitarian attitude that fitted its international image and pleased its own electorate, but at the same time visibly maintained the strict impartiality necessary to protect its neutral status.

Not all foreign soldiers crossing into the Netherlands, however, were liable for internment. In accordance with international law, escaping POWs were allowed to pass through the Netherlands on their way home and were frequently given assistance to speed them on their way. The Dutch press, especially the illustrated press, often carried stories of improbable or exciting escapes, usually supported by a picture of the individuals concerned side by side with the Dutch border guards who had allowed them entry into Holland. Deserters were another problem. Almost exclusively German, the number of deserters increased as the war progressed and presented the Dutch authorities with several problems. Not least was that of identifying a true deserter as opposed to someone merely wishing to avoid internment. In 1917 (the only year for which figures are available) at least 488 German soldiers were interned, then released as deserters.[26] Undoubtedly many more never even reached the stage of being interned. Precise figures are unavailable, but some estimates put the number of German deserters living in the Netherlands by the end of the war as high as 20,000. These were soon to be joined by many former prisoners of war who took the opportunity to escape when being repatriated through the Netherlands immediately after the war, because they had no wish to return to a defeated Germany.

Despite the declaration of neutrality issued at the start of the war, there was never really any serious prospect of the Netherlands remaining unaffected by a general European war. Even if, as seemed very unlikely in 1914, the Dutch Cabinet succeeded in maintaining the neutral position they had adopted, the geographical position of the Netherlands in conjunction with its strong trading links with both Germany and Great Britain meant that it would be involved in many ways. Indeed, it is possible to argue, as some did at the time, that many Netherlanders benefited from the war as the national income rose in real terms despite a fall in the value of the guilder.[27] Henrietta Roland Holst, the revolutionary poetess, writing in 1926 about the Netherlands during the war, said:

'In no other country did the bourgeoisie make capital out of the catastrophe of the war with such shameless cynicism, by all possible means, even the lowest and most despicable.'[28]

While this was an extreme view, Kossmann has argued that Dutch agriculture, industry and navigation did very well in the years 1914-16, and many well-placed people made fortunes from the black market, and in trade with Germany and German-occupied Belgium.[29] Only in the later years, when food supplies ran short and unemployment grew as a result of falling trade and production, were the detrimental effects of the war felt across the whole country. Yet even this often varied between localities. One Dutch serviceman who spent the war years in a country district, living with his wife, recorded that:

'All in all both my wife and I realised that we lived in an oasis. We were scarcely aware of the food shortages which beset the cities or the mobilisation-weariness of the army. But we did know about the continuing export of foodstuffs to Germany, and about the miseries of the export of people: at this time around 20,000 unemployed Dutch workers were forced to find employment in German munitions factories.'[30]

As in the belligerent countries, it was the poor in the cities who felt the effect of the food and fuel shortages the most. Those that did not have the resources to pay for goods on the black market were the ones who spent the last two years of the war cold and hungry. For the wealthier members of Dutch society, rationing was an inconvenience, but as compensation they were able to enjoy the more varied social life brought about by the influx of foreigners to The Hague and other major cities, including many interned officers who, by virtue of their rank, did not have to reside in internment camps. Another similarity with many of the belligerent nations was the increase in the number of women who found employment outside the home in the period 1914-18. Although the traditional breadwinners were not actually fighting, their mobilisation and absence from home meant that their womenfolk were temporarily compelled to take over the responsibilities normally shouldered by men.

It would be wrong to assume that all aspects of Dutch life were disrupted by the war, and sport was one area that blossomed in spite of the conflict. The number of competitions, tournaments and sports events in general increased during the war years, partly with an eye to keeping the mobilised troops occupied. When the 1916 Olympic Games were cancelled because of the war, a national Olympic tournament was held in the Olympic stadium in Amsterdam. Likewise, despite the problems that the very cold winter of 1917 brought, it also provided the chance to stage the *elfstedentocht*, a long-distance skating event that even a World War would not stop the Dutch holding once the ice was available! Politically, even though the war remained a time-consuming and important item on the Government's agenda, it did not completely monopolise Cabinet thinking and time was found for other significant domestic legislation to be debated and passed, including major changes to both tax and suffrage laws.

While these changes were to endure, the majority of the population assumed that other emergency measures taken during the war would be rescinded and that pre-war stability would return. For the most part, these aspirations were met in the months after the armistice. The Belgian refugees and military internees finally returned home and Government centralisation and interference in the economy came to an end. However, even the Netherlands did not entirely escape the revolutionary wave of October/November 1918. Influenced by events in Germany, an increased vote for extreme left-wing parties in the July 1918 general election and a small-scale soldiers' mutiny, the Dutch socialists, led by Pieter Jelles Troelstra, came close to attempting a left-wing takeover, but were soon swamped by a huge wave of demonstrations in favour of fatherland, monarchy and the elected government.[31] After noting that there had been a few 'tense days', the Queen described the scene in The Hague on 17 November:

> '...an immense demonstration of loyalty to the government took place. After unharnessing the horses, the demonstrators pulled the carriage with Hendrik, Juliana and me in it across the parade ground and through the town back to the Noordeinde [Palace].'[32]

Thus the Netherlands' 'revolutionary moment' passed without the upheaval and loss of life experienced elsewhere. In the months and years that followed, the Dutch more or less returned to their pre-war position as a trading and colonial nation in pursuit of profit and largely isolated from events in the outside world.

The snake in the barracks: Sweden and the Second World War

There are some writers who come to enjoy, above all in their own country, the status of secular saint. Their lives and deaths (to which their literary works come to seem brilliant supplements) are read as statements that can illuminate the society and times in which they occurred. D. H. Lawrence, Federico García Lorca, Cesare Pavese, Albert Camus all partake of this identity, and so does the Swedish novelist, short-story writer, essayist and dramatist Stig Dagerman (1923-54), read and respected above all other members of his generation of practitioners of *fyrtiotalismen*, general assumptions about Sweden. Illegitimate, spending his childhood among the rural poor and his adolescence among the urban, embracing anarcho-syndicalism and embarking on an early and passionate marriage to a young German refugee woman of similar political sympathies, he contradicted the hegemonic Swedish belief in a moderate, balanced life by fervent, astonishing and precocious productivity. In addition to his political and journalistic work for the anarcho-syndicalist paper *Arbetaren* (*The Worker*), he was, by the time he was 25, the author of three novels, three plays, one of the finest travelogues of the period, a volume of poems, and a fine book of short stories. The need to find authenticity for oneself and for one's society in a world that war had deprived of ontological certainties – this drove Stig forward and eventually burned him out, prematurely. In this chapter we shall call on Dagerman as a guide in the crossing of difficult territory, a passage made the more hazardous by half a century's obfuscation, some of it intentional, some of it innocent, some of it made at a governmental or institutional level, but a good part the expression of genuine popular perception.[33]

In 1945 Dagerman brought out *Ormen* (*The Snake*)[34], a novel in the form of a sequence of related stories set in wartime Sweden. Its cast of conscripts are all in a state of waiting, 'dangling men' (in Saul Bellow's phrase) in the face of the national military engagement, provoked by German attack that never, of course, comes. Out on exercises in the countryside, one of the conscripts, Bill, finds a snake, and in an existential moment decides to keep it, taking it back to his rural barracks. Later the snake (though is it the same one?) re-emerges in the Stockholm quarters of Bill's regiment, thus linking, through its uncertain dangerous being, disparate people who are nonetheless inextricably bound together by historical circumstances. Inside this second barracks the snake disappears, causing much panic, much activity (much frantic hunting-about all over the place) and a not unwelcome relief from tedium. When, eventually, it is found, it is dead, its back broken. But while it was missing, security and peace of mind were impossible.

Scriber, the significantly named intellectual of *The Snake*, declares: 'It's the tragedy of modern man that he no longer dares to be afraid. That's disastrous, because the consequence is that he's forced to stop thinking.'[35]

At the time of the book's appearance the eponymous snake must have been taken as a symbol of the predicament of Sweden in 1939-45, a neutral country, wondering whether or when it was going to be drawn into the war. Now with hindsight – and Dagerman continues to attract new readers inside and outside Scandinavia – the snake seems more and more to stand for a Swedish malaise over their country's conduct during the Second World War, even for its guilt on this subject. Some are troubled and will use all energies and resources to seek it out. Some will try to scotch it. Others insist (are pretending) that it is not in the barracks at all, and never could have been. During the last decade, the post-Cold War years, however, the position of denial is increasingly difficult to maintain, and certainly the later 1990s saw a wider and bolder approach to the subject of Sweden and the Second World War, extending to the Holocaust itself (though an American journalist in 1997 reported that a third of Swedish schoolchildren in a recent sample were doubtful whether the Holocaust had ever occurred).[36]

For Sweden 1931 was a crisis year and a turning-point; it saw the incident of

Ådalen, up in Västernorrland – about which Bo Widerberg was to make his famous 1969 film[37] – in which timber-mill management had the Army brought in to break a strike and five civilians lost their lives. The shock of this atrocity combined with that occasioned by the spectacular crash of Ivar Kreuger, the 'Match King' (who committed suicide in Paris the following year), galvanised the electorate into bringing about the 1932 victory of the Social Democrats under their charismatic leader Per Albin Hansson (1885-1946). With the exception of a blip in 1936 caused by disagreement over the defence budget, the Social Democrats were to remain in power for the next 40 years, creating an identification between governing party and nation-state in both international and national consciousness hard to parallel in other Western countries. (And the Social Democrat party is indeed in power at the time of writing, May 2000.) As for Hansson, from the working class (the son of a bricklayer) and without formal education, passionately devoted to peace and, at earlier stages of his career, a vocal upholder of disarmament, he was to be the popularly acclaimed, indeed much-loved Prime Minister until his unexpected death in October 1946.

It is with 'Per Albin' that *folkhem* Sweden begins. The term is often used in its definite form, *folkhemmet*, 'the people's home', and cannot be better described than by Hansson himself: 'The good society which functions like a *good* home' [my italics].[38] Swedish society, remarkably homogeneous anyway, and one inhabiting a large country with very considerable natural resources, was to be a family, of which every member could be proud, where none should enjoy undue privilege whether of class, of money, or even of professional and intellectual status – and where, increasingly, differentials of age and gender counted for far less than elsewhere. *Folkhem* is a beautiful ideal but must not simply be written off as that. Careful planning, well-thought-out budgeting, the practice of consensus so that no segment of Swedish society felt itself alienated or marginalised – these, together with certain peculiar circumstances, meant practical and efficient realisation of this widely and consciously held desideratum. Even in our times, when the 'Swedish Model' is yearly declared dead by its friends and enemies alike, Sweden, a prosperous country with a flourishing business sector, can still boast the smallest economic gap between the best-off and worst-off citizens. Hansson was backed up in his policies by truly remarkable colleagues, such as Gustav Möller, Minister of Social Affairs, and Rickard Sandler, who was Foreign Minister in the terrible year of 1939.

Sweden had not participated in any war since 1814, and Social Democrat thinking was peace-orientated, directed towards a rational society for rational people, and consequently favouring low expenditure on defence and trust in the efficacy of international co-operation, particularly the League of Nations. Furthermore, during the 1930s decisions on priorities where defence was concerned were made difficult, as talks between the Scandinavian countries emphasised, by Sweden's geographical position, halfway between Finland, fearful of Russia, and Norway, with its strong relationship to Britain. In 1939 Sweden declined Hitler's offer to all the Scandinavian countries of a non-aggression pact (only Denmark, always nervous of its powerful neighbour, accepted it), but nevertheless – together with Denmark, Norway and Finland – proclaimed neutrality after Britain and France's declaration of war on Germany.

The term 'neutrality' is often used by Swedes and non-Swedes, by politicians, writers and ordinary citizens, as if it refers to an absolute, to some legal and semi-permanent condition. In fact, unilateral declarations of neutrality were made in 1912 and on 3 August 1914, with the First World War imminent, and at no point did Sweden have constitutional or internationally affirmed neutrality – though discussion has often proceeded as if this were the case.[39]

Sweden refused Finland's request for help when attacked by Soviet Russia (then allied with Germany) in November 1939. Many Swedes felt an obligation to help these fellow-Scandinavians, and Rickard Sandler himself resigned when he saw that the Government intended not to honour this. Sweden sent money, weapons and volunteers to Finland, but officially stayed out of the conflict. And Sweden gave a negative reply to Britain and France when they asked if they could send soldiers via Sweden to help the Finns.

In April 1940 Germany invaded Denmark and Norway. Norway resisted the attack, but never had any alternative to surrender. The Norwegian Royal Family and Government requested residence in Sweden until such time as it was possible for them to return. Sweden feared that this would mean German retaliation, and once again made a neighbour an official refusal. Sweden sent no help whatsoever to Norway – but it did accept 50,000 Norwegian refugees. During the fighting in Norway Germany asked if troops and equipment could be sent via Sweden; the Swedish Government felt that this too would be a violation of their neutrality and agreed only to 'humanitarian' passage, to and from Narvik – doctors and medical supplies going one way, the wounded and attendant personnel the other.

But by June Norway had ceded, and the German hold on Europe had intensified. Germany asked again – and more insistently – for permission for troops to go through Sweden into and back from Norway, and this time the Government agreed. These 'transit' train services were to continue for three years. No single act of Sweden's in the war has left such an impression on its people as the permission for this; in over 30 years' experience of Sweden, the author has heard again and again, from a variety of quarters, shame expressed by those who watched these trains pulling their grim-looking carriages through the country – each northward journey spelling some increase in pain for the occupied Norwegians. But nobody did anything, no violent gestures were offered, and that too has been (and still is) a source of shame.

In June 1941 Germany asked Sweden whether it could send military back-up to Finland, which was trying to recover land appropriated in the 'Winter War' by the Soviet Union – now, after Hitler's invasion, on the Allies' side. Sweden agreed to the Engelbrecht Division, of 18,000 men, travelling through. Once again there were protesters (for what did neutrality mean, if this was permitted?) but agreement to German demands – strongly urged by the pro-German King – prevailed.

So much for foreign policy. Economically, Sweden sold Germany iron-ore, ball-bearings (SKF) and other goods, and received German imports in return. In the first years of the war Sweden defied requests from the Allies that certain trades vital to the Nazi war-machine be discontinued. (Later Britain was of the opinion that, because Swedish goods – ball-bearings, for instance – were of such importance for its own war-effort, this two-way traffic between Germany and Sweden should continue; Sweden's unoccupied position must not be endangered.)

In 1943, after Stalingrad and the 'turn of the tide', Sweden's relationship with the Allies was consolidated, and that with Germany deteriorated. The 'transit' trains were stopped, and by 1945 all trade with Germany had finished too. All of this can be put – and over the years more often than not has been put – under a 'What else could we have done?' justification. Sweden kept its lights on all along its southern coast during the years of the German occupation of Denmark, as an aggregate beacon of hope and freedom for the country on the other shore (under curfew). For a neutral country to exist, with no military presence on its terrain, was an inestimable blessing during those grim years, and many availed themselves of it: 6,500 Danish Jews, for example, the entirety of Denmark's Jewish population, and, during the bitter last months of fighting between Germany and the Soviet Union, 35,000 people from the Baltic States. (The not inconsiderable Baltic element in Swedish society dates from this time.)[40]

While there must have been not just a pro-German but a pro-Nazi section of Swedish society (Ingmar Bergman, his father and older brother belonged to it, as his fascinating autobiography, *The Magic Lantern*, reveals with a candour commendable and maybe courageous, but also far from disarming[41]), Sweden had no really significant Fascist movement as such during the 1930s. The great majority of its people, it would seem, even in the face of their justifiable fear of the not-so-distant Russia, had no wish to see the Axis triumph.

Nevertheless Germany was not only Sweden's chief trading partner but also the major country to which she had the closest cultural ties and geographical links. This bore fruit in the days of the 'Greater Germany'. While Germany secured military victory after military victory, in 1940-41, many in the Swedish business sector vigorously pursued lively and lucrative relations with the Germans. Archivist Göran Blomberg[42] has compiled a dossier (mostly from the files of the Swedish Security Police at the National Records Office) of Swedish companies only too anxious to meet German demands – for the 'Aryanisation' of their businesses, for instance. Swedes would assure the German Chamber of Commerce that their particular company was *Judenfrei* (free of Jews). Sometimes, however, the letters are sufficiently ambiguous to suggest that what their writers were saying to their German partners was something that they had no intention of implementing. And it must be insisted that there were numerous Swedish businessmen who would have no truck with any of this. This whole distressing topic finds its way into one of the most distinguished Swedish novels of the 1990s, Kerstin Ekman's *Gör mig levande igen* (*Make Me Living Again*).

Here then is a further area of malaise; here is the presence of the snake at its most destructive of peace of mind. There is more. Many newspapers sought to criticise Hitler's regime and policies. Despite a Freedom of the Press Act dating from 1766, the Government, keen not to get on the wrong side of Germany, keen to do nothing that would provoke any kind of hostility, came down on editors who expressed overtly critical views, and even went so far as to confiscate whole editions of papers that had dared to publish articles in which these were clear. The most famous 'offender' in this instance was Torgny Segerstedt of the Gothenburg paper *Göteborgs Handels-och-Sjöfartstidning*, regularly in trouble – even when he took up admirable causes, such as the exposure of the German use of torture in

Norway. Never, argued Segerstedt, can expediency, assessment of who will be victorious and self-trimming to meet this, be a moral good in itself (as the wartime Government virtually tried to make out). Arne Ruth (born 1943), leading Swedish intellectual and in the very vanguard of those now casting (disconcerting) daylight on to the subject of Sweden in the war, has, in published writing of his own, reminded readers of what Segerstedt said in his editorial 'The Verdict of History': 'When one considers how easily opinions are formed and legends created, how little the version of events that emerges usually has to do with what actually occurred, one is not inclined to place much trust in the testimony of the time, of what the future will call the present.'[43]

In the 'future', however – ie in the post-war years – Sweden occupied itself with the development of *folkhem*, a welfare society more comprehensive than any in history. Its ambitious projects, whether in health or education, in housing or in communications (in all of which it pursued goals with thoroughness and imagination), could be carried out because of the country's extreme prosperity, itself, obviously, a result of its debtless war. During this period Sweden was Europe's richest country per capita after Switzerland (which had passed the war similarly). Though there was, as has been said, moral discomfort (and worse) about the recent past, expression was more often than not confined to behind closed doors. No major Swedish writer tackled the subject of the war as Max Frisch did in Switzerland, not even the politically acute and bold P. O. Enquist, whose 'documentary' novel of 1968 *Legionärerna* (*The Legionnaires*) deals with a morally difficult event after the war – the sending back of Baltic refugees at the Soviet Union's behest.

The main reason for this comparative silence was the demanding pressure of an impressive, benevolent and forward-reaching present, the feeling that – to hark back to Hansson's words – there was something intrinsically good about what Sweden was building up and achieving. The Swedish people had in elections, both at the outset of the war (1939) and immediately after it (1945), enthusiastically endorsed their Government's policies. Surely the success of their society was a vindication of their decisions.

Arne Ruth, in his trenchant and seminal piece 'Post-War Europe: The Capriciousness of Universal Values', written for the review *Daedalus* in 1997, and leading up to an issue of peculiar moral painfulness, puts this situation succinctly and eloquently:

> 'After the war [and his words go beyond the concessions and transactions of the 1940s to shed light on the present] Sweden chose compassion as its own special quality, based on a recently established redefinition of the national project. A form of social change had been instituted in the 1930s that could now be proclaimed as the incarnation of modernity. The communal bodies that had been born in reaction to industrial capitalism had been allowed to share in the management of state affairs. The result was a change not only in the formal division of power but in the moral quality of society. The new social forces, the labour movement and the farmers' association, infused their value systems into the state... The moral basis was enhanced by the Allied victory over fascism. On the one hand, fascist perversion of nationalist

ideology finally rendered obsolete the concept of glorious war as basis for national sentiment. The ideology of participatory democracy as the true legitimation of modern nation-states became firmly embedded in most West European countries... Sweden offered hope for the future; harmony as opposed to chaos, common political action as opposed to paralysing conflicts... Sweden was thought to point the way out of a cumbersome historical tradition.

The idea of being the most emancipated country in the world was integral to the Swedish model. It was traditional nationalism turned upside down. The psychological impact was exactly the same as in the old-fashioned version: Swedish élites could be very proud of their eminence. They became used to feeling morally superior due to the fact that they were no longer fettered by tradition. And leaving nationalism behind was the core of their achievement.

In hindsight, this use of anti-nationalism as a national paradigm must be one of the strangest social paradoxes in political history. Politicians and diplomats were convinced they had a privileged insight into the future of humanity. They projected the Swedish attitude onto the world stage as a special sort of idealism.'[44]

It is possible to put this another way and say that the Swedes converted what war-guilt or communal unease they allowed themselves into a kind of Philoctetes's wound. In Greek mythology it was the pain from the running wound in his side that goaded Philoctetes into being so superb an archer. It was anxiety or embarrassment over their past international role that caused Sweden to establish itself as peace-broker to the world, and a model of harmony for all to look at and profit by. This was certainly the thinking behind the foundation of the admirable (and generous) Swedish Institute. If we cast our minds back to Dagerman's 'snake in the barracks', we recall that the feelings it inspired brought soldiers closer to one another, relieved misery. And Sweden became a responsible society not just to itself but to elsewhere, to the Third World (giving aid with no expectation of trade returns) and seeing itself (or choosing to see itself) as an intermediary between Western and Eastern blocs.

So, riding the mighty wave of *folkhem*, of a society not only just and democratic, but rich and well-respected, Swedes could without strain feel that the past could be allowed to remain where it was, back there. One could not pull it down as one could the old buildings that provided reminders of bad, corrupt old ways (an all too common practice of the 1950s and 1960s – think of old quarters of Gothenburg and Uppsala, for instance) but, in the interests of the future, there was no need to pay it undue attention; indeed, to do so was to detract from the merits of contemporary Sweden. Torgny Segerstedt, except in certain limited circles, did not become a national hero; Raoul Wallenberg, rescuer of thousands of Jews from the deaths Nazi Germany would have arranged for them, was carefully protected by officialdom from too much general awareness of more dubious elements in his personality and life, and was allowed to die, so to speak, probably in Russia's Gulag, to escape too much probing.

The assassination of Olof Palme in February 1986 was a shock from which Sweden has perhaps not yet recovered. 'Our innocence ended then, for ever,' one Swede remarked. The writer Björn Ranelid, born 1949 (one of whose best novels is a recreation of the mind and life of Stig Dagerman), said to the author in conversation: 'After Palme's death we felt, from this time forward anything is possible.' It caused a wave of introspection and intense self-examination enlarged by the end of the Cold War and of Sweden's allegedly non-aligned position during it. The Swedes became far more concerned about their history than ever before; this neutral and detached nation applied for membership of the European Union, was accepted and, unlike Norway, voted to join (and did, on 1 January 1995). This wave involved hard thinking about the war and Sweden's role then. The eminent feminist journalist and social critic, Maria-Pia Boëthius[45], published a storm-provoking study, *Heder och Samvete* (*On My Honour*) in 1991 (revised edition 1999) in which she supplied irrefutable figures of sales and co-operation benefiting Nazi Germany, and named names, challenging convenient apologetic explanations. Reaction was intense; Swedishness itself, it was felt, was under scrutiny – if not attack. One reviewer observed: 'She said right out that Sweden was not neutral during World War Two. That Sweden on the contrary with her official policy helped the Germans in their warfare.'[46]

In the wake of the scandal of the Swiss Nazi gold[47] has come a re-appraisal of key Swedish transactions, and the reaction – Arne Ruth remarked to me – was slow to take off, and inadequately covered in the Swedish media.

Even granting that, for obvious reasons, and, with the equivocal blessing of Britain, Sweden had to trade with Hitler's Germany, we have to consider the payment received. What could the source of that payment have been? Patiently Arne Ruth has reconstructed the negotiations between the Governor of the Swedish Central Bank, Ivar Rooth, and the Deputy Governor of the German Reichsbank, Emil Puhl, later to be convicted – as was, with a life sentence, the President of the Reichsbank and Minister of Economics, Walter Funk – for his acquiescence in transactions involving gold and other valuables appropriated from conquered countries in Eastern Europe and including (to quote from his own testimony of 1946) 'jewellery, watches, eyeglass frames, dental gold, and other gold items in great abundance taken from Jews, concentration camp victims, and other persons, by the SS.'[48]

Puhl's evidence against his minister, because of its implicit indictment of Sweden's wartime financial dealings, was not reported in the Swedish press. And it has taken the best part of three years since the re-opening of this question for recognition of, and concomitant interest in, its implications to become established. But now there has been a conference (October 1999) at which Swedish and Swiss historians reviewed this terrible feature of the pasts of their countries, and the matter was on the agenda of the Spring 2000 Holocaust Conference held in Stockholm itself. A full and detailed report and a summary of it are available from the Swedish Ministry for Foreign Affairs. So now one can perhaps say that the contaminated Swedish gold has entered the Swedish psyche, has become part of a past with which a people realise they must come to terms.

The importance of this is obvious and cannot be underestimated. Equally obvious and impossible to underestimate is the effect of this confrontation on Swedes' vision of themselves and their social achievement, which generations were not only taught to be proud of but were experientially pleased with. Is *folkhem* itself invalidated when we can see that key supports have such morally shaky foundations, that some of those most responsible for its construction and maintenance had truck, and more, with Europe's most heinous crime?

Stig Dagerman, of the Left, intensely committed to social justice, did not in his brief tormented life wholly belong to *folkhem*. His memories of childhood as containing 'a procession of beggars: ragged old men who halted with bent heads inside the door ... bitter youngsters who talked loud and heatedly about the shots at Ådalen'[49], and his awareness of the human capacity for irrational cruelty (his beloved grandfather was murdered) were too strong and consuming for him wholly to accept this national attempt at seamlessness. Again after the war he travelled through war-shattered Germany recording a scene that Sweden had been spared. One of the worst-bombed cities of all, Essen, he described as a 'dream-landscape of denuded, freezing iron-constructions and ravaged factory-walls.'[50] Dagerman ended up, after months of writer's block, inertia and acute depression, taking his life, asphyxiating himself in his own garage; his death has reverberated through the subsequent years.

The reason for this lies in the fact that Swedes have recognised that there was behind much *folkhem* ideology, however humane, something too excluding and exclusive, too determined to keep the pains and disruptions of elsewhere at bay, too Utopian. Elsewhere will always assert itself, and one cannot, and should not, expect it not to.

In truth, in every situation one considers, every nation-state stands compromised; governments have colluded, and worse, in known injustices to save themselves and their people no matter where one looks. There is – it would be patronising to those many hard workers on behalf of the truth to say otherwise – good reason for Sweden to feel guilt. There is also – and in terms of war-conduct itself – good reason for satisfaction; the widespread kindness shown to those, a not inconsiderable number, who came to live in safety and comfort in the country, the bravery of volunteers who went to Norway and Finland, and the demands on Swedish resources this meant, are evidence of a generally and widely beneficent society trying to sustain itself. Some of *folkhem*'s foundations may now be seen in a new and chilling light, but others remain indeed what they have long been supposed to be: hard work, a high level of mutual respect and tolerance, and harmonious organisation of industry and public services alike. The *folkhem* values are still precious to Sweden at the beginning of the 21st century, and their realisation and promulgation have been specifically Swedish achievements.

Recommended reading

Algulin, Ingemar, *A History of Swedish Literature* (Stockholm: Swedish Institute, 1989)

Barnouw, A. J., *Holland under Queen Wilhelmina* (New York: Charles Scribner's Sons, 1923)

Carlgren, Wilhelm M., trans A. Spencer, *Swedish Foreign Policy 1939-1945* (London: E. Benn, 1977)

Child, Marquis, *Sweden: The Middle Way* (New Haven: Yale University Press, 1980)

Dunk. H. W. von der (ed), *Vluchten voor de Groote Oorlog, Belgen in Nederland 1914-18* (Amsterdam: De Bataafsche Leeuw, 1988)

Ekman, Kerstin, *Gör mig levande igen* (*Make Me Living Again*) (Stockholm: Bonniers, 1986)

Flier, M. J. et al, *The Netherlands and the World War: Studies in the War History of a Neutral* (Oxford: Oxford University Press, 1928)

Frey, M., 'Trade, Ships and the Neutrality of the Netherlands in the First World War', in *International History Review* XIX (3) (1997), pp541-62

Kossman, E. H., *The Low Countries 1780-1940* (Oxford: Clarendon Press, 1978)

Scheffer, H. J., *November 1918: Journaal van een revolutie die niet doorging* (Amsterdam: De Arbeiderspers, 1968)

Segerstedt, Torgny, *När stormen klara sikten* (*When the Storm Clears Visibility*) (Stockholm: Ordfront, 1980)

Wahlbäck, Krister, *The Roots of Swedish Neutrality* (Stockholm: Swedish Institute, 1986)

Notes

1. P. H. Ritter, *De Donkere Poort*, Vol I (The Hague: D. A. Daamen's Uitgevers, 1931) p30
2. For an excellent summary of the diplomacy of the Netherlands in 1914, and in the latter stages of the war, see A. S. de Leeuw, *Nederland in de wereldpolitiek van 1900-heden* (Nijmegen, 2nd ed 1975)
3. Just Havelaar, 'Strijdende onzidigheid', *De Amsterdammer*, 13 September 1914
4. P. J. van Munnekrede, 'De Mobilisatie van de Landmacht', in H. Brugmans, *Nederland in Den Oorlogstijd* (Amsterdam: Elsevier, 1920) p5
5. A summary of the conflict between Snijders and the Cabinet can be found in E. H. Kossmann, *The Low Countries, 1780-1940* (Oxford: Clarendon Press, 1978) pp547-9
6. P. H. Ritter, op cit, p54
7. *Uit Bange Oorlogsdagen: Dagboek van een Roosendaaler*, Vol II, p67
8. Wilhelmina, Princess of the Netherlands, *Lonely But Not Alone* (London: Hutchinson, 1959) p100
9. L. G. J. Verberne, *Geschiedenis van Nederland*, Vol III (Amsterdam: Joost van den Vondel, 1938) p340.
10. Fr van de Vrande, *Grensleven* (Velsen: np, nd)
11. Ibid
12. *Panorama*, XIII, 14 February 1916
13. J. A. A. H. Beaufort, *Vijftig Jaren uit Onze Geschiedenis, 1868-1918*, Vol I (Amsterdam: P. N. van Kampen en Zoon, 1928) p247
14. J. H. Hoogendijk, *De Nederlandsche Koopvaardij in den Oorlog (1914-1918)* (Amsterdam: Van Holkema & Warendorf, 1930) p486. See also D. J. Gouda, *De Nederlanse Zeevisserij tijdens de Eertse Wereldoorlog 1914-1918* (Haarlem/Antwerp: Schuyt, 1978) p29, and H. W. von der Dunk, 'Nederland ten tijdevan de eerste wereldoorlog', in D. P. Blok et al (eds), *Algemene Geschiedenis der Nederlanden*, XIV (Haarlem: Fibula-Van Dishoeck, 1979) p46
15. C. Smit, *Nederland in de Eerste Wereldoorlog*, Vol II (Groningen: Wolters-Noordhoff, 1972) p103. A. J. Barnouw, *Holland under Queen Wilhelmina* (New York: Charles Scribner's Sons, 1923) p128
16. *Eindhovensch Dagblad*, quoted in P. H. Ritter, op cit, Vol II, p231
17. The British Government ultimately paid £10,000 in compensation for this incident. J. A. A. H. Beaufort, op cit, p244

18 Charlotte A. van Manen, *De Nederlandsche Overzee Trustmaatschappij: Middelpunt van het verkeer van onzijdig Nederland met het buitenland tijdens den wereldoorlog, 1914-19* (The Hague, 1935). M. Frey, 'Trade, Ships and the Neutrality of the Netherlands in the First World War', in *International History Review* XIX (3) (1997), pp541-62

19 L. G. J. Verberne, op cit, p361, estimates the cost at Dfl350 million up to the end of 1917.

20 Ibid, p361

21 P. W. Klein, 'Krasse Tijden: De Economische en Sociale Situatie in Nederland gedurende de Laatste Oorlogsjaren', p1812

22 Fr van de Vrande, op cit

23 *De Telegraaf*, 13 October 1914

24 *Uit Bange Oorlogsdagen: Dagboek van een Roosendaler Aflevering*, Vol II (Roosendaal: Helvert-Weijermans, nd) p63

25 Much of what has been written about the influx of Belgian refugees into the Netherlands is anecdotal. Academic studies include J. H. van Zanten, 'De zorg voor vluchtelingen uit het buitenland tijdens den oorlog', in H. Brugmans (ed), op cit, pp317-52; H. W. von der Dunk (ed), *Vluchten voor de Groote Oorlog, Belgen in Nederland, 1914-1918* (Amsterdam: De Bataafsche Leeuw, 1988)

26 Figures taken from Algemene Rijksarchief, Record Groups 2.05.04

27 E. H. Kossmann, op cit, p552

28 Henriette Roland Holst-Van der Schalk, *Kapitaal*, Vol II, p118, cited in E. H. Kossmann, op cit, p553

29 E. H. Kossmann, op cit, p552

30 Gerard J. M. van het Reve, *Mijn Rode Jaren: herinneringen van een ex-bolsjewiek* (Utrecht: Ambo, 1967)

31 H. J. Scheffer, *November 1918: Journaal van een revolutie die niet doorging* (Amsterdam: De Arbeiderspers, 1968)

32 Princess Wilhemina, op cit, p108. See also H. J. Scheffer, op cit, pp192-3

33 Laurie Thompson, *Stig Dagerman* (Boston: Twayne, 1983)

34 Stig Dagerman, *The Snake*, translated and introduced by Laurie Thompson (Quartet, 1995)

35 Ibid

36 Alan Cowell, 'Europe Revises Its War Stories', in *The New York Times*, 6 July 1997

37 Bo Widerberg, *Ådalen 31* (Svensk Filmindustri, 1969)

38 Quoted from a 1928 speech in Irene Scobbie, *Historical Dictionary of Sweden* (London: Scarecrow Press, 1995)

39 Gustav Lindström, *Sweden's Security Policy: Engagement – the Middle Way* (Institute for Security Studies Western European Union, October 1997)

40 Ibid

41 Ingmar Bergman, trans Joan Tate, *The Magic Lantern* (London: Hamish Hamilton, 1988)

42 Göran Blomberg, article in *Dagens Nyheter*, 20 May 1997

43 Arne Ruth, 'Post-war Europe: The Capriciousness of Universal Values', in *Daedalus, A New Europe for the Old* 126 (3) (Summer 1997)

44 Ibid

45 Maria-Pia Boëthius, *Heder och Samvete* (Norstedts: Ordfront, 1991, rev ed 1999)

46 Alf Löwenborg, in *Flammen*, 7 October 1999

47 Commission on Jewish Assets in Sweden at the Time of the Second World War, Swedish Ministry for Foreign Affairs, 1997

48 Ibid

49 Stig Dagerman, trans Naomi Watford, *The Games of Night* (Quartet, 1986)

50 Stig Dagerman, trans Robin Fulton, *German Autumn* (Quartet, 1988)

PART II
THE CULTURAL
EXPERIENCE

Chapter 21

'A war of the imagination': the experience of the British artist

Paul Gough

'What did it look like? they will ask in 1981, and no amount of description or documentation will answer them. Nor will big, formal compositions like the battle pictures which hang in palaces; and even photographs, which tell us so much, will leave out the colour and the peculiar feeling of events in these extraordinary years. Only the artist with his heightened powers of perception can recognise which elements in a scene can be pickled for posterity in the magical essence of style. And as new subjects began to saturate his imagination, they create a new style, so that from the destruction of war something of lasting value emerges.[1]

Fundamentally, little changed in the circumstances of British artists during the First and Second World Wars. In both wars the art market shrivelled, prices tumbled, artists' materials – such as fine papers, canvas and pigments – became scarce and expensive. Adventurous and exploratory art forms gave way to rather chastened, reflective work that espoused home virtues and patriotic loyalties. The Government-funded schemes for commissioning official images of wartime were, as we shall see, remarkably similar during both wars; many good artists were commissioned, many others who thought themselves eminently employable were to be disappointed, while others had their skills redeployed into field camouflage, survey and cartography.

Both wars were preceded by frenetic intellectual and artistic activity generated by the modern movement. In the years before the Great War many young British artists were trying to assimilate the new ideas of Cubism and Futurism emanating from Paris and Italy. The period before the Second World War was comparatively calmer, but British art was enjoying a neo-Romantic revival and slowly coming to terms with the challenge of continental surrealism and pure abstraction. Of course, during both periods of war, only a small core of artists was involved in the debates generated by the avant-garde. For many others, their interests were best represented by one of the long-established academies of art that existed in London and in the regions, and during both World Wars the students, graduates and staff of these academies would become the artists, advisors and advocates of the official war art schemes.

Before we examine the key themes that lie behind this century's war art, let us look briefly at two very different artists – Muirhead Bone and C. R. W. Nevinson – who experienced both World Wars and left very different records of their involvement. The Scottish etcher Muirhead Bone was 40 years old when he became the first ever official British war artist in 1916. One year later Christopher Richard Wynne Nevinson, a 27-year-old Modernist painter prone to staging noisy and well-publicised Futurist events, was also appointed. Despite the assertion in his autobiography that his appointment was initiated by a string of generals, Nevinson's chief admirer was in fact Muirhead Bone.[2] Nevinson did, though, have formidable front-line credentials, having already served in France as an ambulance driver with the Belgian Red Cross.

To many observers, Muirhead Bone was a sound, if somewhat predictable, choice as an official war artist. Revered as the 'London Piranesi', he had a reputation for highly detailed and accurate renditions of complex subjects. These ranged from the architectural minutiae of a shipyard or munitions hall, to the uniforms and insignia of groups of soldiers. Although dismissed infamously by one critic as 'too true to be good'[3], Bone was a proficient and prolific worker; during one seven-week visit to the Somme battlefield in late summer 1916 he made 150 finished drawings. By 1917 he had produced 500 highly detailed images for the Government – an effort that drove him to near-collapse. There was, though, an insatiable demand for his work. It reproduced well in black and white, and was widely distributed in print portfolios, booklets and pamphlets aimed at neutral countries such as the United States. Bone travelled behind the front lines in a chauffeur-driven car, stopping occasionally to render the scenery of war. By his own admission he recognised that modern war was an elusive and remote activity:

'I'm afraid that I have not done many ruins… But you must remember that on the Somme nothing is left after such fighting as we have had here – in many cases not a vestige of the village remains, let alone impressive ruins!'[4]

Bone drew the aftermath of the fighting – he was rarely allowed near the front line. As a result his panoramic sketches of the battles of Mametz Wood or the bombardment of Longueval show little more than hazy smoke on a distant horizon. As one critic noted, it was 'like a peep at the war through the wrong end of the telescope'.[5] This was not a criticism that could be levelled at C. R. W. Nevinson.

Nevinson revelled in the role of the front-line war artist. He was described as a 'desperate fellow and without fear [who was] only anxious to crawl into the front line and draw things full of violence and terror'.[6] His war memoir (aptly entitled *Paint and Prejudice*) bristles with exciting incidents such as the time he made an unauthorised visit to Ypres on the eve of the Passchendaele offensive, or another occasion when drawing near the British front line:

'[I] got shelled, had to stick glued against a bank for an hour wondering when Fritz would leave off. I wondered why on earth I had not devoted myself to painting "nice nudes" in a warm studio, instead of risking so much for a picture which will probably not sell, be accused of being faked and certainly be abused by the inevitable arm-chair journalist.'[7]

In fact, the opposite was true. Once exhibited, Nevinson's war paintings and prints attracted huge crowds and, initially, critical acclaim. In part this was due to the artist's energetic publicity campaign, but it was also because his paintings of troops marching, bombs exploding and machine-gunners in action combined figurative realism with simple geometric abstraction. Outwardly his work could not have seemed more different from Bone's; but for all its radical modernism the work remained 'intelligible and unintimidating'[8] especially to soldiers home on leave. A year later, however, just as the *Observer* correspondent asserted that 'he stands alone, in England, as the painter of modern war'[9], Nevinson shed his modernist veneer and turned to a more realistic pictorial style, one intended to evoke suffering, endurance and the stark realities of static warfare.

Working now under the auspices of the Government's Ministry of Information (MoI), Nevinson's brutal realism – no less detailed than Bone's exacting style, but wilfully graphic in its portrayal of pain – fell foul of officialdom. Much of the rest of his involvement in the war is a colourful, but rather tedious, tale of suppressed paintings, censored images and the spiteful correspondence of an aggrieved artist.

Twenty years later, as another World War threatened, both artists again offered their services. Bone, with an embellished reputation as the artist of the industrial sublime, and knighted for his services to the art world, again became the first official British artist to see action in the Second World War. Appointed to the Admiralty with the rank of Honorary Major, Royal Marines, he drew diligently in the shipyards at Portsmouth producing compelling and stirring images of the British fleet. In 1940 he recorded the return of the remnants of the British Expeditionary Force from Dunkirk. Bone had lost none of his eye for telling detail that had made him so useful for propaganda purposes during the Great War. Furthermore, he was extraordinarily versatile and quick to adapt to Government needs. In December 1940, for example, he was summoned from a sketching mission in west Scotland to depict the ruins in London after the devastating raid of 29 December. His drawing 'St Brides and the City after the Fire' is an extraordinary image – quite enormous at 77 inches by 44 inches in dimension – which depicts in microscopic detail the smouldering remains of the City. It was later described as 'the kind of document one would produce as evidence before a commission on bomb damage'.[10]

While Bone flourished, Nevinson floundered. After the Great War his work lost its dynamic energy and polemic intensity; like so much English painting in the 1920s it lacked a distinctive flavour and a guiding principle. In 1940 his application to become an official war artist was turned down and the pictures he submitted were rejected. Although he gained an independent commission from the Royal Air Force, he was deeply upset by official rejection and later suffered a severe stroke. Typically, he continued to argue his case, even applying for a menial clerical post as assistant to the war artist's advisory committee. 'Though an eye is lost,' he wrote in late 1942, 'my hand is not and there is every hope of getting it right back.'[11] Four years later Nevinson died, aged 57, having learned to paint with his left hand.

I have dwelt at length on these two very different British artists because they tell us something of the differences and common themes in the art of the two wars. It has been said of the Second World War[12] that very little art could have been produced unless it was done within the auspices of the Government-funded art scheme. To a lesser extent this was also the case during the First World War. Indeed, one art critic goes so far as to argue that the official war art scheme was one of the British Government's 'few inspired moments' because it recognised the cultural value of artistic records in addition to their propaganda function.[13] Let us look in more detail at these schemes.

The origins of an official war art scheme during the First World War can be traced to a decision made by the Foreign Office, in late August 1914, to establish a secret department to manage and disseminate British propaganda. The department, headed by Liberal politician Charles F. G. Masterman, was known simply as Wellington House, after its office address in Buckingham Gate, London. Working in secret, the department published and distributed clandestine literature aimed at neutral countries across the globe. In April 1916 a pictorial section was established and an extraordinary variety of visual propaganda was commissioned; this included war films, picture cards, calendars, bookmarks, lantern slides as well as photographs and line drawings. An all-picture publication, *War Pictorial*, was produced in five language editions and achieved a worldwide circulation of 300,000.

It soon became apparent, however, that the flow of photographs from the battlefronts could not meet the voracious demands of the department. By late 1915 the illustrated newspapers were also desperate for authentic front-line images and were offering cash incentives to soldiers with suitable sketchbook material.[14] The decision to employ artists, rather than studio illustrators, was partly due to the fact that many of the key staff at Wellington House were established figures in the London art world[15], but also because the new photogravure process of volume printing allowed images of subtle tonal complexity to be well reproduced. By sponsoring war art a government could also appear to be nurturing cultural freedom, as opposed to the vulgar propaganda of German Kultur. Only in the latter stages of the war did the idea of creating an art collection as a permanent memorial emerge as a coherent aim. Credit for this must go to Max Aitken (later Lord Beaverbrook) who brought an organisational flair and entrepreneurial zeal (first honed on the Canadian War Memorials Scheme) to the newly formed Ministry of Information in March 1918.

What was the impact of this complex organisational structure on British artists? In the first instance, it provided a small number of painters and printmakers with regular work. Artists such as William Orpen were in demand:

'About ten minutes past four up breezed a car, and in it was a slim little man with an enormous head and two remarkable eyes. I saluted and tried to make military noises with my boots. Said he: "Are you Orpen?" "Yes, sir," said I. "Are you willing to work for the Canadians?" said he. "Certainly, sir," said I. "Well,' said he, "that's all right. Jump in, and we'll go and have a drink."'[16]

Under Aitken's stewardship the British War Memorials Scheme became systematic and prescriptive: wartime activity was divided into eight subject groupings (Army, Navy, Air Force, Merchant Marine, Land, Munitions, Clerical and other work by Women, and Public Manifestations), and artists were then selected to fit these subjects. By the end of the war more than 130 artists had been conscripted to this purpose, including 16 'soldier-artists' who had been released from active service to paint on the front line.

Commissioning could be quite draconian. The artist Adrian Hill, who had served at the front as a signaller and scout in the 1st Honourable Artillery Company, was told precisely what to draw:

'Towns and localities behind the lines which are specially identified with the British Army ... points of juncture between our line and the line occupied by the French, American, Belgian and Portuguese, so as to show the different nationalities side by side ... labour and engineering work by Coloured Battalions which show the distinct dress of the Chinese etc, and especially some sketches of Tanks HQ showing repairing and the like.'[17]

In time Hill produced an extensive portfolio of 187 pen-and-ink drawings documenting rather mundane and unremarkable activities of the war zone. An active commissioning policy, however, had its drawbacks. Whereas Hill's drawings were encouraged (and, it is said, were highly regarded by General Haig) his oil paintings were flatly rejected: 'The committee was not favourably impressed by your oil paintings and it was thought desirable that you should keep to drawings in future.'[18]

The main thrust of the Ministry (and in turn the newly formed National War Museum) was to create both a record and a memorial through its art collection. Some artists were paid to produce a single picture for an intended Hall of Remembrance (£300 plus materials and studio expenses for one of the larger pictures). Younger, less established artists were offered a rather more modest deal – a salary of £300 per annum in return for their total artistic output during that period. This proposal was accepted by now familiar figures such as Paul Nash, Colin Gill, Bernard Meninsky and John Nash (all aged under 30) but, interestingly, rejected by Nevinson who surmised that it would 'prove a bad business proposition'.[19]

Inevitably, the Hall of Remembrance was not built, nor was the great Canadian Memorial Scheme, which was intended to house Aitken's other collection of war art. Arguably the greatest legacy of the war's art was the scheme itself. Twenty years later it provided the template for the War Artists' Advisory Committee (WAAC) headed by the respected art historian Sir Kenneth Clark, then the Surveyor of the King's Pictures at Windsor and Director of the National Gallery, London. Despite Clark's single-minded ambition to produce an outstanding artistic record of the war by employing many of Britain's finest painters, printmakers and sculptors, he soon became entangled in the political rivalries of Whitehall and the Armed Services. 'Painting of war scenes is publicity and not news,' opined one memorandum from the Ministry, 'and it ought therefore to be our responsibility and not that of the service departments.'[20]

Clark was also restricted by the need to employ artists capable of making representational or illustrative work. In 1942 he looked back on the parameters set by the committee's terms of reference:

'The War Artists collection cannot be completely representative of modern English art, because it cannot include those pure painters who are interested solely in putting down their feelings about shapes and colours, and not in facts, drama and human emotions.'[21]

While not fully representative, Clark trawled far and wide for the best artists. In its first 16 weeks the committee considered some 800 names, including all those employed during the Great War. Few made the grade. Nevinson, as we have seen, was omitted. A few veterans – Paul Nash, Kennington, and Bone – were recruited. The fees offered by the WAAC were lower than those offered in the Great War; £150 to £200 was the average price of an oil-painting, while water-colours might be bought for as little as £10.

In the Second War most art was 'made to order', and although some artists were given commissioned rank and loosely attached to a fighting unit, their output was constantly tailored towards producing a particular portfolio of images. In the Great War the first wave of official artists had been given honorary rank, a vague brief and allowed to roam at will. All this changed as the Beaverbrook reforms took hold and artists were required to conform to the grand scheme of the Hall of Remembrance. Although this produced some fine art it also produced an air of conformity; several landscape painters, for example, agreed to work to a common horizon line. The Government's attempts to make a complete record of military activities also bred an atmosphere of casual overproduction.

Managing the schemes of both wars required logistical prowess, administrative dexterity and, perhaps most crucially, patience. Those in the military who had to deal with the artists seemed to have suffered equally during both wars. In 1917 the Department (later Ministry) of Information had asked that a permanent artists' base be set up in France to cater for greater numbers than the one-at-a-time system so far in place. This did not happen. The BEF Intelligence Chief, Brigadier-General John Charteris, argued that two artists at any time was ample and complained of their unfortunate tendency to 'want to sit down and look at a place for a long time'.[22]

Little had changed by the Second War. The minutes of the War Artists' Advisory Committee (which met weekly between 23 November 1939 and 28 December 1945) relate numerous tales of petty frustrations and restrictions, tinged with some modest successes:

'29.12.1939: Letters to Robert Medley [artist] in ARP offering 50 gns for 8 pictures of scenes at a disembarkation port in France and of "life at the base".

11.1.1940: Medley refused permission to go to France by the War Office and appointed to do Civil Defence.

7.2.1940: John Nash and Eric Ravilious appointed Captain, Royal Marines. Medley authorised to travel third class.

13.9.1943: Home Security: Mr Kenneth Rowntree. This artist has accepted the commission to paint jam-making, which is being done by the Women's Institute.'23

However humble his calling, Mr Rowntree's achievement in gaining the status of an officially appointed artist was considerable. There were a great many others in both wars who yearned for such a position. Those who administered the war artists schemes were inundated with requests from artists who wished to sell war-related work, or who craved official accreditation. Algernon Mayow Talmage, Royal Academician, silver medallist at the Paris Salon, bronze medallist at the Pittsburgh International exhibition, was one such artist. In May 1917 he presented his credentials to the war museum:

> 'No picture that I am aware of, has been really studied on the spot so as to get the real environment and atmospheric conditions and phenomenon. I have been painting in the open all my life and I feel that were it possible to give me opportunities to study this subject I could paint a picture which would be a value as a record and venture to hope as a work of art which would be something entirely different to the usual hackneyed and unconvincing picture.'24

Like so many others he was turned down.

Rowland Hill, by comparison, was an unknown painter who had served out the war as a lance-corporal ('a very unimportant item' as he described it) in the Royal Defence Corps on Home Service. Two months after the Armistice he wrote the first of many letters to the War Museum pleading for 'official leave' to 'make some record of our true battlegrounds, and of the immensely picturesque material before it is all "mended" and tidied up'.25 Despite several rejections Hill eventually gained a passport to travel to France, but failed to gain clearance to sketch in the old war zones. Undeterred he again approached the war museum, only to be rebuffed. Eventually, as restrictions were eased, he gained access and seems to have visited the 'sacred sites' on the old front line – destroyed tanks on the Freyzenburg Ridge, the Cloth Hall at 'Wipers', the Ramparts, etc. We know this because for the following 12 years he wrote regularly to the museum begging them to buy his work: 'Will your people give me two guineas for this drawing of the Ramparts of Ypres?' he wrote in January 1930. 'It is unique in its way. I am pitifully hard up and the money would help me considerably.'26 Deluged with similar requests the museum pleaded lack of funds and a glut of images of ruination. There is, however, a pleasing coda to this tale. Hill's obituary of 1952 relates:

> 'It is difficult to assess the influence of events on the work of a man, but one definite step was achieved in his career. After the war he received a permit to visit the battlefields and one of his works created out of that venture hangs in the Imperial War Museum.'

And this oil-painting, *Ypres*, donated by the painter to the war museum in December 1919, is listed in a dictionary of painters as one of Hill's principal works.27

Similarly, throughout the Second World War the authorities were besieged by earnest but frustrated 'war artists'. In March 1940 the secretary of the WAAC, E. M. O. Dickey, wrote despondently to a fellow committee member:

'There is a man called Richard Ellis who has been plaguing the life out of us here. His trouble is that he wants to be both an official artist and a spy at the same time... I seem to be fated to refer to you people whose handwriting nobody can read.'[28]

What was at the root of this fascination with depicting warfare? Few of those who aspired to become war artists did so to avoid danger; in both wars artists were exposed to discomfort and death. Financial security may have held some attraction, though as we have seen the remuneration was rarely generous. Perhaps we must recognise that many artists wished to be exposed to the privations of war so as to test out and hone their skills in unique and demanding circumstances. To witness, interpret and leave some form of personal testimony was an ambition more pervasive than is commonly thought. In both wars, it appears, artists needed to come to terms with their violent muse.[29] 'I tell you,' wrote the soldier-artist Keith Henderson in October 1916, 'the "subjects" are endless, and in particular I long to do great big stretches of this bleak brown land.'[30] Twenty-five years later, official artist Edward Bawden wrote in a similar vein:

'It often seemed to me unfair that I should enjoy the privilege of remaining an Official War Artist in the Middle East when there are so many competent painters at home ... so many others have not had the privilege of being able to pursue their civilian occupations. I must admit that I thoroughly enjoy the life, that trekking and camping or a long march gives me immense pleasure.'[31]

In 1943 the poet Stephen Spender wrote that 'War Pictures' could mean only one thing: 'Famous ruins ... our historic monuments in their sudden decay ... the bombed city'. The artist of this war, he declared, is 'the Civilian Defence Artist'.

'In the last war we would have meant pictures of the Western Front ... a picture of blasted trees, trenches, mud, shell-holes, shattered Ypres, the straight roads of France with army lorries moving through a landscape of bursting shells, a landscape where no bird sang.'[32]

Despite the many other theatres of war – East Africa, Gallipoli, Salonika and Jerusalem – the trench world of Flanders was, and still is, the leitmotif of that conflict. 'There is a kind of insistence,' concludes Spender, 'a continuity, about the idea of the Western Front, which immediately conjures up the whole of the Great War.'[33]

Artists played their part in reinforcing this condition, though not all of them found it abhorrent. Painters and poets developed a morbid obsession with the phantasmagoric terrain of no-man's-land. David Jones described its strange topography as a place of:

'…sudden violences [sic] and long stillnesses, the sharp contours and unformed voids of that mysterious existence profoundly affected the imaginations of those who suffered it. It was a place of enchantment.'[34]

It is ironic that such a quantity of paintings, prints and drawings (and the occasional relief sculpture) should have resulted from a land that had been so systematically destroyed. Not all artists could translate the desolation into visual terms. John Singer Sargent was dumbfounded:

'The further forward one goes the more scattered and meagre everything is. The nearer to danger, the fewer and more hidden the men – the more dramatic the situation the more it becomes an empty landscape.'[35]

Faced with emptiness artists learned to describe the void. Although Muirhead Bone's drawings of piles of rubble in the midst of a few burnt tree stumps are entitled 'Deniecourt Chateau' or 'Thiepval Village', there is little to prove that he was in the correct location. Instead, many artists fixed on the few remaining architectural icons of the Western Front. The Cloth Hall of Ypres and the ruined Basilica and Leaning Madonna at Albert were favourite motifs; indeed, it would be possible to compile a pictorial record of the tortuous destruction of the Cloth Hall from the hundreds of drawings and paintings made by British artists alone. One painter, David Baxter (serving as an official artist with the Red Cross and St John Ambulance) painted the ragged remains of the Flemish Hall no fewer than 24 times.[36]

Images of the soldier, though numerically fewer, could have a memorable impact. The first painting of the Great War to capture the public imagination was Eric Kennington's reverse painting on glass, 'The Kensingtons at Laventie', which depicted a platoon of dishevelled infantrymen preparing for the trenches. The picture's authority is based in part on its harsh authenticity and extraordinary technical virtuosity, but also on Kennington's experiences as a footsoldier.[37]

Like the soldiers painted by Nevinson, Kennington's weary and dishevelled platoon is a far cry from the heroic youth daily depicted in the illustrated press or hanging from the walls of the Royal Academy every summer – 'castrated Lancelots' as Nevinson lampooned them.[38] Painting a uniformed figure, however, required a level of draughtsmanship that was often beyond the talents of the amateur, and this may in part explain the prevalence of battlescapes in the Great War oeuvre.

Images of ruined towns and buildings were common to both wars. They were especially prevalent during the first years of the Second World War. The reason is obvious: left without a toehold on the Continent, Britain had to endure months of aerial bombardment. Compared to the deserted warscapes of Nash and Nevinson the bombed cities of London, Coventry and Bristol are populated with wardens, construction and demolition teams, firemen and stretcher parties. Here the accent is on dogged resistance, rather than benighted desperation. In the Second War, paintings of the ruined city served as the narrative background to 'the new type of warrior' – the ordinary man, long suffering, but ever determined. 'The hero,' argued J. B. Morton, 'even when he is not in the picture, is Tom, Dick or Harry, and the heroine his wife.'[39] This resulted in a form of popular, democratised portraiture in which the dispatch rider, the auxiliary fire messenger and the air raid warden became the focus of the artists' attention. In the previous war such sittings would have been strictly reserved for high-ranking generals and air 'aces'.

The benighted and blitzed Britain of the 1940s presented a very different challenge to artists normally accustomed to working *en plein air*. Nightshift production, sunken control rooms and dimly lit headquarters offices became legitimate subject matter for artists, giving rise to a sub-genre of claustrophobic, busy interiors. The Blitz also produced a new motif of the administrator as war hero. Meredith Frampton's triple portrait of the Senior Regional Commissioner for Civil Defence in the London Region and his deputies is, as Angela Weight observes, a formidable image of 'administrative sang-froid'[40] providing evidence that 'order, stability and control' are being maintained despite the chaos and darkness above ground.

The Blitz provided artists with an extraordinary narrative of movement, colour and action. The crowded dormitories of London's shelters and underground stations gave draughtsmen such as Felix Topolski and Edward Ardizzone unique opportunities to draw complex forms in subdued lighting. Henry Moore's shelter sketches proved to be a turning point in his artistic development. British painting, though, lacked the painterly language that might match the apocalyptic vision of the Blitz. Composed primarily of illustrators and draughtsmen, many of the WAAC artists were short of the expressive power needed to describe the catastrophic grandeur of the bombing.

For four years the Home Front was the cultural lodestone of the Second World War, just as the Western Front had been during the Great War. This is immediately obvious in the titles of the two series of illustrated booklets *War Pictures by British Artists* funded by the Ministry of Information and published by Oxford University Press in 1942 and 1943. The four booklets in the First Series were entitled 'War at Sea', 'Blitz', 'RAF', 'Army'; the Second Series 'Women', 'Production', 'Soldiers', 'Air-Raids'. Among the 50 pictures reproduced in 'Production', for example, are depictions of tank manufacture, miners at work, barrel testing, and snack-time in a factory.

Such limited subject matter might have dispirited the most innovative artist. But this appears not to have been the case. R. V. Pitchforth's painting 'Snack-time' is, in fact, a typically bold design of three workmen hastily consuming their food. His painting 'Welding Bofors Guns' describes the same men immersed in their work. Pitchforth accentuates the harsh light, the simple repetition of cube and cylindrical forms amidst the theatrical setting of the darkened factory. During the First World War many of the younger war artists had adopted the geometric dynamic offered by Cubist and Vorticist art to shape the industrial scale of the war machine. Painters such as Edward Wadsworth and Nevinson learned to simplify their pictorial language, opting for the diagonal line over the perpendicular, extreme tonal differences over subtle gradations, simplification instead of detail. Wadsworth's images of dazzle ships epitomise this bold and uncompromising method. Thirty years later British artists renewed their interest in the industrial process by bringing together the abstract formal qualities of the built environment but paying greater attention to the role of the individual worker.

This reached its zenith in Stanley Spencer's extraordinary sequence of paintings depicting the shipyards on the Clyde produced between 1940 and 1946. Employed by the WAAC, Spencer thrived in the close-knit community of Port Glasgow and learned quickly to understand the individual tasks of the different workers. His precise drawing style was ideally suited to the visual confusion of the welding shops, the panel beating and the caulking. Having never been taught to sketch rapidly, however, he was not always able to capture the bustling energy of the yards. In 1942 he wrote somewhat dejectedly:

'I wish I could have made more particular studies of the men… What I seriously need is to make a careful series of drawings … of women and men … in their native clothes… It is that subtle variation in their clothes [which is] expressive of their varied character that is so truly full of charm, beauty, and interest. But whenever I have been up there they have all been too busy.'[41]

In both wars artists rapidly learned to make the most of the physical and visual constraints of the workplace. Nowhere was this more evident than when drawing in the blitzed cities. Graham Sutherland had first realised the 'possibilities of destruction as a subject' when drawing in bombed Swansea in 1940.[42] But it was not until he was required to return to the East End of London that he began to appreciate the gravity of events and his responsibilities as an artist:

'I had been attempting to paraphrase what I saw and to make paintings which were parallel to rather than a copy of nature. But now, suddenly, I was a paid official – a sort of reporter and, naturally, not only did I feel that I had to give value for money, but to contrive somehow to reflect in an immediate way the subjects set me.'[43]

Finding the devastation around the City 'more exciting than anywhere else' he made what he called 'perfunctory drawings' as a way of accustoming himself to the weird sights of flattened office blocks, charred buildings, twisted and collapsed lift-shafts 'like a wounded animal'. But like his predecessors in the Great War, Sutherland took to his tasks in a very business-like way:

'…on a typical day, I would arrive there from Kent where we had resumed living, with very spare paraphernalia – a sketchbook, black ink, two or three coloured chalks, a pencil – and with an apparent watertight pass that would take me anywhere within the forbidden area.'[44]

Working sketchbooks show us how Sutherland developed his initial impressions. One drawing made in Fore Street, City of London, in 1941 has been 'squared-up' so that it can be transferred in the studio to a canvas or larger sheet of paper. There is a palpable tension between the ink and charcoal marks that describe the awful devastation, and the precisely numbered transfer lines coolly drawn over the surface of the tortured city. It is as if the artist was trying to use lineal order and control to neutralise the hurt. Notations in other sketchbooks tell us much about the matter-of-fact way many war artists went about their business; Sutherland's drawings of tin-miners in Cornwall are accompanied by brief phrases that evoke the non-visual phenomena:

> 'Miner approaching turns on hearing voice issues from slope below. Walls dripping with moisture. Do paintings sufficiently large to give an impression of the actual scale of the mine tunnel.'[45]

We can learn a great deal from scrawled marginalia and notes in artists' sketchbooks. In First World War drawings we find similar notations – detailed colour notes, vital information about insignia, occasionally the censor's signature and date stamp. In a reconnaissance sketch drawn from a front-line trench by Paul Maze, the phrase 'could not go on through heavy shelling' is scribbled, with appreciable haste, in the corner of the unfinished image.[46]

In both wars artists often had to cope with poor equipment and sub-standard materials – Maze writes in his war memoir of a time when the watercolour brush actually froze on the paper. During both periods there are many stories of artists overcoming difficult, sometimes appalling circumstances. This was especially true of those artists who were captured and confined to prison of war camps. Jack Chalker kept an illicit sketchbook while building the Burma Railway as a prisoner of the Japanese.[47] Official war artist John Worsley was captured in 1943 while taking part in daring raids in the Adriatic. During his imprisonment in Marlag Camp, Bremen, he made water-colours of the camp and an oil-painting of the contents of a Red Cross parcel. Soon after his release, Worsley successfully appealed to the organisers of an exhibition of war art at the National Gallery to exhibit this work:

> 'I took so much trouble, and underwent such considerable hazard (including hiding much from the Germans) to get them out of Germany and in a small way justify my capture, that the disappointment was extreme. I even constructed a container from Red Cross milk tins, which I carried for an eighty-mile march, under strafing from fighter planes, to get them here.'[48]

As we have seen, the second wave of official war artists commissioned during 1917 and 1918 were largely drawn from officers and soldiers with recent front-line experience: Wyndham Lewis had been a subaltern with the 6th Howitzer Battery; Paul Nash and John Nash had served respectively with the Hampshires and the Artists Rifles; William Roberts had been in France with the Royal Field Artillery, and Stanley Spencer was barely surviving as a footsoldier with the Berkshire Regiment in Macedonia. *The Studio* arts magazine regularly published lists of artists, illustrators, poets and draughtsmen serving with the forces.

Front-line experience brought a vigour and edge that had largely been missing from the work of establishment figures such as William Orpen and Muirhead Bone. Once experienced, however, few of these soldier-artists expressed a wish to return to the theatre of war. Lewis might have described modern war as 'the greatest romance', but he also wrote of life in the salient as an unpalatable 'mixture of tedium and acute danger'[49] and most of the young artists painted their memorable pictures while safely ensconced in studios in rural England.

Drawing on the front line was often a hazardous but illuminating experience. In the months before his appointment as an artist, Adrian Hill had served as a scout and sniper. He recalled a typical drawing patrol in no-man's-land:

> 'I advanced in short rushes, mostly on my hands and knees with my sketching kit dangling around my neck. As I slowly approached, the wood gradually took a more definite shape, and as I crept nearer I saw that what was hidden from our own line, now revealed itself as a cunningly contrived observation post in one of the battered trees.'[50]

Many of Hill's later front-line drawings share this same quality – hurriedly drawn eye-witness accounts of lone figures scurrying across the flattened ground, tanks marooned on the battlefield, signallers feeding out wire in a dissipated space.

Hill's fluid and active drawings predict many of the front-line images of the Second War. Artist's output in that war had fallen into several distinct phases: images of waiting and watching during the 'Phoney War' of 1939, paintings of industrial production during the early 1940s, partnered by the powerful drawings of the Blitz by Sutherland, Piper and Moore. Between 1942 and 1943 home-based artists – such as Pitchforth and Vaughan – described periods of intense training and preparation. During 1944, just as the war in Europe exploded into action, artists had to rise (as Hill had done) to the challenge of a fluid, physically demanding and dangerous artistic environment.

Possibly the finest example of the artist-soldier in the Second World War is the young painter Albert Richards. Born in 1919, Richards had already served three years as a sapper, followed by a year as an engineer parachutist before being transferred for official duties as a war artist – the committee having been impressed by batches of drawings and water-colours he had submitted. Unlike many artists faced with the repetitive sights of ruin and blitz, Richards found subjects everywhere: anti-tank ditches, searchlight batteries, camouflaged huts, Bailey bridges and the myriad of physical tasks of the sapper were all recorded. Perhaps Richards's most impressive work of early 1944 was his renditions of parachute training in southern England. Parachuting could not have been more different from the earth-bound duties of a sapper. The experience was exhilarating, bringing weightlessness and release from the tedium of ordinary life. To the artist it introduced a unique new vista:

> 'The ground, once seen with all its ugliness and imperfections, was now a remote drifting region of spilled yellows, greens and brown, the sky tilted and the body freed.'[51]

On midnight before D-Day, 6 June 1944, Richards parachuted into Normandy with 9th Battalion 6th Airborne Division to produce 'paintings of the war and not preparations for it'[52]. This he certainly did. But upon landing it was found that all the officers were injured and Richards, still only an Honorary Captain, had to take command of the platoon and advance on their objective, an enemy battery near Merville, east of Sword Beach. The battery was taken just 2 hours before the beach landings began. Soon after, Richards made four water-colour sketches of 'the landing at H hour minus six', the aftermath of the attack on the battery, 'the constant watch for snipers' at Le Plein, and gliders crash-landed against a bridge. Later in England he was able to develop and refine these hastily drawn images. On 19 July he described the circumstances in which they had been made:

> 'I know the four water-colours I sent in to you were much below what I expected of them. I was in a rather dazed condition when I painted them… The method which the committee suggests I work is the method which I have been brought up to. The Design School at the RCA was a great believer in giving the subject time to develop before putting any statement on paper. I have always felt that if the subject was good enough, it would still be fresh months after seeing it, and probably would have developed in one's mind during that time.'[53]

Richards was an adventurous water-colourist. Often he ignored the customary rules; a favourite technique was to rub a wax candle into parts of the paper so as to animate the picture surface and create a texture that might evoke the surface of a glider canopy or an abandoned vehicle. As well as being an intuitive colourist, Richards had no fear of the colour black: he used it frequently to unify a picture's design or to control the swathes of orange and red that appear so often in his work. Richards' best work bears comparison with the Great War work of Paul Nash; there is a similar ability to animate a picture through surface design, and a keen understanding of the role of outline in the internal scaffolding of the paintings.

Characteristically, Richards had a low opinion of his front-line work. Like many war artists he was torn between his function as an impartial observer and his responses as a friend and colleague. He wrote in 1944:

> 'I am not sure of their value. In painting them my mind was always full of my gallant Airborne friends who gave their lives so readily. It's the first time I have ever witnessed death in this crude from. Somehow I am hoping that it will all help me to paint the pictures that I want to paint yet feel unable to do so. I feel that water-colour transparent and opaque will be the best medium for me to use at this stage of the battle.'[54]

Other artists had landed on the beaches of Normandy. Anthony Gross waded ashore holding his drawing-board high over his head. Barnett Freedman, Stephen Bone and Richard Eurich drew on the beaches during June and July. Hard lessons were learned. Edward Ardizzone, for example, had remembered to protect his precious artist's materials. One year earlier during an amphibious landing in Italy he had lost his balance and fallen into the water. His sketchbook, though, was safe – 'I'd wrapped that up in a F. L. ['French letter'] for protection against the water'.[55]

Stephen Bone arrived in mid-July and spent many weeks recording scenes on sea and shore. Like many oil-painters the dust and sand irritated him. Muirhead Bone, drawing on his experiences of an earlier war, advised the WAAC that artists should use a special box for wet oils: 'I remember Orpen travelled with several of these – he needed them on the Somme – I remember that!'[56]

After the breakout from the beachheads, artists followed close behind the advancing Allied armies – a mobility that was never enjoyed by Adrian Hill or Paul Nash. The rapid advance bought its own problems. Albert Richards found that there was no time to develop his front-line sketches. In February 1945 he wrote to Gregory at the WAAC:

'Advances are happening at different points in the line. So much so, that one is inclined to hop from one sector to another. The landscape is becoming more interesting as we climb out of Holland into Germany. The flooded landscape has brought fresh interest to the warfare... Slowly but surely we are creeping into Germany, one might say into Germany in bottom gear which surely applies to driving in a jeep, for it's not traffic that holds one up, it's the muddy roads. I'm not very good at traffic hold-ups which I suppose are inevitable, and I've developed the bad habit of trying to find a new road.'[57]

His habit had fatal consequences. A few days after writing, Richards turned off the road near the Maas River and drove straight into a minefield. He died later that night, aged just 26.

This terrible loss points us to the single most surprising difference between the artists of the two World Wars. Only one official artist died in the Great War (a minor Naval painter, Geoffrey Allfree) whereas three died in the Second War – Richards on the Maas, Eric Ravilious off Iceland, and Thomas Hennell in Indonesia. These three were artists of quality, still young and with their very best work ahead of them. In an unpublished article, 'The Work of a War Artist', Hennell summarised the dilemma facing his colleagues; he leaves us with a fitting epitaph to this analysis of their experience in the two World Wars:

'The artist has but one duty, to observe and record – the moment he is tempted to interfere or play an active part himself he ceases to perform his duty as an artist.'[58]

Recommended reading

Cork, Richard, *A Bitter Truth: Avant-Garde art and the Great War* (New Haven, CT: Yale University Press, 1994)

Darracott, Joseph and Keegan, John, *The Nature of War* (New York: Holt, Rinehart, Winston, 1981)

Foot, M. R. D., *Art and War: Twentieth Century Warfare as Depicted by War Artists* (London: Headline, 1990)

Fosse, Brian, *Medium and Message: British Identity, National Culture and War Art, 1939-45* (New Haven, CT: Yale University Press, in preparation for 2000)

Harries, Meirion and Susie, *The War Artists* (London: Michael Joseph and Tate Gallery, 1983)

Harrington, Peter, *British Artists and War: The Face of Battle in Paintings and Prints, 1700-1914* (London, 1993)

Ross, Alan, *Colours of War: War Art 1939-45* (London: Jonathan Cape, 1983)

Shone, Richard, *A Century of Change: British Painting since 1900* (Oxford: Oxford University Press, 1977)

Spalding, Frances, *British Art since 1900* (London: Thames & Hudson, 1986)

Notes

1   Flyleaf introduction to *War Pictures by British Artists*, First Series, booklets 1-4 (Oxford University Press, 1942)
2   C. R. W. Nevinson, *Paint and Prejudice* (London: Methuen, 1937) p103
3   George Bernard Shaw quoted in Bone's obituary, *The Times*, 23 October 1953
4   Bone to Ernest Gowers, 30 September 1916, Imperial War Museum Department of Art [hereafter IWM DA], File M999, Part 1
5   *Manchester Guardian*, 30 August 1917
6   C. F. G. Masterman to John Buchan, 18 May 1917, IWM DA, Nevinson file
7   Nevinson to Masterman, 30 July 1917, IWM DA, Nevinson file
8   Meirion and Susie Harries, *The War Artists* (London: Michael Joseph, 1983) p39
9   Paul Konody, *Modern War Paintings by C. R. W. Nevinson* (London: Grant Richards, 1917)
10 Quoted in Harries, op cit, p186
11 Nevinson to Bracken, 31 December 1942, IWM DA, Nevinson file
12 Alan Ross, *Colours of War: War Art 1939-45* (London: Jonathan Cape, 1983) p24
13 Denis Farr, *English Art: 1870-1940* (Oxford: Oxford University Press, 1978) pp226-7
14 See, eg, *Illustrated London News*, 24 April 1915 and 4 September 1915, and *The Graphic*, 8 January 1916
15 Among the staff at Wellington House were Eric Maclagan, later Director of the Victoria and Albert Museum, Campbell Dodgson, Keeper of Prints and Drawings at the British Museum, and Alfred Yockney, one-time editor of *Art Journal*
16 William Orpen, *An Onlooker in France* (London: Williams & Norgate/Ernest Benn, 1923) p42
17 Ffoulkes to Hill, 14 June 1918, IWM DA, File 74/3, Part ii
18 Director-General of National War Museum to General Haig, 1 October 1917; Yockney to Hill, 27 February 1919, IWM DA, File 74/3, Part ii. See also Hill's letters of 4 October 1917 and 12 November 1917 held in the Brotherton Library, Liddle Collection, Leeds University
19 Nevinson to Masterman, 10 March 1918, IWM DA, Nevinson file
20 Deputy Director General to Director General, 6 November 1939, IWM DA, File GP/46/A
21 'War Artists at the National Gallery', *The Studio* CXXIII (January 1942) p586
22 Charteris to Masterman, 12 March 1917, IWM DA, File G4010/17
23 IWM, WAAC Minutes file
24 IWM DA, File 303/7
25 IWM DA, File 156/5, Part ii
26 Hill to E. Blaikley, 28 January 1930, IWM DA, File 156/5, Part ii
27 Grant M. Waters, *Dictionary of British Artists working 1900-1950* (Eastbourne Fine Art, 1975)
28 E. M. O. Dickey to Coote, WAAC Minutes, 6 March 1940
29 For a fuller debate on this topic see Howlett, Jane and Mengham, Rod (eds), *The Violent Muse* (Manchester University Press, 1994)
30 Keith Henderson, *Letters to Helen* (privately published, 1917) p66
31 Bawden to Dickey, 16 October 1941, IWM DA
32 Stephen Spender, *War Pictures by British Artists*, Second Series, No 4 'Air Raids' (Oxford University Press, 1943)
33 Ibid

34 David Jones, *In Parenthesis* (London: Faber, 193) px
35 Charles Serrill Mount, *John Singer Sargent: An Autobiography* (London: Crescent Press, 1957) p297
36 See Paul Gough, 'The Empty Battlefield', *Imperial War Museum Review* No 8 (1993) pp38-48
37 'The Kensingtons at Laventie', IWM DA 15661. See also the essay on the painting by Angela Weight, *Imperial War Museum Review* No 1 (1986)
38 Nevinson to Masterman, 25 November 1917, IWM DA, Nevinson file
39 J. B. Morton, *War Pictures by British Artists*, First Series, No 2 'Blitz' (Oxford University Press, 1942)
40 Angela Weight, 'Night for Day: the symbolic value of light in the painting of the Second World War', *Imperial War Museum Review* (1988) p50
41 Stanley Spencer to Dickey, 4 March 1942, IWM, Spencer correspondence; see also *Stanley Spencer RA* (Royal Academy of Arts, 1980) p193
42 Sutherland quoted in *The Daily Telegraph*, 10 September 1971
43 Ibid
44 Ibid
45 Notes on the artists' drawings held by IWM DA
46 Cited in Paul Gough, 'The Experiences of British Artists in the Great War', in H. Cecil and P. H. Liddle (eds), *Facing Armageddon* (London: Leo Cooper, 1996) p847
47 Jack Chalke, *Burma Railway Artist: War Drawings of Jack Chalker* (London: Leo Cooper, 1994)
48 Worsley, 8 October 1945, quoted in Alan Ross, op cit, p177
49 Wyndham Lewis, *Blasting and Bombardiering* (London: Eyre & Spottiswoode, 1967) p184
50 Adrian Hill, 15 November 1930, in *The Graphic*
51 Richards quoted in Alan Ross, op cit, p104
52 Richards to Gregory, 5 June 1944, IWM DA
53 Richards to IWM, 19 July 1944
54 Richards to Gregory, end of June 1944
55 Edward Ardizzone, unpublished diary entry, 8 July 1943
56 Bone to Gregory, 12 August 1944, IWM, Bone file
57 Richards to Gregory, ? February 1945. This was Richards's last letter to the WAAC.
58 Hennell, unpublished article 'The Work of a War Artist', IWM

Chapter 22

British fiction

Hugh Cecil

It is a common generalisation that nearly all of the worthwhile British literature to come out of the First World War has been poetry. Another generalisation is that this was superior to any British literature inspired by the Second World War, of which there was relatively little. A third generalisation is that other than a few poems early on in the war, by Rupert Brooke and Julian Grenfell, most of the literature of the 1914-18 conflict was thoroughly disillusioned and anti-war. A fourth is that because the struggle against Nazism was manifestly in a good cause, the literature of the Second World War was ipso facto patriotic and triumphalist. One commentator, Michael Paris, has put it thus: 'The elements of protest and revelation, so much a part of the fiction of World War One, are almost entirely missing from the novels of the Second World War.'[1]

To take the first of these popular generalisations, it is undoubtedly true that the Great War was a war of versifiers: there was a vast number of English war poets – in her massive bibliography Catherine Reilly gives a figure of 'no fewer than 2,225'[2]. Most people who wrote fiction after the First World War probably had also written some poetry during it. Poems, like life, came cheap in the trenches. Certainly there were excellent practitioners of the art. It would be a mistake, however, to discount the prose creative writing as unimportant – the fact is that both wars spawned a veritable industry of novel writing by people who had taken part. Hager and Taylor's impressive compilation of titles by novelists in the First World War gives a good idea of the output, as does Michael Paris's more recent volume, which lists around 600 Second World War British novels for the years between 1939 and 1970 alone (Paris's list, which also includes foreign novels in translation, in fact goes up to 1988). The actual number of British Second World War novels published is probably substantially higher even than the figure in Paris's book. Quite a few titles are not on the list – to take a few names at random: Desmond Leslie's *Careless Lives*, Donald Eyre's *Foxes Have Holes*, R. A. Forsyth's *Squadron Will Move*, A. G. Street's *Shameful Harvest* and Barry Sullivan's *Fibre*. Only the latter is outstanding, and this is no reflection on Michael Paris as an editor, simply a demonstration of the enormous task of tracking down all such works.

On the whole, the bulk of war novels by veterans of the First World War came out between 1919 and 1939; the few exceptions – such as Stuart Cloete's crude *How Young They Died* (1969), Carl Fallas's lyrical *St Mary's Village Through the Mind of an Unknown Soldier Who Lived On* (1954), James Lansdale Hodson's *Return to the Wood* (1955), and Henry Williamson's outstanding roman fleuve, *A Chronicle of*

Ancient Sunlight (1954-60) – only prove the rule. War novels by Second World War veterans have continued to be written in considerable numbers beyond the 1970s.

The average Second World War novel is more competent and sophisticated than the average First World War novel. On the other hand, among the better works the Great War line-up is rather more impressive: it includes Siegfried Sassoon's 'Sherston' Trilogy, Frederic Manning's *The Middle Parts of Fortune*, V. M. Yeates's *Winged Victory*, Ford Madox Ford's *Tietjens' Tetralogy*, Richard Aldington's *Death of a Hero* and Henry Williamson's war volumes in *A Chronicle of Ancient Sunlight*. The best Second World War novelists' team is also excellent, but conveys the 'pity of war' with less intensity. It contains writers of great distinction, such as Evelyn Waugh, with the *Sword of Honour* Trilogy, and Anthony Powell, with the war volumes of his novel sequence *A Dance to the Music of Time*. Somewhere in the same list must also go proficient best-sellers such as Nicholas Monsarrat's *The Cruel Sea*, James Clavell's *King Rat* and J. G. Ballard's *Empire of the Sun*, all still read; also less well-known but talented works such as George Millar's sardonic and entertaining *My Past Was an Evil River*, David Piper's *Trial by Battle*, Dan Billany's *The Trap* and Barry Sullivan's *Fibre*.

It should be observed, incidentally, that no fiction in either war written by British ex-servicemen has sold as well as such highly successful foreign novels as Remarque's *All Quiet on the Western Front*, Joseph Heller's *Catch-22*, or Norman Mailer's *The Naked and the Dead*.

There are certainly plenty of reasons for the third, very frequent generalisation: that once the initial flush of patriotic excitement was over, the literature of the First World War became universally disillusioned and pessimistic. The main reason is probably because that is the way people today prefer to view that war. The writings they rated highest are the disenchanted ones, such as the poems of Wilfred Owen and Siegfried Sassoon, and the novels that frequently get a mention, such as Sassoon's *The Memoirs of a Fox Hunting Man* and *The Memoirs of an Infantry Officer*, Richard Aldington's *Death of a Hero*, and Henry Williamson's *The Patriot's Progress*.

Among such novels are some specifically written to draw attention to certain scandals and evils. One that is regularly reprinted is A. P. Herbert's *The Secret Battle* (1919). Herbert, later a Member of Parliament and a leading humorous writer, was in the Royal Naval Division and took part in numerous courts martial, involving cases of desertion and cowardice. During his time of service, one of his fellow officers, one Sub-Lieutenant Edwin Dyett, was found guilty of desertion in the face of the enemy and shot. Herbert believed the charge unjust and that Dyett had been suffering from battle fatigue; he wrote the *Secret Battle* condemning the inhumanity of the system. His book was influential in altering the code of practice, and capital punishment for such offences was virtually dropped. Another well-publicised novel from the same war that also drew attention to the problem was *Rough Justice* (1926) by C. E. Montague, the celebrated journalist and wartime conducting officer. Forgotten now, but in the same genre, was Terence Mahon's *Cold Feet* (1929), which looked sympathetically at the psychology of cowardice, or loss of nerve, as did, more coldly, another forgotten work, *The Coward* (1927), by A. D. Gristwood.

Other war books with a bitter message included Warwick Deeping's best-selling *Sorrell and Son*, about an unemployed ex-officer looking desperately for work after the war, and Peter Deane's *The Victors*, on the same theme. The first-named novel has a happy end, the gentlemanly Sorrell eventually, after a long period of humiliation, finding a satisfactory occupation; in the second, less familiar work, the central character, a young former subaltern, despairs of employment, and gasses himself. These books, and others like them, also had their impact on opinion; in 1945 the British Government tackled the whole question of post-war unemployment properly and demobilised men went back into work.

Several of the most ambitious First World War novels, surveying the effect of the war on society as a whole, also carry a pessimistic or critical message. A good example is R. H. Mottram's prize-winning *Spanish Farm* Trilogy (1924-27), which laments the loss of civilised values. Ford Madox Ford's *Tietjens' Tetralogy* (1924-28) draws an unillusioned portrait of the ruling classes, the High Command and hypocritical Edwardian morality. The hero, Tietjens himself, emerges from the war as an honourable man among rogues, and achieves a precious liberty, but the war itself is seen as a vast agent of oppression over the face of the earth. The five First World War volumes of Henry Williamson's 15-volume *A Chronicle of Ancient Sunlight*, written in the 1950s, present a rich panorama of all England at war, of home and fighting fronts, of town and country, evoked with the aid of Williamson's eye as naturalist and soldier, but it is a picture also of international fratricide, hardship and misery.

Finally, even when it was not necessarily the desire of First World War writers to express disillusion, they rarely avoided tragedy and harrowing scenes, since the most compelling reason for writing, other than money, was to come to terms with their experience. The novelist Richard Blaker tried, in writing *Medal Without Bar* (1930), to expunge the horrors of life in the Royal Field Artillery on the Somme and at Arras, haunted by a sense that all feeling had been driven out of him; as one of his characters says:

> 'If we get through to the end ... there won't be a damned thing left in the world to upset us, and excite us, and make us get the wind up. I dare say we'll be able to smile at things now and again, but it'll take a hell of a lot to get a tear out of us. "These are they which came out of great tribulation..." the generation of the broken hearted.'[3]

Unexpectedly, Blaker, whose style is generally low-key and reticent, like many writers of his generation, introduced into his book what is actually one of the most horrific moments in a First World War novel – when an Australian quartermaster-sergeant is found paralysed and trapped against a red hot stove by shell blast, the inside of his thighs frying.

> 'More stifling shovel work produced for those on the stairway that savour as of fresh cutlets on a frying pan. After the reek, in a moment while the diggers were hushed and listening, there came a string of slow, thoughtful blasphemies:

"God," said one of the diggers, "it's the Quarter," and he fell to, shovelling again, fiendishly.'[4]

To quote Michael Paris again: 'The novels written by the ex-soldiers and airmen sought ... to describe for the uninitiated the reality of war and the true cost of armchair patriotism. All this gives these fictions of World War One a moral indignation and a dynamic strength of purpose which cannot fail to rouse an emotional response in the reader.'[5]

It would, however, be a gross over-simplification to conclude therefore that the majority of the First World War novels were pessimistic and anti-patriotic in tone. In reality most of the fiction that emerged from that war was patriotic, positive and reassuring in its message, as, for example, Patrick Miller's *The Natural Man*, a curious and imaginative book that won a well-deserved prize in 1924. Even Frederic Manning's great novel, *The Middle Parts of Fortune*, is not an anti-patriotic work, though it is hardly a book in praise of war. None of the more 'patriotic' works did as well as the German *All Quiet on the Western Front*, which sold over 2 million in two years; nor are they still in print, as is Robert Graves's disenchanted memoir *Goodbye to All That*. Nonetheless many of them enjoyed very large sales – 100,000-300,000 – and enjoyed a long innings, as, for example, Ernest Raymond's *Tell England* (1922), A. S. M. Hutchinson's *If Winter Comes* (1921), and Gilbert Frankau's *Peter Jackson, Cigar Merchant* (1920).

Such novels conveyed the message that war, however awful, could be a uniquely fulfilling experience in all kinds of unimagined ways. In Gilbert Frankau's book, Peter Jackson's marriage is saved by the war because his wife's buried feelings of love for him are released by seeing her husband shell-shocked and vulnerable. Frankau's own marriage was broken largely by the war, but he devised the outcome to please readers eager for a romantic and soothing conclusion in what was in some ways a subversive and disturbing book. *Simon Called Peter*, by Robert Keable, which sold over 300,000 copies, was based on his real-life love affair with a Women's Auxiliary Army Corps driver when he was a padre with the South African forces. This experience led him to shed his wife and faith, and go to live with his new love on Tahiti. The book was written before these consequences had ensued, and in it the hero simply undergoes a spiritual renaissance. At all events, the image of the war presented is positive – that it provides an opportunity to make a new life.

Wilfrid Ewart's *Way of Revelation* (1921) is another example of a 'non-disenchanted' and highly successful First World War novel. It carries the message that the war has served as a great test of human worth, revealing who is true-hearted and who is superficial and false. A subaltern in the 2nd Scots Guards, Ewart was badly wounded and shell-shocked; he survived the war only to suffer a nervous breakdown afterwards, but not before his solemn novel became a major best-seller.

Such 'optimistic' works had their equivalent in Second World War literature. The evil nature of Hitler's regime was such that to the victors it was self-evident that the struggle had been worthwhile; and much of the Second World War fiction did dwell both on the triumph and on personal development and achievement.

Many British servicemen during the Second World War had 'a good war' and felt that it had conferred benefits on them by giving them the chance to live for a cause other than themselves. Nicholas Monsarrat, in *The Cruel Sea*, for example, stressed the way the war helped stronger and more admirable people to realise their full stature; Ericson, captain of the *Compass Rose* and the *Saltash*, emerges as a heroic figure, like other commanders in the convoys, single-mindedly working to defeat the enemy:

> 'They were men who had become dedicated to a single theme of war ... the men of the Atlantic had become remarkably expert, astonishingly specialist, with no eyes for any theatre of war except their own.'[6]

Such feelings of pride were widespread – for example in Vian Smith's book, with its self-descriptive title *Song of the Unsung: A Story of Sappers* (January 1945), or James Aldridge's *Signed with their Honour* (October 1942), the latter dedicated to Squadron Leader 'Pat' Pattle and Squadron Leader T. S. Hickey, both killed in action in Greece where this novel of the RAF is set. It tells a moving story, its style, like so many war books to emerge from the Second World War, strongly reminiscent of Ernest Hemingway – a major influence on the literature of action for many years to come. Both Smith's and Aldridge's books were written in wartime and their purpose was partly to inspire; nonetheless they were both sincere works, unsparing of painful detail. *Signed With Their Honour* was thought good enough to re-publish in 1954, when there was no need for propaganda.

It would be wrong, however, to imply that there was nothing disillusioned about Second World War novels. People may have been confident that they were fighting for a good cause, but quite as much as in the previous war they saw things that horrified and disgusted them, including bullying, dishonesty and selfishness on their own side. Possibly the Second World War, which was fought in many different situations, may have presented a more bewildering series of moral choices than the monotonous routine of the trenches.

The very fact, too, that by the time the Second World War was over, censorship of what might be thought shocking had significantly relaxed, meant that writers were freer, when trying to describe the indescribable, to go into detail. This inevitably darkened the tone and content of what they wrote. Paul Fussell's influential work *The Great War and Modern Memory* centres on the failure of nearly all First World War writers and poets to find the words to evoke the horror of their situation. He argues with considerable persuasiveness that they were trapped in an old-fashioned literary convention, supported by the censorship, which romanticised and sanitised warfare.

The horror of Richard Blaker's passage about the Australian quartermaster, quoted above, was in fact almost unique in British First World War literature. In Second World War literature such passages are all too frequent. Monsarrat's *The Cruel Sea*, describing a corvette's crew and its part in the Battle of the Atlantic and the war at sea, is unsparing in its details of men's spirits broken, and of unspeakable deaths. There is an element of guilt and shame as well; men are courageous and efficient, but they also die badly, disgrace themselves, or let each other down. One of the most painful passages in the book describes an officer's impotence to help an appallingly burned man, who will not die:

> 'Just before he began he said: "It's a soothing ointment."
>
> I suppose it's natural that he should scream, thought Lockhart presently, shutting his ears: all the old-fashioned pictures showed a man screaming as soon as the barber-surgeon started to operate, while his friends plied the patient with rum or knocked him out with a mallet... The trouble was that the man was so horrifyingly alive; he pulled and wrenched at the two men holding him, while Lockhart, stroking and swabbing with a mother's tenderness, removed layer after layer of his flesh. For the other trouble was that however gently he was touched, the raw tissue went on and on coming away with the cotton-wool.'[7]

Monsarrat seems to have been haunted by cruel images for long after the war, his bad memories revived by the atrocities committed by the Mau Mau in Kenya where he settled. Alan White wrote his book *The Long Day's Dying* (1965) a brutal account of a day in the life of a commando, as a way of getting his unhappy experiences out of his system. In a climactic episode, he describes the filthy business of killing a man, and its shameful aftermath:

> 'He was not dead, but was starting to scream in agony. The air line of his windpipe was severed and no actual sound could come out. A stream of bubbles came from his throat, blowing the welling blood into red iridescent bubbles. His mouth was open, so I put the barrel of my rifle in, and fired three more shots to end his agony.
>
> Then, dazed, I started to walk back to the barn. I hadn't gone five steps when I started to heave, bitter bilious vomit jerking spasmodically from my throat, wrenching its way up my entire body. I staggered and sat in the hedge with my knees open and my head down and still vomited. Then a great convulsion shook me and it was as if all my orifices opened at once. Tears streamed from my eyes, there was a roaring sound in my ears, and my bowels and bladder opened together. Great heaving sobs wracked me, great tortured gasps of horror, hatred, pain, and remorse.
>
> I sat there in my own stink, drawing the back of my hand across my lips, wiping the streaming tears from my cheek with the cuff of my jumping jacket, smelling my own stinking sweat.'[8]

In Second World War literature, there are equivalents of Herbert's *The Secret Battle*, which draw attention to abuses, evils and painful aspects of service life. Shame and guilt pervade these novels; the disgrace of cowardice and of desertion from the Army is a very common theme. Paris lists several titles: R. Llewellyn's *Few Flowers for Shiner* (1950), P. H. Newby's *Retreat* (1953) and N. Fersen's *Tombolo* (1954), for example. The problem of 'Low Moral Fibre' ('LMF'), is sensitively dealt with in Barry Sullivan's quietly distinguished first book *Fibre* (1946), set in North Africa. A pilot is afraid that he is cracking and that his growing fear will become obvious to all. Men dismissed with LMF usually found it impossible to get anything but menial employment after the war, and the dishonourable label could ruin their lives; to survive, it was sometimes necessary to go abroad and 're-invent' themselves. As a psychological study, Sullivan's book goes deeper than Herbert's, which is more concerned with putting over a message than with the inner workings of personality.

Another Second World War novel that centres on a shameful situation is *Execution*, by a Canadian former officer, Colin McDougall, set in Italy in 1943; the crucial episode, which occurs early in the book, is the judicial murder of two harmless Italian deserters, following a general order given on the grounds that such people could be brigands who might attack Allied troops (as had happened several times). The two Italians have been impressed into service as platoon cooks and helpers by the protagonist, Lieutenant John Adam, and the soldiers, in a few days, have become quite attached to these two cheerful, unwarlike boys. After they are shot, revulsion and sorrow linger on in the platoon. It is the writer's clear purpose to highlight an action by Allied troops that would have been declared a crime if their side had lost and to point the lesson that even good men, in a war, cannot always act the way goodness wants them to.

A. G. Street's novel *Shameful Harvest* (1952) deals with a wartime civilian tragedy. It was dedicated 'to the memory of George Raymond Walden of Itchen Stoke, Hampshire, who lost his life on July 22nd 1940, while resisting eviction from his home at the order of the Hampshire County War Agricultural Committee'. In the novel, an eccentric farmer, Jim Hazard VC, is victimised by the local 'War Ag', for failing to carry out their directives. They serve an eviction order on him; a First World War veteran, he decides to fight it out, using Home Guard weapons stored in his home. In the siege that follows, he kills several soldiers and is blown up with his farm, when a mortar bomb hits it.

A very noticeable vein of disenchantment in Second World War literature is associated with sexual episodes. The casual wartime relationships, the long separations from wives and fiancées, were bound to be the cause of much bitterness, which found its way into the fiction, but this was no different from the previous war, where indeed such themes were extensively explored, as in Ewart's *Way of Revelation* and Aldington's *Death of a Hero*, both by men who suffered from the infidelity of the women they loved. The disenchanted treatment of love in Second World War novels, however, reflects also the fact that since the start of the inter-war period, British society had been increasingly exposed to freer ideas about sex without having fully shed Victorian guilt feelings on the subject. In the war novels of the 1940s and 1950s the allusions to sex tend to be either as something idealised and sentimentalised – a dream of home and an antidote to the harsh masculinity of war – or grubby, furtive and dishonourable. *The Cruel Sea* contains both varieties.

In the grubby vein, there is a striking episode in a particularly exciting novel about flying Mosquitoes, *Crispin's Day*, by a former RAF navigator, Leigh Howard. Flying officer 'Candy' Smith, a member of an RAF Operational Film Unit in May 1943, is about to go on an almost suicidal 400-mile, low-level photo-reconnaissance run over the Ruhr dams the day after they have been bombed by

617 Squadron; his WAAF driver bestows her favours on him out of a sort of dogged sense of patriotism because he, like any of the other airmen, may be killed. Although he accepts, he is none too grateful to the poor girl – she is frightened and does not attract him:

> 'He had a kaleidoscopic impression of her thin unwilling flanks; of the mean, pitiful ugliness of her sparse body; of the crucifix slipping up to her throat and falling on to the grass; of the awful agony on her face and of his surging desire to hurt her more and more; he sighed, then he shuddered and opened his eyes. She moaned with pain, turning her head from side to side, and he left her quickly, walking round a corner of the hedge.'[9]

This disagreeable vignette, redolent of sexual disappointment and self-disgust, is far more daring than anything that appears in the British First World War novels between the wars, where characters tend to lose out on sexual activity; a visit to a prostitute by Lieutenant Blaven in Patrick Miller's *The Natural Man* is inconclusive, as it is in V. M. Yeates's *Winged Victory* (1935). In both cases the protagonists change their minds, pay the woman and leave. A kindly actress gives Ronald Gurner's Freddy Mann in *Pass Guard at Ypres* (1930) the necessary tender loving care that he cannot get from his fiancée, but no particulars are given; Robert Keable gets closest to the post-Second War mode with a scene where the Rev Peter Graham has a bath with his girlfriend in a London Hotel. Absent from any such accounts, however, are the kind of physical details to be found, for example, in Monsarrat's *The Cruel Sea*, or James Clavell's *King Rat* (1962), or the above passage, where sexual excitement is mentioned. In none of the pre-war novels is there more than passing mention of homosexuality, whereas in *King Rat* its existence in the prisoner-of-war camp life at Changi is an important element in the story. One of the more tragic figures in that novel is a wartime flying officer called Sean, who becomes a trans-sexual in the camp, losing all sense of his identity, and finally killing himself. Again this contributes in that book to the general feeling of blighted hope at the end.

One of the most striking features in many Second World War novels, as opposed to those of the First, is the strong element of class conflict, feeding into a general feeling of unease about the future. In Clavell's *King Rat*, for example, much of the drama turns on the consuming hatred felt by the working-class officer Lieutenant Grey, rigorously carrying out his duties as Provost Marshal, for Flight Lieutenant Peter Marlowe, a former public schoolboy who makes friends with the chief illicit trader in Changi, an American corporal, 'the King', dedicated to a ruthless philosophy of self-help that gives him enormous power over the other starving inmates. In the end the camp is liberated, the King loses his position and is suspected by the British liberators of collaboration, but Grey never succeeds in humiliating his enemy Marlowe. He takes leave of him with a threat: 'I saw the King cut down to size, and I'll see it happen to you. You and your stinking class! …I'll beat you in the end. Your luck's going to run out.'[10]

The language of class conflict occurs in many other novels, for example George Smith's *The Unfinished Battle* and R. A. Forsyth's interesting account of RAF life in India, *Squadron Will Move* (1947). In the latter work, Sergeant Wheeler listens to his colleague Donaldson's anger that another man who 'went to Eton or Harrow, and knows a few Air Vice-Marshals' has been given promotion. Donaldson continues: 'I can see you're not interested. You may be, if you ever get invited to a Burra-Sahibs' Club and get snubbed by the officers there, or if you ever take your girl to a hotel lounge and they tell you you can't get in, because it is for Officers only. I've had some.'[11] The British, of all classes, by 1945 had become more openly questioning and uncomfortable than the previous generation about their social position, their institutions and their moral values. By comparison, the First World War novels sketch a society far more sure of its values, and at ease with itself. The later change of mood reflected a loss of confidence in Britain's traditional ruling classes and the legacy of the General Strike and the Depression, reinforced by the rise of socialism, and wartime egalitarian propaganda.

This did not mean that there was no class feeling in the 1914-18 period – Other Ranks always resented officer privilege – but as it appears in the Great War novels open class aggression tended to come from above rather than from below, in the form of snobbery rather than resentment. In *The Chronicle of Ancient Sunlight*, Phillip Maddison is the butt of social snubs – 'Blasted little cockney!' – from fellow officers for his lower-middle-class ways and the company he keeps.[12]

The classic work on a changing Britain and the disintegration of values is the three volumes of Evelyn Waugh's *Sword of Honour* trilogy, which the critic Cyril Connolly has described as 'unquestionably the finest novels to have come out of the war'. Waugh tells the story of Guy Crouchback, a genuinely honourable and good man in his mid-30s from an old-established Catholic gentry family, in much reduced circumstances. He has an heroic ancestral background to live up to, and he sees the international crisis before the war as the moment of truth for all he values most: 'The enemy at last was in plain view, huge and hateful, all disguise cast off. It was the Modern Age in arms. Whatever the outcome there was a place for him in that battle.'[13]

Crouchback tries to find that place, but is involved in a series of largely futile training schemes and military adventures, and in spite of being a reasonably efficient officer, gains little credit and takes the blame, unfairly, for irresponsible actions by other people. He takes part in the disastrous British expedition to Crete, arriving just in time to find the British Army in retreat. One of his friends, Ivor Claire, who has a reputation for cool valour, ignominiously abandons his position and takes flight on one of the last boats away from the island, while Crouchback escapes on a small boat to Egypt, its occupants nearly starving on the way. For the rest of the war he is not involved in any front-line fighting.

Claire's failure to live up to the aristocratic code of honour that is the *raison d'être* of his class is only one of many acts of selfishness and betrayal by various characters in the story. Whether they do well or badly, Crouchback's acquaintances are mainly driven by the desire to cut a figure or better themselves in various financial, social, or amorous ways. Crouchback, unassuming and patient, is one of the few in the book to emerge from the war with any integrity; but even he, before the end of the story, has to admit to selfishness. In Serbia, as a Liaison Officer, he takes a group of homeless Jews under his wing, particularly an educated and cultivated couple, the Kanyis, in the knowledge that the communists who are now gaining control in Serbia care as little about their fate as did the Germans. Before he leaves Serbia he asks Mme Kanyi what will happen to her and the others; she replies:

> "'Is there any place that is free from evil? It is too simple to say that only the Nazis wanted war. These communists wanted it too. It was the only way in which they could come to power. Many of my people wanted it, to be revenged on the Germans, to hasten the creation of the national state. It seems to me there was a will to war, a death wish, everywhere. Even good men thought their private honour would be satisfied by war. They could assert their manhood by killing and being killed. They would accept hardships in recompense for having been selfish and lazy. Danger justified privilege. I knew Italians – not very many perhaps – who felt this. Were there none in England?'
>
> "God forgive me," said Guy. "I was one of them."'[14]

At the end of the book he returns to civilian life and marries for a second time, happily. It is no less than he deserves, and the quiet untriumphal end is what Evelyn Waugh feels appropriate for a war where so much truth and honour has been compromised, even on the winning side. For Waugh, as for many, the victory had been vitiated by the triumph of Stalin's tyranny in Europe.

Both wars, then, had their literature of disenchantment as well as of triumph. Both disillusioned and triumphant genres expressed powerful truths: about the imperfection of victory and selfishness of many of the players, and about the steadfastness and warm-hearted devotion among many others. Reading through all that literature today, it strikes one that the strongest feelings of bonding and loyalty do seem to be expressed in the novels of the First World War rather than the Second. If one contrasts Nicholas Monsarrat's *The Cruel Sea*, which gives due credit to loyal and brave members of the ships' crews, with Frederic Manning's account, in *The Middle Parts of Fortune*, of ordinary infantrymen in and out of battle during the Somme campaign, the first thing that impresses one is the warmth, the simplicity and the sense of humour of the latter work, compared with an almost machine-like coldness of the other – despite some compassionate portraits by Monsarrat, of, for example, a young officer, 20 years old, a former bank clerk, who breaks down nervously. And in spite of the fact that nobody more than Manning has conveyed the merciless quality of the trench fighting, one of the officers, Clinton, speaks to Private Bourne just after they have been in action: 'You and I are two of the lucky ones, Bourne; we've come through without a scratch; and if our luck holds we'll keep moving out of one bloody misery into another, until we break, see, until we break.' In Manning's book a close-knit unit of infantrymen from a Midlands regiment is gradually killed off in the fighting, and Private Bourne, after losing one of his closest companions, a boy soldier of 16, throws himself desperately into the fighting until he too receives a fatal wound. What makes the book effective is the human quality of the characters. They are chatty, affectionate, irritable, gloomy, cheerful, kind, often drunk; and they amuse each other. Manning was a well-born Australian, an aesthete, and an interesting minor poet, most unlike the average British soldier, by all appearances; yet he entered into the soul of an infantry battalion as no other writer in the First World War has done.

There is really no equivalent of this for the Second World War, but approaching *The Middle Parts of Fortune* in quality of humour, portrayal of character, and depiction of a unit at war, is *Trial by Battle* by David Piper, later Director of the National Portrait Gallery. Piper tells the story of a young Indian Army officer's initiation and his final death in action. Alan Mart arrives in Malaya in October 1941, on the eve of Britain's disastrous withdrawal, carrying with him impedimenta of his civilian life – a privileged Cambridge outlook, the expectation of some mandarin career and a certain polished flippancy. He finds very quickly that he is among people who have no time for anything unless it helps them to defeat their enemy. They are neither hostile to him nor prepared to accept him on any other terms but their own. Their attitude is personified in that of an extraordinary individual, Acting-Captain Holl, generally known simply as 'Sam'.

Holl is a larger-than-life figure, the son of a baker, without conceit, dedicated, savage, generous-hearted, an intermittent drunk, and a natural-born killer. The author conveys the magnetism of the man so perfectly that it is easy to understand how the sophisticated young hero is very quickly drawn into the spirit of combat that Holl generates. He is borne along by the fighting, as though a will greater than his is driving him. Like *The Middle Parts of Fortune* his own death is preceded by that of a friend – in this case Holl, burned to death in a Bren gun carrier. Impressive and gracefully written though the book is, however, it does not have the pathos and tragedy of Manning's great work.

Fiction, through its descriptive power and ability to get inside character, can in some ways illuminate the nature of war more than any other medium. Yet it is selective, and some types of conflict stimulate the novelist's imagination more than others. Few engagements could be more harrowing than Arnhem, Anzio or Monte Cassino, all of which were scenes of British heroism; yet they have not yet inspired an exceptional novel. Film, undoubtedly, has served the memory of the Second World War better. For all the subtlety, humour and perception of the *Sword of Honour* Trilogy, for all the merciless detail about the Battle of the Atlantic that Monsarrat dispenses in *The Cruel Sea*, for all the acute understanding of the psychology of fear and of leadership in David Piper's *Trial by Battle*, for all the accomplishment of so many English writers of the Second World War, their works do not quite have the same tragic impact as their forerunners, the sometimes artless, sometimes less sophisticated novels that evoke the sombre rituals and carnage of the trenches in France and Flanders.

Recommended reading

Aldington, Richard, *Death of a Hero* (London: Chatto & Windus 1930)
Aldridge, James, *Signed With Their Honour* (London: Michael Joseph, 1942)
Ballard, J. G., *Empire of the Sun* (London: Flamingo, 1995)
Billany, Dan, *The Trap* (London: Faber & Faber, 1950)
Blaker, Richard, *Medal Without Bar* (London: Hodder & Stoughton, 1930)

Bracco, Rosa Maria, *Merchants of Hope; British Middlebrow Writers and the First World War, 1919-1939* (Oxford: Berg, 1993)

Cecil, Hugh, *The Flower of Battle: How Britain wrote the Great War* (South Royalton, Vermont: Steerforth Press, 1996)

Clavell, James, *King Rat* (London: Michael Joseph, 1962; Coronet Books, 1992)

Cloete, Stuart, *How Young They Died* (London: Collins, 1969)

Deeping, Warwick, *Sorrell and Son* (London: Cassell, 1925)

Desmond, Leslie, *Careless Lives* (London: MacDonald, 1945)

Deane, Peter, *The Victors* (London: Constable, 1925)

Ewart, Wilfrid, *Way of Revelation* (London: G. P. Putnam's, 1921)

Eyre, Donald C., *Foxes Have Holes* (London: Robert Hale, 1948)

Fallas, Carl, *St Mary's Village Through the Mind of an Unknown Soldier Who Lived On* (London: Hodder & Stoughton, 1954)

Ford, Ford Madox, *Some Do Not, No More Parades, A Man Could Stand Up, Last Post* (London: Duckworth, 1924, 1925, 1926, 1928)

Forsyth, R. A., *Squadron Will Move* (London: Macmillan, 1947)

Frankau, Gilbert, *Peter Jackson, Cigar Merchant* (London: Hutchinson, 1920)

Fussell, Paul, *The Great War and Modern Memory* (Oxford: Oxford University Press, 1975)

Graves, Robert, *Goodbye to All That* (London: Jonathan Cape, 1929; Penguin Books, 1960)

Gristwood, A. D., *The Somme* including also *The Coward* (London: Jonathan Cape, 1927)

Gurner, Ronald, *Pass Guard at Ypres* (London: J. M. Dent, 1930)

Hager, Philip E. and Taylor, Desmond, *The Novels of World War 1: An Annotated Bibliography* (New York: Garland Publishing Inc, 1981)

Harvey, A. D., *A Muse of Fire: Literature, Art and War* (London: The Hambledon Press, 1998)

Heller, Joseph, *Catch-22* (London: Jonathan Cape, 1962)

Herbert, A. P., *The Secret Battle* (London: Methuen, 1919)

Hodson, James Lansdale, *Return to the Wood* (London: Gollancz, 1955)

Howard, Leigh, *Crispin's Day* (London: Longman's Green & Co, 1952)

Hutchinson, A. S. M., *If Winter Comes* (London: Hodder & Stoughton, 1921)

Keable, Robert, *Simon Called Peter* (London: Constable, 1921)

Mailer, Norman, *The Naked and the Dead* (London: Alan Wingate, 1949)

Manning, Frederic, *The Middle Parts of Fortune* (London: Peter Davies, 1930; 1977 ed)

McDougall, Colin, *Execution* (London: Macmillan, 1958)

Millar, George, *My Past Was an Evil River* (London: Heinemann, 1946)

Miller, Patrick, *The Natural Man* (London: Grant Richards, 1924)

Monsarrat, Nicholas, *The Cruel Sea* (London: Cassell & Co, 1951)

Montague, C. E., *Rough Justice* (London: Chatto & Windus, 1926)

Mottram, R. H., *Spanish Farm* Trilogy (pub as one volume, London: Chatto & Windus, 1927)

O'Connor, Michael P., *Vile Repose* (London: Ernest Benn, 1950)

Onions, John, *English Fiction and Drama of The Great War, 1918-1939* (London: Macmillan, 1990)

Paris, Michael, *The Novels of World War Two: An Annotated Bibliography of World War Two Fiction* (London: The Library Association, 1990)

Piper, David, *Trial by Battle* (London: Peter Towry, 1959; 2nd ed, with Introduction by Frank Kermode, London: Collins, 1966)

Powell, Anthony, *The Music of Time: The Kindly Ones, The Valley of Bones, The Soldier's Art, Military Philosophers* (London: Heinemann, 1962, 1964, 1966, 1968)

Raymond, Ernest, *Tell England* (London: Cassell, 1922)

Remarque, Erich Maria, trans A. W. Wheen, *All Quiet on the Western Front* (London: G. P. Putnam's, 1929)

Reilly, Catherine W., *English Poetry of the First World War: A Bibliography* (London: George Prior Publishers, 1978)

Sassoon, Siegfried, *The Memoirs of a Fox Hunting Man* and *The Memoirs of an Infantry Officer* (London: Faber & Faber, 1928, 1930)

Smith, George, *The Unfinished Battle* (London: Jarrolds, 1958)

Smith, Vian C., *Song of the Unsung: A Story of Sappers* (London: Hodder & Stoughton, 1945)

Street, A. G., *Shameful Harvest* (London: Faber & Faber, 1952)

Sullivan, Barry, *Fibre* (London: Faber & Faber, 1946)

Waugh, Evelyn, *Sword of Honour* Trilogy: *Men at Arms, Officers and Gentlemen, Unconditional Surrender* (London: Chapman & Hall, 1952, 1955, 1961; Penguin Books, 1984)

White, Alan, *The Long Day's Dying* (London: Hodder & Stoughton, 1965)

Williamson, Henry, *A Chronicle of Ancient Sunlight* (London: Macdonald, 1954-60; 1984 ed)
The Patriot's Progress: Being the Vicissitudes of Private John Bullock (London: Geoffrey Bles, 1930)

Yeates, V. M., *Winged Victory* (London: Jonathan Cape, 1934)

Notes

1   Michael Paris, *The Novels of World War Two: An Annotated Bibliography of World War Two Fiction* (London: The Library Association, 1990) Introduction, ppix-x

2   Catherine W. Reilly, *English Poetry of the First World War: A Bibliography* (London: George Prior Publishers, 1978) p5

3   Richard Blaker, *Medal Without Bar* (London: Hodder & Stoughton, 1930) p379.

4   Ibid, p535

5   Michael Paris, op cit, ppix-x

6   Nicholas Monsarrat, *The Cruel Sea* (London: Cassell & Co, 1951) pp324

7   Ibid, p241

8   Alan White, *The Long Day's Dying* (London: Hodder & Stoughton, 1965) p5

9   Leigh Howard, *Crispin's Day* (London: Longman's Green & Co, 1952) p165

10 James Clavell, *King Rat* (London: Michael Joseph, 1962; Coronet Books, 1992) p444

11 R. A. Forsyth, *Squadron Will Move* (London: Macmillan, 1947) pp95-6

12 Henry Williamson, *The Chronicle of Ancient Sunlight* (London: Macdonald, 1954-60, 1984 ed) Vol 5 'A Fox Under My Cloak'

13 Evelyn Waugh, *Sword of Honour* Trilogy (first published by Chapman & Hall as *Men at Arms*, 1952; *Officers and Gentlemen*, 1955; *Unconditional Surrender*, 1961; London: Penguin Books, 1984) p565

14 Ibid, pp565-6

Chapter 23

Classical music

Donald Webster

Though the Second World War was of longer duration, cost more lives, wreaked more destruction, created more severe and longer-lasting political problems and led to more thorough-going social reconstruction than its predecessor, in creative cultural terms its impact was very much less. The rebelliousness of such scores as Walton's *Belshazzar's Feast*, his First Symphony, Vaughan Williams's Fourth and Bliss's music for the H. G. Wells film *Things to Come* clearly anticipated the post-1939 disasters. But many of the 1940s' most striking British compositions were works containing a strong spiritual element, such as Vaughan Williams's Fifth, the most profound work in his symphonic cycle. An intensified spirituality also informs the church compositions of Herbert Howells, such as *Like as the Heart* and his *Evening Canticles* written for the Choir of King's College, Cambridge.

The post-war years were noteworthy for greatly improved performance standards, superior recorded reproduction and greater state munificence for the arts, modest though this was. It reflected a belated acknowledgement of the increasingly important place classical music was playing in the lives of ordinary folk.

Wartime experiences showed how great was the thirst for classical music. Musical appreciation classes and gramophone societies proliferated. Dobson and Young became temporarily a national institution, while they 'sold' the idea that music was part of the 'good life' in numerous radio broadcasts. Ex-servicemen who had served in Italy became aware for the first time in their lives of the joys of grand opera. The establishment of the BBC's Third Programme was a natural consequence of all this, and a response to popular demand, even if it still reflected only a minority taste.

But of changes in idiom there was nothing to compare with what took place post-1919. Composers who had been active in the 1930s and who continued to compose during the 1940s and 1950s did so with remarkable stylistic consistency. Of course, there were enfants terribles, as there are in every age, but many composers were happy to wear the neo-Romantic label. Music's stylistic revolution, including the belated influence of Webern[1], is essentially a child of the 1960s.

By general consent, the decade 1820-30, dominated as it was by the achievements of Beethoven, Schubert, Weber and Mendelssohn, is looked upon as music's greatest. Yet there are those who lay claim to the 1904-14 period as being an era of comparable achievement, and not without cause. The mere recital of the names of some who were active at this time demonstrates the magnitude of the musical creativity, including Jánacek, Suk, Bartok, Dohnanyi, Kodaly, Debussy, Ravel, Dukas, Fauré, Satie, Richard Strauss, Schoenberg, Wellesz, Zemlinsky, Elgar, Parry, Stanford, Vaughan Williams, Delius, Holst, Puccini, Respighi, Glazunov, Medtner, Rachmaninov, Scriabin, Stravinsky, Falla, Sibelius, Stenhammar and Nielsen. All were masters of the technique of composition and most wrote on a big scale. Their achievements represented the climax of the Romantic period. If the First World War had not taken place, some violent cultural reaction would nevertheless have burst the expansionist bubble, though its effect would have been less catastrophic for the course of music in the 1920s and 1930s than proved to be the case. Of those who were active prior to 1914, only Richard Strauss among the major figures was seemingly unaffected by the war. Stravinsky rushed feverishly from one idiom to another, Elgar and Sibelius gave up serious composition in the early 1920s, and others cultivated an austere style from which pre-war artistic luxuriance was rigorously excluded. For most of them the times were truly out of joint.

During the Edwardian period Edward Elgar came to be recognised as Britain's composer laureate, and few Masters of the King's Music have taken their duties more seriously. His *Coronation Ode*, which incorporated the 'Land of Hope and Glory' tune at Edward VII's request, subsequently seemed to encapsulate all the patriotic sentiments of a nation at war. Elgar in wartime wanted more modest words for the tune, but his pleas went unheard. The *Pomp and Circumstance* March No 4 (1907) expresses equally forthright national feeling. His *Spirit of England* (1915-17) tempers such emotions with poignancy. In the first movement, '4 August', the demonic nature of war is expressed in music reminiscent of the 'Demons' Chorus' in *The Dream of Gerontius*. But the highest level of inspiration is evident in *For the Fallen*, in which Binyon's famous words find lustrous setting. The theme of 'Flesh of her flesh they were, spirit of her spirit' induces an emotional reaction from the printed page, without any music being heard. His requiem for all who died in the war and for the civilised values that departed, seemingly forever, is surely the noble Cello Concerto (1920).

In Austria, confidence in her ultimate victory was reflected in the work of the composer Max Reger. His last composition for organ, Op 145 No 7, *Siegesfeier*, foretells of victory for the Central Powers. Perhaps it was fortuitous that Reger, who died in 1916, did not live long enough to witness the outcome. The work's borrowed material includes the chorale *Nun danket alle Gott* and the German/Austrian National Anthem. The former is treated reverentially, seldom rising above mezzo piano; the latter thunders forth triumphantly, leaving the listener in no doubt as to whom the glory of victory really belongs.[2]

There is little doubt that most Britons went to war in 1914 with a light heart and in the expectation that it would be a brief military adventure. This was reflected in some of the war songs, such as the following, which appeared as early as September 1914 and was set to music by Edward Elgar:

'A place in the ranks awaits you
Each one has some part to play
The past and the future are nothing

In the face of the stern today.
Stay not to sharpen your weapons
Or the hour will strike at last
When from dreams of a long battle
You may wake – to find it past.'

A more sober note was struck in the writings of Ernest Newman, a critic who exercised enormous influence, during and between both wars – and beyond.[3] He wrote of a new political delimitation and a new cohesion of social ideals and habits. He deplored the economic suffering that war entailed such as the restriction in publication of 'the better kinds of music' and the cessation of imports of music from German publishers. Whereas many branded all the Germans as equally bad, he was one of the few to draw a distinction between the abundance of German musical culture and a handful of militarists. With remarkable prophetic insight he feared for the effect of war on composers' stylistic evolution. Perhaps more surprising is Newman's following statement, in the light of my list of active composers:

'There is no denying that of late music has lacked truly commanding personalities and really vitalising forces. Strauss has failed us ... German music settled into a complacent tilling of an almost exhausted field. Schönberg [has] aspirations towards something new and personal, but lacks the capacity to realise them. Never has there been an epoch of such general musical capacity but great figures and great ideas are not so plentiful.'

Again with wonderful foresight he feared that a bad political settlement would keep the old national animosities alive until they once more found their inevitable outlet in (another) war. He also feared the consequences of an aggressive musical nationalism between France and Germany, in the wake of the Franco-Prussian War of 1870, wherein the seeds of the 1914-18 conflict had been undoubtedly sown. It was somewhat alarming to read advertisements as early as those in the September 1914 edition of the *Musical Times* promoting anthems and hymns 'for use in time of war'. Some were newly composed. In October 1914 Newman lamented: 'It is [as much] the fault of composers as of the peoples that national songs are as a rule such poor stuff. Why should our soldiers in France go marching to the most wretched of music hall songs when we have composers of the calibre of Elgar and Bantock.'[4] Yet there was something infinitely more wholesome in 'A Long Way To Tipperary', 'Pack Up Your Troubles', 'Keep The Home Fires Burning' and 'Roses of Picardy', all of which have enjoyed a sturdy survival, than in the tasteless emptiness of the Elgar song already quoted.

The career of the English organist Herbert Willoughby Williams suffered as a consequence of the musical nationalism so deplored by Newman. Although Williams occupies no place in any British work of reference, his career shows the tragedy of being caught between two flags in wartime.[5] After a distinguished career at Dresden's Royal Conservatorium, Williams stayed on to become Organist at the American Church and later Repetiteur at the Royal Dresden Opera in 1901. His duties included training choruses and soloists and having charge of the assisting orchestra. Because he feared the outbreak of a European conflict and because he desired an English education for his growing family, he was encouraged by Basil Harwood and Sir Alexander Mackenzie, then Principal of the Royal Academy of Music in London, to apply for the post of Organist of Leeds Parish Church, which had become vacant in 1913 following the appointment of Dr Edward Bairstow to York Minster.

At that time Britain nursed a musical inferiority complex towards its music, when comparisons were made with German achievements, and consequently the appointment of Williams to Leeds represented a considerable coup. However, once war was declared all that changed. His wife, who by all accounts was a charming German lady, was treated with much hostility, and it was believed that having lived in Germany for more than 20 years he nursed German sympathies. His daughters, then in their early teens, had to contend with hostile jostling as they left the family pew at church. From the time of his appointment it had been Williams's custom to play extended voluntaries after the Sunday evening service, and a large congregation stayed behind to hear them. Soon after the war started, the congregation expressed its displeasure towards Williams by almost stamping out of church, and generally making so much noise as to bring the recitals to an end.

Notwithstanding his vast experience at the highest level in Germany, no 'extramural' conducting appointments came Williams's way in Leeds. As early as 15 December 1914 one of the curates, the Reverend W. H. Elliott, later a famous Vicar of St Michael's, Chester Square, wrote, 'Just a belated line to say that I honestly feel that in five years experience of the Parish Church, I have never heard anything more beautiful than the Anthem last Sunday night. I know hundreds feel the same. Go on and prosper.' The tone of this letter is clearly as much an expression of encouragement as of congratulation. It is not without significance that the five years included nearly four when the formidable Dr Bairstow was in charge. Yet this treatment told heavily on Williams's self-confidence and his marriage. He was required to resign in 1919 and his marriage ended in divorce.

Wagner evenings at the Proms were an early war casualty[6], but they were quickly re-instated, and an American Cinematograph version of *Tannhauser* was shown with a cleverly contrived mosaic of passages taken from the opera, devised by two Harrogate musicians, Julian Clifford and Ernest Farrar.

In 1915 a Music in Wartime Committee[7] was set up under the Chairmanship of Sir Walford Davies[8]. The Carl Rosa Opera Company presented in Blackpool a season of ten operas in a fortnight, including such comparative rarities as *The Jewels of the Madonna* by Wolf Ferrari, Nicolai's *Merry Wives of Windsor*, *Tannhauser* and Verdi's *Aida*. Praise was lavished on the singing, acting and scenery, but the contributions of the orchestra and chorus left much to be desired. The visits of Moiseiwitsch to Wakefield[9] and the performance of Beethoven's Third Piano Concerto in Leeds, by Arthur Rubinstein, showed the determination of the provinces to keep music alive.[10] The enthusiastic local secretary of the Music in Wartime Committee, Herbert Bacon Smith[11], made a handsome contribution to this work. He was closely associated with Leeds Parish Church where the musical establishment of 30 boys, 11 altos, eight tenors and 13 basses was sustained by the congregation, without any external support, at a cost of £700 per annum. There was no cathedral establishment of remotely comparable size. In Harrogate[12] the newly formed municipal choir under the direction of Ernest Farrar announced the visits of Cowen, Somervell, MacLean and Fletcher to conduct their own compositions.

Julius Harrison[13] took a party of seven musicians under the auspices of the YMCA to visit the troops in France amidst their hardship and suffering.[14] Rosa Newmarch visited Russia and wrote that she could confidently affirm that the war had not visibly affected any of the established musical organisations there.

One of Sir Thomas Beecham's motives in promoting opera seasons in Birmingham, Manchester and London was to give employment to more musicians than other genres afforded. An account of an opera in Blackpool makes astonishing reading: 'Before today, Tetrazzini, Melba, Kubelik and Kreisler have all been engaged at the different places of amusement on the same night'[15], and it was the town's boast that one did not need to spend more then sixpence to hear any of them: 'Opera they have had at all seasons of the year, but not on the Beecham scale, nor at the Beecham prices ... packed every night, but the matinees could not lure the crowds from breeze and sunshine, pies and promenade. Probably at no theatre in the country can opera-going be indulged with equal satisfaction.' Beecham's role was strictly that of impresario, and the conducting was in the hands of Eugene Goossens (senior and junior), Percy Pitt and Wynn Reeves. Praise was given to Frank Mullings's *Faust* and Robert Radford's *Mephistopheles*, but it was surprising to read that 'one cannot think that *Trovatore* and *Samson* [Saint Saens?] have really enduring qualities, but they are worth seeing as "shows"'.

Sir Henry Wood said: 'There ought to be after the war a tremendous uplift for orchestral and choral music. There is a tremendous lot of character about Russian music. German music is at a standstill. Outside Richard Strauss, who is a genius, there are no notable German composers.'[16] In another interview, Wood said: 'All the great continental names in music belong to the past generation. I could mention at least six English composers of today who write for orchestra whose work cannot be touched by any continental contemporary. I attribute this glorious outlook for our future – in part at least – to the decay of the Festival, with its passion for the academic.'[17]

But even amidst the rigours of war, time could be found for amusement. A performance of Haydn's 'Toy' Symphony was given at the Queen's Hall on 28 October 1918.[18] Its performers included Albert Sammons, Sir Alexander Mackenzie, Edward German, York Bowen, Beatrice Harrison, W. H. Squire (strings); Arthur de Greet (piano); Sir Edward Elgar (cymbals); Benno Moiseiwitsch (triangle); Frank Bridge and Sir Frederick Cowen (rattles); Myra Hess and Irene Scharrer (nightingales); Mesdames Albani, Crossley and Tubb (cuckoos); and Mark Hambourg (castanets). One wonders if a performance by artists of comparable stature could be arranged today.

A number of notable composers and musicians undertook active service during 1914-18. Paul Wittgenstein, the Austrian pianist, was an outstanding young virtuoso, who, after a successful debut in 1913 joined the Austrian Army. He was severely wounded in action, and this necessitated the amputation of his right arm.

He was a prisoner of war in Siberia in 1916, but after his repatriation later the same year he devoted himself to playing with the left hand. His devotion to playing thus allowed him to acquire an amazing virtuosity, which enabled him to overcome difficulties that would have been formidable even to a two-handed pianist. In addition to his own adaptations he commissioned a series of works from famous composers, the most important of which were Richard Strauss's *Panathendaenzug* and *Parergon zur Symphonia Domestica*, Ravel's Concerto for the Left Hand, Britten's *Diversions on a Theme* and Prokofiev's Fourth Piano Concerto, a work he never played. Many other compositions for solo piano, chamber ensemble and concerti were written for him. The Ravel is one of the 20th century's masterpieces, and the difficulties of playing it with one hand contribute significantly to the work's overall expressive effect. In a two-handed adaptation these would be lost.

Douglas Fox suffered a similar injury. As both organist and pianist he had made a profound impression prior to the 1914-18 war. He won an Organ Scholarship to the Royal College of Music and to Keble College, Oxford. By extraordinary persistence and by developing a skill in using both feet simultaneously he was able to overcome this disability to a very remarkable extent. As Director of Music at both Bradfield and Clifton Colleges he acquired an almost legendary teaching reputation, and many outstanding musicians passed through his hands. He became Organist at Great St Mary's Church, Cambridge, in 1957 after leaving Clifton. The choral repertoire at the school included such demanding works as Holst's *Two Psalms*, and Dvorak's *Te Deum*. Fox's organ-playing skill, notwithstanding his disability, can be judged from the recital he gave at Glasgow Cathedral in July 1945. The programme included Parry's Toccata and Fugue, *The Wanderer*, Debussy's *The Blessed Damozel*, Stanford's Postlude in D Minor and a group of Bach Chorale Preludes.

George Butterworth, the British composer, was born into a family of considerable social standing and material resource. At Eton he showed much musical promise, and soon after arriving at Trinity College, Oxford, to read Greats he found that music was the supreme absorbing interest of his life. Meeting Cecil Sharp and Vaughan Williams reinforced this. He wrote musical criticism for *The Times* and became increasingly active in the English Folk Song and Dance Society. Even so, despite a busy professional life, which encompassed a variety of activities, Butterworth was often tormented by a sense of purposelessness in his life. Like many more in a similar situation, service in the Army offered a solution and he immediately enlisted in the Durham Light Infantry. He abandoned all thoughts of music, and destroyed many of his manuscripts. In September 1915 he first went into the trenches and was the recipient of a posthumous Military Cross the following year. His *A Shropshire Lad* settings, his orchestral rhapsody of that name, his *On the Banks of Green Willow* and the *Two English Idylls* reflect, in their soft-spoken, poignant lyricism a fine, sensitive and artistic mind.

The dominant quality in the music of Ralph Vaughan Williams is that of an inward spirituality and a peaceful pastoral feeling. Yet despite the mystical quality that distinguished his church music and the numerous photographs of him as an English country gentleman, he was never a professing Christian and there was also a turbulence in much of his music. He was nearly 42 when the First World War began, yet he felt bound to serve, first as a wagon orderly with the Royal Army Medical Corps in France and on the Salonika front. He later returned to France as an artillery officer. Soon after the Armistice he became Music Director for the First Army of the British Expeditionary Force. Thus he was responsible for organising amateur music-making among the troops. The flair that he showed in this was manifest later in his involvement with such groups as the Leith Hill Festival, and in the promotion of much amateur activity. His wartime experiences no doubt contributed to his sense of a fundamental tension between traditional ideas of belief, morality and spiritual anguish. All these qualities are strongly evident in his late cantata *Hodie*.

The British organist and composer, Ernest Bristow Farrar, was one of many young musicians, on the verge of highly promising careers, who were claimed by the 1914-18 conflict. The importance of Farrar rests on the impact that his generous personality made upon others. First, there was Ernest Bullock, who came to Leeds in 1906 with the Bairstows and lived as an adopted son. In 1908 he became Organist at Micklefield Parish Church, near Tadcaster, where Farrar's father was Vicar, and a warm friendship developed between the two young men. Bullock, though five years younger than Farrar, was clearly the more musically gifted of the two in an intellectual sense, leaving Farrar far behind, obtaining his Durham MusB in 1908 at the age of 18 and his Doctorate six years later. He rose to the rank of Captain in the Army. Yet a recently issued CD of Farrar's orchestral music leaves one in no doubt as to his superiority as a composer.

In 1912 Farrar was appointed Organist of Christ Church, Harrogate, and soon afterwards the 13-year-old Gerald Finzi became his pupil. The actual period of his teaching was a short one, because Farrar joined the forces, and Finzi then became a pupil of Bairstow in York, but it was to Farrar that Finzi wrote when faced with a musical or a personal problem. The spiritual intimacy between the two men is reflected in a certain idiomatic similarity in their compositions. It was certainly the death of Farrar following the loss of a succession of close relatives that strengthened Finzi's pacifist resolve and his introspective bent, which is reflected in his music, and which endears it to a growing number of people.

Farrar's commanding officer wrote to his widow, 'He was a magnificent example to all in courage and devotion to duty and was beloved by all ranks in his battalion.' Equally warm-hearted tributes came from Sir Charles Stanford and J. B. Priestley, the novelist.

But the most significant memorial by far is Frank Bridge's Piano Sonata (1921-24). It is an agonised and far-reaching reaction to the tragedy of war, and a sense of inconsolable personal loss seems to emerge in this violent and radical work. A comparison of the Sonata with Bridge's organ works written ten years earlier shows how the composer's feelings called forth an entirely new idiom and formed the starting point of an entirely new phase in his output. No doubt it was the new Bridge idiom that so attracted the young Benjamin Britten in the late 1920s to become a composition pupil, and it contributed to his uncompromising pacifism.

It was not only musicians from combatant nations who fell victim to the war. The career of Enrique Granados, the Spanish composer and pianist, came to an abrupt and premature end as a direct consequence of war conditions combined with an ill-judged desire to accede to a request from President Wilson. Granados's most famous and lasting success came with the Piano Suite *Goyescas*, which was received with enormous enthusiasm when the composer played it in the Salle Pleyel in Paris on 4 April 1914. He was elected to the Legion d'Honneur, and was encouraged to give operatic treatment to *Goyescas*. The Paris Opera accepted this, but as a result of the war delay was inevitable. Granados therefore took the opera out of their hands and gave it to the New York Metropolitan, where it received tremendous acclaim on 26 January 1916. President Wilson requested that Granados should give a recital at the White House, causing him to miss the boat on which he had booked a passage, and which would have taken him directly to Spain. He therefore took a ship to England, and in Liverpool boarded the *Sussex* for Dieppe. The *Sussex* was torpedoed by a German U-boat in mid-Channel. A lifeboat picked up Granados, but seeing his wife struggling in the water he dived in to save her, and both were drowned.

In France the composer Alberic Magnard was another victim of the war. He was born into a comfortable home, and, following early professional success, grew up into a man who was taciturn, humourless and did not suffer fools gladly. Composition never came easily to him. Many of his works are thickly scored and show the influence of César Franck. Though he enjoyed only limited popular success, he remained true to his ideal of artistic truth and formal classical perfection. His end was thoroughly consistent with his personality. He spent much of the summer of 1914 in his large country house at Baron. When war was declared, he sent his family off to a safe place, but he remained behind, and was working in his study when, during the German advance on Paris, a party of German cavalry entered his estate. From an upstairs window Magnard fired, killing two of them. The Germans retaliated by returning his fire and setting the house ablaze, destroying several of Magnard's manuscripts, as well as killing the composer himself.

When the First World War began Sergei Rachmaninov was already an established figure in Russia's musical life, but found war conditions in the country increasingly unbearable. By 1916 Russia was gripped by strikes and successive governments, which only served to increase ill-feeling towards the Tsar. Rachmaninov's attempts to obtain a visa to leave the country were unsuccessful and he was on the verge of despair. He then received an invitation to play in Stockholm, and at once travelled to Petrograd to arrange the journey. His family followed a few days later, and just before Christmas the whole family left Russia for the last time, leaving behind practically all their money and possessions.

The First World War had a greater impact on music and musicians' lives than had been anticipated in 1914. Many composers' careers were brought to a premature end, while others' work took a new direction as a consequence of the war. In Britain, a retrospect of the conflict was provided by the *Musical Times*:

'Most of us anticipated a short war, with an almost entire cessation of musical activities on the part of the belligerents. Instead we have had a long war, and in this country at all events an unprecedented amount of music making ... great activity in Chamber Music circles ... demand for cheap reprints. Whilst due credit must go to Sir Thomas Beecham and others, we think that the presence in our midst of so many foreign and colonial friends must have had not a little to do with the increased interest in [opera], an art form that has never so far appealed much to the average Englishman. There has been an unlooked for activity on the part of our native composers and large sums of money have been raised for war charities.'[19]

It is interesting to note that even at this comparatively late date, music was looked upon as a financial contributor to Britain's national well-being rather than as a recipient of subsidy to promote higher artistic standards. The patriotic feeling of the war years, however, clearly led the writer of the above extract to make exaggerated historical claims when he wrote that, 'It is safe to say that never in her history has England been so rich in composers of unquestioned talent as she is today.'

Although the outbreak of the Second World War was not unexpected, it found the BBC, the nation's principal patron of classical music, singularly unprepared. Most of the Corporation's activities were transferred to Bristol, and there was heavy reliance on unstructured programmes of gramophone records. A glance at a pre-war record catalogue shows the pitifully small amount of music from the standard repertory that was available.[20] Familiar complaints were made about the snobbery shown by concert-goers, and there was a plea for Reginald Foort, a popular theatre organist, to be invited to give a recital in St Paul's Cathedral. In fact, Foort was a Fellow of the Royal College of Organists.[21] Although some of his colleagues maintained that he had sold his soul, there is abundant evidence to show that he was thoroughly at home with the classical organ repertoire.

Despite the blackout, London's concert season began enthusiastically, if a little late.[22] Sadlers Wells opened on 30 September with a performance of Gounod's *Faust*; the London Symphony Orchestra's season began on 8 October; Wigmore Hall recitals began on 7 October; and, most influential of all, were Myra Hess's National Gallery lunchtime concerts from 10 October. W. R. Anderson complained about the generally doleful nature of post-1918 music[23], and at this juncture one may compare the opulence of pre-1914 ultra-Romanticism with the austerities of the 1920s.

The war years of 1939-45 saw no similar abrupt stylistic divide. The determination to preserve the status quo was nowhere more apparent than in church music[24], where, despite depletion caused by war service, strenuous attempts were made to maintain standards. Church attendance, though lower than in pre-1914 days, maintained pre-1939 levels, and National Days of Prayer were supported faithfully. A stream of books giving help to amateur choirmasters reflected this, and though he was in his middle 60s when war broke out, Sir Sydney Nicholson, the founder of the School of English Church Music, toured the land giving practical help. It was significant that in areas where there were many reserved occupations, choral standards fell hardly at all. Thanks to the sterling work of Conductor Malcolm Sargent and Chorus Master Herbert Bardgett, the Huddersfield Choral Society attained world status. Its 1945 recording of Elgar's *Dream of Gerontius* contains what is, by common consent, the finest choral singing of any recorded performance of the work. An equally famous choir, Leeds Philharmonic, only 15 miles away, and conducted by the eminent Sir Edward Bairstow, suffered severe depletion.

In February 1940 we read the following extraordinary statement: 'Sibelius, who is fortunately safe, despite the Russo-Finnish war, has released for performance his eighth Symphony.'[25] He was quoted as saying, 'It will help to sustain my valiant countrymen in their fight against the invader.' In fact, no such score has ever been found. Whether there once was one, which was later destroyed by the composer, is something we shall never know.

The invasion of Russia in 1941 stirred Dmitry Shostakovich into patriotic activity, which encapsulated the determination of his nation to resist the German invasion. Prior to 1939 he had had a chequered relationship with the Soviet authorities, who accused him of departing from the canons of Soviet realism in certain works. His Fifth Symphony of 1937 is subtitled 'A Soviet artist's reply to just criticism', and was looked upon at the time as a measure of the Government's control over the lives and thinking of composers. It is now regarded as a supreme masterpiece. At the time of Hitler's invasion of Russia, Shostakovich's star was in the ascendant. He was besieged in Leningrad during the early months, and at this time he composed the first three movements of his gigantic Leningrad Symphony. He dedicated his work to the city, and it seeks to express the heroism and sacrifices of its citizens. In October 1941 he was evacuated to Kuybishev and completed the work two months later. Performances took place on 5 March 1942 at Kuybishev, on 29 March in Moscow and on 5 August in Leningrad. A microfilmed score was flown to America, where Toscanini conducted the NBC Symphony Orchestra for an audience of millions. The work became the symbol of resistance against Nazism – 'Music written with the heart's blood,' wrote Carl Strindberg – and during the 1942-43 season there were 62 performances in the USA alone. Truly, if the war produced an international composer laureate, it was assuredly Shostakovich.

The power of music as a sustainer of morale was well known[26] and the study of musical appreciation in the forces as well as in civilian life developed apace, often in the most unlikely places, thanks to individual initiative. In the *Musical Times* of July 1941 Sir Percy Hull wrote about receiving a letter from a former chorister who was then a prisoner of war. It told of how he had conducted a performance of Bach's *St Matthew Passion* on Good Friday. The choir of 30 and the orchestra of 25 were made up of fellow prisoners. The letter also told of 'leading the orchestra and trying to play viola in a String Quartet'. He was also hopeful of taking up the cello in six months' time. 'We try to arrange a revue and a danceband once a month.' The YMCA, in Geneva, had supplied some instruments, while others were paid for by prisoners from their pay. Such humane treatment of prisoners gave some hope for the retention of civilised values in the post war-world. Olivier Messiaen, the great French composer, was taken prisoner in 1940, and while in captivity he was inspired to write one of his most famous works, the *Quartet for the End of Time*. It received its first performance in a Silesian camp before an audience of 5,000 fellow prisoners.

To most young musicians in Britain it was clear where their duty lay in wartime. Sir David Valentine Willcocks[27] writes:

'As almost all my Cambridge contemporaries during the academic year 1939-40 (except those in "reserved occupations", eg studying Medicine) were in the same position, I did not mind particularly having my studies being interrupted. I would certainly have felt very uncomfortable if I had not joined the forces along with my friends. I think that most of us thought that the war would not last long, despite the fall of France; we never envisaged a world-wide conflict lasting another five years... I think that all those with whom I served felt that we were engaged in a just war and that there was no alternative method of stopping Hitler's aggression in Europe... There were of course conscientious objectors, but they were few and far between, and there was generally a strong feeling of patriotism throughout the nation.'[28]

Willcocks served with the 5th Battalion of the Duke of Cornwall's Light Infantry. By the invasion of Normandy he had been promoted to Captain, and was Battalion Intelligence Officer throughout the campaign in North West Europe. His gallantry was revealed in numerous dispatches and recognised by the award of the Military Cross. While many musical servicemen found opportunities to use their professional skills to entertain their comrades, for Willcocks war service meant the exclusion of other considerations:

'During the war I gave no thought to my post-war career, though I imagined that it would be in music. It was only when I was due in November 1945 for "Class B" release (a category which gave priority of demobilisation to those whose Higher Education had been interrupted by service in the Forces) that I gave some consideration to the possibility of remaining in the Army for a few years, then retiring with a pension and embarking on a musical career with no financial worries... In general I know that I derived great benefit from my years of service in the Army. I met people from many different family backgrounds and I came to enjoy the comradeship and mutual trust that came from shared danger and discomfort. I appreciated the value of discipline and I learned how to make the best of difficult situations. I recognise how fortunate I was not to be killed or wounded nor to have suffered mental illness as a result of my war experience; accordingly I hope that I have learnt to count my blessings. I found many examples of self-sacrifice and unselfishness from people who looked for no reward other than the satisfaction of feeling that duty had been well done.'[29]

In comparison with musicians who believed that their patriotic duty transcended all other considerations, there were those, like Benjamin Britten, who, as the clouds of war threatened, expressed their conscientious objection by going to the United States of America with a view to settling there permanently. His left-wing political views were hard to reconcile with this action, and, it was claimed, represented a mockery of the sociological ideals he formerly professed.[30] In *The Sunday Times*, 8 June 1940, Ernest Newman described Britten as a 'thoroughbred' reckoning that he had been fighting the 'Battle of Britten'. George Baker, the well-known British baritone, reflecting the sentiments of many, replied, 'There are a number of musicians in this country who are well content to let Mr Newman have this dubious honour. Mr Britten is in America ... most of our music "thoroughbreds" are stabled in or near London and are directing all their endeavours towards winning the City and Suburban Victory Stakes, two classic events that form part of the programme called the "Battle of Britain", a programme in which Mr Britten has no part.' A letter from Pilot Officer E. R. Lewis asked if composers were the only ones that mattered. Were there not others who wished to work undisturbed? There was little virtue in saving one's skin at the cost of failing to do one's duty.

Others pointed out that the right to exercise one's conscience was one of the ideals for which Britain was fighting the war, and that Britain recognised conscientious objection to a degree unknown elsewhere. Nevertheless, it was remarkable how Britten and his friend Peter Pears were able to live a life of comparative comfort while fellow composer Michael Tippett underwent a prison sentence for his pacifist beliefs.

Other musicians, such as Alfred Melville Cook, while sympathetic to Tippett's stance, felt unable to follow his example. Cook was born in Gloucester, and at an early age became a chorister and later an articled pupil of the then cathedral organist, Herbert Sumsion. In 1937 he was appointed to the important post of Organist and Master of the Choristers at Leeds Parish Church. It says much for the humane attitudes at the War Office that Cook was granted deferment from National Service until he had completed his Doctorate, which he received from Durham University early in 1941. Cook's entire philosophy of life was non-violent, but he was prevented from registering as a conscientious objector partly out of a sense of patriotic duty, and partly because he feared professional consequences in the post-war world. Such fears were entirely justifiable. In these respects he was typical of many young men of his generation.

He saw war service in East Africa and in India, where he was brought face to face with sincere believers of other religions. There was something in Cook's make-up that made him sympathetic to Hinduism. Such experiences caused him to question the universal claims of Christianity, and for a long period he ceased to be an Anglican communicant. At Leeds the Vicars he served sympathised deeply with his position, realising that but for the war Melville Cook's Anglican orthodoxy would not have been threatened in this way, and they looked upon him as an earnest seeker after truth. Cook always maintained that his years at Leeds were the happiest of his life.

After ten less than happy years as Organist at Hereford Cathedral he became the much loved and highly respected Organist of the United Metropolitan Church, Toronto. On his return to England he lived in Cheltenham. He joked that since local church music standards were so poor he would join a denomination where there was no music, and became a Friend. But it has always seemed likely that he was drawn to Quakerism by a freedom from doctrinal constraints, and by the opportunity to uphold his pacifist principles.

A comparison was also made with those above military age who chose to remain in Britain, in the firing line. At the outbreak of war Myra Hess cancelled a lucrative overseas concert tour and stayed behind to promote the National Gallery Concerts. The departure of Sir Thomas Beecham, who in 1940 toured Australia, then went to the United States, where he remained until 1944, left the orchestra he had founded, the London Philharmonic (LPO), in dire financial straits. An appeal was made to Sydney Beer, a wealthy racehorse owner and amateur conductor, who had occasionally paid for the privilege of conducting the orchestra. He replied that such help would be forthcoming if he were made sole artistic director. To the LPO's great credit, the offer was turned down, whereupon Beer promptly formed his own orchestra, the National Symphony, securing some of the capital's best players by paying higher fees.[31] The LPO's vicissitudes were the subject of a film, *Battle for Music*, and received detailed mention in Thomas Russell's books, *Philharmonic* and *Philharmonic Decade*.

Help for the LPO came from an unexpected source. The bandleader Jack Hylton acted as impresario, and arranged for the orchestra to tour towns and cities where the appearance of a live orchestra was a rarity. Many such places lacked a suitable hall and the orchestra did some twice-nightly stints at Music Halls where such arrangements were the normal pattern. One such theatre was the Empire in Leeds. Programmes consisted of popular works, and during one of the Leeds concerts an air raid warning siren sounded. No one left the theatre and during Tchaikovsky's *1812* Overture it was difficult to distinguish between heavy orchestra percussion and the sound of anti-aircraft fire! The conductor who was most closely associated with these enterprises was Malcolm Sargent, whose work in the service of music was incalculable. He was able to relate to new audiences who realised for the first time that classical music had some appeal for them. Thomas Armstrong[32], later Principal of the Royal Academy of Music, described an audience of which he had been part in Llandudno as 'one of the most invigorating I have ever seen. The future of music lies in the hands of this new and young public.' Wigan, with a population of 100,000, heard its first live concert – a feast for the eye as much as for the ear – for 25 years. Sargent's frequent appearances with some of the country's leading intellects, like Julian Huxley and Bertrand Russell, in the popular *Brains Trust* radio programme, brought new respect for the profession, but the day when to admit that a lack of musical knowledge or interest reflected on a person's general education was many decades away.

Sir George Dyson, who had served in the First World War and was the author of *A Manual of Grenade Fighting*, which soon became a standard army textbook, was appointed Director of the Royal College of Music. In his address to his students, in September 1941, he reassured them about fears of lost technique while serving in the Forces: 'Brains, not muscles, determine quality. You will be all the better musicians for being willing helpers in the defence of the world.'[33] Certainly, for some individuals the war offered opportunities to take new musical directions. When Francis Alan Jackson, the distinguished organist, joined the forces he looked upon it as a resented interference in his personal and professional existence. However, war service enabled him to indulge in another musical interest, which has remained with him throughout his life, the Big Band. During the war Jackson expressed no desire to return to the humdrum life of a minor church musician, and there is little doubt that had he not been appointed Master of Music at York Minster, in 1946, the Big Band world would have found a new leader, and classical music would have lost one of its greatest organists.

Before the war John Barbirolli had attracted notice as a promising conductor, and whenever he directed provincial ensembles he invariably raised them above their customary standard. Even so, a ten-week contract as guest conductor of the New York Philharmonic Symphony Orchestra followed by a three-year stint as permanent conductor, in succession to Arturo Toscanini, raised many eyebrows. Yet Barbirolli's New York years showed him to be an undoubted world-class conductor. After the expiry of his second contract he returned to England in 1943 as permanent conductor of the Halle Orchestra, a post unfilled since the departure of Hamilton Harty in 1933. A Herculean task awaited him. During the war many of the Halle players also served as members of the BBC Northern Orchestra, and early in 1943 the BBC offered many of them permanent contracts in return for the Corporation's right to their exclusive services. In a time of great financial uncertainty the BBC offer was very tempting, and many players accepted it. This left the Halle seriously depleted, and on his arrival in Lancashire Barbirolli auditioned many unlikely players, including Norman Beatty, trombonist in the orchestra of an Oldham Music Hall, who was almost wholly unfamiliar with the symphonic repertory, and Enid Roper, a horn player with the amateur Leeds Symphony Orchestra. Both gave wonderful service to the Halle for many years. As early as the summer of his first year the Halle's concerts, under Barbirolli's direction, set new standards for wartime orchestral playing. His ability to create rich orchestral sonorities concealed the inevitably depleted numbers of the string section.

Though Barbirolli was a Londoner through and through, there was a deep-seated belief among British audiences that artists with foreign names were essentially better than our own. This prejudice created especial problems in wartime. There was much sympathy shown towards refugees, especially Jews, but letters in musical journals expressed fears that their presence would lead to unemployment among British artists. Officially, a distinction was made between escapees from friendly and enemy countries, and it was pointed out that no foreign artist could accept work from British nationals or societies without a work permit. The mechanical reproduction and broadcasting of music was seen as a real threat to live music, and the work of such bodies as ENSA and the Carnegie and Pilgrim Trusts saved many whose income had been reduced to almost starvation point.

There was no outright ban on the music of enemy countries, but because of the complexity of the music, and the lack of availability of scores, little post-1930 music from either Germany or Italy was broadcast.[34] The vacuum was filled by Russian cultural contacts and the music of Gliere, Khachaturian, Krannikov, Miaskovsky and Shostakovich, little of which had been heard in Britain pre-war. Curiously enough, the music of Alan Bush, a composer of avowed communist sympathies, failed, both then and subsequently, to establish itself in British musical life in a way that his talents undoubtedly justified. His Symphony's first movement describes capitalism, the second the middle class and politically conscious working class, and the finale the politically conscious and scientifically minded working class.[35] Critics commented on Bush's use of 12-note techniques in the first two movements, and 'wholesome diatonicism' in the third. It was generally agreed that there was a lack of inspiration behind the composer's scorn for the politically non-conscious, and the indignation was insufficiently eloquent to hold our attention. Of his *Fantasia on Soviet Themes*, the *Musical Times* described his intentions as better than his deeds.

A greater political maturity was shown generally during the Second World War in attitudes to the middle verse of the National Anthem, which became a source of indignation and embarrassment for tender consciences. However, the difference in attitude during the two World Wars is indeed striking. Harvey Grace, a man of much charm and sound Christian belief, wrote in 1915: 'If we could not and should not pray for the confounding of such politics as the violation of Belgium and the frustration of such knavish tricks as piracy and the use of poison gas and liquid fire, we have no right to be fighting them.'[36] Yet in 1944 Bernard Shaw, no less, offered an alternative verse:

'O Lord our God arise,
All our salvation lies
In Thy great hands.
Centre his thoughts on Thee
Let him God's captain be
Thine to eternity
God save the King.'

It never caught on. Elgar was happy to set all three verses of the original. Britten, characteristically, set verse one dolefully and left out verse two entirely, in his 1962 setting.

Berta Geissmar, who had been Wilhelm Furtwangler's secretary, published her controversial book, *The Baton and the Jackboot*, soon after her arrival in this country. She pointed out that 'Goebbels thinks War every minute and shouts Peace every second!' During the Weimar Republic the arts had been starved, but under Hitler there was lavish endowment of those works of art that upheld Nazi tastes. Festivals, theatrical weeks, exhibitions and literary congresses were arranged to disguise to foreigners the Government's true intentions. Yet even after the war began the Nazis' financial support for music in Germany put that of the British Government utterly to shame.

Furtwangler maintained that he had supported the Nazis because he was apolitical (as did Richard Strauss), and in order to save Jewish members of the Berlin Philharmonic Orchestra. Yet he must have known that while he was conducting Beethoven's Ninth Symphony, thousands were being put to death.

While during the immediate post-war period some German musicians were suffering the odium of their past, others whose admiration for the Nazi philosophy was more overt, such as Clemens Krauss and Elizabeth Schwarzkopf, escaped censure. Despite his immense wealth and the astronomic sales of his recordings, critical reviews of Herbert Von Karajan's performances were undoubtedly tinged by prejudice against him.

In the *Musical Times* of September 1945 it was reported that there were weekly concerts by either the Berlin Philharmonic or the Opera Orchestra. A concert billed for 22 July had to be postponed for five days because of the failure of the electricity supply. The programme consisted of Handel's *Concerto Grosso* in D Minor, Ravel's *Spanish Rhapsody*, Mussorgsky's *Night on the Bare Mountain* and Rimsky-Korsakov's *Scheherezade*. Though the Opera House was badly damaged, local artists put together concerts of operatic excerpts most weeks. It says much for the human spirit and for the capacity of music to heal sores that, notwithstanding the material and other damage that Berlin suffered, such strenuous attempts were made immediately after the war to restore the city's musical life.

Music also expressed widespread feelings of shock and incomprehension concerning the sheer scale and inhumanity of the conflict. Probably unique in music is *Memorial to Lidice*, the work of Bohusla Martinu, the Czech composer. *Memorial to Lidice* uses dissonant language to express the pity and horror of that tragedy. The village of Lidice was situated a few miles north-west of Prague, and before 1939 had a population of around 450. It was liquidated on 10 June 1942 as a reprisal for the assassination of Reinhard Heydrich, the brutal Nazi ruler of the Protectorate of Bohemia and Moravia. All the men were shot (about 200), the women were deported, mainly to Ravensbrüch concentration camp, and the children sent to German institutions. Many disappeared without trace. The choice of Lidice appears to have been an entirely arbitrary one, and as an act of brutality has few equals in the annals of modern war.

Recommended reading

Scholes, P. A., *The Oxford Companion to Music* (London: Oxford University Press, 1970)
Walker, E. P., *A History of Music in England* (Oxford: Clarendon, 1952)
Young, P. M., *A History of British Music* (New York: W. W. Norton, 1967)

Notes

[1] Webern himself was a victim of the Second World War, shot by a US soldier on the balcony of his home in Austria, after misunderstanding orders to obey a curfew.
[2] Programme note from John Scott Whiteley's organ recital in York Minster given during the 1999 York Early Music Festival
[3] *Musical Times* [hereafter MT], 1914, p571
[4] Ibid, p605
[5] D. F. Webster, *Parish Past and Present* (Leeds: 1988) p81
[6] MT, 1914, p625
[7] MT, 1915, p104
[8] Ibid, p107
[9] Ibid, p176
[10] Ibid, p113
[11] MT, 1917, p410
[12] MT, 1915, p305
[13] Ibid, p400
[14] Ibid, p521
[15] MT, 1918, p468
[16] Ibid, p446
[17] Interview in the *Sunday Telegram*, 18 August 1918
[18] MT, 1918, p554. This was a 'Fun Concert' arranged by Sir Landon Ronald in aid of War Charities.

[19] MT, 1919, p9

[20] MT, 1939, p712

[21] Ibid, p721

[22] Ibid, p728

[23] Ibid, p747

[24] Ibid, p760

[25] MT, 1940, p90

[26] MT, 1941, p274; 1944, p300

[27] Organist of King's College, Cambridge, 1957-74; Director of the Royal College of Music, 1974-84

[28] Sir David Valentine Willcocks, letter to the author, 3 March 2000

[29] Ibid

[30] MT, 1944, p234. Correspondence on this controversial matter was closed on p376.

[31] Ibid, p78

[32] Ibid, p10

[33] Ibid, p378

[34] MT, 1942, p283

[35] Ibid, p275

[36] MT, 1915, p541

Chapter 24

Leisure and entertainment

Matthew Taylor

The provision of entertainment in wartime has always been controversial. In both World Wars the idea of widespread participation in sporting pursuits and other forms of entertainment caused considerable debate. Some insisted that it was inappropriate, or simply immoral, to 'play' while others were laying down their lives for the country. A football match or a visit to the theatre could easily be regarded as an unnecessary and frivolous distraction from the more important focus on the front line. At best, those involved in the provision of wartime entertainment were accused of having misjudged the national mood; at worst they were chastised for lacking patriotism. Those who advocated 'carrying on', on the other hand, emphasised the role of entertainment in ensuring normality. By providing people with a break from the drudgery of war work or deflecting their minds from anxiously waiting for news from the front, entertainment was an essential part of the business of maintaining morale. Continuing to 'play' could also be interpreted as an act of defiance against the external enemy; a way of signalling a determination to protect established traditions and cultures. Pelham Warner, Deputy Assistant Secretary of the Marylebone Cricket Club (MCC) during the Second World War, commented that 'if Goebbels had been able to broadcast that the War had stopped cricket at Lord's it would have been valuable propaganda for the Germans'.[1] Few pretended that life could go on as before, and most accepted that sacrifices had to be made, but 'sacrifice' could be interpreted in a variety of ways.

The disposition to 'carry on' was more pronounced in the Second World War than it had been in the First. In 1939-45 organised leisure was less frequently viewed as counterproductive, and was increasingly regarded as complementary to the war effort. Much of this can be explained by the fact that while the First War was focused on the trenches of the Western Front, during the second conflict the entire population, civilian and military, experienced war at first hand. Entertainment itself was profoundly affected by the enhanced circumstances of 'total war', which led to a level of state intervention that had not been witnessed in the earlier conflict. Yet while 1939-45 might well be considered a 'good' war for the entertainment industry as a whole in a way that 1914-18 had not been, it would be a mistake to submerge the diversity of wartime experience (in this as in so many other areas) beneath the search for general trends.[2] And it is equally important to recognise comparisons as to draw contrasts. Indeed, in many spheres of leisure activity the Second World War seems to have been approached as if it were essentially a replay of the First. The Ivanhoe Cricket Club in Leicester was certainly not the only organisation to decide to 'follow the procedure of the last war' when it suspended its programme of fixtures in 1940.[3] The First War provided models to be copied as well as lessons to be learned.

Clearly a distinction needs to be made between entertainments such as cinema, radio and, to some extent, music and theatre, which were particularly susceptible to state control, and organised sport, which remained relatively free from outside influence. The Defence of the Realm Act of 1914 guaranteed wide state powers, particularly in the nationalisation of key industries like mining, shipbuilding and the railways, and in the control of labour. However, leisure and entertainment were generally left untouched.[4] The propaganda opportunities offered by the theatre and cinema, in particular, were utilised by the Government but not as a fundamental prop of domestic policy. A committee for propaganda in theatres and music halls was created, and the Government sponsored the production of patriotic plays and films, but a Ministry of Information was not established to oversee this activity until 1918. Through the Films Division of the newly formed MoI, cinema became much more closely supervised during the Second War, both as a propaganda tool and a means of boosting morale; the BBC played a similar role in broadcasting. Quasi-governmental bodies such as the Entertainments National Service Association (ENSA) and the Council for the Encouragement of Music and the Arts (CEMA) provided an official framework for the entertainment of service and civilian personnel, as well as for the employment of actors, musicians and other artistes.[5]

Sport, however, less obviously a source of propaganda, managed by and large to resist the wartime trend towards state intervention and in both periods continued to be run mainly according to the principles of voluntarism. There was some debate towards the end of the First World War over the creation of a Ministry of Recreation, but the idea generally received short shrift among sports administrators anxious to protect their independence.[6] Organisations like the Football Association (FA) were more closely involved with the wartime authorities in the Second World War, particularly by contributing to the 'Fitness for Service' scheme and the establishment of training centres for the Civil Defence service. And while FA Secretary Stanley Rous's chairmanship of the Civil Defence Sports Committee was a concrete sign of that sport's commitment to the war effort, innovations of this kind by no means challenged the tradition of British sport to govern itself.[7] We are not directly concerned here with the relationship between entertainment and propaganda, or the role of the cinema and broadcasting. Our focus is on the varied experiences of individuals and groups involved mainly in sport, but also in the popular theatre, under the peculiar circumstances of war.

The relationship between leisure activities and the state becomes clearer if we consider the different responses to the outbreak of war in 1914 and 1939. With little guidance from the authorities, the governing bodies of sport and many entertainment establishments were left to decide for themselves whether to continue. Expecting a short war, amateur sports such as hockey, golf, rugby union and lawn tennis discontinued competition immediately in 1914 and dedicated their resources and manpower to the war effort. By contrast, commercial operations like the theatre and music hall and sports like football, racing, rugby league and cricket, which employed professional staff and were run along business lines, felt that they had little choice but to carry on until hostilities ceased. The FA, for one, offered to stop playing immediately in a letter to the War Office, but was advised that any decision was 'a matter for the discretion of the Association'. There was no compulsion from the Government, which recognised 'the difficulties involved in taking such an extreme step and ... would deprecate anything being done which does not appear to be called for by the present situation'.[8]

With no conscription during the first two years of war, the worlds of sport and entertainment were publicly judged on their attitude to the enlistment of recruits. For the authorities and players of rugby union, in particular, this was the perfect opportunity to display moral superiority over the businessmen of professional spectator sport. The amateur Rugby Football Union (RFU) appealed to national, county and club sides to suspend fixtures indefinitely and for its players to join up. Its Welsh counterpart felt confident that its players, as 'the very pick of men eligible for service in the Army, and considering that Welshman have the reputation of not wanting either in patriotism and pluck', would enlist in large numbers.[9] London's Blackheath club was more forthright: 'It is the duty of every able-bodied man of enlistable age to offer personal war service to his king and country, and ... every Rugby footballer of the present day comes within the scope of Lord Kitchener's appeal.'[10]

Cricket was also seen to be answering the call. Wisden reported that some 1,200 officers had been notable public school cricketers and there were clearly many more working-class players represented in the rank and file.[11] County cricket, with the additional concerns of wage bills for its professionals, completed the remainder of its 1914 season. W. G. Grace's famous letter to *The Sportsman* on 27 August 1914 – in which he considered it 'not fitting at a time like the present that able-bodied men should play day after day and pleasure-seekers look on' – is often interpreted as heralding the end of county cricket, but it was not until late January that the 1915 championship was officially abandoned.[12] Notwithstanding some criticism, the county game's contribution to the recruitment drive was well publicised. In December 1914 *The Times* published a list of 186 county cricketers serving in the forces, including 'many test players' and five England captains. By May 1915, 2,100 of the 5,300 MCC members had apparently enlisted, the remainder probably being too old for military service. In addition, well-known amateur batsmen such as Gilbert Jessop and Archie MacLaren addressed potential volunteers at recruitment drives.[13]

The number of volunteers from the theatrical profession was proudly recorded in the journal *Era*. Some 170 actors had enlisted by the end of September 1914, a figure that had risen to 1,500 (possibly 15 per cent of the profession) by the following July. Enlistment was facilitated by the creation of the Artists' Rifles for actors, musicians and artists, which acted as a form of pre-training for voluntary recruits.[14] Sportsman's Battalions were also formed, such as that under Edgar Mobbs, the Northampton and England rugby international. Mobbs is possibly the most celebrated sporting recruit of the Great War. Initially denied a commission because of his age, he enlisted 250 members for his battalion, was wounded twice and received the DSO, but was eventually killed at Zillebeke in July 1917. His enthusiasm and self-sacrifice epitomised the role of the public-school-educated amateur sportsman, whose contribution to the war was measured by enlistment and casualty figures.[15] By contrast, professional football was widely criticised for continuing its programme during the first year of the war and the allegedly poor recruitment record that resulted from this.[16]

In 1939 the immediate introduction of conscription and the risk of air attack restricted the decision-making power of sporting and entertainment institutions. At the outbreak of hostilities on 3 September the Government issued an order that 'all places of entertainment and outdoor sports meetings' be closed.[17] Many organisations and clubs thus hardly had any choice but to suspend operations and cancel programmes. With the experience of 1914 in mind, the football authorities were among the first to act. Three days after the official declaration, the Scottish FA suspended all football played under its jurisdiction, and, on 8 September, the English FA followed suit, announcing that all football, except that organised by the armed forces, was abandoned 'until official notice is given to the contrary'.[18] The RFU had cancelled its fixtures by 12 September, while the close season in cricket meant that public gestures were more necessary than actual decisions. Below the national associations and the professional establishments, a range of local committees met in the first weeks of war to consider the moral and practical implications of continuing. The vast majority appears to have decided to stop, for the short term at least. A writer for Mass-Observation described the traumatic effect of this initial ban on competitive sport. It was like

> '…a knock-out blow, a complete scattering of the sport world to a standstill… The magic habit of recurring matches and pools and all that the other elaborate weekly cycles brought out in the press, was broken. As anthropologists know, the breaking of an established habit which occurs at regular intervals, can have deep repercussions. People become "conscious" of what they are doing instead of taking it for granted each week as an essential part of the routine of living.'[19]

Yet there was little obvious consternation from within sporting circles and few objections to the Government's decision. The response from the theatrical world was more critical. In a letter to *The Times*, George Bernard Shaw wrote that the closure of theatres and picture houses was 'a masterstroke of unimaginative stupidity'. In a more balanced communication, the director and producer Basil Dean pointed out that 'entertainment cannot be turned on and off like a tap', and suggested that the decision to open or close places of entertainment be taken out of the hands of local authorities and delegated to a central entertainment authority consisting of representatives of metropolitan and provincial theatre, cinema exhibitors, sporting bodies as well as the civil defence authorities.[20] In the event, agitation from outside interests and, no doubt, recognition that the initial order had been excessive, led to the ban soon being lifted. Cinemas and theatres located outside cities, and sports grounds in low-risk areas, were permitted to re-open on 9 September, and five days later opening was extended to city venues, providing they closed at 10 o'clock, and West End theatres, which were to shut at 6.[21] On 21 September the Home Office agreed to a revised programme of football, but placed some restrictions on attendances. Crowds were limited to 8,000 for most clubs in evacuation areas, or 15,000 for those with large stadiums, and all matches were subject to authorisation by the local police.[22] In addition, the requisitioning of buildings and playing fields, the scarcity of equipment as well as transport and blackout restrictions had an immediate and dramatic impact on the nature of leisure activity. Angus Calder thought that 'no national institution of comparable importance had been so badly hit by the outbreak of war' as sport, but, as we shall see, in most cases the recovery was swift, if not always complete.[23]

The imposition, then relaxation, of Government restrictions in the first three weeks was to be repeated during subsequent phases of the war.[24] Spectacular entertainments like the theatre, football and racing were particularly sensitive to the changing fortunes of war, which forced them to adapt and re-evaluate policy at every stage. In this respect we should keep in mind that we are not simply comparing two single events, but charting the ebb and flow of wartime experience and the implications this had on what people did, said and felt in this area as in others. The remainder of the discussion will focus more specifically on the way in which different types of sport and commercial entertainment managed in wartime.

More than any other sport, cricket was symbolic of a particular notion of Englishness represented by images of morality and tradition and by the values of sportsmanship and fair play, characteristics that were particularly apposite during wartime.[25] Yet while cricket in both 1914-18 and 1939-45 was unequivocally patriotic and dedicated to the war effort, there was more to the game than this. Wartime cricket took a variety of forms. At the head of the administrative structure, the MCC adopted a policy of self-sacrifice during the First World War. Lord's and other club buildings were used to accommodate various military units, while those staff who had not enlisted busied themselves in the pavilion making haynets for Army horses. £50,000 was also invested by the club in 5 per cent war loans. The MCC continued to send sides to compete against the public schools, and some cricket was still played at Lord's, but these were restricted to service and charity matches.[26] The journalist Alfred Gibson was struck at first by the desolate atmosphere when he visited Lord's in May 1915 to interview MCC secretary F. E. Lacey. He left convinced that 'cricket was not dead but only hibernating'.[27]

County cricket tended to follow the MCC lead. The pavilions at Derbyshire, Lancashire and Nottinghamshire functioned as military hospitals, while Leicestershire's Aylestone Road ground became the headquarters of the Leicestershire Volunteer Regiment and a remount depot. The suspension of first-class cricket in 1915 meant that, as at Lord's, most counties only hosted school and military matches on a regular basis. Charity fixtures involving celebrated cricketers were arranged, but these were few and far between, amounting to only eight days' play in 1917 and 17 in 1918.[28] There is some evidence, however, that the wartime break in first-class cricket had a beneficial effect on the finances of county clubs. Professionals were no longer employed, there was fewer ground staff, match expenses diminished and inflation reduced the burden of debt repayments. A significant proportion of members were persuaded to continue subscription payments, and additional appeals for funds allowed counties like Derbyshire, Hampshire, Leicestershire and Somerset to pay off pre-war debts and others to record profits. The picture was less rosy for Essex, Northamptonshire and Warwickshire, whose financial record had deteriorated marginally, while Gloucestershire's financial crisis was eased when it sold its ground at Bristol to Fry's for £10,000.[29]

At the lower level of league and club cricket, survival was equally (and often more) precarious. In the prestigious leagues of the North and the Midlands, the impact of the war was mixed. Most chose to continue, but crowds were reduced and the increased travel difficulties meant that as the war progressed clubs either closed down or shortened their fixture lists. The Lancashire League, for example, abandoned its junior competition in 1915, outlawed professionalism in 1916 and shut down completely in 1917 and 1918.[30] The most successful competition was the Bradford League, which maintained a full programme throughout the hostilities and took advantage of county cricket's inactivity to entice some of its best players. The limit of one professional per team was relaxed for the duration of the war, allowing a club like Saltaire to acquire Sidney Barnes, and Idle to engage the famous Surrey and England batsman Jack Hobbs. At the start of the 1917 season, no fewer than 17 county players were employed by Bradford League clubs, and Keighley was apparently so well stocked that some professionals had to play for the second team.[31] Attendances shot up. Undercliffe and Great Horton both recorded crowds of over 3,000 on one May Saturday in 1916, which would have been unthinkable before the war, and one newspaper estimated that gate receipts had increased six-fold between 1914 and 1916.[32] But generally league cricket limped along as best it could.

Club cricket, without a fixed competitive structure, could stop more easily. Many clubs at town, village and neighbourhood level did not play at all after 1914, but the more established managed to stay afloat by arranging occasional social events and eliciting the help of members and benefactors. Ivanhoe CC in Leicester decided initially to run only its First XI for the 1915 season, but the loss of players to the forces led the club to resolve that 'we do not carry out any Fixtures under the name of the Ivanhoe CC'. A depleted committee gathered twice in May 1915 to confirm the cancellation of its matches for that summer but did not meet again until February 1919. After the war, Huyton CC in Liverpool simply tried to repeat its 1914 fixtures using the same opponents and the same dates.[33] Not surprisingly, less is known of those clubs who for various reasons were unable to resume activities in 1919.

More top-level cricket was played in the Second World War. Pelham Warner's suggestion that 'cricket enjoyed a boom' was perhaps exaggerated, but the game certainly flourished in a way that it had not in the previous war.[34] The MCC once again strove to ensure normality as far as was practical by continuing to stage representative and charity matches and fulfilling its public school fixtures. But there were also some innovations, most notably the British Empire and London Counties XIs, which drew on leading cricketers to play one-day charity matches throughout the war. Most importantly, perhaps, cricket (like football, rugby and boxing) was dominated by the services. The 'Phoney War' period, especially, and the fact that service personnel spent a fair proportion of their time in Britain, placed the military at the centre of the domestic sporting scene. Sides representing the Army, the RAF and the Dominions services – along with the Civil Defence organisations – were prominently featured at Lord's and the other major grounds, as well as in the pages of the press and the cricket bible, *Wisden*. The County Championship was once again scrapped and most counties took a similar stance regarding recruitment and the payment of members' subscriptions as in 1914-18. Kent went so far as to quote its 1915 appeal in a circular letter. Despite the loss of players to the forces and munitions work, some counties endeavoured to play on. Nottinghamshire managed to arrange six matches at Trent Bridge during the summer of 1940, and organised local home and away matches with Derbyshire and Leicestershire in 1942. Lancashire, another relatively active county, proposed a modified regional competition, but the MCC rejected this as impractical and inappropriate.[35]

League cricket was equally active but possibly less prominent than before. The Bradford League repeated its policy of bringing in stars of county and league cricket like Len Hutton and Learie Constantine. In 1943 the League engaged more than 70 county cricketers, 14 of whom were test players.[36] Elsewhere, those competitions that suspended the payment of professionals were often able to field locally based 'guest' players engaged by the services or in war work. Even if it is true that more people had access to the game as players and spectators than ever before, the obstacles to cricket in towns and villages were undoubtedly greater than in the First World War. What seemed to have changed was the will to 'carry on'. The Club Cricket Conference, which represented the more socially exclusive clubs in the Home Counties, noted the likelihood of private grounds being commandeered by the military or Government authorities but resolved that 'where it is practicable clubs should carry on cricket in 1940'.[37] Shepshed Town CC played in a local competition until this was closed down in 1942, but still managed to complete 19 friendlies the following season with the help of a number of players who were prepared to cycle long distances for a game.[38] Rugby CC survived to celebrate its centenary season in 1944 by organising 'games with Clubs in the town and immediate vicinity'. The club's Souvenir Programme summed up the difficulties faced:

> 'The inevitable restrictions of these days preclude us from arranging a programme as extensive and varied as would be possible in normal times. Journeys must be restricted to essential purposes, food rationing ... does not permit dispensing hospitality on the traditional scale, and we know that many to whom we should delight to extend welcome will be unable to be with us.'[39]

War obviously had a greater impact on professional cricketers than it did on amateurs. It ought not to be forgotten that the suspension of contracts left dozens of players out of work. With a wife and four children to support, Jack Hobbs was one who faced immediate financial problems in 1914. He took a job in a munitions factory and, as we have seen, supplemented his income by appearing regularly in the Bradford League, a decision that provoked widespread comment and a fair amount of criticism. Lord Hawke, the aristocratic President of the MCC and Yorkshire CC, thought that the engagement of cricketers of military age was 'scandalous'. The northern weekly *Athletic News* debated the issue at great length on its front page, but concluded that until conscription was introduced players like Hobbs had every right to receive a wage for playing cricket.[40] When he finally enlisted in 1916, Hobbs would have found the distinction between gentlemen and players neatly replicated in the division between the officer class and the other ranks. This was less evident in the Second War, when a number of professional cricketers managed to obtain commissions alongside their amateur colleagues. The RAF was especially open to promotion by merit, allowing both the Kent wicket-keeper Leslie Ames and the Middlesex batsman William Edrich to become Squadron Leaders. This apparent social levelling, along with the end of the symbolic use of separate changing-rooms at Lord's, led the professional Dennis Brookes to suggest that the relationships between amateurs and professionals 'could never be the same again'. Even *Wisden's* editor called for the end of a social distinction that he considered to be 'humbug' and 'vastly absurd'.[41]

What is more, war had a profound effect on many cricket careers. After the cessation of first-class cricket in 1915, there was some discussion of providing county matches for professionals above the military age, players whose careers were effectively finished with the outbreak of war. The continued but haphazard nature of Second World War cricket also contributed to doubts about the future. One player recalled: 'I think my greatest worries came during the war. Although I managed to play some cricket in the meantime, it was difficult to know what was going to happen in 1946. Would I still be good enough? There was no way of knowing whether another one hundred good players would suddenly spring up.'[42] Don Kenyon, meanwhile, just 15 years old in 1939, considered himself to be one of 'a new breed of professional cricketer' for whom the wartime game had provided valuable experience and accelerated promotion opportunities. After the war, Kenyon's Worcestershire side was apparently split into two factions, representing the 'old' professionals who had played before 1939 and the 'new' intake.[43]

Commentators were similarly divided on the nature and value of wartime cricket. It is not uncommon for cricket writers and historians to regard the war years primarily as an 'interruption' in the careers of players and the development of the game. A spectator at a match between teams representing England and the Dominions at Lord's in 1918 commented that, 'There were moments …when it was possible to forget that it was war cricket, but the moments were few'.[44] Despite the greater numbers who watched cricket in the Second World War, R. C. Robertson-Glasgow did not regard the wartime game as comparable to what had preceded it: 'For most of us the mere sight of such players is enough. It reminds us of what has been and what soon will be again … it has been cricket without competition; a snack not a meal.'[45] By contrast, David Lemmon has written that the significance of wartime cricket matches

'…cannot be overemphasised. For a young generation growing up in desperate circumstances, they created an everlasting love of the game, and they brought alive cricketers whose previous existences had only been as pictures on cigarette cards. For an older generation, they, like the concerts given by Myra Hess in the National Gallery, had a richer significance.'[46]

After its 'crisis season' of 1914-15, top-level football in Britain survived by modifying its rules and truncating its competitions. In England there was to be no League Championship, no FA Cup and no international fixtures, and trophies and medals were not awarded. Neither was the remuneration of players permitted, although football employees were free to guest for other clubs 'as a matter of convenience of work and residence'.[47] For the 1915-16 season 30 Football League clubs competed in regional competitions based around Northern and Midland sections, while the leading metropolitan clubs joined together to form the London Combination. Newcastle United, Middlesbrough and Sunderland, relatively isolated in the North East and with a majority of players engaged in war work, chose not to compete, as did clubs like Aston Villa, West Bromwich Albion and Blackburn Rovers, which considered the organisation of competitive football both financially impractical and immoral. Nevertheless, these skeletal competitions continued throughout the war, partly as a result of the imposition of income-sharing arrangements whereby the richer and better-supported clubs helped out the weak. The Scottish League, meanwhile, abandoned its second division, but the top division continued to function throughout the war years. However, certain sacrifices had to be made: wages were reduced in 1915 from a maximum of £4 10s to £1 per week, and in 1917 Aberdeen, Dundee and Raith Rovers (from Kirkcaldy) were persuaded to retire so as to reduce travel expenses for the majority of clubs based in the central belt between Glasgow and Edinburgh.[48]

If the basic pattern of regional competition, guest players and transport difficulties was repeated during the Second World War, the details were very different. In England and Wales football initially reverted to a series of regional groupings, which included all but six of the Football League's 88 member clubs, while special wartime cup competitions were established. The decision in 1942 to divide clubs into simple north-south sections was less well received, especially by clubs from the capital, which broke away to form their own London War League.[49] Additionally, there were regular home internationals, representative matches and, of course, inter-service games. But despite improvements in the planning and formalisation of arrangements, organised football was much more directly affected by wartime conditions than had been the case in 1914-18. Even if the immediate threat of air attack failed to materialise, disruption was often caused in areas where air raids were frequent. At first the Home Office had ordered that play must stop every time an alert was sounded, a situation that could cause delays and even lead to the abandonment of matches. At the height of the Battle of Britain, one match at Stamford Bridge apparently took three hours to complete; one of the players, Joe Mercer, remembered that the sirens were heard so often that 'we were in and out, in and out'.[50] Even so, the adoption of the 'spotter' system at most grounds and the reduction of daylight bombing after 1942 led to a significant increase in attendances and a safer atmosphere at most matches.[51]

Travel restrictions were less easily solved. Rail services were limited and could be withdrawn from time to time, while professional teams were only permitted to travel by road within a 50-mile radius (25 miles for amateur teams). The transport authorities were loath to make special arrangements for football teams. One representative of the Ministry of War Transport informed a Football League deputation in December 1941 that the game ultimately had 'to bow to more essential considerations'. Another asked the deputation 'to consider the effect on public opinion in the USA, where petrol had been rationed so that it could be sent to England, if it were known that the petrol was being used to convey football teams'.[52] Under these circumstances, players were known to arrive at matches by any means necessary, some finding lifts on milk lorries, fire engines and even in planes.[53]

As we have seen of cricketers, the outbreak of war had major consequences for professional footballers. Although most did not lose their jobs in 1914, the wages of professionals in England were cut, with the savings put into a central fund to support clubs struggling to meet wage bills. The union objected to this, and some players refused to sign new contracts, but eventually agreed to the scheme because 'throughout the country workers … were having to sacrifice in a similar manner'.[54] The termination of contracts the following season caused greater distress and, despite the increasing severity of the war in Europe, calls for the re-introduction of payment were not uncommon. In August 1916 the former Union Chairman, Charlie Roberts, opined that, 'If a player is ineligible for the army or working on munitions he should not be debarred from picking up a few shillings extra… I do feel that the player has been the MUG too long. Some are only earning now about 3s a week instead of their £4/£5… Players, come along and show your British pluck – for heavens sake, stick up for your rights!'[55] Similarly, in September 1939 the future for many looked bleak and uncertain. As Peter Doherty, an inside-forward with Manchester City, later recalled:

> '…the cleavage was a harsh one; contracts were automatically torn up, and for those players who had families to support and no savings to fall back on, the immediate prospect was grave. It was a grim lesson for the professionals… Without a scrap of consideration or sentiment, our means of livelihood were simply jettisoned, and we were left to find fresh ones as best we could.'[56]

When football resumed on an ad hoc basis, the rewards for players were limited. They could receive no more than 30 shillings per match in England (£2 in Scotland), in contrast with the pre-war limit of £8. The players' union reported that 'many players could not get a game nor find employment' and that some 'had no income whatsoever'.[57] Few players had other skills to fall back on. Only one of Heart of Midlothian's eight internationals, for example, had an occupation other than football.[58]

Not all footballers suffered to the same extent. Some of the leading players became Physical Training Instructors (PTIs) in the Army or the RAF. By January 1940 the FA could report that 74 footballers had successfully passed out as Army Sergeant-Instructors and that a further 40 had been accepted for RAF training.[59]

Matt Busby, a 31-year-old Scottish international when the war began, was one of the first batch to undergo training at Aldershot. In 1944, when the Allies invaded Italy, Busby was made Officer-in-Charge of the British Army team sent to entertain the troops in battle areas. He was responsible for the training, tactics and selection of the team and also for the general discipline of the footballer-soldiers under his command. This proved to be invaluable experience for Busby's subsequent position as manager of Manchester United, which he began a month after demobilisation in October 1945.[60] Joining up did not prevent suggestions that footballers (and sportsmen in general) were having it easy. Indeed, while the playing of football was no longer considered unpatriotic, it remained a sensitive issue both at home and abroad. Even in the course of defending football's contribution to the war effort, the editor of the West Bromwich Albion club programme could comment that 'some famous footballers who had joined the army seem to be doing more football than military service'.[61] Willie Watson, a member of Busby's Army team in Italy, remembered being derided by shouts of 'come on the D-Day Dodgers' during one match, and Tom Finney also admitted that during his time with the Royal Armoured Corps in Egypt and the Middle East he 'often wondered if it was right that I should go on playing while others were fighting'.[62]

As an industry based on a considerable labour force, an extensive railway network and the use of vast areas of land (not to mention a close association with gambling), it was inevitable that horse racing would be subject to wartime curtailment. That it was able to continue in some form during both wars was testament to the social influence of the Jockey Club and the leading breeders and owners, together with their ability to adapt to changing circumstances. Rail problems and the use of racecourse facilities by the military led to the cancellation of a series of major meetings during the first months of the Great War. In October 1914 the Jockey Club resolved that racing should continue 'where local conditions will permit and where the feeling of the locality is not adverse to the meeting being held'.[63] Press objections crystallised in opposition to the Ascot Festival, the social side of which was considered particularly incongruous with a country at war. In the event, the practical considerations of transportation led to a compromise in 1915 whereby the majority of courses, including Ascot, Epsom and Doncaster, were closed, but Newmarket, the industry's headquarters, stayed open. The Derby, the Oaks and the St Leger were thus transferred to Newmarket, while the Grand National also moved in 1916 from Aintree in Liverpool to Gatwick.[64]

Racing's primary justification to continue in 1914-18 – its role in bloodstock breeding for the cavalry – was of less significance during the Second World War.[65] Moreover, its function alongside football and cricket in sustaining morale was challenged by Mass-Observation, which reported in April 1942 that over half the population thought racing should discontinue 'mainly due to the feeling that it is a minority sport for the rich'.[66] Even Lord Rosebery felt that the necessity for racing was not recognised 'outside the circle of owners and breeders'.[67] Under these circumstances, it was hardly surprising that National Hunt Racing closed down completely in September 1942, only to be revived in January 1945.[68] Flat racing was once again centred on Newmarket and a handful of local meetings. Trainers, jockeys and the vast majority of racecourse companies suffered substantial financial losses. At Leicester, the requisitioning of facilities by the military led to the cancellation of the 1941 racing programme and the immediate reduction of directors' fees and staff salaries. The course was not de-requisitioned until April 1946.[69]

According to the referee Eugene Corri, 'Of all sports during the [First World] War none lived a more lusty life than boxing, none thrived so, none ate itself more surely into the affections of the people.'[70] Boxing had reached a peak of popularity in the years preceding 1914, and in many respects was remarkably unaffected by the outbreak of war. Between 1914 and 1916 the heavyweight 'Bombardier' Billy Wells competed as often as he had before, including three fights against Dick Smith. The Welshman Jimmy Wilde won and lost the British flyweight title over the course of two bouts in late 1914 and early 1915. Both boxers resisted enlistment and defended their stance publicly, but seem to have lost little popularity as a result.[71] Neither did Freddie Welsh, who moved to America, where he offered to arrange boxing shows to fund a sportsmen's regiment, or Ted 'Kid' Lewis, who spent the entire war in the United States, fighting 88 bouts.[72] In Britain, Monday evening shows continued at the National Sporting Club in Covent Garden, later supplemented by weekly 'American nights' involving US service troops, but by the second half of the war boxing programmes were less frequent and generally less well-attended.

The resilience of professional boxing during the Second World War has barely been recognised by historians. Calder's only comment on boxing was that it became a 'minor butt of public opprobrium'[73], but there is a great deal of evidence that the sport thrived in certain areas. Liverpool, for instance, seems to have become a centre for wartime boxing. The city hosted an average of 37 shows a year between 1939 and 1945, reaching a peak of 61 in 1942. With admission prices reduced and good publicity, many of these shows sold out. The boxers themselves either worked locally in 'preferred' industries such as docking or the Merchant Navy, were stationed close by with their military units, or boxed while on leave. Additionally, promoters could call on refugees and military personnel from France, Czechoslovakia, the United States and Canada.[74] Boxing flourished in the services as it had done in the First World War. Civilian professionals were segregated from amateurs but were permitted to box on the same bill and to spar with one another in exhibition contests.[75]

Based around private clubs and often played on secluded courses, golf was an activity that theoretically could continue away from the public gaze. In 1914 major tournaments were cancelled and club professionals were encouraged to join up, but the game did not stop altogether. At Stoke Poges 'the normal course of life was completely suspended … but that is not to say that the club stood idle'. Members played at the weekend, but during the week the course was deserted save for the occasional injured military officer.[76] One journalist dismissed the accusation that middle-aged men 'might be more profitably employed' than in walking around a golf course: 'They have done their duty and deserve their entertainment just as much as … their critics, who prefer to spend hours in picture-house, music hall or theatre.'[77] The Second World War witnessed a similar suspension of competition, and many courses were given over partially or completely for agricultural purposes. Where they could, clubs remained open, but during this 'people's war' many felt less justified to exclude on grounds of status and class. Walsall Golf Club agreed to allow all officers, NCOs and men billeted locally 'who have at any time been members of a Golf Club and have been in possession of an official handicap' to play on the course free of charge and to use the club house.[78] Similarly, at Stanmore Golf Club in London, American army officers were admitted, but these moves towards democratisation were only taken, it seems, with reluctance.[79]

Although cycling faced its restrictions, as a pastime and a sport it was well suited to wartime. The National Cyclists' Union (NCU) was able to carry on with the usual limited programmes and patriotic gestures in the First World War, but the sport was much more prominent between 1939 and 1945.[80] The bicycle became an obvious alternative means of transportation that had the joint benefit of saving fuel and improving physical fitness. In a leading article, *The Times* celebrated the wartime renaissance of the bicycle: 'Many a cobwebby corner of an old stable has given up its dead ... the forgotten veterans have taken to the road... Those who have been long absent from the saddle have probably tasted one of the joys of life in recapturing a sensation.'[81] As a competitive sport, cycling had many forms but was restricted by the NCU's self-imposed prohibition of road racing. In defiance of the ban, a mass-start road race between Llangollen and Wolverhampton took place in June 1942, leading to the creation of a breakaway British League of Racing Cyclists.[82] The loss of members to the forces naturally affected many local clubs, but most continued to organise recreational and competitive events. The Walsall Cycling & Running Club, for example, launched a membership drive in March 1940 that had reached 61 members by 1942, including 21 serving in the forces and 16 ladies. In the summer of 1944 it recorded in its wartime bulletin that the racing section was 'sadly depleted', although there were still regular club runs, tours, road races and time trials.[83] The Loughborough Cyclist's Touring Club informed its scattered membership in April 1943 that it was 'probably stronger, in both numbers and spirit, than at any previous time'. Looking to the future the following September, the club proclaimed its wish to continue cycling's wartime role as a 'common-leveller' and 'a necessity for business and pleasure'.[84]

In certain respects, the effect of the First World War on the theatre and music hall was comparable to that on sport. By September 1914 poor attendances had led to the closure of many London theatres, while as many as 200 companies were forced to stop touring. The salaries of music hall performers in the West End were cut by 50 per cent and a fund established by the Variety Artistes Federation for struggling members. A similar distress fund for unemployed actors had collected £1,062 by the end of 1914 and aided 84 actors.[85] Yet while most sports pared down their operations or stopped altogether, the theatre boomed as the war progressed. Not only did it benefit from increased prosperity among the working and lower-middle classes, but also, especially in London, a new, more diverse theatre-going public emerged. And despite initial reservations, an evening at the theatre did not seem to generate the same moral indignation as an afternoon at the football or a day at the races.

Between 1939 and 1945 the role of the acting profession in the war effort was recognised by the state. The Home Morale Emergency Committee was determined to 'Tell actors that they are counted on to keep people cheerful'[86], but it was the Ministry of Labour that secured priority status for the profession through the deferment of its key performers. By February 1941 the cases of some 137 actors whom 'it was felt were more use in the theatre than in the forces' had been approved.[87] Yet it tended to be specific wartime bodies – ENSA under Basil Dean, along with CEMA and the Army and RAF revues – that dominated the provision of theatrical entertainment. ENSA alone arranged over 2½ million shows during the war, and despite some criticism concerning the quality of performances, launched a number of post-war careers. [88] Despite the boom in variety, some performers who had enlisted in the early weeks of war believed that they had been squeezed out. Rikki McCormick commented bitterly that, 'The real performers and pros were flying aeroplanes and transporting munitions ... and they got left out of it [ENSA, etc]... Many of them never recovered from the war.'[89]

Expenditure on entertainment rose by an incredible 120 per cent between 1939 and 1945. Activities such as going to the pictures and listening to the wireless enjoyed unprecedented popularity, and other more traditional pursuits, such as drinking and pub-going, flourished. But despite the stories of those who resolutely carried on under difficult circumstances, both the First and Second World Wars were for many little more than intervals in the 'normal' pattern of recreational and sporting activity. On 27 April 1946, over 98,000 watched Derby County beat Charlton Athletic in the first post-war FA Cup Final. As *The Times* football correspondent noted: 'Here at last ... after seven years is the real thing again.'[90]

Recommended reading

Baker, Norman, 'A More Even Playing Field?: Sport During and After the War', in Hayes, Nick and Hill, Jeff (eds), *'Millions Like Us'?: British Culture in the Second World War* (Liverpool: Liverpool University Press, 1999)

Birley, Derek, 'Sportsmen and the Deadly Game', in *British Journal of Sports History* 3 (3) (December 1986) pp288-310

Playing the Game: Sport and British Society, 1910-45 (Manchester: Manchester University Press, 1995)

Collins, L. J., *Theatre at War, 1914-18* (London: Macmillan, 1997)

Dean, Basil, *The Theatre at War* (London: George G. Harrop, 1956)

Lanfranchi, Pierre and Taylor, Matthew, 'Professional Football in World War Two Britain', in

Kirkham, Pat and Thoms, David (eds), *War Culture: Social Change and Changing Experience in World War Two* (London: Lawrence & Wishart, 1995) pp187-97

McCarthy, Tony, *War Games: The Story of Sport in World War Two* (London: Queen Anne Press, 1989)

Midwinter, Eric, *The Lost Seasons: Cricket in Wartime, 1939-45* (London: Methuen, 1987)

Veitch, Colin, '"Play Up! Play Up! and Win the War!": Football, the Nation and the First World War, 1914-15', in *Journal of Contemporary History* 20 (3) (July 1985) pp363-78

Williams, Jack, 'Cricket and the Great War', in *Stand To!* 51 (January 1998) pp6-9

Notes

1   Sir Pelham Warner, *Lord's, 1787-1945* (London: White Lion, 1946) p245
2   See Jose Harris, 'War and Social History: Britain and the Home Front during the Second World War', in *Contemporary European History* 1 (1) (1992) pp17-35
3   Ivanhoe CC Committee Minutes, 1932-49, newspaper cutting (undated), Leicester Record Office (LRO), DE 1565/3
4   Ian F. W. Beckett, 'Total War', in Colin MacInnes and G. D. Sheffield (eds), *Warfare in the Twentieth Century: Theory and Practice* (London: Unwin Hyman) pp1-23
5   Michael Sanderson, *From Irving to Olivier: A Social History of the Acting Profession, 1880-1983* (London: Athlone Press, 1985); Ian McLaine, *Ministry of Morale: Home Front Morale and the Ministry of Information in World War II* (London: George Allen & Unwin, 1979); Philip M. Taylor (ed), *Britain and Cinema in the Second World War* (London: Macmillan, 1988); Sian Nicholas, *The Echo of War: Home Front Propaganda and the Wartime BBC, 1939-45* (Manchester: Manchester University Press, 1996); F. M. Leventhal, '"The Best for the Most": CEMA and State Sponsorship of the Arts in Wartime, 1939-45', in *Twentieth Century British History* 1 (3) (1990) pp289-317
6   John M. Osborne, '"To keep the life of the Nation on the old lines": The Athletic News and the First World War', in *Journal of Sport History* 14 (2) (1987) pp137-50
7   See 'Fitness for Service' Scheme, Report of Progress, Reference Minute 5(b), Football Association (FA) War Emergency Committee Minutes, 29 July 1940; CCPR Report on Association Football, Reference Minute 51(e), FA War Emergency Committee Minutes, 20 May 1944; Stanley Rous, *Football Worlds: A Lifetime in Sport* (London: Faber & Faber, 1978) pp104-14; Geoffrey Green, *The History of the Football Association* (London: Naldrett Press, 1953) p367
8   F. J. Wall to War Office, 8 September 1914; B. B. Cubitt to FA, 10 September 1914 (FA Minute Books, 1914-15)
9   David Smith and Gareth Williams, *Fields of Praise: The Official History of the Welsh Rugby Union, 1881-1981* (Cardiff: University of Wales Press) p201
10   Quoted in Derek Birley, *Playing the Game: Sport and British Society, 1910-45* (Manchester: Manchester University Press, 1995) p59
11   Jack Williams, 'Cricket and the Great War', in *Stand To!* 51 (January 1998) p5
12   *The Sportsman*, 27 August 1914; *The Times*, 29 January 1915
13   *The Times*, 11 December 1914; Jack Williams, op cit, p6
14   Michael Sanderson, op cit, pp157-61
15   Derek Birley, 'Sportsmen and the Deadly Game', in *British Journal of Sports History* 3 (3) (December 1986) pp292-3
16   See Colin Veitch, '"Play Up! Play Up! and Win the War!": Football, the Nation and the First World War, 1914-15', in *Journal of Contemporary History* 20 (3) (July 1985) pp363-78
17   Norman Baker, 'A More Even Playing Field?: Sport During and After the War', in Nick Hayes and Jeff Hill (eds), *'Millions Like Us'?: British Culture in the Second World War* (Liverpool: Liverpool University Press, 1999) p128
18   *The Times*, 9 September 1939
19   Quoted in Tony McCarthy, *War Games: The Story of Sport in World War Two* (London: Queen Anne Press, 1989) p34
20   *The Times*, 5 September 1939
21   Angus Calder, *The People's War: Britain 1939-45* (London: Jonathan Cape, 1969) p64; *Birmingham Mail*, 9 September 1939
22   *Birmingham Post*, 21 September 1939; 'Football in Time of War', Memo No 3, 21 September 1939 (FA Minute Books, 1939-40)
23   Angus Calder, op cit, p374
24   On this, see Norman Baker, op cit, pp125-55
25   For an excellent discussion of the values and images associated with cricket, see Jack Williams, *Cricket and England: A Cultural and Social History of the Interwar Years* (London: Frank Cass, 1999)
26   Sir Pelham Warner, op cit, p171; Benny Green, *Wisden Anthology, 1900-1940* (London: Queen Anne Press, 1980) pp436, 439-40
27   *Athletic News*, 10 May 1915

28 E. E. Snow, *A History of Leicestershire Cricket* (Leicester: Edgar Backus, 1949) p243; Jack Williams, 'Cricket and the Great War', op cit, p6

29 Jack Williams, 'Was the First World War Beneficial to County Cricket?', in *Journal of the Cricket Society* 15 (2) (Spring 1991) pp27-31

30 Jack Williams, 'Cricket and the Great War', op cit, p6

31 *Athletic News*, 16 April 1917; Fred Root, *A Cricket Pro's Lot* (London: Edward Arnold, 1937) p180

32 *Athletic News*, 8 May, 24 July 1916

33 Ivanhoe CC Committee Minutes, 26 October 1914, 29 March, 10 May 1915, 14 February 1919, LRO, DE 1565/1; Neil Wigglesworth, *The Evolution of English Sport* (London: Frank Cass, 1996) p121

34 Sir Pelham Warner, op cit, p246

35 Eric Midwinter, *The Lost Seasons: Cricket in Wartime, 1939-45* (London: Methuen, 1987)

36 See Gerald Howat, *Len Hutton: The Biography* (London: Heinemann Kingswood, 1988) pp51-64, and *Learie Constantine* (Newton Abbot: Readers Union, 1976) pp120-41

37 *The Times*, 2 November 1939. The Club Cricket Federation had in fact originated in 1915 as the London and Southern Counties Club Cricket Conference. It functioned in the First World War as a fixture bureau to arrange games at short service, particularly for servicemen. Jack Williams, *Cricket and England*, op cit, pp36-9; Eric Midwinter, op cit, pp64-5

38 Anon, *A Century of Cricket: A History of Shepshed Town Cricket Club from 1869 to 1968* (Shepshed: Freeman Press, 1969) p27

39 Rugby Cricket Club Centenary Souvenir Programme, Ivanhoe CC Committee Minutes, 1932-49 LRO, DE 1565/1

40 *Athletic News*, 7 June 1915

41 Michael Marshall, *Gentlemen and Players: Conversations with Cricketers* (London: Grafton Books, 1987) pp128-9. For the limits to change in the post-war period, see Norman Baker, op cit, pp140-55

42 Christopher Brookes, *English Cricket: The Game and its Players through the Ages* (Newton Abbot: Weidenfeld & Nicolson, 1978) pp162-3

43 Michael Marshall, op cit, pp133-4

44 Quoted in Sir Pelham Warner, op cit, p173.

45 Quoted in Tim Heald, *Denis Compton* (London: Pavilion Books, 1996) pp83-4

46 David Lemmon, *Changing Seasons: A History of Cricket In England, 1945-1996* (London: Andre Deutsch, 1997) p4

47 *Athletic News*, 26 July 1915

48 Bob Crampsey, *The First 100 Years: The Scottish Football League* (Glasgow: Scottish Football League, 1990) pp57-70

49 Simon Inglis, *League Football and the Men Who Made It* (London: Collins Willow, 1988) pp165-70

50 John Ross Schleppi, 'A History of Professional Association Football in England During the Second World War' (unpublished PhD Thesis, Ohio State University, 1972) Vol 2, p412

51 FA Consultative Committee, 15 October-10 December 1940; Anthony Bristowe, *Charlton Athletic Football Club, 1905-50* (London: Voice of the Valley, 1992 (reprint)) pp49-50

52 Report of Interview with the Ministry of War Transport, 3 December 1941 (Football League Minute Books, 1941-42)

53 Sam Bartram, *His Autobiography* (London: Burke, 1957) pp101-2; John Ross Schleppi, op cit, pp405-8

54 Football Players' Union Minutes, 2 November 1914

55 John Harding, *For the Good of the Game: The Official History of the Professional Footballers' Association* (London: Robson Books, 1991) pp120-1

56 Peter Doherty, 'Footballers at War', reprinted in Stephen Kelly (ed), *A Game of Two Halves* (London: Mandarin, 1992) p27

57 Football Players' Union Minutes, 2 October 1939

58 *Birmingham Post*, 12 September 1939

59 'Football and the Forces', Reference Minute 4, FA War Emergency Committee, 22 January 1940

60 Eamon Dunphy, *A Strange Kind of Glory: Sir Matt Busby and Manchester United* (London: Heinemann, 1991) pp80-3

61 Quoted in John Ross Schleppi, op cit, p329

62 Willie Watson, *Double International* (London: Stanley Paul, 1956) p27; Tom Finney, *Football Round the World* (London: Sportsman's Book Club, 1955) p30. [The jibe recalled by Watson was likely to have been collectively self-mocking re service in Italy – Editor]

63 Wray Vamplew, *The Turf: A Social and Economic History of Horse Racing* (London: Allen Lane, 1976) p63

64 Michael Wynn Jones, *The Derby* (London: Croom Helm, 1979) pp151-4

65 *The Times*, 25 September 1939

66 Neil Wigglesworth, op cit, p125; Angus Calder, op cit, p374

67 *The Times*, 4 December 1940

68 Roger Munting, *Hedges and Hurdles: A Social and Economic History of National Hunt Racing* (London: J. A. Allen, 1987) p66

69 Leicester Racecourse Directors' Meeting Minutes, 28 February, 19 June 1941, 4 April 1946, LRO, DE 2805/4

70 Eugene Corri, *Refereeing 1,000 Fights: Reminiscences of Boxing* (London: C. Arthur Pearson, 1919) p167

71 Stan Shipley, *Bombardier Billy Wells* (Tyne & Wear: Bewick Press, 1993) pp109-39

72 Dai Smith, 'Focal Heroes: A Welsh Fighting Class', in Richard Holt (ed), *Sport and the Working Class in Modern Britain* (Manchester: Manchester University Press, 1990) p215; Morton Lewis, *Ted Kid Lewis: His Life and Times* (London: Robson Books, 1990)

73 Angus Calder, op cit, p374

74 Gary Shaw, 'To what extent was Liverpool's experience of professional boxing during the Second World War duplicated in Manchester?' (unpublished MA Research Essay, De Montfort University, 1999)

75 *The Times*, 12 October 1939

76 N. L. Jackson, *Sporting Days and Sporting Ways* (London: Hurst & Blackett, 1932) pp256-7

77 *Athletic News*, 17 May 1915

78 Walsall Golf Club Committee Minutes, 5 November 1940, Walsall Local History Unit (WLHU), 188/2

79 Richard Holt, 'Golf and the English Suburb: Class and Gender in a London Club, c1890-c1960', in *The Sports Historian* 18 (1) (May 1998) pp81-2

80 *Athletic News*, 16 April 1917

81 *The Times*, 5 July 1943

82 Tony McCarthy, op cit, p98

83 Walsall Cycling & Running Club (WCRC) Minutes, 20 March 1940, WLHU, 303/1; WCRC Wartime News Bulletin, April 1943, July 1944, WLHU, 303/11

84 *The Cyclist's Companion: Organ of the Loughborough Section of the Cyclist's Touring Club*, April 1943, September 1944, LRO, DE 3469/33/1-69

85 Michael Sanderson, op cit, pp161-2; *The Times*, 10 August 1914

86 Ian McLaine, op cit, p63

87 Michael Sanderson, op cit, p258

88 On ENSA, see Basil Dean, *The Theatre at War* (London: George G. Harrop, 1956)

89 Roger Wilmut, *Kindly Leave the Stage!: The Story of Variety* (London: Methuen, 1985) p138

90 *The Times*, 27 April 1946

PART III
THE MORAL
EXPERIENCE

Chapter 25

Keeping faith and coping: belief, popular religiosity and the British people

Michael F. Snape and Stephen G. Parker

The significance of religion in Britain during the First and Second World Wars has received scant attention from either military or social historians. Additionally, and more surprisingly, few historians of religion have explored the nature and significance of religious faith for the British people during these conflicts. When religious life has been examined, the discussion rarely extends much beyond its implications for pacifism, the dilemmas of the religious hierarchy, or the experiences of the clergy and the religious intelligentsia.[1] This chapter sets out to redress this imbalance, seeking to present a survey of war's impact upon some key aspects of popular religious faith in Britain during these years. Unlike many previous studies, the essay's aim is not to focus on Christian pacifism or on the churches' leadership, but to investigate the broad range of religious belief and religious commitment in Britain and to illustrate the multi-faceted response of millions of religious believers to the ordeal of the two World Wars.

According to the best available statistics, in 1914 the major Christian denominations in mainland Britain had approximately 8,071,000 active adherents out of a total population of nearly 42 million.[2] In 1914 there were also around 250,000 British Jews[3], 58,000 members of smaller churches and sects[4], and a mere 2,881 subscribers to the secularist Rationalist Press Association[5]. Generally speaking, Ireland, Wales and Scotland had higher levels of church attendance and participation than had England, a function of the strong association of certain religious traditions with the cultural identity of these regions.[6] These regional variations in religious practice were to be fully reflected within the British Army during the First World War and even persisted, albeit to a lesser extent, into the Second World War.[7] Besides these regional variations, the preponderance of female worshippers in most churches and synagogues was also characteristic of British religious life.[8] Although regional and gender differences were to remain abiding features of the British religious landscape, active participation in mainstream church life within the nation as a whole was in decline in relative terms by 1946, the number of active church members and churchgoers among the major denominations having risen to only 8,124,000 out of a population that now approached 48 million.[9]

By the mid-1940s new patterns of religious practice and affiliation were clearly asserting themselves. However, not all of these were indicative of a decline in religious belief. While fewer than 5,000 people subscribed to the Rationalist Press Association in 1946[10], as many as 20 per cent of the adult population tuned in to the BBC's *Sunday Half Hour*, a statistic that demonstrates the huge impact made by the rise of religious broadcasting in the inter-war period.[11] Moreover, these years saw steady growth for the Roman Catholic church in mainland Britain while also witnessing the rapid expansion of more marginal Christian groups such as the Jehovah's Witnesses and the Seventh Day Adventists.[12] In addition, the 1930s and the war years greatly increased Britain's Jewish population, which had grown to number around 450,000 by the mid-1950s.[13] Overall, however, the statistics present a sombre picture, for Britain's mainstream Protestant churches, of a slow but gradual decline in active membership relative to the population as a whole between 1914 and 1945.

Nevertheless, what these figures tend to obscure is the continuing vitality of faith within and beyond the confines of organised religion. Undisclosed by these statistics, which highlight the active religious affiliation of several million Britons, are the nature and the extent of the religious faith of many millions more. Usually, when judged upon the criteria of churchgoing and church membership, this latter group often appears to be indifferent to religion, but, as Sarah Williams's recent study of working-class religion in London has demonstrated, theirs was often a religious outlook that defied the norms of religious practice as prescribed by clergymen and other representatives of the churches.[14] Clearly, and particularly in the light of such work, for the purposes of this chapter and for the religious and cultural history of 20th-century Britain in general, the boundaries between the religious and the irreligious need to be re-examined and the role and importance of religious faith for the population of Great Britain during the war years needs to be reappraised.

Personal religious faith is a problematical concept, its various manifestations being notoriously hard to assess and interpret. During the 19th century, the commonly accepted measure of personal and national religiosity was church attendance, a criterion that served as the basis for Britain's only official census of religious practice in 1851. However widely employed in more limited surveys thereafter, the inadequacy of churchgoing as an index of personal faith was brought home to many devout laymen and chaplains during the course of the First World War, a realisation that presented them with the daunting challenge of turning tacit believers into active churchgoers after the coming of peace, and which gave rise to a radical reformist discourse among many of the Church of England's military chaplains.[15] The salience of an ethically based, non-dogmatic form of Christianity that the much-vaunted 'soldier-saint' Donald Hankey portrayed as 'The Religion of the Inarticulate'[16], and which D. S. Cairns described as a 'dim and instinctive theism'[17], is undoubtedly the most complicating factor of a study such as ours, the situation being productive of a mass of contradictory verdicts as to the nature and importance of religion for the nation at large. From Cairns's perspective, namely that of a Scottish Presbyterian academic with some YMCA experience, a state of 'spiritual anarchy' had prevailed within the Army during the First World War[18], a view that had already been neatly summarised by one chaplain's conclusion that, 'The Soldier has got Religion; I am not sure that he has got Christianity.'[19] Significantly, these verdicts on evidence garnered from the ranks of Britain's citizen army in the First World War are mirrored by the findings of several Mass-Observation reports from the Second World War. One report, which was based on a survey of religious attitudes in a London borough in 1944, was emphatic in its conclusion that:

'The keynote of the whole investigation was confusion. The ordinary person has not a logically arranged system of beliefs and doubts. Nor has he even a consistent set of prejudices… His beliefs are a mixture of convictions and habits, independent thought and the relics of what he was taught as a child… These beliefs and prejudices are often put into narrow pigeon holes so that one scarcely influences the other.'

One constant in this investigation, however, was that, 'To many people … religion means neither belief in a particular doctrine, nor going to church, nor even a belief in God. To these, religion consists of living a good life… It is the Christian ethic they speak of, which has become so much a part of the ideas of this country that it is taken for granted.'[20]

Among church commentators, it was broadly accepted that the prevailing state of religious confusion among a substantial section of British society was primarily due to the churches' failure to create a sound system of religious education. Among Protestant commentators during the First World War, this failure was variously ascribed to the secularism of council schools, to the careless non-denominationalism of parents, and also to the fact that Sunday Schools themselves generally failed to retain their scholars beyond adolescence.[21] By the time of the Great War, so one of Cairns's sources maintained, these factors had conspired to produce a generation of men who were deeply ignorant of Christian doctrine while being remarkably well-versed in Christian hymnody[22], men for whom, so another of Cairns's informants argued, God was 'the clear relic of their days in Sunday school'[23]. Even grammar and public schools were accused of failing to teach religion effectively, the latter being blamed for stifling religious enthusiasm at an early age by reducing religious education to a routine attendance at chapel and for utterly failing to inculcate 'an intelligent interest in religion for its own sake apart from school discipline'.[24] However, these failings were not confined to Protestant schools alone, one Catholic chaplain admitting that:

'The war has proved the enormous value of Catholic elementary schools, and has shown their chief weakness, religion not made spontaneous enough, too much part of school discipline. In a religious sense, crowds of our men have never grown up at all – their religious ideas, their prayers and their ideas of sin remain just as they were at, say, thirteen years old.'[25]

If pundits were right to ascribe widespread religious ignorance to the shortcomings of religious education at this time, this situation could only deteriorate during the inter-war years. For the principal Protestant denominations during this period, the number of children at church day schools and Sunday Schools decreased not only as a function of a declining birth rate but also as a result of the improvement of council schools and the increasingly 'home-based recreational pattern' of the inter-war British Sunday.[26] Moreover, in addition to the inherently eclectic quality of popular religion, the inter-war religious landscape was complicated by a new interest in Indian philosophy and mysticism, which was popularised by Theosophists such as Annie Besant, and also by the growth of profoundly secular ideologies such as Communism and Fascism. Certainly, from the standpoint of the religiously committed, the net results of popular ignorance, pluralism and eclecticism were unsettling, being productive of a popular religious outlook that was scarcely characterised by an informed and committed Christian orthodoxy. Peter Mayhew, an Anglican Army Chaplain during the Second World War, insisted that he and his colleagues were 'dealing with a pagan generation'[27], while Raleigh Trevelyan, who was also a practising Anglican, noted the irony of British graves near Anzio being marked by 'crazy imitations of the Christian symbol', particularly when these were 'the graves of men who most likely have never heard of Jesus except as a swear-word in American gangster novels'.[28]

Despite the complexity of the contemporary religious milieu, religious commentators could at least console themselves about one of its most important aspects, namely the minority status of articulate atheism within it. The investigations conducted for the church-sponsored Army and Religion Report led D. S. Cairns to assert that atheism had only a marginal appeal among British soldiers between 1914 and 1918; belief in God was, he concluded, 'almost universal'.[29] Significantly, during the Second World War Mass-Observation surveys conducted on a nationwide basis consistently found that three-quarters to four-fifths of the British people still believed in God. If these surveys found that only one-tenth of the population could be classed as actively churchgoing, only a small minority of the British public regarded themselves as outright unbelievers. In fact, in 1944 Mass-Observation investigators found that 'only one person in twenty was willing to say frankly and definitely that he believed there was no God, whereas thirteen out of twenty were quite definite about their belief in Him'. Ironically, however, the same survey found that, of those 'who doubted or denied the existence of a God, over a quarter said they prayed on occasions to a God whose existence they doubted. One in twelve had been to church within the past six months [and] over half thought there should be religious education in schools.' Such idiosyncrasies were also to be found among regular and occasional churchgoers, somewhat more than a quarter of Anglican churchgoers being prepared to discount the divinity of Christ. From such statistics and anecdotal evidence, the report drew the conclusion that, for organised Christianity at least, the principal problem was 'not the 5 per cent who disbelieve, but the 32 per cent who are not quite certain and the still larger number who do believe but are confused about the implications of their belief.'[30]

Despite strong indicators of religious confusion and of the long-term decline of church membership and attendance, British society nevertheless remained identifiably and self-consciously Christian between 1914 and 1945. Throughout this period Christian moral values continued to exert a strong and defining influence on British society, a fact evinced by the Abdication Crisis of 1936, and one that was also manifest in the country's laws on homosexuality, abortion and Sabbath day observance. Indeed, it is arguable that, in the form of the religious provisions of the Education Act of 1944 and of the identification of its cause with the defence of 'Christian civilisation'[31], the experience of the Second World War momentarily strengthened rather than weakened the Christian self-consciousness of British society.

During the war years, moreover, Britain's Christian culture furnished the nation's leaders and propagandists with a rich repertoire of imagery and metaphor, which placed the country's tribulations within a broader framework of providential history, and which grounded its struggles in the universal battle between good and evil. From the conduct and pronouncements of the nation's leaders at this time, it would appear that the same God who had watched over the affairs of Britain since the Reformation remained on hand to support the nation in its present crises. In the centuries-old tradition of national days of fast and humiliation, both King George V and George VI called national days of prayer throughout the war years and led the nation in thanksgiving after victory had been won. Indeed, one Anglican clergyman said of these days of prayer that they were like 'calling on the old tribal gods for help'.[32] In a similar vein, the wartime speeches of Lloyd George and Winston Churchill were spiced with biblical and providential allusions, the latter ascribing to divine mercy, for example, Allied success in outstripping the Germans in nuclear technology.[33] In terms of Britain's military leadership, both Douglas Haig and Bernard Law Montgomery were convinced that Britain's struggles were divinely aided and that a militant religiosity would play a key role in ultimate victory.[34]

In ecclesiastical quarters, too, such assumptions of divine assistance were echoed and endorsed. According to Bishop Percival of Hereford in 1915, Britain and her allies were none other than 'the predestined instruments to save the Christian civilisation of Europe from being overcome by a brutal and ruthless military paganism'.[35] Likewise, on the third anniversary of the Battle of Britain, Archbishop William Temple, in terms that were clearly coloured by his concerns for post-war reconstruction, opined, 'We may and must believe that He Who has led our fathers in ways so strange and has preserved our land in a manner so marvellous, has a purpose for us to serve in the preparation of His perfect Kingdom.'[36] Other appeals to Britain's Christian consciousness were made by less distinguished propagandists. During the First World War the widespread destruction of churches in France and Belgium and the alleged crucifixion of a Canadian prisoner were used to great effect in inciting anti-German feeling both in Britain and in Allied countries.[37] On a slightly different note, Allenby's capture of the Holy City of Jerusalem in 1917 was a tonic to the nation after a year of terrible losses and repeated frustrations on the Western Front. In the Second World War, and largely through the endeavours of the Ministry of Information's Religions Division, the Nazi euthanasia programme and the persecution of Christianity in Germany and in occupied Europe received widespread coverage, largely through a weekly publication entitled 'The Spiritual Issues of the War'. In both conflicts, therefore, Britain's Christian identity helped to define the character of Britain's struggle against its enemies, whether they were neo-pagan Huns, Muslim Turks or heathen Japanese.

Finally, and although treated with caution by many church leaders, the language of holy war was commonly used during both conflicts. The Bishop of London, Arthur Winnington Ingram, famously described Britain's war with Germany and the Central Powers as a 'holy war' in 1915.[38] However, similar crusading rhetoric was also employed by Lloyd George, who claimed in 1916 that the young men of Britain had flocked 'to the standard of international right, as to a great crusade'.[39] When the Second World War came, this idiom naturally re-emerged. Archbishop Cosmo Lang damned Nazi ideology as 'an insult upon all that Christianity means, or has meant in the life of nations' and declared that, in the new war with Germany, 'a supreme moral and indeed spiritual issue' was at stake.[40] In a similar vein, a BBC Dominion Day broadcast to Canada in 1940 spoke of the numerous Empire and free European troops then in Britain, a concourse that reminded the broadcaster, Vincent Massey, of 'the warfare against the infidel, when Christian men from every part of Europe were gathered to fight for the deliverance of the Holy Sepulchre.'[41]

Despite some evidence of popular scepticism (one Mass Observer was told in late 1942, for example, 'No good mixing up religion with war. What about Russia? They're all atheists and Stalingrad hasn't fallen yet'[42]), the rhetoric of Britain's wartime leaders and propagandists undoubtedly reflected and reinforced convictions that were widely held within British society. The currency achieved by accounts of miraculous intervention on behalf of the BEF at Mons, and, indeed, on other occasions during the early years of the First World War, is indicative of the extent to which the public readily seized upon any evidence of divine favour at large.[43] The same phenomenon recurred during the Second World War, especially with regard to the 'miracle' of Dunkirk. In a letter to *The Times* of 6 June 1940, a Lowestoft clergyman reminded readers that the prevailing calm that had facilitated the Dunkirk evacuation had persisted since the national day of prayer on Sunday 26 May, concluding his letter with an apposite scriptural reference, '"Why are ye fearful, O ye of little faith? Then He arose and rebuked the winds and the sea: and there was a great calm."'[44] Four years later, in response to 'a very clear Vision of the Cross' being seen in the skies above Suffolk, the Rev Harold Green of Ipswich placed the event firmly in the context of recent signs and wonders appointed by God for the preservation of the nation, signs and wonders that included the Dunkirk evacuation, the Battle of Britain and Germany's turning eastwards to Russia.[45]

In view of the widely accepted belief in the rectitude and sanctity of Britain's cause in the two World Wars, it is not surprising that the concept and rhetoric of crusading should appeal to many. Sometimes the parallels were fairly obvious, as they were to Bryan Cooper, an officer with the Connaught Rangers at Gallipoli, for whom the Turkish enemy were still 'the old enemy of Christendom', and the spirit of his comrades was still 'the spirit of Tancred and Godfrey de Bouillon, as they fitted themselves to take their places in the last of the Crusades.'[46] Although the religious connotations of crusading appear to have been only dimly grasped by the public at large in 1940[47], it would appear that British Catholics were particularly susceptible to such sentiments at this time, many of them having supported the Nationalist 'crusade' during the recent civil war in Spain and reviling the current alliance between the godless Nazi and Soviet regimes.[48] If, for fighting men in the Second World War, crusading parallels were less convincing, then they were still well to the fore. The Eighth Army had two official newspapers, the daily *Eighth Army News* and the weekly *Crusader*, and Raleigh Trevelyan, a subaltern in Italy in 1944, distinctly remembered how a fellow officer once complained that, 'All this talk about crusades made him retch'.[49]

However, the most significant expression of the assumption that Britain was indeed on the side of the angels during both World Wars was the positive response that the national days of prayer elicited during the course of both conflicts. Proclaimed by the monarch, these Sundays were widely observed during both conflicts, wartime anxieties and popular monarchism combining to produce notable expressions of public religiosity. Even after the losses and disappointments of previous years, *The Times* could report how the churches, chapels and synagogues of the capital had been 'thronged with worshippers' during the national day of prayer held on 6 January 1918.[50] However, even in the capital in the supposedly more secular atmosphere of the 1940s, such enthusiasm was still very much in evidence. One Mass-Observation survey of 1941 demonstrated that the national day of prayer, called for Sunday 23 March, produced a far higher level of church attendance at churches in Paddington than did the following Easter Sunday, when overall church attendance fell by one-third.[51] The mood that such days of prayer could engender was captured by Winston Churchill himself, who wrote that there was a palpable sense of 'pent-up, passionate emotions' in Westminster Abbey on 26 May 1940.[52] Even towards the end of the war, and in the relatively secure backwaters of rural Warwickshire, Clara Milburn, a middle-class housewife, could write in her diary for Sunday 3 September 1944:

'It has been a day of National Prayer and the King and his People have been to their respective churches and chapels to join in prayer and thanksgiving … and to show their dependence on Almighty God, to ask His help and to give Him praise. It is a wonderful feeling to worship in such an atmosphere. The church was pretty full today, and didn't we sing the good old hymns with vigour!'[53]

Illustrative of the power of wartime circumstances to elicit more spontaneous expressions of popular religiosity was the Big Ben Minute Association, which dedicated the chimes of Big Ben at 9.00pm each evening to a moment of private prayer.[54] This popular religious impulse was also instanced by the nationwide response to the news of the D-Day landings. Despite the lack of official warning and 6 June being a weekday, across the country churches were opened and impromptu services were held as news of the invasion emerged. That evening, the King's broadcast, which called the nation to prayer, was followed by a solemn service of dedication led by the Bishop of London.[55]

Evidence for the significance of religion as an aid to morale is abundant at an individual as well as at a national level. If the dualism of Christianity aided propagandist interpretations of both World Wars as manifestations of the cosmic struggle between the forces of good and evil, then it also coloured and strengthened more personal perceptions of the nation at war. On 21 March 1915 Philip Bryant, a sailor on board the battleship *Queen Elizabeth*, wrote from the Dardanelles to his old Bible class teacher in Bournemouth: 'I would not be risking my life now if I did not think ours was a just cause… You say if Germany win you will emigrate but with God's Almighty help we shall all live in England as rulers of the Sea again.'[56]

During the war years numerous individuals also drew inspiration and comfort from such mainsprings of British religious culture as the King James Bible and *Pilgrim's Progress*. For the more educated, these often served as repositories of language and metaphor with which to express the depth and significance of their wartime experiences.[57] In March 1917, a despondent Anglican chaplain wrote, 'No truer book was written than the *Pilgrim's Progress*. One must press on, or try to, very stumblingly and helplessly at times, and in such terrible isolation.'[58] Similarly, 27 years later, only the words of the psalmist could express the sentiments felt by Raleigh Trevelyan prior to an attack on the Italian town of Arezzo.[59] However, by this time such consolation could be found in other media beside the great classics of English religious literature. On 28 May 1940 John J. Simpson, a gunner with the 56th Anti-Tank Regiment, wrote to the vicar of Millom from the beaches at Dunkirk expressing his pleasure at having heard a religious service broadcast during the national day of prayer: 'I heard the wireless service on Sunday morning and my thoughts turned to the Old Church at once and I thoroughly enjoyed every minute of it.'[60]

Naturally, in all too many cases, religion also offered dignity for the deceased and a measure of consolation for the bereaved. With regard to the former, chaplains often made strenuous efforts under difficult conditions to ensure the burial of the dead, a solemn imperative that could produce expressions of practical ecumenism seldom matched in civilian life. On the battlecruiser HMS *Tiger* following the battle of Jutland, for example, the dead of the ship's company were, of necessity, buried at the same time by the ship's Roman Catholic and Anglican chaplains. As Fr T. F. Bradley recalled:

'Word came through that they would be buried at 6.30. A row of mess tables were placed with one end over the starboard side of the quarter deck & the bodies were laid [out]… A six-inch shell was placed under their heels and tied on to their sea boots to ensure the bodies remaining at the bottom … the C of E padre first of all said the burial service, then I said mine and then we both said our words of committal together.'[61]

In terms of comfort for the bereaved, friends and relatives of J. K. Brown, a soldier of the London Scottish killed near Cambrai, readily invoked the Christian concept of the hereafter in October 1918. As one letter confided to his family, 'Christ is the only comforter at these awful times… The Separation is hard to bear but it is only for a time, then we shall all meet around the Heavenly throne, with

Jesus and our loved ones never to part again.'[62] Religion also proved of some comfort to Mrs Min Skinner of Brighton, whose son, an RAF crewman, was posted missing in the late summer of 1940: 'We are all very sad and anxious but still hopeful that our dear Eric is still alive and well,' she wrote that September. 'He has an even chance and by God's help we shall hear good news of him soon … there is nothing for us to do only leave it in God's hands. Our vicar wrote me a Prayer and I find it a great help, he has also asked for prayers in Church for him.'[63]

Wartime captivity could also bring about a rekindling of religious faith and a sense of purpose for some British prisoners of war. Although this was not unknown on an individual basis during the Great War[64], the internment and prison camps of the Far East during the Second World War provide the most striking collective illustrations of this phenomenon. Although British historians have recognised that the calamitous defeat of the secular Third Republic in 1940 prompted a religious revival in France and among French prisoners of war in Germany[65], it has not been recognised that a similar religious revival was also experienced among the many thousands of Britons who fell into Japanese hands following the fall of Hong Kong, Malaya and Singapore. The reasons behind this revival were manifold, but the perils and uncertainty of captivity, the presence (in civilian camps at least) of numerous missionaries, the lack of alternative recreations and the pressing need for the kind of mutual co-operation fostered by the Christian ethic, all played their part. The need for reassurance in isolation induced bids to procure good news from the super-empirical sphere. At one extreme, among civilian inmates of Stanley internment camp in Hong Kong, promising news was gleaned via Ouija boards and the reading of tea leaves.[66] At the other, among soldiers in Singapore's Changi prison, great importance was attached to the revelatory powers of the Bible following the fall of the island in 1942. As Ernest Gordon, an officer in the 2nd Argyll & Sutherland Highlanders recalled:

> 'The Bible [was] viewed as having magical properties; to the man who could find the right key all would be revealed. One group assured me with absolute certainty that they knew that the end of the war was at hand. When I asked them for proof they told me that they had found it in the books of Daniel and Revelation.'[67]

Among civilian internees, missionaries played a vital role in sustaining morale through welfare work and through providing some much-needed recreation. According to Joseph Sandbach, a Methodist missionary interned in Stanley camp after the fall of Hong Kong, 'I can honestly say I came through that camp buoyant, optimistic, glad I had a job to do … when it was all over I was greatly, greatly moved at the number of people who took the trouble to write to me and say a word of thanks for that sort of thing.' Significantly, Stanley's ecumenical United Congregations held services that were, in Sandbach's words, 'crowded, absolutely crowded', a result not only of the consolation that internees sought, but also, as he conceded, of the fact that these services at least provided somewhere to go and something to do.[68] According to Ernest Gordon, the revival of religion in the appalling conditions of the work camps on the Kwai was part of a process of the re-organisation of camp life by the prisoners themselves, a re-organisation that followed a period in which morale had practically collapsed and 'the law of the jungle' had prevailed among them.[69] As Gordon recalled, 'We were seeing for ourselves the sharp contrast between the forces that made for life and those that made for death.' This realisation, he argued, led not only to the creation of camp education groups, workshops and libraries but also to a renascent religious consciousness owing to the identification of these 'forces that made for life' with Christianity itself.[70]

Given the prominence of a religiosity that defied neat categorisation, to pose the question of whether war was conducive to the increase or diminution of faith seems somewhat inappropriate in relation to the nation at large. Indeed, even from the perspective of individual churches it could prove impossible to establish whether the experience of war had had a positive or negative influence on the faith of their members. In 1919 not even Roman Catholic chaplains were unanimous as to their verdicts on the general effects of the war on Roman Catholic servicemen, notwithstanding a well-publicised stream of conversions to Catholicism among British soldiers in France during the war years.[71]

Nevertheless, during both World Wars there existed a substantial core of church members and churchgoers who were able to reflect critically upon their experiences of war in the light of an informed Christian faith. In a recent article, Rich Schweitzer postulated a 'spectrum model' in order to illustrate the range of religious responses that the ordeal of the First World War induced among British soldiers, the model being useful in illustrating the often nuanced shifts in religious belief during both World Wars.[72] For Hubert Worthington, for example, an infantry officer who had been wounded on the Somme on 1 July 1916 and who had been 'through a lot of religious or anti-religious phases' since being at school, his ordeal strengthened rather than diminished his developing Christian faith. Writing to his brother nearly six months later, Worthington told how he had recently been confirmed by the Bishop of Oxford and announced how he was now firmly convinced of the doctrine of the communion of saints: 'My 70 odd dead boys are always near me,' he wrote. 'Practically all died as heroes. The best men were Christians.'[73]

Similarly, for Lavinia Orde, who was at that time a driver in the Auxiliary Territorial Service, the gruesome sight of a plane crash in Oxfordshire in the spring of 1940 did not so much diminish her faith as underline its consoling aspects: 'There was practically nothing left of the two pilots,' she recalled. 'I left thanking God that we had souls and not only bodies to end up like that.'[74] According to Harry Levy, an Orthodox Jewish chaplain with the British Army in Germany in 1945, not even the experience of Belsen could obliterate the faith of Jewish soldiers under his care: 'I can't say with certainty that it affected them religiously but it certainly intensified their Jewish identity because these were our brothers ... we managed to see hundreds who had survived ... you had a feeling ... Israel lives.'[75]

These cases all illustrate an important point, namely the tendency for war to strengthen rather than undermine the religious faith and identity of many. As Alan Wilkinson has pointed out, the experience of war was not necessarily corrosive of faith in Britain between 1914 and 1918.[76] The 1920s, indeed, saw a short-lived resurgence in formal religious observance, and the ordeal of war benefited Roman and Anglo-Catholicism, Spiritualism and also progressive elements within the Church of England.[77] In a similar fashion, despite the calamities of the Second World War, these years were productive of the 1944 Education Act, which paved the way for religious worship and religious education in all state-funded schools, and the 1950s also saw a modest upturn in formal religious observance in Britain.[78] Mass-Observation reports provide some valuable insights into the dynamics of this phenomenon. In January 1940 a Mass-Observation poll found that 14 per cent of respondents claimed that their religious faith had been altered by the impact of war, nearly two-thirds of whom 'gave answers indicating loss of faith'. The rest of the poll was equally divided between those individuals whose faith had not been affected and those who were indifferent to the matter. This situation obtained despite the increased coverage given to religious matters in papers such as the *Daily Mail* and *Daily Express* and despite the fact that 16 per cent of all radio programmes were now concerned with religion.[79]

However, in 1941 a further survey of Mass-Observation's National Panel of 1,500 voluntary informants (who, in theory at least, represented 'a cross-section of more thoughtful and informed opinion' and were drawn from 'all parts of the country, working in all sorts of jobs, and holding all sorts of beliefs') found that the apparent trend towards religious disillusionment had not only been arrested but reversed. Under the impact of the deepening war, 9 per cent of the National Panel now claimed that their faith had been weakened, while 16 per cent claimed that it had been strengthened. Only 'a negligible proportion' was reported as having lost their faith. A year later, in 1942, this emerging trend was confirmed by 26 per cent of the Panel claiming that their faith had been strengthened, while only 9 per cent still claimed that it had been weakened.[80] Such statistics are, of course, significant, particularly as these years saw some spectacular defeats for British arms, some of the heaviest German bombing of the war, and what has been described as the most complete military mobilisation of any Allied nation with the sole exception of the Soviet Union.[81]

However, according to these same reports the strengthening of faith was generally more 'qualitative' than 'quantitative', being largely confined to 'the more thoughtfully and consciously religious'. Moreover, this process was coterminous with an overall decline in church attendance, the significance of which should not be overstated given the widespread destruction of churches and the displacement and disruption consequent upon evacuation, conscription and the blackout.[83] Clearly, faith survived and even flourished despite these adverse circumstances. Significantly, among the armed services the move towards religion was more pronounced than among civilians. A poll of RAF personnel in 1941 found that, in comparison with the male members of Mass-Observation's National Panel, there was a greater trend towards the strengthening of faith (25 per cent as opposed to 18 per cent) and that far fewer men in the RAF claimed to have no religion or to be indifferent to it (11 per cent as opposed to 35 per cent of men on the National Panel).[84] In a similar vein, a 1942 report on the situation of Army

Chaplains indicated that servicemen in 'direct contact with the enemy tend to have more time for religious matters', a perception that its author supported with various illustrations of what he termed 'some sort of "religious revival" in the Middle East'.[85] Among the religiously uncommitted on the Home Front, on the other hand, the tendency was for the war to erode what residual faith remained, questions of theodicy deepening the doubt of the agnostic and hardening the scepticism of the atheist. As one report on faith and wartime conditions dated January 1943 put it, 'Among all the samples studied, never more than a tiny proportion of 1-4 per cent say they have lost their faith. In general the effect of war has been to confirm pre-existing attitudes, to strengthen faith where it existed before, but also to confirm and strengthen attitudes of scepticism, agnosticism and indifference.'[86]

As these Mass-Observation surveys indicate, if the loss of personal faith was a relatively rare phenomenon, far more common was a sense of its degradation under the impact of war. This degradation appears to have been very much a function of wartime upheaval, with servicemen and women being particularly – although by no means exclusively – susceptible to it. Private Frank Richards of the 2nd Royal Welch Fusiliers recalled an extreme example of religious decline in his memoir *Old Soldiers Never Die*. In 1917, he recalled,

> 'A dozen new signallers joined us… One of them was a bit religious and told me that he had been studying for the ministry but had joined up at his country's call… In three months time he was the only one left out of the twelve… His bad language won universal approval and he also became highly proficient in drinking a bottle of ving blong [sic]. He was killed in December on Passchendaele Ridge.'[87]

Although such a story might be expected from Richards, who freely admitted that he had little time for either churches or 'parsons'[88], such deterioration of faith was no doubt widespread. With good reason, the sources for *The Army and Religion* report fretted about the very different standards of morality that appertained in the Army, particularly when soldiers were exposed to every kind of moral temptation in bases and rear areas. According to a clergyman who had worked with the Army in Salonika, 'Sins of the body are not felt to be disgraceful. The cheeriest bunch of men I ever met perhaps were patients in a venereal hospital at Marseilles… Public opinion in the Army does not condemn a man for drunkenness, impurity, or profanity. It does not condemn him because of its sense of the conditions of his life.'[89] However, moral deterioration was not only a function of profanity, drunkenness and sins of the flesh, but was for some a corollary of the brutality of war itself. F. R. Barry, an Army Chaplain and a Fellow of Oriel College, was all too aware of these corrupting influences, observing in an essay published in 1917 that

> '…the most horrible thing about war in the end – worse than all the physical disgusts so carefully kept from you by the papers – is that it means the cancerous destruction of the highest spiritual faculties and a progressive lowering of standards. Of course it is not in the least surprising. A life that

varies between infernal monotony and unnameable obscenity, with never any privacy, leisure or comfort, is not very fruitful soil in which to seek for new growths of spiritual power.'[90]

Service life during the Second World War posed identical spiritual and moral challenges. For Tom Wilson, an Anglican evangelical serving with the RAF in Northern Ireland in 1942, the funeral of an Australian pilot shook his pre-war evangelical convictions to their foundations:

> '...the service was absolutely miserable, the Northern Irish, Church of Ireland vicar ... couldn't see that an Australian fighter pilot had much chance of not being damned... I was absolutely fed up after the service and I felt, "Right, if that chap doesn't want our lot in Heaven with him I'd rather stay with Junior."'[91]

For 20-year-old Paddy Devlin, one of thousands of Roman Catholic volunteers from Eire who served in the British forces during the Second World War, the distribution of contraceptives among his battalion prior to the Normandy invasion came as a similar test of civilian values:

> 'I refused them [he recalled] and said to the Major, "I thought we were going to France to fight, Sir" ... to prevent further embarrassment I took them and gave them away... I often wondered would we have been issued with the condoms if we had been invading any other country than France.'[92]

In view of such circumstances, one Mass-Observation report considered separation from hearth and home as the litmus test for genuine religious commitment and concluded that not all coped as well as Devlin appears to have done:

> 'Reports have shown many cases of people who in "civvy" street were fairly keen church-goers, and now keep very little connection at all. Many of these people were members of a church dance band, leading lights in the tennis club, regular attenders at the social club, etc. One man, who now goes nowhere near a church, avoids church parades whenever he can [and] swears like a trooper, was the vigorous leader of a Boys Brigade group before joining up – and intends to go back to it after the war!'[93]

Notwithstanding the inimical effects of wartime conditions to the faith of many, the factors that gave rise to the positive development of religious faith during wartime are not hard to identify. As Mass-Observation established in 1942, not only did war have a tendency to 'harden people to the idea of death', rendering some almost indifferent to it, but it also helped to focus a good many minds on the subject.[94] Significantly, during the First World War mass mortality helped not only to stimulate a heightened interest in spiritualism[95] but also served to dissolve centuries-old Protestant taboos concerning prayers for the dead, the Church of England in particular being compelled to adjust its public prayers in order to allow the bereaved to intercede for the deceased.[95] Even from among the ranks of the Church of Scotland, the experience of the First World War elicited calls for the formulation of a Protestant doctrine of purgatory.[96]

In a similar vein, during the Second World War Mass-Observation noted the popularity of films like *Smiling Through*, which represented the afterlife in 'an optimistic way' and which 'showed the dead in heaven still very much as they always had been and taking a deep interest in their loved ones below'.[97] If religion helped to put a more positive gloss on death and its corollaries, then it also helped to provide some means of explanation, support and even vicarious control over difficult circumstances. In this regard, the limited revival of British religion during the Second World War was symptomatic of the same uncertain circumstances that encouraged a strong sense of fatalism, a widespread recourse to intercessory prayer, the common use of amulets, and the observance of sundry protective rituals. Moreover, the war years also sustained a strong interest in astrology, particularly, so Mass-Observation recurrently noted, among women on the Home Front.[98] Although by no means absent from the Home Front during the First World War, all of these phenomena (with the possible exception of astrology) were, of course, very much in evidence among British servicemen of 1914-18, uncertainty and the proximity of death generating a range of responses that was practically identical to that produced on a broader scale in the Second. What must be borne in mind, of course, is that the promiscuous eclecticism, which has characterised popular religion in Britain during the 20th century, ensured that, however conflicting they may have been in theological terms, such beliefs and practices were by no means mutually exclusive; indeed, one Mass-Observation report on astrology dated July 1941 even suggested 'a positive correlation between churchgoing and astrology, in the sense that there is a higher probability of astrological belief among the minority who go to church than among those who do not.'[99]

A conspicuous feature of religious practice in both World Wars was the resort to intercessory prayer, a form of prayer that was routinely observed by parishes and congregations throughout the country (particularly for their members serving with the forces) and which was also a keynote of the national days of prayer.[100] However, such prayer was also private, often routine and by no means confined to occasions of public worship. As one First World War chaplain put it, 'Most men say their prayers before going into action. Some who come out safe never say them again until they are in like danger. But some do, and make prayer a habit.'[101] Although such prayer was sometimes dismissed by rigorists as mere 'funk religion', some churchmen, such as D. S. Cairns, took a more sympathetic view, preferring to acknowledge the often vestigial faith that gave rise to it.[102] However, prayer was not only offered on behalf of oneself but was frequently offered on behalf of others. In an echo of the famous street shrines erected at clerical instigation in the East End of London during the First World War[103], a round of outdoor prayers by the vicar of 'a large industrial parish' in Bristol met with a ready response from its inhabitants in the early summer of 1940. As one letter to *The Times* described it:

'As he stands there with his little crucifix held up against the sky people gather round, or open their doors and windows, not it seems in any vague curiosity but with some understanding and reverence. Names of absent husbands and sons are handed in for special remembrance; and the gratitude of these wives and mothers is very moving.'[104]

Moreover, there is plenty of evidence to show that those who were prayed for often derived considerable comfort from this fact. A week before his death on the Somme on 1 July 1916, Private Walter Shaw of the Leeds Pals wrote to his fiancée telling her that 'it is a welcome thought when one knows his loved ones are commending him to the care of the Almighty'.[105] Similarly, another Yorkshireman, Douglas Firth, recalled that on leaving Great Britain for the Far East in 1941, 'Amidst my own mixed feelings I felt wonderfully aware that many of my family and Christian friends on "the home front" were praying for me.'[106] Of course, apart from the prayers of the living, Catholics in both World Wars also derived comfort from the prayers of the dead. Among saints and putative saints, the young Carmelite nun Therese of Lisieux became popular among Catholic soldiers throughout the Allied armies in the First World War by virtue of her role as intercessor, a role that greatly aided the process of her own canonisation in 1925.[107] Among Protestants, popular hymnody often expressed what more personal prayers could not, a reflection of the great importance of hymnody in popular culture.[108] For a deserter and ex-convict from the East End, the contents of an Army hymn book, which he sang together with an Anglican padre, provided the main source of religious consolation on the eve of his execution in July 1917. As the padre in question, Julian Bickersteth, recalled:

> 'To him, hymn singing meant religion. Probably no other aspect or side of religion had ever touched him, and now he was "up against it" he found real consolation in singing hymns learnt in childhood – he had been to Sunday school up to twelve or thirteen. Anyhow, that was the point of contact I had been seeking for.'[109]

Similarly, as Alfred Castle watched the SS *Yorkshire* slip beneath the surface of the Atlantic in the autumn of 1939, the words of 'Abide with Me' stole into his mind: 'Fast falls the eventide, the darkness deepens, lord with me abide…'[110] Naturally, because of their dramatic context, there is a danger of equating the popularity of intercessory prayers too closely with wartime conditions; as Sarah Williams has shown, routines of private and domestic prayer were commonplace even among non-churchgoers in the borough of Southwark in the period 1880-1939.[111] Again, Mass-Observation reports contextualise this phenomenon. In 1941 and 1942 the members of Mass-Observation's National Panel were asked to specify whether they prayed and what they prayed for, their answers revealing an essential continuity with peacetime routines and concerns. Among the 50 per cent who admitted to praying either regularly or occasionally[112], the surveys found that, although prayers for peace, victory and those in 'wartime danger' were offered by a small minority,

> '…the basic things which people pray about appear to be unaltered by the war… Prayer is thus very largely directed towards the personal well-being,

spiritual and material, of individuals, especially those close to the person praying. They concentrate almost entirely on the present, on physical safety, spiritual goodness and ability to grapple with life's problems.'[113]

Another characteristic feature of religious sentiment in Britain during both World Wars was a strong sense of fatalism, an outlook that, in its orthodox form, was a function of a strong Christian belief in the sovereign hand of providence and, in its more heterodox manifestations, could be more redolent of an atheistic scientific determinism, of the Islamic concept of 'kismet' or of the bleak nihilism of the *Rubáiyát of Omar Khayyám*.[114] Indeed, the case of Douglas Wilson, an officer with the 5th Cameron Highlanders, illustrates that these conflicting attitudes could even co-exist, Wilson confessing in his post-war memoirs that, 'I carried in my tunic pocket two slim paper-covered books held together by a single elastic band – the *Rubáiyát of Omar* and the New Testament. Their covers touched but their content remained worlds apart.'[115] So widespread among British soldiers in the First World War was the '"sure-to-be-hit" sensation' that it was even the subject of a wryly humorous piece by a Private J. Hodson in the *Daily Mail*, in which the author confessed that the sensation was 'mighty unpleasant' and that 'everything you do seems to make death doubly certain'.[116] Among the devout, a sense of fatalism could often take the form of a sense of vocation, with those who survived being convinced that providence had spared them for some special purpose. For Joseph Sandbach, service with the RFC led him to the Methodist ministry after the end of the First World War, the death of a close friend having led him to reflect, 'Well, there's Kenneth, he's gone, it could easily have been me, my life has been saved, what ought I to do with it?'[117] Likewise, for Tom Wilson, an RAF navigator shot down during the Second World War and an avid worker for peace thereafter, 'the statistics were ... of every ten airmen shot down, one survived, and so I've felt since that I've got the burden of the other nine to carry and try and make the world a better place.'[118]

Naturally, the churches were disposed to capitalise on such sentiment. During the First World War 'Tubby' Clayton persuaded prospective ordinands to sign the following pledge: 'If God decides to bring me through this war, I vow to take it as a hint from Him that I shall help and serve the Church in future throughout the life that He gives back to me.'[119] Mass-Observation noted that one evangelical poster of the 'Phoney War' period capitalised on fatalism in civilian circles by proclaiming that 'Not a single shaft can hit, till the love of God sees fit'.[120] Although it is clear that fatalistic sentiment could be exploited by the churches, they were at the same time genuinely concerned about the nature and currency of such convictions among the mass of British soldiers, the SPCK even publishing a pamphlet in 1917 entitled *Christian Fatalism: A conversation between a Soldier and a Chaplain* at the request of Bishop Gwynne, the Army's Deputy Chaplain General. According to one source for *The Army and Religion* report, such fatalism was neither self-consciously Christian nor self-consciously non-Christian, rather 'it is an active philosophy, that if there is a bullet made for you, it will get you some time. It is only a philosophy like this, heathenish though it sounds, that enables many men to stick it.'[121] Similarly, one Roman Catholic chaplain was prepared to discount the significance of such sentiments among men of his own flock: 'Catholics make the same remarks as other men in the same circumstances, but I don't think it can be dignified by calling it the expression of fatalism. It's just jargon.'[122]

Certainly, under comparable circumstances during the Second World War, there was a recrudescence of fatalism among many servicemen. According to a Mass-Observation report of 1941, 'A sort of mystical fatalism' seems to have had 'a very considerable vogue'. According to its author, 'something over 50 per cent profess faith in it', these being divided 'between "Fatalists" and "Scientific Determinists"', who often argued about their conflicting interpretations of human destiny.[123] Whatever their nature, the consequences of such perspectives were clear enough. Thomas Illman recalled how, while serving with the 1st Royal Scots in north-east India in 1944, a stretcher-bearer told him, 'Tomorrow I'm going to die.' The next day, while on patrol, 'there was a shot, and he got shot through the forehead and I always remember before he died he crossed himself... I don't put any significance in the fact that he said he was going to die, it might have just been coincidence but he obviously felt he was.'[124]

Co-existent with a strong sense of fatalism and a firm belief in the power of intercessory prayer was the common observance of protective rituals and the use of protective amulets, or 'mascots' as they were generally referred to by this time. As with the case of personal prayer, the use of such rituals and mascots was already widespread in civilian life, the war serving to accentuate their use.[125] Concerning fatalism, it was often difficult to judge how far such observance and use was emblematic of genuine religious sentiment and how far they were related to the more secular notion of ensuring good luck. Notwithstanding this, many rituals and amulets had a clear Christian derivation. In terms of Christian ritual, soldiers about to go into battle readily attended sacraments such as confession and Holy Communion. In 1917, for example, Hubert Worthington wrote that 'before the last show practically the whole battalion took the Communion.'[126] The same phenomenon re-emerged in the Second World War, with Eric Gethyn-Jones, a padre with the 43rd Reconnaissance Regiment, noting a 'remarkable' turn-out for voluntary services held for the regiment prior to its first action in Normandy in July 1944.[127] Besides formal services, the blessing of the clergy was often sought, particularly (although by no means exclusively) by Catholics.[128] Fr Rudesind Brookes, chaplain to the 1st Irish Guards in 1943, remembered how, before an attack in Tunisia, 'first one soldier, then another, and then another slipped out of the ranks and knelt in front of me for my blessing before quietly returning to their places.'[129]

In both World Wars, the paraphernalia of Catholic devotion – rosaries, crucifixes, miraculous medals and scapulars – was widely seen in the hands of even Protestant Britons. According to Fr Willie Doyle, then writing to his father from the Western Front in 1917, 'There are few men, no matter what their belief, who do not carry a rosary or a Catholic medal around their necks.'[130] In the Second World War, this phenomenon appears to have repeated itself. Although an Anglican by upbringing and wholly impatient of his Roman Catholic sergeant and his 'gaudy pictures of saints'[131], Raleigh Trevelyan was himself presented with a St

Christopher medal by his mother before leaving England, a medal to which he subsequently ascribed his survival on several occasions while serving in Italy.[132] Significantly, for more Bible-conscious Protestants, there was reassurance in the protective value of the Good Book itself. For Arthur Smith, a staff officer on the Western Front during the First World War, a Bible given to him by his father proved to be life-saving. Inscribed with a text from the Psalms ('Because thou hast made the Lord thy refuge. There shall no evil befall thee…') Smith recalled that on one occasion a shell splinter 'cut right through the Bible until that page in the Psalms from which that text was taken … that to me was a very significant thing and encouraged my faith.'[133]

Closely related to this belief in the protective efficacy of personal religious artefacts was a widespread belief in the providential survival of public religious images and buildings. This was strongly evidenced by the multitudinous observations made during the First World War on the survival of crucifixes in ruined churches and wayside calvaries on the Western Front. As one scarcely literate soldier wrote to his old Bible class teacher in Bournemouth, 'I visited a certain place the other week out here, the church there was all in ruins, the stain glass windows were all smashed and broken … the Alter [sic], it was all smashed and broken about, but the Crucific of our "Almighty Father" left intact. It being left suspended on two or three remaining pieces of plaster left from the ruined brickwork of the Alter [sic].'[134] Similar observations were to resurface three decades later. In 1944, for example, Charlie Wakeley, a private in the 1st Worcesters, noted the survival of calvaries amidst the shattered landscape of Normandy, a phenomenon that so impressed him that he raised the matter with his chaplain.[135]

Similarly, on the Home Front from as early as September 1939, a Mass-Observation observer noted how a labourer had commented to his workmates 'that it is, "Mervyllous how these 'ere Virgin Marys ain't broken after an air-raid on a church."'[136] This sense of the providential immunity of sacred sites partly accounts for the use of churches as air raid shelters in both World Wars[137] and also accentuates the religious significance of the famous propaganda image of St Paul's Cathedral standing intact in the midst of the London Blitz (the 'war's greatest picture' as the *Daily Mail* styled it[138]) and helps to account for why the destruction of Coventry Cathedral came to symbolise the ordeal that the city experienced on the night of 14 November 1940. Whereas, on 31 December 1940, a *Daily Mail* correspondent described St Paul's as 'an island of God, safe and untouched'[139], Clara Milburn wrote on the day after the blitzing of Coventry, 'The casualties are in the neighbourhood of a thousand, and the beautiful 14th-century cathedral is destroyed. I feel numb with the pain of it all.'[140] However, despite its currency, contemporary churchmen often found this fervent attachment to religious artefacts and buildings to be disturbing rather than encouraging. First, this tendency could prove ultimately damaging to faith, particularly given the demonstrably indiscriminate nature of death and destruction.[141] Second, not even the Catholic church, which was naturally sensitive to charges of this kind, taught that devotional items had any intrinsic value as mascots, Catholic chaplains being keen to emphasise that devotional objects should be seen and used as devotional aids, as emblems of denominational allegiance and as tokens of their owners' dedication to that divine power in whom the fate of all things rested.[142]

Although the misuse and misperception of religious artefacts and rituals clearly posed problems for orthodox religion, the use of more secular amulets and rituals was just as widespread. Evidence from both World Wars shows that there was an endless variety of mascots and rituals, many being seen as effectual only by their owners. Besides the rabbits' paws and four-leaf clovers sanctioned by popular custom, virtually anything could become a mascot. During the First World War Philip Gibbs had a small piece of coal pressed upon him by an Irish officer who described it as his 'lucky charm', and Gibbs remembered having felt much safer for possessing it.[143]

The same accentuated belief in luck was also apparent during the Second World War. Kenneth Lee, a fighter pilot during the Battle of Britain, kept a 'Jiminy Cricket' mascot in the cockpit of his Hurricane and ensured that he always urinated on its tailwheel before take-off.[144] Although it has been estimated that one out of three British servicemen and women carried some form of mascot during the Second World War[145], belief in luck and the observance of related rituals was also endemic on the Home Front at this time. Mass-Observation reports from the war years consistently found that, even among the members of the organisation's National Panel, four-fifths of women and half of men observed rituals or held beliefs that were deemed to be 'superstitious'.[146] Again, as with the case of mascots, many of these rituals and beliefs were highly personalised, one Mass-Observer admitting:

'Since serving in the [Auxiliary Fire Service] I have become superstitious about cleaning my rubber boots. After cleaning my boots we generally suffer a blitz, and I am out all night fighting fires. The same thing occurs if I am short of cigarettes while on duty. It has occurred so often.'[147]

Besides artefacts and rituals, even people could be regarded as fundamentally lucky or unlucky. During the First World War Guy Chapman invested considerable faith in his battalion's commanding officer, who became a 'talisman which could soothe frayed nerves and call up new strength'.[148] Chapman was not alone in entertaining such beliefs. One Mass-Observer serving with the RAF in 1941 noted how some of his colleagues regarded themselves as 'attracting danger', whereas others thought of themselves as 'dispelling danger'.[149] Naturally enough, the clergy tended to take a dim view of these attitudes and practices, a fact that can be illustrated by the case of the 5th Gloucestershire Regiment and its direct descendant in the Second World War, the 43rd Reconnaissance Regiment. In 1915 the chaplain-editor of *The Fifth Glo'ster Gazette* wrote, 'It is high time that attention be drawn to the childish belief in "mascots". It is nothing less than rank paganism and silly superstition to believe that the "lucky charm" is going to protect one from danger.'[150] Twenty-nine years later, just prior to the Normandy invasion, Eric Gethyn-Jones was faced with a similar problem, being compelled to give a talk to the 43rd Reconnaissance Regiment on 'the foolishness of superstition', a talk that had been occasioned by an apparent unwillingness to tempt fate that had manifested itself in 'the reluctance of some to wear their identity discs'.[151]

This chapter has investigated hitherto neglected aspects of popular religious behaviour and attitudes in Britain during the two World Wars. In doing so it has illustrated both the resilience and complexity of popular religious culture and also the accuracy of the observation that 'the religion of the British people ... did not fit securely and simply into the ecclesiastical or theological categories of the main-line churches'.[152] In these respects, the two World Wars would certainly appear to be but 'two acts ... in a single drama'.[153] There are, however, important differences between the two cases. During the inter-war period, churchgoing and Sunday school attendance were on the decline while religious broadcasting became a significant new element in the religious life of the nation. There are differences, too, in the sources available to the historian, Mass-Observation's surveys comprising a broader synthesis of the religious life of the nation between 1939 and 1945 than any church-sponsored survey of the Army between 1914 and 1918. Nevertheless, given the similarities between the two contexts, it may be that this delineation of religious life during the Second World War provides a useful interpretative model for those investigating its dynamics between 1914 and 1918.

Recommended reading

Brown, Stewart J., '"A Solemn Purification by Fire": Responses to the Great War in the Scottish Presbyterian Churches', in *Journal of Ecclesiastical History* xlv (1994) pp82-104

Hastings, Adrian, *A History of English Christianity 1920-1990* (London: SCM, 1991)

Hoover, A. J., *God, Germany, and Britain in the Great War: A Study in Clerical Nationalism* (New York: Praeger, 1989)

God, Britain, and Hitler in World War II: The view of the British Clergy, 1939-1945 (Westport, CT: Praeger, 1999)

Marrin, Albert, *The Last Crusade: The Church of England in the First World War* (Durham, NC: Duke University Press, 1974)

Johnstone, Tom and Hagerty, James, *The Cross on the Sword: Catholic Chaplains in the Forces* (London: Cassell, 1996)

Robbins, Keith, 'Britain, 1940 and "Christian Civilisation"', in Beales, D. and Best, G. (eds), *History, Society and the Churches* (Cambridge: Cambridge University Press, 1985)

Schweitzer, R., 'The Cross and the Trenches: Religious Faith and Doubt Among Some British Soldiers on the Western Front', in *War and Society* xvi (1998) pp33-57

Sheils, W. J. (ed), 'The Church and War', in *Studies in Church History* xx (1983)

Wilkinson, Alan, *The Church of England and the First World War* (London: SPCK, 1978)

Dissent or Conform?: War, Peace and the English Churches 1900-1945 (London: SCM, 1986)

Notes

[1] See, eg, Martin Ceadel, *Pacifism in Britain 1914-1945* (Oxford: Clarendon Press, 1980); Adrian Hastings, *A History of English Christianity 1920-1990* (London: SCM, 1991); A. J. Hoover, *God, Germany, and Britain in the Great War: A Study in Clerical Nationalism* (New York: Praeger, 1989); A. J. Hoover, *God, Britain, and Hitler in World War II: The view of the British Clergy, 1939-1945* (Westport, CT: Praeger, 1999); Albert Marrin, *The Last Crusade: The Church of England in the First World War* (Durham, NC: Duke University Press, 1974); Stuart Mews, 'Religion and English Society in the First World War' (unpublished PhD thesis, Cambridge: 1973); Keith Robbins, 'Britain, 1940 and "Christian Civilisation"' in D. Beales and G. Best (eds), *History, Society and the Churches* (Cambridge: Cambridge University Press, 1985); W. J. Sheils (ed), 'The Church and War', *Studies in Church History* xx (1983)

[2] The former figure comprised 2,437,000 Episcopalians, 1,242,000 Scottish Presbyterians, 2,003,000 Nonconformists, and 2,389,000 Roman Catholics. Robert Currie, Alan Gilbert and Lee Horsley, *Churches and Churchgoers: Patterns of Church Growth in the British Isles since 1700* (Oxford: Clarendon Press, 1977) p31

[3] Geoffrey Alderman, *Modern British Jewry* (Oxford: Clarendon Press, 1998) p120

[4] These figures include older groups such as Quakers and Moravians as well as 19th-century arrivals from the United Sates such as the Mormons and the Seventh Day Adventists. Robert Currie et al, op cit, pp157-60

[5] Ibid, p194

[6] See David Hempton, *Religion and Political Culture in Britain and Ireland* (Cambridge: Cambridge University Press, 1996)

[7] D. S. Cairns, *The Army and Religion: An Enquiry and its Bearing upon the Religious Life of the Nation* (London: Macmillan, 1919) pp189-91

[8] Callum G. Brown, *Religion and Society in Scotland since 1707* (Edinburgh: Edinburgh University Press, 1997) pp196-204; Hugh McLeod, *Religion and Society in England, 1850-1914* (Basingstoke: Macmillan, 1996) pp156-68

[9] The former figure now comprised 1,987,000 Episcopalians, 1,297,000 Scottish Presbyterians, 1,746,000 Nonconformists and 3,094,000 Roman Catholics. See Robert Currie et al, op cit, p32

[10] Ibid, p194

[11] Ibid, p235

[12] Ibid, pp157-9. The Seventh Day Adventists increased their membership from 2,671 in 1914 to 6,268 in 1946. The Jehovah's Witnesses, who first made converts in Britain in about 1914, numbered 11,395 in 1946.

[13] Geoffrey Alderman, op cit, p321

[14] S. C. Williams, *Religious Belief and Popular Culture in Southwark c1880-1939* (Oxford: Oxford University Press, 1999) p10

[15] See, eg, F. B. MacNutt (ed), *The Church in the Furnace: Essays by Seventeen Temporary Chaplains on Active Service in France and Flanders* (London: Macmillan, 1917); L. Creighton (ed), *Letters of Oswin Creighton, C. F.* (London: Longmans, Green & Co, 1920)

[16] Donald Hankey, *A Student in Arms* (London: Andrew Melrose, 1918) pp12, 89-102

[17] D. S. Cairns, op cit, p30

[18] Ibid, p200

[19] D. S. Cairns, op cit, pxiv; Alan Wilkinson, *The Church of England and the First World War* (London: SPCK, 1978) p161

[20] Mass-Observation [hereafter MO] FR 2274. All Mass-Observation material is reproduced by permission of Curtis Brown Ltd, London, © the Trustees of the Mass-Observation Archive at the University of Sussex

[21] D. S. Cairns, op cit, pp100-21; P. C. T. Crick, 'The Soldier's Religion' in F. B. MacNutt (ed), op cit, pp352-5

[22] D. S. Cairns, op cit, p115

[23] Ibid, p116

[24] P. C. T. Crick, op cit, p356

[25] Charles Plater (ed), *Catholic Soldiers by Sixty Chaplains and Many Others* (London: Longmans, Green & Co, 1919) p34

[26] John Stevenson, *British Society 1914-45* (Harmondsworth: Penguin, 1990) pp148, 361; Adrian Hastings, op cit, pp75, 254

[27] Alan Wilkinson, *Dissent or Conform?: War, Peace and the English Churches 1900-1945* (London: SCM, 1986) p296

[28] Raleigh Trevelyan, *The Fortress* (London: Buchan & Enright, 1985) p81

[29] D. S. Cairns, op cit, p2

[30] MO FR 2274

[31] Keith Robbins, op cit; A. J. Hoover, *God, Britain, and Hitler in World War II*, op cit, pp97-117

[32] N. Longmate, *How We Lived Then* (London: Hutchinson, 1971) p398

[33] Alan Wilkinson, op cit, pp26-8; Paul Chilton, 'Nukespeak: nuclear language, culture and propaganda' in C. Aubrey (ed), *Nukespeak: The Media and the Bomb* (London: Comedia, 1982) pp99-100

[34] Nigel Cave, 'Haig and Religion' in Brian Bond and Nigel Cave (eds), *Haig: A Reappraisal 70 Years On* (Barnsley: Pen and Sword, 1999) pp242-3; B. L. Montgomery, *The Memoirs of Field-Marshal the Viscount Montgomery of Alamein* (London: Collins, 1958) pp227-30

[35] Alan Wilkinson, *The Church of England and the First World War*, op cit, p26

[36] A. J. Hoover, op cit, p103

[37] Paul Fussell, *The Great War and Modern Memory* (Oxford: Oxford University Press, 1977) p117; Annette Becker, *War and Faith: The Religious Imagination in France, 1914-1930* (Oxford: Berg, 1998) pp15-7

[38] Albert Marrin, op cit, p139

[39] Elizabeth Sibbery, 'Images of the Crusades in Recent Times' in Jonathan Riley-Smith (ed), *The Oxford Illustrated History of the Crusades* (London: BCA, 1995) p382

[40] MO FR 23

[41] Cited in Keith Robbins, op cit, p285

[42] MO FR 1566

[43] Paul Fussell, op cit, pp115-6; Albert Marrin, op cit, p137; Stewart J. Brown, '"A Solemn Purification by Fire": Responses to the Great War in the Scottish Presbyterian Churches', *Journal of Ecclesiastical History* xlv (1994) pp82-104, pp88-9

[44] Matthew 8:26

[45] Harold G. Green, *The Sign of the Cross* (Ipswich: 1944) pp8-9. The authors are grateful to Ms Violet Connell for this reference.

[46] Bryan Cooper, *The Tenth (Irish) Division in Gallipoli* (Blackrock: Irish Academic Press, 1993) p107

[47] MO FR 363

[48] James Flint, '"Must God Go Fascist?": English Catholic Opinion and the Spanish Civil War', *Church History* lvi (1987) pp364-74; 'English Catholics and the Proposed Soviet Alliance, 1939', *Journal of Ecclesiastical History* xlviii (1997) pp468-84; MO FR 23

[49] Raleigh Trevelyan, op cit, p75

[50] *The Times*, 7 January 1918, p4

[51] MO FR 658

[52] N. Longmate, op cit, p398 footnote

[53] Peter Donnelly (ed), *Mrs Milburn's Diaries: An Englishwoman's day-today reflections, 1939-45* (Glasgow: Fontana, 1980) p290

[54] N. Longmate, op cit, p428

[55] J. Gardiner, *D-Day: Those Who Were There* (London: Collins & Brown, 1994) pp178-80

[56] Imperial War Museum Department of Documents (hereafter IWM Documents), Mrs L. Hayman, 88/51/1

[57] Paul Fussell, op cit, pp137-44

[58] L. Creighton (ed), op cit, p180

[59] Raleigh Trevelyan, op cit, p. 196

[60] IWM Documents, Miscellaneous 169, Item 2601

[61] IWM Documents, Fr T. F. Bradley, 91/38/1

[62] IWM Documents, J. K. Brown, 94/46/1

63 IWM Documents, Miscellaneous 158, Item 2446

64 See, eg, IWM Documents, T. B. Butt, 90/18/1; Liddle Collection, Percival Arthur Brown

65 Gavin White, 'The Fall of France' in W. J. Sheils (ed), op cit, p432

66 Bernice Archer, '"A Low-Key Affair": Memories of Civilian Internment in the Far East, 1942-1945' in M. Evans and K. Lunn (eds), *War and Memory in the Twentieth Century* (Oxford: Berg, 1997) p53

67 Ernest Gordon, *Miracle on the River Kwai* (London: Collins, 1972) p69

68 Interview with Joseph Sandbach, IWM Sound Archive, 4784 /8, 1980

69 Ernest Gordon, op cit, pp87-91

70 Ibid, pp121, 142-5

71 Charles Plater, op cit, pp144-53; Tom Johnstone and James Hagerty, *The Cross on the Sword: Catholic Chaplains in the Forces* (London: Cassell, 1996) p109

72 R. Schweitzer, 'The Cross and the Trenches: Religious Faith and Doubt Among Some British Soldiers on the Western Front', *War and Society* xvi (1998) pp33-57, p36

73 Liddle Collection, Sir Hubert Worthington

74 IWM Documents, Lavinia Orde, 96/34/1

75 Interview with Harry Levy, IWM Sound Archive, 11572/2, 1988

76 Alan Wilkinson, *The Church of England and the First World War*, op cit, pp290-1

77 Robert Currie et al, op cit, p31; Jay Winter, *Sites of Memory, Sites of Mourning: The Great War in European Cultural History* (Cambridge: Canto) pp54-77; Stuart Mews, 'Religious Life Between the Wars, 1920-1940', in Sheridan Gilley and W. J. Sheils (ed), *A History of Religion in Britain* (Oxford: Blackwell, 1994) pp449-53

78 Adrian Hastings, op cit, p444; Callum G. Brown, op cit, p64

79 MO FR 23

80 MO FR 1566

81 A. Danchev, 'The Army and the Home Front 1939-45', in D. Chandler (ed), *The Oxford Illustrated History of the British Army* (Oxford: Oxford University Press, 1994) p311

82 MO FR 1525; FR 1566

84 MO FR 622

85 MO FR 1870A

86 MO FR 1572

87 Frank Richards, *Old Soldiers Never Die* (London: Anthony Mott, 1983) p239

88 Ibid, pp11-3; 88-91

89 D. S. Cairns, op cit, p148

90 F. R. Barry, 'Faith in the Light of War' in F. B. MacNutt (ed), op cit, p53

91 Interview, authors' collection, 27 January 1999

92 IWM Documents, P. R. Devlin, 89/13/1

93 MO FR 1870A

94 MO FR 1315

95 Jay Winter, op cit, pp54-77

95 Alan Wilkinson, *The Church of England and the First World War*, op cit, pp175-8

96 Stewart J. Brown, op cit, p94

97 MO FR 2190E

98 MO FR 23; FR 769

99 MO FR 769

100 Alan Wilkinson, *The Church of England and the First World War*, op cit, p67; N. Longmate, op cit, p386

101 D. S. Cairns, op cit, p166

102 Ibid, p12

103 Alan Wilkinson, *The Church of England and the First World War*, op cit, p170-1

104 *The Times*, 10 June 1940, p7

105 Liddle Collection, Walter Shaw

106 Douglas Firth, *The Spirit of the River Kwai* (Keighley: Richard Netherwood, 1995) p7

107 Annette Becker, op cit, pp83-5; Benedict Williamson, *'Happy Days' in France and Flanders* (London: Harding & More, 1921) pp84-5; 92

108 S. C. Williams, op cit, pp149-54

[109] J. Terraine (ed), *The Bickersteth Diaries* (London: Leo Cooper, 1996) p193

[110] IWM Documents, A. V. Castle, 97/38/1

[111] S. C. Williams, op cit, pp142-3

[112] MO FR 1566

[113] MO FR 1525

[114] D. S. Cairns, op cit, p162

[115] Liddle Collection, D. J. B. Wilson

[116] Frederick Treves (ed), *Made in the Trenches* (London: George Allen & Unwin, 1916) pp183-4

[117] Interview with Joseph Sandbach, IWM Sound Archive, 4784/8, 1980

[118] Interview, authors' collection, 27 January 1999

[119] Cited in Alan Wilkinson, *The Church of England and the First World War*, op cit, p277

[120] MO FR 23

[121] D. S. Cairns, op cit, p161

[122] Charles Plater, op cit, pp19-20

[123] MO FR 569

[124] Interview with Thomas Tillman, IWM Sound Archive, 18438/2, 1998

[125] S. C. Williams, op cit, pp61-75

[126] Liddle Collection, Hubert Worthington

[127] Eric Gethyn-Jones, *A Territorial Army Chaplain in Peace and War* (East Wittering: Gooday Publishers, 1988) p106

[128] Charles Plater, op cit, p20

[129] A. Wheatley, *Father Dolly, the Guardsman Monk* (London: Henry Melland, 1983) pp132-3

[130] Alfred O'Rahilly, *Father William Doyle SJ* (London: Longmans, Green & Co, 1932) p497

[131] Raleigh Trevelyan, op cit, p68

[132] Ibid, pp24, 77-8

[133] Liddle Collection, Arthur Smith

[134] IWM Documents, Mrs L. Hayman, 88/51/1

[135] Interview, authors' collection, 28 June 1999

[136] MO FR 23

[137] Alan Wilkinson, *The Church of England and the First World War*, op cit, pp67-8; N. Longmate, op cit, pp387-8

[138] *Daily Mail*, 31 December 1940, p1

[139] Ibid, p3

[140] Peter Donnelly (ed), op cit, p80

[141] Charles Plater, op cit, p10

[142] Ibid, pp24-32

[143] Philip Gibbs, *Realities of War* (London: Heinemann, 1920) p117

[144] Tim Clayton and Phil Craig, *Finest Hour* (London: Hodder & Stoughton, 1999) p230

[145] Geoffrey Gorer, *Exploring English Character* (London: Cresset Press, 1955) p265

[146] MO FR 975; FR 2112

[147] MO FR 975

[148] Guy Chapman, *A Passionate Prodigality* (Leatherhead: Ashford, Buchan & Enright, 1990) pp195-6

[149] MO FR 569

[150] J. G. Fuller, *Troop Morale and Popular Culture in the British and Dominion Armies 1914-1918* (Oxford: Clarendon Press, 1990) p157

[151] Eric Gethyn-Jones, op cit, p81

[152] Keith Robbins et al, 'Religion', in Dear, I. C. B. (ed), *The Oxford Companion to the Second World War* (Oxford: Oxford University Press, 1995) p938

[153] Michael Howard, 'A Thirty Years' War?: The Two World Wars in Historical Perspective', in *Transactions of the Royal Historical Society* Sixth Series (iii) (1995) p172

Chapter 26

Ethics and weaponry

Edward M. Spiers

In the two World Wars controversies erupted over the introduction of poison gas, submarine attacks on merchant shipping, and the bombing of civilian communities. Those engaged in these forms of warfare may not have understood the distinctions between *jus ad bellum* and *jus in bello* (the laws governing the causes of war and the conduct of war respectively)[1], but they were not oblivious of the ethical issues involved, even if some chose to dispute their significance, justifying their actions on more pragmatic grounds, or found little opportunity to act in accordance with any ethical reservations. Nor were these servicemen normally knowledgeable about the finer points of ethics and theology, although they would sometimes express their views in religious terms. In some cases their ethical perspectives derived from hazy notions of what constituted chivalrous behaviour in warfare, prompting J. B. S. Haldane (one of the leading scientists involved in chemical warfare for Britain in the First World War) to condemn 'this ignorance' as 'one of the most hideous forms of sentimentalism … the attachment of the professional soldier to cruel and obsolete killing machines'.[2] Nevertheless, ethical sentiments were expressed by servicemen in both wars, often colouring attitudes towards the enemy, the war, and the mode of combat involved.

The introduction of poison gas on the battlefield, particularly the first major chlorine attack by the Germans at Ypres on 22 April 1915, aroused fierce indignation. Allied soldiers were appalled by the spectre of gas clouds rolling inexorably towards Allied trenches, the inability at first to counter this threat, the indiscriminate and surreptitious effects of the gas (attacking the body from within), and the appearance of the victims. The latter, as Sergeant Elmer Cotton (5th B[attalio]n Northumberland Fusiliers) recalled, were 'all gassed – their colour was black, green and blue, tongues hanging out and eyes staring – one or two were dead and others beyond human aid, some were coughing up green froth from their lungs'.[3] Soldiers had already suffered horrendous wounds, and died in far greater numbers (and probably in as much agony) from conventional ordnance; what appalled survivors of the early gas attacks was the new mode of warfare. As Private E. A. Shephard (1st Bn Dorset Regiment) reflected, 'Had we lost as heavily while actually fighting we would not have cared as much, but our dear boys died like rats in a trap, instead of heroes as they all were.'[4]

Like many of his officers and men, Sir John French, Commander-in-Chief of the British Expeditionary Force, deplored the gas attacks as unchivalrous and underhand. 'It was a very dirty "low down" game to play,' he wrote, 'shooting out that damnable "gas".[5] Several German commanders shared these misgivings: Crown Prince Rupprecht of Bavaria and Colonel-General Karl von Einem, commanders of the Sixth and Third Armies respectively, regarded the use of gas as distasteful, unchivalrous, and likely to redound on the Germans (whenever the Allies retaliated in kind and exploited the prevailing westerly winds).[6] By breaking the norms of warfare, the Germans had intensified the resentment against them. 'This was no clean war,' argued Private Young (9th Bn Royal Scots). 'The enemy had burned their boats, and now it was war to the end, bitter and implacable.'[7] Second Lieutenant A. D. Gillespie (2nd Bn Argyll & Sutherland Highlanders), who acted as censor for the letters of his men, noted that nothing had done more to rouse the men's spirits than these 'dirty tricks'. Not only had gas made him feel 'less and less scrupulous about fighting to the bitter end', but it had also enhanced the righteousness of the Allied cause. He now lost 'all regret, except the personal one for lives lost on our side in this war; they are necessary sacrifices for the lives of all the rest, and for finer principles.'[8]

Commendably for one who believed that the German infraction of *jus in bello* had enhanced the Allies' *jus ad bellum*, Gillespie hoped that the Allies would not retaliate in kind. All war, he conceded, was a 'a bloody business' but it was only 'by sticking to the few rules that men have agreed to keep, that we can prevent ourselves from descending lower than beasts'.[9] His views contrasted sharply with those of Lance Corporal George Ramage (1st Bn Gordon Highlanders): 'All war is foul,' he declared. 'Why object to gas & not bullets… We are arrant humbugs … we object to the Germans using chlorine scientifically. Why the hell don't we use it? Humbug, hypocrisy & want of a clear intelligence I expect.'[10] Many others, from Sir John French downwards, agreed that the Allies had to retaliate in kind. As the Honourable William Fraser (1st Bn Gordon Highlanders) observed, 'They are dirty devils… But we must play their own dirty game as far as gas goes.'[11]

Soldiers of the Special Brigade (formed to deliver the British gas offensive) commonly described their task as one of meting out deserved retribution. 'We feel rather keen,' recalled Richard Gale on the eve of the first British gas attack at Loos, 'at the prospect of giving the Hun some of his own medicine … we feel no humanitarian scruples on the subject'.[12] Lieutenant Charles Ashley (Royal Engineers) concurred; he doubted that 'gas was more objectionable on moral or any other grounds than high explosive'.[13] Adrian E. Hodgkin, who still regarded gas as 'a vile method of warfare', consoled himself with the thought that 'the Bosches have brought it on themselves'.[14] Even Captain Norman P. Campbell, a deeply religious officer, admitted that

'…except for a few days at the very beginning … I have never had any doubts about it [gas warfare] being right… The only real rules seem to me to be:
1. Not to harm non-combatants.
2. Not to do more damage even to combatants than corresponds to the military advantage gained … if one feels that one's cause is just, one may go ahead cheerfully with a clear conscience, not bothering about any other rules than these.'[15]

Although Sir Douglas Haig had justified recourse to gas as a means to an end, namely breaking the deadlock of trench warfare at Loos[16], gas never proved a decisive weapon on the Western Front (and had only localised successes on other fronts). Despite improvements in the methods of delivery and the introduction of more effective gases, particularly mustard gas on 12 July 1917, gas became just another means of inflicting casualties or of harassing the enemy (by forcing him to wear respirators in the vicinity of chemical attacks). While Major Charles H. Foulkes, commander of the Special Brigade, argued that, 'We are not concerned with the ethics of the use of gas in civilised warfare'[17], others could still be incensed at the new methods employed by the enemy. After the Germans introduced mustard gas, Lieutenant J. B. MacLean (1st Bn Cameronians) wrote:

'Honestly, it is a rotten war and some of the things one sees here make one want to choke the Kaiser and all the rest of them. They have a new gas on this sector, the result of which is to produce broncho-pneumonia combined with boils and blisters. Pleasant, isn't it, especially as the stuff usually lies about for a bit before anyone know's [sic] it's there.'[18]

The casualties inflicted by mustard gas only fuelled further demands for retaliation in kind, with Sir Henry Rawlinson pressing for the production of British mustard gas shells to boost morale and assist the defensive battle by creating 'a selected area of ground impossible to attack over'.[19]

Unlike the politicians and propagandists, however, soldiers learned that gas was not an excessively cruel weapon, and that it inflicted a far smaller proportion of fatalities than conventional ordnance. John Singer Sargent's famous painting of 11 blindfolded gas victims hobbling along the road to Amiens failed to convey the reality that some 75 per cent of mustard gas victims suffered only temporary eye irritation and could return to the front within three months or less.[20] A. L. Robins was gassed twice in the last year of the war: the first time was '[as] if I had a bad cold and sore throat' for which he had to go to bed for a week; the second was 'a heavy dose of gas' but only involved hospitalisation for 'about a month' without any 'permanent damage'.[21] In September 1918 Captain H. A. Siepman also tried to reassure his mother that he had suffered 'a touch of gas and the trouble with gas is that it is apt to get at your eyes a bit … they don't even think it is serious enough for me to be sent down to the Base. Within about 3 days I expect to go back to the Battery.'[22] Chemical warfare, in short, had become only one facet of a deeply unpleasant war. It was neither strategically decisive nor peculiarly cruel, but once introduced – breaching the spirit, if not the letter, of the pre-war Hague Conventions on gas warfare – it stimulated the impulse to retaliate in kind and ensured that gas was employed extensively by the major belligerents.

In the wake of the war there were repeated attempts to proscribe chemical warfare, culminating in the Geneva Protocol (July 1925) that banned the first use of chemical and bacteriological methods of warfare but left the signatory powers with the right to retaliate in kind if attacked with these weapons. Following the employment of gas by Italian forces in the Italo-Abyssinian War (1935-36), including the extensive use of aerial gas attacks, most European states endeavoured to prepare their defences against gas warfare and enhance their retaliatory capabilities. Although the principal belligerents declared their willingness to abide by the Protocol at the outset of the Second World War, the first use of gas was considered by some powers, not least Britain after the fall of France (when a German invasion seemed imminent) and after the demoralising effects of the German V-bomb attacks. On both occasions the first-use option was rejected, and on both occasions ethical considerations were raised. On 16 June 1940 Major-General Kenneth M. Loch, the Director of Home Defence, objected to any first use even in the event of invasion lest Britain throw away 'the incalculable moral advantage of keeping our pledged word for a minor tactical surprise', and, five days later, Brigadier Crawford, Inspector of Chemical Warfare, objected on more substantive grounds, but gave moral turpitude as the first disadvantage, particularly lest it offend opinion in the United States.[23] In 1944, when Winston Churchill sought to re-open the issue following the V-bomb attacks on southern England, he exhorted his military advisers to refrain from any moralistic considerations and make a 'cold-blooded calculation' about whether it would pay Britain to launch gas attacks. The Chiefs of Staff duly provided a host of pragmatic reasons for not resorting to gas warfare, but Churchill, though willing to heed their advice, was unconvinced: 'Clearly,' he reflected, 'I cannot make head against the parsons and warriors at the same time.'[24]

Submarine attacks would also provoke ethical debates, particularly when launched without warning against merchant shipping or passenger liners. Merchantmen were legitimate targets, and little ire was aroused by the conventional mode of attack involving German surface ships in the early months of the Great War. Warnings were given, merchant seamen – regarded as civilian non-combatants – were allowed to take to their boats before their ships were sunk, then taken on board the intercepting ship (and often landed at a neutral port). Although submarines could and did intercept ships on the surface, allowing crews to leave before sinking their ships by gunfire, torpedo or planted explosive, exposure exacerbated the risks taken by submariners. Once anti-submarine defences evolved, particularly the use of Q-boats and convoys, submarines had to rely increasingly on submerged attacks without warning, often conducted further out into the Atlantic. Survivors of sunken ships then had to make longer voyages, often in conditions far more hostile than those encountered by ships sunk in coastal waters. As Tony Lane has argued, the 'brutalities' allegedly committed by submarines were essentially 'acts of omission. It was not the case of acts perpetrated but of rescues not undertaken.'[25]

German naval commanders, including Admiral von Pohl, Admiral Reinhard Scheer and Admiral von Holtzendorff, justified the submarine attacks as retaliation for the British blockade of Germany, the only means by which the German Navy could try to end the war quickly (and so save more lives in the longer term), and the only means of maximising the military utility and the peculiar characteristics of the submarine itself. Even in November 1914, before the policy of unrestricted submarine warfare was officially approved, von Pohl asserted that, 'The gravity of the situation demands that we should free ourselves from all scruples which certainly no longer have justification.'[26] The submarine, argued

Scheer, as adopted by all major states, was a peculiarly offensive weapon (unable to rescue large numbers of seamen). It was ideally suited to making war on commerce because it could appear unexpectedly, cause fear and panic, and scare away trade while at the same time escaping the pursuit of the enemy. If it sank merchant vessels, including any crews and passengers, 'the blame,' he asserted, 'would attach to those who despised our warnings and, open-eyed, ran the risk of being torpedoed…' He also queried if it made

> '…any difference, purely from the humane point of view, whether those thousands of men who drown wear naval uniforms or belong to a merchant ship bringing food and munitions to the enemy, thus prolonging the war and augmenting the number of women and children who suffer during the war?'[27]

These views were not widely shared. At the outbreak of the war, Captain R. W. Blacklock (then a Lieutenant) recalled that 'senior officers in the Royal Navy regarded the submarine as a completely caddish way of behaving in warfare and disapproved of it altogether'.[28] His Majesty's submarines, nonetheless, were soon in action with commanders displaying few inhibitions about their missions. As Lieutenant N. D. Holbrook wrote from the Dardanelles on 21 December 1914, 'I hear I sent 100 Turks & many Germans to sleep. I am afraid it lies very lightly on my chest. I very nearly sunk another steamer of sorts today, the dirty dog just managed to escape me.'[29]

Yet the newness of submarine warfare, coupled with the difficulty of taking prisoners or of providing for the security of ships' crews without endangering the submarines concerned, posed acute difficulties. These proved politically embarrassing because the U-boats could inflict substantial civilian casualties. When the Cunard liner *Lusitania*, which was carrying munitions, was sunk on 7 May 1915, 1,198 lives were lost, including 119 Americans. The outrage of the neutral United States and a further outcry over the sinking of the White Star liner *Arabic* (19 August 1915) prompted the imposition of temporary curbs on U-boat operations, but in February 1917 Germany again approved unrestricted submarine warfare. Towards the end of the war, after the mail packet *Leinster* was sunk with the loss of 527 lives (10 October 1918), Arthur Balfour described the Germans as, 'A people with the heart of beasts. Brutes they were, and brutes they remain.'[30]

Many U-boat sailors, though, regarded their work as thoroughly justified. 'If we were to starve like rats in a trap,' claimed Claus Bergen, 'then surely it was our sacred right to cut off the enemy's supplies as well.'[31] Artificer Karl Wiedemann agreed that, 'Swift counter-measures were essential if Germany were not to lose the war almost before it had begun', and, if further justification for submarine operations were necessary, German sailors were incensed, as Leading Seaman W. Schlichting recalled, by the use of armed decoy ships. By employing these vessels, he argued, the British had displayed both 'duplicity and cowardice'.[32] Although U-boats were given orders not to place themselves at risk by surfacing to examine enemy ships[33], many German submarines, like their Allied counterparts in the Baltic, either gave warning or enabled crews to embark on their lifeboats (and sometimes, as in the case of SS *Armenia*, sent out SOS signals, asking any ships in the vicinity to pick up survivors).[34]

Atrocities were committed on both sides, not least in firing on helpless crews in the water, which happened to the crew of the submarine *E13* after it was stranded in Danish waters (19 August 1915) and the crew of *U-24* by Royal Marines from the Baralong (21 August 1915). Similar incidents occurred when some merchant ships were torpedoed without warning – Lieutenant-Commander Wilhelm Werner of *U-55* being renowned for his savagery in the killing and drowning of 100 seamen on one patrol.[35]

As inter-war attempts to prohibit the use of submarines as 'commerce destroyers' foundered with the French refusal to ratify the Washington Treaty (6 February 1922), German and British submariners entered the Second World War bound by the London Protocol (1936). Under these Prize Regulations submarines could sink troopships, warships and ships escorted by warships or aircraft without warning, but were supposed to surface, stop and search unarmed ships, and allow their crews and passengers to escape in boats prior to sinking the vessels. As early as 4 September 1939 the *U-30* sank the liner *Athenia* without warning, and, by the end of the month, the Admiralty announced a general fitting-out of British ships with anti-submarine weapons. On 30 September U-boats were freed from any constraints in the North Sea and the Baltic; on 4 October they were allowed to attack armed merchant ships without warning. From 17 August 1940 onwards they were required to enforce a total blockade around Britain. Quite apart from the intrinsic difficulties of enforcing the Prize Regulations (and British and US submarines would later wage war on merchant shipping without warning), the Germans regarded their U-boat fleet as a crucial strategic weapon. On 28 September 1939 Fleet Officer U-boats wrote 'that the U-boat is still our most effective weapon against Britain, provided sufficient boats are available'.[36] U-boat commanders agreed: Herbert Werner (*U-557*) described the shipping he had sunk in 1941 as 'a vital contribution toward the defeat of Great Britain', and Wolfgang Hirschfeld (a U-boat NCO) recalled the exhortation of Admiral Karl Dönitz in 1942 that, 'The outcome of the war depends on your success.'[37]

The idea of the end justifying the means of submarine warfare (and by ending the war more quickly actually helping to save lives in the longer term) was widely shared. Lieutenant Ian McGeoch, when serving with *P228* in the Mediterranean, believed that if British submarines could cut the supply lines to Rommel's Afrika Korps, 'our army could beat him'. He also refrained from the custom of flying the Jolly Roger on the return from successful patrols, claiming that it was 'no more piratical to sink an enemy destroyer by torpedo from a submarine than, say, by gunfire from a cruiser'.[38] Many Royal Navy boats, nonetheless, flew the Jolly Roger, so demonstrating a sense of separateness about their activities, a pride in their kills (or claimed kills), and a recognition of their distinctively offensive role.[39] Submarine warfare may have become a standardised form of naval conflict, but in waging 'a war of concealment and cunning against defenceless cargo and passenger ships', submarines could arouse feelings of profound loathing in the minds of their enemies. Midshipman Volkmar Konig was very grateful for military protection when the captured crew of *U-99* was landed at Liverpool.[40]

Submariners reacted quite differently to the tensions and pressures involved in tracking a potential prey, launching a salvo of torpedoes (and awaiting upon the result), and, if successful, coping with all the pressures of becoming the hunted instead of the hunter. Lieutenant George Colvin, in command of *Sunfish*, never relished the task of sinking merchant ships, and on one occasion, after firing three torpedoes at a merchant ship making for Kirkenes, was heard to say, 'God, how I hate doing this.' Lieutenant (later Commander) Edward Young reckoned that Colvin had not acquired 'the crust of emotional indifference towards his targets which would have been natural in one whose business was war', and noted that the Torpedo Gunner's Mate aboard the same boat only had one ambition in life, namely 'to kill Germans'. Lieutenant-Commander Malcolm Wanklyn, commander of the *Upholder*, was also described as having 'no qualms' at all about putting 'an end to any number of Huns'.[41]

Between these extremes were a myriad of disparate feelings. Some felt morally numb; as Kapitänleutnant Heinrich Müller-Edwards wrote to his parents:

> 'One is in such a state of nervous tension when one has overcome all sorts of obstacles, avoiding all the destroyers and crept upon one's victim that one has no other thoughts; just like the enemies who have no moral scruples when they want to take our lives with depth charges and bombs.'[42]

All submariners were trained for their profession, and each knew that as part of tightly knit crews they could ill afford any personal distraction lest it jeopardise the safety of the boat itself. Many felt that they had little option on patrol; they had to kill and avoid being killed. Even when there were only 11 U-boats operating in the Atlantic against huge Allied battle fleets (and accompanying aircraft), 'We in the German Navy,' recalled Kapitän Peter Cremer, 'saw ourselves as David being sent out to do battle with Goliath.'[43]

Atrocities occurred on all sides. Some Japanese crews beat prisoners (including the few survivors of the British submarine *Stratagem*), deprived them of food, and reportedly hacked some merchant seamen to death with swords.[44] After the US submarine *Sculpin* had sunk a Japanese fishing-patrol boat, *Miyashiyo*, on 19 June 1943, American sailors took 'pot shots' at the Japanese in the water.[45] There were instances of a British submarine and a U-boat firing on enemy crews in the water, and Kapitän zur See Wolfgang Lüth paid scant attention to the safety of any survivors during his shelling of the sailing ship *Notre Dame du Chatelet*, and the Greek freighter *Cleanthis*.[46] Nevertheless, there were plenty of examples of nautical chivalry prevailing, even when it placed the submarines at some risk to themselves. U-boat commanders, like their British counterparts, passed bandages, supplies, cigarettes, cognac or whisky, and other supplies to shipwrecked crews, gave them courses to steer by if close to land, or released standard SOS signals to draw attention to the position of survivors adrift on the open seas. Roar Boye Börrenson, a stoker from the Norwegian vessel *Ringstad*, paid tribute to Cremer after he had sunk his ship: 'The man was very humane … he was a seaman, one of the type that we produce. He behaved according to the code of seamen who take no oath on it but know: help one another when in trouble at sea!'[47] After vessels had been sunk, many sailors sympathised with the plight of their victims, floundering in the water. 'Once you did get them [U-boat crews] up,' opined Wally Riley (HMS *Starling*), 'you felt sorry for them because of the ordeal they had been through.' Petty Officer Ian Nethercott agreed: 'I don't really see how you could hate them. You just treated them like you would any other half-drowned sailor.'[48]

In view of the limited aerial resources available during the Great War, only a few belligerents could bomb the countries of their enemies. While much of Germany remained inaccessible to Allied aircraft (and Berlin was never bombed), Germany possessed as early as January 1915 an aerial capability unrivalled in range and bomb-carrying capacity. However, Kaiser Wilhelm II and Admiral Alfred von Tirpitz were reluctant to despatch their Zeppelins L3 and L4 on indiscriminate bombing raids, with Tirpitz describing this tactic as 'repulsive', especially if the bombs 'hit and kill an old woman', but he reckoned that 'If one could set fire to London in thirty places, then the repulsiveness would be lost sight of in the immensity of the effect'.[49] Count Zeppelin had also urged the use of his dirigibles in accord with his philosophy: 'the hottest war is the kindest war'.[50] In the subsequent assault by airships and later aeroplanes against 'military' and 'government' targets in London, Paris and elsewhere, the German High Command also attacked enemy morale. Two German lieutenants, captured after their Gotha aircraft came down on the evening of 5-6 December 1917, admitted 'that if bombs went astray it was of no consequence, as one of the objects in raiding England was to demoralise the civilian population, particularly in the East End of London'.[51]

Aerial bombing aroused intense emotions. German pilots were dubbed 'baby-killers' and British pilots professed few scruples about retaliatory bombing. Although Lieutenant H. S. Walmsley preferred to attack Zeppelin sheds, aerodromes and army billets, and did not want 'to go & drop bombs on Hun towns, just to satisfy public opinion', he readily bombed the enemy because 'the Boche … started the game first & is such a complete & utter bounder that I have little sympathy for him & his'.[52] The ends justified the means for Lieutenant Frederick Williams, who refused to consider that German children could suffer from his bombing errors: 'To me, Germany represented a huge fighting machine, which we were bound to resist with every means in our power, if we were not to be crushed.'[53] Lieutenant W. H. Greaves, flying in a Handley Page, was delighted whenever the bombs were dropped, 'knowing as I do, the rotten work the Huns used to do on innocent people and towns in dear old England'. He justified these reprisals, by claiming, 'How different is our work from theirs. We bomb important military circles and they, the first thing they find.'[54]

Despite the effort expended, and the sacrifices of the pilots involved, aerial bombing neither inflicted massive civilian casualties nor posed a strategic threat during the Great War. In both scale and purpose, bombing proved a strategic, if not a decisive, option during the Second World War, with Bomber Command dropping some 1 million tons of bombs on Germany (about 70 per cent of the Allied bombing effort).[55] Although the bombing was not inhibited by any inter-war legal convention, Bomber Command entered the war with instructions that forbade the intentional bombardment of civilians, that stressed the importance of identifying targets, and that required any bombing be conducted with a 'reasonable expectation' of hitting the target and not civilians in the neighbourhood 'through negligence'.[56] However, after the German bombing in Poland, Churchill's appointment as Prime Minister (10 May 1940), and the Luftwaffe's destruction of much of Rotterdam (14 May 1940), the British authorities showed few scruples about launching Bomber Command in attacks upon German targets east of the Rhine. Although the indiscriminate bombing of civilians was still prohibited, the area bombing of oil supplies, air installations, communications and industrial targets was authorised and civilian casualties were only too likely to occur.[57] Sir Charles Portal, when Commander-in-Chief Bomber Command, assumed that Anglo-American bombing could incidentally kill some 900,000 civilians (and seriously injure another 1,000,000) in the course of destroying one-third of German industry, diverting more and more of the German war effort to home defence, and so handicapping German operations by land, sea and air in all other theatres.[58]

Inevitably, in view of the vast numbers of service personnel involved, area bombing aroused mixed emotions. Many would agree with Air Vice-Marshal Jack Furner that 'I felt no guilt at the time – and I feel none now' (20 November 1991).[59] Ron A. Read DFC, regarded war as an 'excuse for abandoning morality … [and in] a business of inflicting nastiness and horror upon the enemy, morality quickly deserts the combatants'.[60] Some admitted that they had never really reflected on the ethical issues involved in area bombing. 'I must confess,' wrote Eric H. Woods (a former navigator, Bomber Command) that 'like a lot of my colleagues … concern at the consequences never entered my head. We had all seen what had happened to London and most of the other large cities and so our attacks seemed fully justified…'[61] More pragmatically, Stephen Claud Masters, a Lancaster navigator, would reply to post-war criticism of Bomber Command by arguing:

> 'If I am to worry about what I am doing, then I can't do what I am supposed to be doing. I knew what they were going through… We weren't interested in people, we were interested in a target… We felt quite justified in what we were doing.'[62]

The special nature of bombing, and the peculiar demands imposed upon small bomber crews during a mission, imposed peculiar constraints and forged fierce bonds of loyalty and comradeship. Many insisted that we were only 'doing our job'; and, whatever the emotions of exhilaration or fear experienced by individuals, 'once airborne,' recalled Frederick Fish, 'we became strictly professional to do a good job, swallow our fear and not to show it, and try to keep calm during dangerous moments.'[63] Neither the Luftwaffe nor Bomber Command ever mentioned people in their preparatory briefings, and the technical demands of flying a mission consumed collective energies. Peter Stahl, a Ju88 pilot, recounted the list of 'military' targets catalogued before his first raid on London and the reassurance that in 'modern war it is hardly possible to determine a clear dividing line between military and non-military targets'.[64] In any event, the dropping of bombs at night from 20,000 feet was a remote impersonal exercise. 'Our destructive efforts,' observed Robert S. Raymond (an American volunteer with Bomber Command), 'are never identified with the people themselves. Even when I see buildings blowing up and in flames as at Milan, I can't imagine people in them. It's like looking at a picture on the screen.'[65] Norman Lee, an air gunner in Halifax bombers, added, 'It was just a technical job, delivering the bombs ... letting them go and then returning home again. We didn't think about the people we were killing, because we didn't see them.'[66] Group Captain H. Gordon Davies conceded that it was only after the war, when he took passengers in his Lancaster on low-level daytime flights over Germany, that 'the true horror became real and we saw the price the German people had paid for their mesmerisation by Hitler and the Nazi party'.[67]

Some airmen, nonetheless, were concerned about the sufferings of their victims. Pilot Rupert D. Cooling claimed that he had doubted the precision of area bombing, and, while admitting that it improved towards the end of the war, he preferred attacking single targets in the desert such as airfields, ports and harbours.[68] On his first operational mission, Sergeant Les Bartlett wrote in his diary: 'I say a prayer to ask forgiveness for the murder of so many human beings by the dropping of my bombs.'[69] A long-serving Pathfinder navigator reportedly 'hated the thought of indiscriminate bombing and always thought of women, children, hospitals and suchlike. But, to whom could you express such doubts?'[70]

Many others regarded their task as one of meting out retributive justice. Luftwaffe pilots professed growing anxiety about the increasingly extensive effects of Anglo-American bombing in Germany. While some recognised that pilots on both sides were trying to discriminate between military and non-military targets, others like Hajo Herrmann saw themselves engaged in 'revenge attacks' on London.[71] Similarly, Flight Lieutenant Kenneth M. Pincott recalled that there was a resolve in Bomber Command to 'avenge the blitzkrieg that took place on our towns and cities'[72], sentiments sometimes compounded by feelings of personal vengeance. In November 1943 Richard Dyson volunteered to serve as aircrew because German bombing appalled him: 'In my mind, at that particular time, there was only one good German, and he had to be a dead one!'[73] James C. Richardson, a bomb-aimer on board Halifax bombers, wanted retribution after his wife was nearly killed during an air raid in London, while Norman Winch, a Stirling pilot, having lost his father in the First World War and his wife and sister in an air raid in 1940, admitted, 'I didn't mind who I killed as long as they were Germans.'[74] Pilot V. Hartwright, who had seen cities burning from some 50 miles out over the North Sea, could only imagine 'what untold horror, misery and suffering the Nazi bombers have caused'. Retaliation in kind could not suffice: 'Germany as a nation,' he argued, 'must be destroyed, and before we lay down our arms it should also be punished.'[75]

However much the claim of Air Chief Marshal Sir Arthur Harris that the Nazis had 'sowed the wind – and now they are going to reap the whirlwind'[76] resonated through the ranks, the aircrews of Bomber Command also recognised that their bombing missions represented the only way of striking directly at Germany for much of the war. This was recognised not only as a means of bolstering public morale and of fulfilling various strategic and tactical purposes (including deflecting attention from the much-delayed launching of the Second Front), but it also served a fundamental ethical purpose. If Bomber Command was, as Flight Lieutenant Charles E. Smith asserted, 'the essential prong at the heart of Hitler', then the endeavours of allied aircrew were thought likely to assist in ending the war more quickly and so saving lives in the longer term.[77]

In both wars serving personnel grappled with the ethical implications of employing new weapons, especially those that had extensive, indiscriminate effects and a potential strategic significance. If some discounted the significance of these concerns, and many were too preoccupied with their duties, tired, or distracted by other fears and emotions to worry unduly about them, soldiers, sailors and airmen on both sides perceived the importance of justifying their actions at the time and in retrospect. These justifications embraced notions of chivalrous conduct in battle, respecting the lives of non-combatants (or at least of not deliberately targeting them), proportionate reprisals often in the guise of retaliation in kind, retributive punishment, and employing various means to terminate the war more quickly. Inevitably these aims could not be pursued in an absolute sense, and at times the pursuit of one aim would contradict another, particularly if dependent upon weapons that lacked the necessary accuracy and precision. Under the pressures of war and small group solidarity, few individuals felt able to express any ethical reservations openly, still less allow them to detract from their duties in a gun battery, on board a submarine, or during a bombing mission. Nor did the victims of bombs or torpedoes discern much difference between those that were delivered with a sense of remorse or vengeance. Ultimately, though, these ethical feelings testified to the endurance of humanitarian sentiments even under the most exacting of circumstances, and contributed to the post-war debates about the propriety of particular forms of combat.

Recommended reading

Best, Geoffrey, *Humanity in Warfare* (New York: Columbia University Press, 1980)

Garrett, Steven A., *Ethics and Airpower in World War II: The British Bombing of German Cities* (New York: St Martin's Press, 1993)

Haldane, J. B. S., *Callinicus: A Defence of Chemical Warfare* (New York: Garland, new ed 1972)

Howard, Michael (ed), *Restraints on War: Studies in the limitation of armed conflict* (Oxford: Oxford University Press, 1979)

Howard, Michael, Andreopoulous, George J. and Shulman, Mark R. (eds), *The Laws of War: Constraints on Warfare in the Western World* (New Haven: Yale University Press, 1994)

Walzer, Michael, *Just and Unjust Wars: A Moral Argument with Historical Illustrations* (London: Pelican Books, 1980)

Wells, Mark K., *Courage and Air Warfare: The Allied Aircrew Experience in the Second World War* (London: Frank Cass, 1995)

Notes

[1]　G. Best, *Humanity in Warfare* (New York: Columbia Press, 1980) pp8-11

[2]　J. B. S. Haldane, *Callinicus: A Defence of Chemical Warfare* (New York: Garland, new ed 1972) p28

[3]　Sgt E. W. Cotton, Diary, 24 May 1915, Imperial War Museum [hereafter IWM], P262T

[4]　Pte E. A. Shephard, Diary, 2 May 1915, Liddle Collection, Brotherton Library, University of Leeds [hereafter LC]

[5]　Sir J. French to Winifred Bennett, 27 April 1915, IWM, PP/MCR/C33

[6]　Kronprinz Rupprecht von Bayern, E. von Frauenholz (ed), *Mein Kriegstagebuch*, 3 Vols (Berlin: 1929) Vol 1, pp304-5; U. Trumpener, 'The Road to Ypres: The Beginnings of Gas Warfare in World War 1', in *Journal of Modern History* 47 (1975) pp460-80

[7]　Anonymous [Rev W. P. Young], '9th Royal Scots (TF) B Company on Active Service From a Private's Diary February-May 1915' (1915) pp66-7; see also Shephard, Diary, op cit, 2 May 1915, and Lt R. L. Mackay, Diary, 12 October 1916, Argyll & Sutherland Highlanders Museum, Stirling Castle, N-E11.MAC

[8]　2nd Lt A. D. Gillespie, *Letters from Flanders* (London: Smith Elder, 1916) pp115-6, 146-7, 149

[9]　Ibid, pp147, 257

[10]　L Cpl George Ramage, Diary, 15 May 1915, National Library of Scotland [hereafter NLS], Ms 944

[11]　Hon W. Fraser to his father, 3 May 1915, in D. Fraser (ed), *In Good Company: The First World War Letters and Diaries of The Hon William Fraser, Gordon Highlanders* (Salisbury: Michael Russell, 1990) pp51-2; see also French to Winifred Bennett, 24 May 1915, IWM, PP/MCR/C33

[12]　R. Gale, Diary, 22 September 1915, IWM, 66/163/1

[13]　Lt C. A. Ashley, Diary, 19 July 1915, IWM, 85/22/1

[14]　A. E. Hodgkin, Diary, 30 January 1916, IWM, P399

[15]　Mrs N. P. Campbell, *Norman P. Campbell: Scientist, Missionary, Soldier* (Cambridge: W. Heffer & Sons Ltd, 1921) pp35-6

[16]　Sir D. Haig, Diary, 16 September 1915, Haig Mss, NLS, Acc 3155, Vol 102

[17]　Maj C. H. Foulkes, 'Lecture on the employment of Gas in the Offensive', 23 December 1916, Foulkes Mss, Liddell Hart Centre for Military Archives, 6/10

[18]　Lt J. B. MacLean to A. MacLean, 15 August 1917, LC

[19]　Sir H. Rawlinson to W. S. Churchill, 22 April 1918, Rawlinson Mss, National Army Museum, Acc 5201-33-21

[20]　Major V. Lefebure, *The Riddle of the Rhine: Chemical Strategy in Peace and War* (London: Collins, 1921) p237

[21]　Robins, 'Gas', Robins Mss, LC

[22]　Capt H. A. Siepman to his mother, 16 September 1918, LC

[23]　Director of Home Defence to Director of Military Operations and Planning, 16 June 1940; and Brigadier Crawford, 'Memorandum on the use of gas in the defence of United Kingdom', 21 June 1940, Public Record Office [hereafter PRO], WO 193/732

[24]　General Ismay for Chiefs of Staff Committee, 6 and 29 July 1944, PRO, PREM 3/89

[25]　T. Lane, 'The British Merchant Seaman at War', in H. Cecil and P. Liddle (eds), *Facing Armageddon: The First World War Experienced* (London: Leo Cooper, 1996) pp148-9

[26]　Admiral Scheer, *Germany's High Sea Fleet in the World War* (London: Cassell, 1920) pp222-3; see also pp228, 236, 240, 247, 249-52

[27]　Ibid, pp218, 220-1

[28]　Capt R. W. Blacklock, recollections, tape 445, LC

[29]　Lt N. D. Holbrook to Sam, 21 December 1914, LC

[30]　Rear Adm W. Jameson, *The Most Formidable Thing: The Story of the Submarine from its earliest days to the end of World War 1* (London: Rupert Hart-Davis, 1915) pp163-4; J. Terraine, *To Win a War* (London: Sidgwick & Jackson, 1978) p198; H. Nicolson, *Peacemaking 1919* (London: Constable, 1933) p24

[31]　K. Neureuther and C. Bergen (eds), *U-Boat Stories: Narratives of German U-Boat Sailors* (London: Constable, 1931) p49

[32]　Ibid, pp49, 59

33 Admiral Scheer, op cit, p227

34 Neureuther and Bergen, op cit, pp84, 93, 138, 146-7; T. Lane, op cit, pp148-9

35 Lt-Cdr K. Edwards, We Dive At Dawn, London, Rich & Cowan, 1939, pp. 196-7; Jameson, The Most Formidable Thing, pp. 220-1; P. H. Liddle, The Sailor's War 1914-18, Poole, Dorset, Blandford, 1985, pp. 99-100.

36 Ministry of Defence (Navy), German Naval History: The U-Boat War in the Atlantic 1939-1945 (London: HMSO, 1989) pp10, 40-6

37 H. A. Werner, Iron Coffin: A personal account of the German U-boat attacks of World War II (London: Arthur Baker, 1969) p45, and W. Hirshfield, as told to Geoffrey Brooks, Hirschfield: The Story of a U-boat NCO 1940-1946 (London: Orion, 1996) p132

38 I. McGeoch, An Affair of Chances: A Submariner's Odyssey 1939-44 (London: IWM, nd) pp62, 76; on stopping supplies from reaching Africa, see also interview with Lt M. Crawford, IWM Sound Archive, 11763/3, Reel 1, 1991

39 See pictures of returning crews in D. J. Quigley, Under the Jolly Roger: British Submariners At War 1939-1945 (Portsmouth: Portsmouth Publishing and Printing Ltd, 1988) pp39, 57, 63, 104; on submarines as 'purely offensive weapons', see interview with Lt M. Wingfield, IWM Sound Archive, 9153/5, Reel 2, 1985

40 Quoted in 'The Battle of the Atlantic' video (Luther Pendragon, 1995); see also Capt S. W. Roskill, The War at Sea 1939-1945 (London: HMSO, 1961) Vol III, Part II, p306, and W. Hirschfield, op cit, p216

41 E. Young, One of Our Submarines (London: Rupert Hart-Davis, 1952) pp69, 76-77; see also a recollection of Lt-Cdr Wanklyn's views in J. Winton (ed), The Submariners: Life in British Submarines 1901-1999: An Anthology of Personal Experience (London: Constable, 1999) pp121-5

42 CaptLt H. Müller-Edwards to his parents, 22 March 1943, reproduced in M. Middlebrook, Convoy: The Battle for Convoys SC.122 and HX.229 (London: Allen Lane, 1976) p297

43 P. Cremer, U333: The Story of a U-Boat Ace (London: The Bodley Head, 1984) p214; see also interview with Lt-Cdr A. Piper, IWM Sound Archive, 13298/3, Reel 1, 1993; P. Kaplan and J. Currie, WOLFPACK: U-Boats at War 1939-1945 (London: Aurum, 1997) p7

44 J. Winton, The Forgotten Fleet (London: Michael Joseph, 1969) p243; E. Young, op cit, p272

45 Rear Adm C. Mendenhall, Submarine Diary (Annapolis: Naval Institute Press, 1991) p145

46 Kaplan and Currie, op cit, pp193-4; J. Vause, U-Boat Ace: The story of Wolfgang Lüth (Annapolis: Naval Institute Press, 1990) pp141, 143-4

47 P. Cremer, op cit, pp42-3; see also H. A. Werner, op cit, p38; W. Hirschfield, op cit, p173; Kaplan and Currie, op cit, p194; interviews with Petty Officer I. Nethercott, IWM Sound Archive, 11068/4, Reel 2, 1989, and Crawford, IWM Sound Archive, 11763/3, Reel 3, 1991

48 W. Riley, 'The Battle of the Atlantic' video, and interview with Nethercott, loc cit

49 Quoted in E. Dudley, Monsters of the Purple Twilight: The True Story of the Life and Death of the Zeppelins (London: G. G. Harrap, 1960) p34

50 Ibid, p76

51 Quoted in G. Best, op cit, p269; see also E. Dudley, op cit, p34

52 Lt H. S. Walmsley to his father and mother, 6 and 31 October 1917, RAF Museum [hereafter RAFM], AC 1998/23/10; see also C. M. White, The Gotha Summer (London: Robert Hale, 1986) p157

53 Lt F. Williams, memoirs, p48, RAFM, DC 74/135/6

54 Lt W. H. Greaves, Diary, 3 October 1918, reproduced in A. White, The Hornet's Nest: A History of 100 Squadron Royal Air Force 1917-1994 (Worcester: Square One, 1994) p208

55 S. A. Garrett, Ethics and Airpower in World War II: The British Bombing of German Cities (New York: St Martin's Press, 1993) pp21, 193

56 Air Ministry, 'Instructions Governing Naval and Air Bombardment', 22 August 1939, PRO, AIR 8/283

57 R. Overy, Bomber Command 1939-1945 (London: Harper Collins, 1997) pp30, 33; M. Hastings, Bomber Command (London: Michael Joseph, 1979) pp123-5; 'Plans for Attack on German War Industry...', 15 May 1940, PRO, AIR 8/283

58 Sir C. Portal, 'Memorandum prepared for the British Chiefs of Staff', 3 November 1942, PRO, AIR 14/739A

[59] D. Richards, 'Bomber Command Reminiscences': Air Vice-Marshal J. Furner, RAFM, AC 96/5/7; see also R. Rodley, P. Hinchliffe and Sir J. Curtiss in R. Overy, op cit, pp194, 198 and 200

[60] D. Richards: R. A. Read to the Editor, Sun in English, 18 February 1945 [SIC, 1995], RAFM, AC 96/5/3

[61] D. Richards: E. H. Woods, RAFM, AC 96/5/7; see also C. Patterson in R. Overy, op cit, p201

[62] S. Claud Masters in 'Bomber' (DD Video, 1999)

[63] D. Richards: F. F. Fish; see also R. T. Newbury and S. E. Adams, RAFM, AC 96/5/7, and Pilot Officer G. J. A. Smith in M. Middlebrook, *The Berlin Raids: RAF Bomber Command Winter 1943-44* (London: Penguin, 1988) p331

[64] P. Stahl, *The Diving Eagle: A Ju88 Pilot's Diary* (London: William Kimber, 1984) p128; see also H. Herrmann, *Eagle's Wings* (Shrewsbury: Airlife, 1991) p66

[65] R. S. Raymond to Betty, 31 October 1942, RAFM, ARD/1977/83; see also H. Nash in R. Overy, op cit, p198

[66] N. Lee, 'Lower-Crust War', LC

[67] D. Richards: H. Gordon Davies, RAFM, AC 96/5/2

[68] D. Richards: R. D. Cooling, RAFM, AC 96/5/2

[69] Sgt L. Bartlett, Diary, 22 November 1943, LC

[70] Quoted in M. Middlebrook, *The Battle of Hamburg: Allied Bomber Forces against a German City in 1943* (London: Penguin, 1984) p349

[71] H. Herrmann, op cit, p66; see also P. Stahl, op cit, pp128-30 and D. Baker, *Adolf Galland: The Authorised Biography* (London: Windrow & Greene, 1991) p133

[72] D. Richards: K. M. Pincott, RAFM, AC 96/5/7; see also M. Middlebrook, *The Battle of Hamburg*, op cit, p348, N. Lee, 'Lower-Crust War', op cit, and C. Patterson in R. Overy, op cit, p201

[73] R. Dyson, tape-recorded interview 1243 and 1244, LC

[74] D. Richards: J. C. Richardson, RAFM, AC 96/5/5, and N. Winch in 'Bomber' (DD Video, 1999)

[75] Sgt Pilot V. Hartwright to Julie, nd, RAFM/DB 335

[76] Quoted in 'Bomber Command: Reaping the Whirlwind' (DD Video, 1997)

[77] D. Richards: Fl Lt C. E. Smith, RAFM, AC 96/5/7; M. Middlebrook, *The Battle of Hamburg*, p350; Sir J. Curtiss quoted in R. Overy, op cit, p200

Chapter 27

The opposition to war

Martin Ceadel

The experience of opposing the World Wars did not differ only between the two conflicts, but also varied enormously from country to country; and even within Second World War Britain, with which this chapter mainly deals, it varied considerably according to the motives, temperaments, and social and religious positions of the opponents themselves. Even so, in respect of democratic countries it is possible to offer one generalisation about how the experience of opposition to the Second World War differed from that of opposition to the First. Physically, it was easier: liberal democracies had become more tolerant of dissent on this issue, and opponents of the war were less harshly treated. Psychologically, however, it was harder – the war was widely held to be a definitively just one, and its opponents often felt misgivings about their own stand.

In many countries opposition to war has been a dangerous, even fatal experience. As a historian of conscientious objection from 1939 to 1945 has noted: 'Openly declared objectors in Austria, Belgium, Bulgaria, Czechoslovakia, Finland, France, Germany, Hungary, Italy, Poland, Portugal, Spain, Russia and Yugoslavia risked imprisonment and execution.'[1] The most dangerous of these countries, predictably, was Nazi Germany, where in consequence conscientious objection was confined to a tiny core of Christians, almost all of them members of millenarian sects. By far the most numerous were Jehovah's Witnesses, whose leading role in refusing military service during the 20th century has not received the recognition it deserves. (This is both because they have been too ill-educated and socially marginal to have left records of their collective experience in the way Quakers in particular have, and because their objection to war has been neither pacifist nor political – 'They are willing to fight for the Lord at Armageddon but not for the temporal powers here and now', as a major study of modern conscientious objection has put it[2] – and so has caught the imagination of neither the peace movement nor progressive opinion.) Of the just over 280 men known to have claimed a conscientious objection to fighting for Hitler, more than 250 were Jehovah's Witnesses. Many were executed; the leading historian of world pacifism, Peter Brock, has noted in Germany 'the objector faced almost certain death, even if in rare cases capital punishment was commuted into long-term imprisonment'.[3]

To oppose war in a defeatist or defeated country, however, was to find oneself going with the grain of public policy or international events to an almost embarrassing degree. The Danish pacifist organisation Aldrig mere Krig (No More War) applauded its Government's 'bravery' in not offering military resistance to

Germany's invasion on 9 April 1940, and subsequently was able to enjoy what has been described as 'a kind of everyday life'.[4] Similarly, one of France's small number of Christian pacifists, Henri Roser, who had been imprisoned for four years as a conscientious objector at the outbreak of war, suddenly found himself at liberty in June 1940 owing to the collapse of his country's military effort and the imminent arrival of German troops in the area in which he was being held, which caused his gaolers to release him.[5]

In Britain, opposing war has been comparatively easy in respect of the state's willingness to tolerate dissent. Yet during both World Wars there was a wide range of British anti-war experiences. For one thing, selective objectors – those who did not oppose all wars but refused to support this particular one – found less sympathy for their position than did pacifists, who opposed all wars. In the First World War, for example, the ugliest assaults on its opponents were on socialist meetings, held following the convention at Leeds on 3 June 1917, to welcome the overthrow of the Tsar and call for an end to the war; on 28 July 1917 Bertrand Russell only narrowly escaped assault at one such meeting in the Brotherhood Church in Hackney, and was more deeply shaken than the humorous account in his autobiography implied.[6] The next day Arthur Horner had his teeth knocked out in an even more violent meeting in Swansea.[7] In the Second World War, moreover, as Fascists, Communists and members of the Independent Labour Party (ILP) found, selective opposition was psychologically harder because of the near consensus that Britain had gone to war for better reasons than in 1914.

Britain's Fascists experienced even greater unpopularity during wartime than their controversial political allegiance had already accustomed them to. They opposed the Second World War, despite an ideological predisposition in favour of martial glory, on the grounds that a conflict with Germany was neither ideologically nor geo-strategically necessary; a sympathetic view should be taken of the anti-communist aims and achievements of the Third Reich; and Germany should be allowed to dominate Europe since this would not endanger Britain's vital interests, which were centred upon its Empire. Fascists were too few to make much impact during the 'Phoney War', when the Government estimated the paid-up membership of Sir Oswald Mosley's British Union of Fascists at 9,000, of whom only 1,000 were active.[8] Nonetheless, although it made clear its willingness to resist invasion during the military emergency of 1940, Mosley's organisation was suppressed, and about 800 Fascists were imprisoned under Defence Regulation 18B. Mosley's wife, who 'was put in a dirty cell with the floor swimming with water … and only a thin mattress on the dirty, wet floor', was told that she could take either her 11-week-old or her 19-month-old child into Holloway Prison with her but not both, and decided that conditions were suitable for neither. Adding insult to discomfort was the widespread public belief that she was enjoying special privileges, which caused the conductor of a bus that stopped outside the gaol 'to direct his passengers: "This way for Lady Mosley's suite"'.[9]

A member of Mosley's rank and file, John Charnley, argued that the Government's treatment of the Fascists amounted to discrimination, pointing out that whereas Britain had a tradition dating back to the 18th century of tolerating dissenters from its wars, 'this was the first time that opponents had been arrested and imprisoned'.[10] Moreover, Fascists who claimed conscientious objection were rarely successful. Their experience has seldom been recorded, but many years later a Sunday newspaper journalist came upon Derek Talbot Baines, a long-standing Mosleyite of mixed German and English parentage. Denied exemption, and sentenced to imprisonment for an attempt to evade the military authorities, he escaped from custody in Leeds and spent the rest of the war on the run in London and on the South Coast, the prelude to a miserable post-war existence spent on the margins of society.[11]

For Britain's Communists, the experience of opposing the Second World War was unexpected and tentative, but mercifully short-lived. A tight-knit party with 18,000 members at the outbreak of war, it had been calling since the mid-1930s for the formation of a 'peace front' of the Soviet Union and the democracies against the Fascist states. However, the Soviet Union's decision to conclude the Molotov-Ribbentrop pact of 22 August 1939 called this policy into question. For the next six weeks the party in Britain was in intellectual turmoil, its General Secretary, Harry Pollitt, refusing to believe that war resistance was what Moscow now wanted. On 2 October 1939, however, it loyally espoused this policy on instructions brought directly from Moscow by the British representative at Comintern headquarters, Dave Springhall, who was later imprisoned for spying on behalf of the Soviet Union.[12] Pollitt was replaced by R. P. Dutt, a theoretician who from the start had welcomed the pact as 'the logical and inevitable' response to the 'sabotage of the Peace Front' by both the National Government and the Labour Party, and who now condemned what he called 'the second imperialist war'.[13] The party issued a new policy statement with the message: 'Stop the War! The people must enforce the terms of a lasting peace'.

This change of tack created considerable difficulties even for those obedient to the new line. The party's one MP, Willie Gallacher, found himself 'a sort of pariah in the House of Commons' and was thought by his friends to be at risk of a breakdown because of the psychological pressure upon him.[14] Its Sussex area organiser, Ernie Trory, had to use emollient techniques learned in a previous career as a vacuum-cleaner salesman to minimise the hostility that Communists ran into at public meetings.[15] Party members working under cover in front organisations were obliged for the first time to show their hand, which proved a testing experience. In October 1939 Gabriel Carritt, an employee of the youth section of the League of Nations Union since the autumn of 1935 and an activist in the British section of the International Peace Campaign – both of them broadly based organisations that were strongly committed to collective security against Germany – began calling for an international peace conference rather than for a vigorous prosecution of the war. Carritt was taken aback by the hostility with which his obviously Communist-inspired demand was received by liberals and socialists with whom he had previously enjoyed warm relations; he complained that 'he had been charged as being a Moscow agent and a Goebbels agent'.[16] Despite their new unpopularity, he and his fellow Communists stuck to their task. Their '"Stop the War" group', as its critics called it, succeeded in influencing the youth groups of the League of Nations Union to such an extent that its leadership suspended them altogether.[17] And although they failed similarly to capture the

British section of the International Peace Campaign, they paralysed and effectively destroyed it.

However, the Communist Party stopped short of sabotaging the war effort. It instructed its members to enter the armed forces rather than claim conscientious objection. It gradually switched its emphasis to economic grievances, since, as a party historian later acknowledged, 'Building an anti-war movement among ordinary people was proving to be uphill work. By contrast, developing struggle on bread and butter issues offered quite new opportunities.' During the military crisis of 1940, it toned down its peace message, calling in June for a people's government on the grounds that this would lead the German workers to overthrow Hitler.[18] In July it also launched a new front organisation, the People's Vigilance Committee, which demanded a change of government, friendship with the Soviet Union, and better living standards.[19] This cautious policy won support from those denied their usual outlet for protest by the Labour Party's participation, after May 1940, in Churchill's Coalition Government. When therefore a People's Convention was held in London on 12 January 1941, it attracted the surprisingly large total of 2,234 delegates. However, many of these later felt that they had been duped; for example, the celebrated actor Michael Redgrave, a socialist, discovered that the Convention had been controlled by Communists and was therefore linked with revolutionary defeatism only when the BBC dropped him for taking part in it[20]; and the future television scriptwriter Ted Willis, previously an activist in the Labour Party's League of Youth but at that time a soldier, later described his decision to make a speech to the Convention as 'almost the only political decision in my life which I regret'.[21] The Government responded to the Convention by immediately banning the Communist newspaper *Daily Worker*.

For most Communists the anti-war experience was thus one of constant intellectual unease and evasiveness. When Hitler launched 'Operation Barbarossa' in late June 1941 and the Soviet Union became perforce an ally of Britain, Communists threw themselves with evident relief into supporting the war effort, forgetting about their 20 months as war resisters, albeit of a hesitant kind; and the *Daily Worker* resumed publication.

For the ILP, the experience of opposition was a largely formalistic one, the application of an ultra-left purism, which by then had become the party's sole reason for existence. It had been one of the groups that had set up the Labour Party in 1900, but in 1932, finding its creation too moderate, it had disaffiliated in expectation of an imminent social revolution. This had proved a serious error – the ILP had rapidly dwindled into a fringe group, except in its Glasgow heartland where a strong sense of the class struggle had enabled it to return four MPs. Moreover, after the Spanish Civil War broke out its attitude to war had become incomprehensible to many; most of its members – including former absolutist conscientious objectors such as Fenner Brockway – had supported the armed struggle against Franco, while nonetheless claiming that a war against Germany would be an imperialist one unless Britain became a socialist country first.

When the Second World War broke out, some ILP members became conscientious objectors, and the party's anti-war stand helped it gain much-needed publicity at by-elections. But it lacked either the numerical strength or the ideological confidence to resist the war effort substantively. Increasingly, the ILP's anti-war stand, which ideological rigidity prevented it from abandoning, became a symptom of the party's loss of contact with political reality. By 1945 its membership had fallen to a mere 2,500, and the party stood on the brink of extinction as a parliamentary force.[22] Its opposition to the Second World War thus offered a pitiful comparison with its opposition to the First, when it had supplied some of the peace movement's most inspirational leaders.

By contrast, Britain's pacifists found that their motives for opposing any war were generally understood even by that overwhelming majority of their fellow citizens who thought them misguided in this particular case. Partly because of the long-term influence of the Quakers, who had been committed to non-resistance since as early as 1661, the state had made generous statutory provision for conscientious objection when it had first introduced conscription in 1916; in particular, it had catered for total exemption, as well as exemption from combatant service only, and for objections of a non-religious kind as well as religious ones. However, public hostility to those unwilling to fight had been so strong that only 16,500 men had availed themselves of the conscience clause, a mere 0.33 per cent of those who had either enlisted voluntarily or been conscripted.[23] Moreover, their cases had been judged by tribunals that had originated as part of the recruiting process, were initially under War Office control, and applied the law in a restrictive fashion. Thus although the tribunals had offered some kind of exemption to four-fifths of applicants, they had given only 350 total exemptions, almost all of them to Quakers, and had shown little sympathy towards non-religious objectors. As a result, there had been a significant number of dissatisfied objectors who consequently took a defiant stand; some of those who had been refused any kind of exemption defied the military authorities, which attempted to induct them into the Army; and some of those who had been offered 'alternative' service instead of total exemption chose to go to prison rather than accept this lesser concession. Although only about a thousand objectors had stuck to these 'absolutist' positions, their suffering – in several well-publicised cases they wrecked their health in prison – had captured the imagination of the public and contributed to a better understanding of pacifism.

With the development during the inter-war years of military aviation, which brought a significant threat to Britain's homeland for the first time, a fear of war had developed from which pacifism benefited, particularly after the collapse in the mid-1930s of hopes that the League of Nations would be able to prevent aggression. The Peace Pledge Union, founded in May 1936 by the influential churchman Canon Dick Sheppard, had become the world's largest pacifist association ever, attracting support from prominent intellectuals such as Vera Brittain, Aldous Huxley, John Middleton Murry and Bertrand Russell, and soon acquiring a six-figure membership. But from the end of 1937 it had grown only slowly, which meant that it had never posed a threat to the defence effort; most of its leading thinkers had accepted that pacifism was not a practical technique for war prevention but a faith that could be implemented only in the very long run. In consequence, the existence of a sincere, respectable and unthreatening pacifist minority had become widely accepted.

When conscription was re-imposed in 1939, the provisions for conscientious objection enjoyed greater public support than they had in the First World War. The local tribunals were placed under civilian control from the start and were chaired by a judge in an effort to ensure a better understanding of the law. The public mood was one of resigned acceptance of the war rather than the startled emotionalism of 1914 with its attendant heresy-hunting. More conscientious objectors came forward; they comprised 2.2 per cent of the first wartime batch of conscripts, and though the figure declined steadily thereafter, with a particularly sharp dip in the summer of 1940, they eventually numbered nearly 60,000, 1.2 per cent of those called up. Only in two respects did the state take a harder line than in the First World War. First, in January 1941 it made fire-watching compulsory in urban areas, and, insisting that this was a wholly civilian activity, provided no conscience clause. This resulted in 475 prosecutions. Second, at the end of 1941 conscription was extended to women for the first time. However, the measure applied only to single women aged 19 to 31 (and in practice only those born between 1918 and 1923 were called up); they could opt for industrial or civil defence work if they preferred, and if they chose the armed services they could not be obliged to use a lethal weapon without their written consent. Approximately 1,000 women became conscientious objectors.[24]

Compared with the First World War, therefore, the British state had seized the moral high ground in two respects. First, it was fighting a war that was in political terms impeccable. Indeed, a leading Christian pacifist, C. J. Cadoux, published a book in 1940 that argued that pacifists should, without recanting their faith, admit that the war was 'relatively justified' and therefore better 'victoriously carried through' than 'discontinued before the undertaking is completed'.[25] Second, it was treating conscientious objectors as well as they could reasonably expect to be treated. As the Peace Pledge Union's weekly paper, *Peace News*, was soon to acknowledge, there was an 'almost complete absence' of the 'scorn and hatred for COs' manifested in the last war.[26] However, for pacifists this created its own problems. As *Peace News* was to put it in the latter part of the conflict: 'There has not been a simple form of pacifist action, such as existed in 1914-18, in the refusal of conscription and the acquiescence in imprisonment for the duration.'[27]

Many pacifists felt guilty about their comparatively privileged position and anxious to repay their debt through service rather than adopt an attitude of intransigence. As the chairman of the Peace Pledge Union soon noted, 'The absolutists are relatively less numerous than in the last war.'[28] The 'alternativists' – who now preferred to call themselves 'humanitarians' – were more self-confident, the Peace Pledge Union deciding at the first wartime meeting of its national council 'that the demand of members for opportunities of service to their fellows, under pacifist auspices, should be met.'[29] After Dunkirk, these anxieties understandably increased, as social resentments against those not helping with the defence effort increased significantly. Many employers, including local authorities, refused to employ objectors, and wholesale newsagents refused to distribute *Peace News*, even though the Government tolerated it. An objector admitted early in 1941 that it was 'not easy nowadays for pacifists to avoid the feeling that they are in the wrong with society, and because of this to prevent a cautious, even diffident manner, from creeping into their relations with others'.[30] Another, the writer James Byrom, whose unusually varied wartime experience included travelling to Finland as a volunteer fireman and being parachuted into France as a stretcher-bearer, felt 'full of appreciation of the fairness' of the tribunal, which recognised his plea to be allowed to undertake non-combatant service, and 'could not help reflecting that a country so tolerant towards the liberty of the individual conscience was a country that richly deserved to be fought for. The wave of patriotism nearly carried me into the nearest recruitment office.'[31]

Such diffidence might have been even greater had the war not been one in which, simply as civilians facing air bombardment, pacifists bore a share of the risks run by combatants. Thus Vera Brittain noted in her diary that at a Peace Pledge Union meeting during the Blitz 'everyone much below their best through air raids'.[32] The Union's local groups organiser, John Barclay, a veteran of the First World War, 'remembered the forgotten horrors of Passchendaele' during the 20 seconds in which he thought that a bomb, which fell only yards from his house, was going to kill him as he did the washing-up.[33] And its treasurer, Maurice Rowntree, died from a fall attributable to the blackout.[34] Even so, pacifists were aware of consuming food that had to be shipped in at considerable risk. In 1942, therefore, some members of the Peace Pledge Union went on a five-day fast in order to 'aid seamen'.[35] And a Quaker undertaking non-combatant service 'felt that to be a bomb-disposer would lessen the stigma of being a Conchie'.[36]

Some objectors were unable to maintain their stand. The Quaker just mentioned joined the Army. Clifford Simmons, who believed that he was 'making some contribution' while undertaking relief work in London during the Blitz of 1940-41, felt differently thereafter: 'The inactivity of my pacifist role became increasingly irksome. I still believed that the position of the pacifist was ultimately right but I was beginning to realise that, at the same time, I could not stand aside from the struggle which was engulfing my contemporaries.' In May 1942 he therefore enlisted.[37] And many of those who remained objectors for the duration of the war suffered frequently from self-doubt. Alex Bryan, a devout Christian pacifist, remembered the years 1939-45 as being 'full of great difficulty and great uncertainty. They were a time of testing and of considerable challenge. Many a time I asked myself if the course I had chosen was really the right one for me.'[38]

How keenly these uncertainties were felt depended to a considerable degree on temperament. The sensitive, like Len Richardson, an insurance agent who belonged to the Christadelphian sect, liked 'to be thought well of, and to go with the crowd', and therefore found isolation difficult. Richardson soon found that the question on everyone's lips early in the war, 'When are you going?', became an embarrassment to him after he had decided to be a conscientious objector. He later recalled that his

'...weekly round of calls, collecting insurance premiums, became an increasingly traumatic experience; explaining why I was NOT going, to people whose sons and husbands had already, in many cases, gone. The sense of being an outcast, disliked and ridiculed, is undoubtedly one of the greatest crosses that the CO has to endure, depending on its intensity. There are people (I have known some) to whom opprobrium seems almost welcome, and public disfavour an honour… In my own case, however … I squirmed uncomfortably throughout the wartime experiences. I well recall seeing notices outside public houses in those days, reading "No Coaches", yet it was some time before I realised the true import of these signs, my tortured imagination having translated it as "No Conchies".'[39]

Withdrawn personalities could ignore unpopularity. One of the most prominent and controversial of pacifists, the Marquess of Tavistock (after August 1940 the 12th Duke of Bedford), was a withdrawn and unhappy man, whose miserable private life had become public knowledge when his wife, whom he had left in 1934 because of her close friendship with their children's tutor, had unsuccessfully sued him for restitution of conjugal rights.[40] His son and heir, no admirer of 'his many cranky notions', was later to offer the harsh observation: 'I don't think that all his life he really knew what it was to give affection to anybody, though he demanded it from others.'[41] Tavistock was a Christian pacifist who had become chairman of the Anglican Pacifist Fellowship and a supporter of the Peace Pledge Union, yet was also an anti-Semite prepared to work alongside Fascists in organisations such as the British Council for a Christian Settlement in Europe.[42] Apparently imperturbable, he was a regular contributor to *Peace News* throughout the war.

Aggressive personalities – in other words, contrarians by temperament – found the opportunity to defy majority opinion a positive attraction of pacifism. For example, when some years ago the author of this chapter addressed an academic conference on pacifism in the era of two World Wars, he was criticised by a distinguished professor in the audience, who had been a conscientious objector during the Second World War, for ignoring the extent to which he and others had been motivated by simple bloody-mindedness rather than non-violent scruple.[43] The chairman of the Peace Pledge Union, the Cambridge physicist Dr Alex Wood, soon concluded that the principal cleavage within the pacifist movement in wartime was not an ideological disagreement between the religious and the political objector, but a 'fundamental psychological division between the introvert and the extrovert'.[44] Revealingly, when a team of pacifist orderlies working in Winford Hospital near Bristol developed a private vocabulary, one of its most important terms was a 'tusker', which denoted an 'aggressive pacifist' as distinct from a 'blossom'.[45]

 This tension between contrasting personality types caused problems for some attempts to create pacifist communities. 'Community' had become a pacifist catchphrase in the late 1930s, as many in the Peace Pledge Union had retreated from their initial belief that it could prevent war. Pacifist communities had been expected not only to meet the practical needs of conscientious objectors required to undertake agricultural work, but also to constitute the nuclei of the non-violent society that pacifists had hoped to build. In the words of John Middleton Murry, who bought a farm in 1942 and established a community there:

'I was convinced that the pacifist has a peculiar duty to the national society that he must try to fulfil. He must try to prove that a society of peace is a real possibility and not an idle dream. The primary cell of such a society is a farm community or a co-operative farm. If a group of pacifists, justly ordered by the State to work on the land, take a neglected farm and make it flourish, and in this effort become a group of people knit together by a new social morality, they would have done something to justify their privilege.'

However, Murry soon discovered that a community became a magnet for 'negative egocentrics who seek a refuge from the demands of social existence which they are incapable of meeting'. The one saving grace was that these 'parasitic incapables crack fairly quickly. Their accumulated resentment at the steady exposure of their insufficiency does not take long to explode.' They tended therefore to leave the farm, though this eventually left it short of labour and dependent – ironically for a pacifist enterprise – on hiring gangs of German and Italian prisoners of war.[46] Murry's fellow pacifist and writer Ronald Duncan had already been through a similar process of disillusionment, having started his farm community shortly before the outbreak of war. By September 1941 he was wondering sardonically: 'Perhaps community is an experiment which might be repeated when the farm is in such good order that one has only to lean against a switch to milk the cows with cream from one teat and butter and cheese from the other.' A year later he had parted company with the last of his communitarians and was preparing to run the farm 'entirely by myself'.[47] Explicitly Christian communities were more harmonious, however; members of the Christian Pacifist Forestry and Land Units, established by Henry Carter, a leading Methodist minister, in 1940, liked each other well enough to flourish and even hold post-war reunions, despite 'moments of friction, when in our human weakness we "got on each other's nerves"'.[48]

The experience of opposition was easiest for those whose position in society gave them the most support. Wealth and social standing were particularly helpful. Charles Kimber, educated at Eton and Oxford, possessed private means and was the heir to a baronetcy. In the autumn of 1938 he had co-founded Federal Union, a peace association that campaigned for the replacement of the discredited League of Nations by a federation. A year later, unlike most of his fellow federalists, Kimber declared himself a conscientious objector. His tribunal generously exempted him on condition that he continued working for Federal Union, which he evacuated for a time to his country home at Lulworth Cove in Dorset; later it gave him permission to set himself up as a market gardener in Devon, which he had the resources to do.[49]

The playwright William Douglas Home, third son of the 13th Earl of Home and brother of a Conservative politician who was later to become Prime Minister, had decided at the outbreak of war that he was ineligible to be a conscientious objector because his objection 'was political rather than religious'. He therefore volunteered for military service in a cause he thought mistaken. After fighting several by-elections as a critic of the war, he refused to take part in the battle of Le Havre because he believed that insufficient care had been taken to protect the local civilians. His commanding officer was willing to turn a blind eye to this aristocratic mutiny – only the fact that Douglas Home announced it in a letter to a British newspaper caused him to be court-martialled. He escaped with imprisonment, an experience eased by visits from friends and relations.[50]

Vera Brittain, a well-off member of the upper middle class, maintained a courageous and energetic witness against the Second World War and suffered economically because some members of the public did not like buying books written by pacifists. Even so, her lifestyle was so obviously comfortable that half a century later the editors of her wartime diary felt obliged to apologise for her 'upper-middle-class' position and 'the degree to which the upper levels of that society "enjoyed" a qualitatively different war from their "social inferiors"'.[51] Indeed, it cannot be denied that a much more depressing experience of opposition was undergone by those at the other end of the social scale, such as the working-class objector whose predicament was summarised by a pacifist friend during the summer of 1940: 'Window-cleaner, married; owing to being a CO his trade has slackened, and he is earning about £1 per week. Living on his savings, prospects nil.'[52]

Many of the humblest objectors were members of millenarian sects. An academic philosopher who sat on the South-Western Tribunal, G. C. Field, encountered members of 51 religious groups, including some who believed either that the Bible had originally been written in English, or that the Dunkirk evacuation was a divine miracle, or even, in the case of one sect, that they could not serve as firemen because they might be asked to extinguish blazes in chapels or churches belonging to other denominations.[53] Such objectors were often protected from self-doubt by their simple verities and sense of detachment from the secular world; the writer Edward Blishen, who as a conscientious objector was intrigued to find himself doing agricultural work alongside 'cussed adherents of strange types of Puritanism', formed the view that in some cases they were to be 'complacent spectators at what they took to be Armageddon'.[54]

To give a more detailed idea of the ups and downs of life as an opponent of the war, this account will conclude with the experiences, as recorded in hitherto private family papers, of two thoughtful and articulate pacifists, the sons of the headmaster of Birkenhead Grammar School, who was himself a supporter of the war.[55] The elder, John Ure, born in 1912, had won a scholarship to Wadham College, Oxford, in the early 1930s, but, being of left-wing opinions, had turned his back on a conventional career in the professions and taken a series of casual jobs in London instead. He became a pacifist, and became secretary of the Putney branch of the Peace Pledge Union. As the Second World War began, he presciently warned his mother: 'I shall not in any case fight. My position is going to be pretty difficult.'[56] He told the telephone rental company that then employed him that he would be unable to take on the increasingly profitable part of its business that involved the armaments industry. The company initially accepted this reservation, but after the fall of France it feared that employing a local official of the Peace Pledge Union would damage its reputation, and dismissed him because he would not resign from that association.[57] Obliged to find another means of support at a difficult time, he obtained various jobs, including briefly that of waiter at a West End hotel during the Blitz, where he was expected to find his way home in the small hours through air raids and return in time to serve breakfast. At this time he poured out his political resentments to his brother, who, with the licence of a fraternal fellow pacifist, retorted bluntly: 'The most striking sentence in your letter, about the war being merely a quarrel between two sets of business-men with a third looking on, is so gross an oversimplification as to be really silly.'[58]

John Ure and his wife decided to move to Cornwall to seek agricultural employment. His age cohort having been called up, he went before the South-Western Tribunal, chaired by Judge Wethered, in November 1940. Even though this was one of the most generous in granting total exemptions[59], John Ure found its chairman hostile and felt obliged to stand up to him, reporting to his mother afterwards: 'I must have said a lot of silly things, but the things he said were sillier.'[60] He was refused the total exemption that he sought, and required instead to work in agriculture, horticulture, forestry, or land drainage and reclamation. Though in any case seeking such work, he challenged this decision on principle. His brother was horrified, partly because of the risk that the Appellate Tribunal would impose the even less satisfactory requirement of non-combatant service in the Army, and implored him not to 'be so foolish as to appeal against a decision which, after all, recognises your essential claim'.[61] John Ure eventually compromised – he withdrew his appeal, and accepted his tribunal's ruling.

He therefore spent the rest of the war in a succession of mainly agricultural jobs. In one he made the painful discovery that his employer, who had advertised his willingness to hire pacifists in *Peace News*, was in reality 'not in the least sympathetic to COs but obtaining them was one of his bright ideas for getting cheap labour'.[62] In another – as a resident gardener, with his supportive wife as a housemaid – he found himself working for the celebrated campaigner for birth control, Dr Marie Stopes, which proved an unhappy experience. Moreover, because she lived in what was classed as an urban area, John Ure was required to register for fire-watching. He refused – an absolutist act that owed something to his irritation with his employer. His brother, who by then had served two prison sentences, was outraged because he thought this an extreme, libertarian position inconsistent with the moderate one previously taken:

'You are, if I may say so, behaving like an idiot. You cannot possibly do any good by going to clink for refusing to fire watch… It simply isn't worth while as I know you don't feel strongly about the conscription side of the question – if so why did you go to a tribunal? It looks from your letter merely as if you were doing it out of annoyance with the Stopes regime, which is absurd… Don't be a BLOODY fool. You make me so annoyed. I assure you that it simply isn't worth undergoing the unpleasantness of prison, difficulties about getting another job and so on, in such a trivial and slapdash way… I went to prison merely because it was the only way I could get registration as a CO and be enabled and free to do useful work as I hoped. Only in exceptional cases can one do any good through the mere fact of going to prison, and then it is usually good of the "witnessing" kind, with which I'm sure you don't agree.'[63]

In the event, John Ure escaped both compulsory fire-watching and prison by moving back to a rural area to work in a home for refugee children. As the war went on and labour shortages increased, he found it easier to obtain employment. With the war drawing to a close, however, he was unable to secure official guidance as to when his obligation to undertake agricultural work would expire. He took a job as a schoolteacher anyway, and heard no more from the authorities.

His younger brother, Peter Ure, born in 1919 and in later life a Professor of English Literature at Newcastle University, had on leaving school been sent by his parents to work for Selfridges in London, but had disliked the firm, and in 1937 began reading English at Liverpool University instead. There he became a convinced pacifist; and on the outbreak of war, as he reported to his brother John, he

> '…distributed handbills in at people's front doors calling for PEACE, and was pursued by a little man who asked me what else I was doing for my country besides distributing handbills. After I had patiently explained several things to him, he called me a coward and went away without saying goodnight. That was the only encounter I had.'[64]

Though exempted from military service for the duration of his course – he was sitting his finals as France collapsed – he had registered as a conscientious objector. However, his local tribunal was unimpressed by the excessively literary manner in which he presented his beliefs, and refused him exemption of any kind, a decision upheld on appeal.[65] He therefore refused to undergo his army medical, and, while waiting to be arrested, undertook voluntary work with a Pacifist Service Unit in a Liverpool air raid shelter. He explained to his brother:

> 'Personally I suffer from a restless desire to help civilian sufferers in some way or other, and it is the cruellest of fortunes that I am kept here in semi-idleness through the inefficiency and indifference of the blasted bureaucracy. Either I want to be in prison or I want to be free to help people (not the war).'[66]

However, his first experience of incarceration, for a fortnight spanning Christmas 1940, was – unsurprisingly in view of being trapped on his own in a dark cell – dominated by 'sheer terror of death as Walton Gaol was the object of dive-bombing attacks'.[67]

On his release, Peter Ure moved to London and undertook voluntary work for the Friends' Ambulance Unit in Stepney. His father refused to have him in the house for Christmas 1941, causing him to observe wryly that 'it doesn't look as though I shall be going to visit the ancestral mansion until the perfumed Hun is driven into the North Sea'.[68] Following a second refusal of a medical examination, he was imprisoned for nearly two months in Wormwood Scrubs in the spring of 1942, which he also found a psychological ordeal, reporting shrewdly: 'Most of the COs in here are really nice blokes but are few of us I'm afraid precisely the stalwart type of the last war.'[69] Under a procedure designed to prevent the repeated cat-and-mouse prosecutions of the First World War, he was allowed to go back to the Appellate Tribunal in May 1942. This time he was exempted subject to undertaking ambulance or hospital work. Taking the view that the formal recognition of his conscientious scruples was what mattered most, he accepted this condition. He joined the Friends' Ambulance Unit as a cook and medical auxiliary. He complained of the war having 'produced a vast slagheap of days through which we must shovel'[70], disliked some of the Quaker officials he met as 'loungers and sybarites'[71], and was depressed by some of his work with a relief team in Egypt and Greece during 1944-46, but concluded the journal he kept of his time away from Britain with the positive observation that 'on the whole I have "fait un bon voyage" and am content'.[72]

Peter Ure's great friend since their student days together as pacifists reading English at Liverpool, Frank Kermode, later a distinguished literary scholar too, remembered an episode in 1940 that occurred shortly before he – unlike the Ure brothers – decided to rescind his registration as a conscientious objector and join the Navy. His and Peter Ure's local Peace Pledge Union branch

> '…had the bad luck to have scheduled its annual general meeting on 10 May, the day when the Germans invaded Belgium and Holland. A pack of Conservative Party members attacked the meeting and were carrying away the passively resisting pacifists when the Boxing Club arrived, resolved to defend to the death our right to snivel about our despicable opinions without interruption. There was a brawl, for which we sanctimoniously blamed not our assailants, the Tories, but our deliverers, the boxers.'[73]

Though perhaps improved in the telling, Kermode's anecdote encapsulates a central experience for many British pacifists during the Second World War, namely that of being simultaneously despised as politically foolish and accepted as morally legitimate.

Recommended reading

Barker, Rachel, *Conscience, Government, and War: Conscientious objection in Great Britain 1939-45* (London: Routledge & Kegan Paul, 1983)

Goodall, Felicity, *A Question of Conscience: Conscientious Objection In The Two World Wars* (Stroud: Sutton, 1997)

Rae, John, *Conscience and Politics: The British Government and the Conscientious Objector to Military Service 1916-1919* (London: Oxford University Press, 1970)

Notes

[1] Rachel Barker, *Conscience, Government, and War: Conscientious objection in Great Britain 1939-45* (London: Routledge & Kegan Paul, 1983) p121

[2] Charles C. Moskos and John Whitley Chambers II, *The New Conscientious Objection: From Sacred to Secular Resistance* (New York: Oxford University Press, 1993) p204

[3] Peter Brock, 'Conscientious Objectors in Nazi Germany', in Peter Brock and Thomas Socknat (eds), *Challenge to Mars: Essays on Pacifism from 1918 to 1945* (Toronto: University of Toronto Press, 1999) pp370-9

[4] Peter Kragh Hansen, 'Danish War Resisters under Nazi Occupation', in Brock and Socknat (eds), op cit, pp380-94, at pp385, 388

5   Peter Farrugia, 'The Conviction of Things Not Seen: Christian Pacifism in France, 1919-1945', in Brock and Socknat (eds), op cit, pp101-16, at p108

6   Ray Monk, *Bertrand Russell: The Spirit of Solitude* (London: Jonathan Cape, 1996) pp501-2; Bertrand Russell, *Autobiography*, 3 Vols (London: George Allen & Unwin, 1967-9) Vol 2, p501

7   David Egan, 'The Swansea Conference of the British Council of Soldiers' and Workers' Deputies, July 1917: Reactions to the Russian Revolution of February 1917, and the Anti-War Movement in South Wales', *Llafur* 1 (4) (1975) pp12-37, at pp22-3

8   Robert Benewick, *Political Violence and Public Order* (London: Allen Lane, 1969) p110

9   Sir Oswald Mosley, *My Life* (London: Nelson, 1968) pp408-9

10 John Charnley, *Blackshirts and Roses: An Autobiography* (London: Brockingdale, 1990) p98

11 David Egan, 'A fascist comes in from the cold', *Observer*, 26 November 1979

12 Keith Laybourn, '"About Turn": The Communist Party of Great Britain and the Second World War, 1939-45', in Keith Dockray and Keith Laybourn (eds), *The Representation and Reality of War: The British Experience* (Stroud: Sutton, 1999) pp218-34

13 *Labour Monthly*, September 1939, p516; and October 1939, p581

14 William Gallacher, *The Last Memoirs of William Gallacher* (London: Lawrence & Wishart, 1966) p272

15 Ernie Trory, *Imperialist War: Further Recollections of a Communist Organiser* (Brighton: Crabtree Press, 1977) pp45-59

16 Minutes, Executive Committee of British section of International Peace Campaign, 16 November 1939, Noel-Baker Papers 5/152, Churchill College, Cambridge

17 Minutes, LNU general council, 19-20 June 1940 (fos 6-7), League of Nations Union Papers, British Library of Political and Economic Science

18 Noreen Branson, *History of the Communist Party of Great Britain 1927-1941* (London: Lawrence & Wishart, 1985) pp281, 288-91

19 D. N. Pritt, *A Call to the People: A Manifesto of the People's Vigilance Committee* (London: People's Vigilance Committee, nd [cAugust 1940])

20 Michael Redgrave, *In My Mind's Eye: An Autobiography* (London: Weidenfeld & Nicolson, 1983) pp135-41

21 Ted Willis, *Whatever Happened to Tom Mix?: The story of one of my lives* (London: Cassell, 1970) pp192-3

22 Peter James Thwaites, 'The Independent Labour Party 1938-1950' (PhD thesis, London School of Economics, 1976) fos 104-51

23 John Rae, *Conscience and Politics: The British Government and the Conscientious Objector to Military Service 1916-1919* (London: Oxford University Press, 1970) p71

24 Rachel Barker, op cit, pp107-11

25 C. J. Cadoux, *Christian Pacifism Re-Examined* (Oxford: Basil Blackwell, 1940) p216

26 *Peace News*, 3 November 1939, p8

27 Ibid, 24 March 1944, p2

28 Ibid, 2 February 1940, p1

29 Ibid, 22 September 1939, p6

30 Ibid, 21 February 1941, p3

31 James Byrom, *The Unfinished Man* (London: Chatto & Windus, 1957) p118

32 Alan Bishop and Y. Aleksandra Bennett (eds), *Vera Brittain: Wartime Chronicle, Diary 1939-1945* (London: Victor Gollancz, 1989) p60

33 *Peace News*, 29 November 1940, p3

34 Ibid, 25 August 1944, p1

35 Ibid, 8 May 1942, p3

36 F. R. Davies, *Some Blessed Hope: Memoirs of a Next-to-Nobody* (Lewes: The Book Guild, 1996) p42

37 Clifford Simmons (ed), *The Objectors* (Douglas, Isle of Man: Times Press, 1965) p16

38 Alex Bryan, *'Bloody Conchie...!'* (London: Quaker Home Service, 1980) p33

39 Cited in Felicity Goodall, *A Question of Conscience: Conscientious Objection In The Two World Wars* (Stroud: Sutton, 1997) pp88, 91

40 *The Times*, 14 November 1935, p4

41 John, Duke of Bedford, *A Silver-Plated Spoon* (London: Cassell, 1959) pp3, 33

[42] The best account is in Richard Griffiths, *Patriotism Perverted: Captain Ramsay, the Right Club and British Anti-Semitism* (London: Constable, 1998) pp55-6, 68, 180-3, 220-9

[43] The occasion was a session of the Ecclesiastical History Society's conference in Reading, on 23 July 1982: my talk was published in W. J. Sheils (ed), 'The Church and War' (*Studies in Church History*, Vol 20) (Oxford: Basil Blackwell, 1983) pp391-408

[44] *Peace News*, 26 April 1940, p1

[45] Stanley Smith, *Spiceland Quaker Training Centre: Cups Without Saucers* (York: William Sessions, 1990) p35

[46] John Middleton Murry, *Community Farm* (London: Peter Nevill Ltd, 1952) pp34, 110, 116

[47] Ronald Duncan, *Journal of a Husbandman* (London: Faber & Faber, 1944) pp94, 117

[48] Lewis Maclachlan, *CPFLU: A short history of the Christian Pacifist Forestry and Land Units* (London: Fellowship of Reconciliation, 1952) p53

[49] Richard Mayne and John Pinder, *Federal Union: The Pioneers: A History of Federal Union* (London: Macmillan, 1990) p17. Interview with Sir Charles Kimber Bt, 28 July 1977

[50] William Douglas Home, *Half Term Report: An Autobiography* (London: Longmans, Green & Co, 1954) pp146-209

[51] Bishop and Bennett (eds), op cit, p11

[52] *Peace News*, 9 August 1940, p3

[53] G. C. Field, *Pacifism and Conscientious Objection* (Cambridge: Cambridge University Press, 1945) pp5, 86

[54] Edward Blishen, *A Cackhanded War* (London: Thames & Hudson, 1972) p24

[55] I am grateful to Ms Janice Ure for allowing me to see and use this material in her possession, and for advising me about the careers of her father and uncle.

[56] John Ure to his mother, 1 September 1939, Ure Papers [hereafter UP]

[57] John Ure to his mother, 12 June 1940, UP

[58] Peter Ure to John Ure, 10 October 1940, UP

[59] Rachel Barker, op cit, p42

[60] John Ure to his mother, 28 December 1940, UP

[61] Peter Ure to John Ure, 2 January 1941, UP

[62] John Ure to his mother, 29 July 1941, UP

[63] Peter Ure to John Ure, 10 February 1943, UP

[64] Peter Ure to John Ure, 7 October 1939, UP

[65] Frank Kermode, 'Peter Ure, 1919-1969', in C. J. Rawson (ed), *Yeats and Anglo-Irish Literature: Critical Essays by Peter Ure* (Liverpool: Liverpool University Press, 1974) pp1-39, at p10

[66] Peter Ure to John Ure, 5 December (with postscript dated 8 December) 1939, UP

[67] Peter Ure to John Ure, 2 January 1941, UP

[68] Peter Ure to John Ure, 18 December 1941, UP

[69] Peter Ure to John Ure, 29 April 1942, UP

[70] Frank Kermode, op cit, p15

[71] Peter Ure to John Ure , 22 July [1943], UP

[72] Peter Ure's journal entry for 20 November 1946, UP

[73] Frank Kermode, *Not Entitled: A Memoir* (London: HarperCollins, 1996) pp69-70

PART IV
REFLECTIONS

Chapter 28

Reflections on total war in the 20th century

Imanuel Geiss

Total war in the 20th century has its roots in traditional war, for Historical Realism, a universal reality of the past.[1] Ultimate 'pursuit of power'[2] through war ('ultima ratio') is governed by the *pleionexia* of the ancient Greeks: power wants more power, ending in defeat by a superior power and collapse. Aristotle's definition of power in his *Politics*, distinguishing 'quantity' (territory, population) from 'quality' (nobility, education, wealth) and *pleionexia*, helps to analyse wars. Germany and Russia are telling examples: United Germany suffered from too much quantity and quality in Europe as a Great Power and too little quantity as a would-be World Power; Russia always from too much quantity and too little quality. In fatal zero-sum games, both tried to overcome their deficit by conquest in two World Wars against each other – Germany seeking territories, mainly to the east, Russia seeking industrial quality to her west.

In both terms, total war has become the hallmark of the 20th century – quantity (extent of war theatres, number of people involved) and quality (war technology). Above all, it has wiped out the differentiation between fighting armies and enemy civilian populations in limited war, as it had emerged in the 18th and 19th centuries. Ludendorff, the Kaiser's leading general in the First World War, first conceived total war in his inter-war writings (1935), projecting 'lessons' of the First World War into the future Second World War, which made them reality, to the extreme of Auschwitz, symbol of industrialised genocide. The decisive structural break came in the First World War, with powerfully industrialised mass armies, outdone by the Second World War. Between them, the two Great Wars covered most of the first half of the 20th century, while most of its second half was taken by the Cold War, with regional 'hot' sub-wars.

Yet the First World War, the 'seminal catastrophe' of the 20th century (George F. Kennan) did not come out of the blue, but was preceded and followed by small wars, just as the Second World War, after Decolonisation and the Cold War, was followed by small successor wars. However peripheral they may look, they are nigh ubiquitous, number into the hundreds, had cumulative effects comparable with the more spectacular Great Wars, and heralded or practised total war. Both war types are linked in a complex dialectical relationship: small wars paved the way for Great Wars, which absorbed older regional conflicts and released them, as their deadly legacies, post-imperial and post-colonial successor wars, on the ruins of dynastic and colonial empires – followed, after the fall of the Imperium Sovieticum and the Cold War, by post-communist successor wars. Some are even indispensable for understanding recent wars, such as that in Yugoslavia. Understanding them can broaden historical perspectives beyond the two World Wars.

The historical background to total war can be subdivided into periods of unequal length and structurally different content – traditional and civilised war. Both together explain total war.

Under the shell-shock of modern total war, it is easy to belittle traditional war for its cosy limitations in space and level of military technology, to fall for the 'myth of the peaceful savage'.[3] Instead, even a quick glance reveals striking parallels: if modern total war does not spare the enemy civilian population, nor did traditional war. After a brief spell of civilised war, modern total war is a continuation of traditional war with different means (*pace* Clausewitz).

Although wars, with proper names and dates, emerged only with Civilisation, there is no need to idealise violence before Civilisation, which carried on 'barbarous' warfare. First, captured enemies were sacrificed on the battlefield to victorious gods, then later put to work as slaves. Cities stormed were 'punished' by massacres of males and the enslavement of women and children. Enemies conquered at imperial peripheries were often spared, their leaders re-installed as vassals to the overlord under indirect rule. Burning crops and houses (Latin: 'devastatio') was common practice to terrorise enemies into submission through 'scorched earth', for example in the Peloponnesian War. Traditional war was just old-fashioned total war with limited means.

Yet centres of civilisation and imperial power slowly did evolve rules – declarations of war, armistices, peace treaties, safe conduct for envoys – which gradually also filtered even into far-distant Black Africa.[4] After 1000, feudal wars in Latin Europe were mellowed by moral strictures of the Church: *Pax Dei* on regional and proto-national levels restricted local feuds and protected women and children. Still, Christian chivalry was for peers only, not for Muslims or Jews, for example after the capture of Jerusalem in the First Crusade in 1099. The Thirty Years War (1618-48) was a last peak in outrages of European armies against non-combatants.

We are so used to the ideal of differentiation between belligerents and civilian populations that it requires a special intellectual effort to realise its uniqueness in time and space. It developed only in Europe in the 18th and 19th centuries, as an ideal of 'gentlemen's war' and a reaction against atrocities of traditional war. After the traumatic Thirty Years War, mercenaries, highly valued as living assets, were not to be lightly squandered in pitched battles, and prisoners were often enlisted into victorious armies or kept as pawns for peace negotiations. Ideally, subjects should not notice that war was taking place, with disciplined armies fed from state magazines, making living on the land unnecessary. Looting became rare, as in Lombardy by Bonaparte's Army in 1794. The greatest crime of which Napoleon's worst enemies accused him was to have 1,200 Turkish prisoners shot in Jaffa during his Egyptian campaign in 1799, because he could not feed them.

If Ludendorff was the theorist of unlimited total war, Clausewitz was the theorist of limited civilised war. Its rules were even codified in Red Cross Conventions since 1864 and in the 'Hague Convention Respecting the Laws and Customs of War on Land' in 1907: combatants had to wear uniforms, at least 'a fixed distinctive emblem recognizable at a distance', had 'to carry arms openly' (art 1), treat prisoners of war 'humanely' (art 4), expressly forbidden 'to declare that no quarter will be given' (art 23 e); and they had to spare civilian populations, and respect their civil rights and properties, which 'cannot be confiscated' (art 46). 'The pillage of a town or place, even when taken by assault, is prohibited' (art 47). And 'The right of belligerents to adopt means of injuring the enemy is not unlimited' (art 22).

In historical hindsight, there reigned almost world peace around 1900. Since 1815 wars in Europe and colonial wars to impose *Pax Colonialis* had been rare, brief and limited, while those after 1900 appeared as mere regrettable relapses into traditional war, to be overcome by bold paragraphs patiently listed on paper. However, against solitary trends to civilise war in Latin Europe in the Age of Reason, Reason in its dreams also bred 'monsters' (Goya) of its own. Since civilised war happened only in Europe, ongoing traditional war spilled over, wearing down the walls that protected enemy civilian populations from fighting armies. The Industrial and French Revolutions, together with the fervours of nationalism, generated a momentum of power and pleionexia. Some pre-1914 wars showed the imminent future – 'better' weapons, undeclared wars, ill-treatment of prisoners of war, massacres of civilian populations pell-mell, ethnic cleansings, and genocides.

In yet another way, the calm of near world peace in 1900 proved deceptive. In that year Max Planck inaugurated quantum physics, which literally turned our world view upside down, followed by Albert Einstein's relativity theory in 1905. One of its consequences was the atom bomb, which thereafter stalked as a theoretical ghost through science fiction, and was made practical reality through Einstein himself when, in the Second World War, fearing that Nazi Germany was building one herself, he pleaded with the American President to build an American atom bomb.

At colonial peripheries, civilised warfare petered out; technical superiority and military discipline turned colonial wars into one-sided massacres of Africans. On the other hand, *Pax Colonialis* first imposed internal peace in Africa. Revolts were put down, most savagely in King Leopold's Congo and German East and Southwest Africa in 1904-07, violating most brutally the rules of civilised war at home. At worst, colonial armies conformed to levels of traditional indigenous atrocities, but largely kept well below them.

America withheld civilised war from the Red Indians, who obstructed moving frontiers on their jubilant march with Progress and Christianity, from Atlantic to Pacific. The coming World Power on the western fringe of the European system grew up in blissful isolation and safety, with ever-expanding frontiers, into a huge power vacuum. Without serious rival, but with sufficient quantity and quality at hand, it felt invincible, ever victorious: 'God's own country' stood for righteousness, adding religious zeal to quality, to make the world safe for Democracy.

When expanding Russia ran into resistance against fulfilling her 'manifest destiny', to make space between Latin Europe and the Pacific safe for Russian power, she established her own tradition of massacres and mass deportations, from the Caucasus to Central Asia, from Tsars and Stalin to Yeltsin and Putin, all for redeeming mankind through Orthodoxy or Communism. Her power was always more extensive ('quantity') than intensive ('quality'). The rival missions of the superpowers in the Cold War can be summed up symbolically in their capitals – Third Rome (Moscow) vs Fourth Rome (USA) – whatever the ideological disguise.

In the Balkans, mountainous regions bred ethnic and political fragmentation and invited conquest to impose imperial peace (Rome, Byzantium, Ottoman Empire). Thus, the region remained outside the pale of civilised war in Europe after 1700, with archaic structures – clan (*zadruga*), vendetta, irregular warfare of *hajduks* ('semi-brigand, semi-revolutionary mountain chiefs'[5]) and their Greek counterparts, *klepths*, against Turks. Industrialism and revolution in the 19th century politicised religious and dynastic loyalties into modern nationalisms, still crystallised around Orthodox national churches. The 'Eastern Question' (1774-1923)[6], the agony of the Ottoman Empire, released a chain of revolts and wars, culminating in the Eighth Russo-Turkish War of 1877-78, a pandemonium of mutual massacres, sweeping half a million distracted Muslim refugees ('mohadjirs') to Constantinople, the Russian Army hard on their heels. This traumatic shock aroused the furor of assimilationist Turkish nationalism *à la française* to preserve the Ottoman Empire, only to whip up more violence from above and below, first against Armenians, with the climax of genocidal Armenian massacres during the First World War, in 1915-16.

Meanwhile, 'progress' – economic and demographic growth – provided warfare with growing power in terms of quantity and quality. Since the French revolutionary *levée en masse*, continental mass armies had been based on general conscription, and were bigger, with ever 'better' weapons. Nationalism, the secularised modern civil religion, led increasingly towards wars 'of the people'. In the European Revolution of 1848-49, railways first appeared as vehicles of greater mobility and a key to industrialised warfare. Railways first moved troops in an international war, against Austria, in 1859. In the American Civil War (1861-65) mass armies, moved sometimes by rail, fought with modernised weapons. The submarine was born and trenches proliferated, both developments of prophetic significance for the future. Iron-clad warships heralded fleets of 'Dreadnought' (1905) and 'Invincible' battleships, packed with the high technology of their time. Sherman's march through Georgia broke the South by sheer terror of a classical 'devastatio' – ex-colonial New Europe in the New World showed Old Europe her future from the peripheries – the return of traditional war.

The Franco-Prussian War of 1870-71 led directly to the founding of the Second German Empire, and, indirectly, in the course of crises and small short wars, to the First World War. Germany, as it was uniting, proved superior to Napoleon III's Second Empire both in quantity (numerical strength of armies) and quality (better maps, staff work, railways). In 1870 Moltke, the Prussian Chief of Staff, could read Napoleon's war plans from the structure of the French railway system.[7] The shades of a *francs-tireurs* war of embittered Frenchmen against Germans – real or imagined – lingered on to the First World War, especially in Belgium, at least in the imagination of invading German armies in August 1914. The bombardment of both Strasbourg in 1870 and Paris in 1871 by German heavy artillery made no military sense, but pointed to air bombardment in the future.

The intervention of 14 powers into the last dynastic cycle of Imperial China, the 'Boxer War' of 1900, was really a show of 'civilised' imperialism. But Wilhelm II saw off the German contingent from Bremerhaven with his notorious 'Hun' speech to inspire his soldiers with the model of Attila's Huns during the invasion of the barbarians, not to take prisoners, thus violating a basic rule of civilised warfare. The 'Hun' propaganda label stuck to Germans in the First World War and subsequently. More important than the flamboyant knight errant posing as Kaiser was Japan's expansion against her neighbour in agony. Civil War in China after the fall of the Manchu Dynasty in 1911 seduced Japan into filling the huge power vacuum with an overseas empire of her own, which drew her into the First World War and, even more disastrously, into the Second World War.

The Boer War (1899-1902), a hangover from imperial conquest in the 19th century, heralded 'novelties' and contributed to the constellation of 1914; early Boer victories in 1899 provoked regular war with massive mobilisation of imperial troops, followed by guerrilla war by Boer commandos. The British answered with the first concentration camps to separate Boer commandos from civilian infrastructures – Mao Tse-tung, with his fish-in-water theory, was still an obscure boy in rural China. Those camps were different from later Nazi and Soviet concentration camps, but conditions were so appalling that public outcry robbed the Tories of their military victory and gave political victory to the 'brave, gallant Boers'. The Boers were released by liberal largesse into the cul-de-sac of Apartheid, from which they could retreat only into black majority rule by an Afrikaans *perestroika* in striking parallel with that in the Soviet Union in 1985-91. The international repercussions of the Boer War were dramatic: Irish Republicans sent two Irish brigades to fight the British. The Boer War raised questions about Britain's 'splendid isolation', her need for allies and for Haldane's Army Reform. J. A. Hobson was inspired to write his seminal book *Imperialism*, the fountainhead of all Marxist theories of imperialism.

Soon thereafter, the Russo-Japanese War of 1904-05 confronted a European power with the first emerging Asian great power, modernised on European lines. Japan opened hostilities without a declaration of war and mass armies, first entrenched on a large scale, used machine-guns. The fate of Russian prisoners of war in Japanese hands gave a grim foretaste of the Second World War.

The first outburst in the new century of the Balkan tradition of irregular war came with the Macedonian Uprising (1903-08).[8] The Congress of Berlin in 1878 had restored Macedonia to Turkey, but cut off edges to the advantage of Serbia and Bulgaria. Still, they and Greece wanted more, for 'historical' reasons: Macedonia had belonged to past empires – Alexander's and Byzantium, two 'Great' Bulgarian Empires in the Middle Ages, and the 'Great' Serbian Empire of 1346-55. Since the diplomatic skirmishes at the Berlin Congress, Macedonia had become the great prize in the ensuing three-cornered fight. The territorial claims of Serbs and

Greeks did not clash, but Bulgarian ambitions with Serbia did conflict to the west and with Greece to the south. This fact explains the friendships and enmities of Balkan nations in pursuit of neo-imperial ambitions through a series of Balkan wars ever since.

The Macedonian Uprising of 1903 was an unofficial prelude to the Second Balkan War of 1913. Both were prepared by a war of statistics and maps, giving the majority of the population to Greeks, Serbs and Bulgarians respectively.[9] The Uprising was a confused affair, befitting an extremely mixed ethnic situation, which explains the French and Italian label *Macedonian* for mixed fruit salad. Ignited by Bulgarian anarchists, it turned into a nightmare of massacres by each side in a weird war of everyone against everyone. Irregular bands ('comitadjs') in the traditions of *hajduks* and *klephts*, sent by Greece, Serbia and Bulgaria, produced as many 'co-nationals' as possible for future elections or plebiscites by killing off 'enemy' civilians. Between all 'fronts' stood the Turkish Army with its own tradition of atrocities. Army officers from Macedonia, among them the future Kemal Ataturk, took power as the 'Young Turks' in 1908 to save the Ottoman Empire.[10] However, the repressive assimilationism of the Young Turks made the situation only more explosive.

After Italy's attack on the Ottoman Empire in 1911-12, the official return of traditional warfare to Europe began with the Balkan Wars of 1912-13. Once the post-Ottoman successor states had driven the Turks to Constantinople in the First Balkan War of 1912, they fought each other in the Second – Bulgaria against the rest. The Balkans exploded in an orgy of carnage, committed by 'comitadji' and regular armies. 'Ethnic cleansings' first became a euphemism for massacres and genocide. Pan-Germany chauvinists took them up as a cue for their version of expansion and 'Germanising' in the First World War, pressing for a border strip of Polish territory about 100km wide along the German-Russian frontier to be germanised.[11] Though still conceived without bloodshed, their plans became a prelude to Nazi 'ethnic cleansings' in the Second World War – in fact, genocide.

The Balkan Wars of 1912/13 heralded future conflicts, including Kosovo, then still part of Macedonia. Thousands of Muslim Albanians were killed when confronted by Orthodox Serbs with the fatal alternative – enforced baptism or death.[12] When a few lonely journalists reported the outrages, Austria-Hungary took up the matter for power politics of her own and asked the Great Powers for humanitarian intervention, but only drew upon herself the ill-reputation of bullying 'gallant little Serbia'. Serbs committed the macabre precedent for what Catholic Croats did to Orthodox Serbs in the Second World War in the Ustache State.

The 20th century knew so many different wars that the time-honoured differentiation between external (ie international) and internal (ie civil war) is no longer sufficient. New categories have to do justice to new forms of war, but only to provide rough orientation as ideal types in the Weberian sense, for historical realities are mixed in endless complexity.

As a first point of departure it may help to distinguish between global Great Core Wars (the two 'hot' World Wars and the Cold War[13]) and small Peripheral Wars.

Most Peripheral Wars were fought by new post-imperial (-colonial, -communist) successor states, often with discarded Great Power arms, before, between and after Core Wars. But their historical roots plunged far back into the past. In Europe, many ethnic conflicts had first burst on the scene during the European Revolution of 1848-49, linked to each other in a global system of communicating pipes through mass media, economic and financial bonds, and shaped by national or regional modifications, by general historical mechanisms and precedents. Comparable situations bred comparable patterns of actions and reactions – what one nationalism or ruler did, others could do as well, *con variazone, da capo al fine, ad infinitum*.

Neo-imperial *Reconquista* Wars sought to regain 'lost' parts of empires – *membra disiecta*: French Vietnam War 1946-54, Tibet 1950-51, Falklands War 1982, the Yugoslavian War 1991-99, and the Chechen Wars 1994-96, 1999-2000.

Modern partisan war, first introduced by the Spanish *guerrilla* against Napoleon (1808-12), unfolded its cruelties during and after the Second World War, with its characteristic of sharing time and space between opposing parties – day and town/city for occupant/ruler, night and countryside for guerrillas. Its return to traditional warfare often consciously violated rules of civilised warfare to provoke a superior enemy into excessive outrages, to swell the ranks of partisans. Guerrilla wars could also include elements of civil war.

Geographically in Europe, but historically outside the pale of civilising war, remained the wars in the Balkans, both irregular and regular. Here modern war was traditional, pure and simple.

A new category was given currency by Alan Bullock – Stalin's 'war against his own citizens'[14] – and it is useful also for comparable cases, eg post-1945 wars, declared 'internal affairs'.

The two World Wars were fought over hegemony and domination between rising powers – Germany, Serbia, Russia, young and hungry, offensive in their drive for more power – and older Great Powers – Britain, France, largely defensive in being established – but started over peripheral conflicts with a small power (Serbia) and a middle-sized power (Poland). The First gave birth to the Second World War. Only a few farsighted contemporaries, left and right, had warned of modern war as a catastrophe for Civilisation as such – before 1900 the elderly Friedrich Engels, Field Marshal Moltke and lonely pacifists, in 1914 the younger Moltke and Chancellor Bethmann Hollweg.[15] Grey's famous image of lights going out over Europe amounted to the same. Norman Angell's 'Great Illusion' had banked on the hope that a Great War would be so disastrous that it would never occur. Yet it did come in August 1914, for structural reasons.

After all the murderous preludes, 'the great seminal catastrophe of this century'[16] started the erosion of civilised war on a global scale, less through deviation from its rules than through the sheer weight of industrial war technology in quantity (manpower) and quality (firepower, mobility). Before 1914 World War had become thinkable, if all the Great Powers of the European Pentarchy were at war against each other at the same time after the dissolution of the Ottoman Empire or the death of Emperor Francis Joseph.[17] Diplomatic crises between 1875 and 1913 had postponed the Great War only at the price of coalitions to fight actual war on military fronts forecast by pre-war diplomatic fronts – Germany in the west against France and Britain, Austria-Hungary and Germany in the east against Russia and Serbia.[18] Escalating tensions exploded in general war, triggered by the Balkans.[19] Europe's dominance in the world made it the first truly global war.

As in most wars, the First World War in essence started with the weapons and the strategies of the last major war in Europe, the Franco-Prussian War of 1870-71, with dashing cavalry attacks, so dear to the Kaiser's heart, and infantry advancing in thick columns under fire. Yet the defender had a supreme advantage in the machine-gun. Losses were correspondingly high in the first months of the war, especially among officers. In August 1914 all offensives failed, on all fronts. Still, Imperial Germany, quantitatively and qualitatively growing by leaps and bounds before 1914, was powerful enough almost on her own, with weak allies of only doubtful military value (Austria-Hungary, the Ottoman Empire and Bulgaria), to fight France and Britain into stalemate in the west, and to fight Russia into revolutionary breakdown on the Eastern Front in 1917. Finally, the balance of war was tipped by the USA against the Central Powers.

Some technical developments were at modest disposal at the beginning of the war – machine-guns, heavy artillery. Others followed in rapid succession – increasingly specialised aeroplanes, airships, barbed wire, gas, flame-throwers, tanks and mechanised transport for troops. The only real innovation for war was the telephone, at first much overrated, because it still had many technical shortcomings. Also, in a war zone, telephone lines were vulnerable to shellfire, and in occupied zones to sabotage. With strategic stalemate in trench warfare, intensive and prolonged artillery barrages were traumatic experiences for those cowering in trenches and dugouts. In different countries the great but disadvantaged offensives had different names: Verdun in 1916 for French and Germans; the Somme in 1916 and Passchendaele/Flanders in 1917 for Britons, soldiers of the Commonwealth and of Germany; and Isonzo for Italians and Austrians. Gallipoli (1915-16) had a special ring for Australians and New Zealanders. Success there for Turkish defenders under German guidance ensured that Tsarist Russia remained cut off from crucial Allied supplies through the Straits and the Black Sea, and thus collapsed only one year later in the March Revolution of 1917.

Some 65 million men, mostly conscripted, were equipped with weapons deadlier than ever before, mainly in Europe, on the Western and Eastern Fronts. Also, Allied colonial empires were drafted into the war effort, both in economic and military terms. Not only in Africa, but also in Europe on the Western Front, French and British colonial troops served, with the British also having the support of the Indian Army. In the end, 8.5 million men were killed, 21 million wounded, and 8 million made prisoners of war or reported missing, not counting civilian victims, including millions who fell to the terrible influenza during the winter of 1918-19. So far, this had been the most destructive war in history, a quantum leap in warfare, beggaring all description.

By and large, the First World War still roughly adhered to the rules of civilised war. But soldiers surrendering on the battlefield were too often killed, with or without orders not to take prisoners, apparently first by Germans on the Western Front, but also by Scottish regiments, correspondingly feared by German troops.[20] Gas had been expressly banned by the Hague Convention. In an uncanny irony of history, the German scientist who invented German gas weapons, Professor Haber, was a Jew, later to suffer under the Nazi regime. Germany's invasion of neutral Belgium violated an international treaty of 1839 (Chancellor Bethmann Hollweg having referred to it as 'a scrap of paper'), and the German Army acted in an atmosphere of hysterical reaction to real or alleged Belgian *franc-tireurs* in a way to justify the German 'Hun' image of Allied war propaganda. The systematic policy of 'scorched earth' during the retreat in October 1918, after suing for armistice, violated the Hague Convention and was an act of exemplary stupidity. Still, as in the Second World War, apart from those excesses Germany behaved in the west less brutally than in the east. Here also the scope of envisaged annexations and vassal states was much larger than in the west, where 'only' half of Belgium, Luxembourg and the small iron-ore district of Longwy-Briey were earmarked for incorporation into the Reich.[21] The Allied blockade against the Central Powers violated international law and made for total war, as did, of course, the German countermeasure, unlimited submarine war (1915, 1917-18), which, in the end, only provoked America's entry into the war against Germany, an entry of decisive influence.

Civilian populations suffered directly on a greater scale than since about 1700, in particular refugees in France, Serbia and on the Eastern Front. Jews were deported as unreliable from behind the Russian Front, suspected of leaning towards Germany for cultural and language affinities (Yiddish). Their lot was mild compared with that of the 2 million Armenians killed by order of the Young Turk Government, their pro-Russian sympathies taken as an excuse for the first genocide of the century. Hunger and undernourishment had a crippling effect on the Central Powers and on Russia, where hunger revolts initiated, first, general strikes in Austria-Hungary, then in Germany in January 1918, then the first Russian Revolution in March 1917.

In another respect, the First World War was still conventional, sticking to formalities of international law. It began with declarations of war and ended with armistices in October-November 1918[22] and fully fledged peace treaties in 1919-20 – Versailles with Germany, St Germain with Austria, Trianon with Hungary, Neuilly with Bulgaria, and Sèvres with the Ottoman Empire, repudiated by the Young Turk Republic, with Soviet help, and replaced by the Peace of Lausanne in 1923.

But the vanquished of 1918 were excluded from the peace negotiations – they had to take peace conditions or face total *debellatio*. The sudden way in which the war ended for most Germans in November 1918, after they had been lulled into the illusion of final victory, after four years of embellished war bulletins, helped to prepare the second war only 21 years later. The German 'stab in the back' legend and the claim not to have lost the war on the battlefield (*im Felde unbesiegt*) gave room to the obvious lie that Germany had succumbed only to a sinister plot of treacherous socialists and communists ('Marxists'), pacifists and Jews. In fact, the German Revolution of November 1918 was a classical collapse revolution after military defeat, and armistice terms with disintegrating Austria gave Allied troops free passage through Bohemia and Tyrol for the threatened invasion of Germany in the spring of 1919, just as in early 1945.

The overall results of the First World War were interlinked: totalitarianism, successor wars and total war in 1939-45. But they took their time to unfold in grim concerted action. Although total war was not yet formally declared, the huge furnace of the First World War changed all the elements of the time – families, society, economy, technology, literature, the arts, music, women's emancipation. Nothing remained unchanged. The war effort even reached down to villages in Black Africa. The Great War had wrought such havoc that its wounds could not be healed at one attempt by the Versailles Settlement. Hence, the Paris peacemakers were hopelessly overtaxed. The collapse of dynastic empires in revolutions had created huge power vacua, which rival successor states tried to fill, leaning on France. The vanquished sought, as usual, to revise, that is to destroy, the Versailles Peace, France to defend it by restoring her former near-hegemony lost in 1815. After Versailles the United States withdrew completely, and Britain largely so, from the Continent. Ethnic situations in post-imperial successor states were too complex, rivalries between them too bitter, to satisfy anyone with new frontiers, drawn allegedly after the principle of national self-determination, but dubiously against vanquished nations.

Instant offshoots of the First World War were revolutions within the great losers – Russia was first in 1917 with two revolutions. Hungary, Austria and Germany followed suit after their final military defeat in late 1918. The Bolshevik October Revolution established the first totalitarian system, one that proved the most durable, until 1991. In 1919 Lenin hoped to escalate socialist collapse revolutions within the former Central Powers into communist revolutions, to save his revolution in backward agrarian Russia by merging it with revolution in industrialised Germany. Marrying Russian quantity with German quality would make World Revolution, under his leadership, irresistible, to enforce eternal peace on mankind.

All such hopes misfired. In Germany and Austria, weak though unpopular republics, scapegoats for defeat and post-war dislocations held down all communist aspirations, but gradually slipped from the socialist left to the right. By January 1933 Hitler took power, openly fusing, after Mussolini's fascism, his right-wing totalitarian National Socialism with traditional imperialism and anti-semitism, in contrast to Soviet left-wing totalitarianism, which joined International Socialism furtively with traditional imperialism and anti-semitism. Hostility between these totalitarian regimes largely produced the Second World War. In vain Stalin had tried to woo Hitler in 1939-40 into everlasting comradeship against Western capitalism and democracy, by offering to merge German quality with Russian quantity. Together they would become invincible. For that they had to crush weaker successor states between them, above all Poland, the greatest of all. But the dialectics of power politics also cleared the decks for becoming neighbours again – and enemies, according to Machiavelli's terrible realism: the neighbour is the enemy.

The twisted relationship between the two great totalitarianisms leads straight to post-imperial successor states after the First World War. Successor states are, by their very nature, unstable in their struggle for territorial and political definition. Modern nationalisms demand ethnic purity, according to the French Jacobin doctrine, *la nation une et indivisible* – the one nation, not to be divided by vertical (social, class) and horizontal (ethnic, religious) divisions. Because most post-imperial successor states are just as heterogenous as their 'mother' empire had been, post-imperial successor wars fought by post-imperial successor states inexorably blend with civil war. And civil war, even more so if blended with ethnic war, when the civilian population become hostages or prime victims, knows no rules of civilised war. When women take to arms, any distinction between armies and civilian populations finally breaks down. Since the Red Khmer genocide against their own people in 1975-78, but also in recent African civil wars, children soldiers add another twist to the spiral of escalating violence beyond pre-1914 civilised warfare.

Post-imperial successor wars in Europe after the First World War consisted of many-cornered fights of new nationalisms against imperial nations, hostile neighbouring fellow-nationalisms and communism, fretting themselves through the belt between the four great losers – Germany and Austria-Hungary to the west, Russia and Turkey to the east[23], with structural parallels in the Caucasus, Central Asia and Arab Middle East. Theirs was a strange twilight of international and civil wars, where ethnic minorities became internal enemies. At least they were concluded by formal peace treaties. The Greek-Turkish War (1918-23) was the first and last successor war. Finland, Estonia and Latvia had a mix of civil war between 'Red' and 'White', in the wake of the Russian Revolution, and wars of national liberation. The remains of German military power upheld 'Whites', seeking to carve out new 'Lebensraum' for German Freikorps soldiers in Latvia. Lithuania had to assert herself against Germans, Russians and Poles. The Hungarian Soviet Republic stuck to old Greater Hungary and clashed with Romania over Transylvania, and Czechoslovakia over Slovakia ('Upper Hungary'). After the collapse of Austria-Hungary, Yugoslavia arose more by a military campaign of the Serbian Army than by Croat peaceful assent. War between Turks and Armenians continued and escalated Ottoman massacres against Armenians. The Turkish Republic repudiated the Treaty of Sèvres, because it gave autonomy to Armenians (and Kurds). With Soviet aid, it was about to deliver the *coup de grâce* to Armenians, who were saved from certain genocide in late 1920 by a *deus ex machina* – the former Russian Armenia around Erevan became a Soviet Republic. The Anglo-Irish War of 1919-21 ended with the division of Ireland in 1922, but spilled over into civil war in Southern Ireland in 1922-23 and the Ulster 'Troubles', on and off ever since.

The Polish-Soviet War of 1919-20 compressed great issues of the 20th century: the resurrected Poland, the biggest post-imperial successor state, clashed with most of her neighbours over her return to the historic frontiers of 1772 before the First Partition. While the Polish advance to Kiev under Pilsudski failed in 1920 because Ukrainian peasants were loath to have their Polish overlords back, the Soviet counter-offensive over Poland to Berlin, to ignite world revolution through the German proletariat, also failed in the face of Polish resistance to Russian rule in 'progressive' disguise. Stalin's hatred of the popular Marshal Tuchachevsky made him the most prominent victim of deadly purges in 1937. Poles felt Stalin's wrath in acts of bloody revenge for the setback before Warsaw in 1920 – carving up Poland with Hitler in 1939, killing and deporting Poles by the hundreds of thousand, and denying help to the Warsaw Uprising of the *Armija Krajowa* against German SS units from August to October 1944. Stalin's blood-letting of the non-communist Polish nation in the Second World War obliquely opened the Cold War.

The Second World War was, of course, linked to the First World War by innumerable threads, above all the two great totalitarianisms, in Russia from 1917, and in Germany from 1933 after the interregnum of the weak Weimar Republic. They can be compared for what they had in common – structures, personality and flag cults, ideologies, means of repression – without overlooking their differences. Their attitudes to each other oscillated between the extreme poles of bitter ideological hostility and opportunistic collaboration, both against the West and Poland, which each hated equally. Between them they opened the Second World War as comrades in arms, although Nazi Germany undoubtedly, as the apparently more powerful and dynamic partner, had the overall initiative.

Reactions to the traumatic carnage that the emerging total war provoked were varied – in Britain and France, the prevailing abhorrence of a repeat performance largely explains their policy of appeasement. Italy and Japan felt slighted by the Versailles Settlement. Germany remained unwilling to accept the defeat of 1918 against the proverbial 'world of enemies', which she herself had provoked into alliance by her 'Weltpolitik'. Her general will to more power can be summed up as to 'do better next time'. For that purpose, internal unity had to be forged in the totalitarian Nazi one-party state. But it drove the best brains, about half a million intellectuals, scholars, and artists with their families, out of Germany, many of them Jews. Germany, until 1933 the greatest power in terms of intellectual, scholarly and cultural quality, suffered irreparable loss as Hitler funnelled a powerful brain drain to the world, mostly to the USA, the classical immigration country: Einstein, Thomas Mann and Paul Hindemith may stand here as symbolic names. Even so, with the rest of Germany's intellectual quality remaining in the Reich, she was powerful enough to set up, within a few years, the most formidable war machine the world had yet seen.

In the first phase of its war of revenge, to 1941, the Third Reich overran most of the Continent, while Britain held on in insular isolation, covertly upheld in her overseas lifelines by the USA. Japan had made huge inroads on China since 1931 and 1937, and overran, after Pearl Harbor, South East Asia by early 1942, provoking the United States into war. Thus, the Second World War had two main theatres – Europe, with the Mediterranean and Atlantic as the two maritime flanks, and the Far East and Pacific. Since the shores of the USA are washed by both oceans, she was inexorably drawn into the Second World War as well.

The Second World War was indeed the first total war. Fighting fronts were supported by 'home fronts', fully mobilising female as well as male potential usefulness for the state. Total war became a euphemism for inhumane warfare. It was no longer the continuation of policy by other means, keeping a tolerable peace settlement in mind during limited war, but an absolute end in itself, most fitting for totalitarianism, of the left and the right. It began as a mix of conflicts, with and without declarations of war, and surpassed the First World War in all possible ways, quantitatively by the geographical expansion of war theatres, in particular the

Pacific, culminating and ending in the dropping of the two atom bombs on Hiroshima and Nagasaki, and the number of victims killed (27 million soldiers and 25 million civilians), wounded or dislocated as refugees, by deportation or forced labour, inside or outside concentration camps.

Protective walls between combatants and non-combatants broke down on an even greater scale. Mass murder of civilians by Nazi Germany started in Poland in September 1939, most viciously against unsuspecting Jews who had feared pogroms more from Poles than Germans, for whom traditionally they had great respect, if only for their economic and cultural achievements. Massacres escalated in the West after May 1940 with systematic hunts for German émigrés, especially Jews, in German-occupied countries, even more so in the (undeclared) war against the Soviet Union, with the killing of political commissars of the Red Army and Jews by special units (*Sondergruppen*) behind the front. Hitler's rejection of Stalin's offer to respect international rules of war fitted into the Nazi war of destruction against 'subhuman' Jews and Slavs. The Holocaust became the most systematic, institutionalised and industrialised form of genocide in total war against unarmed people. In fascist Italy, basically not anti-semitic, the Army strove to shield Jews from persecution in their occupation sectors in the Balkans, until it was disarmed after Mussolini's fall on 25 July 1943.[24]

Partisan war, in the Balkans and behind the Eastern Front, further blurred the distinction between combatants and non-combatants: in Yugoslavia it merged with civil and ethnic war, mainly between Croats and Serbs, in the Balkan tradition. Massacres of at least 300,000 Orthodox Serbs, unwilling to accept enforced conversion to Catholicism, were answered by revenge massacres of Croats in 1944-45. There also raged an equally bloody civil war between (mostly Serbian) communist partisans and Serbian royalist right-wing Chetniks.

Even the Allies contributed to total war, though their cause was just: Winston Churchill in a speech in America in 1941 pleaded for waging total war. Saturation bombing of civilian quarters in cities, to arouse the working class into revolt, killed about 300,000 German civilians alone, by huge firestorms in Hamburg and Dresden. Its military value was limited, if only because army barracks and industrial plants were largely spared. Bombing did not crack German morale, but directed popular anger more against the Allies than Hitler.

In the 'Great Patriotic War', Stalin ostentatiously suspended his internal war against Soviet citizens, but carried it on furtively against populations falling under his rule in his new West: thousands from East Poland, the Baltic states and Moldavia (Bessarabia) were deported to Siberia or Kazakstan, and 'class enemies' in prison were shot before the German invasion or the arrival of the Wehrmacht in June 1941. Minorities were deported and massacred for 'collaboration', such as Volga Germans, Crimean Tatars and Chechnians. In Russian tradition, Soviet prisoners of war were, on Stalin's order, considered as defectors and, when handed over to him by Western Allies in 1945, treated as such. At best, they landed in the Gulag system. With Germany's collapse, German refugees were attacked, wounded and killed by the Soviet Army, as has recently happened in Chechniya. In 1945 the clearing of German enclaves in East and South East Europe, provinces east of the Oder-Neisse-frontier and the 'Sudeten' regions of Czechoslovakia, amounted to revenge 'ethnic cleansings', with 3 million dead out of 12 million refugees and deportees. In their different ways, the German Holocaust, Stalinist terror, Dresden and the American atom bombs, as modern versions of *devastatio* in traditional war, were the highest stages of breaking down the differentiation between armed forces and civilian population in war.

A logical consequence of looming total war had been Ludendorff's panicking battle-cry for the finale of the First World War. By trying to whip imperial Germany into a desperate last stand, worthy of *Götterdämmerung* – 'Rather an end in terror than terror without end'. What level-headed German politicians had prevented in late October 1918 – a whole nation cannot commit collective suicide – was taken up one World War later by Hitler in his hour of final defeat. While he let loose the furies of total war on Germany's neighbours in a series of 'blitz' wars, he tried to wage them in such a way that the German civilian population should not feel the material pinch. One way was to fix food rations at the beginning of the war above the peacetime living standard of the lower classes – producing 'guns and butter' at the same time, as Goering had boasted even before war. Only after Stalingrad did Hitler change gear to total war, cynically and theatrically proclaimed by Goebbels in a pseudo-plebiscital setting in the *Sportpalast*, in Berlin, in February 1943. In the final stages, old men up to 60 and, in the spring of 1945, boys born before 31 December 1930, were drafted into hastily improvised units of *Volkssturm*, a kind of militia. By the spring of 1945, Hitler swung round full cycle to the opposite extreme against the German nation with his self-destructive 'Nero' order: his cynical version of 'war against his own citizens' was to destroy civilian infrastructures, robbing Germans of all means of survival in a grandiose inferno accompanying his own end *à la Rienzi*.

Japan faced defeat in August 1945, for the first time in her history, after the traumatic shock of 'conventional' saturation bombing and the two atom bombs. Before, she had grossly violated rules of civilised war by starting wars against China, the USA, Britain and Holland without declarations of war, treating prisoners of war inhumanely, and slaughtering about 300,000 Chinese after the capture of Nanking in 1937.

The defeat of Nazism in 1945 by the victorious Western Allies and the Soviet Union paved the way for both Democracy and the spread of Communism. It also ushered in Decolonisation and the Cold War, when the unequal 'anti-Hitler coalition' fell apart after the end of the Third Reich.

With the fall of right-wing totalitarianism, the triumphant left-wing totalitarianism of Stalin and his successors tried to fill the huge power vacua in Europe and Asia that Germany and Japan had left behind. It was done directly by the Soviet Army, and indirectly through communist-led revolutions and anti-colonial wars of liberation, or by strong communist parties even in the West (Italy, France). The Cold War emerged as a late phase of ideological 'global civil war' (*Weltbürgerkrieg*, Ernst Nolte), because the United States took up the challenge of 'containing' communism and its attempts to spread World Revolution. Mankind was spared a Third World War, even if often enough some conflicts moved dangerously to the brink of nuclear war – Korea (1951), Vietnam (1954), Berlin (1961), the Middle East (1956), and Cuba (1962). Nuclear weapons, though produced in an arms race between West and East, reached absurd heights of innumerable 'overkills' that effectively deterred their use. The relative rationality of both the hegemonial superpowers and the East-West conflict bloc discipline ensured that small 'hot' conflicts within the Cold War were fought only with 'conventional' weapons, those of the Second World War, 'improved' by modernisation – cold comfort to those stricken by them. Prepared by the repercussions of the First World War on European colonies, relatively rapid dismantling of colonial empires after the Second World War became the equivalent of the collapse of the dynastic empires following the First World War. The overall effect was similar – successor wars between post-colonial independent states, together with anti-colonial wars of liberation.

Hiroshima had opened the nuclear age, and the reaction against the Holocaust opened a new awareness for human rights, as enshrined in the 1948 UN Convention against genocide: all UN members pledged their countries to respect human rights. Yet many violated them, mostly communist countries and post-colonial successor states. Practically all wars since 1945 made civilian populations suffer most. Within the framework of the Cold War and Decolonisation, unfolded under the global umbrella of nuclear arms, about 150 regional wars took place after 1945, some by proxies, and interlocking in many ways. Anti-colonial and post-colonial successor wars could merge, for example, with the East-West conflict and neo-imperial *Reconquista* Wars. Decolonisation and the spread of communism (from one-sixth to one-third of mankind) had dialectical effects, that is to the contrary of what the victors could have wished – wars in and between post-colonial successor states, after the collapse of the Soviet Empire in 1989-91, and wars in and between post-communist successor states.

The Greek Civil War of 1944-49 was a radical continuation and intensification of the war against the Axis powers of 1940-44. A communist victory in Greece ran against the Yalta Agreement, which had 'given' Greece to Britain. The struggle for Greece definitely merged with the Cold War, when the USA took over in the spring of 1947 and opened 'Containment' by upholding Greece and Turkey against Soviet pressure. Yugoslavia's break with Stalin on 28 June 1948 ended her support for the Greek communists, who were defeated in isolation. Also, anti-colonial liberation movements under communist leadership strengthened the communist camp. In China, a common national effort against Japan in 1937 had only suspended the civil war following the fall of the Manchu dynasty in 1911. It was resumed in 1946, and the communists won in 1949.

The Korean War began as an attempt by communist North Korea to re-unite all Korea, in June 1950, through force. It was repelled by the USA with a UN mandate and contingents of other Western UN members. Both the Korean and Vietnam wars conjured up the spectre of nuclear war, first, in early 1951, when General MacArthur called for atom bombs against the masses of Chinese 'volunteers' driving back the UN Army from the boundary between China and North Korea, the Yalu River; then in May 1954 after Dienbienphu, when the USA obliquely hinted at the use of atom bombs against the victorious Vietminh. The American Vietnam War of 1965-74 and the Afghanistan War of 1979-88 are later examples of 'hot' wars during the Cold War.

In the hour of triumphant Decolonisation, conflicts between neighbouring hostile post-imperial successor states dashed again any hopes for a peaceful post-war order. In general, post-colonial wars can be understood against the background of pre-colonial structures, changes under colonial rule and the universal mechanisms of successor states and 'nation-building'.

Decolonisation and its dialectics began in 1946 with independence for India, which then also included Burma and Ceylon. While Indian nationalists strove to keep 'Greater India' intact, India was split up in 1947 with the secession of Muslim Pakistan ('State of the Pure') in reaction against Nehru's vision to create a socialist unitarian state, which would have denied autonomy to Muslims. Mutual massacres of Hindus and Muslims cost half a million lives, and set about 10 million refugees on the move in both directions, where they have caused havoc to this very day. A chronic bone of contention is Kashmir, with a Muslim majority but a Hindu ruler, claimed by India on shadowy 'historical' grounds as the home of the ancestors of the Brahmin Nehru family. Partitioning Kashmir solved nothing: the smouldering conflict flared up into three wars between India and Pakistan and drove them to build atom bombs of their own.

Answering the Indian Question raised the Burma and Singalese Questions, answered with independence for both countries in 1948. They were faced with internal nationalisms of their minorities; if autonomy were denied, they demanded independence, through violence from below. Burma, in self-chosen isolation imposed by military dictatorships, is beset by constant wars against peripheral minorities. Sri Lanka/Ceylon has reeled under a war of independence (or secession) by the Tamils since 1983. India, Pakistan, Burma and Sri Lanka have become sad models of instant wars in and between post-colonial successor states.

Sovereignty for Arab countries after 1945 was over-shadowed by conflict, since 1948 with modern Israel and Zionism, the Jewish version of modern nationalism since 1882-97. Answering the Jewish Question automatically raised the Palestinian Question. In four Middle East Wars (1948-49, 1956, 1967, 1973) qualitatively superior Israel ('David'), backed by America, held its own against quantitatively superior Arabs ('Goliath'). The Middle East conflict, deeply rooted on both sides in history and religion, is the stuff of which Armageddon is made.

On the whole, Decolonisation proceeded peacefully, even if occasionally under the threat of anti-colonial liberation wars, as in India in 1946, which war-weary Britain shunned, or in Morocco and Tunisia in 1955-56, on the wings of the Algerian War, which also hastened the advent of Decolonisation in Black Africa. But in extreme cases, the vested interests of the colonial powers (Indonesia, Vietnam) and/or the European settlers on the spot (Kenya, Zimbabwe, South Africa) blocked peaceful independence. Repression from above provoked revolutionary resistance from below, escalating to anti-colonial wars, also conditioned by the Cold War.

In a formal sense, some were not wars at all, because colonies had been annexed as *départements* (Algeria by France in 1848) or 'Overseas Provinces' (by Portugal in 1951). Despite all legalistic tricks to avoid 'intervention' from abroad, the 'colonial situation' did exist and bred anti-colonial wars, in an inexorable chain reaction: Vietnam I (1946-54), Kenya (1952-60), Algeria (1954-62), Angola (1962),

Mozambique (1963), Vietnam II (1963-75), Zimbabwe (1965-77), Namibia, South Africa. They also acquired a social revolutionary dimension, if they were supported by the Soviet Union and China, and later also Cuba. Logically, since the Korean War in 1950, the colonial powers were backed by the USA.

Japanese occupation in 1942-45 had encouraged nationalism in Vietnam and Indonesia. Holland's colonial *Reconquista* War after 1945 raised the fear that Sukarno might seek Soviet help. To stop Indonesia from going communist, the USA pressured Holland into conceding independence in 1949. But following the Korean War, Washington encouraged France to hang on in her *Reconquista* War to reconquer Vietnam against the communist-led Vietminh under Ho Chi-Minh, supported by the Soviets and, since 1949, communist China. The Fourth Republic conceded military defeat after Dienbienphu in May 1954 and withdrew in agony.

With the Algerian revolt of 1 November 1954, partly under the leadership of seasoned soldiers from the French Army in Vietnam (Ben Bella), the anti-colonial chain reaction reached the Maghrib. Here traditions of revolt were twofold – in the mountainous regions of Kabylia, the Kabyls, Algerian Berbers, had revolted against France in 1870 during the Franco-Prussian War, and in neighbouring Morocco unruly Rif-Berbers had risen against the Spanish and French Protectorate Powers in 1922, under Abdel Kerim. After defeat in 1926, the latter had found asylum in independent Egypt in 1947, and he and Nasser supported revolt in Algeria from 1954. Its first mass basis, outside Arab cities of the coastal plain, lay in notoriously rebellious Kabylia. The Anglo-French Suez campaign in 1956, co-ordinated with Israel during the Second Middle East War, failed to cripple anti-colonial forces. The Algerian 'dirty war' (*la guerre sale*) finished the Fourth Republic: the Generals' Coup in Algeria in May 1958 brought General De Gaulle back into power, but the Fifth Republic had to give up *Algérie Française* in the Peace of Evian, 1962. Independent Algeria later drifted into the usual internal troubles – with a major ethnic minority (Kabyls) and fundamentalist Islamists, and a morass of corruption and misuse of power.

Salazar's masking of Portuguese colonies as Overseas Provinces had the same result as in Algeria. Bitter wars, between 1962 and 1974, in Angola and Mozambique ruined both 'motherland' and colonies. Only the downfall of the authoritarian system in 1974, Portugal's 'return to Europe' and the collapse of her colonial empire ended the anti-colonial wars. They spilled over into even bloodier civil wars between left-wing governments and right-wing rebels, complicated by material interests (diamonds, oil) and Cold War interventions (South Africa, USA; Soviet Union, Cuba).

After the French retreat and the provisional partitioning of Vietnam in May 1954, the USA tried to fill the power vacuum in South Vietnam. Soon after the Algerian War came the American Vietnam War, sliding into escalating involvement, from 'military advisers' to combat units in 1963, still under President Kennedy, into hidden war against the communist Vietcong and North Vietnam in 1964. The USA got itself involved in bombing North Vietnam and openly sending combat troops into South Vietnam from early 1965 onwards, to stop the 'row of falling dominoes' into communism (J. F. Dulles). But even the rich USA could not produce 'guns and butter' at the same time, as President Johnson boasted at the beginning of 'escalation'. Economic costs were immense – inflation, leaving the gold standard, devaluation of the dollar, rapid increase of state debt, and social evils (drugs, first widespread in the US Army in Vietnam).

The American Vietnam War confirmed a lesson taught by the Boer War – however successful an army may have been on the battlefield against partisans fighting for independence, moral losses could count more on the political field than sheer military power. Recklessness against helpless civilians, from napalm and mass bombing to defoliating chemicals, brought home by the first instantly televised war in history, eroded the American claim of moral superiority. A further escalation of the Civil Rights issue for Afro-Americans produced the most serious crisis in the USA since the Civil War of 1861-65. The Vietcong Tet offensive, their self-inflicted military disaster, coincided dramatically with Easter riots in 1968 after the murder of Martin Luther King. The humiliating retreat from South Vietnam in 1974, the collapse of the South Vietnamese regime in 1975, and communist takeovers in Laos and Cambodia heightened the malaise within the USA (Watergate) and a loss of prestige. But the USA was strong enough in terms of quantity and quality to take the post-Vietnam crisis in her stride and to stumble into victory in 1989-91 over the Soviet Union in the Cold War.

Communist victory in 'Indo-China' (Vietnam, Laos, Cambodia) had disastrous dialectical results – for communism. Instantly traditional mechanisms of power politics, hidden by 'progressive' ideology and the common front against the external enemy, returned with a vengeance in the first clashes over off-shore islands as early as 1975. Vietnam's overthrow of the genocidal Red Khmer in Cambodia in 1978 provoked the most twisted 'hot' sub-war of the Cold War; the humanitarian action also coincided with Vietnamese pre-colonial aspirations for regional hegemony over 'Indo-China' and unveiled the Machiavelli-mechanism, in uncanny purity, speed and brutality. Vietnam, always in ambivalent relations with the giant neighbour China, hovering between long periods under direct or indirect Chinese rule and shorter phases of precarious independence, felt emancipated from Chinese tutelage and aid after her victory over the USA in 1974-75. While united Vietnam committed 'ethnic cleansing' by evicting from its newly won South citizens of Chinese extraction ('boat people') as class enemies, its invasion of a fellow communist state in Cambodia offended traditional claims of Chinese suzerainty over all 'Indo-China'. The attack of the Chinese Army to 'punish' Vietnam demonstrated the instant return of traditional, pre-colonial mechanisms of power politics through war, even between ideological comrades-in-arms against 'world imperialism'. Historical neighbours resumed their normal enmities. For China, Cambodia was the neighbour of the hostile neighbour – Vietnam to the south. In her humanitarian-cum-hegemonial intervention to stop carnage in the Red Khmer 'killing fields', Vietnam sought help from China's hostile neighbour to the north, the Soviet Union, locked with Mao's China in an ideological power struggle over the purity of communism since the Great Schism of World Communism in 1960. China, in her turn, took the bloody Pol Pot regime under her dragon's wing, just to spite upstart Vietnam and the 'revisionist' Soviet Union. Furthermore, the Soviets remained the Cold War arch-enemy of the United States, which championed universal rights of man under President Carter.

On a high moralising pitch, the USA sided against Vietnam, the Soviet ally, thus upholding 'Red China', even the genocidal Pol Pot regime, in its guerrilla war against the Vietnamese and collaborating moderate Cambodian communists.

The last regional 'hot' war of the Cold War began as a Soviet military intervention in Afghanistan in late 1979 to stem the mounting tide of fundamentalist Islamism following the rise of the theocratic Islamic Republic in Shi'a Iran, in early 1979. Propping up a faltering communist regime failed for several reasons. The Soviet invasion hurt the fiery Afghan love of independence, which had twice defeated military interventions by Britain in the 19th century. The Anglo-Russian Agreement of 1907 had neutralised Afghanistan as a buffer state, and the invasion plunged the Soviets into international isolation and gave scope to recalcitrant Poland in the west of the *Imperium Sovieticum*. Afghanistan rapidly turned into the Soviet Vietnam War – against guerrillas, equipped by the ideological enemy in the Cold War, the USA, via Pakistan, the American client state pitted against India, the furtive ally of the Soviet Union. Decisive was the supply of anti-aircraft and anti-helicopter Stinger rockets to the Afghan Mujaheddin, which crippled Soviet air superiority. Also the Soviet Union lost less on the military battlefield than in terms of morale, economic costs and political isolation, inaugurating the end of the Soviet Union. After the humiliating retreat under Gorbachev in 1988 and the fall of the Berlin Wall in late 1989, the Soviet Union imploded in 1991.

Even in the 'African Year', 1960, post-colonial conflicts, rooted in colonial and pre-colonial pasts, exploded in Black Africa. Legacies of the colonial state were the first structures of modern statehood, rule of law, the idea of the nation state, and, inevitably, new boundaries. The Congo troubles in the hour of independence demonstrated instantly the uncanny mechanism. But in retrospect, future clashes had been building up, largely obscured by the Cold War, most clearly in the biggest African states in terms of quantity – population (Nigeria) and territory (Sudan).

In the advent of Decolonisation, tensions rose in Nigeria over who would take power – the more Christian modernised south or the traditional Muslim north. Muslim leaders wanted to complete the march of Islam to the coast, interrupted by English missionaries in 1840, who had supplied fire-arms to Yorubas against the victorious Jihad from the north. This basic tension escalated after independence in 1960 into the first military coup in 1966, and the Biafran War of 1967-70. Later military regimes, dominated by the north, took Nigeria into the Islamic League, and the introduction of the Sharia in the north is provoking more violence, which would dwarf the Biafran War.

The same mechanism worked in Sudan. It had been conquered in two phases by Egypt (1820-22, 1874-75), which, just like Indian neo-imperial nationalists in 1946 vis-à-vis Burma and Ceylon, wanted to keep Sudan after independence. Yet Sudanese northern nationalists seceded in 1956 and wanted to keep their south in a Muslim unitarian state, although the Negroid south is structurally different – mostly animist, with Christians since colonial rule. As the south was refused autonomy, Sudan was instantly wrecked by civil, ethnic and religious war, a neo-imperial *Reconquista* Jihad to enforce Sharia and Islam on the south. It is complicated by neo-imperial aspirations of the greatest southern people, the

Shilluk, on smaller peoples, some of them siding, in despair, with the Muslim Central Government.

Sudan is but one segment from a huge belt of internal wars that rent post-colonial successor states straddling the Southern Sahara and the Sahel zone: Mauretania, Mali, Niger, Chad. The geographical dichotomy bred one of ecology, living conditions and social structures, political and historical antagonisms – the perennial clash between cattle-raising, slave-raiding, light-skinned desert nomads (Berber, Tuareg, Arab) and black subsistence peasants as their victims. Colonial rule turned the tables on them by sheer modernisation: Sahel black peasants took more easily to modernisation, through Christianity as its vehicle, whereas desert nomads resisted, aloof in proud isolation and backwardness. Their former slaves took political power after independence to administer sweet revenge on their latter-day slave-drivers and masters by discriminatory measures. Final abolition of slavery robbed nomads of part of the traditional nomadic livelihood, and disastrous droughts in the 1970s and 1980s enabled the new masters to allow the hated nomads silently to starve in the desert simply by withholding external relief from them. Nomad revolts were ruthlessly put down by central governments of modernising black peasants. The civil war in Chad (1966-91) was complicated by neo-imperial territorial claims of Ghadaffi's Libya.[25]

More African post-colonial successor states have been wrecked by internal conflicts, along the same pattern: heterogeneous 'national' societies thrown together by history, and the colonial state exploding if one group, usually the strongest in terms of quantity and/or quality, tries to impose homogenisation for nation-building by centralisation and assimilation from above. Pre-colonial power structures of a hegemonial or quasi-imperial character fired the imagination, as aspirations or fears, as in Uganda, Togo, Rwanda and Burundi. Nightmares of chaos raged, indeed in some cases continue to rage in Zaire/Congo, Somalia, Sierra Leone and Liberia, some with intervention from abroad. A UN peacekeeping force ('blue helmets') was sent into the Congo, including a Ghanaian contingent, as early as 1961. Idi Amin's attack against Tanzania in 1978 provoked the latter's counter-offensive, which overthrew Amin in 1979 and prolonged Uganda's anarchy until 1986. African peacekeeping troops, dominated by Nigeria, tried to stem chaos in Liberia and Sierra Leone, where modernised Afro-Americans and Africans had apparently enjoyed a flying start into modernisation since the early 19th century. In reality, they were privileged oligarchies swept away in bloody convulsions, which only created real chaos, with, presently, no end in sight. In Somalia, where colonial rule had first introduced modern state structures, defeat against Ethiopia in the Ogaden War in 1978 made the state as such collapse and dissolve into the Hobbesian natural state of clans and tribes – *bellum omnium contra omnes* – with appalling consequences for the population. But a clumsy UN military intervention only made things worse.

After Mobutu's overthrow in Zaire/Congo in 1997, several African countries intervened with armed forces on both sides of the ensuing conflict, including neighbouring Uganda and Rwanda, but also far-distant Zambia and Namibia. The results are of the kind of Egypt's military intervention in the Yemen (1962-67) or India's in Sri Lanka (1988-89): they weakened the intervening side, without resolving anything. In Zimbabwe, President Mugabe has ruined the country by autocratic rule, military intervention in the Congo and, recently to divert tensions from his failures, by inciting the occupation of white farms, his one goose to lay the golden eggs. In short, about half of Africa suffered from post-colonial successor wars in one form or another.

Conflicts in and around Ethiopia are particularly complex and fit into several categories. Eritrea's annexation by Ethiopia as a province in 1962 provoked an instant war of liberation (1962-91), spreading also to northern provinces, in particular Tigray. Brutal attacks by the army made it another 'war against citizens of one's own state'. Imperial Ethiopia's *Reconquista* War was carried on by the new republican, soon communist, regime under Mengistu after the fall of the monarchy in 1974, as all revolutionary regimes since 1789 did with traditional lines of expansion pursued by their respective Ancien Régime. But the Ogaden War of 1977-78 over a half-desert, opened by pro-communist Somalia in pursuit of a Greater Pan-Somalia, made it also a late 'hot' Peripheral War of the Cold War, because of the sudden *renversements des alliances*: Somalia switched over to America, and Ethiopia drifted into the Soviet camp. Mengistu survived only thanks to Soviet arms and Cuban 'volunteers', but continued the *Reconquista* War against Eritrea and Tigray until its own collapse in the wake of the fall of the Soviet Union in 1991. After a few honey years of brotherly understanding, the frontier war since 1998 between Eritrea and Ethiopia about a barren piece of half-desert (with suspected or prospected oil reserves) is the next round in neo-imperial *Reconquista* War, now of a Marxist left-wing regime against the Eritrea regime of kin ideological complexion, as in the three-cornered contest involving Vietnam-Cambodia-China. The new Ethiopian regime, ostentatiously indulging in 'ethnic federalism', is shifting 'ethnic cleansing' to the level of autonomous regions being made 'homogeneous'. The result is clear – internal conflicts that might end in Ethiopia falling apart. Ethiopia also demonstrates a macabre way of continuity through successive regimes of varying ideological shades; Negus, Mengistu and the present Ethopian regime all waged their *Reconquista* War to hold or hold down Eritrea at the cost of letting part of their population starve in frequent famines, in their particular versions of war against their own citizens.

The First Gulf War between Iraq and Iran in 1980-88 is the most recent turn of the age-old conflict between Plain and Mountains/Highland since the Ancient Orient, with its offensives and counter-offensives. Changing imperial and ideological/religious disguises took the form of intra-Muslim conflict between Sunni and Schiite from the beginnings of Islam, now fought with modern weapons. Iraq, under the modernising National Socialist Ba'ath ('rebirth', ie of the Califate) regime of Saddam Hussein, took advantage of turmoil in Iran after the victory of Khomeini's Islamic Revolution and hoped to score an easy victory to gain hegemony in the Gulf region with its oil wealth. When Iran struck back and threatened to break the Iraqi front, Saddam Hussein appealed successfully to the West by posing as a moderniser against Schiite fundamentalism. He used gas against his own Kurd population and rockets against Iranian cities. The war of attrition ended in stalemate, but Saddam Hussein's attempt to recoup his immense losses by taking Kuwait in 1990 provoked the Second Gulf War in 1991, the first exclusively high-tech air war with an element of virtuality.

Another conflict burst on the world scene in East Timor in 1999: after Portugal's retreat in 1974, a short-lived independent East Timor state had been overrun by giant Indonesia, which annexed it under no 'historic' pretext whatsoever, through sheer post-colonial neo-imperial aggression. Indonesia provoked instant and constant guerrilla war for independence, which she answered with massacres. When she had to quit East Timor in 1999 under international pressure and after a free vote of the surviving population, she practised 'scorched earth' and 'ethnic cleansing' on Serbian lines, holding the ring for 'militias', equipped, trained and paid by the army, to commit atrocities in a war against its own civilian population.

Wars in the post-communist era of globalisation, since 1989-91, have also been fought without atomic, biological or chemical weapons. However, despite efforts to banish or curb them, they are getting out of hand, floating through parts of the 'Third World' and the post-Soviet former 'Second World'. 'Democratic' Russia even reminded the world recently that she still is a nuclear power, when former President Yeltsin rejected criticism of Russia's second Chechniya War in late 1999. Iraq was threatened with non-conventional weapons during the Gulf War of 1991, and international UN inspections of its industrial capacities to build them remain one of the critical issues between Saddam Hussein and the world community. Recently, after nuclear tests, India and Pakistan rattled their atomic sabres over Kashmir.

The fall of the Soviet Empire and Yugoslavia in 1989-91 also re-opened for Europe and adjacent regions (the Caucasus, Trans-Caucasia, ex-Soviet Central Asia) Pandora's box of post-imperial successor wars. They began in 1988 between Armenia and Azerbaijan over the enclave of Berg-Karabach, for which sullen Armenian public opinion had clamoured even in the outgoing Soviet period. After independence, Georgia was wracked by civil war and wars with neighbouring peoples, who had been supplied with modern arms by the retreating Soviet Army. Also in 1988, the Soviet retreat from Afghanistan left behind chaos and a power vacuum. After the collapse of the local communist regime in 1992, which rival forces tried to fill by imposing brands of tribal hegemony (Pashtan, Tadschiks) or ideological (Islamic) theocracy, the Taliban ('Students of Koran') militias won. They recruited, trained and equipped from Pashtan refugees in Pakistan, with Saudi and American money. Their fiery Islamic regime is frightening even the theocractic Islamic Republic of Iran, which has been mellowing recently.

Communist Yugoslavia, with some modifications a version of the Soviet Empire *en miniature*, had profited from the Cold War since her break with Stalin in 1948. With Tito's death in 1980 she drifted into a loose confederation of nation states with ill-defined internal boundaries. Perennial tensions between quantitatively and qualitatively the strongest national factors – Serbs against Slovenes and Croats – were exacerbated by mutual atrocities, which from the Balkan Wars to the Second World War had been pushed into a collective underground, where they poisoned relations between the peoples of Yugoslavia. No public debate, which might have acted like a collective psychoanalysis, had allowed genuine reconciliation. Historic resentments, smothered with an iron hand by Titoism, rebounded with a vengeance, and pent-up hatred exploded with the end of the Cold War after 1991. In a chaos of international and internal wars, neighbours literally reverted to deeply rooted Balkan traditions of individual and mass atrocities. After the brief prelude against peripheral Slovenia, the Yugoslav War fretted itself through Croatia, Bosnia-Herzegovina and Kosovo, threatening Macedonia and Montenegro, which had latterly tried to steer clear of Milosevic's Serbia.

NATO's air war against 'rump-Yugoslavia' in March-June 1999, to stop 'ethnic cleansing' of Kosovo Albanians, incited Milosevic into stepping up his war against his Kosovo-Albanian people. But NATO's war got out of hand as a bombing war against the Serbian people, for it destroyed the very basis of its livelihood, even with radioactive uranium ammunitions. When Milosevic yielded to international pressure and gave up Kosovo, revenge massacres by Albanians against Kosovo Serbs opened the next round of 'ethnic cleansings'. Stronger than before in Bosnia-Herzegovina, UN contingents are trying to prevent a renewal of a people's war between Albanians and Serbians, along the lines of traditional Balkan atrocities.

Russia tried to protect fellow Orthodox Serbia, although her two Chechnian Wars (1994-96, 1999-2000) are classical *Reconquista* Wars of annihilation, in the worst Tsarist and Stalinist tradition. Grosny was the byname of Ivan IV, 'the Terrible', and Chechnians had been massacred by Tsars and Stalin. The army of 'democratic' Russia is using a modernised version of the Second World War; pretending to fight terrorism by indulging in Russian state terrorism, Russians, proud of their partisan war in the Second World War, are now behaving as any conquering occupant when confronted with armed resistance from below, violating rules of civilised war and the Hague Convention of 1907. Dialectical consequences will be the same as the Soviet-Afghanistan War – self-destruction. It also brings about that 'clash of civilisations' after the end of the Cold War, which has so often been denied; when Muslim Chechens in the battle for Grosny shouted *Allah Akbar* ('Allah is great') Russian soldiers answered with their battle-cry, the Orthodox Eastern salute – 'Christ has risen'.

Fittingly, the 20th century ended with 'ethnic cleansings' through undeclared wars (East Timor, Chechniya) in two great states of imperial dimensions and pretensions. More internal wars are bred by neo-imperial nationalisms, denying autonomy to minorities in heterogeneous unitarian states. A Chinese *Reconquista* War against Taiwan is looming on the horizon.

It would be rash to spread undue optimism about the chances of returning at least to civilised war, since war seems to be irrepressible. Civilised war in itself had only been a brief interlude in world history, for two centuries in Europe, and was even then full of contradictory trends that brought about its end again after 1914 – successively and progressively. The structural reason is obvious: total war, in its traditional as well as in its modern form, has ruled supreme, so far, in the world. Of course, as long as we live, we ought to uphold as a minimum ideal at least civilised war, perhaps as a first timid step towards making war superfluous altogether, if only in the enlightened self-interest of all. But we ought to refrain from facile illusion: only Political Realism, based on Historical Realism, may – perhaps – effect a turn for the better.

Notes

[1]   For a general survey in a systematic, not chronological, order, see John Keegan, *History of Warfare* (New York: 1993); since pertinent literature is immense, with no pretence to having read but a tiny fraction of it, this chapter mentions only works from which it profited directly or indirectly, or which might be helpful as further literature; also my own titles, where I myself went more into details. No titles are given to generally known wars, as the Boer War or the Russo-Japanese War 1904/5, or revolutions in the wake of defeats, because the flood of titles would become unmanageable.

[2]   William H. McNeill, *The Pursuit of Power* (London, Chicago: 1982)

[3]   For an instructive antidote against any romanticism, see now Lawrence Keeley, *War before Civilization: The Myth of the Peaceful Savage* (New York: Oxford University Press, 1997)

[4]   Robert S. Smith, *Warfare and Diplomacy in Pre-Colonial West Africa* (London: James Currey, 2nd ed 1989)

[5]   'The Other Balkan Wars: 1913 Carnegie Endowment Inquiry in Retrospect with a New Introduction and Reflections on the Present Conflict by George F. Kennan' (Washington, DC: Carnegie Endowment of International Peace, 1993) p31

[6]   M. S. Anderson, *The Eastern Question 1774-1923* (London: 1978)

[7]   Arden Bucholz, *Moltke, Schlieffen and Prussian War Planning* (New York, Oxford: Berg, 1991) p53

[8]   Firet Adanir, *Die Makedonische Frage: Ihre Entstehung und Entwicklung bis 1908* (Wiesbaden: 1979)

[9]   'The Other Balkan Wars', op cit; for rivalling statistics see pp28, 30; for map of rivalling aspirations of Serbia, Bulgaria and Greece, see p38

[10] Feroz Ahmed, *The Young Turks: The Committee of Union and Progress in Turkish Politics 1908-1914* (Oxford: 1969)

[11] Imanuel Geiss, *Der polnische Grenzstreifen 1914-1918: Ein Beitrag zur deutschen Kriegszielpolitik im Ersten Weltkrieg* (Hamburg, Lübeck: 1960; Polish ed, Warszawa: 1964)

[12] Hanns Christian Löhr, *Die Albanische Frage: Konferenzdiplomatie und Nationalstaatsbildung im Vorfeld des Ersten Weltkrieges unter besonderer Berücksichtigung der deutschen Außenpolitik* (Bonn: Diss, 1992)

[13] Gabriel Kolko, *Century of War* (New York: The New Press, 1994) concentrates on what is called here the Great Core Wars

[14] Alan Bullock, *Hitler and Stalin: Parallel Lives* (HarperCollins, 1991) p447 in Fontana 1993 ed

[15] Stig Förster, 'Der deutsche Generalstab und die Illusion des kurzen Krieges, 1871-1914: Metakritik eines Mythos', in Johannes Burkhardt et al, *Lange und kurze Wege in den Ersten Weltkrieg: Vier Augsburger Beiträge zur Kriegsursachenforschung* (Munich: Verlag Ernst Vögel, 1996) pp115-58

[16] George F. Kennan, *The Decline of Bismarck's European Order: Franco-Russian Relations, 1875-1890* (Princeton: Princeton University Press, 1979) p3

[17] Marian Kent, *The Great Powers and the End of the Ottoman Empire* (London: 1984)

[18] For a long-term global analysis, see I. Geiss, *Der lange Weg in die Katastrophe: Die Vorgeschichte des Ersten Weltkrieges 1815-1914*, Serie Piper 943 (Munich: Piper, 1990)

[19] For the outbreak of the First World War, see I. Geiss, *July 1914: Selected Documents* (London: 1967)

[20] Niall Fergusson, *The Pity of War* (London: The Penguin Press, 1998) (pp339, 353 in the German edition)

[21] For details, see Fritz Fischer, *Germany's War Aims in the First World War* (New York: W. W. Norton, 1967)

[22] For November 1918 see Hugh Cecil and Peter Liddle (eds), *At the Eleventh Hour: Reflections, Hopes and Anxieties at the Closing of the Great War 1918* (Barnsley: Leo Cooper, 1998)

[23] For a survey in some more (relative) detail, see I. Geiss, 'Armistice in Eastern Europe and the Fatal Sequels: Successor States and Wars 1918-23', in Hugh Cecil and Peter Liddle (eds), op cit, pp237-54

[24] Jonathan Steinberg, *All or Nothing: The Axis and the Holocaust 1941-43* (London: Routledge, 1990)

[25] Albert Wirz, *Kriege in Afrika: Die nachkolonialen Konflikte in Nigeria, Sudan, Tschad und Kongo* (Wiesbaden: Steiner-Verlag, 1982)

Chapter 29

Apprehending memory: material culture and war, 1919-39

Nicholas J. Saunders

Anthropologists have long been interested in the cultural dimensions of war.[1] However, attention has focused mainly on conflicts among tribal peoples, from the lowlands of South America[2] to the Pacific[3] and Africa[4]. Such studies have been concerned mainly with social process, ie matters associated with ethnicity, trade and politics, rather than an analysis of the materiality of conflict. Even more rare are anthropological studies of the material culture of 20th century warfare.[5] The beginnings of a serious and broadly archaeological concern with modern warfare and its consequences[6] is forcing an interdisciplinary re-evaluation of this kind of material culture from a wide variety of perspectives.[7]

Hitherto, the majority of studies of the 20th century's two World Wars have focused on aspects of military history[8] (ie formal history and personal accounts), and the economic, social and political consequences of these conflicts. Nevertheless, there are signs of more anthropologically inflected approaches at least to the First World War[9], and which draw, variously, on archaeology, geography, art history and psychology, as well as history – though interestingly none of these has been written by anthropologists. Other recent work on the Great War has contributed valuable insights that inform an anthropological approach and widen our interpretive horizons.[10]

It is clear that, as first-hand memory of these two events disappears with the passing away of those directly involved, history increasingly becomes archaeology, and our view of the past enters a new realm – that defined by interpretations of material culture by those who had no part in its production or original purpose. It is here that anthropology, and particularly that part which focuses on materiality, offers new ways of exploring and understanding the multi-dimensionality of industrialised war on a regional as well as global scale. Modern conflicts are, after all, defined by their technologies, and all can be considered wars of matériel.

War can be seen as the transformation of matter through the agency of destruction. In other words, war creates as well as destroys. This point, obvious and subtle by turns, is one element in the application of theories of material culture studies to the analysis of war.

The study of materiality sees objects as possessing important and variable social dimensions beyond (as well as including) their original design purpose.[11] Objects may be small (eg a bullet or a dog-tag), intermediate (eg a tank, aeroplane or bunker) or large (eg a trench system or a whole battlefield landscape). All share a defining characteristic by virtue of being the product of human action rather than natural processes. The Western Front of the Great War of 1914-18 is as much an artefact as a Second World War V2 rocket, as is the symbolic terrain of war memorials or the production, sale and consumption of war-associated artefacts as souvenirs. Seeing material culture in this way enables us to construct a biography of the object[12] – to explore its 'social life' by assessing the changing values and attitudes attached to it by different people over time.[13]

Adopting this approach, objects can be regarded as objectifying individual and collective ideas and emotions, for, as Miller[14] notes, the variability of artefacts is social in origin. Objects are part of, and at the same time constitute, the physical world, which in turn structures perceptions, constraining or unleashing ideas and emotions of the people who live within it.[15] The changing attitudes in Britain towards the commemorative association of war memorials, Armistice Day, and the observance of the 2 minutes silence between 1919 and the present is a case in point.[16] Here, physicality, spirituality, symbolism and emotion link the living with the dead in a complex interplay of past and present.

We all interact with the objects that surround us, and, in one sense, objects make people just as much as people make objects.[17] However, the passage of time and generations creates different interpretations of, and responses to, this materiality. While objects possess inalienable qualities by virtue of their physical existence, it is their contextualisation – the shifting values recorded in written documents, oral testimony, or film – that allows us to follow their individual trajectories through social, geographical and symbolic space. For example, a museum's collection of artefacts only comes alive through interpretive contextualisation, for this identifies the object with an individual or a succession of individuals who came into contact with it, and thereby adds layers of meaning or chapters to its biography.

In this materiality-based view of the world, an individual's social being is determined by his relationship to the objects that represent him – the object becoming a metaphor for the self, a way of knowing oneself through things.[18] In this way, the study of the material culture of war – and the tracking of its materiality beyond war – offers new ways of exploring the human experience of conflict and its consequences.

The courses and consequences of the two industrialised World Wars has, to a considerable extent, defined the 20th century, transforming technologies, national boundaries, and social, political and cultural attitudes. In many respects, the modern world is an artefact forged in the crucibles of war. The materiality of these two events (together with that of subsequent conflicts – most notably the Cold War) surrounds us today, but is too large a topic to be dealt with here.[19] Consequently, in order to keep a meaningful focus, I will concentrate here on one aspect that I call the 'memory bridge'.

The memory bridge is one way of conceptualising the effects of the materiality of the First World War on those who lived during the inter-war years. Objects, ideas and attitudes linked the two World Wars during a period of dramatic social, economic and cultural change, forming a bridge composed of materiality, emotion and memory. Within the physical and symbolic space spanned by this bridge was a world that not only shaped people's everyday lives, but also their perceptions of the past (ie the Great War) and of a hoped-for future. These perceptions became increasingly ironic as a second conflict loomed during the 1930s.

From this viewpoint, the inter-war world can be seen as composed, to a considerable extent, of physical and symbolic objects and attitudes to the Great War. While attitudes to the war, its ending, and the commemoration of the dead, were diverse rather than monolithic[20], the materiality of 'the past in the present' was taking similarly diverse, often ambiguous, and certainly ironic forms. Some of these forms have been investigated extensively in recent years, eg war memorials, while others have been virtually ignored, eg 'trench art'.

In Britain, the physicality of the post-Armistice world was everywhere apparent in commemorative materiality. The obvious and well documented objects and attitude-shaping events – such as Sir Edwin Lutyens's Cenotaph in London's Whitehall[21], the tomb of the Unknown Warrior in Westminster Abbey[22], and the annual Armistice Day events[23] – were either restricted in time or applicable only to that part of the population who resided in or occasionally visited the capital. More significant on an everyday basis were other objects and realities that intersected the lives of the wider populace.

Arguably the most obvious, and ironic, physical aspect of everyday life was the absence on the street of large numbers of young men together with the presence of a significant quantity of damaged men – the war-maimed. As Jim Wolveridge[24] observed:

'…there was a Mr Jordan who'd lost his right arm, my old man who'd been gassed, and the man at the top of the street who was so badly shell-shocked he couldn't walk without help. And there were lots of one-armed and one-legged old sweats begging in the streets.'

Even in the period just preceding the outbreak of the Second World War, there were 640,000 officers and men receiving disability pensions.[25]

Related to this powerful visual referent of the war were the numbers of widows, single women, and incomplete families. Although in a statistical sense the numbers of the dead and wounded were perhaps less significant demographically than might at first appear, it is nevertheless true that many of the basic social structures of pre-war British society had been subverted. Certainly the physical and psychological aspects of a civilian population reduced by four years of war was an integral part of post-war social realities and interactions. In the inter-war years, people were missing from the nation's streets and the war-maimed were ever-present.

This new kind of street life took place against a changing background of architecture and objects that contributed to changing perceptions of space and emotion. Vivid reminders of the war appeared in many towns and villages in the form of artillery pieces and tanks placed in town centres, and the so-called street shrines. The movement towards constructing these had started during the war, particularly from 1916 onwards, and was aimed at encouraging the association of military self-sacrifice with the cross. Street shrines could take a variety of forms, sometimes home-made, sometimes professionally produced. One example, seen in St Pancras, London, describes a colourful scene – an old kitchen table as a base, on which was placed a red cloth and an apron embroidered with 'God Bless Our King', a frame containing lists of servicemen and the dead, two green flags each decorated with an Irish harp entwined with Union Jacks and surrounded by flowers, and at the base, white and blue tissue paper, photographs of Lord Kitchener, Admiral Jellicoe and Sir John French, together with local heroes – Tommies smoking in their shirtsleeves.[26]

The power of these ephemeral but highly visual examples of materiality to affect people's actions and emotions is seen in the fact that local people made and maintained these shrines, and they were widely held in respect. The flowers were not stolen, and even the roughest men and boys raised their hats as they passed by.[27] These shrines were often aimed especially at women, and were seen by the Anglican church clergy who supported them as '…an opportunity to present to them [ie women] the idea that citizens in arms were bearers of special moral worth, and that their sufferings were achievements of public significance'.[28]

Reinforcing this commemorative materiality were the 'Rolls of Honour' that had also first appeared during the war, displayed prominently in public places, and innumerable, mainly post-war local memorials – the politics, design and placement of which have been explored at length by Borg[29] among others. In addition to this transformation of public space was the founding of memorial hospitals, public halls, playing fields, and, in places such as Stockport, Aberdeen and Hereford, museums that were themselves, or combined elements of, commemorative war memorials.[30] Associated with this development was the establishment of a new kind of museum, the regimental museum. During the inter-war period large numbers of these were formed, though by and large they were only infrequently open to the public, failed to cultivate public support, and were developed on an ad hoc basis usually by serving or retired officers.[31] Ironically, these same museums are now a unique and virtually untapped resource for research into the materiality of war, though they remain chronically underfunded, only occasionally open to the public, and staffed by dedicated but often part-time unpaid personnel. On 9 June 1920, the Imperial War Museum collections were opened by the King and Queen at Crystal Palace, and acted as a national focus for the commemorative materiality of war-related objects.[32]

A hitherto largely unacknowledged dimension, which added to the re-casting of Britain's physical and symbolic landscape, was that associated with the increase in motoring and road construction. This part of the built environment shaped and perpetuated memories of the war by virtue of the belief that local war memorials were expected to be of interest and accessible to the rising number of leisure motorists. The notion of commemorative materiality is well caught by the view of Ian Hay[33] that '…every English highway is now one continuous memorial avenue. The cumulative effect upon the traveller's mind is almost unendurable in its poignancy.'

If street life was now different, then related physicalities also existed in the domestic sphere. During and after the war, soldiers brought or sent home large quantities of battlefield souvenirs – either unaltered mementoes of war, such as bullets, helmets and lumps of shrapnel, or a category of objects known collectively as 'trench art'. These items appeared in many different forms – from engraved and decorated artillery shell cases, bullet-crucifixes, pens and writing sets made from cartridges and scrap brass, to picture frames, embroideries, and carved wood, bone and stone objects.[34]

'Trench art' is a complex kind of material culture for many reasons. Some objects were made by soldiers, others by civilians, some during the war and others in the inter-war years. What united all was their capacity to objectify soldiers' experiences of war and their potential to act as embodiments of loss if the soldier didn't return. Leaving aside that part of the objects' social lives at or near the battlefield, when 'trench art' items entered the domestic space of the home they became an integral part of the house-worlds of their owners and descendants.[35] As such, '…they mediated between past and present lives, moving history into private time by juxtaposing it with a personalised present…'.[36]

The capacity of 'trench art' objects in the home to objectify, release and stimulate memories was not restricted to those who participated in the conflict. In *Auntie Mabel's War*[37] – an account of a nurse who served with the Scottish Women's Hospital in Northern France and the Balkans during the Great War – we have a unique insight into how memories can be triggered by objects. It was the presence of an artillery shell case punch-decorated with flowers that 'released' the memory of Auntie Mabel in the mind of her niece, Mrs Turner, and led to a flood of memories that became the book. As she told Marian Wenzel:

'Yes, that thing by the fireplace with the flowers on it is really a shell case… She brought that back from France for her parents; I thought it was an awfully morbid thing… It got to Granny's house and then it came here… I often look at it and wonder how many men its shell killed.'[38]

The presence of such objects in the home altered physical space, changed emotional surroundings, and was a constant reminder of the absence of loved ones. A pair of decorated shells on a mantelpiece, a bullet letter-opener on a desk, or a shell dinner-gong sounded at mealtimes, were ever-present physical manifestations of grief and loss for the bereaved, and feelings of relief or guilt for those who had survived. Such objects were often the only material reminder of the dead – whether a family member, or a mate. As Stewart[39] says, in the distancing process between rememberer and remembered, 'the memory of the body [was] replaced by the memory of the object'[40].

Furthermore, there was a multi-sensorial dimension to these objects.[41] Many were made of brass and '…tarnished quickly, giving rise to a domestic routine of cleaning and polishing which probably had therapeutic effects for the bereaved'[42] – a behaviour that sometimes became an obsessive compulsion. The smell of brass polish, the sound of the dinner-gong, and the feel of carved wood or embroidered textiles all produced sensations that added texture to the memories constrained or unleashed by frequent encounters with these kinds of materials. These private encounters yielded the realisation that the human body is a way of relating to and perceiving the world.

Reinforcing this, and in a sense extending the poignancy of the objects, was the fact that many examples of the genre were made during the inter-war years and were bought by battlefield pilgrims and tourists as souvenirs, thereby enabling '...them to carry home a tangible link with the memory, or even the spirit, of the dead'.[43] Visitors to the battlefields and associated cemeteries and commemorative monuments were forever separated from the immediacy of war, yet were able to 'authenticate' their experiences through purchasing souvenirs[44], whether 'trench art' or unworked battlefield debris.

'Trench art', together with other objects such as heraldic china[45], the wearing and display of campaign medals, and a host of miscellaneous ephemera[46], were an important part of the memory bridge that transported and transformed emotions via the physical alteration of domestic space. In mainland Europe such objects functioned similarly, but could also take different forms. In Germany, for example, private ways in which the living reconciled themselves with the dead and resolved the sense of loss, is seen in the fact that many homes had a '...little memorial shrine, a picture of husband, son, or father on the wall or mantel, draped in mourning at the proper times...'.[47] Mourning or Sweetheart jewellery, often made from recycled war matériel, also played its part in reconstructing the individual.[48] In Catholic France, ex-voto paintings (often with a photograph and the individual's name) were placed in churches and cathedrals, thanking saints for their intercession in saving a soldier's life.[49]

Also part of this constructed physical reality were objects that represented what might be termed 'background noise', in the form of books and films about the war. A host of now famous publications, such as Robert Graves's *Goodbye To All That* (1928), Edmund Blunden's *Undertones of War* (1928), and Erich Maria Remarque's *All Quiet on the Western Front* (1929), together with films such as *Dawn Patrol* (1930), *Westfront 1918* (1930), and the celluloid version of Remarque's novel (1930), all contributed in potentially powerful ways to the cultural memory of the war. Whatever their literary or cinematic merit (which is now their main claim to fame or otherwise), these artistic and technological creations were definitively material culture, existing in the world and available, for those who were interested, to reinforce or challenge their own views of what the war had been about. These creations had an often powerful effect on emotions and could shape attitudes accordingly. In the case of books, they crossed the boundary between public and private space, existing in bookshops and libraries, but also could join other examples of war-related materiality in the home.

Occasionally, the trauma of loss was so deeply felt that some individuals felt drawn to supposedly inexplicable materialisations of spirituality in the form of visitations from their dead loved ones, either directly or, more often, through a medium. As Jay Winter[50] points out, the Great War triggered an avalanche of interest in spiritualism, though it had begun to wane by the 1930s. Nevertheless, in the 'psychic photography' of Mrs Ada Emma Deane, which purported to show the faces of the dead hovering above the living at Armistice ceremonies during the

1920s[51], we have a strange inversion of materiality. In this instance, material objects did not produce feelings of loss or spirituality through apprehending the object – rather the individual's willingness to believe in spirits created the need for physical proof in the form of altered photographic images. The invisible were made visible, the spiritual rendered material.

A quite different dimension that contributed to the materialisation of cultural memory and the shaping of individual and collective identities during the inter-war years was the advent of battlefield pilgrimages and tourism. Spurred on by the British Government's refusal to allow the repatriation of British war dead[52], this phenomenon added foreign travel, personal experience of landscape and its indigenous inhabitants, souvenirs, and poignancy to the texture of life for large numbers of the bereaved and curious.

Between 1919 and 1939, foreign battlefields, and the old Western Front especially, quickly became landscapes of remembrance for hundreds of thousands of battlefield pilgrims and tourists. This phenomenon has been the subject of detailed original research in recent years[53], yet its implications for the materiality of cultural memory has not yet been fully acknowledged.

Large numbers of people from Britain, Australia, New Zealand and Canada visited the old battlefields during the inter-war years. Their experiences changed them irrevocably and these changes – of perception and attitudes – re-made them as individuals when they returned home. In so far undocumented ways, these experiences altered, or had the potential to alter, their relationship with other people and the homes that had previously been 'complete' but now were not. Key to the appreciation of such issues is that battlefields (and associated areas of destruction and commemoration) are multi-vocal and multi-dimensional landscapes[54] where personal and cultural identities are explored and created.[55] In other words, people created or re-created themselves in relation to their personal experiences of 'being in' the place(s) where their menfolk suffered and died.

When the bereaved visited the old Western Front, for example, they entered a long imagined symbolic landscape replete with memories of loved ones – '…located and glimpsed through letters, postcards, souvenirs sent home, and (sometimes) home-leave conversations'.[56] Wartime censorship of soldiers' written communications meant that relatives at home could not locate soldiers in geographical space. 'Somewhere in France' was a common address, so in post-war visits to the battlefields pilgrims located themselves according to an imaginative grid laid over a symbolic landscape.

Throughout the inter-war years, much reconstruction took place on the Somme and in Flanders, further confusing the battlefield visitor in search of specific locations – vainly attempting to correlate the images of destruction in battlefield guides with the rapidly reconstituted landscape in which they found themselves. As the years went by, commemorative edifices arose – most notably the monuments to 'The Missing' at Thiepval in France and Tyne Cot and The Menin Gate in Belgium. These acted as a focus for visitors (especially relatives of the missing), their imposing and emotion-laden materiality becoming a shared 'image' in the collective memory of visitors who took these experiences home (along with booklets, photographs and postcards), thereby adding to the shrine-like propensities of domestic space.

For many, this elusive and slippery kind of connection in turn affected the materiality of everyday life. The inhabitants of many British towns were so affected by their battlefield visits that, having already sacrificed their menfolk, they now donated money for reconstruction in France and Belgium – a gesture formalised by the official twinning of towns such as Birmingham and Albert, and Ipswich and Fricourt. By such actions, as with the acquisition of small souvenirs, a symbolic link was established between the home town and the battlefield – part of the Western Front was brought to Britain, and part of Britain (ie the dead and their survivors' donations) sent abroad. The inter-war experiences of battlefield visitors added significantly to the complex mix of domestic (private and municipal) space, architecture, and the shaping of a post-war generation for whom the visual and textual cues of their environment were part of the 'natural order'.

The First World War was largely a conflict of stasis and entrenchment, during which the civilian population of Britain did not suffer to any significant extent in terms of direct enemy action. The 'distant' nature of the war kept first-hand experiences at bay for British civilians, and only for those who travelled abroad after 1918 did the scale of physical devastation become apparent. Their sense of loss was also distanced after the war with the bodies of the dead separated from family and motherland by geographical and symbolic space. Partly as a consequence, the materiality of the period 1919-39 in Britain was largely commemorative in nature.

Although a detailed analysis is beyond the scope of this chapter, a brief exploration of issues associated with the materiality of the Second World War is appropriate. This is partly because of the complex and varied differences of this later conflict, and partly due to the fact that, despite its great potential, even less has been published from an anthropological and material culture perspective for the Second World War than the First.

The Second World War was much more one of movement, was more globalised in extent, possessed deep and multifaceted ideological dimensions, and involved large-scale atrocities against civilians and vast damage to civilian landscapes. For the British, and, in different ways for the Germans, Japanese, Russians and the Jewish people in Occupied Europe, the materiality of cultural memory of this Second War was of a different order from that of the Great War. While the First World War's 'trench mentality' was largely avoided from mid-1918, the Second World War's capacity for targeting urban centres and civilian populations set the tone for most subsequent 20th-century conflicts – where its varied legacies still resonate in areas of the former Yugoslavia and in Chechnya, to mention but two striking examples.

Where the defining material culture of the First World War in Britain lay in small objects brought or sent home during or after the conflict, and a burgeoning number of national and local memorials, its analogue post-1945 was a heterogeneous mix of objects and memories that recalled metropolitan bomb damage and civilian casualties, such as that caused by the Blitz in London and Coventry. Elsewhere, the consequences were even more severe: Stalin's purges and the Gulags, the Holocaust, the pan-European displacement of civilians as refugees, and extensive bomb damage at, for example, Dresden, Hamburg, Hiroshima and Nagasaki. All of these activities killed, maimed, damaged and destroyed large numbers of civilians and their corresponding civilian landscapes, thereby affecting the nature of the memories and attitudes of a post-1945 generation in ways undreamed of after 1918.

In contrast to these distinctive features of the Second World War, the Great War had been the last to limit conflict to traditional, mainly open-country, battlefields – albeit partly 'domesticated' by trench systems and 'industrialised' by heavy weapons. In one sense, Ypres in Flanders and Albert on the Somme are notable as exceptions for being urban centres on that most bucolic of battlefield landscapes, the Western Front. In the inter-war years, and again since the mid-1960s, this rural setting formed part of the reflective poignancy of areas whose materiality was constituted of war matériel, bodies of the missing, war cemeteries, remembrance monuments, and areas saturated with unexploded ordnance.[57] By and large, destruction and death in the Great War took place away from centres of civilian population, whereas between 1939 and 1945 the opposite was true. This difference created a materiality whose emotional referents were distinct from those of the period 1919-39.

The physical landscape of Britain from 1945 onwards was more akin to parts of France and Belgium after the Great War than to post-1918 Britain. Clearly, the destruction of war was also a creation, a rebirth that saw the opportunities of remodelling the world in terms of new social attitudes, mores and ideas. The materiality of the legacy of the 1939-45 conflict was less in memorials to the dead than in a 'rush to the future', whether in Britain, Germany, Japan or the United States. Ironically, at the same time many of the distinctive aspects of First World War commemorative materiality in Britain were increasingly lost by virtue of changes in society and a conflation of memorial activities, where the war dead of both conflicts were commemorated now in joint acts of remembrance, often at Great War memorials whose physical surfaces had been altered by inscriptions that added the names and dates of the second global conflict.

At the beginning of a new millennium, the consequences of the Second World War in terms of the materiality of militarism lay to a great extent in the huge outlay and investment of money in objects and buildings – now largely redundant – associated with the Cold War.[58] From the point of view of anthropology and archaeology, this is a vast and largely unexplored aspect of 20th-century materiality that affected physical and symbolic space as well as people's ideas and attitudes.[59] The Berlin Wall, for example, was a construction born out of the Second War's destruction of that city, and which in turn 'created' differing generations of West and East Germans during its 'lifetime'. More widely, by its physical partition of a city, the wall came to symbolise the so-called Iron Curtain, with 'Checkpoint Charlie' as an ambiguous iconic doorway between two post-war worlds.

Material culture changes its values and significances through time, affecting, and being affected by, changing cultural conditions and individual and collective beliefs and attitudes. In this sense, it is appropriate to mention the trajectories that some kinds of Second World War objects have taken since 1945, and especially during the four decades from the 1960s. In Europe and the United States, and with Vietnam being the exception that proves the rule, a lack of large-scale wars in which to participate has contributed to the development of a burgeoning market in militaria (and the associated interest in battle re-enactment) – where the material objects of 20th-century war are increasingly bought, sold, traded and exchanged in what today is financially a seven-figure industry. Increasingly these objects are auctioned on internet websites in cyberspace – the internet itself ironically being the commercial application of a Cold War computerised command system.

There has also been a renewed interest in battlefield tourism, to the Western Front and beyond, partly as a result of changes to school curricula, but also to a general increase of interest and curiosity – itself possibly a partial response to the lack of any direct connection to war by younger generations. Although to date this has tended to focus on the First World War, there is increasing interest also in the Second World War – especially where monumental materiality is present to connect people to landscape and historical events, such as the gigantic German concrete bunkers and gun emplacements overlooking the Normandy beaches.[60] Nazi concentration camps have more sinister resonances, but are none the less prime examples of how one aspect of war's extreme materiality can physically and metaphorically destroy and create at the same time, adding texture to memory, and guilt and hope to different social groups.

At the same time, there has been a move within the museum world away from simply collecting and displaying 'things' and towards contextualising objects, increasingly in terms of the common soldiers' and civilians' experiences of war.[61] Part of this movement has been the development of a new kind of museum – that which converts places of historical significance into unique museum experiences, such as Winston Churchill's War Room in London, and Bletchley Park.[62]

All of these things have one thing in common – they are different treatments of, and objectify different attitudes to, our cultural memory of war – both the Second World War, and, via the memory bridge, the First World War. This trend continues apace with memories and interpretations of the 20th century's many conflicts being materialised at an ever-increasing rate in print and film – and being tragically reproduced, in miniature, and in reality, in a seemingly endless number of small but bitter conflicts from Rwanda to Kosovo and Chechnya. Whatever historical, political, ethnic and psychological imperatives are at work in these conflicts, all are embodied to a greater or lesser degree in the largely untold biographies of the physical intermediaries between human thoughts and action – material culture.

The personal experience of war goes beyond diaries, regimental histories and oral testimony. It includes these dimensions but also encompasses the materiality of conflict and its many intersections with the ways in which individuals and societies conceptualise themselves, during conflict and afterwards. The anthropological and archaeological study of the material culture of 20th-century war is in its infancy, but, by its very nature, offers a powerful new way of exploring the momentous events that occurred over the past hundred years, which still linger in the minds of the living, and which have the power to shape our views of the past in an ever-changing present.

Recommended reading

Becker, Annette, *War and Faith* (Oxford: Berg, 1998)

Bourke, Joanna, *Dismembering the Male: Men's Bodies, Britain and the Great War* (London: Reaktion Books, 1996)

Clout, Hugh, *After The Ruins: Restoring the Countryside of Northern France after the Great War* (Exeter: University of Exeter Press, 1996)

Derez, Mark, 'A Belgian Salient for Reconstruction: People and Patrie, Landscape and Memory', in Peter H. Liddle (ed), *Passchendaele in Perspective: The Third Battle of Ypres* (London: Leo Cooper, 1997) pp437-58

Kavanagh, G., *Museums and the First World War: A Social History* (Leicester: Leicester University Press, 1994)

King, Alex, *Memorials of the Great War in Britain: The Symbolism and Politics of Remembrance* (Oxford: Berg, 1998)

Liddle, Peter H., and Richardson, Matthew, 'Passchendaele and material culture: the relics of battle', in Peter H. Liddle (ed), *Passchendaele in Perspective: The Third Battle of Ypres* (London, Leo Cooper, 1997) pp459-66

Miller, Daniel, *Artefacts as categories* (Cambridge: Cambridge University Press, 1985)

Saunders, Nicholas J., 'Bodies of Metal, Shells of Memory: "Trench Art" and the Great War Re-cycled', in *Journal of Material Culture* 5 (1) (2000) pp43-67

Schofield, J. (ed), *Monuments of War: The Evaluation, Recording, and Management of Twentieth-Century Military Sites* (London: English Heritage, 1998)

Winter, Jay, *Sites of Memory, Sites of Mourning: The Great War in European cultural history* (Cambridge: Cambridge University Press, 1995)

Notes

The author would like to acknowledge the encouragement and support of the Department of Anthropology, University College, London. This chapter, and the research from which it is drawn, was made possible by the British Academy, London, through its award of an Institutional Fellowship.

[1] Morton Fried, M. Harris and R. Murphy (eds), *War: The Anthropology of Social Conflict and Aggression* (New York: Doubleday, 1968); M. Nettleship, R. D. Givens and A. Nettleship (eds), *War, Its Causes and Correlates* (The Hague: Mouton, 1974); Jonathan Haas (ed), *The Anthropology of War* (Cambridge: Cambridge University Press, 1990); J. Groebel, J. and R. Hinde (eds), *Aggression and War* (Cambridge: Cambridge University Press, 1989)

[2] Napoleon A. Chagnon, 'Yanomamo Warfare, Social Organization and Marriage Alliances' (PhD dissertation, University of Michigan; Ann Arbor: University Microfilms, 1966); Napoleon A. Chagnon, *Yanomamo: The Fierce People* (New York: Holt, Rinehart & Winston, 3rd ed 1983)

[3] Andrew Vayda, *Maori Warfare* (Wellington: Polynesian Society Maori Monographs No 2, 1960); Andrew Vayda, *War in Ecological Perspective: Persistence, Change, and Adaptive Processes in Three Oceanian Societies* (New York: Plenum, 1976)

[4] B. Oget (ed), *War and Society in Africa* (London: 1972)

[5] Nicholas J. Saunders, 'Bodies of Metal, Shells of Memory: "Trench Art" and the Great War Re-cycled', in *Journal of Material Culture* 5 (1) (2000), pp43-67; Peter H. Liddle and Matthew Richardson, 'Passchendaele and material culture: the relics of battle', in Peter H. Liddle (ed), *Passchendaele in Perspective: The Third Battle of Ypres* (London: Leo Cooper, 1997) pp459-66

[6] Franky Bostyn, *Beecham Dugout: Passchendaele 1914-1918* (Zonnebeke: Association for Battlefield

Archaeology in Flanders, Studies 1, 1999); C. Dobinson, J. Lake and A. J. Schofield, 'Monuments of War: Defining England's twentieth century defence heritage', in *Antiquity* 71 (1997), pp288-99; Nicholas J. Saunders, *Archaeology and War: The Great War* (unpublished ms, nd)

7   B. Lowry (ed), *Twentieth-century defences in Britain: An introductory guide* (London: Council for British Archaeology, 1995); J. Schofield (ed), *Monuments of War, The Evaluation, Recording, and Management of Twentieth-Century Military Sites* (London: English Heritage, 1998); John Schofield, William Gray Johnson and Colleen Beck (eds), *Materiel Culture: The Archaeology of 20th Century Conflict* (London: Routledge, 2001)

8   Martin Gilbert, *Second World War* (London: Weidenfeld & Nicolson, 1989); Martin Gilbert, *First World War* (London, Weidenfeld & Nicolson, 1994); John Keegan, *The First World War* (London: Hutchinson, 1998)

9   Joanna Bourke, *Dismembering the Male: Men's Bodies, Britain and the Great War* (London: Reaktion Books, 1996); Hugh Clout, *After The Ruins: Restoring the Countryside of Northern France after the Great War* (Exeter: University of Exeter Press, 1996); Mark Derez, 'A Belgian Salient for Reconstruction: People and Patrie, Landscape and Memory', in Peter H. Liddle (ed), op cit, pp437-58; Jay Winter, *Sites of Memory, Sites of Mourning: The Great War in European cultural history* (Cambridge: Cambridge University Press, 1995)

10   John Keegan, *The Face of Battle* (London: Pimlico, 1996); Modris Eksteins, *The Rites of Spring: The Great War and the Birth of the Modern Age* (New York: Anchor Books/Doubleday, 1990); Paul Fussell, *The Great War and Modern Memory* (New York: Oxford University Press, 1977)

11   Editorial, *Journal of Material Culture* 1 (1) (1996) pp5-14

12   I. Kopytoff, 'The Cultural Biography of Things: Commoditization as Process', in Arjun Appadurai (ed), *The Social Life of Things* (Cambridge: Cambridge University Press, 1986) pp64-91

13   Arjun Appadurai, Introduction: 'Commodities and the Politics of Value', in Arjun Appadurai (ed), op cit, pp3-63; Nicholas J. Saunders, 'Bodies of Metal, Shells of Memory', op cit

14   Daniel Miller, *Artefacts as Categories* (Cambridge: Cambridge University Press, 1985) p1

15   Ibid, pp204-5

16   Matthew Richardson, 'A Changing Meaning for Armistice Day', in Hugh Cecil and Peter H. Liddle (eds), *At The Eleventh Hour: Reflections, Hopes and Anxieties at the Closing of the Great War, 1918* (Barnsley, Pen and Sword, 1998) pp347-56; Alex King, *Memorials of the Great War in Britain: The Symbolism and Politics of Remembrance* (Oxford: Berg, 1998)

17   Daniel Miller, Introduction, in Daniel Miller (ed), *Material Cultures: Why some things matter* (London: UCL Press, 1998) pp3-21; P. Pels, 'The Spirit of Matter: On Fetish, Rarity, Fact, and Fancy', in P. Spyer (ed), *Border Fetishisms: Material Objects in unstable spaces* (London: Routledge, 1998) pp91-121

18   Janet Hoskins, *Biographical Objects: How Things Tell the Stories of People's Lives* (London: Routledge, 1998)

19   W. G. Johnson and C. M. Beck, 'Proving Ground of the Nuclear Age', in *Archaeology* 48 (3) (1995) pp43-9; W. G. Johnson, 'Cold War architecture: A reactionary cultural response to the threat of nuclear war', and C. M. Beck, 'The archaeology of scientific experiments at a nuclear testing ground', both in Schofield, Johnson and Beck (eds), op cit

20   Alex King, op cit; Matthew Richardson, 'A Changing Meaning for Armistice Day', op cit; Jay Winter, op cit

21   E. Homberger, 'The Story of the Cenotaph', *The Times Literary Supplement*, 12 November 1976, pp1429-30; Jay Winter, op cit

22   Alex King, op cit, pp139-41

23   Matthew Richardson, 'A Changing Meaning for Armistice Day', op cit

24   Joanna Bourke, op cit, p35

25   Ibid, p33

26   Alex King, op cit, pp20-6, 216-8

27   Ibid, p52

28   Ibid, p55

29   A. Borg, *War Memorials* (London: Leo Cooper, 1991)

30   G. Kavanagh, *Museums and the First World War: A Social History* (Leicester: Leicester University Press, 1994) pp155-6

31 Ibid, pp157-9, 174

32 Ibid, p146

33 Alex King, op cit, p23

34 Nicholas J. Saunders, 'Bodies of Metal, Shells of Memory', op cit

35 J. Sixsmith and A. Sixsmith, 'Places in transition: The impact of life events on the experience of home', in T. Putnam and C. Newton (eds), *Household Choices* (London: Futures Publications, 1990) pp20-4

36 Nicholas J. Saunders, 'Bodies of Metal, Shells of Memory', op cit, pp59-60

37 Marian Wenzel and John Cornish (comps), *Auntie Mabel's War: An account of her part in the hostilities of 1914-18* (London: Allen Lane, 1980)

38 Ibid, p8

39 Susan Stewart, *On Longing: Narratives of the Miniature, the Gigantic, the Souvenir, the Collection* (Durham: Duke University Press, 1994) p133

40 Ibid

41 D. Howes, Introduction, 'To Summon All the Senses', in D. Howes (ed), *The Varieties of Sensory Experience* (Toronto: University of Toronto Press, 1991) pp3-21

42 Nicholas J. Saunders, 'Bodies of Metal, Shells of Memory', op cit, p60

43 D. W. Lloyd, 'Tourism, Pilgrimage, and the Commemoration of the Great War in Great Britain, Australia and Canada, 1919-1939' (PhD thesis, Cambridge University, 1994) p188

44 Susan Stewart, op cit, p134

45 R. Southall, *Take Me back to Dear Old Blighty: The First World War through the eyes of the Heraldic China Manufacturers* (Horndean: Milestone Publications, 1982) pp7-8, 44-51

46 M. Rickards and M. Moody, *The First World War: Ephemera, Mementoes and Documents* (Jupiter, 1975)

47 R. W. Whalen, *Bitter Wounds: German Victims of the Great War, 1914-1939* (Ithaca, NY: Cornell University Press, 1984) p183

48 B. Maas and G. Dietrich, *Lebenszeichen: Schmuck aus Notzeiten* (Köln: Museum für Angewandte Kunst, 1994); Marcia Pointon, 'Wearing Memory: Mourning, Jewellery, and the Body', in G. Ecker (ed), *Trauer Tragen* (Munich: 1998)

49 Annette Becker, *Croire* (Péronne: Historial de la Grande Guerre) pp60-1

50 Jay Winter, op cit, pp 54, 76

51 Ibid, p74, Fig 9; p75, Fig11

52 Ibid, pp23, 27

53 D. W. Lloyd, op cit; D. W. Lloyd, *Battlefield Tourism: Pilgrimage and the Commemoration of the Great War in Britain, Australia and Canada, 1919-1939* (Oxford: Berg, 1998)

54 Nicholas J. Saunders, 'Matter and Memory in the Landscapes of Conflict: The Western Front, 1914-1999', in Barbara Bender and Margot Winer (eds), *Contested Landscapes: Landscapes of Movement and Exile* (Oxford: Berg, 2001)

55 Christopher Tilley, *A Phenomenology of Landscape, Places, Paths and Monuments* (Oxford: Berg, 1994)

56 Nicholas J. Saunders, 'Bodies of Metal, Shells of Memory', op cit

57 Nicholas J. Saunders, 'Matter and Memory in the Landscapes of Conflict', op cit

58 Nick McCamley, *Secret Cold War Nuclear Bunkers* (London: Leo Cooper, 2000)

59 Mandy Whorton, 'Evaluating and Managing Cold War era historic properties: The cultural significance of US Air Force defensive radar systems', in Schofield, Johnson and Beck (eds), op cit; David Uzzell, 'The hot interpretation of the Cold War', in J. Schofield (ed), *Monuments of War*, op cit, pp18-20

60 Tim Kilvert-Jones, *Sword Beach* (London: Leo Cooper, 2000); Carl Shilleto, *Utah Beach* (London: Leo Cooper, 2000)

61 Susan Pearce, *Museums, Objects, Collections* (London: Routledge, 1992) and *Interpreting Objects and Collections* (London: Routledge, 1994); Yvonne M. Cresswell, *Living with the Wire: Civilian Internment in the Isle of Man during the two World Wars* (Douglas: Manx National Heritage, The Manx Museum & National Trust, 1994)

62 Maurice Freedman, *Bletchley Park and Ultra* (London: Leo Cooper, 2000)

Chapter 30

The Obligation of Remembrance or the Remembrance of Obligation: society and the memory of World War

Bob Bushaway

'Have you forgotten yet?
…Look up, and swear by the green of the spring that you'll never forget.'[1]

Those who looked on the Cenotaph in Whitehall when it was unveiled for the first time as a permanent memorial on 11 November 1920 regarded Lutyens's masterpiece from a viewpoint impossible for most of us in Britain now to share, that of bereavement in war. Those who reflect on the Cenotaph and its meaning, in this new 21st century, must do so with the perspective of Britain's unprecedented experience in two World Wars and in the knowledge of Britain's transition from global imperial power to hesitant European nation. Other combatant nations, while sharing the experience of loss and suffering common to the wars of 1914-18 and 1939-45, as to all wars, have developed other historical perspectives to understand what had happened to them. For some countries, emerging from the conflicts, nationalism was nourished through the memory of war and its commemoration. For those countries, such as Australia and Turkey after the First World War, remembrance became an affirmation of national self-confidence. Defeat brought for other countries bitter memories and little opportunity for memorialisation, leaving only the assimilation of loss through internalised private rituals or their tumultuous expression in extreme political forms.[2]

For other countries the memory of war was invested with triumphant significance for their political ideologies or value systems, as in the cases of federal democracy in post-First World War America, republicanism in France after 1918, or communism in Soviet Russia at the end of the Second World War.

Not forgetting means remembering. To remember something requires that the object of remembrance is comprehended and can be unequivocally recognised.

The memory of war and its consequences became universal for most of the world in the 20th century. It has been estimated that 100 million people have been killed or have died as a result of war in the decades since 1900. Memory of war is, therefore, one of the most familiar aspects of social memory, and social memory is given form and meaning by memorialisation, commemoration, sanctification, formal record, informal reminiscence and remembrance. These forms are part of the landscape and language of the memory of war throughout the world.[3]

Remembering war and celebrating peace have become acceptable collective, public and outward manifestations in most countries, while simultaneously providing a forum for personal, private and inward expression of loss for many individuals and their families. Remembering war can be part of a process of reconciliation, grieving and healing as well as a political act designed to reinforce other meanings. Germany commemorates its dead in two World Wars and the victims of Nazi oppression on the second Sunday before Advent, *Volkstrauertag*, which embraces simultaneously German national war dead and the dead of the Holocaust and those whose deaths were caused by the tyranny of German National Socialism. The modern democratic state that is Deutschland since unification thus provides a space for reflection on the German dead of two World Wars while acknowledging the duty to remember those killed by Nazi policy. The popular memory of war is sometimes referred to as 'remembrance', a term that has come to be applied in a special sense to the collective rituals commemorating war dead as in the British experience of Armistice Day after the First World War and Remembrance Sunday after the Second. The rituals of remembrance in Britain – language, liturgy, hymnody, landscape – have the appearance of being timeless and changeless, yet were created consciously for political reasons at a precise point in time. Notwithstanding the fact that remembrance is intended to be both of the moment and for all time, its purpose can encompass different meanings for different groups in society or provide a terrain for their debate in different political, cultural and national contexts, remaining subject to change in form and meaning through time.

Remembering war has been a major factor in the formation of social memory in Britain and elsewhere throughout the 20th century. The series of 50th anniversary commemorations of the principal events of the Second World War through the first half of the 1990s, beginning, for Britain, with Dunkirk and the Battle of Britain, passing through El Alamein and D-Day and ending with VE and VJ days, and the revival of popular interest in the rituals of remembrance as illustrated by the sustained campaign to restore the national 2 minutes silence to Armistice Day (11 November), indicate how powerful is the popular memory of war in forming collective identity.[4]

Remembering war could scarcely have been less familiar for British society than during the Victorian period, when martial experience was confined to the specialist recall of battles at the beginning of the 19th century, such as Trafalgar and Waterloo, by professional soldiers and statesmen or the grandiloquence of British popular patriotism and imperialism. British society saw little of war other than at a distance or in the peacetime activities of the voluntary movement, whose memories were of military camps on Wimbledon Common, musketry in city drill-halls, or marching through the streets of Britain's towns and cities to Sunday church parades.[5] War was left to a handful of professional soldiers garrisoning the outposts of Empire supported by locally recruited auxiliaries and sustained by the Royal Navy. Unlike the experience of much of Europe or of the United States of America, Britain had no direct knowledge of modern war on the scale foreshadowing the coming of 'total war'.[6] Elsewhere in Europe and in America, the popular experience of war, whether in modern democracies or imperial states, had already witnessed mass conscription, heavy casualties and the effects of the application of force through sustained modern economic and industrial power. In America, popular memory of war sprang from the experience of five years of bitter civil conflict, in which large numbers of people served either in the armies of the Union or the Confederacy and in which the battlefields in every theatre of operations were marked by casualties on an unprecedented scale. Such was also the experience of the wars in Europe between France of the Second Empire, Prussia and the German states, emerging Italy and the Austrian Empire.

Memorialisation of ordinary citizen-soldiers, as opposed to their generals, first arose in America and in Europe at this time and thereafter.[7] For example, it has been estimated that there are no fewer than 1,300 monuments and memorials on the Gettysburg battlefield, making it the most memorialised battle landscape in the world. Its administration was established in the care of the Gettysburg National Military Park under the supervision of the War Department in 1895, but its early 'monumentation', as the process is called in America, was begun by veterans' associations, first those of the Union regiments, then by similar Confederate groups. Most southern dead had been removed for burial in the south in the years after the battle, leaving the National Cemetery on Cemetery Hill largely to the Union dead.[8]

Britain's brief glimpse of the realities of modern warfare in alliance with France and the Ottoman Empire against Russia did not prepare British society for the scale of what was to come. Even the immediate impact of more contemporary conflicts between world powers such as the wars between Russia and the Ottoman Empire in the 19th century or between Russia and Japan at the beginning of the 20th were barely noticed in Victorian and Edwardian Britain.

The coming of war in 1914 changed Britain's attitude to her own war dead because of the numbers and because, for the first time, the whole of society was involved, as Lloyd George recognised when he wrote of Britain's New Armies in January 1915:

> 'It is a force of a totally different character from that which has hitherto left these shores. It has been drawn almost exclusively from the better class of artisans, the upper and lower middle classes … the people of this country will take an intimate and personal interest in its fate of a kind which they have never displayed before in our military expeditions.'[9]

Britain's involvement in the First and Second World Wars transformed British popular memory of war by making the experience of modern warfare universal for

Britain's armed forces and citizens alike. As Reginald Arkell wrote in 1928, reflecting on the writings of Rudyard Kipling:

> 'He told us tales of soldier men –
> We hadn't all been soldiers then!
> But now we know as much or more
> As Rudyard Kipling did before.
> We leave his volumes on our shelves
> And tell those soldier tales ourselves.'[10]

Or as Mrs Dalloway thought, looking into Hatchards window in Piccadilly during her morning walk in the early 1920s:

> 'This late age of world's experience had bred in them all, all men and women, a well of tears. Tears and sorrows, courage and endurance, a perfectly upright and stoical bearing.'[11]

The universal experience of loss in war was new to British society in the 1920s in a way that it was not throughout Europe and America, to which the landscape of memorialisation in those countries already testified.

The world of memory of the survivors of World War – ex-servicemen and women, grieving relatives and the public at large in Britain and in other countries – has been largely left unrecorded other than in the form of the national recognition of individual duty in the award of medals for service. In Britain, after the First World War, many were entitled either to the trio of the 1914 or 1914-15 star, the British War Medal and the Allied Victory Medal, known universally as 'Pip, Squeak and Wilfred', or a duo of the last two (without one of the service stars) called popularly 'Mutt and Jeff'. After the Second World War medals were awarded for service in different theatres of operations, together with the Defence Medal and the War Medal as appropriate.[12] After 1918 every next of kin who had lost an individual family member received a large bronze medal, the National Memorial Plaque designed by E. Carter Paxton, and a scroll from the King. The King's scroll was dispatched by Buckingham Palace with the following note: 'I join with my grateful people in sending you this memorial of a brave life given for others in the Great War.'[13] Such reinforcement of loss was not repeated in Britain at the end of the Second World War, nor was its suggested meaning that Britain's First World War dead should be regarded in terms of Christ-like sacrifice.

Attitudes to death and customary rituals of mourning in British society, strained by the scale of loss in the First World War, were totally altered by the coming of the Second World War.[14] Ordinary personal memory of war has now been left to the occasional oral history, rare memoir or reminiscence, or private recollection at annual gatherings of ex-servicemen and women. For the First World War in thousands of homes domestic shrines were created throughout Britain from photographs, medals, private rolls of honour, mementoes and artefacts. The scale of personal memory, expressed in these informal ways, was enormous, and is largely unknown outside the circle of friends and relatives with whom such personal loss was shared. The number of those who remembered in this way has been steadily eroded through time. Such personal/private memory was expressed in ephemeral ways. The annotation of printed rolls of honour or other published material or of photographs usually perishes with the death of the individual responsible for the annotations. Only in rare cases does such personal remembrance survive. For example, an annotated copy of the Dulwich College Roll of Honour 1914-19 in the author's possession contains marginal reference to some of those commemorated. Of Wing Commander Frank Brock an annotation records:

> '"Old Fireworks" blew up the stove in the 3rd Engineers' Form Room with powdered fire and was sent up to the Old Man who let him off as he was so fond of fireworks.'

Brock originally joined the Royal Artillery, served with the Royal Naval Air Service and, working with the Board of Invention and Research, was responsible for the development of the Dover Flare, for anti-submarine warfare, the Brock colour filter, for naval use, the Brock Bullet, an incendiary bullet for use against airships, and the smoke screen used in the Royal Navy's raid on Zeebrugge, where he was killed on 23 April 1918. In this example, annotation by an unknown school contemporary has enriched with personal anecdote the formal act of remembrance undertaken by Dulwich College in its printed record.[15]

Remembrance in British society after the First World War saw the creation of a pervasive mythology that emphasised not triumphs but disasters, in which the ultimate victory of 1918 was not remembered as much as the sacrifice on the battlefields of the Somme and Passchendaele. In this mythology the progress of war was chronicled by accounts of bungle and muddle rather than as a history of the mobilisation by the state of the resources of the national economy in the process of learning from experience how to conduct a war on a global scale. In part, the genesis of this particular mythology arose from the need to explain the losses of the First World War when their initial justification no longer bore scrutiny.

As George Orwell wrote of the First World War: '...the four names which have really engraved themselves on the popular memory are Mons, Ypres, Gallipoli and Passchendaele, every time a disaster. The names of the great battles that finally broke the German armies are simply unknown to the general public.' To these, Orwell might have added 1 July 1916 – the first day on the Somme – which retains its morbid fascination to our own time.[16]

The tenth anniversary of the First World War's end marked an important stage in the completion of the language and landscape of remembrance for British society, for 1928 was the year of the British Legion's and the British Empire Service League's 'Great Pilgrimage' to the battlefields of Belgium and France. Armistice Day at the Cenotaph on 11 November was first broadcast by the BBC and, in January, Earl Haig had died.[17] Many reflected on the scale of Britain's contribution to the war and set the victory in the context of that loss and of its resultant impact on the British Empire:

'Of many nations, of all languages, of all religions, men to the number of one million and more died for the cause. They died in England, Scotland, Ireland, Wales; in France and Belgium, in every country of Europe, in every continent of the world, and in the islands of every ocean; and many died upon the seas. They were women too. They also took, in thousands, their lives in their hands for the tending and helping of the men who fought, and of them also many paid the price. On Armistice Day the Empire honours in public ceremony, and each of its citizens in private commemoration, the glorious company, their immortal memory, their victory, their great achievement.'[18]

But what was 'the cause' and was there consensus about the nature of 'their great achievement'? Was this acknowledged in a similar way on the tenth anniversary of the Second World War or by other nations who had also taken part in both World Wars?

Many countries hold commemorations on 11 November. Armistice Day is still officially marked as a day of commemoration in Australia, Bermuda and Canada as Remembrance Day, and in Belgium and France and elsewhere as Armistice Day. In the United States the date is commemorated as Veterans Day.

Australia, New Zealand, Samoa, and Tonga mark 25 April as ANZAC Day with great ritual and remembrance. In Portugal the same date is commemorated as Revolution Day, marking the Portuguese Revolution of 1974, and in Italy as Liberation Day, from the country's freedom in the Second World War. In Poland 11 November is commemorated as Independence Day, marking the end of the German occupation of Warsaw in 1918.

The experience of Warsaw illustrates the changing mood. At the heart of communist-controlled Poland, Warsaw's massive Tenth Anniversary Stadium was constructed in 1954-55 using rubble from the destroyed city in its foundations and was intended for the World Festival of Youth. After 1989, and long since having fallen into disrepair, the stadium is now home for a large open-air market called the Saxon Fair.

The memorials in the 1940s and 1950s convey the spirit of freedom and hope for the future and concentrate on the expectations of the living, rare in the memorials of the post-First World War period. This was the case with the democratic abstraction of the West, as in the reconstruction of Rotterdam and Ossip Zadkine's defiant monumental bronze 'To a Destroyed City' (completed in 1953 and standing at the gateway to the Port of Rotterdam), and in the socialist monumentalism of the East, seen in the rebuilding of Warsaw. The attempt to unify the meaning of remembrance in the form of the language and landscape that came into being after 1918 was not repeated in the same way after 1945.[19]

Remembrance in the 20th century has been shaped by historical perspective. The experience of the City of Cardiff, as illustrated by its public memorialisation of war, demonstrates that popular commemoration of war has not remained unchanged. In close proximity to each other in Cathays Park, three war memorials have been created.[20] The Welsh South African war memorial by Albert Toft presents the embodiment of peace bearing a crown and carrying an uprooted olive tree and a dove of peace. On each side are figures representing 'war' and 'grief'. The names of nearly 900 Welsh men and women (two nursing sisters are included) from 100 units in the British Army who died in South Africa between 1899 and 1902 are commemorated on the memorial, which was unveiled on 25 November 1909 by Sir John French. Sir Ivor Herbert MP, who presided, emphasised in his address, given in both Welsh and English, the role of small nations in the British Empire. French referred to the customs of the Napoleonic Armies of calling the roll, including the names of those long since killed. When their names were called, he reminded his listeners, the response was made 'Dead on the field of honour'.[21] The aspiration of glorious nationhood within the British Empire as well as military glory are therefore enshrined by the memorial in Cardiff, which had only recently been elevated to city status in 1905.

The second monument, by Sir Ninian Comper, takes the form of a classical circular colonnade or triodos in the park setting of Alexandra Gardens. With three porches representing victory by land, sea and air, and with a central winged figure representing the bringer of victory, raising a sword, the memorial was unveiled in 1928, amid controversy, as the Welsh National War Memorial. Complete with an inner court set below ground level with benches to permit personal and private contemplation, the public memorial includes, within the circle of columns, a fountain with dolphins' and lions' heads in the general shape of a trefoil. The inscription, in Welsh, dedicates the memorial 'To the sons of Wales who gave their lives for the country in the war, 1914-1918'. There are also English language inscriptions different from the Welsh inscriptions.[22]

A little way off from the Welsh National War Memorial stands a rugged stone of remembrance to the 'Welsh volunteers who defended democracy' and who fought in the Spanish Civil War, on which is inscribed Herbert Spencer's words: 'None can be free till all are free'. This memorial was unveiled by the Lord Mayor and Michael Foot in October 1992.[23]

The first memorial was created when Cardiff was a regional city in a Britain at the heart of the wider British Empire. Popular memory commemorates the Welsh contribution to a far-off imperial conflict while seeking a national identity that sits comfortably within both a British and an Imperial identity. When the second memorial was unveiled, Cardiff aspired to be identified as a sub-national capital, not without opposition from other parts of Wales, and had constructed a national memorial to the memory of the Welsh contribution to British victory in 1918, but which allowed space for those who wished to grieve on an individual basis. The memorial to the Welsh in the Spanish Civil War commemorates a fierce, independent radicalism that cut across national identities in support of an international European democracy.

A bound volume, containing the names of the Welsh men and women who died in the First World War, was first deposited in the National Library of Wales but is now located in Cardiff's Temple of Peace and Health. The Welsh National Book of Remembrance contains 35,000 names of those of Welsh birth or parentage or who served in Welsh regiments. It was inscribed by Edward Prince of Wales on 12 June 1928.[24]

To mark the difference in moods, after the Second World War the Welsh Book of Remembrance commemorating those who died in the Second World War resides in the Glamorgan building nearby but is temporarily in store because of building work. The First World War memorial was re-dedicated to include the Welsh dead from the Second World War. No further monument was erected.

Warsaw is a city whose experience of war in the 20th century is unparalleled. The tomb to the Polish unknown soldier is constructed as a raised slab with an eternal flame in a surviving triple-arch fragment of the remains of the Saski Palace. Created on 2 November 1925 by the interment of an unknown victim of the defence of Lvov, panels commemorate the names and dates of Poland's military contributions, including Arras in 1915. The monument to the Polish dead on the Western Front in the First World War was erected by the French at La Targette. The tomb also commemorates the Second World War, and the invasion of Poland in the battles of 1939 and, after Poland's occupation, Monte Cassino and the Falaise Gap in 1944, as well as the Fall of Berlin and the battles of the Eastern Front. Since 1989 new memorials have appeared in Warsaw, including a monument to commemorate Polish soldiers deported or killed by Soviet forces after the occupation in 1939. The memorial takes the form of a railway truck loaded with crosses on a track where each sleeper bears the place name of a labour camp or place of execution, including Katyn. A second memorial, designed by Jergy Jarnusykiewiez, is a bronze statue of a small boy in a hopelessly oversize uniform and carrying a machine-gun, which commemorates Polish children's role in the rising of the Home Army in 1944. The memorial to the Heroes of the Warsaw Uprising, designed by Wincenty Kucma, was unveiled in 1989, and on the 50th Anniversary Commemoration of the Warsaw Uprising, in 1994, the German President visited the memorial and made apology to the Polish nation for the Nazi oppression of Poland and the destruction of the City of Warsaw. The memorial to the Deported, the memorial to the Heroes of the Uprising, and the Monument to the Young Insurgent, would have been impossible under the pre-1989 Polish regime. These monuments now stand alongside existing memorials to the soldiers of the Red Army killed during the liberation of Warsaw, dedicated in 1949, and known ironically by Warsaw's inhabitants as 'the monument to the sleeping soldiers', referring to the Red Army's inactivity during the Home Army's uprising in 1944. Together with the memorial to the Ghetto Heroes, commemorating the rising of the Warsaw Ghetto, both memorials were created in the post-war period of communist authority in Poland.[25]

Poland's experience of war in the 20th century has left unresolved issues and, in a similar way to the argument over memorialisation that can be seen in disputed regions such as Alsace-Lorraine between 1871 and 1945, the position of ethnic Germans in Polish Silesia has been reflected in political tensions over war memorials. One report states that, 'For Poles, it has been a shocking experience to see war memorials go up that display German eagles and iron crosses. But for the Silesian Germans, this has been the simplest way to express their long-suppressed identity.'[26]

The geographical location of ethnic populations, as well as the nature of governing regimes, are reflected in Silesia over the memory of war. Unresolved issues also concern Poland's experience of the nation's remembrance for the genocidal destruction of its Jewish population by the Nazis in the Second World War. The commemoration of the Holocaust in Poland remains controversial.

The Warsaw Ghetto uprising, which began on 19 April 1943, was commemorated by a monument to the Ghetto Heroes dedicated in 1948 on the fifth anniversary of the uprising. Designed by Nathan Rapaport, it was constructed from Swedish granite blocks that had been previously cut for Hitler's proposed victory monument in Berlin. In 1983 unofficial demonstrations took place before the Warsaw Ghetto Memorial during the period of martial law following the setting up of the Solidarity Trade Union.[27]

In the United Kingdom, Cardiff also illustrates the memory of Poland at war. One of the pylons in front of Cardiff City Hall is affixed with a plaque commemorating Polish forces in the Second World War. It was erected by Poles living in South Wales and their Welsh friends.

Remembrance remains a terrain contested by those who wish to be certain that particular meaning is fixed in social memory to ensure that, as far as formal memorialisation of the past is concerned, the act of remembrance is a political act for the present, as the memory of war in Cardiff and Warsaw illustrate.

Cardiff also contains many other memorials and rolls of honour listing participants in both World Wars and where the common bond between the individuals whose names are recorded, beyond their military service, is the affiliation, organisation, place of work, place of education or of worship, locality and community.

Community memorials are more vulnerable to change through time as building function changes or demolitions have occurred. Street memorials appeared during the First World War, from the popular street shrines in many working-class communities in towns and cities in Britain to the street memorials created after the war as a permanent record of the names of those who served in the war.[28]

From 1915, when the earliest discussions in Britain concerning the form of war memorials took place, the argument often raged between those who favoured a utilitarian form of memorial and those who wished to erect commemorative memorials with symbolic figurative or allegorical meaning. Memorialisation took many forms, although no British national memorial project, either at the end of the First World War or the Second, ever came to fruition.[29] It is remarkable how similar were the debates in Britain about memorialisation at the end of the 1914-18 war and at the end of the 1939-45 war.[30] The outcome, however, was very different. In comparing the relative merits of the Cenotaph in Whitehall and the Scottish National War Memorial in Edinburgh Castle, one critic observed in 1927: 'While England has made an ethereal monument of her inarticulateness, Scotland has seized the occasion to mobilise all the resources of her national art into a visible monument with form and colour.'[31] A United Nations' War Memorial, in the form of an international university, was proposed in 1945[32] and, more recently, the National Memorial Arboretum has been proposed as an area to be planted on reclaimed land north of Lichfield and Tamworth in Staffordshire with the theme of remembrance and reconciliation. The Arboretum, it is suggested, should include separate gardens such as the Avenue of the Western Front, the Royal British Legion poppy field and the Burma Star Gardens. Consciously based on the experience of America's National Arboretum and the Arlington National Cemetery, such vision may yet bring into being a national memorial to Britain's war dead.[33] In the meantime, another project, co-ordinated by the Imperial War Museum, itself a form of war memorial, has established a National Inventory of War Memorials, and the Association for the Friends of War Memorials was founded in 1998.[34]

The memorials in Britain that provide the functions closest to those of a national focus for remembrance were the Cenotaph in Whitehall and the Tomb of the Unknown Warrior in Westminster Abbey. Both are derived from the nature and scale of British loss in the First World War. As a contemporary account expressed it: 'The Unknown Warrior's grave commemorates the average of the men who died; the Cenotaph in Whitehall commemorates the whole of those men.'[35] 'The Glorious Dead', as the Cenotaph proclaims, embraces the total of British and Empire dead in the First World War, and it was natural simply to extend that meaning to the dead of the Second World War, as was the case with most town and village memorials throughout Britain after the Second World War.

Herein lies a difference in approach. The experience of the First World War produced two great projects in British society. The first took the form of the obligation of remembrance for the dead expressed by local communities in the process of memorialisation and the rituals of remembrance. The second was expressed as the obligation of remembrance for the dead in the attempt to commemorate every single name or known grave through the work of the Imperial War Graves Commission.[36] While the former was not to be repeated to the same extent after the First World War, the work of the second great project was indeed continued and extended to include the commemoration of British and Empire dead of both World Wars. Some 1.75 million British and Empire dead are recorded in this way, 750,000 as names on memorials to the missing and about 950,000 in identified graves. The Commonwealth War Graves Commission has charge of 85 memorials to the missing of the First World War and 42 memorials to the missing of the Second World War. These memorials include naval forces memorials at British ports, land forces memorials associated with particular campaigns and particular periods, air forces memorials in particular theatres of war, and Merchant Navy memorials.[37]

The Imperial War Graves Commission, building on the earlier work of graves' registration undertaken by Sir Fabian Ware, was incorporated by Royal Charter in April 1917. Its first 20 years of work was presented in a report to the Imperial Conference of 1937. The Commission remained true to its aim 'to reflect the spirit of equal sacrifice in which all had fought and died and yet to remember the individual among the multitude'. The Commission's final task after the First World War had been the construction and dedication of the last memorial, the Australian National Memorial, unveiled by King George VI at Villers-Bretonneux on 22 July 1938. Just over a year later, Britain was at war for a second time, and, in 1940, advancing German armoured units shelled the memorial, whose tall tower offered an ideal observation point.

The Imperial War Graves project made – and continues to make – an enormous impact on social memory in Britain with its scale of endeavour matching the scale of British losses. As Stanley Baldwin put it: 'So great was our sacrifice in the war that no human effort could erect memorials commensurate with our loss, but the

Imperial War Graves Commission has come nearer to this, in the work that it has accomplished in the last ten years, than would have seemed possible… Nothing on a similar scale has ever been attempted by any people in the world.'[38] The experience of Gallipoli is, perhaps, typical. On the Gallipoli peninsula there are 31 Commission cemeteries containing 22,000 graves, of which it was possible to identify by name only 9,000. A further 14,000 names are recorded on memorials to the missing at Helles, Lone Pine, Twelve Tree Copse, Hill 60 and Chunuk Bair. The design of the cemeteries and memorials was the work of Sir John Burnet, except for the memorial to the New Zealand missing at Chunuk Bair, which was undertaken by a New Zealand architect, S. Hurst Seager. Construction was undertaken between 1923, after the Chanak crisis had passed and access was permitted, and 1926, when the first pilgrimage of bereaved relatives took place.

In accordance with the Commission's practice, the cemeteries were constructed either where existing clusters of burials were to be found, or by major fields of action where remains were recovered, or by bringing together scattered graves from elsewhere on the peninsula or the adjacent islands. Only one lone grave was permitted to remain, that of C. H. M. 'Dick' Doughty-Wylie (Royal Welsh Fusiliers) on Hill 141 above Seddülbahir, the capture of which on 26 April 1915 he did so much to bring about. The smallest cemetery is Plugge's Plateau Cemetery, containing 21 burials. It is only reached after a stiff climb above Shrapnel Valley at ANZAC Cove. The largest is Twelve Tree Copse Cemetery, containing 3,359 burials largely from the fighting in front of the village of Krithia (Alcitepe), a first-day objective on 25 April and never taken.[39] Probably the most difficult to reach is the Farm Cemetery, below Chunuk Bair, which contains 652 burials and marks the site of bitter fighting on the morning of 10 August 1915 during the Turkish counter-attack that secured the summit of Chunuk Bair. Of the Sixth Battalion, Loyal North Lancashire Regiment, a New Army battalion formed in September 1914 from men from Bolton and Preston, the commanding officer, nine other officers and nearly 500 men were reported missing. The Farm plateau itself was left 'forsaken by both sides … held by the dying and the dead'.[40] Describing the Helles memorial to the missing in 1926, T. J. Pemberton wrote:

> 'It will be seen that no portion of the inscriptions bears a hint of the gallant actions of the dead. There is no word of triumph, there is no mention of what was accomplished, nor of the purpose of the campaign. It was not for these things that the monument was erected, but as a tribute in all humility to the sacrifice which was made, and can be made, by men raised on British soil the world over.'[41]

He also noted the peculiar 'Britishness' of the idea of commemoration in this plan. 'The Turks, whose dead lie in Gallipoli soil in equal numbers to those of their erstwhile enemies, have made no attempt whatever to mark their places of burial.'[42]

Turkish memorialisation of the Gallipoli Peninsula was not immediate and has proceeded at different times since the formation of the Republic in 1923. The main phases of Turkish commemoration took place in 1934, 1985, 1991 and 1995.

Indeed, the process continues as new panels are being carved into the sides of the Turkish memorial overlooking Morto Bay 'to the memory of all Turkish martyrs'. Mustafa Kemal Ataturk stands on Chunuk Bair and other memorials have been erected at different places to indicate the main points where the Turkish defenders contained the British, ANZAC and French landings.[43]

In 1940 the Commission received a supplemental charter to extend its duties 'in like manner' to the commemoration of the new generation of war dead. The first cemetery relating to 1939-45 was the Dieppe cemetery completed in 1949 and the first memorials to the missing were the extensions to the naval memorials. The last memorial, to the missing in the Greek Campaigns, was inaugurated in Athens in 1961, a year after the Commission had adopted its new title as the Commonwealth War Graves Commission. The dates of the World Wars relevant to the Commission's work are 4 August 1914 to 31 August 1921, which represents the dates of the British declaration of a state of war with Germany and the official date for the end of the First World War, and 3 September 1939 to 31 December 1949, which represents the dates of the state of war between Britain and Germany and an equivalent period of 34 months after the end of the Second World War to match that of the First World War.[44]

The memorialisation of the British and Canadian part in the Normandy campaign by the Commission is typical of the Second World War. There are 22,421 graves in the 18 Commission cemeteries in Normandy, and a further 1,805 names are recorded on the Bayeux memorial to the missing. The largest cemetery is the Bayeux War Cemetery itself, containing 4,648 burials. This is the largest British Second World War cemetery in France. The smallest cemetery is the Jerusalem War Cemetery at Chuain, which contains only 47 British war graves. Among the 1,222 interments in the Tilly-sur-Seulles war cemetery is the grave of the poet Keith Douglas, who was killed while serving with the Sherwood Rangers (the Nottinghamshire Yeomanry) on 9 June 1944 in the fighting to take the village.

In combat alongside the British was the 1st Polish Armoured Division, which, with the 4th Canadian Division, advanced south of Caen towards Falaise and was the unit that sealed the Falaise pocket in August 1944. The Polish cemetery at Grainville-Lagannerie is not maintained by the Commonwealth War Graves Commission but by France's Ministry of Anciens Combatants. There are also six large German war graves cemeteries created after 1953, but many German burials are also to be found in the Commonwealth War Graves Cemeteries in Normandy.[45]

If the work of the Commission continued following the Second World War, the war memorials project largely did not. There was no attempt to cover the land in new memorials. Indeed, changes in taste saw the disappearance of some. St Agatha's Parish Church in Sparkbrook, Birmingham, had created a memorial chapel after the First World War with an altar lit by candles of remembrance and a perpetual light hung in an upturned steel helmet. Behind the altar was a large fresco connecting Christ's salvation to the acts of those who had fought in the war. It was reported:

'...the picture in tempura, covering the whole of the north wall, representing the vision of Christ in glory. At the foot of the picture, on each side of the altar, which will be of marble, will be shown the kneeling figure of a mother and a husband and wife and, flanking each side of the altar, will appear groups of sailors, soldiers, and members of the airforce, bearing the standards of the Warwickshire, Worcestershire and Staffordshire regiments. The remainder of the chapel will be painted in white, and on the west wall, between the windows, alabaster slabs inscribed with the names of regiments of the fallen, will be fixed.'[46]

Little of this remains. After damage by enemy action in 1940, most of chapel was removed by 1957 and was not restored. The panels remain, affixed to the altar, but the fresco was overcovered with whitewash, the altar was covered and the candles and lights were withdrawn from use.

The memorial had been financed by donations to a Memorial Fund and was dedicated on 9 December 1918. A solemn requiem for those who fell in the war was sung on Sunday 14 December 1918 and the Advent sermons were given on the subject of the Problems of Peace. The series included Sir Gilbert Barling, Vice-Chancellor of Birmingham University, on Peace in the world. The events were accompanied by a Victory Memorial Fair on 29 November to 2 December.[47]

In the main, existing memorials were modified by the addition of new panels and new dates and lettering to encompass the commemoration of the dead of the Second World War. The debate about war memorials that took place during and after the First World War was replicated during and after the Second World War. Some favoured preserving the remains of 'blitzed' churches as memorials, or their restoration alongside new buildings, of which the new Coventry Cathedral, consecrated in 1962, is, perhaps, the best example.[48] Others favoured a scheme for establishing a National Memorial with gardens around St Paul's Cathedral. The Royal Academy favoured a redevelopment along more modernist lines, while the County of London planners favoured a precinct for Westminster.[49] A War Memorial Advisory Committee was formed and recommended:

'Let us make our war memorials, of whatever type they may be, things which can never be mistaken for anything but what they are. It would, for instance, be entirely wrong to imagine that any project becomes a fitting war memorial merely by attaching the label "war memorial" to it. Again, any project likely to be soon undertaken by national or local government seems undesirable; we must resist any inclination to use war memorial funds for such things as will be provided for Social Service as part of the State's responsibility. The permanence of a war memorial will only be assured if the fact that it is built as a remembrance dominates the minds of those who erect it.'[50]

There was no rush to erect new memorials whether utilitarian or monumental. That is the essential difference between the experience of the First and Second World Wars in Britain's social memory. It is well illustrated by the example of the remarkable war memorial at Ledbury in Herefordshire. Constructed as a memorial to those killed in the First World War, the memorial takes the form of a series of panels of names with mosaic depictions of a soldier, sailor and airmen. A flaming torch is born aloft. After the Second World War, further panels were added, but the two inscriptions from the First and Second World Wars illustrate the difference in meaning. The inscription from the First World War makes it clear that the dead had died in the patriotic defence of the nation: 'To the Glory of God and to the immortal memory of the gallant men from this town who gave their lives for their country in the Great European war 1914-1919' and is concluded by 'Greater love hath no man than this'. The inscription from the Second World War simply states: 'Let us remember before God the men of this parish who gave their lives in the cause of freedom 1939-1945'.

After the First World War a landscape of war memorials was created in place of the 'land fit for heroes' promised at the time, whereas British society in 1945 strove to create the 'New Jerusalem' rather than a further new national war memorial project. The recording of the names of the dead from later wars on existing memorials has become the usual form of commemoration. An example is the war memorial at Martock in Somerset, which has panels commemorating the dead from the village in the First and Second World Wars, Korea, and the Falklands. After the First World War British society was persuaded or was willing to accept the obligation of remembrance for its own sake to deflect criticism or political debate. After 1945, British society acknowledged that remembrance was an act designed to recognise obligation undertaken during the war rather than to be an end in itself. The rhetoric of remembrance established during and after the First World War was no longer suitable for repetition, and, in the mood of confidence, a new vision for society in which the principles of the welfare state were put into practice, enabled Britain to commemorate the victory over fascism as an obligation discharged. The gritty realism, devoid of allegory or supranational symbolism, such as the Commando War Memorial at Spean Bridge by Scott Sutherland, revealed the new sense of confidence. Utilising the motto 'United we conquer' and the descriptive phrase referring to the rugged surroundings of the memorial, 'This Country was their training ground', a new confidence is demonstrated. The memorial was unveiled on 22 September 1952 with an address by Lord Lovat, who had famously led Commando units in the Second World War, and the playing of the pipe lament 'Flowers of the Forest'.[51]

For Britain, the principal reasons for the transformation of the social memory of war was not that the experience of war was any less horrible in the Second World War than in the First, but that the two global conflicts differed in the scale of British losses, their causes, outcomes and consequences. First, casualties in the First World War, as experienced by Britain and not including civilian deaths as a result of the influenza pandemic, were overwhelmingly military and combatant. In the Second World War, Britain's civilian population was more directly in the front line and more deaths resulted. For the world as a whole, non-combatant casualties were on similar scales in both World Wars. The Central Statistical Office has calculated that Britain suffered only 8,389 civilian casualties in the First World War compared with 63,635 in the Second. Worldwide, the equivalent figures for both wars were estimated as 13 million and 13.2 million respectively.[52]

From information presented in 1949-50, a comparison between the casualties of the two World Wars was made. British and Empire dead in the First World War amounted to 1,089,900, with approximately 2.4 million wounded and only 191,650 prisoners of war. The equivalent figures for the Second World War were 353,652 killed, 475,070 wounded, and the much larger figure of 326,459 for prisoners of war.[53]

Second, British combatant casualties were far larger in the First World War than in the Second, and, while the experience in 1914-18 had been predominately one of infantry fighting in rifle platoons supported by artillery, the 'sharp end' for British servicemen and women in 1939-45 could range across many varied situations. The horizon for the First World War British infantry soldier was mainly that glimpsed through the trench periscope or fleetingly in open ground and, for a far smaller number, open sea or air. In the Second World War, British servicemen or women could expect to see anything from an illuminated radar screen to the enclosed world of the tank, or the high-altitude vista of a burning town at night to the monotony of the storage depot. The difference between the World Wars in the military service of British officers is well illustrated by a comparison between the relevant volumes of the war records of Britain's public schools. The pages of the *Stonyhurst War Record of the Great War*, published in 1927, are filled with portraits of men who served and died as infantry or artillery officers, of whom Second Lieutenant Harold J. Lynch is typical. Born in 1895, best all-round athlete at Stonyhurst in 1914, Company Sergeant-Major in the Officers Training Corps, enthusiastic choir member, he was commissioned in the Royal Welsh Fusiliers in 1914 and killed in action during the Battle of Festubert in 1915. Lynch is described as having 'laid down his life as a gallant gentlemen' by his Company Quarter-Master Sergeant in a letter to his mother.[54]

The equivalent volume for the Second World War was not published until 1989 and the range of service is much more varied, as Squadron Leader Michael J. Casey's war experience illustrates. Shot down on 17 October 1939 while on operation over Ems, he was captured and, after several escape attempts, took part with 75 men in the mass escape of 22 March 1944. He was recaptured and shot by the Geheime Staatspolizei (Gestapo).[55]

Third, Britain's forces in the 1914-18 war were composed of regular soldiers, Territorials, volunteers and, after 1916, conscripts, whereas in 1939 a national scheme for mobilisation was implemented at the outset of war with conscription to the armed forces being managed in a systematic manner. The years 1939-40 did not see the element of voluntary enlistment to the so-called 'Pals' Battalions – the service battalions formed in the First World War from men who volunteered and served together in units associated by place or other affiliation. Morale in the Second World War was fostered by the dynamics of the unit rather than through the mutual association of school, community, sport or place of work.

Fourth, at the end of the Second World War any ambiguity concerning the war's outcome was removed in the circumstances of the unconditional surrender of Germany and Japan. Victory in Europe (VE) and Victory against Japan (VJ) days were clear end dates. The Armistices in 1918 at the end of the First World War (30 September with Bulgaria, 30 October with Turkey, 3 November with Austria-

Hungary and 11 November with Germany) left uncertainty and ambiguity even after the conclusion of the successive Peace Treaties in 1919, 1920 and 1923.

Fifth, the circumstances of victory for the Allies in the Second World War left no doubt in the popular mind as to the nature of the enemy regimes being fought. The liberation of the concentration camps in Europe and the Allied prisoner of war camps in the Far East exposed the truth for all. The Holocaust altered the nature of remembrance, and the justification beyond patriotism was clear. The transfer from Armistice Day to Remembrance Sunday in Britain, aided by the fact that in 1945, 11 November fell on a Sunday, passed with little discussion. As Adrian Gregory has written of the ritual of the 2 minutes silence:

> 'The mood of 1945 was sceptical of the high ideals and high-flown phrases that had marked the year which saw the beginning of the silence. The disillusionment that had begun during the last years of the 1930s had come to fruition. There was a new silence in 1945, the silence after Auschwitz and the silence after Hiroshima, the silence in which nothing meaningful could be said.'[56]

In 1918 the popular mood accepted the obligation of remembrance in order to assuage mass grief. An over-arching meaning of sacrifice developed to give meaning and justification to Britain's losses. In 1945 the completeness of victory and the evident justification for the Allied cause, emphasised in the war's final months, meant that the remembrance of obligation discharged was the dominant mood, especially as, for Britain, the immediate cost in lives appeared to be far less than had been endured in the Great War. The war of 1914-18 for British society retained the title 'Great' simply because of the scale of British losses. After the Second World War, new national interpretations developed in popular culture around the notions of Britain's circumstances in 1940 – the 'Dunkirk spirit', 'Britain Stands Alone' and the Blitz – essentially sustaining notions of collective ideology. The memory of the Holocaust is a significant element in the popular memory of war since 1945 throughout the world. In Britain, the treatment of Allied prisoners of war by Japan remains a source of bitterness for many veterans of the conflict in the Far East and it is, perhaps, significant that one of the exceptions to the general lack of new memorials has been the case of the efforts of the Burma Star Association to memorialise their 'forgotten' war.[57]

Finally, the appearance of the atomic weapon and its chosen use by the Allied democracies against the Japanese cities of Hiroshima and Nagasaki changed popular conceptions about war and thereafter the nature of the popular memory of war by appearing to negate the individual in war, making irrelevant the memory of the individual dead. Death in atomic war meant obliteration of individuals and oblivion for their memory. The First World War had come close to this, but atomic then nuclear war suggested the impossibility of the remembrance of sacrifice on its previous basis. Only by remembering the act itself, the mass destruction of humanity by a single act of war or genocide, can humanity begin to remember the individuality of death in war. In the world after the Second World War, the rituals of Hiroshima Day or Holocaust Memorial Day or *Volkstrauertag* represent an attempt to overcome these difficulties.[58]

Even those ritual acts of remembrance are more likely to achieve their purpose than cases when there is no commemoration possible because the circumstances of killing are on a genocidal scale and have an anonymity that defies memory, such as in the killing fields of Cambodia, or in Rwanda, or in the former Yugoslavia. Only a universal memorial such as Michael Sandle's *Twentieth Century War Memorial* will serve.[59] Perhaps remembrance in the form of cemeteries with individual graves and names on memorials to the dead has only been possible in the historical period from the mid-19th century to the end of the Second World War and in wars between industrialised nation states. The modern nation state has both the means to wage war and to construct the social memory of the nation's dead when peace returns. Perhaps remembrance of individual war dead is one of the defining marks of the nation state, rather than the tribe or race or geo-economic block. The aftermath of genocidal conflicts that have taken place since the end of the Second World War suggest that the memory of individual war dead is no longer possible in such conditions where there are no survivors left to raise memorials or to perform acts of remembrance. Those who remain do not have the luxury of the means for permanent commemoration in the struggle to survive. There are only the missing.

Recommended reading

Bushaway, Bob, 'Name upon Name: The Great War and Remembrance', in Porter, Roy (ed), *Myths of the English* (Cambridge: Polity Press, 1992) pp136-61

Evans, Martin and Lunn, Ken (eds), *War and Memory in the Twentieth Century* (Oxford, New York: Berg, 1997)

Gaffney, Angela, *Aftermath: Remembering the Great War in Wales* (Cardiff: University of Wales Press, 1998)

Gibson, Major Edwin and Kingsley Ward, G. (eds), *Courage Remembered* (London: HMSO, 1989)

Gillis, John R. (ed), *Commemoration: The Politics of National Identity* (Princeton: Princeton University Press, 1994)

Gregory, Adrian, *The Silence of Memory: Armistice Day 1919-1946* (Oxford, Providence: Berg, 1994)

King, Alex, *Memorials of the Great War in Britain: The Symbolism and Politics of Remembrance* (Oxford, New York: Berg, 1998)

Mosse, George, *Fallen Soldiers: Reshaping the Memory of the World Wars* (New York, Oxford: Oxford University Press, 1990)

Winter, Jay, *Sites of Memory, Sites of Mourning: The Great War in European Cultural History* (Cambridge: Cambridge University Press, 1995)

Young, James E., *The Texture of Memory: Holocaust Memorials and Meaning* (Newhaven, London: York University Press, 1993)

Notes

[1] 'Aftermath' by Siegfried Sassoon, dated March 1919, in Rupert Hart-Davis (ed), *The War Poems of Siegfried Sassoon* (London: Faber & Faber, 1983) p143. Sassoon relinquished his acting rank of

Captain and was placed on the retired list, on account of ill-health caused by wounds, on 12 March 1919.

2   See Jay Winter, *Sites of Memory, Sites of Mourning: The Great War in European Cultural History* (Cambridge: Cambridge University Press, 1995) pp78-116, on the role of war memorials and the mourning process. Winter's work is part of a significant new interest in memorialisation and commemoration of war in the 20th century.

For other studies, see Annette Becker, *Les Monuments Aux Morts: Patrimoine et Mémoire de la Grande Guerre* (Paris: Editions France, 1994); Bob Bushaway, 'Name upon name: The Great War and Remembrance', in Roy Porter (ed), *Myths of the English* (Cambridge: Polity Press, 1992) pp136-61; Angela Gaffney, *Aftermath: Remembering the Great War in Wales* (Cardiff: University of Wales Press, 1998); Adrian Gregory, *The Silence of Memory: Armistice Day 1919-1946* (Oxford, Providence: Berg, 1994); Alex King, *Memorials of the Great War in Britain: The Symbolism and Politics of Remembrance* (Oxford, New York: Berg, 1998); D. W. Lloyd, *Battlefield Tourism: Pilgrimage and the Commemoration of the Great War in Britain, Australia and Canada, 1919-1939* (Oxford, New York: Berg, 1998); and Martin Evans and Ken Lunn (eds), *War and Memory in the Twentieth-Century* (Oxford, New York: Berg, 1997), in particular the articles therein: Jane Leonard, 'Facing the "Finger of scorn": veterans' memories of Ireland in the Great War', pp59-72; Catherine Moriarty, 'Private Grief and Public Remembrance: British First World War Memorials', pp125-42; William Kidd, 'Memory, Memorials and Commemoration of War: Memorials in Lorraine, 1908-1988', pp143-59; and Barry M. Doyle, 'Religion, Politics and Remembrance: A Free Church Community and its Great War Dead', pp223-38

For Australia, see Michael McKernan and Peter Stanley (eds), *ANZAC Day: Seventy Years on* (Sydney: Collins, 1986) and Alistair Thomson, *ANZAC memories: Living with the legend* (Melbourne: Oxford University Press, 1994)

Something of modern Turkish perceptions can be seen from the recent guide by Hüseyin Uluarslan, *Gallipoli Campaign* (Istanbul: Kerskin, nd [c1995])

3   Recent work on the politics of memory has been greatly influenced by Pierre Nora, *Realms of Memory: The Construction of the French Past*, I 'Conflicts and Divisions', II 'Traditions', and III 'Symbols' (New York: Columbia University Press, 1996, 1997, 1998). These volumes are an abridgement and English translation of Nora's monumental work *Les Lieux de Mémoire* (Paris: Editions Gallimard, 1992)

See also: Chris Wickham and James Fentress (eds), *Social Memory* (Oxford: Blackwell 1992); Raphael Samuel, *Theatres of Memory* (London: Verso, 1994); Paul Fussell, *The Great War and Modern Memory* (New York: Oxford University Press, 1975); Michael Kammen, *Mystic Chords of Memory: The Transformation of Tradition in America Culture* (New York: Alfred A. Knoff, 1991); George Mosse, *Fallen Soldiers: Reshaping the Memory of the World Wars* (New York, Oxford: Oxford University Press, 1990); John R. Gillis (ed), *Commemorations: The Politics of National Identity* (Princeton: Princeton University Press, 1994), especially Part Three: 'Memories of War and Wars over Memory', pp127-211; James E. Young, *The Texture of Memory: Holocaust Memorials and Meaning* (New Haven, London: Yale University Press, 1993); Serge Barcellini and Annette Wieviorka, *Passant, Souviens – Toi! Les Lieux du Souvenir de la Seconde Guerre Mondiale en France* (Paris: Plon, 1995)

4   The movement to restore the 2 minutes silence to the anniversary of the actual time and date of the Armistice in 1918, 11 o'clock am on 11 November, was began in 1995 by the Royal British Legion. Employers are invited to offer their employees the opportunity to take part and, in 1996, it was estimated that over two-thirds of adults in Britain commemorated the moment. See *The Guardian*, 12 November 1996

5   For the voluntary movement, as a typical example see Col H. A. R. May, *Memories of the Artists Rifles* (London: Howlett & Son, 1929) pp3-70 and illustrations pp71-117

6   See Stig Förster and Jörg Nagler (eds), *On the Road to Total War: The American Civil War and the German Wars of Unification, 1816-1817* (Cambridge: Cambridge University Press, 1997)

7   See Annette Becker, 'War Memorials: A Legacy of Total War', in Förster and Nagler (eds), op cit, pp657-80

8   For Gettysburg, see Kent Gramm, *Gettysburg: A Meditation on War and Values* (Indianapolis: Indiana University Press, 1994)

9   David Lloyd George, *War Memoirs* (London: Odhams Press, 1938) Vol 1, p220

10 Reginald Arkell, *Meet these People* (London: Herbert Jenkins, 1928) p18

11 Virginia Woolf, *Mrs Dalloway* (London: Hagarth Press, 1925) p10 in the Penguin 1991 ed

12 For service medals, see Maj L. L. Gordon, *British Battles and Medals* (London: Spink & Son, 1971) pp309-14, 339-51

13 For the National Memorial Plaque, see *The Studio* 73 (1918) p136, and *The Architectural Review* 43 (1918) pp84-5. The words of the King's letter, accompanying the memorial scroll, are taken from that which commemorates Private Dennis Holloway, the Worcestershire Regiment.

14 See David Cannadine, 'War and Death: Grief and Mourning in Modern Britain', in Joachim Whaley (ed), *Mirrors of Mortality: Studies in the Social History of Death* (London: Europa Publications, 1981) pp187-242

15 For Wing Commander Frank Brock, see *Dulwich College War Record 1914-1919* (London: The Marshalsea Press) pp26-7). Pencil annotation in copy in the author's possession

16 George Orwell, 'England Your England', in *Inside the Whale and other Essays* (London: Penguin, 1972) p69. On the Battle of the Somme, see Geoff Dyer, *The Missing of the Somme* (London: Penguin Books, 1995)

17 For the 'Great Pilgrimage', see *Battlefields Pilgrimage 1928 Handbook* and *The Story of an Epic Pilgrimage* (both London: British Legion, 1928)

18 *War Graves of the Empire*, reprinted from the special number of *The Times*, 10 November 1928 (London: The Times Publishing Company, 1928) p8

19 For Warsaw, see Malgorzata Omilanowska and Jerzy Majewoki (eds), *Warsaw* (London: Dorling Kindersley, 1997) and Boleslaw Bierut, *The Six-Year Plan for the Reconstruction of Warsaw* (Warsaw: Ksiazka and Wiedza, 1949). For Rotterdam, see Arnold Whittick, *European Architecture in the 20th Century* (Aylesbury: Leonard Hill, 1974) pp546-9

20 For a description, see John Newman, *The Buildings of Wales: Glamorgan* (Cardiff: Penguin and University of Wales Press, 1995) pp221-33

21 For a description of the dedication ceremony and the speeches of Sir John French and Sir Ivor Herbert, see *Cardiff Times and South Wales Weekly News*, Saturday 27 November 1909, p3, col 3

22 John Newman, op cit, p223. The controversy surrounding the memorial is fully explored by Angela Gaffney, *Aftermath: Remembering the Great War in Wales* (Cardiff: University of Wales Press, 1998) pp44-68

23 *Wales on Sunday*, 1 November 1992, p12

24 For the Welsh National Temple of Peace and Health, see John Newman, op cit, p232

25 Information on Warsaw from personal field notes and Omilanowska and Majewski (eds), op cit

26 See *The Independent on Sunday*, 16 May 1993, p12

27 See James E. Young, op cit, pp155-86, 185-208, and also Michael Steinlauf, *Bondage to the Dead: Poland and the memory of the Holocaust* (New York: Syracuse University Press, 1997)

28 See, as an example, Alice Goodman, *The Street memorials of St Albans Abbey Parish* (Hertford: St Albans & Hertfordshire Architectural & Archaeological Society, 1987)

29 See Bob Bushaway, op cit, for a full discussion of the debate

30 For the Second World War, see Arnold Whittick, *War Memorials* (Glasgow: The University Press, 1946) pp1-6, 12-33

31 Sir Lawrence Weaver, quoted in Arnold Whittick, op cit, pp14-5

32 Ibid, pp144-62

33 See 'After a Century of War, a Vision of Peace' in *Weekend Telegraph*, Saturday 6 April 1996, p3

34 On the origins of the Imperial War Museum itself, see Gaynor Kavanagh, *Museums and the First World War: A Social History* (Leicester: Leicester University Press, 1994). For the Association for the Friends of War Memorials, see Newsletter, 1998

35 Sir J. A. Hammerton, *A Popular History of the Great War*, Vol VI 'Armistice and After' (London: The Fleetway House, nd [c1933]) p499

36 For the work of the Imperial (now Commonwealth) War Games Commission, see Maj Edwin Gibson and G. Kingsley Ward (eds), *Courage Remembered* (London: HMSO, 1989); also Bob Bushaway, op cit, pp144-5, 149-50

37 Gibson and Kingsley Ward (eds), op cit

38 *War Graves of the Empire*, op cit, p3

39 Details from the Commonwealth War Graves Commission's Information Sheet, *The Gallipoli Peninsula, Turkey* (Maidenhead: Commonwealth War Graves Commission, 1998)

40 Brig-Gen C. F. Aspinall-Olgander, *Military Operations in Gallipoli*, Vol II 'May 1915 to the Evacuation' (London: Heinemann, 1932) p307

41 T. J. Pemberton, *Gallipoli To-day* (London: Ernest Benn, 1926) p115

42 Ibid, p20

43 See Hüseyin Uluarslan, op cit

44 Gibson and Kingsley Ward (eds), op cit, pp58-63

45 For Normandy, see Tonie and Valmai Holt, *Normandy Landing Beaches* (Ashbourne: Moorland Publishing, 1994), which reproduces the Commonwealth War Graves Commission's Guide to the Commonwealth War Cemeteries and the Bayeux Memorial, Normandy, June-August 1944, pp234-43. For Keith Douglas, see Desmond Graham, *Keith Douglas, 1920-1944: A Biography* (Oxford: Oxford University Press, 1988)

46 'Striking memorial scheme', in *Handsworth Herald*, 8 February 1919

47 Illustration in Souvenir Programme: Christmas Fayre and Fete, December 1923, St Agatha's Church, Sparkbrook, Parish Archives. See also 'Church Notes and News' in 'Parish Magazine – Church of St Agatha, Sparkbrook, Birmingham' 6 (12) (December 1919), Parish Archives

48 Arnold Whittick, *War Memorials*, op cit, p10, which quotes correspondence in *The Times* of September and August 1944. On Coventry Cathedral as a war memorial, see Alan Borg, *War Memorials: From Antiquity to the Present* (London: Leo Cooper, 1991) pp83, 137

49 Arnold Whittick, op cit, pp15-6

50 Ibid, p8

51 See Derek Boorman, *For Your Tomorrow: British Second World War Memorials* (York: Derek Boorman, Dunnington Hall, 1995) p46, and John Gifford, *The Buildings of Scotland: Highlands and Islands* (London: Penguin Books, 1992) p264

52 Central Statistical Office, *Fighting with Figures: A Statistical Digest of the Second World War* (London: HMSO, 1995) pvi

53 Articles 'Casualties in the First World War' and 'Casualties in the Second World War' in Athelstan Ridgway, *Everyman's Encyclopaedia: The Third Edition* (London: J. M. Dent, 1949-50) Vol 3, pp343-6. Discussion of British casualty figure remains controversial. For a discussion of the position regarding the First World War, see J. M. Winter, *The Great War and the British People* (London: Macmillan, 1986)

54 Rev Francis Irwin, *Stonyhurst War Record* (Derby: Authorities of Stonyhurst College, 1927) pp190-1

55 R. Raymond Walsh, *Stonyhurst College War Record 1939-45* (Blackburn: THCL Books, 1989) p20

56 Adrian Gregory, op cit, p222

57 Derek Boorman, op cit, pp60-6

58 For the Holocaust see James E. Young, op cit

59 For the 50th Anniversary of VE Day, the Tate Gallery Liverpool promoted an exhibition of Michael Sandle's work, including his 'Twentieth Century War Memorial' (1971)

Chapter 31

Bibliographic sources for the study of the two World Wars

Peter T. Scott

'A great many profound secrets are somewhere in print, but are most easily
detected when one knows what to seek'

Sir Lewis Namier

This is a purely personal guide to some of the bibliographies and related sources
for the study of the two World Wars that I have used in my work as a military
historian and as a bookseller handling new, second-hand and rare books in the field
of 20th-century warfare. It deals principally with English language materials and
concentrates on British resources. Despite this limited, selective and
Anglocentric approach, I hope that those working in other countries and other
languages will find it of value, discovering parallels in their own bibliographical
research. However, this survey takes little account of the resources of the
internet/world wide web, which, by its very nature, changes from second to
second. Free and subscription 'on-line' access to the catalogues of libraries and
special collections around the world can provide a wealth of raw information, but
the printed bibliography, and especially the annotated bibliography, no matter
how old, remains an indispensable tool for the researcher.

The first step for any researcher is to refer to the bibliographies and source notes
appended to their works by any recent authors writing in the same or allied fields.
Time employed enquiring about a library's acquisitions of relevant newly
published books is never wasted. The full citation of primary and secondary sources
is invaluable, and this existing spadework can often save the new researcher hours
of labour repeating work already done, and can point the way along entirely new
and unsuspected lines of enquiry.

Such sources having been exhausted, the researcher will necessarily turn to the
relevant bibliographies, some of which are recorded here.

The First World War, or Great War, 1914-1918

The outbreak of war in 1914 was accompanied by an immense literary offensive on
every possible front. No aspect of the conflict, its causes, course, or likely outcome
was left unexplored. Booksellers offered blanket-order programmes tailored to the

specific interests of their private and institutional clients, thereby relieving them of the fear that they might miss a vital book, pamphlet, periodical or map. All kinds of organisations produced checklists, handlists and readers' guides, and the professional bibliographers were not far behind.

The first to attempt a systematic subject bibliography were F. W. T. Lange and W. T. Berry, with their four-volume series *Books on the Great War: An Annotated Bibliography of Literature issued during the European Conflict* (1915-16). There are subject and author indexes, and the annotations, such as there are, occasionally provide a useful gloss. The coverage of foreign language material and particularly German books and pamphlets is surprisingly good.

Concurrent with Lange and Berry's efforts, Professor George W. Prothero was busily accumulating material for his *Catalogue of War Publications*, issued initially in pamphlet form, then as a cumulation comprising works published to June 1916. Its compilation was part of Prothero's work for the Central Committee for National Organisations, ostensibly a private venture set up and run by Prothero and ex-Conservative MP Henry Cust, which was coeval with and later subsumed by Wellington House, the British Government's covert War Propaganda Bureau.

Prothero's editorship of the handbooks prepared by the Foreign Office Historical Section for the Paris Peace Conference fatally weakened his health, and the final edition of his bibliography, now titled *A Select Analytical List of Books Concerning the Great War*, and edited by Stephen Gaselee, appeared posthumously in 1923.

The *Subject Index of the Books Relating to the European War, 1914-1918, held by the Library of the British Museum* had appeared in 1922 and, although useful in its own right, it is best seen as complementary to Prothero's *Select Analytical List*. The American equivalent is *A Check List of the Literature and Other Material in the Library of Congress on the European War (1918)*. Compiled under the direction of H. H. Meyer, the library's Chief Bibliographer, it includes excellent coverage of posters, broadsides, prints, photographs (including stereoscopic views), and a truly remarkable collection of wartime sheet music from all combatant nations.

Official British Government wartime publications are best traced through the Stationery Office's *Monthly List of Official Publications*, and Parliamentary Papers through its *Monthly List of Parliamentary Papers*, though it is probably easier to trace these through the *General Index* (1960), which also covers the Second World War. There is also the *Catalogue of War Literature issued by HM Government, 1914-1919* (1921), which is particularly valuable for its listing (albeit partial) of the Parliamentary Recruiting Committee Posters, Irish Recruiting Posters, Parliamentary War Savings Posters, War Loan Posters, reproductions of drawings by Muirhead Bone and other war artists, and a number of related books and pamphlets.

All of the drawings and at least some of the books and pamphlets in this catalogue were covertly financed, wholly or partially, by the previously mentioned Wellington House, using the imprints of established publishing houses, and in 1916 and 1917 one of the largest distributors of printed matter in the world. Fortunately, there is a *Schedule of Wellington House Literature*, a printed confidential list produced 'in house' in April 1917 and supplemented by

'Continuations' to just beyond the end of the war. Arranged in rough chronological order of distribution, it is without any form of index, but the majority of entries include the ostensible publisher and a synopsis of the contents. Very few copies of the original lists are known to have survived, but photocopies are available on repayment from the Department of Printed Books of the Imperial War Museum.

For those works perceived by the Allies to be German war propaganda, a major source is the catalogue of the *Library of German War Literature attached to MI7(B)*. It is divided into ten subject classifications and, despite minimal bibliographic information, is particularly useful on German-language material distributed throughout the Deutschtum, pro-German English-language literature published in America and for those works translated for the benefit of neutral readers. Only 100 copies were printed, but a photocopy should be available from the Imperial War Museum. The catalogue should be used in conjunction with the MI7(B) *Report on the Propaganda Library* and its two separate Appendices (1917). Written by Sir Peter Chalmers Mitchell, but issued anonymously, copies were sent to a number of libraries under the strict injunction that they were 'not for public circulation during the war'. A third appendix 'dealing with the use of English Authors in Enemy Propaganda' was prepared in typescript but not printed or circulated.

The British Series in the Carnegie Endowment's *Economic and Social History of the World War* includes M. E. Bulkley's *Bibliographical Survey of Contemporary Sources for the Economic and Social History of the War* (1922), which remains an absolutely invaluable guide within its remit, with excellent subject classifications and a thorough index. It is especially useful for its coverage of Acts of Parliament, official publications and periodical literature, and Bulkley's annotations and summaries are pertinent. Other worthwhile volumes in the Carnegie British Series are N. B. Dearle's *Dictionary of Official War-Time Organizations* (1928), Hilary Jenkinson's *Archive Administration, including the problems of War Archives and Archive Making* (1922) and Hubert Hall's *British Archives and the Sources for the History of the World War* (1925). In the American Carnegie series, the *Introduction to the American Official Sources for the Economic and Social History of the World War* by Waldo G. Leland and Newton D. Mereness (1926) is especially valuable. It provides an excellent guide to the structure of the wartime Federal legislature, judiciary and executive departments, with numerous bibliographic references, together with a survey of State War History Collections.

Creative writing, whether poetry or prose, received little bibliographical attention in the inter-war period. Exceptions are the *Catalogue of the War Poetry Collection of the Birmingham Public Libraries Reference Collection* (1921) – an important source, even in the light of Catherine Reilly's *English Poetry of the First World War* (see below) – and *European War Fiction in English and Personal Narratives – Bibliographies* by Dawson and Huntting [sic] (1921), whose selection and classification gives point to the perennial dilemma as to where personal narrative ends and fiction begins. Their coverage does at least have the merit of including those narratives that appeared only in periodicals.

War Books: A Critical Guide by Captain Cyril Falls (1930), the best-known and most respected of all the readers' guides to the literature and history of the Great War, covers personal narrative as 'Reminiscence' and 'Reminiscence – Foreign'. Falls's selections under these and the other classifications he employs are actually less important than his comments about each book. As R. J. Wyatt recorded in the introduction to his new edition of *War Books* in 1989: 'Falls wrote with clarity and precision, always with great consideration for the general reader and not just for the specialist; he was careful with his research and above all, he took part in the momentous events himself.'

Falls was a co-compiler with Edmund Blunden and H. M. Tomlinson of *The War 1914-1918 – a booklist* [1930], which generally succeeded in its aim of presenting 'a representative selection of books for those who would know why the War was and what it was', but has greater value for Blunden's introduction. Similarly, Tomlinson's introduction to Catalogue 47, *Rare Books in English Literature and a supplement of War Books*, of Elkin Mathews Ltd, the London booksellers, is worth seeking out. His 1932 opinion that if 'you look over a bibliography of the war ... it is astonishing to be reminded of so much that is not only good to read, but good in itself' is now true of both World Wars.

The three French bibliographies to which I have had recourse most frequently are Jean Vic's *La Littérature de Guerre: Manuel Methodique et Critique des Publications de Langue Française* (5 Vols, 1918-23) and the *Catalogue raisonné of the Collection Henri Leblanc* (8 Vols, 1916-22). The former has proved particularly useful in locating works that deal with the French view of her allies and English-language works (particularly propaganda) that were translated into French. For details of French first-hand accounts there is Jean Norton Cru's *Témoins: essai d'analyse et de critique des souvenirs de combatants édités en francais de 1915 á 1928* (1929). With its remarkable biographical and bibliographical data and numerous analytical indexes, it would provide an admirable pattern for a similar work on first-hand accounts in English. Wartime German publications can be traced through J. L. Kunz's *Bibliographie Der Kriegsliteratur* (1920) and the *Catalogue Méthodique du Fonds Allemand de la Bibliothèque* by Jean Dubois (4 Vols, 1921-23). A companion volume to this is the *Catalogue Méthodique du Fonds Italien de la Bibliothèque* (1923).

For Canadian material, Professor W. B. Kerr's *Historical Literature on Canada's Participation in the Great War* (1933), a review article with appended bibliography reprinted in pamphlet form from *The Canadian Historical Review*, remains a useful guide.

Study of the First World War, overshadowed and overwhelmed by the events of the Second World War, remained dormant until the mid to late 1950s, when a slow trickle of works developed into a flood, then into a deluge as the approach of four years of 50th Anniversary commemorations from August 1964 coincided with the release in Britain of substantial tranches of public records and the unveiling of documents in private hands. Alex Danchev's essay, '"Bunking" and Debunking: The Controversies of the 1960s' in *The First World War and British Military History* (1991) serves as an excellent annotated bibliography for the period, and the same work contains a valuable 'Chronology of Publications on the Military History of the First World War'.

With one major exception there was no advance in bibliographical publication during the 1960s and 1970s. However, the exception, the *Subject Catalog of the World War I Collection of the New York Public Library Reference Department* (4 Vols, 1961), is one of the most important and most useful published bibliographical sources for the study of the Great War. Reproduced from the library's original catalogue cards, it provides some 58,000 subject entries for a major collection in its field. The NYPL's policy of giving its 'European agents standing instructions to send everything of consequence that appeared abroad' from the outbreak of war provided the collection with a particular strength in German and French material, and its excellent holdings of periodicals are valuably indexed with entries for individual articles. Moreover, the catalogue's terminal date of 1958 usefully marks the end of the long dry season in First World War studies. Once researchers find their way around the catalogue's occasionally eccentric and irritating subject subdivisions (including references to headings that do not exist, at least not in this printed form) and come to terms with its somewhat unwieldy format, they will find it a true mine of information that repays any time spent with it, whether making a deliberate and systematic search or just casually turning its leaves. It is reputedly still in print.

A. G. S. Enser's *A Subject Bibliography of the First World War: Books in English 1914-1978* (1979), the companion to his Second War bibliography (see below), was marred by avoidable errors due to unfamiliarity with the subject matter compounded by an over-reliance on secondary sources rather than first-hand knowledge of the books themselves. While the revised edition of 1990 incorporates a number of corrections, has an extended terminal date of 1987 and can be counted an improvement over its predecessor, it should still be used with care.

Bibliographically speaking, American involvement in the Great War has been well covered. Ronald Schaffer's *The United States in World War I: A Selected Bibliography* (1978) and *America and World War I: A Selected Annotated Bibliography of English-Language Sources* (1985) by David R. Woodward and Robert Franklin Maddox are both excellent, but the Woodward and Maddox annotations are especially valuable. The title of Charles V. Genthe's *American War Narratives 1917-1918: A Study and Bibliography* (1969) is somewhat misleading in that the bibliography also includes British personal narratives published in America. The US Military History Institute's Special Bibliographic Series of important surveys (see also Second World War, below) includes No 20, Vol I, 'World War I Manuscripts [and] The World War I Survey' by Hermine Scholz (1986). Arranged by Order of Battle, the Survey lists the respondents to questionnaires sent to 94,000 Army and Navy veterans between 1977 and 1983.

The war novel in English is analysed in *The Novels of World War I: An Annotated Bibliography* by Philip E. Hager and Desmond Taylor (1981), which lists 900 adult and 370 juvenile novels and includes a valuable bibliography of critical materials. Catherine W. Reilly's *English Poetry of the First World War: A Bibliography* appeared in 1978.

The first war in the air has been the subject of more books and articles than virtually any other aspect of the Great War, and by way of proof James Philip

Noffsinger's *World War I Aviation Books in English: An Annotated Bibliography* (1987) lists 1,663 books and pamphlets. For naval operations Arthur Marder's annotated bibliography appended to the final volume of his magisterial *From the Dreadnought to Scapa Flow* (1970) is, to apply a naval term, first rate.

The catalogue of the substantial and broad-based Joseph M. Bruccoli Great War Collection, established by Matthew J. Bruccoli at the University of Virginia in 1965 in honour of his father, a Great War veteran, is a very recent addition to the bibliography of the war and, as well as straightforward printed matter, includes film and video material.

The Second World War

On the whole the Second World War has been less well served by bibliography than has the Great War. The flood of printed matter from 1939 to 1945 exceeded that of 1914 to 1918, but there appears to have been less desire to record, classify, describe and prepare readers' guides and checklists.

Janet Ziegler's 1971 compilation *World War II: Books in English, 1945-1965* was apparently the first attempt at something approaching a major bibliography, and even this omits all wartime publications, works of less than 50 pages and several other categories. Arthur Funk's *A Select Bibliography of books on the Second World War Published in the US 1966-75* (1978) acts as a supplement to Ziegler.

A. G. S. Enser's *A Subject Bibliography of the Second World War: Books in English 1939-1974* (1977) has the immense advantage over Ziegler of including wartime publications, but as with his First World War bibliography (see above) it should be treated with care. A supplementary volume covering 1975-83 appeared in 1985.

The massive contribution of the Soviet Union to the defeat of Nazism is only becoming properly appreciated in the West now that the Soviet Union itself is dead and its archives are being opened to historians. For published Soviet works, *The USSR in World War II: An Annotated Bibliography of Books Published in the Soviet Union, 1945-1975, with an Addenda for the Years 1975-1980* by Michael Parrish (2 Vols, 1981) provides comprehensive reference. The partisan war is covered in Alexander Dallin's *The German Occupation in World War II: A Bibliography* (1955).

The Third Reich, especially its armed forces down to the last nut and bolt, and Nazism, continue to provide apparently endless subjects for books, many attempting to square the circle of the contradictions inherent in a demonstrably invincible military force that went down not just to defeat but to virtual extirpation. Despite its age, *The Nazi Era 1919-1945 – A Select Bibliography of Published Works from the Early Roots to 1980* by Helen Kehr and Janet Langmaid (1980) remains a key source for works in English and German, not least because the compilers had personal knowledge of almost all the books they describe.

The work of the Ministry of Information, the public face of British propaganda, included the publication by the Stationery Office of around 60 wrapped booklets in different formats describing various aspects of the British, Commonwealth and Allied war effort. *A Bibliography of WW2 HMSO Paperbacks* by A. R. James (1993) reveals their diversity and makes clear their probable value to the historian, not least for their pictorial content.

Naval operations are dealt with by Derek G. Law in his *The Royal Navy in World War Two: An Annotated Bibliography* (1988) and by Myron J. Smith in *World War II at Sea: A Bibliography of Sources in English* (3 Vols, 1976).

The fiction of the war is carefully delineated in *The Novels of World War Two: An annotated bibliography of World War Two fiction* by Michael Paris (1990), which is arranged in an annotated chronological list of over 2,000 novels with subject, author and title indexes. Catherine W. Reilly's *English Poetry of the Second World War: a biobibliography* [sic] appeared in 1986.

I have not used the US Army Military History Institute's four-volume *Second World War bibliography* (1977-79), but it has been reported as being both comprehensive and sensibly arranged.

Finally, although not a bibliography, the Third Revised Edition of *The Second World War: A Guide to Documents in the Public Record Office* by John D. Cantwell (1998) is indispensable, not only as an archive guide, but also as a guide to the structure of the British Government in wartime and the interrelation between its departments.

Both World Wars and general sources

Despite its age, the *Bibliographic Guide to the Two World Wars: An Annotated Survey of English-Language Reference Materials* (1977) by Dr Gwyn M. Bayliss, remains an outstandingly useful work of reference. It is logically arranged, provided with comprehensive author, title, regional/country and subject indexes and, most important of all, has incisive annotations by Dr Bayliss who, as Keeper of the Department of Printed Books at the Imperial War Museum, had practical experience of the books he describes.

Of much the same vintage and of equal value is *The Two World Wars: A Guide to Manuscript Collections in the United Kingdom* by S. L. Mayer and W. J. Koenig (1976), which surveys primary source material in libraries, archives and record offices.

As well as having its Library Catalogs, listing 1.3 million volumes, reproduced in over 70 volumes in the 1960s and 1970s, the Hoover Institution on War, Revolution and Peace, founded at Stanford University in 1919 by President Herbert Hoover, has produced numerous checklists and bibliographies based on its holdings, including a comprehensive Guide to its remarkable archive (1980). Not surprisingly, North American material makes up more than 50 per cent of the collection, but it does have strong Russian and East European holdings, and among the British materials are over 180 boxes of propaganda material from the Ministry of Information Library given to the Institution by the Foreign Office in 1920.

The substantial holdings of the Liddell Hart Centre for Military Archives at King's College, London, including 1,000 boxes of Sir Basil Liddell Hart's own papers, are noted briefly in its *Consolidated List of Accessions* (1986) and a Supplement (1990).

Although out of date in certain respects, *A Guide to the Sources of British Military History* (1972) and *Sources in American Military History* (1975), both edited by Robin Higham, continue to have far more than a curiosity or antiquarian value. Revised and enlarged editions would be a boon to military historians, as would an updated version of the same editor's *Official Histories: Essays and Bibliographies from around the World* (1970). A *Handbook of American Military History* (1996), edited by Jerry K. Sweeney, arranged in six chronological sections, each provided with an introductory essay, biographical notes and annotated select bibliography, is a useful concise reference, but suffers from the lack of an index.

For those who not only wish to study the books they have identified but also wish to own them, there are the ranks of booksellers specialising in out-of-print military history. Fearing that I will leave myself open to the quite justified accusation of blowing the trumpet of the trade to which I belong, I offer instead the opinion of Michael Sadleir, the noted publisher, book-collector and bibliographer. He wrote of the 'highly individualised class of Specialist Bookseller, to whom you will learn to apply when the needs of your collection chance to correspond with the scope of his speciality ... who knows the difficult titles under his particular heading, who is more likely than anyone else to have the exact book you're looking for. *This man can help you more than any reference book.*' (My italics)

A growing number of dealers specialising in military history (both new and second-hand) now list their stock on the internet, and sophisticated searching by many criteria is becoming easier and easier. However, for most dealers the printed catalogue remains the main platform of their business and, even when thoroughly out of date as a record of stock in hand, such catalogues remain valuable sources of information. The catalogue of the Barry D. Maurer Collection, *The Literature of the Great War*, produced by the William Reese Company in 1995, is a case in point.

Endnote
The scope for further detailed bibliographical research on the two World Wars is almost limitless and, like Sidney Webb, 'I stoutly maintain that every orderly arranged bibliography, however incomplete, will be of use to somebody'.

Checklist

'A selected list of books of which it may be useful to know the correct titles.'

Major-General Sir J. F. Maurice

The following works are listed in the order in which they appear in the chapter. All are published in London unless otherwise stated.

First World War
Lange, F. W. T. and Berry, W. T., *Books on the Great War: An Annotated Bibliography of Literature issued during the European Conflict*, Vols I-III [in one vol] (Grafton & Co, 1915)

Lange, F. W. T., *Books on the Great War: An Annotated Bibliography of Literature issued during the European Conflict*, Vol IV (Grafton & Co, 1916)

Prothero, Sir George W., *A Select Analytical List of Books Concerning the Great War* (HMSO, 1923)

Subject Index of the Books Relating to the European War, 1914-1918, Acquired by the British Museum, 1914-1920 (British Museum, 1922)

Meyer, Herman H. B. (comp), *A Check List of the Literature and Other Material in the Library of Congress on the European War* (Washington: Government Printing Office, 1918)

Monthly List of Official Publications (HMSO, 1897-1922)

Monthly List of Parliamentary Publications (HMSO, 1897-1922)

General Index to the Bills, Reports and Papers Printed by Order of the House of Commons and to the Reports and Papers Presented by Command 1900 to 1948-49 (HMSO, 1960)

Catalogue of War Literature issued by HM Government, *1914-1919* (HMSO, 1921)

Schedule of Wellington House Literature [and 'Continuations'] (Wellington House, 1917-18)

Library of German War Literature attached to MI7(B) (War Office, 1917)

Report on the Propaganda Library [War Office, 1917]; Appendix I: 'Propaganda Chiefly Relating to Nationalities'; Appendix II: 'Germany and America' [War Office, 1917]

Bulkley, M. E., *Bibliographical Survey of Contemporary Sources for the Economic and Social History of the War* (Oxford: Clarendon Press for The Carnegie Endowment for International Peace, 1922)

Dearle, N. B., *Dictionary of Official War-Time Organizations* (Oxford University Press for The Carnegie Endowment for International Peace, 1928)

Jenkinson, Hilary, *Archive Administration, including the problems of War Archives and Archive Making* (1922)

Hall, Hubert, *British Archives and the Sources for the History of the World War* (1925)

Leland, Waldo G. and Mereness, Newton D., *Introduction to the American Official Sources for the Economic and Social History of the World War* (New Haven: Yale University Press for The Carnegie Endowment for the Economic and Social History of the World War, 1926)

Catalogue of the War Poetry Collection (Birmingham: Birmingham Public Libraries Reference Department, 1921)

Dawson, Loleta I. and Huntting, Marion Davis, *European War Fiction in English and Personal Narratives – Bibliographies* (Boston: F. W. Faxon Co, 1921)

Falls, Capt Cyril, *War Books: A Critical Guide* (Peter Davies, 1930; 2nd ed, with new intro and additional entries by R. J. Wyatt, Greenhill Books, 1989)

Blunden, Edmund, Falls, Cyril, Tomlinson, H. M. and Wright, R., Intro by Edmund Blunden, *The War 1914-1918: a booklist* (The Reader [1930])

Rare Books in English Literature and a supplement of War Books, Intro by H. M. Tomlinson (Catalogue 47, Elkin Mathews Ltd, 1932)

Vic, Jean, *La Littérature de Guerre: Manuel Méthodique et Critique des Publications de Langue Française* (Paris: Payot, 1918-23)

Leblanc, Henri, *Collection Henri Leblanc: La Grande Guerre: Iconographie – Bibliographie – Documents Divers. Catalogue Raisonné…*, 8 Vols (Paris: Emil-Paul Frères, 1916-22)

Cru, J. N., *Témoins: Essai d'analyse et de critique des souvenirs de combattants édités en française de 1915 á 1928* (Paris: 'Les Étincelles', 1929)

Kunz, Dr J. L., *Bibliographie Der Kriegsliteratur (Politik, Geschichte, Philosophie, Volkerrecht, Friedensfrage)* (Berlin: Hans Robert Engelmann Verlag, 1920)

Dubois, Jean, *Catalogue Méthodique du Fonds Allemand de la Bibliothèque* (Paris: Etienne Chiron (Vol I); Alfred Costes (Vols II-IV), 1921-23)

Michel, Paul-Henri, *Catalogue Méthodique du Fonds Italien de la Bibliothéque* (Paris: Alfred Costes, 1923)

Kerr, W. B., *Historical Literature on Canada's Participation in the Great War*; reprinted from *The Canadian Historical Review*, December 1933. Supplements were published in the same journal in June 1934 and September1935.

Bond, Brian (ed), *The First World War and British Military History* (Oxford: Clarendon Press, 1991)

The New York Public Library Reference Department Subject Catalog of the World War I Collection, 4 Vols (Boston: G. K. Hall & Co, 1961)

Enser, A. G. S., *A Subject Bibliography of the First World War: Books in English 1914-1978* (Andre Deutsch, 1979; 2nd ed, rev and enl to 1987, Aldershot: Gower, 1990)

Schaffer, Ronald, *The United States in World War I: A Selected Bibliography* (Santa Barbara, Ca: Oxford, 1978)

Woodward, David R. and Maddox, Robert Franklin, *America and World War I: A Selected Annotated Bibliography of English-Language Sources* (New York, London: Garland Publishing, 1985)

Genthe, Charles V., *American War Narratives 1917-1918: A Study and Bibliography* (New York: David Lewis, 1969)

Scholz, Hermine, 'World War I – Manuscripts – The World War I Survey' (Special Bibliography 20, Vol I) (Carlisle Barracks, Pennsylvania: US Army Military History Institute, 1986)

Hager, Philip E. and Taylor, Desmond, *The Novels of World War I: An Annotated Bibliography* (New York, London: Garland Publishing, 1981)

Reilly, Catherine, *English Poetry of the First World War* (Prior, 1978)

Noffsinger, James Philip, *World War I: Aviation Books in English: An Annotated Bibliography* (Metuchen, NJ, London: Scarecrow Press, 1987)

Marder, Arthur J., *From the Dreadnought to Scapa Flow: The Royal Navy in the Fisher Era, 1904-1919*, Vol V: 'Victory and Aftermath (January 1918-June 1919)' (Oxford University Press, 1970)

Berkeley, Edmund (comp), *The Joseph M. Bruccoli Great War Collection in the University of Virginia Library* (Columbia, SC, M. J. B[ruccoli]., 1999)

Second World War

Ziegler, Janet (comp), *World War II: Books in English, 1945-1965* (Stanford, Ca: Hoover Institution Press, 1971)

Funk, Arthur L. (ed), *A Select Bibliography of Books on the Second World War published in the US 1966-75* (New York: MA-AH, 1978)

Enser, A. G. S., *A Subject Bibliography of the Second World War: Books in English 1939-1974* (Andre Deutsch, 1977)

A Subject Bibliography of the Second World War: Books in English 1975-1983 (Aldershot: Gower Publishing, 1985)

Parrish, Michael E., *The USSR in World War II: An Annotated Bibliography of Books Published in the Soviet Union, 1945-1975, with an Addenda for the Years 1975-1980* (New York, London: Garland, 1981)

Dallin, Alexander, *The German Occupation of the USSR in World War II: A Bibliography* (Washington: Department of State, Office of Intelligence Research, External Research Paper No 122, 1955)

James, A. R., *A Bibliography of WW2 HMSO Paperbacks: Being a Bibliography of His Majesty's Stationery Office series of publications in paperback and wrappers dealing with contemporary aspects of World War Two...* (Southwick, Sussex: A. R. James, 1993)

Law, Derek G., *The Royal Navy in World War Two: An Annotated Bibliography* (Greenhill Books, 1988)

Smith, Myron J., *World War II at Sea: A Bibliography of Sources in English*, 3 Vols (Metuchen, NJ, Scarecrow Press, 1976)

Paris, Michael, *The Novels of World War Two: An annotated bibliography of World War Two fiction* (Library Association, 1990)

Cantwell, John D., *The Second World War: A Guide to Documents in the Public Record Office* (Kew: Public Record Office, 1998, 3rd ed, rev)

US Army Military History Institute, Special Bibliographic Series No 16, *World War II*, Vol I 'General Histories' by Roy Barnard and others (1977); Vol II 'Pacific War' by Duane Ryan (1978); Vol III 'Eastern and Balkan Fronts' by Laszlo M. Alfoldi (1978); Vol IV 'Western Europe – Mediterranean' by Louise Arnold (1979) (Carlisle Barracks, Pennsylvania)

Both World Wars and general sources

Bayliss, Gwyn M., *Bibliographic Guide to the Two World Wars: An Annotated Survey of English-Language Reference Materials* (London, New York: Bowker, 1977)

Mayer, S. L. and Koenig, W. J., *The Two World Wars: A Guide to Manuscript Collections in the United Kingdom* (London, New York: Bowker, 1976)

Library Catalogs of the Hoover Institution on War, Revolution, and Peace, Stanford University, 63 Vols (Boston: G. K. Hall & Co, 1969). A supplement covering Serials and Newspapers was published in 1969 (3 Vols) and first and second general Supplements in 1972 (5 Vols) and 1977 (6 Vols).

Palm, Charles G. and Reed, Dale, *Guide to the Hoover Institution Archives* (Stanford: Hoover Institution Press, 1980)

King's College, London, Liddell Hart Centre for Military Archives, *Consolidated List of Accessions* (University of London, 1986); Supplement 1 August 1985-1 November 1990 (University of London, 1990)

Higham, Robin (ed), *A Guide to the Sources of British Military History* (Routledge & Kegan Paul, 1972)

(ed), *Sources in American Military History* (Hamden, CT: Archon Books, 1975)

(ed), *Official Histories: Essays and Bibliographies from around the World* (Manhattan, Kans: Kansas State University Library, 1970)

Sweeney, Jerry K. (ed), *A Handbook of American Military History: From the Revolutionary War to the Present* (Boulder, Col: Westview Press, 1996)

The contributors

Professor Margaret Atack, The University of Leeds, UK
Vol 1, Chap 30 The experience of occupation: Northern France
Margaret Atack is Professor of French at the University of Leeds. Her publications include *Literature and the French Resistance: Cultural Politics and Narrative Forms 1940-1950* (1989), *Contemporary French Fiction by Women: Feminist Perspectives* (co-editor, 1991) and *May 68 in French Fiction and Film: Rethinking Society, Rethinking Representation* (1999).

Dr Stephen Badsey, Royal Military Academy, Sandhurst, UK
Vol 1, Chap 3 The experience of manipulation: propaganda in press and radio
Stephen Badsey is Senior Lecturer in the Department of War Studies at the Royal Military Academy, Sandhurst. He is the author or editor of more than 30 books and articles on military history and defence studies covering the period from the mid-19th century to the present day, including *The Gulf War Assessed* (with John Pimlott) and *The Media and International Security*.

Dr Niall J. A. Barr, Joint Services Command and Staff College, UK
Vol 1 Chap 7 The Desert War experience
Dr Barr is a Lecturer at King's College, London, based at the Joint Services Command and Staff College. He is an authority on the history of the British veterans' movement and has a deep interest in the history of both World Wars. Having recently worked with J. P. Harris on a collaborative study, *Amiens to the Armistice: The BEF in the Hundred Days Campaign 8 August-11 November 1918*, he is currently researching the Alamein campaign of 1942.

Lieutenant-Colonel Sir John Baynes Bt, independent military historian
Vol 1, Chap 2 Preparing for war: the experience of the Cameronians
Sir John Baynes served in the British Regular Army with the Cameronians (Scottish) Rifles and the Queen's Own Highlanders. He has written numerous military biographies and related books, and is best known for his outstanding work, *Morale: A Study of Men and Courage: The Second Scottish Rifles at the Battle of Neuve Chapelle* (1987)

Professor Joan Beaumont, Deakin University, Victoria, Australia
Vol 2, Chap 13 Australia
Joan Beaumont is Professor of History and Dean of Arts at Deakin University, Victoria, Australia. Among her publications are *Australia's War, 1914-18* (1995)

and *Australia's War, 1939-45* (1996), *Gull Force: Survival and Leadership in Captivity, 1941-45* (1988), and *The Defence Centenary History: Sources and Statistics* (forthcoming, 2001). She is a fellow of the Academy of Social Sciences of Australia.

Dr Eric M. Bergerud, Lincoln University, San Francisco, USA
Vol 1, Chap 8 War in the Pacific
Eric Bergerud received a PhD at the University of California, Berkeley, in 1981. He is now Professor of History at Lincoln University in Oakland, California. His works include *Dynamics of Defeat: The Vietnam War in Hau Nghia Province* (Boulder, CO and Oxford: Westview Press, 1991); *Red Thunder, Tropic Lightning: The World of a Combat Division in Vietnam* (Boulder, CO, and Oxford: Westview Press, 1993); and, most recently, *Fire in the Sky: The Air War in the South Pacific* (Boulder, CO, and Oxford: Westview Press, 2000).

Dr Sanjoy Bhattacharya, Sheffield Hallam University, UK
Vol 2, Chap 12 Colonial India: conflict, shortage and discontent
Sanjoy Bhattacharya is a Wellcome Research Fellow attached to the Department of History and the Cultural Research Institute, Sheffield Hallam University. He has published a number of articles on colonial India, and has recently completed a monograph, *'A Necessary Weapon of War': State Policies towards Propaganda and Information in Eastern India, 1939-45* (Richmond: Curzon Press, 2000). He also contributed to *At the Eleventh Hour*. He is currently working on a jointly authored book, *The Control and Eradication of Smallpox in India, 1900-1975*.

Paul M. Binding, independent author, Ludlow, UK
Vol 2, Chap 20 The Netherlands and Sweden: the experience of neutrality
Paul Binding lectured in a Swedish University (Umeå) in the 1970s and has maintained a regular relationship with Sweden ever since, visiting it during the 1990s, frequently under the auspices of cultural and press organisations, to lecture and to report, as often as three times a year. He covered the pivotal 1994 Swedish elections for the *New Statesman*. In 1996 he was awarded a prize by the Swedish Writers' Union for his work promoting interest abroad in Swedish literature. He edited and wrote the greater part of the *Babel Guide to Scandinavian Fiction in Translation* (1999). A novelist, critic and memoirist, he is a frequent contributor to the *Times Literary Supplement* and the *Independent on Sunday*, and is a Senior Associate Member of St Antony's College, Oxford, for 2000.

Professor Nick Bosanquet, Imperial College, University of London, UK
Vol 1, Chap 18 Casualties and British medical services
Nick Bosanquet is Professor of Health Policy at Imperial College. He is a health economist and formerly worked at the Centre for Health Economics at the University of York. He is a special advisor to the House of Commons Select Committee on Health Services. He contributed to *Facing Armageddon* (1996) and lists among his leisure pursuits visiting battlefields, and brainstorming with Americans and others about military history.

Professor Joanna Bourke, Birkbeck College, University of London, UK
Vol 1, Chap 16 The experience of killing
Professor Bourke is the author of *Dismembering the Male: Men's Bodies, Britain and the Great War* (1997) and *An Intimate History of Killing* (1999), as well as books on Irish history and the British working classes. She is currently writing a history of fear in the 19th and 20th centuries.

Dr J. M. Bourne, The University of Birmingham, UK
Vol 1, Chap 1 A personal reflection on the two World Wars
John Bourne has taught History at the University of Birmingham since 1979. He thought that the publication of *Britain and the Great War* (London: Edward Arnold, 1989, 1991) would be his first and last on that conflict, but he was mistaken. During the last ten years his work has become increasingly focused on the British Army during the First World War and he is currently completing a revisionist study of the British Western Front generals.

Dr Bob Bushaway, The University of Birmingham, UK
Vol 2, Chap 30 The Obligation of Remembrance or the Remembrance of Obligation: society and the memory of World War
Dr Bushaway is Director of Research Support and Business Development at the University of Birmingham. He is best known for his work on popular culture. He is the author of *By Rite: Custom, Ceremony and Community in England 1700-1880* (198?), but he has long been fascinated by the Great War. His article 'Name upon Name: The Great War and Remembrance' was published in *Myths of the English*, edited by Roy Porter, in 1992. He broadcasts regularly on radio and television and is an associate member of the Department of Modern History at the University of Birmingham. He is a fellow of the Royal Historical Society and of the Royal Anthropological Institute.

Peter Caddick-Adams, Cranfield University, UK
Vol 2, Chap 8 The Western Balkans
Peter Caddick-Adams was educated at Shrewsbury School. He was commissioned in the Staffordshire Regiment in 1979 and joined the Territorial Army in 1985. He took a degree in War Studies at the University of Wolverhampton as a mature student. He did two tours in Bosnia with the peacekeeping forces, including a stint as official historian. He is currently Lecturer in the Strategic Studies Institute at Cranfield University. He is the author of *By God They Can Fight! A History of 143rd Infantry Brigade 1908 to 1995* (1995). He is currently working on a study of the Yugoslav wars for London Books.

Professor George H. Cassar, Eastern Michigan University, Ypsilanti, Michigan, USA
Vol 1, Chap 21 Political leaders in wartime: Lloyd George and Churchill
Professor Cassar's extensive publications on various aspects of the First World War include *Asquith as War Leader* (1994) and the *Forgotten Front: The British Campaign in Italy 1917-18* (1998). He is currently completing a study on *Kitchener and British Strategy, 1914-1916*.

Dr Martin Ceadel, New College, University of Oxford, UK
Vol 2, Chap 27 The opposition to war
Martin Ceadel has been Fellow and Tutor in Politics at New College, Oxford, since 1979 and is currently Acting Head of the Department of Politics and International Relations at Oxford University. He has published three books on various aspects of the British peace movement, including most recently *The Origins of War Prevention: The British Peace Movement and International Relations, 1730-1854* (1996). His next book is *Semi-Detached Idealist: The British Peace Movement and International Relations, 1854-1945*, to be published in December 2000.

Dr Hugh Cecil, The University of Leeds, UK
Vol 2, Chap 22 British fiction
Hugh Cecil is Senior Lecturer in History at Leeds University and a Fellow of the Royal Society of Literature. His works include *The Flower of Battle: British Fiction Writers of the First World War*, and (with his wife Mirabel) *Clever Hearts*, the life of the journalist Desmond McCarthy, which won the 1990 Duff Cooper Memorial Prize and the Marsh Biography Award. He was co-editor, with Peter Liddle, of *Facing Armageddon: The First World War Experienced*. He and his wife are currently writing a joint life of Lord Edward Cecil and Lady Edward Cecil.

Professor Emeritus James J. Cooke, University of Mississippi, Oxford, Mississippi, USA
Vol 1, Chap 13 The experience of being abroad: doughboys and GIs in Europe
Vol 2, Chap 10 America
Professor Cooke is the author of *The Rainbow Division in the Great War* (1994), *The US Air Service in the Great War* (1996), *Pershing and His Generals* (1997) and *The All-Americans at War* (1999). He contributed to *Facing Armageddon* (1996) and *At the Eleventh Hour* (1998). He is a Fellow of the Royal Historical Society.

Mark Derez, The Catholic University of Leuven, Belgium
Vol 1, Chap 29 The experience of occupation: Belgium
Mark Derez is an archivist whose speciality is the history of the University. He contributed to *Facing Armageddon* (1996), *Passchendaele in Perspective* (1997) and *At the Eleventh Hour* (1998).

Dr Philip Dine, Loughborough University, UK
Vol 2, Chap 18 The French Empire
Philip Dine is Senior Lecturer in French, Department of European Studies, Loughborough University. His research centres on the political, social and cultural reordering of France since 1945, with particular reference to the representations of decolonisation, sport and leisure, and popular culture. He is the author of *Images of the Algerian War: French Fiction and Film, 1954-1992* (Oxford: Clarendon Press, 1994) and is currently completing a social history of French rugby football.

Professor John Erickson, The University of Edinburgh, UK
Vol 1, Chap 24 General Brusilov and Marshal Zhukov, June 1916 and June 1944
John Erickson FBA FRSE FRSA is Emeritus Professor of Higher Defence Studies

and Honorary Fellow in Defence Studies in the University of Edinburgh. He is the author of *The Soviet High Command 1918-41* (1962; 1984), *The Road to Stalingrad, The Road to Berlin* (1975, 1998, 2000), *The Soviet Armed Forces 1918-1992: A Research Guide to Soviet Sources* (1996) (with L. Erickson) and editor of *BARBAROSSA, The Axis and the Allies* (1994) (with David Dilks).

Professor M. R. D. Foot, formerly Professor of History, University of Manchester, UK
Vol 1, Chap 19 Spies, codebreakers and secret agents
M. R. D. Foot, an army officer all through the war against Hitler, sometime Professor of Modern History at Manchester University, has written on Gladstone, resistance, escape, and the SOE. He helped Ian Dear with the *Oxford Companion to the Second World War* (Oxford: Oxford University Press, 1995).

Professor Imanuel Geiss, University of Bremen, Germany
Vol 2, Chap 22 Reflections on war in the 20th century
Imanuel Geiss became known to an international audience for his work on the origins of the First World War, *July 1914*, first published in English in 1967. His recent work includes a multi-volume world history, *Geschicte griffbereit* (1993). He also contributed to *Facing Armageddon* (1994) and *At the Eleventh Hour* (1998).

Professor Guy S. Goodwin-Gill, Wolfson College, University of Oxford, UK
Vol 1, Chap 32 The experience of displacement: refugees and war
Guy Goodwin-Gill is an international lawyer and Director of the Centre for Socio-Legal Studies, Oxford. He is the author of *The Refugee in International Law* (Oxford: Clarendon Press, 1983, 1996) and *The Role of the Child in Armed Conflict* (Oxford: Clarendon Press, 1994) (with Ilene Cohn).

Professor Paul Gough, University of the West of England, Bristol, UK
Vol 2, Chap 21 'A war of the imagination': the experience of the British artist
Paul Gough is a painter, broadcaster and writer. As a painter he is represented in many public and private collections, including the Imperial War Museum and the National War Museum, Ottawa. Since completing his PhD on First World War British art (1991) he has published widely on war art, commemoration and the aesthetics of conflict. Among his broadcasting work he has made documentaries on military sketching and on the photographer Don McCullin. He was appointed Dean of the Faculty of Arts, Media and Design at the University of the West of England in January 2000.

Dr Christina J. M. Goulter
Vol 1, Chap 6 War in the air: the bomber crew
Christina J. M. Goulter was educated at the University of Canterbury, New Zealand, and King's College, London, where she took her PhD in 1993. She worked for two years as a historian at the Ministry of Defence, London, and was later Associate Visiting Professor of Strategy at the United States Naval War College. She is the author of *A Forgotten Offensive: Royal Air Force Coastal Command's Anti-Shipping Campaign, 1940-1945* (London: Frank Cass, 1995).

Dr Irene Guerrini, The Library, Genoa University, Italy
Vol 2, Chap 7 Italy: extreme crisis, resistance and recovery
Irene Guerrini works collaboratively on Italian popular writing during the 20th century and has published articles on the 'organisation of consent' during the Fascist period. Her book on the celebrated Italian fighter pilot, Francesco Baracca, is to be published in 2000. She is currently working on a book about Italian military justice during the First World War.

Dr Heinz Hagenlücke, Heinrich Heine University, Düsseldorf, Germany
Vol 2, Chap 4 The home front in Germany
Heinz Hagenlücke has published on aspects of German party political activity in the 19th and 20th centuries, *Die Deutsche Vaterlandspartei* (1996). He contributed to *Passchendaele in Perspective* and *At The Eleventh Hour*. He is currently working to produce a published edition of Wolfgang Kapp's 1914-18 papers.

Professor Eric Hopkins, The University of Wolverhampton, UK
Vol 2, Chap 1 British children in wartime.
Eric Hopkins has taught in secondary schools, in teacher training and in the University of Birmingham, where he is an Honorary Senior Research Fellow in Economic and Social History and a Fellow of the Institute for Advanced Research in the Arts and Social Sciences. He is currently Visiting Professor at the University of Wolverhampton. His latest book is a biography of the politician and First World War propagandist, *Charles Masterman, Politician and Journalist: The Splendid Failure* (Lampeter: Edwin Mellen Press, 1999).

Dr David Jordan, Joint Services Command and Staff College, Bracknell, UK
Vol 1, Chap 5 War in the air: the fighter pilot
Dr Jordan is a Lecturer at King's College London, based at the Joint Services Command and Staff College. He was educated at St Edmund Hall, Oxford, and the University of Birmingham, where he took his doctorate. He specialises in air power and international relations and is currently writing a book on the development of tactical air power in the First World War.

Professor Tarif Khalidi, King's College, University of Cambridge, UK
Vol 2, Chap 19 The Arab world
Tarif Khalidi is Sir Thomas Adams Professor of Arabic and Fellow of King's College, Cambridge. His most recent publication is *Arabic Historical Thought in the Classical Period* (Cambridge: Cambridge University Press, 1994). *The Muslim Gospel: The Sayings and Stories of Jesus in Arabic Islamic Literature* is due to appear in early 2001, published by Harvard University Press.

Dr Sergei Kudryashov, Editor-in-chief of the archival journal *Istocnik*, Moscow, Russia
Vol 2, Chap 6 The impact of war on Russian society
Sergei Kudryashov trained as a military historian at the Russian Academy of Sciences and has published extensively on the history of the Second World War. His major study, *German Occupation of the USSR and Collaboration*, is due for publication in 2001.

Professor Tony Lane, Cardiff University, UK
Vol 1, Chap 4 The merchant seaman at war
Tony Lane is Director of the Seafarers International Research Centre at Cardiff University. He has written extensively on merchant seafarers in the 19th and 20th centuries, including *The Merchant Seaman's War* (1990).

Dr Diana Lary, University of British Columbia, Canada
Vol 2, Chap 11 China
Diana Lary is Professor of Modern Chinese History at the University of British Columbia and the Director of the Centre of Chinese Research.

Dr Klaus Latzel, University of Bielefeld, Germany
Vol 1, Chap 14 German soldiers in victory, 1914 and 1940
Klaus Latzel is a member of the Faculty of Sociology at the University of Bielefeld. His main areas of research are the history of the First and Second World Wars, and the history and theory of sociology. His most recent books are: *Deutsche Soldaten – nationalsozialistischer Krieg? Kriegserlebnis-Kriegserfahrung 1939-1945* (Paderborn: Schoeningh, 1998) and, as editor, *Georg Simmel, Aufsätze und Abhandlungen 1908-1918,* Vol 1 (Frankfort/M: Suhrkamp, 2000). He is co-editor-in-chief of *Simmel Studies.*

Dr Mark Levene, The University of Warwick, UK
Vol 1, Chap 33 The experience of genocide: Armenia 1915-16 and Romania 1941-42
Mark Levene is Senior Lecturer in History at the University of Warwick, where he specialises in Jewish history and comparative genocide. His publications include *War, Jews and the new Europe: The Diplomacy of Lucien Wolf, 1914-1919* (Oxford: 1992) and *The Massacre in History* (Oxford: 1999), co-edited with Penny Roberts.

Dr Peter H. Liddle, Director of the Second World War Experience Centre, Leeds, UK
Vol 1, Chap 17 The experience of captivity: British and Commonwealth prisoners in Germany
Peter Liddle was appointed Director of the Second World War Experience Centre in 1999, having been founder and Keeper of the Liddle Collection in the University of Leeds. The Centre's mission is to save and make available evidence of personal experience in the 1939-45 war. Dr Liddle has written or edited many books on the Great War, including studies of Gallipoli, the Somme and Third Ypres. His most recent book, with Richard Campbell Begg, is on the Second World War, *For Five Shillings a Day.*

Professor S. P. MacKenzie, The University of South Carolina, Columbia, USA
Vol 1, Chap 17 The experience of captivity: British and Commonwealth prisoners in Germany
S. P. Mackenzie is Associate Professor of History at the University of South Carolina. He is the author of several war-related books, among them *The Home Guard* (1995) and *British War Films* (2000), as well as a number of articles on POW affairs. He is currently examining the development of the Colditz phenomenon.

Malcolm Mackintosh CMG, independent historian and author
Vol 1, Chap 12 Partisans and guerrillas
Malcolm Mackintosh saw service in the Middle East, Italy and the Balkans during
the Second World War, latterly as a British Liaison Officer with the Soviet Army
in Bulgaria. He later worked for the BBC Overseas Service, then the Foreign and
Commonwealth Office and finally the Cabinet Office, specialising in Soviet and
East European affairs. He is a graduate of Glasgow University and the author of
books on the foreign policy of the Soviet Union and the Soviet armed forces.

Dr Bob Moore, University of Sheffield, UK
Vol 2, Chap 20 The Netherlands and Sweden: the experience of neutrality
Bob Moore is Lecturer in Modern History at the University of Sheffield and has
recently published extensively on the history of The Netherlands and on the Second
World War. Recent works include *Victims and Survivors: The Nazi Persecution of the
Jews in the Netherlands* (1997) and *Resistance in Western Europe* (2000).

Dr Bill Nasson, University of Cape Town, Republic of South Africa
Vol 2, Chap 16 South Africa
Bill Nasson is a Professor of History in the Department of Historical Studies at the
University of Cape Town. He has published on the South African War, 1899-
1902, and on South African experience in the First World War, including *The
South African War 1899-1902* (1999) and *Uyadela Wen'osulapho: Black
Participation in the Anglo-Boer War* (1999). He contributed to *Passchendaele in
Perspective* and *At the Eleventh Hour*.

Robin Neillands, independent historian and author, Marlborough, UK
Vol 1, Chap 15 The experience of defeat: Kut (1916) and Singapore (1942)
Robin Neillands is a journalist, writer and popular historian. Hs books include *A
Fighting Retreat: Military Campaigns in the British Empire 1947-1997* (1997), *The
Conquest of the Reich, 1945* (1995) and *The Great War Generals on the Western Front*
(1998). His next book concerns Sir Arthur Harris and the combined bomber
offensive.

Dr Dean F. Oliver, Canadian War Museum, Ottawa, Canada
Vol 2, Chap 15 Canada: fact and fancy
Dean F. Oliver is Senior Historian at the Canadian War Museum and an Adjunct
Research Professor at the Norman Paterson School of International Affairs,
Carleton University. He is the contributor on foreign and defence policy for the
Canadian Annual Review of Politics and Public Affairs, editor of *Studies in Canadian
Military History* and co-author (with Laura Brandon) of *Canvas of War: Painting the
Canadian Experience, 1914-1945* (Vancouver: Douglas & McIntyre, 2000).

Stephen Parker, The University of Birmingham, UK
Vol 2, Chap 25 Keeping faith and coping: belief, popular religiosity and the British people
Stephen Parker is a postgraduate student at the University of Birmingham,
Westhill, researching a doctoral thesis 'Faith on the Home Front', a study of the
role of the churches and the significance of religious belief in Birmingham during
the Second World War.

Professor Phillip Parotti, Sam Houston State University, Huntsville, Texas, USA
Vol 1, Chap 9 War in the Tropics: East Africa and Burma.
Professor Parotti graduated from the United States Naval Academy in 1863, served four years at sea, and enrolled at the University of New Mexico to pursue graduate studies, receiving his PhD in 1972. In addition to having published essays, professional articles, poetry and short fiction, he is the author of *The Greek Generals Talk: Memoirs of the Trojan War* (1986), *The Trojan Generals Talk: Memoirs of the Greek War* (1988), and a novel, *Fires in the Sky* (1990).

Cliff Pettit, independent historian and author, Alnwick, UK
Vol 1, Chap 2 Preparing for war: the experience of the Cameronians
Cliff Pettit is a retired solicitor who served as an infantry platoon commander in North West Europe in the later stages of the Second World War. He has an extensive knowledge of the First and Second World War battlefields of Western Europe, and has presented, advised and assisted in television documentaries on Gallipoli, the Somme and Third Ypres.

Dr William J. Philpott, London Guildhall University, UK
Vol 1, Chap 27 Coalition war: Britain and France
William Philpott is Principal Lecturer in International History at London Guildhall University. He has published *Anglo-French Relations and Strategy on the Western Front, 1914-1918* (Macmillan, 1996) and many articles on Anglo-French relations in the era of the two World Wars. He is currently co-editing a volume on *Anglo-French Defence Relations Between the Wars* with Professor Martin Alexander. He is a Fellow of the Royal Historical Society and a Member of the Council of the Army Records Society.

Dr Marco Pluviano, Italian Federation of Archives of Popular Writing, Genoa, Italy
Vol 2, Chap 7 Italy: extreme crisis, resistance and recovery
Marco Pluviano collaborates with the historical museum of Trento and has published widely in the area of soldier welfare and worker compliance in the First World War, and on the Italian people under Fascism. His book on the celebrated Italian fighter pilot, Francesco Baracca, is to be published in 2000. He is currently working on a book about Italian military justice during the First World War.

Dr Anita J. Prazmowska, London School of Economics, UK
Vol 1, Chap 31 The experience of occupation: Poland
Dr Prazmowska is Senior Lecturer in the Department of International History, London School of Economics. She is the author of *Britain, Poland and the Eastern Front, 1939* (Cambridge: Cambridge University Press, 1986), *Britain and Poland 1939-1943* (Cambridge: Cambridge University Press, 1995) and *Eastern Europe and the Outbreak of the Second World War* (Basingstoke: Macmillan, 2000). She is currently working on the establishment of communism in Poland, 1943-48.

Dr Christopher Pugsley, independent historian, Armidale, NSW, Australia
Vol 2, Chap 14 New Zealand: 'from the uttermost ends of the earth'
Christopher Pugsley is a former officer in the New Zealand Army and has

published widely on aspects of New Zealand military experience, including *Gallipoli: The New Zealand Story* (1984), and *On the Fringe of Hell: New Zealanders and Military Discipline in the First World War* (1991).

Dr Nicholas Saunders, University College, London, UK
Vol 2, Chap 29 Apprehending memory: material culture and war
Nicholas Saunders is a Lecturer in Material Culture in the Department of Anthropology, University College, London. He is currently also British Academy Institutional Fellow in the Department, making a study of the material culture of 20th-century war, especially 'Trench Art' of the Great War and inter-war years.

Peter T. Scott, independent historian and author, Sanderstead, UK
Vol 2, Chap 31 Bibliographic sources for the study of the two World Wars
Peter Scott has assisted the research of many through his knowledge of published work on the First World War. He was founding editor of *Stand To!: the Journal of the Western Front Association* and published his own highly regarded journal, *The Great War, 1914-18: an illustrated journal of First World War history* [1988-91]. His books on the First World War are *Home for Christmas: Cards, Messages and Legends of the Great War* and *Dishonoured: the 'Colonel's surrender' at St Quentin*.

Professor Gary W. Shanafelt, McMurry University, Abilene, Texas, USA
Vol 1, Chap 28 Coalition war: Germany and her Allies, Austria-Hungary and Italy
Professor Shanafelt received his doctorate from the University of California, Berkeley, in 1977. Since 1981 he has taught modern European history at McMurry University. His book *The Secret Enemy: Austria-Hungary and the German Alliance, 1914-1918* deals with Austrian political relations with Germany during the First World War. In addition to his interest in the Habsburg Monarchy, he has also published work on Edith Durham and her life in the Balkans before the war.

Ingrid Sharp, The University of Leeds, UK
Vol 2, Chap 5 'Frauen und Fraß': German women in wartime
Ingrid Sharp is Lecturer in German at the University of Leeds, where she has worked since 1989. Her areas of interest are in women's history, ranging from the birth and development of the women's movement in Germany, gender and culture at the *fin de siècle*, gender relations and two World Wars, to the position of women in the German Democratic Republic. Supported by funding from the AHRB, she is currently exploring the influence of Abolitionist ideas on attitudes to the regulation of sexuality in Germany from 1898 to 1933. She has published a number of articles on gender-related topics; her five-volume edition on the life and work of Josephine Butler, *Diseases of the Body Politic*, will be published in 2001 by Routledge as part of their *Feminist Forerunners* series.

Dr G. D. Sheffield, Joint Services Command and Staff College, Shrivenham, UK
Vol 1, Chap 25 Reflections on the experience of British generalship
Gary Sheffield is Senior Lecturer at King's College, London, based at the Joint Services Command and Staff College, where he is Land Warfare Historian on the Higher Command and Staff Course. He has written widely on the history of the two World Wars. His most recent publication is *Leadership in the Trenches: Officer-*

Man Relations, Morale and Discipline in the British Army in the era of the Great War (Basingstoke: Macmillan, 2000).

Dr Naoko Shimazu, Birkbeck College, University of London, UK
Vol 2, Chap 9 The experience of middle-class Japanese women
Naoko Shimazu is Lecturer in Japanese History at Birkbeck College, University of London. Her publications include *Japan, Race and Equality: The Racial Equality Proposal of 1919* (London: Routledge, 1998). She is currently working on a cultural history of the Russo-Japanese War, and on an international art exhibition project on Taiwanese cultural identities in the Japanese colonial period.

Professor Dennis E. Showalter, Colorado College, Colorado Springs, USA
Chapter 26 Coalition war: the Anglo-American experience
Dennis Showalter is Professor of History at Colorado College. He is President of the Society for Military History, joint editor of 'War in History', and a Patron of the Second World War Experience Centre. His relevant publications include *History in Dispute: World War II*, 2 Vols Detroit: St James, 2000) and *Tannenberg: Clash of Empires* (Hamden, CT: Archon, 1991).

Adam Smith, Scottish Museum of Flight, East Fortune, UK
Vol 2, Chap 2 The British experience of bombing
Adam Smith is Curator of the Scottish Museum of Flight, East Fortune, UK.

Dr Michael Snape, The University of Birmingham, UK
Vol 2, Chap 25 Keeping faith and coping: belief, popular religiosity and the British people
Michael Snape has published on the social history of religion in 18th-century England and is currently working on a social history of religion in the British Army from the War of the Spanish Succession to the end of the Second World War.

Professor Edward M. Spiers, The University of Leeds, UK
Vol 2, Chap 26 Ethics and weaponry
Edward M. Spiers is Professor of Strategic Studies at Leeds University. He has written several books on military history and contemporary strategic studies, including *Haldane: An Army Reformer* (1980), *The Army and Society, 1815-1914* (1980), *Radical General: Sir George de Lacy Evans, 1787-1870* (1983), *Chemical Warfare* (1985), *Chemical Weaponry: A Continuing Challenge* (1989) and *The Late Victorian Army, 1868-1902* (1992). He has been Chairman of the School of History at Leeds University and is currently Dean of Research for the Faculty of Arts.

Dr Matthew Taylor, De Montfort University, Leicester, UK
Vol 2, Chap 24 Leisure and entertainment
Matthew Taylor is Research Fellow in the International Centre for Sports History and Culture at De Montfort University, Leicester. He has published work on various aspects of British sport and recreation and is co-author of a forthcoming book on the international migration of professional footballers.

Professor Philip Taylor, The University of Leeds, UK
Vol 2, Chap 3 The experience of manipulation: propaganda in press and radio
Philip M. Taylor is Professor of International Communications and Director of the

Institute of Communications Studies at the University of Leeds. He is the author of numerous articles and books relating to military-media relations and propaganda. His most recent books are *Global Communications, International Affairs and the Media Since 1945* (Routledge, 1997) and *British Propaganda in the Twentieth Century: Selling Democracy* (Edinburgh University Press, 1999).

Major-General Julian Thompson, King's College, University of London, UK
Vol 1, Chap 11 British Special Forces operations behind enemy lines
Major-General Thompson served in the Royal Marines for 34 years in many places round the globe. His commands included a Royal Marines Command, the Commando Brigade in the Falklands War of 1982 and Royal Marines Special Forces. He has been visiting professor at the Department of War Studies, King's College, London. He has published seven books on military history subjects, and contributed to four others.

Commander Jeff Tall OBE RN, Director of the Royal Navy Submarine Museum, Gosport, UK
Vol 1, Chap 3 Waging the undersea war: a British perspective
Commander Jeff Tall is the Director of the Royal Navy Submarine Museum in Gosport, a post he has held since August 1994 when he retired from the Royal Navy. A submariner for 28 years, he served all over the world including a two-year tour of Exchange Service with the United States Navy in Pearl Harbor, Hawaii, in the late 1970s/early 1980s. In 1974 he passed his Submarine Command Qualifying Course (Perisher), and during the next 20 years he commanded four submarines: HMS *Olympus*, HMS *Finwhale*, HMS *Churchill* and, finally, the nuclear-powered Polaris missile submarine, HMS *Repulse*. He served as Admiral Sandy Woodward's submarine staff officer during the Falklands Conflict in 1982. He was co-author, with the naval historian Paul Kemp, of *HM Submarines in Camera* (Alan Sutton & Co), he wrote the historical element of the CD-ROM *The RN Submarine Service – Past, Present and Future*, produced jointly with the Royal Naval Submarine School, which is available to the general public, and was the author of *The Snapping Turtle Guide to Submarines* (Tick Tock Publishing).

Professor Geoffrey Till, Joint Services Command and Staff College, Bracknell, UK
Vol 1, Chap 10 Hitting the beach: the amphibious experience
Professor Till is Dean of Academic Studies at the Joint Services Command and Staff College, Bracknell, and Head of the Defence Studies Department. He is also Visiting Professor in Maritime Studies in the Department of War Studies, King's College, London. In addition to many articles and chapters on various aspects of defence, he is the author of a number of books. His work has been translated into eight languages and he regularly lectures at defence and academic establishments around the world.

Professor Frank E. Vandiver, Texas A&M University, College Station, USA
Vol 1, Chap 23 Foch and Eisenhower: Supreme Commanders
Frank Vandiver is Emeritus Professor at Texas A&M University. He is the author

of numerous books on the American Civil War, is the biographer of General John J. Pershing and is currently writing a biography of Field-Marshal the Earl Haig.

Hugo Vickers
Vol 1, Chap 20 Monarchy in wartime: King George V and King George VI
Hugo Vickers is a biographer and writer, who has specialised in the 20th century and is an acknowledged expert on the British Royal Family. He was born in 1951 and educated at Eton, and Strasbourg University. His works include *Gladys, Duchess of Marlborough*, *Cecil Beaton*, and *The Kiss* (winner of the Stern Silver Pen for Non-Fiction, 1996). His authorised biography of The Duke of Edinburgh's mother, *Alice, Princess Andrew of Greece* will be published in November 2000.

Dr G. T. Waddington, The University of Leeds, UK
Vol 1, Chap 28 Coalition war: Germany and her Allies, Austria-Hungary and Italy
G. T. Waddington took his BA and PhD at the University of Leeds, where he is currently Lecturer in International History. He has published articles and essays on Ribbentrop, Anglo-German and German-Soviet relations, and his translation of the memoirs of Reinhard Spitzy appeared in 1997 as *How We Squandered the Reich* (Norwich: Michael Russell). He is currently completing a monograph on Ribbentrop and German foreign policy for Cambridge University Press. He is also working on a book on Anglo-German relations between the wars with Dr Frank Magee of Coventry University.

Dr Bernard Waites, The Open University, Milton Keynes, UK
Vol 2, Chap 17 Black men in white men's wars
Bernard Waites is Senior Lecturer in History at the Open University, where he has taught since 1972. He is the author of *A Class Society at War* (Berg, 1997) and *Europe and the Third World* (Macmillan, 1999). He is currently working on a study of post-colonialism in historical perspective.

Dr Donald Webster, musicologist, Askham Bryan, York, UK
Vol 2, Chap 23 Classical music
Donald Webster began his musical career as a chorister at Leeds Parish Church. After some years as a schoolmaster, he became a lecturer in Higher Education, teaching at Bradford and Falkirk, and at Huddersfield and Napier Universities. He has been chorus master and conductor of a number of choral societies in Leeds, Bradford, Halifax and Huddersfield. More recently he has been active as a university extra-mural tutor, having a long association with the Open University. His books include *Our Hymn Tunes*, based on his doctoral thesis; *Parish, Past and Present*, a history of the music at Leeds Parish Church; *The Hymn Explosion*; and *A Hymn Book Survey 1980-1993*. He has made substantial contributions to numerous journals.

Professor Peter Wetzler, East Asia Institute, Ludwigshafen Business School, Germany
Vol 1, Chap 22 Erich Ludendorff and Tôjô Hideki: some comparisons
Professor Wetzler received his doctorate from the University of California, Berkeley, in 1977. He is currently Professor of Japanese Business, Politics and

Language at the East Asia Institute, Ludwigshafen Business School, Germany. His writings include *Hirohito and War: Imperial Tradition and Military Decision Making in Prewar Japan* (Honolulu: University of Hawai'i Press, 1998).

Dr Ian R. Whitehead, The University of Derby, UK
Vol 1, Chap 18 Casualties and British medical services
Ian Whitehead is Lecturer in Modern British History at the University of Derby. He has recently completed a book, *Doctors in the Great War* (Leo Cooper, 1999), and has also contributed chapters to *Facing Armageddon, Passchendaele in Perspective* and *Medicine and Modern Warfare*.

Susanne Wolf, University of Sheffield, UK
Vol 2, Chap 20 The Netherlands and Sweden : the experience of neutrality
Susanne Wolf is a doctoral candidate at the University of Sheffield, where she is completing a thesis on Dutch internment policy during the First World War.

Dr Benjamin Ziemann, Ruhr University, Bochum, Germany
Vol 1, Chap 14 German soldiers in victory, 1914 and 1940
Dr Ziemann's main fields of research are the social history of German Catholicism in the 20th century, German military history and the social history of the two World Wars.

Index